An Introduction to World Politics

An Introduction to World Politics

Conflict and Consensus on a Small Planet

RICHARD OLIVER COLLIN
AND
PAMELA L. MARTIN

ROWMAN & LITTLEFIELD PUBLISHERS, INC.
Lanham • Boulder • New York • Toronto • Plymouth, UK

Published by Rowman & Littlefield Publishers, Inc.
A wholly owned subsidiary of The Rowman & Littlefield Publishing Group, Inc.
4501 Forbes Boulevard, Suite 200, Lanham, Maryland 20706
www.rowman.com

10 Thornbury Road, Plymouth PL6 7PP, United Kingdom

British Library Cataloguing in Publication Information Available

Library of Congress Cataloging-in-Publication Data
Collin, Richard.
 An introduction to world politics : conflict and consensus on a small planet / Richard Oliver Collin
and Pamela L. Martin
      p. cm.
 Includes bibliographical references and index.
 ISBN 978-1-4422-1803-1 (pbk. : alk. paper) — ISBN 978-1-4422-1804-8 (electronic)
 1. International relations—Textbooks. I. Martin, Pamela, 1971– II. Title.
 JZ1242.C634 2013
 327—dc23
                                                                      2012010252

∞^{TM} The paper used in this publication meets the minimum requirements of American
National Standard for Information Sciences—Permanence of Paper for Printed Library
Materials, ANSI/NISO Z39.48-1992.

Printed in the United States of America

Contents

PART II: HOW THE WORLD FUNCTIONS: FREEDOM AND POLITICAL CONFLICT

PART III: KINDS OF CONFLICT: THE WORLD WHEN THINGS GO WRONG

Preface

The Rationale

This preface is addressed primarily to our professorial colleagues using *An Introduction to World Politics* for their courses. If your office looks anything like ours, there are hundreds of books on politics standing at attention on your shelves. Many of them are remarkably good, and most were written by authors who are smarter than we are. Does the world really need another textbook? Has this army of academics left anything unsaid?

Perhaps not, but twenty-five years ago, when I, Richard Oliver Collin, started teaching Coastal Carolina University's "Introduction to World Politics" course, I couldn't find a textbook that met my teaching needs. After struggling along with books by other authors, I began to create my own set of notes, and this homemade material eventually evolved into a manuscript. When Pamela L. Martin joined the Coastal Carolina University Department of Politics, the two of us began field-testing chapters one-by-one to get a sense of what did and didn't work in an actual classroom. Gradually, Pamela became such an important collaborator in the development of this book, that it made sense to add her as a full-fledged coauthor.

Our first goal was to capture and communicate the pleasure we both derive from teaching a course that combines an introduction to political science with a preliminary look at contemporary world politics. The study of world politics, as other scholars have noted, is not always defined by borders and states. Often, it's the people—their language and culture—and things that happen above and below the level of the state that impact politics. In this book, we do not separate comparative politics from international relations. We treat the disciplines as fluid and complementary, while still noting their traditional sub-disciplines within political science. In our view, politics are not isolated by international and domestic levels of analysis, but rather a complex and messy mix of multiple levels and actors that influence peace and conflict on the planet.

We political scientists are blessed with a natively fascinating subject; there is no excuse for a boring book about an exciting discipline. After genocidal massacres in Rwanda, uncivil wars in the Balkans, terrorist attacks on American cities, and controversial campaigns in the Middle East, it can be tough to get a chuckle out of this sorry planet, but we've done our best to keep it all from being too grim.

There have always been some good general introductions to politics on the market, but many of them are too difficult and too theoretical for the average American university student. They are also U.S.-centric and lack a personal application of the political in a student's daily life. In writing *An Introduction to World Politics*, our first concern was to find a way of speaking directly and intelligibly to the actual students who turn up in our classes, many of whom have only just graduated from high school.

We teach in a better-than-average regional university that is moving rapidly toward national status. Our students are usually clever young people with limitless potential. More often than not, however, their earlier academic training has made them into political illiterates who are weak in world history and geography and economics, and hopeless at current events. Unpersuaded that the subject of world affairs has any relevance to their lives, they, in general, do not follow international news in any coherent fashion until the awful day they enroll in our class.

What these students need is a book that builds upon their intelligence and their eagerness to learn, and offers them enough supportive material to do the catching up that needs to be done. This shouldn't involve oversimplifications of complicated issues; it does mean building the intellectual foundations upon which they can achieve a sophisticated understanding of world politics and the general field of political science. There are many maps in the text because students need a constant geographic frame of reference. Similarly, there is a lot of history in these pages; budding political scientists need to anchor themselves in the past before they can understand the present and speculate about the future.

What frustrates many beginning students of politics is the use of so many specialized terms, acronyms, and abbreviations. There is no alternative to learning the language of politics; as T. S. Eliot's Sweeney observed, "I gotta use words when I talk to you." We have avoided inventing idiosyncratic definitions and acronyms for difficult elements in political science, however, trying in every case to adopt and explain, warts and all, the terminology that is already commonly used in both the media and the discipline. When a new term or key phrase is introduced, we've printed it in bold, and defined it in the glossary.

We also wanted to provide a book that could be used in a variety of ways by our creative colleagues in the university world. As far as possible, the fourteen chapters in *An Introduction to World Politics* have been structured to be independent of one another, so they can be assigned and read in any order. *An Introduction to World Politics* lends itself to a variety of approaches and a range of teaching situations.

Context and Content

Let's think about practical teaching needs for a moment and explore how we can use the study of world politics as an introduction to political science. Nearly every university in the United States offers two separate first or second year introductory political science courses, one of which is the venerable American national government course. The second is often less clearly defined and is sometimes called either "Introduction to Political Science" or "World Politics," or something nebulous like "Global Problems" or "Contemporary Issues." Whatever their titles, these courses normally all have the dual purpose of presenting the discipline of political science and of introducing world politics in a way that provokes interest in the field. While individual instructors are free to adapt this book for whatever teaching situation they wish, *An Introduction to World Politics* was primarily written to satisfy the textbook needs of professors teaching a first or second year introduction to political science and/or world politics, and/or one of the "global studies" courses that have become so popular in recent years.

More practical than theoretical, *An Introduction to World Politics* looks at a conflict-stricken planet and tries to explain why we spend so much of our time and energy brawling with our neighbors, both nationally and internationally. The table of contents and the introduction give a fuller sense of the book's ingredients, but we have divided our narrative into four separate parts, each addressing a different aspect of conflict. Without taking the student reader too deeply into the arcane theoretical disputes within the field, *An Introduction to World Politics* explains how political scientists approach global political realities. Each chapter in the text prepares the student for one or more of the classic subfields within the discipline of political science.

We have a lot of thank-yous to give. Enormous thanks go to the patient people at Rowman & Littlefield, especially Susan McEachern, Grace Baumgartner, Carrie Broadwell-Tkach, and Alden Perkins. Gratitude goes to Professor Richard W. Coughlin for his sensitive review of the manuscript. Thanks also go to our students who contributed editorial help: Jonathan Young, Tyler Greatorex, Jonathan Morales, Andrea Lizarzaburu, and Dominique de Wit. We thank our spouses, Bill Martin and Thea Collin, for not divorcing us during the protracted composition of this book. We thank Matthew E. Collin for his review of our work on economics and development. And thanks go to Gabriella and William Martin for understanding when Mommy closed her door to work.

We think that a professor is a kind of temporal ambassador who represents the past to the future. As authors and academics, our respective intellectual lives were influenced strongly by the scholars who taught us, and whose insights and wisdom we have tried to transmit to our students and to the readers of this book. Pamela Martin wants to take this moment to thank Ted Robert Gurr and Virginia Haufler of University of Maryland, College Park for their inspiration. Richard Oliver Collin wishes to honor the memory of Christopher Seton-Watson of Oriel College, Oxford University, who taught him so much about history, politics, and life.

All our students pitched in with enthusiasm, making comments, gently complaining when material wasn't clear enough, and generating their own ideas for improvements and features. Political science is tough enough to learn without simultaneously having to help the teacher write the textbook, but their assistance, cooperation, and encouragement were crucial. Our love and thanks to all our past and present Coastal Carolina University students, to whom this book is affectionately dedicated.

Richard Oliver Collin, D. Phil (Oxon.)
Pamela L. Martin, Ph.D.
Coastal Carolina University

/

Introduction

We've never been convinced that students actually read authors' introductions, but stay with us for just a few pages, and we'll give you a sense of where we're going and what we'll try to learn along the way.

Every book reflects the life experience of its authors. Richard came to the formal study, and later the teaching of political science, only after several decades of living and working in Europe, North Africa, and the Middle East, followed up by an Oxford University doctorate. For him, politics is primarily the practical business of moderating conflict, organizing democracy, avoiding bloodshed, and arranging food and shelter for needy people. After teaching in the United States for a quarter century, Richard and his wife, Thea, have retired to Yorkshire in Britain. Pamela Martin, who lives with her husband, Bill, and their children in South Carolina, has a deep background in Latin American affairs with a special intellectual and emotional connection to the Republic of Ecuador. She has written widely about environmental affairs and the politics of indigenous peoples. Her recent book *Oil in the Soil: The Politics of Paying to Preserve the Amazon* appeared in 2011 from Rowman & Littlefield. A fluent Hispanist, Pamela completed her doctorate at the University of Maryland.

In the pages that follow, therefore, we've tried to harmonize diverse but complementary intellectual traditions. As experienced travelers who have spent years in the field, we have also attempted to strike a balance between the theoretical and the practical. We need to read Plato's thoughts on the ideal society, and we also need to figure out how to keep our Israeli and Palestinian friends from killing each other. The debate between Adam Smith and Karl Marx exposes central questions about the equitable distribution of resources; after we've understood economic theory, however, we need urgently to start feeding all those malnourished kids in Africa, Latin America, and South Asia.

We are interested in the why and wherefore of human conflict and have tried to explore how political systems broker, channel, and re-dimension conflict in an increasingly interconnected world. Conflict is an integral part of the human experience. It can be as humble as a happily married couple watching CNN over coffee and toast in the morning and discovering that they have slightly differing views about the United Nations. It can be as awful as Rwanda's Hutu majority raping, mutilating, and murdering more than half a million members of the Tutsi minority in central Africa. In functioning democracies, conflict is normally resolved through open discussion, arbitration and ne-gotiation, lawyers and judges, and decisions reached by elected public officials. In less fortunate societies, internal domestic conflict sometimes translates into military seizures of power, terrorism, or civil war. When two sovereign governments discover they differ on some significant issue, the results can range from a friendly chat among diplomats, or nuclear war, or one of the thousand waypoints in-between.

In the twenty-first century, the increased interconnectedness of the world compli-cates all conflict, and this book is an effort to help you identify and understand the subtle interrelationships in world politics. For example, the September 11 terrorist attack on the World Trade Center and the Pentagon may have changed American society funda-mentally, focusing U.S. attention on the ways that religion, electoral politics, petroleum economics, and climate change can all be fatally related.

An Example from the Middle East of Interconnected Political Conflict

Conflict can be hard to understand when a given feud involves multiple linkages or connections to other conflicts and other factors. For a half century now we have been watching the Israeli-Palestinian conflict on our television screens, and this Middle East-ern imbroglio is a good example of the kind of interconnections that make conflict both fascinating and hard to understand.

Consider the factors in this exasperating blood feud. Europe's historical inability to deal reasonably with its Jewish population contributed to the establishment of a Jewish political state in the Middle East after World War II. Israel came into existence, how-ever, against the will of its indigenous Palestinian population and its Arab neighbors, and without an international agreement over its ultimate boundaries. American political culture demands U.S. diplomatic support for the Jewish state, despite the hostility of Israel's Islamic neighbors. During the Cold War, the Arab-Israeli conflict blended with the hostility between the United States and the Soviet Union.

Wealthy industrial societies, such as Europe, Japan, and North America, however, all possess an unquenchable thirst for petroleum, an uncomfortable economic fact that involves them intimately with oil-producing but Israel-hating dictatorships such as Saudi Arabia. Furthermore, as we have been learning since September 11, 2001, many Saudis despise both their own government and the United States for its role in supporting both the Saudi regime and Israel. Indeed, the cultural, commercial, social, and military pres-ence of the United States in the Middle East serves as a perpetual irritant to militant Islamic fundamentalists, who wish to restore the mythic purity of their civilization.

The American desire to be simultaneously agreeable to Jewish Israelis and Muslim Arabs makes a coherent Middle Eastern foreign policy impossible, helping to explain why nothing much has worked in the region for sixty-five years. But even if we could sort out the politics, there would still be a crucial environmental dimension. Most Middle East-erners regarded the American invasion/liberation of Iraq as motivated completely by the desire to control Iraqi oil. Whatever the truth, Americans are convinced that they need a lot of oil, although the scientific community is approaching unanimity in its belief that continuing reliance on the combustion of natural gas, oil, and coal for energy is creating potentially devastating environmental problems such as rapid climate change.

Retooling our economy to run on some other power source would allow the United States to retreat from the troublesome Persian Gulf and create jobs in North America. It would also necessitate sweeping changes in domestic politics, international economics, and energy technology. And, at least in the short term, it would be expensive, since we would have to redesign our entire industrial system to run off sustainable and renewable power resources. While this might be a good idea in the long run, democracies aren't very good at persuading their citizens to take bad-tasting medicine (such as giving up SUVs and cheap gas and electricity).

Osama bin Laden is gone, but his al-Qaeda followers live in the pockets of these contradictions. The point of *An Introduction to World Politics* is to help us learn to think about seemingly separate dilemmas as parts of the same puzzle. Foreign and domestic conflicts are connected to commercial and environmental factors, and linked in turn to acts of terrorism and war. In the twenty-first century, the increased pace of globalization ensures that almost everything is connected to almost everything else.

Expanding Political Science

There is more to politics than just politics and we need to venture into areas where politicians never go. We'll be looking, therefore, at topics that are sometimes left out of the equation, even though they are quintessentially political: health care, the status of children in global society, the changing roles of women in the developing world, and the complicated interplay among population growth, resources, pollution, the environment, and sustainable development. We'll see that a growing imbalance between resources and population is the source of much contemporary conflict. That 1994 genocidal slaughter of the Tutsis, for example, is often cited as an ethnic conflict, but we'll see that its roots lay in Rwanda's environmental degradation, the shortage of arable land, and rampant overpopulation in a region of limited resources. Kenya's late Wangari Maathai won the 2004 Nobel Peace Prize for showing us the connection between preserving the environment and keeping the peace.

While political science is the central organizing discipline in understanding world politics, we should not hesitate to knock down those departmental barbed-wire fences to borrow and integrate data from history and sociology and environmental science and economics and a dozen other fields in the social and applied sciences.

As the title of this book implies, a world politics/political science text needs to be about the whole planet. This is a book by two American authors designed mostly for use in North American colleges and universities, but we don't want to see the human condition in terms of Americans and foreigners. The United States is a big and important country, but it is only one of nearly two hundred sovereign states on the planet, and its citizens constitute less than 5 percent of the world's population. An increasingly interconnected world demands that we see ourselves in a global context. In this book, therefore, words like "we" and "us" refer to the human race, not to the population of the United States.

What's Coming Your Way

PART I

In chapters 1 through 4, we start with a look at how we achieve global literacy, examining the ways both students and professional political scientists learn about world politics. We then move on to study the raw ingredients of conflict in human society with a diagnostic snapshot of the planet. People feud and sometimes fight over language, religion, and kinship, and we'll study all these factors. International conflict happens between countries or sovereign states, and we need to observe the complicated distinctions among nations, states, multinational states, and stateless peoples. This first portion of the book concludes with a look at nationalism and the politics of nationalism.

PART II

Having examined some of the sources of conflict in human society in part I, part II tackles the whole vexing connection between conflict and human freedom. When we're lucky, international conflict is managed and brokered by factors like international law and diplomacy. In this light, we take a look at the organization of the United Nations and its peacekeeping operations. Then, we study the creation of the European Union and how it works. Next, we study human freedom and different ideologies, and describe the left-right dimension in both domestic and international politics. Finally, we study how freer societies have created electoral mechanisms to avoid violence by controlling, moderating, and channeling conflict. Along the way, we feature a case study of modern China, which is involved in domestic political conflict over the issue of its evolving economic system, and a case study of India and its improbable democracy.

PART III

Undemocratic societies are normally less free precisely because they are less able to grapple successfully with conflict; in this light, part III opens with an examination of oligarchies, royal dictatorships, theocracies, and military regimes. Venturing into the realm of the unruly, we then look at violent conflict. We'll start by doing some analytical work on violence and then move to a series of ideological conflicts, looking at Marxist movements, Cuban-American animosities, right-wing and neo-Fascist groups, and finally, the fundamentalist Islamic rage that led to the terrorist assault on the United States in September of 2001. This portion of the book concludes with four detailed case studies on ethnic and national conflict, providing an analysis of the former Yugoslavia, Israel/Palestine, South Asia (Kashmir and Sri Lanka), and Northern Ireland. Along the way, we also feature a case study of contemporary Russia and its struggle with its evolving economic system.

PART IV

The fourth and final part of this book zeros in on the economic heart of politics. In most countries most of the time, the essential core of political discourse in domestic politics is a debate over the allocation of money and resources. Despite the importance of economic conflict, we sometimes fail to understand how decisions we make (or decisions that are quietly made for us by others) affect the quality of our daily lives. So we'll start by looking at the connection between money and politics in the developed world. Then we'll focus on the planetary poor, examining the causes and impact of economic deprivation. After a look at the politics of population change, the book concludes with a consideration of the arguments over environmental politics, resource conservation, and the whole question of sustainable development.

The book occasionally takes a break from formal text to illustrate some real-world aspect of global politics. For that purpose, we have created some specifically themed subsections, as follows:

TOUGH CHOICES

A university classroom is an easier place to make moral judgments than is a desk in the Pentagon, a desert battlefield in the Middle East, or an indigenous village in the Andes. Many textbooks tend to simplify decisions that—in the real world—are gut-wrenchingly complex. In an interconnected planet, every local policy decision will have global ramifications, which means that there are never any easy decisions. A bold moral stand in defense of an ethical principle sometimes gets many innocent people killed. An unpalatable alliance with an undemocratic regime might prevent the emergence of an even more horrific regime. As we've tried to illustrate in our series of "Tough Choices" features, all political choices are tough, and all solutions are inevitably provisional.

PARALLEL LIVES

Politics is about people and the ways in which they interact with one another and with the political systems that govern their lives. The "Parallel Lives" sections demonstrate how private citizens and public officials all over our planet face essentially very similar problems but view them from different perspectives.

PORTRAITS OF THE REAL WORLD

We've tried to keep this book free of war stories, but since the two authors have traveled expensively in impoverished and occasionally trouble-prone parts of the globe, we have occasionally used a personal reminiscence to hammer home an important point.

One note on the use of statistics: too many numbers can make our eyes glaze over, but beginning political scientists need to get used to the way we sometimes quantify political realities. Governments, educational institutions, and international agencies, such as the United Nations, all generate statistics. These institutions often use differing mathematical approaches, so a number from the World Bank may be a long way from a comparable number crunched by the U.S. Bureau of the Census or Treasury Department.

In order to bring some consistency to the statistical information provided in this book, *An Introduction to World Politics* uses data wherever possible from the most recent edition of the annual *United Nations Human Development Report* published by the United Nations Development Programme (UNDP). We'll talk about money in chapter 12, but all foreign currency figures are expressed as U.S. purchasing power parity Dollars (PPP US$), which means they are adjusted to account for differences in the cost of living in different countries. As a way of classifying countries, we have employed the UN Development Programme system first summarized in chapter 3, and explained in greater detail in chapter 12. This system for dividing the world into wealthy, moderately prosperous, developing, and underdeveloped societies has been adopted by the *New York Times* and is gradually becoming standard in both the press and the academic community. In the various figures and tables presented in the text, we have arranged countries according to their standing on the most current UN human development index.

Why It's Important

As *An Introduction to World Politics* should demonstrate, there are threats to our health and prosperity in the early years of this new millennium that are every bit as serious as anything we have faced in the past: the environment is in jeopardy, our energy supplies are threatened, and the Western world has slipped into a protracted conflict with Islamic society. The global political situation has never been more chaotic or less-well understood by the general public. Nor has it ever been more important, since the challenges ahead are fearsome. You are not studying political science and world politics because there is a new book to read and a final examination to pass. You are, or ought to be, studying politics because your life and the lives of your children depend upon it.

We're going to talk a lot about the three-sided tension among economic prosperity, population growth, and dwindling resources, and you will notice the common use of 2050, some forty years from now, as a target date. Environmental scientists and population experts have learned not to push their projections too far into the future because predictions get very wobbly after a few decades of volatile history.

But the "crystal ball" year of 2050 will strike a chord with many readers. Students come in all ages, but many readers of this book are now in their late teens or early twenties and—with expanding life expectancies—should still be here in four decades, perhaps with graying hair and a few wrinkles. Today's generation of university students will live their lives through what everyone expects to be a population-versus-resources crunch of some kind. We may be wrong in some or even all of our predictions, but something dramatic is going to happen, and most of the readers of this book will be around to see the results.

If you are twenty-two in 2012, you will be sixty in 2050. Ultimately, political decisions we make today will influence your political and physical environment in thirty-eight years. Will you live in a peaceful and prosperous democracy, or an economically deprived and authoritarian society? Will international organizations such as the United Nations have developed techniques to defuse political violence, or will you grow middle aged in a war-torn world, not much different from the one you are living in as a young person? Globally speaking, how many other people will there be on the planet when you have sixty candles on your birthday cake?

Back when they were still all alive and as young as many of the readers of this book, the Beatles wondered lyrically, "Will you still need me, will you still feed me, when I'm sixty-four?" Will there be enough birthday cakes for everybody? Will anybody still need or feed you, and your generation, when you're all sixty-four?

We may not know the answer. We may not even have the question right. But we need to start thinking now. What kind of world you inhabit when you have sixty-four candles on your birthday cake is largely up to you.

Part I

INTRODUCTION
TO A SMALL PLANET

CHAPTER 1

Global Literacy
UNDERSTANDING A COMPLICATED WORLD

"Have you guessed the riddle yet?" the Hatter said, turning to Alice again.
"No, I give it up," Alice replied. "What's the answer?"
"I haven't the slightest idea," said the Hatter.
"Nor I," said the March Hare.
Alice sighed wearily. "I think you might do something better with the time," she
said, "than wasting it in asking riddles that have no answers."

Could a nineteenth-century children's book be a good place to start the study of **politics** in the twenty-first century? In fact, Lewis Carroll (the pen name for Charles Lutwidge Dodgson) had a lot to say about riddles as well as politics. Carroll was born in 1832 as Europe was recovering from the Napoleonic wars and Britain was in the middle of the Industrial Revolution, which was making a few Englishmen very rich and many others very poor. While Carroll taught mathematics at Oxford University most of his life, he became famous as the author of *Alice's Adventures in Wonderland* (1865) and *Through the Looking Glass* (1871), in which he commented trenchantly and humorously on the politics of his era.

Lewis Carroll was part of a generation that experienced an unending succession of small-to-medium nationalist conflicts, an era not dissimilar to our own. During his lifetime, Germany and Italy fought wars to assemble themselves into modern nation-states and Britain evolved into a wealthy global empire, deploying forces all over the world to stitch together its far-flung colonial realm. While the British Empire would last until after World War II, other empires were already fragmenting under the onslaught of angry nationalisms. Lewis Carroll died just over a century ago, but his barbed comments on people and politics continue to be relevant in the opening years of this new millennium.

In the course of this book, we'll check back with Lewis Carroll from time to time because anyone scanning a daily newspaper or catching the evening television news will find plenty of questions with no obvious solutions. Alice wonders if we are wasting our time in contemplating riddles with no answers, but—on this side of the looking glass—we don't have the option of ignoring puzzling questions. We need to face the real political questions of our times in order to feed our children, stay out of wars, and organize education and medical care for our families.

In this preliminary chapter, we're going to take a swing at several global riddles, covering the following topics:

- *Why does the world seem so complex and daunting?* We'll try to appreciate why there are crucial gaps in our knowledge because some important information isn't available. We'll see why we probably need to know more history and geography than we do.
- *What are the principal nonacademic media through which we can learn about the political universe?* We'll do a quick survey of the print and online media, trying to distinguish good from bad, and then we'll see why—with some exceptions—television is mostly a waste of good electrons. Finally, we'll glance at one old-but-still-valuable medium, radio, and one relatively new, but occasionally misused channel for political information, the Internet.
- *In a media-cluttered universe, what can we actually believe?* There are some deep structural problems with the way Western societies get information about the world, and

we'll try to understand why the commerciality and size of some media empires detracts from their ability to do the job we want them to do. We'll move on to look at what has sometimes been called the "New Media" (blogs, social networking sites, etc.) and close this chapter by trying to decide how we can construct an informational diet for ourselves so that we get adequate news nourishment.

1. Why It's All So Confusing

Thinking about our planet and all its conflicts and problems, most of us are confused some of the time, even those of us who make planet watching a lifetime pursuit. Unfortunately, the "experts" often make as much sense as the March Hare and the Mad Hatter who entertained Alice in Wonderland. Politicians make speeches. Pundits pontificate. And professors explain—sometimes in bewildering detail—why the politicians and pundits are wrong.

This confusion comes from a variety of sources. At the risk of creating confusion about why we're confused, it might be worth asking why we spend so much time feeling perplexed when we think about global issues. Let's start by looking at some of the intellectual tools we need (but might not possess) to understand our battered old planet.

TERRIBLE TERMINOLOGY AND DEADLY DETAILS

Some world-affairs issues are relatively straightforward at a conceptual level but are routinely expressed in technical phraseology or obscure abbreviations or arcane acronyms. Writers are sometimes just showing off, but difficult political situations do have a way of producing difficult nomenclature. Consider, for example, the issue of world hunger. On the conceptual level, the essence of the problem can sometimes be relatively simple. Sometimes there is not enough food to go around. Sometimes, there is enough food on the market, but people with empty stomachs sometimes also have empty pockets. To get beyond a superficial understanding of the situation, however, we need to master the language of world politics. In the context of famines, this means acronyms such as the PC/GDP (per capita gross domestic product), RPG (rapid population growth), and IMF (International Monetary Fund), all of which we'll tackle later.

Conflict can generate even more jargon. The UN weapons inspectors who were monitoring alleged weapons production in Saddam Hussein's Iraq before the 2003 war originally worked for UNSCOM (UN Special Commission), which then evolved into UNMOVIC (UN Monitoring, Verification, and Inspection Commission). They were later joined in the field by inspectors from the IAEA (International Atomic Energy Agency), making some Americans more confused by acronyms than by Iraq itself.[2]

Even mass-circulation newsmagazines make sometimes surprising assumptions about the vocabularies of the general public. If you've missed the point of an article in your local newspaper because you didn't know that OECD stood for Organization for Economic Cooperation and Development (a kind of club of rich countries), then you're suffering from "awful acronym syndrome."[3] This is curable, but it's going to take some work.

Don't worry too much: once we've made our way through the phraseology, the jargon, and the abbreviations, the actual problem can often be fairly simple.

Riddles within Mysteries

We often take for granted that somebody—a professor in a university or a spy in the bowels of the CIA—understands the problems that torment us.[4] We assume, therefore, that our comprehension of world events depends upon our willingness to do the same hard intellectual work needed to achieve the same level of expertise.

Unfortunately, our own local mini-confusion is sometimes a manifestation of global mega-confusion; some issues are not well understood by anybody. Some planetwide problems are hard even for scholars to process intellectually because they cross the kind of subject-matter picket fences that universities erect between academic departments. An issue like **global climate change**, for example, demands more science than most students of politics can muster, and a greater mastery of global political life than most scientists have at their disposal.

Sometimes crucial information about a given policy dilemma is classified; it can be tough to talk about America's **national missile defense** program, for example, when key facts about nuclear warfare are locked away in **government** laboratories. There can be a huge gap between secret knowledge (the world as seen by the Pentagon and the CIA) and public knowledge (the world as understood by scholars and journalists). We could perhaps live with the fact that so much important information is classified if we had some guarantee that all the secret stuff was actually correct, but a lot of evidence suggests that the CIA is sometimes as mystified by world events as are the rest of us.[5] The custodians of America's secrets certainly have money and power at their disposal, but they have routinely failed to anticipate major international political developments. The CIA, for example, discovered that the Soviet Union was collapsing about the same time the *New York Times* did. Defense Intelligence Agency (DIA) spies didn't know about the September 11 attacks until a hijacked aircraft slammed into the Pentagon. In his essay, "Fixing Intelligence," Richard Betts maintains that a great deal has gone wrong with our intelligence-gathering apparatus and making it right is going to be expensive and time-consuming.[6]

Understanding other issues can be hampered by the sheer enormity of the field. For example, discussions on whether the U.S. government's budget is balanced or will be balanced in the future get shipwrecked by the fact that economists and political scientists cannot agree on what numbers belong in the equation, or even what it means conceptually to balance a budget.

The Horrors of History

Some news stories seemingly come out of nowhere, but most of the problems that bedevil us today have been around for a long time, a simple way of saying that every crisis has a temporal or historical dimension. And we won't understand an emerging crisis unless we have some sense of its history. The Germans have long words for tough concepts: *Vergangenheitsbewältigung* means "mastery of the past," a phrase that suggests that we need to come to grips with our history before we can grapple successfully with the future.

Understanding today's world requires a rough grasp of world history, particularly the major political and social events of the nineteenth and twentieth centuries. This doesn't mean memorizing long lists of dates, but we need to carry a general chronology around in our heads. It is tough to understand contemporary Europe, for example, without knowing when the two world wars began and ended and who was on which side.

Our current perception of history always conditions our political behavior. In 1992, the United States became militarily committed to an attempt to reverse the collapse of Somalia, only pulling out when the citizens of Mogadishu slaughtered a large number of American soldiers. Two years later, Rwanda's Hutu majority slaughtered hundreds of thousands of Tutsis, but the United States was disinclined to intervene because memories of Mogadishu were too strong. After absorbing brutal criticism about America's neglect of central Africa, however, the Clinton administration was shamed into intervening in Bosnia in 1995 to halt genocide there. The relatively quick success in Bosnia created enough optimism to support intervention again in Kosovo in 1999. Finally, Washington policy makers considered the relatively smooth invasion of Afghanistan in the winter of 2001–2002 when deciding to attack Iraq in 2003. When embarking on a new foreign policy adventure, it can be tough to decide which chapter in the history book ought to be required reading.

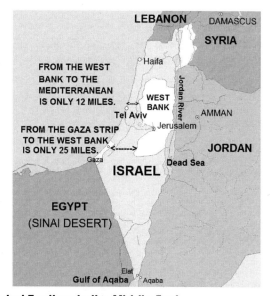

Map 1.1. Tormented Territory in the Middle East
Israel is the dominant military power in the Middle East but has always seemed nervous about its national security. One of the reasons is geographical. The original Israel was a long, narrow country, and it is not far at all from the West Bank, populated mostly by Palestinians, to the Mediterranean Sea. When Palestine becomes an independent state, it will want to link the Gaza Strip with the West Bank, and here too, the distance is not great. In politics and real estate, it's location, location, location.
Map by R. O. Collin.

Tormented Territory

Humans have long fought over politics and nationalism, but it is clear today that many conflicts really revolve around more mundane issues, such as land and water and access to vital resources. To understand almost any conflict, therefore, we need to comprehend its spatial dimension, and this means knowing more geography than most people remember from high school. There is an unfunny old joke about war being God's way of teaching geography to Americans, but it doesn't seem to work. In the weeks before the United States invaded Iraq in the spring of 2003, for example, the National Geographic Society produced a poll showing that only 13 percent of Americans between 18 and 24 years in age could find Iraq on a map.[7] In 2006, the National Geographic Society bravely produced a blank map of the Middle East, and asked members of a test group to locate Iraq, Saudi Arabia, Iran, and Israel. Three years after the United States had invaded the country, 63 percent could not identify Iraq; 63 percent could not find Saudi Arabia; and an impressive 75 percent failed to locate either Iran or Israel.[8]

And the names of cities, provinces, and even countries keep changing, typically after revolutions or radical regime changes. As we'll see in chapter 8, the dictatorial Burmese government insists upon calling the country "Myanmar." You can't go back to Bombay because it's now "Mumbai," and in the summer of 2005, the black majority government of South Africa decided to change the name of its executive capital from "Pretoria" (named after a Dutch general who was good at slaughtering black Africans) to Tshwane (the name of a historic black African king).

Location is said to be everything in real estate, and it's even more important in politics. Geography in tiny places where there isn't enough land can affect politics in ways that can be difficult for people who live in big spacious places, such as the United States, to understand. Despite their overwhelming military strength, for example, Israelis are nervous about national security because their state is so narrow at certain points (see map 1.1). Depending on how suicidal **Israeli** traffic is on a given day, the drive from the West Bank to the Mediterranean Sea takes just a few minutes. A dozen miles isn't much when there are hostile armies to the north, northeast, east, southeast, and southwest, as well as the West Bank itself and the Gaza Strip. The Israeli-Palestinian situation is complicated, and geography is part of that complexity.

Mr. Nixon and the Ambassador from Wherever

The interconnection between geography and politics is always there, but you need to get it right, especially if you live in the White House. President Richard M. Nixon once received a visit from the ambassador from Mauritius (a warm, wet island in the Indian Ocean). Unfortunately, the White House staff confused Mauritius with Mauritania (an arid sub-Saharan society in Arab Northwest Africa). Unaware that he had the two countries mixed up, a muddled Mr. Nixon launched into a discussion of dry-soil agriculture. Since Mauritius has one of the heaviest rainfalls in the world, dry soil isn't a big problem. The ambassador was too polite to say so, but he must have gone away wondering if the globe was in good hands.

Source: Henry Kissinger, *Years of Renewal* (New York: Simon & Schuster, 1999), 72.

In the largest sense of the word, geography includes not only land, bodies of water, and terrain features, such as mountains and deserts, but also the human inhabitants of the territory in question. The United States and its allies, for example, have fought two wars in little more than a decade against the Republic of Iraq. In chapter 9, we'll talk more about the politics of these wars, but in the meanwhile, Iraq serves as an example of how much there is to know about a country and an ongoing political crisis.

Iraq sits on real estate once called Mesopotamia, controlled in ancient times by Sumerians and Babylonians. As you can see in chapter 9, the Tigris and Euphrates rivers bring both water and conflict to the region. They begin in Turkey and pass through Syria on their way to Iraq, and both Turkey and Syria want more of that water for irrigation. Before spilling into the Persian Gulf, these two historic rivers unite and then splinter, making it hard to know where Iran begins and Iraq ends.

To understand the Iraqi people, we need to study the various mutually antagonistic ethnic communities within its borders. Iraq's people are far from homogenous and since 2003, the world has been taking a crash course on Sunnis and Shi'ites, two branches of a religion known as **Islam**. The bottom line is that we can't put what we need to know about Iraq onto a three-by-five card or into a one-paragraph executive summary. It's complicated and detailed. Oversimplification of an inherently complex problem turns a crisis into a cartoon, and we don't want to study (or conduct) foreign policy on the basis of cartoons. In order to unravel the complex web of contemporary political realities, we need to borrow information from wherever we can find it: history, geography, social psychology, comparative religion, and even—as we'll see in chapter 13—from the physical sciences.

Growing Out of Political Illiteracy

We are all illiterate in many areas of knowledge. At various stages in our lives, we make decisions (sometimes unconsciously) about the kind of information we need to have to do what we want to do. Some topics interest us; others bore us. How open are you to news about the world? If you purchase a morning newspaper, do you skip the front page and the editorial columns to turn first to the sports or the comics? Watching television over dinner, do you look at *Seinfeld* reruns or the Public Broadcasting System's *NewsHour*? You can absorb a certain amount of information through sheer osmosis, but if you don't read the newspaper or listen to news broadcasts, your grasp of global realities is likely to be primitive.

At various places in this book we'll encounter the effects of **cognitive isolation**, a situation in which people are cut off (or cut themselves off) from the global mainstream of thought and information on a given topic. The North Koreans, for example, suffer from cognitive isolation because their closed, secretive, totalitarian government executes people caught listening to foreign radio stations. Even in free societies, however, someone who never bothers with the news is going to be as cognitively isolated as a North Korean. Either way, a cognitively isolated person is intellectually deprived, wandering blindly in a political world that makes no sense and where everything comes as a surprise.

Some areas of human knowledge come in neat and fairly predictable packages. For example, if you got an A in Math 101, you should have the intellectual equipment to start Math 102. But the study of global politics (or any other kind of social science) doesn't work that way. There isn't anything precise or easily packaged about it. A political science course may have no formal prerequisites, yet you are expected to have mastered a vast but imprecise body of data before the first day.

It hardly seems fair. It's the first day of Politics 101, and your instructor suddenly lurches through WTO agreements and the infant mortality rates (IMR) as if those arcane terms were part of your everyday vocabulary.[9] Even worse, the professor has some difficulty accepting that you have never heard of Vladimir Putin or Angela Merkel. In the individual case of a freshman politics student, political illiteracy may involve a painful F, but at a collective, global level, this kind of ignorance might mean defeat in war, national bankruptcy, or a ruined economy.

The Existentialist Defense Secretary

In the middle of an impassioned 2003 debate about the imponderables of going to war against Iraq, Secretary of Defense Donald Rumsfeld delivered a thoughtful observation about the nature of human knowledge that struck some observers as a cross between poetry and existentialist philosophy. "There are known knowns," said the defense secretary. "There are things we know we know. We also know there are known unknowns; that is to say we know there are some things we know we do not know. But there are also unknown unknowns—the ones we don't know we don't know." Whatever our individual views on the wisdom of the 2003 Iraq War, Mr. Rumsfeld's meditation is worth our consideration. What we know we don't know, we can find out or at least tiptoe around the area of our ignorance. In politics, however, what blows up in our face is usually something we didn't know we didn't know, and never dreamed we needed to know.

Beyond the practical business of passing a course, is there any reason you should care about world politics? Isn't there someone in Washington, D.C., getting paid to keep track of foreign affairs? Professors who make a living teaching world politics are typically so fascinated by the planet and all its complexities that it can come as a shock to encounter students who frankly don't care.

2. Where We Start: World Politics and the Media

"Talk Politics like Hillary Clinton in Three Easy Weeks!" Don't you love those advertisements for quickie courses, promising a painless way of mastering the piano or a foreign language? The bad news is that there is no shortcut to learning what the professor teaching your intro to politics course assumes that you already know about the planet and its politics. If you don't have some fundamental background, you're going to find even an introductory course to be heavy going. Regrettably, there is no fast and facile way of learning everything you need to know about global politics, particularly if you have made cognitive isolation a way of life. A book like this one can provide only a preliminary platform upon which to build.

In this section, we need to look at the role played by the wire services in gathering and disseminating the news. Then we'll look at the news media in general, particularly newspapers and magazines in print and online formats. We'll do a critical review of television as a source of news, and go on to suggest that the older medium of radio might do a better job. Next, we'll take a look at the emerging and significant role of social media and see why the social media are beginning to become so popular. Finally, we'll think about the Internet as a whole, including wire service data, newspapers online, radio broadcasts from around the world, access to social media sites, and television coverage.

The suggestions presented below should be thought of as minimalist, since it would take much longer to survey the length and breadth of what is available. Here we are looking for basic political literacy and this is how to start.

WIRE SERVICES, NEWSPAPERS, AND MAGAZINES

Before talking about specific newspapers, let's remember that most newspapers, magazines, and TV newsrooms get their out-of-area news from international news-gathering organizations usually called **wire services**. The Associated Press (AP), Reuters, United Press International (UPI), and similar information services are popularly called wire services because—when they began in the midyears of the 1800s—their stories were carried in Morse code along copper telegraph wires.[10] Today, of course, satellites, cellular phones, e-mail, and social media are the preferred methods of communication, and these same companies now sometimes bill themselves as information agencies, because their functions have expanded with advances in computer technology. Wire services, newspapers, and magazines are some of the oldest forms of mass media; so we need to start by seeing how they interconnect.

"Hot off the Wire!" Modern Information Agencies

Today, the larger wire services maintain teams of reporters around the world to cover the news. The stories are edited in New York or London or Washington and then sold to newspapers, radio and television stations, Internet providers, and sometimes to private consumers.

Several of them claim to be the world's biggest, but the real global information giant is probably the Associated Press, whose stories reach an estimated one billion readers, viewers, and listeners a day. When you see AP at the start of a news story in your hometown paper, you know that it was filed by an Associated Press journalist and not a local reporter. Reuters also covers normal political and social events, but specializes in economic and corporate news. Some of the larger national papers (such as the *New York Times*) double as wire services, sending out reporters to write stories to print in their own pages as well as to retail to smaller newspapers and magazines.

The Associated Press, Reuters, United Press International, the *New York Times,* and a few others try for global coverage, reporting stories from everywhere to everywhere on virtually every possible topic. Most countries have one or more wire services. Agence France-Presse brings us stories from Paris while ANSA tells us what's happening in Italy. The Kyodo News Agency of Japan is dominant on the Pacific Rim and ITAR-TASS covers Russia and the former Soviet Union. Most European wire services operate independently of their governments and have high journalistic standards, but some African and Asian wire services are controlled by dictatorial regimes and say precisely what they are told to say. For example, the good news from North Korea's P'Yongyang comes to us courtesy of the Korean Central News Agency of the Democratic People's Republic, which reports whatever North Korea's communist government wants to see in print.[11]

In evaluating the news, it's important to remember that your regional or local newspaper does not maintain journalists around the world to cover events in Africa and South Asia. In fact, only a handful of newspapers have any correspondents abroad; the *New York Times* and the *Washington Post* have only twenty to thirty apiece at any given time and rely upon the Associated Press and Reuters for extended coverage. In fact, your local paper might not even have a reporter in Washington. As a consequence, the bulk of the national and international news you read in the morning paper has been sold to your editor by one of the three or four biggest news services.

National, Regional, and Local Newspapers

In that golden era before World War II and before television and the Internet came to dominate our lives, a daily newspaper was the fundamental source of information about the world. In the United States, there were many more newspapers than there are today and even fairly small cities typically had two rival papers, often one in the morning and one in the evening.[12] Today, a handful of giant media corporations own most newspapers, and few communities have more than one. After World War II, 80 percent of American newspapers were independent and locally owned; by the 1990s, 80 percent were owned by national media conglomerates.[13] Local newspapers are still important in local politics, however, and in the United States, major national papers are still crucial for creating a public consciousness, particularly among the elite.[14] The average American may not read the *New York Times* editorial page, but Washington's political leaders all do, so those editorials still carry tremendous clout. A series of articles in the *Washington Post* exposed the Watergate scandal and effectively brought the Nixon presidency to a premature end.[15]

In Europe, there are still a lot of newspapers, and they compete ferociously with one another for commercial and ideological supremacy, in the process often printing information and points of view that never appear in the American media. After the September 11 attacks on the United States, for example, many Americans turned to British newspapers such as the London-based *Guardian* for a European perspective on U.S. news.[16]

While newspapers sell briskly in most parts of the world and the business is absolutely booming in the developing world, newspaper sales are in moderate decline in Europe and significantly down in the United States. Why don't more Americans read a daily paper? The first answer might be technical: finding the paper version of the *New York Times* can be complicated if you don't live in a big city and it may be easier to read it online. Also people on the move are able to access papers such as the *New York Times* from applications on newer smart phones such as the iPhone or Android. Most European countries have a truly national press, that is, comprehensive, high-quality newspapers edited in a major city and then distributed around the country in time for first-thing-in-the-morning consumption. The British, for example, can have the *Times* or the *Guardian* delivered to their doorsteps with the morning milk no matter where in the United Kingdom they live. From Palermo to Milan, Italians can drink their first espresso of the day while pondering *La Repubblica* or Milan's *Corriere della Sera*. In the United States, only *The New York Times*, *The Washington Post*, *The Wall Street Journal*, and *USA Today* (criticized by some as intellectually lightweight) try for this kind of nationwide coverage, and the sheer size of the North American continent means that none of them succeeds the way European papers do.

From time to time, all of these national newspapers find themselves criticized for being too left wing or too right wing (chapter 6 will clarify these terms), but they are all essentially mainstream publications. Usually, they are competent and comprehensive. Read any one of them every day for a year, and you will be tolerably well informed about the world.

There is a second category of regional newspaper (such as the *Atlanta Constitution* or the *Los Angeles Times*) that attempts a mix of international, national, and regional news, but—if you live some distance from the hub—you may find a regional paper too much of a compromise.[17] On one hand, the paper may not tell you what's playing at the local motion picture show, nor will it report the recent developments in Kosovo or Kashmir in much depth. And finally, strictly local papers have their uses, but they aren't much good for keeping track of the world, since advertisements, sports and human interest stories, horoscopes, classified ads, announcements, and cartoons take up a lot of room, leaving little room for foreign stories.

Political Periodicals

If you can't get your hands on one of the quality national papers, you definitely need to read one of the three comprehensive American weekly newsmagazines: *Time*, *Newsweek*, or *US News and World Report*. An annual student subscription to any of these magazines in print runs about $24 for fifty-two issues, although the cost for individual copies at your newsstand will be much higher. You can also access these newsmagazines online for free through many university and public libraries.

Which one is best for you? As an experiment, buy all three of them the same week to see what stories they carry and how they handle them. In 2009, *Newsweek*—which has been losing money badly—evolved from being a strictly news-oriented weekly to one offering more commentary, making it less of a *Time* clone. In 2010, it joined forces with an Internet site called The Daily Beast. Insiders still claim, however, that *Newsweek* appeals to liberals, while *Time* is the preferred reading of moderate Republicans.

There is actually a fourth weekly newsmagazine you might want to consider if your interests include international corporate and financial news. Britain's *Economist* might bust your budget (although digital versions are less costly), but intellectually, it's streets ahead of the three American weeklies, featuring very detailed coverage of the world scene, including stories about countries *Time* and *Newsweek* assume you haven't heard of and don't care to follow. The editorial tone is Anglo-American and business oriented.[18]

Figure 1.1. *The Economist*
Providing very solid reporting of world political and financial affairs, Britain's *The Economist* magazine makes two-thirds of its total global sales in the United States, appealing to business leaders and academics. Courtesy of *The Economist*.

TELEVISION: THE MEDIOCRE MEDIUM

No matter how good newspapers and magazines are, most Americans and many Europeans regard television as their favorite medium for both entertainment and news. TV is unquestionably popular. Is it any good?

The tube is inherently great at punching home certain highly visual realities. For example, most historians believe that TV was pivotal in ending the war in Vietnam, since viewers around the world were treated to a dose of Southeast Asian awfulness every night before dinner. In 1992, Americans watched members of the Los Angeles Police Department deliver a savage beating to an African American suspect named Rodney King, communicating a message about police brutality more succinctly than a thousand newspaper stories. In 2003, American armored units raced from Kuwait to Baghdad, and the world went along for the ride, thanks to "embedded" journalists traveling with the attacking Anglo-American coalition.

On the other hand, there is near-universal agreement among media specialists and professional political analysts that commercial television has increasingly become a relatively poor medium for the dissemination of serious news, with a few partial exceptions.

What's Wrong with TV?

Overwhelmingly, Americans get their news from one of the three network news services (ABC, NBC, and CBS) or one of the cable news channels such as CNN, MSNBC, or Fox News. Except during emergencies and presidential elections, ABC, NBC, and CBS all present snatches of news during their morning shows, and then an evening thirty-minute main program, supplemented by a variety of specials, late-night interview shows, and Sunday-morning panel discussions.

Despite the popularity of the networks, they do not really offer much content for the student striving to achieve political literacy. Try this experiment. Join NBC's affable Brian Williams some weekday evening at 6:30 with a stopwatch in hand and try to determine precisely how much of a typical thirty-minute evening broadcast is actually news. Typically, there will be about seventeen minutes of news and thirteen minutes of commercials and fluff. Nor is there any point in switching over to see what the other networks are doing. CBS and ABC are virtually synchronized, telling the same stories at almost the same time and pausing for commercials at nearly the same instant. These shows are oriented toward older Americans, who are accurately believed to be more interested in serious news than young people, and the advertisements promise remedies for arthritis and incontinence and acid reflux.

There isn't very much news on commercial television, and it isn't very good. Information is presented in a hurried, choppy manner, interrupted relentlessly with aggressive commercial breaks, leaving the viewer dazed and bewildered rather than educated or informed. Dedicating only a few seconds to each story, television suggests to us that the world and all its myriad complexities can be reduced to tiny nuggets of information, data-bullets fired at the viewer. Since airtime is expensive, television never has the luxury of exploring the interconnectedness of global issues. Network news editors assume that viewers are not very bright and seldom allow anchors to go into much depth.

Programming decisions are increasingly made on the basis of purely financial consid-erations, eliminating real news in favor of sitcoms. This trend may have begun in 1966 when CBS began covering Senate hearings on the expanding American military commit-ment in Vietnam. When CBS mandarins decided that more money could be made with reruns of the *I Love Lucy* show, they cancelled TV coverage of the Senate hearings pre-cisely when the world might usefully have learned a little more about the war in Southeast Asia.[19] One study done by media maven Andrew Tyndall suggests that the coverage of foreign news by the three networks declined by more than 60 percent between 1988 and 2000.[20] Coverage rose in response to the terrorist attacks of September 11, but this was almost entirely reporting on American military activities abroad.

Ever since television was invented, educators and psychologists have been arguing that television changes the way we think and erodes our critical facilities.[21] In his 1964 classic *Understanding Media*, Marshall McLuhan argues that TV does most of our think-ing for us and does it badly.[22] There is some empirical evidence to suggest that television actually renders viewers less able to deal with political realities. Media critics Martin Lee and Norman Solomon report a University of Massachusetts study about reactions to the 1991 Gulf War. According to the study, the more hours of television people watched, the less they actually knew in terms of basic facts about the conflict, but the more likely they were to support the U.S. government's position.

Network television is a money-making business enterprise, not a charity or a public service. If there is less news on television today than there was in the 1950s, it is because television news generates less revenue today than it did a half century ago. The networks still broadcast a little news every day because enough people tune in and sit through the commercials to make it barely worth their while. But from the stockholders' point of view, the commercials are the object of the exercise, and news stories are selected and edited on the basis of their anticipated capacity to keep you watching until it's time for the next commercial. The kind of news you need to live intelligently and participate meaningfully in the political life of your planet may not be the same news that will keep you glued to your seat between advertisements, and this is the core problem with com-mercial television as a source of serious news.

TV for News Addicts: CNN and PBS

If you're one of those people who simply must spend an hour a day in front of the televi-sion set, let's think about some positive alternatives to the intellectual wasteland of com-mercial network television. Despite some flaws, CNN and PBS are two alternative, albeit rather different, options.

With its aggressive reporting team and around the clock availability, CNN emerged as a favorite among viewers during the 1990–1991 Gulf War. A second channel, CNN Headline News, presents shortened versions of the same stories; the value of Headline News consists in its instant and endless availability. At any time, CNN has about thirty foreign correspondents, more than the combined total of CBS, NBC, ABC, and Fox News.[23]

CNN-International is now available nearly everywhere in the world and is watched by opinion makers on every continent. CNN's global presence gives it enormous international importance and helps create a global American perspective on the news. As Keohane and Nye observe, "When Iraq invaded Kuwait in 1990, the fact that CNN was basically an American company helped frame the issue, worldwide, as aggression . . . rather than as a justified attempt to reverse colonial humiliation."[24]

CNN's domestic American programming is intellectually a little lighter and has received mixed reviews. It is clearly significant that a major corporation has decided that news is important enough to be the sole basis for an entire network. Without question, CNN features more information about events at home and abroad than do any of the networks, and the Atlanta-based reporting team achieves a significantly greater level of sophistication than do any of the network newscasts. Complicated issues, however, are sometimes still rushed-by viewers in thirty-second sound bites. CNN tends to follow a lead story obsessively, which is fine if you happen to be interested solely in a presidential election or the latest military engagement in the Middle East. When there is a juicy Hollywood scandal, however, CNN promptly forgets about the rest of the world.

On the other hand, none of CNN's rivals does quite the same job. NBC has mounted a competitive challenge in the form of CNBC, which generally follows the CNN format, but delivers a greater emphasis on economic and business news. Fox News combines news with a more distinctly conservative political comment and occasionally riotous debates. And MSNBC is the liberal answer to Fox News.[25]

C-Span's two channels belong in a class by themselves. With live broadcasts of Senate subcommittees and debates in Britain's House of Commons, C-Span is wonderful for seasoned political sophisticates and news junkies, but if you are just starting your search for political literacy, this is the deep end of the pool.

Almost every serious student of world affairs will be at least an occasional watcher of the Public Broadcasting System (PBS). Created in 1967, the Public Broadcasting System is a nonprofit corporation based in Alexandria, Virginia, and supported by government grants and contributions from a variety of other sources (especially viewers). Each of the fifty states has a PBS affiliate organization. Programming varies somewhat from state to state although most key programs originate nationally.

During the day, PBS concentrates on children's and educational programs, but in the evening and on weekends there is a series of high-quality news shows, of which the premier is the *NewsHour*, offering sixty minutes of news presented without commercial breaks. If ABC/NBC/CBS offers tenth-grade news analysis and CNN is aimed at a high-school audience, *NewsHour* anchor Jim Lehrer and his colleagues assume a university level of sophistication.

The *NewsHour* is not without its critics. Conservatives complain of an automatic bias against the right, while radicals maintain that the show stages debates between mainline Democrats and mainline Republicans, presenting an essentially centrist point of view. PBS is essentially free of commercials, but a lot of public television funding comes from corporate giants such as AT&T and Archer Daniels Midlands; businessmen would drop the *NewsHour* like a stone were the program to become too antiestablishment. Nevertheless, *NewsHour* is about as good as news on television gets. PBS also presents a series of hour-long investigative programs called *Frontline*, delving into specific topical political issues.

Figure 1.2.   PBS's Judy Woodruff
At PBS from 1983 to 1993, Judy Woodruff was the chief Washington correspondent for *The MacNeil/Lehrer NewsHour*. From 1984 to 1990, she also anchored PBS's award-winning weekly documentary series, *Frontline with Judy Woodruff*. Woodruff also served as a chief correspondent for CNN and has worked at NBC. Courtesy of PBS NewsHour. Photo by Robert Severi (http://www.robertseveri.com/).

RADIO AS THE ULTIMATE NEWS SOURCE

Radio has been with us since the beginning of the twentieth century, and we tend to think of it as old-fashioned, a substitute medium for moments when we can't watch television. However, as a technology, radio is actually advancing more rapidly and in more dramatic ways than television. Radio transmission is inexpensive when compared with television and its relative cheapness encourages broadcasters to take chances that would horrify a risk-averse television producer. Let's look at four noncommercial radio news sources.

The Public Radio System

Most commercial radio is a vehicle for popular music and sports and the average Top-40 station will not bring us much nuance during its two-minute news bulletin. Public radio, however, is in many ways a superior medium for people who want fast and accurate news from around the world.

Public radio in the United States sprang up locally in the 1950s and 1960s, often in connection with universities or other regional groups. While it has received some financial assistance from state and federal governmental sources, public radio derives much of its income from listener contributions. Virtually every state has a statewide public radio organization, often (but not always) in partnership with the PBS organization described above. For technical reasons, these state-based public radio stations use slightly different frequencies for each individual city, but their broadcasts can generally be found on the far left of your FM dial between 88 and 92 MHz.

At the national level, much of the programming for public radio is supplied by a Washington-based nonprofit organization called National Public Radio (NPR).[26] Broadcast times and programs will also vary from state to state and sometimes even from city to city, but news coverage begins in most areas about 5:00 a.m. with a very successful NPR program called *Morning Edition*, which lasts until 8:00 or 9:00 a.m. depending upon the area. Some NPR local affiliates spend much of the day with classical music and return to hard news in mid-afternoon; others have gone over to an all-news-all-talk format.

NPR has a hardcore audience of perhaps eight million influential listeners, who earn about twice the national average and are mostly university graduates. National Public Radio is a very earnest attempt to provide a thorough and nuanced view of the world, delivered with humor and sophistication. Hard political news is interspersed with culture and sports but never interrupted with commercials, so that an hour's news means sixty minutes of solid programming. NPR has its own reporters in the United States and abroad, and often shares overseas correspondents with the British Broadcasting Corporation.

Short-Wave Radio and the BBC

Despite its crucial importance for Europeans, Asians, and Africans, few Americans are interested in the unique coverage of the world available on **short-wave** (SW) radio. Since the 1920s, nearly every national government and many nongovernmental organizations have aired SW broadcasts in an effort to educate and influence world opinion. These broadcasts are delivered in every language and dialect under the sun, and students trying to master a foreign tongue often find it useful to have a steady supply of news, music, and drama in that language. It may be that the ultimate instrument of freedom is the short-wave radio. All governments lie sometimes, and some governments lie all the time, but with a short-wave radio you can sit in Zagreb or Minsk or Soweto or Sao Paolo or Detroit and scrutinize the airwaves for truth.

Nearly all commentators agree that the premier news service in the world is still provided by the venerable British Broadcasting Corporation, which maintains more than two hundred full-time correspondents outside the UK. As Keohane and Nye remark, "The BBC . . . maintains credibility in an era of white noise." In addition to its domestic services for British listeners, the BBC World Service broadcasts around the clock in English and a wide variety of other languages to virtually every population group around the world.[27]

The BBC is a public corporation owned by the British government, but its editorial staff has maintained a rigorous tradition of policy independence from Britain's political leadership. During global crises, BBC coverage routinely races ahead of U.S. television. During both wars against Iraq (1990–1991 and 2003), the BBC maintained a full team in Iraq and produced news ahead of the American media. In the United States, you can pick up the BBC World Service with a short-wave radio, over your computer (see below), and via satellite and public radio, which relays BBC transmissions at night.

Portraits of the Real World:
The Virtues of a Bug-Out Bag

Okay, you've been traveling through one of those picturesque but politically unstable countries your politics professor warned you about. One day, you hear the sound of incoming artillery rounds as the insurgents shell the presidential palace, and the last Delta flight leaves the airport without you. There are tanks in the streets as well as an angry mob of men with assault rifles who are shouting . . . well, it does seem to be "Death to America!" That would be you.

Only you can make the decision about "bugging out," and it might be that your best option is to stay put and order from room service until the shooting stops. Experienced travelers to these restless regions typically use the U.S. State Department's Internet site (www.state.gov/) to get the number of the local American embassy and the name of a consular official who can give you good advice. Also check http://www.icrc.org to find addresses and phones for the International Red Cross in your area. Remember to do this *before* the revolution; the Internet is likely to be the first casualty in a guerrilla war.

Is this ever going to happen? With varying degrees of seriousness, it happens all the time, and you could be there the next time the tear-gas canisters start flying. Pamela Martin lived through three separate extralegal coups d'état in Ecuador with roads blocked, tires on fire, drunken mobs looting stores, and food supplies getting low. Richard Collin survived guerrilla wars in Lebanon and the Sultanate of Oman during which he pretended to be from Ontario. No one hates Canadians.

If you decide to run for it, you should have what seasoned travelers call a "bug-out" bag, a small leather or canvas satchel with a shoulder strap, filled with what you'll need on the day when the electricity goes off. It should contain some or all of the following items: your passport and a photocopy in case the original gets confiscated; as much bottled water as you can carry and a plastic jar of peanut butter (lots of protein and it doesn't spoil); suntan lotion; a deet-based insect repellent; a waterproof jacket; a hat; any prescription drugs you need plus a bottle of painkillers; a generic antibiotic in the quinolone class; band-aids for blisters; an antiseptic like bacitracin; a small flashlight; a handheld compass and a good map showing terrain features like mountains and swamps, because you may want to stay off the main roads to avoid police checkpoints; and an English–local language dictionary, unless you're already fluent.

This isn't going to be the senior prom; wear your oldest jeans and take one change of underwear and socks. Leave everything else behind, especially brand-name sneakers unless you want to be murdered for your Nikes. Wear ordinary shoes or boots, not sandals. Stash away two or three hundred dollars in ones and fives for bribes and incidentals. If you're a woman, abandon the cosmetics bag and dress like your grandmother. There are moments when plain is sane, and this is one of them.

Richard's customized personal bug-out bag also includes a whiskey flask and a knife for cutting bread and spreading peanut butter (and/or stabbing people). Wrong-side-of-the-tracks travelers argue about weapons, but a pistol might get you arrested if you're searched by the cops, and you're not going to shoot your way past a platoon of Kalashnikov-armed insurgents. Since information is power, forget about guns and take an AM-FM short-wave radio instead. The BBC will tell you if the insurgents are north or south of you, if Washington is sending in the Marines, and who is winning the civil war—all vital information.

One bit of happy news: the size and weight of short-wave radios has decreased enormously in recent years, and these days you can rely on something like the Grundig Mini World 100 PE. Running about thirty bucks retail, they're about the size of an iPod but capable of bringing in the BBC and the Voice of America just about anywhere. Pamela travels often for research to South America and the Amazon, in particular, where mosquito netting and malaria pills can be added to the bag. As an academic researcher interested in political conflict, Richard still travels to restless parts of the developing world, keeping his bug-out bag handy, fresh batteries in that radio, and his whiskey flask filled.

Satellite and Computer Radio

Censorship is generally simple for hard copy such as newspapers and magazines, the distribution of which can easily be blocked by local governments. Electronic transmission is more difficult to interrupt, but television and FM radio are limited in range, and governments can simply shut down an offending station on their own territory. To kill a short-wave radio signal is a real technological job, but it can be done by "jamming" an objectionable transmission, that is, broadcasting random noise on the same frequency. In Havana, for example, it's hard to hear the BBC World Service, because the Castro government jams it with an annoying electronic buzzing sound.

At the top end of the market, remember that your computer or smart phone may be the best radio in the house. After connecting to the Internet, you can use programs such as Microsoft Windows Media Player or RealPlayer to hear radio stations from around the world. The entirety of the BBC's very-high-quality radio content is available for free over your computer. Some television stations have even begun providing video material over the net, so that you can now also see television programs from overseas.

As an answer to censorship and a sign of advances in radio technology, we have satellite radio. News providers such as Fox News, CNN, and MSNBC all have stations on Sirius/XM radio, giving listeners more-exclusive access to news without the barrier of local radio restrictions. The same stations on satellite radio can be accessed anywhere nationwide. These stations have no commercial interruption, a perk that comes with a cost however, generally between $15 and $30 a month depending on the package chosen.

Podcasts are another emerging method for citizens to get their daily news on their own time. Podcasts can be downloaded from the Internet and through tools such as iTunes and Zune. They can be stored on an iPod or MP3 player, allowing people to listen to them anytime, anywhere. All the major news providers have podcasts available on iTunes and Zune, as well as on their respective websites.

THE INTERNET AS A SOURCE FOR POLITICAL NEWS

The bad news here is that computer-based information collection-dissemination has become a corporate jungle. The good news is that Internet technology can give you unparalleled access to certain kinds of information, although it means venturing into that jungle all by yourself. You don't need to know much about computer technology to surf the net, and the technology is changing too rapidly to explain it all here. Almost every university library and most community public libraries provide free access to computers, courses on computer use and the Internet, and personalized instruction from competent information-technology specialists.

And much of it is free! Some information companies make a significant portion of their products openly available online, so you can read—for example—the *New York Times*, Britain's *Guardian*, France's *Le Monde*, and Spain's *El País* on the screen, or store them on your hard disk, or print them out. Virtually every major newspaper and magazine and radio and television network in the world now has a presence on the Internet. The service gives you detailed world news in the comfort of your home and informational resources that would have been hard to duplicate just a few years ago in a major research library.

How do you find what you're looking for? At the end of every chapter in this book, you will find endnotes that identify online where you can find Internet resources that amplify topics covered in the chapter. Keep in mind, however, that almost anyone can establish a presence on the Internet. Reading something on the Web isn't much different from going into a bar and talking to the person on the next stool. He might be a towering genius or actively psychotic or just creatively drunk. Meeting the same guy in cyberspace does nothing to improve his credibility; he may still be neglecting to take his medication.[28]

A conventional book on politics written by a professor at a recognized university and produced by a well-known publishing company is reviewed and checked for accuracy by a variety of experts. It may be wrong, but it will be at least *authoritatively* wrong. In contrast, the World Wide Web has no system for checking the accuracy of information online, which makes it very democratic and full of unreliable information.

To find accurate data on the Internet, be sure that you know who or what institution is responsible for creating and updating a given site. Avoid sites that do not have a known and trustworthy sponsor. Use Internet sites that have been created by well-known institutions, such as universities, governments, the United Nations, and other international organizations, and reliable national newspapers and magazines. With a little more care, you might consult some governmental sites and some activist organizations, such as Amnesty International and Greenpeace.[29]

A variety of technological advances now makes it possible for residents of North America to have direct access to sources of information that are distinctly unfriendly to—for example—the United States. Both satellite television and the computer bring the Qatar-based al-Jazeera news source to Americans, providing a distinctly anti-American perspective on the Middle East. Indeed, even terrorist groups now have their own websites, and you can read the words of al-Qaeda leaders online, even if American editors are disinclined to print them.

THE SOCIAL MEDIA EMPIRE

Perhaps the most revolutionary resource for accessing the news is social media. We have most certainly ushered in the Facebook and Twitter eras, and they have spread like wildfire. Since starting as a small social-media network on the campus of Harvard in 2003, Facebook now has over nine hundred million members all over the world, with the ability to contact each other wherever there is access to the Internet at the touch of a button. Facebook has evolved from simply a networking website into a one-stop shopping center for information, including news access. Users can simply become a fan of a news network on Facebook, or "follow" them on Twitter. Upon doing so, they are updated with all breaking news right there on their profiles. They are even able to customize different news interests to their liking to specify the information they desire to receive updates about. YouTube, a website where people can upload videos of virtually whatever they wish, has taken many parts of the world by storm. Clips from all different news agencies around the world can be found by simply searching a topic. Many college professors have even begun incorporating YouTube as a significant teaching aid within their classroom instruction. Social media is the preferred method for many college students to gain access to the news in a more convenient way.

In addition to being able to access social media networks on their computers, people are now even able to access them from their cellular phones, or as they are better known now "smart phones." iPhone, Blackberry, and Android, among others, allow users to access networks such as Facebook and Twitter from their cellular phones. These phones have market places at their disposal to add hundreds of mobile applications, most for free and some for a reasonable price. News networks such as CNN, Fox News, and MSNBC, as well as newspapers including the *New York Times* and *USA Today* all have "apps" available to download to these various devices. Once downloaded, users have access the most up-to-date news being reported and can even access videos from the major news networks at the touch of a button from anywhere. These applications can also be customized to add alerts for breaking news, an important example being The Weather Channel application, where you can have your phone update you with severe weather warnings in your area.[30]

Social media recently has proven itself as a political super power. In the Middle East, Facebook and Twitter have been credited with organizing the string of major revolts taking place throughout the spring 2011, coordinating where, when, and how to strike simply by making it an event on Facebook or posting it on Twitter. Their use in coordinating revolts was so effective it forced the government in Egypt to shut down all Internet access around the country in an attempt to cut off rebel coordination.

Another crucial change stems from the fact that tiny digital cameras are now being built into mobile phones and other handheld devices. Once upon a time, nothing got filmed unless there was a camera team there prepared to shoot the footage. Now the news can be collected by anyone.

This use of the new media was graphically and tragically illustrated on June 20, 2009, when crowds gathered in Tehran to protest against the repressive Iranian government. Apparently fired by a police sniper, a shot rang out and a lovely young woman named Neda Agha-Soltan fell down dead. The whole dreadful scene was recorded by someone with a mobile phone, who flashed it around the world on the Internet.[31] The footage told the world more about Iran's dictatorship than could a million newspaper editorials.

3. Evaluating the News and Thinking about the Media

Social critic Marshall McLuhan once predicted that communication technology would someday create a global village in which we would all be connected to one another. Technology has gone a long way toward the creation of McLuhan's "global village," but we still sometimes have problems finding out what's happening in other parts of the world. In the following section, we'll look at a series of problems created by "merger mania" in the media establishment, by attempts by interest groups to control or "spin" the news, and by the effect nationalist or patriotic feelings can have on news reporting. And finally, we'll ask ourselves how much trust we can place in the news that comes to us from television, radio, and the Internet.[32]

Ultimately, we all need better access to quality information about the planet. We'll conclude this chapter with a look at an appropriate "news diet."

The WGIS Factor

Political scientists like to devise confusing acronyms for simple concepts. Let's create the WGIS (White-Guys-in-Suits) Factor to describe the tendency (common in Europe and North America) to view the world exclusively from the perspective of the prosperous Caucasian males who dominate the communications industry in particular and society in general. Television sometimes seems to express the WGIS perspective to the exclusion of all other points of view. For example, the media watch group FAIR (Fairness and Accuracy in Reporting) did a classic study of Ted Koppel's *Nightline*. Over a period of forty months (865 programs and 2,498 guests), 90 percent of Koppel's political guests were male, 95.5 percent were Caucasian, and nearly 100 percent were American citizens. A similar study was done on the Fox News Service, which produced similar results, except that the White Guys in Suits were overwhelmingly members of the Republican Party. The next time you hear that we must be doing great because the stock market or the gross domestic product is up, remember the WGIS Factor; if you're not a white guy in a suit, it may not make a lot of difference.

Note: See Fairness and Accuracy in Reporting at http://www.fair.org/index.php.

MEDIA MADNESS: PROBLEMS WITH THE NEWS

The last two decades have seen several major changes in the way news and information about the world come to us, not all of them entirely positive. Once it was possible to make a valid distinction between electronic journalism (radio and television) and the print media (newspapers and magazines). They were different approaches to journalism, employing different technologies and generally different people.

The 1980s, however, saw the development of generic information companies linked by the Internet that supply information to a wide range of different customers. Radio, television, magazines, and newspapers all began to purchase their news from the same relatively small range of sources. Furthermore, there is a distinct tendency for a wide variety of what seem to be different information sources to be owned by the same restricted group of companies. Their names will be familiar: Time-Warner, Hollywood's Disney, Rupert Murdoch's Australia-based News Corporation, Viacom, Japan's Sony Corporation, Germany's Bertelsmann, and the French Vivendi/Universal. Companies like these have been called the "Lords of the Global Village."

We are not accusing these media conglomerates of journalistic malpractice, but their senior management teams answer to tens of thousands of individual stockholders who demand profits in return for their investments. This means that crucial decisions will be made by accountants with an eye on the bottom line of a spreadsheet, not by crusading journalists who are prepared to take a chance to bring you some crucial (but perhaps uncomfortable) piece of news. As giant corporations, they have economic interests all over the map, and it is difficult to separate them. If the Hearst-owned William Morrow Company publishes a really awful book, will it get an appropriately awful review in the Hearst-owned *Esquire Magazine*?[33]

The discipline of critical media studies, primarily based in communications departments in U.S. universities with overlap in political science, sociology, and psychology departments studies the impacts of corporate ownership and advertising on politics, economics, and society. More recently, critical media studies have analyzed the role of new media, such as YouTube, Twitter, and Facebook, on political events, such as the Arab Spring and U.S. voting patterns. This group of scholars, which highlights Noam Chomsky from MIT as a leader in the field, examines corporate ownership of the media and the production of knowledge in democratic societies. While listening to CNN may give you the news coverage you think you need, reading Chomsky's work might make you take a second look at the TV screen or the front page of the *Washington Post*.[34]

And the role of government also needs to be considered. It has often been said that, in war, truth is the first casualty. When we try to use the media to follow a conflict somewhere in the world, we need to tread carefully, because the parties to the quarrel will both attempt to use a sometimes pliant press to bolster their respective positions. There are several general ways this can happen: the provision of information that is accidentally or deliberately inaccurate, censorship, the "**spinning**" of the news, and an overly intense focus on domestic news.

• Misinformation: From terrorist groups to sovereign governments, organizations occasionally generate wildly inaccurate information and disseminate it to the press, often with authoritative assurances that the data are correct. To err is human, and occasionally someone adds up the numbers incorrectly without a specific intent to deceive. In politically charged situations, however, it can be difficult to believe that a mistake is an honest one.

For example, on July 3, 1988, the U.S. Navy shot down an Iranian passenger aircraft, killing 290 people. In a televised press briefing delivered by Admiral William Crowe, then chairman of the Joint Chiefs of Staff, the U.S. government blamed the incident on the Iranian government. In the fullness of time, every substantive statement made by this bluff old sailor turned out to be wrong, including some "facts" he must have known at the time to be incorrect. The accident was the responsibility of the U.S. Navy, which had managed to mistake a passenger aircraft making a scheduled flight over international waters for an attacking Iranian fighter jet.

Sometimes a false news story can linger for a generation before it is exposed. Back in the 1950s, the Pentagon believed that President Eisenhower was spending too little on strategic missiles. In fact, the United States enjoyed a twenty-to-one missile advantage over the USSR, but rumors were deliberately leaked to the *New York Times* that we had fallen behind the Russians in nuclear striking power. John Kennedy used the rumor to help win the 1960 presidential elections, and by the time the *New York Times* admitted its error, Eisenhower and JFK were long in their respective graves.

In the aftermath of the September 11 attacks, the American government suggested openly that Osama bin Laden and Iraq's president Saddam Hussein had conspired to attack the United States. Since bin Laden and Hussein were each other's worst enemies, the linkage was inherently improbable, and no evidence has ever emerged of collusion between America's two least-favorite Arabs. Long afterward, however, most Americans still believed that Iraq was involved in the devastating 9/11 assault.

One closely related problem is the growth in "not-for-attribution" stories in the media. There have always been times when a senior government official wanted a story—true or not—to be disseminated without leaving a trail back to the source. These leaks have often been important for the breaking of huge stories such as the Watergate scandal. In recent years, however, the percentage of "not-for-attribution" stories has increased so dramatically that a substantial amount of our news comes indirectly from government officials or intelligence agencies that are not prepared to be identified with the "information" they have generated. At best, these "leaks" slant the news to reflect the views of specific politicians; at worst, they are deliberate attempts to misinform the public.

- Censorship: Another problem is censorship. If one party to a conflict is a sovereign government, it may use its security or military forces to prevent journalists from getting access to the news. During the 1990–1991 Persian Gulf War, for example, the American government controlled and manipulated an all-too-willing press. Pentagon policy had shifted enormously by the Iraq War twelve years later, when the U.S. government decided to "embed" reporters within actual combat units. The spectacle of TV journalists dodging bullets on the front lines gave viewers the sense of presence and participation. While the practice has many advantages, embedded reporters tended to self-identify with their units, and military commanders were able to control the flow and character of news reports.

  Sometimes censorship is aimed at preventing the press from printing unfavorable information; in other cases, it can involve punishing a journalist after the publication of a story that displeased the government. In 2002, the central African country of Zimbabwe endured a tumultuous election during which President Robert Mugabe blatantly cooked the electoral books in a successful drive to retain power. His parliament obligingly passed legislation making it illegal to criticize the president, and the security forces promptly locked up journalists who tried honestly to cover a dishonest election. One hundred ten reporters were murdered in 2009 for attempting to do their job. Too many governments resort to shooting the messenger in order to kill the message.[35]

- Spinning: A less-violent way of shaping reality is a practice sometimes called "spinning." There is nothing very subtle about slapping a journalist in prison; in democracies, governments, corporations, and activist groups normally try to influence the news with less-emphatic techniques. Officials are said to be spinning the news when they brief journalists, often "off-the-record," in an attempt to put the best possible light on a breaking story. Spinning the news is often accomplished by arranging a private interview between a senior official and a favored or sympathetic journalist. The chat may be a formal public interview, an off-the-record conversation, or a covert telephonic leak, but the reward for the journalist is a good story. In return, the government's position is normally treated with some sympathy.

A classic example of a spin occurred in the 2008 presidential campaign. The North American Free Trade Agreement (NAFTA) opened up commerce among the United States and Canada and Mexico, pleasing most Americans but upsetting some labor and commercial interests in the protectionist Midwest. When campaigning there in 2008, candidate Obama suggested that NAFTA needed to be renegotiated. When the Canadians began to fret, Obama economics advisor Dr. Austan Goolsbe met privately with them, explaining (accurately) that the candidate's statement "should be viewed as more about political positioning than a clear articulation of policy plans."[36] Goolsbe's spin cycle worked; his candidate went on to win the election; and President Obama never did reopen the question of free trade in North America.

Examples like these are not hard to find: the violent antagonisms between Israelis and Palestinians continue to involve ceaseless efforts on both sides to spin the news. Israeli governmental spokesmen insist that Palestinian violence is terrorism, while Israeli violence is legitimate law enforcement. The Palestinians desperately spin back, arguing that the violence is killing many more Arabs than Israelis and portraying themselves as an embattled and persecuted people defending their ancestral territory in the West Bank and Gaza. The Israeli spin generally works for Americans who have traditionally been pro-Israeli. Europeans often believe that the Palestinian view is more persuasive. Spinning the facts of a conflict is easier than solving it, however, and most consumers of media products continue to find the quarrel a confusing one.

- Nationalism: In the United States, news about America can often obliterate news about the rest of the world. There is nothing abnormal about being interested in your own country. RAI-TV, for example, tells Italians what's happening in their corner of the Mediterranean before moving on to the European Union, and then the rest of the world. Britain's BBC produces stories about the queen and the prime minister before shifting to North America, Africa, and Asia. However, because they believe that their audiences are interested in the rest of the world, the European and Asian media spend a lot of time on international stories, accepting that what happens in the world beyond their borders is critically important to them.

U.S. news media, however, tend to focus overwhelmingly on domestic American concerns. American television and print reporters will venture abroad when American interests are threatened overseas or the American armed forces are in action in some foreign military intervention, but many half-hour newscasts will contain no overseas news at all. When something dramatic occurs abroad, an international story appears suddenly and briefly before abruptly disappearing.

WHAT CAN WE BELIEVE?

Thus far, we have discussed what are essentially mainstream news sources, and a critical but steady reliance on these sources will keep you in tune with what is sometimes called the mainstream or conventional wisdom. It might or might not be true, but it is the *New York Times* version of reality. You read it over breakfast in the morning, and so do the folks in the White House, so if the *Times* gets it wrong, at least you're in good company. Let's pause for a moment, however, to look at some alternative-reality news sources not everybody reads. Then, to avoid becoming too skeptical about the news business, we'll look at two journalists who have actually done some brilliant reporting in recent years. Then we'll ask ourselves some very general questions about our "information diet."

Alternative News Sources

There are groups in every society that reject the conventional wisdom of the mainstream in favor of specialized news sources, and these alternative versions of reality need to be considered. For example, evangelical or fundamentalist Christian news sources sometimes work in tandem with those who hold ultraconservative political perspectives. American talk radio, for example, has offered hospitality to commentators who offer a vision of America and the world that is difficult to reconcile with the mainstream reality perceived by conventional politicians, professors, and political pundits.

Most of us spend too much of our lives behind the wheel, and talk radio is a comfortable way of waiting out a traffic jam. This is also another instance where the use of iPods and MP3 players containing podcasts are relevant. Most car manufacturers are building cars with auxiliary inputs that allow people to plug these devices into their radios with a simple cord.

Evangelical and fundamentalist news sources, for example, operate from a specifically religious perspective, rejecting much of the information generated by major universities, governments, and mainstream book and magazine publishers. Instead, they regard information as correct if it conforms to scriptural sources like the Bible or the Koran.

The most prominent example of a successful and influential "fringe" talk-show host might be radio chat-show commentator Rush Limbaugh, whose passionate message reflects the views of the right wing of the Republican Party. While he seems to care little about the world beyond America's borders, Limbaugh's relentless abuse of liberals resonates with conservatives across the country, and his listeners remained faithful even after he underwent treatment in 2003 for drug addiction.

There is, of course, an important religious content to much of the news. Many Israeli citizens, for example, believe that the deed to Judea and Samara (biblical terms for what is today called the West Bank) was granted to them by God. If you are ignorant of the book of Genesis, you will miss their point. Unfortunately, if you know only Genesis, you may fail to see many other perspectives, since few mainstream analysts think that the complicated skein of Middle Eastern politics can be unraveled solely on the basis of one religious text. In India, Muslims and Hindus have engaged in deadly conflicts over a ruined temple site in Avodhya, each side basing its claim to this real estate on separate ancient books that are sacred to one side and not the other.

Other alternate realities are provided by those on the fringes of the right and the left. These organizations range from racist groups such as the Ku Klux Klan and the Aryan Nation to political groups such as the anticommunist John Birch Society and some militia clubs, many of whom see world politics as an interlocking clutch of conspiracies. There is, for example, a pervasive belief among some ultraconservatives that liberal conspirators have yielded American sovereignty to the United Nations, allowing international bureaucrats to command U.S. armed forces.

Similarly, European and Latin American Marxist groups have often immersed themselves in "hard left" political literature, a process that in some cases has led them to embrace terrorism as a political tool. Interviews with captured European terrorists reveal that they had largely given up paying any attention to mainstream media and were operating cognitively on the basis of the writings of fellow activists who were as ill informed as they were.[37]

Having jumped into world news, we need to think briefly about ways of evaluating what we see, hear, and read. In philosophy, this is called **epistemology**, the business of asking questions such as these: How do I know what is really true? Am I being conned by the press and the politicians? Does that professor behind the lectern actually understand what's going on? There is a difference between being cynical and skeptical. It is cheap and easy to be universally cynical, assuming that all politicians are crooks and all journalists are ignorant. Since some politicians are honest, and journalists do occasionally get it right on the nose, we need to work toward a healthy, balanced skepticism.

Parallel Lives: Christiane Amanpour and Marie Colvin

This critique of journalism might leave readers with the impression that writers and reporters are all servants of big business who are less interested in truth than corporate profits. In fact, there are some extraordinarily competent journalists operating today, and their reporting has materially improved the quality of our understanding of the political world. While they were very different in personal style and approach, two of the best were Christiane Amanpour (who works both for CNN and ABC) and the late Marie Colvin of the *London Sunday Times*.

These two hard-working journalists had a few things in common. They were arguably the two most famous contemporary war correspondents. They both studied in the United States (Amanpour did journalism at the University of Rhode

Island, and Colvin majored in English at Yale). Within a few months of the same age, they were friends and both covered wars (often the same wars) for the past two decades. Both women focused on the politics of conflict and the effects of war on civilians; neither displayed much interest in military strategy or weapons systems. They both systematically took physical risks by going to dangerous places to report important stories.

Growing up in London, Christiane Amanpour is the daughter of an Iranian father and a British mother, a family that gave her both a taste for internationalism and a distinctive accent. After she graduated from college, she began a brilliant television career as a foreign correspondent, covering virtually every international crisis since 1983 when she started work for CNN. Amanpour is a scholarly journalist who appears to understand the issues at an unusually sophisticated level.

Her real fame began in the 1990s when Yugoslavia broke up, and Muslim peoples began to be slaughtered in Bosnia; see chapter 11 for the details. Focused on domestic concerns, the Clinton administration initially ignored the crisis, hoping it would go away, or be resolved by the European Union. Describing her as "utterly fearless," commentator David Halberstam remembers her "exceptional sensitivity to the plight of ordinary people caught in the pull of cruel historical forces" and notes, "She did not believe that being a good reporter in a time of genocide meant neutrality."[38] In a relentless series of broadcasts from the besieged Bosnian capital of Sarajevo, Amanpour kept the spotlight on the suffering endured by women and children. In a televised interview with President Clinton, she bluntly accused him of stalling on the issue. Clinton bristled at the accusation, but the resulting attention helped lead to U.S. involvement in Bosnia and the 1995 Dayton Accords.

Amanpour's top-level interviews with political leaders around the world have continued to change global political perspectives. Her remarkable 1997 dialogue with Iran's then president Khatami, for example, is regarded as pivotal in the West's perception of Iranian politics.

While Ms. Amanpour is a British woman employed by an American company, Marie Colvin was a feisty American who wrote for Britain's *Sunday Times*. While she did some notable television work, Colvin was primarily a writer who specialized in battlefield coverage. Amanpour and Colvin both represented prestigious newsgathering organizations, but their operating styles were different. Christiane Amanpour has become an establishment figure whose interviews are edgy but ultimately polite. Marie Colvin, in contrast, was a journalistic guerrilla warrior; for a famous PBS *Frontline* program, Ms. Colvin badgered the late Yassir Arafat so relentlessly that the PLO chieftain threatened her on camera and ultimately terminated the interview in a fury.

Ms. Colvin found most of her stories in war zones with soldiers and civilians caught up in tumultuous situations. In pursuit of hard-to-get information, she routinely displayed almost suicidal levels of courage. In 1999, East Timor (then part of Indonesia) degenerated into complete mayhem over the issue of independence. As marauding gangs began massacring civilians in the capital city of Dilli, almost all foreigners left. Partly because she wanted the story and partly to protect with her presence a large group of women and children sheltering with her in an abandoned UN compound, Colvin stayed behind. During the worst days of the fighting, she was the only senior Western correspondent on the ground to tell the story.

Two years later in Sri Lanka, she covered the civil war that was raging between Hindu Tamils in the North and the Buddhist-dominated Sinhalese government in Colombo (see chapter 11 for the background). The Sri Lankan government attempted to isolate the Tamil Tigers by forbidding journalists to travel through the rebel-held North, but Marie Colvin slipped into enemy territory to gather material for her story. On the way out, she was caught in an ambush, losing an eye to shrapnel from a hand grenade. In 2002, wearing her famous eye patch, she infiltrated the Palestinian city of Ramallah while it was being attacked by Israeli forces, only to be jolted by a stun grenade thrown at her by angry Israeli troops. In 2005, she explored the clandestine channels of communication between the Gaza Strip and Egypt by crawling through a tiny and dangerous tunnel dug by HAMAS supporters to bring weapons into what was then Israeli-controlled territory. The year 2011 found her in the besieged city of Misrata as the Libyan government battled with insurgents there.

To the enormous sadness of the journalistic community, her luck ran out in February of 2012. She was covering the Syrian government's brutal, even genocidal, repression of anti-regime protesters in the city of Homs. Slipping illegally into the city on the back of a motorbike, Marie Colvin reported on the unfolding massacre as the Syrian Army brutally shelled civilian neighborhoods. "Sickening. Cannot understand how the world can stand by and I should be hardened by now," Marie Colvin wrote to her editor from an impromptu clinic, "Watched a baby die today. Shrapnel. Doctors could do nothing. His little tummy just heaved and heaved until he stopped. Feeling helpless . . . will keep trying to get out the information."[39] On February 22, the Syrians—perhaps deliberately—fired an artillery shell directly into the apartment where she was sheltering with some other reporters, abruptly silencing the most passionate journalistic voice of a generation.

Are you as smart as Christiane Amanpour or as brave as Marie Colvin? What made these two women representative of the best of Western journalism is personal integrity, physical courage, the ability to empathize equally with princes and paupers, a capacity to use the language forcefully and well, and—perhaps most important—an ability to understand and explain complex political realities. If you can develop any of these characteristics, then perhaps you should contemplate a career as a foreign correspondent.

Designing Your Personal News Diet

This may sound like a nutritionist talking about the four basic food groups, but you need to balance and select your news intake in a way that relates reasonably to your need for news and your personal lifestyle. Unless you are terribly wealthy, you will also want to compare prices, since all news costs something and some information sources are terribly expensive. In ordering up your news diet, try to combine the four ingredients listed below.

Designing Your Personal News Diet

1. Daily News Appetizer: Choose a serious news broadcast like National Public Radio every morning at 7:00 a.m. or (if you absolutely cannot break the television habit) the *NewsHour with Jim Lehrer* every night over dinner.
2. A Quality Newspaper Main Course: Remember, to contain as much cognitive nutrition as an hour of National Public Radio, your newspaper is going to have to be very tasty indeed. Sample the *New York Times* or the *Washington Post*.
3. International Salad: To see the world as others see it, make sure there is some imported produce in your diet. Choose the *Guardian Weekly* or Radio Moscow or the BBC World Service or (if you have the linguistic skills) a weekly newsmagazine from another language culture, like *L'Express* from Paris or *Panorama* from Italy. For a fresh look at the Israeli-Palestinian conflict, get the Arab perspective from the *Middle East Review* or a conservative Israeli viewpoint from the *Jerusalem Post*.
4. One Dissident Dessert: A steady diet of conventional wisdom can cause severe mainstream indigestion, so try something spicy from time to time. Sip *The Nation* until you think you might be a socialist, and then digest a few issues of the *National Review* to remind yourself of the virtues of capitalism. If you find yourself still trusting the *New York Times,* have a curative helping of *Mother Jones* or *Harpers*.

---

4. The Wrap: What Have We Learned?

Are you less confused about why you're confused? Putting it another way, you should by now have a sense of the ingredients of world politics, understanding how geography, history, and the social sciences all combine to help us focus on a given issue or area. There wasn't much terminology in this chapter, but there are lots of acronyms and abbreviations and special terminology headed your way, and part of the intellectual task of learning about world politics is mastering the language of political science. We've made the point that no course and no textbook on politics can compensate for a lifetime of ignoring the affairs of the planet. If you've decided that it's time for you to become politically literate, we've provided some suggestions about using media to stay connected to the world.

You should now understand the relationship between wire services and newspapers, and be aware of some of the benefits and dangers of global information services. There are no right or wrong answers here, and the point of this chapter was merely to get you to think about your global cognitive intake and try a new diet if you're intellectually undernourished. There's more at stake than just passing a course; if you're going to hang around on this planet for a while, you really need to know what's going on.

We've introduced for you several different resources available in today's media-infused world. You can choose to be more traditional by listening to the radio and reading the newspaper or magazines. You can find your news on television, where you have the choice of different networks covering the news from different perspectives. Or finally, you can get your daily dose from social media websites like Facebook, which you can access from both your computer or even from your cellular phone, and customize your preferences so you receive the news you want to receive.

If nothing else, this chapter should have acquainted you with the intellectual dangers of relying solely on television to meet your informational needs. You should by now know what the alternatives are in terms of print media like national newspapers and periodical newsmagazines, as well as public radio and short-wave radio. Chances are you're an old hand at search engines and websites, but if you are a cyber-incompetent, get busy. Your university library probably has programs and facilities to get you surfing the net in pursuit of political wisdom, but you need to walk in the front door and ask.

Next stop? In chapter 2, we'll take a preliminary look at the field of political science, which is the scholarly approach to the study of politics.

Notes

1. Lewis Carroll, *Alice's Adventures in Wonderland* (Boston: Lee and Shepard, 1869), 100–101.

2. See the United Nations website at www.un.org; see the UNMOVIC website at www.unmovic.org; the IAEA can be located at www.iaea.org.

3. Organization for Economic Cooperation and Development, www.oecd.org.

4. The U.S. Central Intelligence Agency (CIA), www.cia.gov.

5. James Bamford, *Body of Secrets* (New York: Anchor, 2002), 474–75.

6. Richard K. Betts, "Fixing Intelligence," *Foreign Affairs* 81, no.1 (2002): 43–59.

7. National Geographic Society, www.nationalgeographic.com.

8. The Roper Public Affairs—National Geographic Education Foundation, "2006 Geographic Literacy Study," (Washington, D.C.: The National Geographic Education Foundation, 2006).

9. The World Trade Organization, www.wto.org.

10. *The Associated Press*, www.ap.org; *Reuters*, www.reuters.com; *United Press International*, www.upi.com.

11. For information about the rest of the world, start with the U.S. Department of State at http://www.state.gov before moving on to the CIA's site at www.cia.gov. The CIA's unclassified World Fact Book is located at https://www.cia.gov/library/publications/the-world-factbook (the site is encrypted, so in order to access it directly from this address you must type https://), but some entries are out of date and all publications by the United States or any other government reflect the bias of the administration in power.

12. Stanley J. Baran, *Introduction to Mass Communications* (Mountain View, Calif.: Mayfield, 2001), 111–17.

13. Benjamin Barber, *Jihad vs. McWorld* (New York: Random House, 1995), 123.

14. For a listing of non-U.S. newspapers available online, check out www.newspapers.com/ and click on "International." A similar site is www.thelocalpapers.com.

15. The *New York Times* on the Web is www.nytimes.com; the *Washington Post* online edition is www.washingtonpost.com.

16. Glance at http://www.lemonde.fr. *Le Monde* is France's answer to the *New York Times* and it's—of course—*en français*. Britain's combative *Guardian* has a popular website at www.guardian.co.uk.

17. Find the *Atlanta Constitution* at www.ajc.com, and the *L.A. Times* at www.latimes.com.

18. The Council on Foreign Relations publishes the venerable bimonthly *Foreign Affairs* to tell you what the establishment is thinking. Somewhat more academic in tone, Princeton University's *World Politics: A Quarterly Journal of International Relations* is worth reading. Published nine times a year, *Current History*

is the best way to bridge the gap between history-book history (several years old before it hits the stands) and yesterday's newspapers. Each issue focuses on a region of the world or a hot topic in contemporary history and a series of well-written and easy-to-read articles by top experts. Check out their website at www .currenthistory.com.

19. Dan Rather, *Deadlines & Datelines* (New York: Morrow, 1999), 161.

20. Ken Auletta, "Battle Stations: How Long Will the Networks Stick with the News?" *The New Yorker*, December 10, 2001, 61.

21. Jerry Mander, *Four Arguments for the Elimination of Television* (New York: William Morrow, 1974).

22. M. McLuhan, *Understanding Media: The Extensions of Man* (New York: McGraw-Hill, 1964).

23. Auletta, "Battle Stations: How Long Will the Networks Stick with the News?" 61.

24. Robert O. Keohane and Joseph S. Nye, *Power and Interdependence*, 3rd ed. (New York: Longman, 2001), 224.

25. Many major communications companies distribute a portion of their product for free via the Internet. Perhaps the most-visited site for international news is CNN's www.cnn.com. Fox News (www.foxnews.com) provides news and commentary for people who hate the entire Clinton family. The AP (www.ap.org) makes its money by selling news to paying customers; so it doesn't give you much for free, nor does Reuters at www.reuters.com. See www.washingtonpost.com for a lot of well-organized wire-service content. The British Broadcasting Corporation (http://news.bbc.co.uk) not only relays stories from the BBC news service, but also leads you to schedules and programming information. It also allows you to hear the BBC on your computer. National Public Radio (www.npr.org) provides not only schedules for NPR high-quality radio programming but also text versions of NPR news stories.

26. National Public Radio, www.npr.org.

27. Keohane and Nye, *Power and Interdependence*, 224.

28. The Internet has given us a variety of high quality and sometimes radical magazines that exist only in cyberspace. Microsoft's Slate Magazine (http://slate.msn.com) is mainstream and competent. For the anthologized commentary of America's most serious naysayers, see the Independent Media Institute's Alternet at www.alternet.org. Common Dreams (www.commondreams.org) is similar in inspiration.

29. Find Amnesty International at www.amnesty.org and Greenpeace at www.greenpeace.org.

30. Social-media websites: www.facebook.com, www.twitter.com, www.youtube.com.

31. See http://www.youtube.com/watch?v=CfrfEtW2aT4.

32. Accuracy in Media (www.aim.org) hunts for evidence of what it regards as an automatic liberal bias in the press, while the rival Fairness and Accuracy in Reporting (www.fair.org) worries about tilts to the right. The *Columbia Journalism Review* is both a respected magazine and a popular website (www.cjr.org), providing a neutral, scholarly view of the issue. Reporters sans Frontières is an activist group demanding intellectual freedom and physical safety for journalists; see www.rsf.org.

33. Ben H. Bagdikian is the leading critic of the commercial structures behind the production of news and his *The Media Monopoly: With a New Preface on the Internet and Telecommunications Cartels*, 6th ed. (Boston, Mass.: Beacon Press, 2001) is a classic in the field. Also look at an older but still pertinent book by Martin A. Lee and Norman Solomon called *Unreliable Sources: A Guide to Detecting Bias in New Media* (New York: Lyle Stuart, 1991). The following texts are all relevant: John R. MacArthur, *Second Front: Censorship and Propaganda in the Gulf War* (Berkeley, Calif.: University of California Press, 1993); Robert Waterman McChesney, *Rich Media, Poor Democracy: Communication Politics in Dubious Times* (Champaign, Ill.: University of Illinois Press, 1999); Jan P. Vermeer, ed., *In "Media" Res: Readings in Mass Media and American Politics* (New York: McGraw Hill, 1995). A classic look at reporters and war is Phillip Knightley's *First Casualty: From the Crimea to Vietnam* (New York: Harcourt Brace, 1975). Paul Ginsborg has described how the media in otherwise-democratic Italy fell almost exclusively under the control of its richest man in his *Silvio Berlusconi: Television, Power, and Patrimony* (New York: Verso, 2004). Another classic in the field is James Fallows' *Breaking the News: How the Media Undermine American Democracy* (New York: Vintage, 1997). A pessimistic James Ledbetter suggests that even NPR isn't that good anymore in his *Made Possible By: The Death of Public Broadcasting in the United States* (New York: Verso, 2005).

34. For an interesting look at Chomsky's work, try Noam Chomsky, *9–11: Was There an Alternative?* new ed. (New York: Seven Stories Press, 2011).

35. Anthony Mills, *Press Freedom in an Age of Barbarity*, WPFR: Global Overview, IPI, (February 9, 2010), http://www.freemedia.at/publications/world-press-freedom-review/singleview/4761/ (accessed November 1, 2011) .

36. See *The Slate*, http://www.slate.com/id/2185753/.

37. Richard Oliver Collin, "When Reality Came Unglued: Antonio Savasta and the Red Brigades," *Violence Aggression Terrorism* 3, no. 4 (1989): 269–96 (reprinted in Bernard Schechterman and Martin Slann, *Annual Editions: Violence and Terrorism 91/92* [Washington: Dushkin, 1991]); Richard Oliver Collin, "When Irish Eyes Stop Smiling," *International Counterterrorism*, Winter 1990/1991: 18–26.

38. David Halberstam, *War in a Time of Peace: Bush, Clinton, and the Generals* (New York: Scribner, 2001), 165–66.

39. *The Guardian*, "Marie Colvin," February 23, 2012, 18.

CHAPTER 2

Levels of Analysis

THE PEOPLE, PLACES, AND THINGS WE STUDY

1. How the Professionals Do It

POLITICAL SCIENCE

Political science is the central organizing academic discipline involved in the analysis of governments, political movements, and the ordering of public affairs. While authors since Aristotle have contemplated the political universe, political science flowered as a distinct and important area of scholarly endeavor only in the early twentieth century. Today, every university campus in the United States and Europe has a department of political science staffed by professors with doctorates in that specialization. In the United States, there are several national organizations, of which the American Political Science Association (APSA) is the best known, and there are lots of academic journals dedicated to the scholarly study of the political universe.[1] Around the world, virtually every university has an analogous department, although not everyone believes that political "science" is really a science, and some institutions prefer to call it simply "politics" or "government." Wherever they work, scholars in this field sometimes differ about how best to approach their subject, and we'll explore some of these disagreements below.

At the global level, political scientists and others who study international politics, organizations, economics, movements, and cultures gather professionally through the International Studies Association (ISA) and its regional affiliates around the world.[2] This association is a reflection of the multidisciplinary approach that you will see is needed to study the world today. Scholars who study the international landscape look at environmental issues that require knowledge of climate change and science; those who study how politics and economics intersect will need a background in economic and financial institutions; and those who are interested in the politics of a particular region of the world or country will need to learn its language and cultural practices before they delve into that area's politics, economics, and social systems. If the world interests you, or even if you are the slightest bit curious about things global, you will quickly realize that understanding the governmental structure of a country is only a small part of explaining its politics.

If political science involves the study of "politics," surely we ought to be able to offer a simple definition of this commonly used word. Unfortunately, there seems to be an iron law of scholarship that the more important something is, the harder it is to define and the less helpful our definition will be when we finally concoct it.[3] Can we produce a precise definition of happiness? How about love? Perhaps not, but we can recognize love and happiness when they're happening to us.

Conflict is one of the core concepts in the study of politics, and some famous scholars have produced enigmatic definitions to illustrate this point. Political systems deal with conflict by making binding decisions about the division of resources, a concept David Easton expressed in his famous one-liner: "Politics is the authoritative allocation of values." While Easton's formulation is actually very profound, those seventeen obscure syllables might (at the Politics 101 level) make less sense than a Japanese haiku.[4] Harold D. Lasswell's equally famous dictum that politics is "who gets what, when, and how" is linguistically neat but might not kick-start our investigation of the field.[5] Let's start with something simple. At least for the purposes of this book, "politics" is the set of structures and procedures human societies use to order or organize public affairs and moderate conflict. Politics can include issues of public goods, such as health and education, or private issues, such as marriage and religion. We'll take a look at the contestability of politics below.

Of course, avoiding and/or resolving conflict toward peace is the primary goal of scholars in this field. Some scholars, namely John Mearsheimer or George Quester, would argue that peace can never be attained and security can only be guaranteed through managed nuclear weapon systems.[6] Those who disagree argue that peace and security can be attained through cooperative organizations, such as the European Union.[7] Still other scholars view a peaceful world as attainable through citizen organizations and social movements and see the future of democracy as global citizenship and cosmopolitanism.[8] Ultimately, everyone wants to live in a free and secure world. The challenge of studying international politics is understanding the road blocks on the way toward such a goal and clearly defining how you view yourself within the larger global landscape. Are you a global citizen? How do world politics and the peoples of other countries affect you?

More basically, the definition of politics involves the questionable assumption that we can create precise distinctions between public and private. For example, sex ought to be the most private thing we can do, and yet there is even public conflict about what goes on between the sheets: abortion, birth control, homosexuality, and marriage are all subjects of legislation and controversy in every human society. Governments have always made rules about sexual behavior, but no one had ever gone quite so far as the ruler of Swaziland. Concerned about the AIDS epidemic in his African kingdom, King Mswati III ordered all Swazi girls to practice abstinence for five years, making an exception only for his own large harem of wives.

Yet the public and private blurs even in areas that seem, at first, clear-cut. For example, Virginia Haufler, in her book entitled *A Public Role for the Private Sector*, finds that multinational corporations (MNCs), once thought of as solely in the realm of the private (profit-producing) sector, do provide social and very public goods to people— such as schools, potable water, and malaria nets.[9] For example, bond-ratings agencies are private companies that rate the level of risk of investment in a company or country. If a bond-rating agency drops the rating of investment in a country (as happened to the United States in the summer of 2011), typically the country's economy is impacted. This, in turn, affects political elections and policies in the country. Likewise, an oil company like Shell in Nigeria, which has had a controversial history, might sponsor a school for Ogoni peoples or provide scholarships to university. It might also use Nigerian military forces to protect its oil fields. These activities go beyond the realm of profit making for companies and directly affect politics and peoples. This begins the debate that Hall and Biersteker (2002) and others in political science have considered: what is public and what is private nowadays in the international realm?[10]

Benjamin Barber, in his book *Consumed*, finds that the most innocent and private members of our planet, our children, are inundated with advertising from game, toy, and clothing companies, going so far as to value brand over all else.[11] David Vogel, on the other hand, sees virtue in the market place as MNCs increasingly provide social and environmental benefits.[12] Still, Yale theologian Harvey Cox views "the market as God." Cox criticizes the invasion of the market into our lives and argues that the market itself has become a religion and CEOs are its ministers.[13] You may disagree with these views, but understanding your place within them will help you navigate the waters of world economics and politics, and their intersection. When Pamela Martin went to a small Ecuadorian Amazonian town, called Shushufindi, to view oil extraction sites, she noticed schools that were built by oil companies and indigenous peoples who dressed in Adidas T-shirts and Nike sneakers. Have the politics of the market blurred our most private of values—family, cultural, and spiritual? We'll seek answers to this question and others throughout this book.

GLOBALIZATION AND WORLD POLITICS

We've just introduced you to a few terms within the alphabet soup that political scientists use to more clearly define the players in the game of international affairs. The study of world politics today requires an understanding of the globe that is quite different (some would argue) from what was required during the nineteenth century. To be sure, today we communicate more quickly than ever before, using Facebook, Twitter, and YouTube to not only interact socially but to display real-time world politics to the global stage. We can also travel more easily to a greater range of destinations, allowing more citizens of the world to connect with others. All of this is facilitated by technology and financial flows that have outpaced previous decades and seem to be advancing at lightning speed. This interconnectedness will be illustrated throughout this book and is characterized by the term **globalization**. We will discuss globalization in more detail later in this book, but the process that defines it—interconnectedness across peoples and places that increases the effects of events and ideas on us all—is the prime reason world politics cannot be easily placed in a box that separates what statesmen and diplomats do from what protesters in the streets do. This process of linking the individual in her respective state to the global is often referred to as *glocal* politics, or as we will later call it, *intermestic* politics.[14]

Given the complex web of connections that binds us all, possibly as global citizens in some senses, it helps to provide a context to the connections and the levels at which we can and do interact. Globalization is often viewed by scholars and policy makers through three lenses: (1) the political, (2) the economic, and (3) the social. In the political arena, states and citizens interact through international treaties, such as the Law of the Sea, as well as through international institutions, such as the United Nations.[15] At the economic level, we interact on a daily basis through financial institutions. Banks are global as they invest their funds in bonds and stocks around the world. That means your hard-earned cash may be invested in bonds to pay the debt of another country. Likewise, other countries buy U.S. debt in the form of U.S. Treasury bonds. Loans are given out through the **World Bank** and the **International Monetary Fund (IMF)**, and international trade negotiations occur through the **World Trade Organization** (WTO).[16] The largest group of economies around the world, the G-20, sets policies in place that can affect our economy at home.[17] Finally, societal globalization is so prevalent that oftentimes we miss its subtleties. University students in London and New York often read the same newspapers and blogs online and listen to the same music on their iPods. Increasingly, our students are familiar with both Hollywood and Bollywood (India's burgeoning film industry) movies and their actors. Questions around these incipient forms of influence surround the literature on globalization, including whether such societal influences impact cultures and traditions. Some argue that today's War on Terror is a response to Western societal impacts on Muslim cultures, while others argue that such influences are as old as the spice routes of the Middle Ages. Questions like these will be examined throughout the book.

2. Viewing the World

LEVELS OF ANALYSIS

While globalization is connecting us in many ways, the world can still be divided, in some sense, into levels, what academics typically call levels of analysis. These levels are ways to view the world hierarchically from bottom to top or vice versa. Traditionally, scholars have viewed the world from the individual level to the state (or national) level and on to the international level, as displayed below in figure 2.1. The terminology here can be confusing at first. In the United States, the word "state" is used to represent one of the fifty constituent elements of the whole country (New York, California, etc.) In analyzing global politics, on the other hand, we commonly use the word "state" as a synonym for country, that is, referring to an independent, self-governing (or sovereign) state. Canada, Russia, Bolivia, Nigeria, and Denmark are all states in this sense of the word, that is, they are self-governing sovereign countries. In figure 2.1 and elsewhere in this book, we have used "state" in this sense of the word, as is customary in political analysis.

We have also added the category "Global Issues" to the traditional levels of analysis to include issues that transcend state boundaries. For example, global climate change is an issue that impacts us all, down to the smallest of living creatures on our planet. While certain state policies, such as water pollution policy, individually help or hinder the overall status of climate change, water knows no boundaries, nor does air. For example, excessive carbon emissions from the United States and China (the largest carbon emitters) are helping to melt the glaciers in Antarctica. Other global issues include health issues,

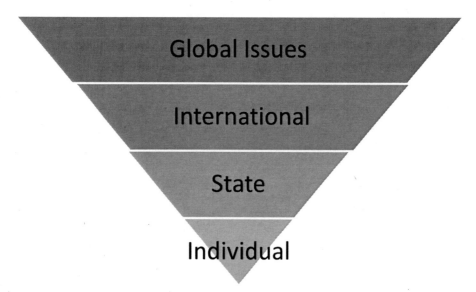

Figure 2.1. Levels of Analysis

such as the outbreak of the H1 N1 influenza or HIV/AIDS, education, nuclear policy, science and technology, and terrorism.

At another level, we can analyze the planet through interstate relations. For example, the United States and Colombia have negotiated various policies to deter drug trafficking and coca growing in Colombia. The United States has provided economic support for such initiatives in Colombia. Countries often negotiate trade policies, visa policies, and aid policies on bilateral or multilateral levels. This would be considered the international level—meaning between or among states. Scholars who emphasize this level of analysis study alliances among states, international organizations, trade agreements, war and peace, and diplomacy.

At the state level, countries can form policies to respond to international-level events. For example, U.S. foreign policy is often driven by U.S. concerns and responses around the world. An example of this kind of response would be the Patriot Act. The Patriot Act was passed in 2001 and altered in 2006 for the purpose of lessening law-enforcement restrictions on obtaining information from telephone, e-mail, and other communications, as well as lessening foreign intelligence gathering restrictions.[18] This U.S. law was created in response to the September 11, 2001, attack on the United States. It is a state-level policy that responds to an international event. Scholars who study this level of analysis tend to look at types of government (i.e., democratic or authoritarian), political parties, military and industrial complexes, and public opinion data.

Finally, the individual level of analysis has become increasingly important as the process of globalization reaches its grasp. Whereas scholars used to only study individuals as engaged in diplomacy or state-level interactions, nowadays, CEOs of corporations accompany the president on trips abroad and individual citizens can impact policies from thousands of miles away with the click of the send button on their cellular telephones. Scholars who study this level of analysis might look at the psychological character of a leader to determine the policies he or she might make. They might look at citizen participation, such as voting, or they might look at social movements or other citizen groups and how they seek to influence international policy.

THE ACTORS IN THE GAME OF POLITICS

Before we go on explaining the dynamics among and between these levels and its integration with the process of globalization, we should take a moment to better understand the specific actors involved in world politics. These actors include people and institutions. The people involved are either diplomats, heads of state and/or government, chief executive officers (CEOs) of corporations, or general citizens. At an institutional level, the actors could include not only states (territorial boundaries that include citizens and governments, such as the United States, Germany, or Nigeria) but also international intergovernmental organizations (IGOs), such as the United Nations (UN) or the World Trade Organization (WTO). These IGOs are institutions that make international policies in specific areas and are composed of states as their members.

Outside of the governmental realm, private, non-state actors can make a difference in the world today too. Multinational corporations (MNCs) span various states and employ thousands of citizens around the world. Their actions affect us not only

Table 2.1.   List of Actors

States
International Intergovernmental Organizations (IGOs)
Multinational Corporations (MNCs)
International Nongovernmental Organizations (INGOs)
Individuals

economically but also politically, socially, and environmentally. The 2010 oil spill in the Gulf of Mexico in the United States by BP international oil company, which is British based, has impacted oil prices, international drilling policies, state offshore drilling policies, science and technology, as well as the health of people and the environment.[19] The former CEO of BP, Tony Hayward, became a household name given his regular appearance on the nightly news.

Other non-state actors are important as well. They include nongovernmental organizations (NGOs), such as Greenpeace and Amnesty International.[20] Nongovernmental organizations are organizations formed outside the realm of the government. International NGOs include members from a multitude of states and their issue areas vary from the environment to human rights and sustainable development. International NGOs number somewhere near 40,000, which is a dramatic increase from the nearly 1,083 that were registered in 1914. NGOs can be funded by a variety of means, including private citizen funding, government funding, or a combination. While students of international relations and politics have traditionally sought employment in government or corporate arenas, NGOs have become another source of employment for recent university graduates.

The complex interaction of these actors on the world stage today has been categorized by some as global governance. This term refers to the creation of policies at global and local levels that have been formed by a network of actors across the world. For example, the 1997 Landmine Ban Treaty (formally known as the Convention on the Prohibition of the Use, Stockpiling, Production, and Transfer of Anti-personnel Mines and on Their Destruction) was the product of an international campaign of NGOs, eventually named the International Campaign to Ban Landmines (ICBL), interstate negotiations among Canadian foreign minister Lloyd Axworthy, then U.S. president Bill Clinton, and U.S. senator Patrick Leahy, plus the personal activism of England's Princess Diana and a multitude of UN meetings.[21]

In the end, Jodi Williams, the ICBL director won the 1997 Nobel Peace Prize for her work on this issue, and the treaty became international law, albeit with various states (including the United States, Iran, and North Korea) refusing to sign the treaty. Still, such an example is a powerful reminder that citizen organizations, governments, and individuals can play a significant role in shaping global, national, and local policies. Lacking the necessary two-thirds majority in the Senate, the Obama administration has not pushed for U.S. confirmation of the Landmine Ban Treaty.[22]

Intermesticity

There is a strong argument for starting politics at home, and it is hard to miss the importance of local affairs; our state and county leaders raise and lower taxes, pave our

Figure 2.2.   Clearing Mines in Mozambique
Getting the civil war in Mozambique stopped was tough, and getting all the land mines out of the ground is even tougher. Here an ordinance technician undertakes the dangerous work of locating and removing still-primed mines. Courtesy of Michael Kendellen, photographer for International Convention to Ban Landmines, http://www.icbl.org/index.php/icbl/image_folio_wrap_frame/wrap (accessed July 4, 2010).

roads, fund or defund our schools, and provide either police protection or police brutality, depending on the circumstances. Perhaps we should then concentrate on domestic problems, the troubles we find in our own backyard. Unfortunately, in an increasingly interdependent world, it is becoming harder to make a clear-cut distinction between what is international and what is domestic. Dr. Bayless Manning has even coined an irresistible phrase, "**intermestic**," to describe an issue that seems domestic at first glance but turns out to be international upon closer inspection. As we will see below, virtually every important sociopolitical problem is intermestic.[23]

3. Political Facts and Political Values

Political science has generated a substantive body of facts that are broadly agreed upon by professionals within the field. If we are all looking at the same data, why don't we all come to the same conclusions? Like everyone else, students of politics make judgments on the basis of **values**, deeply held philosophical positions on the nature of the human condition. Let's look at some of these value systems.

VALUE SYSTEMS

Imagine, for example, a discussion among three professors of political science. One is from Britain's Oxford University, a second from Cuba's Universidad de Habana, and a third from Egypt's Al-Azhar University. If these three scholars are typical representatives of their respective cultures, they are likely to have violently contrasting personal philosophies. The Oxford don might be a **secularist**, a Western rationalist who prefers science to religion and believes in free societies and **free markets**. The equally secular Cuban could be a Marxist who thinks the government should control commerce and who resents European and North American domination of the globe. The devout Muslim Egyptian is likely to dislike both Cuban Marxism and British capitalism, thinking that the Islamic religion provides a better guide to human life. If they're talking about world politics, however, and they've all done their homework, they ought to be able to reach a core agreement on certain basic nuts-and-bolts political realities.

For example, they would all concur that the executive branch of the post-1958 French government is based on a merging of presidential and parliamentary principles (you'll agree when you've read chapter 7). They would achieve unanimity in thinking that the devastating decline of the Russian economy in the 1990s was due more to high levels of defense spending, corruption, and mismanagement than to a genuine shortage of material resources. While they might disagree enormously in their personal assessments of President Bill Clinton (1993–2001), they would agree that the constitutional procedure for removing an American president works and perhaps even why and how Mr. Clinton survived impeachment.

The trouble would start when they began to discuss the moral significance of Mr. Clinton's behavior, as they would probably disagree on whether private vice necessarily corrupts public virtue. An emotionally charged political event like the September 11 terrorist attacks on the United States would almost certainly get them shouting at one another. Politics provokes raw emotions. While there are controversial issues within every academic field, biologists should be able to achieve some emotional distance between themselves and bacteria; astronomers can talk about black holes without acquiring black eyes. But virtually every aspect of politics is personal and controversial. How we feel about the shattering of the World Trade Center, for example, depends a lot on how close we were, emotionally or geographically, to ground zero.

In fact, we all react to world politics on the basis of our core values. These values differ dramatically from individual to individual and from society to society, and even political scientists can be prisoners of their own cultures. To illustrate this point, let's compare two influential political leaders who dominated the political life of their respective countries in the recent past. When **Ayatollah** Ruhollah Khomeini seized power in Iran in 1979, the Iranian people found that they had submitted themselves to the rigid, brutal rule of a religious leader who happened also to be an astute politician. What made Khomeini hard to understand in the West was the utter primacy of his religious beliefs. He felt with total conviction that the unique purpose of all human life was to qualify the individual for personal salvation in the hereafter. Since life was a transitional testing experience, rather than a crucial value in itself, he was less concerned with how well or how long his people lived and more focused on what ultimately became of their souls.

An even craftier politician was elected to power in 1981, ruling for fourteen years as president of France. François Mitterrand had no firm religious convictions; indeed, he had love affairs while in office, and had produced at least one illegitimate daughter with a long-standing mistress. As a secular leader, he saw religion as something inherently separate from public life. On the other hand, he was sincerely disturbed by poverty and social injustice and wanted France to live in peace and prosperity, goals he pursued with some measure of success. In a poll conducted a decade after his death, the French named Mitterrand France's greatest president.

Both Khomeini and Mitterrand were men of considerable personal ambition and even vanity. Each was a consummate politician, capable of twisting and maneuvering and even compromising to get what he wanted. Neither political career, however, makes much sense without a consideration of their respective core values. Although it apparently held no great personal relevance for him, Mitterrand was occasionally prepared to use religion as a tool to accomplish political goals. In contrast, Khomeini saw politics as merely an instrument of religion. Western political scientists were good at predicting how Mitterrand would behave because many of them shared his core values. Khomeini, on the other hand, surprised us every time.

WAYS OF LOOKING AT THINGS: PERSPECTIVES, THEORIES, AND IDEOLOGIES

Studying the world is something that scientists try to do with accuracy in terms of the use of certain methods of analysis. While we will discuss such methods below, you should know that there is a great debate within political science and international relations (one of its subfields) about whether the "science" should be taken out of political science. That being said, any analysis of an issue needs some logical order of thinking to examine the events, people, and places about which we study and in which we interact on a daily basis.

Perspectives

Let's start with perspectives. **Perspectives** are ways of seeing the world—like the lens in eyeglasses. Your way of seeing the world can be influenced by a myriad of factors, such as your values (as discussed above), your experiences, and your vision of reality. Noting that something is a perspective means that you agree it is not the only way to view something. Thus, if you argue that you align with a particular perspective (to be discussed below) in world politics, you also imply that you agree that there are contending perspectives out there. A good example through which to see this is to imagine yourself saying to someone, "My perspective on the war in Afghanistan is . . ." That statement is qualified by your acceptance that your perspective may not be the only one out there, nor the "truth."

Theories

Some scholars, though, argue that political science and its study of world politics should be about predicting what will happen. They contend that the only use of studying world events is to be able to determine when and if they will happen before they do. This way of analyzing the world is based on Thomas Kuhn's scientific method in which he argues that the purpose of science is to find the truth. In seeking the truth, scientists build theories, test them with hypotheses, and find their flaws (called anomalies), so that they can reformulate their theories.[24] The goal is to develop the truth about reality and be able to predict events. When a theory is tested over and over again and no one can find an anomaly (problem or flaw in it), it becomes an accepted truth. We call these accepted truths in science **paradigms**. Creating paradigms is a scientist's ultimate goal.

So, then, how would you go about the scientific method? You would first select a theory that you would like to test. A **theory** is "a set of propositions and concepts that seeks to explain phenomena by specifying the relationships among the concepts."[25] The purpose is to predict the phenomena. If a theory is successful, we can test it with hypotheses and verify its validity or accuracy. **Hypotheses** are statements that posit the relationship between concepts within the theory. If the hypothesis that you create and test verifies the tenets of the theory, you have strengthened the theory and its ability to predict. If your hypothesis finds a problem with the tenets of the theory, then you have found an anomaly and must refine the theory to adapt to it. If scholars continuously test a theory and find no anomalies, it is usually accepted as a truth, or a paradigm in the discipline. A good example of this is the law of gravity. Sir Isaac Newton tested a series of hypotheses surrounding the theory of gravity. As he and others could never disprove the theory, it is a paradigm in the world of science.

The question in the study of world politics is "Do we have paradigms?" Some scholars argue that we come close to science in some areas, such as the democratic peace theory that states that democracies are less likely to go to war with one another. But others contend that the study of the world and its peoples is too complex to determine static variables and test them as you would chemicals in a test tube in a controlled environment. As we will discover later, other scholars posit that the theories that we have today are misguided and have been since the beginnings of their creation, which some say go back as far as the days of Greek city-states and Aristotle, Plato, and Thucydides. In any event, understanding the so-called theories in world politics is important, as they shape foreign policies around the world and will continue to do so. Once you understand these theories and who writes them, you'll understand major world policies and have a better grasp on what is behind state actions.

To sum it up, world politics has some strong theories in which scholars test hypotheses. We really don't have paradigms in our field of study, although some would disagree with that. We will review the major theories later in this chapter so that you can relate them, and even create hypotheses to test them, if you like. Still, some scholars argue that all this talk of theory is rubbish and what we have is differing perspectives in a complex world. We'll let you be the judge.

Ideologies

Your personal values, feelings and experiences of the world, and your political views all add up to what is called an **ideology,** the sum total of your beliefs about politics. Ideologies are different from theories because they are not tested with hypotheses but are based on feelings and personal values, not scientific method. If you've spent a lot of time thinking about politics, you may have a fairly precise and elaborate ideology. If politics has always bored you rigid, your ideology may be latent, although we can bring it to the surface by asking questions. Why do you think poor people are poor? Do you think abortion should remain legal? Should the United States have made war on Iraq in 2003? In the 2008 election, did you vote for Senator Obama or Senator McCain? Did you vote at all? The answers to these and other probing questions would give us a sense of your ideology, even if you weren't previously sure you had one.

Every member of humankind has a separate and individual ideology, but ideologies tend to fall into clusters, and we will look at the more important ones in the course of this book. If you live in Cuba, there is a good chance that your personal ideology has been influenced by the thought of Karl Marx, who mistrusted businessmen and private enterprise. Many Arab Muslims believe that their ideology should be based upon their religion and want no daylight between religious and political thought. Most Europeans, North Americans, Japanese, and Indians generally believe that a free enterprise system acting under some level of governmental control is the best route to prosperity. These are all ideologies, and we'll discuss them in greater detail in part II of this book.

REALISTS

Basic worldview or perspective has influenced a number of theories in the study of international relations. For the purposes of introduction to these views of the world, we will divide them into four categories: (1) realism, (2) idealism, (3) constructivism, (4) Marxism, and other critical theories. These theories are not explanations of the domestic politics of a state, but, rather, they seek to represent interactions at the global level. Members of the same political party may have different thoughts on how the world works. Some may ascribe to a more realist stance and others to a more idealist stance. When thinking about your view of the world, try not to get bogged down in the domestic politics of your country, but rather try to see if the theory you are examining best represents the way you see the planet in its entirety.

Some of us, for example, doubt that humans will ever devise ways to live peacefully together. In political science, **realists** anticipate a future as dominated by conflict and violence as in the past. When they become political scientists, realists tend to be impressed by the concept of power in politics and often build political theories around the idea that politics involves a relentless struggle for power. Realists assume that the international system is chaotic and lacks a central authority, making it anarchic. Given such assumptions, states concern themselves then with security and gaining power in comparison with other states. Those who study realist theories, analyze states as unitary actors in the international system.

Realists tend to see the world through the struggle for power among states. They often use the phrase "balance of power" to describe how states shift in their positions of power. When one state is dominant in the international system, realists call this a unilateral system and the state with sole power is the **hegemon**. Some argued that the United States became the global hegemon following the fall of the Soviet Union in 1990. The Cold War from 1945 to 1990 is commonly represented as a **bipolar** system in which the United States and the Soviet Union were the two dominant poles of power. Some scholars view the concert of Europe from 1815 to the early twentieth century as a **multipolar**

Figure 2.3. Fareed Zakaria
Host of the popular CNN program *GPS*, editor-at-large of *Time Magazine* and author of *The Post-American World*, the India-born Zakaria is a realist who argues that the United States is in decline as a hegemon and needs to refocus its policies as a broker of global agendas with other emerging global powers. Reprinted with permission of Cable News Network, a Time Warner Co.

system in which Austria, Prussia, Russia, and Great Britain balanced their power among each other through the concert of Vienna. Realists differ on which system they think is the most peaceful, but most agree that power is housed in the state and that conflict in the international system is unavoidable.

Realist scholarship dates back to Thucydides' study on the Peloponnesian War and is one of the two (with idealism) dominant theories in world politics. While previous realist scholars, such as John Mearsheimer and George Kennan (who devised the U.S. containment policy regarding the Soviet Union; see also chapter 5), have approached power through the lens of military and security strength, neorealist scholars, such as Robert Gilpin, view power in military and economic terms.[26] Finally, feminist political scholars have also contributed to the conception of power within realist thought. They argue that power does not have to be only the ability of states to act in conflict of one another but can also be the ability of states to work together. As we review concepts, cases, and themes in this book, you should be able to examine them with the theoretical tools we give you in this chapter.

IDEALISTS

In contrast to realists, some people, in and out of the world of politics, optimistically believe that humankind is capable of behaving altruistically and peacefully, and look forward to a day when large-scale violence will be eradicated. Often called **idealists** (or liberals), they place their trust in international law and organizations such as the United Nations. Idealists also study the state and agree with realists that the world has no central authority. Where they differ is in the outcome of the anarchical system in which we live. Idealists contend that cooperation is a possible outcome.

Idealist theory became popular during the Enlightenment through the writings of Baron de La Brede et de Montesquieu (1689–1755) and Immanuel Kant (1724–1804). These scholars argued that collective action among states could eventually avoid war. U.S.

Figure 2.4. Harvard's Joseph Nye
Perhaps the leading "idealist" in contemporary political analysis. Courtesy of Kennedy School of Government, Harvard University, http://belfer center.ksg.harvard.edu/experts/3/joseph_s_nye .html (accessed July 4, 2010).

president Woodrow Wilson also ascribed to liberal theory and proposed the League of Nations (which the U.S. Senate rejected) as a collective security organization to prevent war. Idealists also view international trade and free market interaction as a means of interdependence among states, which they argue will lead to a more peaceful world.

Following World War II, states' cooperation strengthened and formalized in a myriad of ways, which interested scholars. Cooperation among states in the World Bank, the International Monetary Fund (to be discussed in more detail in chapter 12), and the United Nations (chapter 5), among others, merited further study to better understand under which conditions states cooperate. Scholars such as Robert Axelrod, Robert Keohane, and Joseph Nye found that it was in the interest of states to cooperate to protect their security.[27] Through international institutions, such as the North Atlantic Treaty Organization (NATO), states overcame the necessary outcome of conflict, realists would argue, with a cooperative organization. The European Union (EU) is the only example that we have in the international system in which state cooperation goes beyond the security and economic realms to cultural and legal issues. Idealists often refer to the European Union as the closest thing we have today in the international system to Kant's "perpetual peace," or world without war.

As idealist scholars honed their theory, they also found that states were cooperating with other actors, such as multinational corporations (MNCs), nongovernmental organizations (NGOs), and international intergovernmental organizations (IGOs). They found that states actually form networks of interactions among themselves and other international actors.[28] In finding this, idealists posed an interesting question to realists: does power reside solely within the state, or do we have to study other actors (e.g., MNCs, NGOs, IGOs) to accurately determine authority and power in the world? As we watch the importance of MNCs in international economic policies and the increasingly important influence of NGOs, idealist theory may help explain just how influential these actors are.

CONSTRUCTIVISTS

While in the Western industrialized world, realism and idealism are the main theories on which most foreign policies of states are based, constructivism is a serious approach (and relative newcomer) to the study of world politics. Whereas realists look at states as sources of power in the international system and idealists view cooperative institutions and states as sources of power, constructivists think that relying on structures (such as states and international institutions) as a unit of analysis only explains part of the story. Constructivists study the normative (or ethical) foundations and identities of states and world leaders to better understand relationships. For example, Alexander Wendt, a well-known constructivist scholar, contends that "anarchy is what states make of it."[29] According to Wendt and other constructivists, the process of interaction among states and actors (MNCs, NGOs, IGOs, etc.) is what determines the structure of the system. So, if states interact in an anarchical way without higher authority, then that is the structure they form. The emphasis here is on the actions, and the norms and values that underlie them. For realists and idealists, the world stage is already determined. For constructivists, we (represented by states, NGOs, MNCs, IGOs, etc.) determine what happens in the world.

Constructivists see the world as complex and not so easily explained by theories of states that act solely to gain power (i.e., in their own interest). For a constructivist, situation is everything. For example, if your professor walks into the room and tells everyone they are stupid, it is likely that the structure and dynamics of the class will be altered. However, if the professor walks into the room and says how brilliant everyone is, the interactions among students and professor, and outcomes of the class will likely be different from the previous negative scenario. Constructivists argue that states and world leaders learn from their interactions, which creates norms and identities that form structures, such as international institutions or new foreign policies and international treaties.

Constructivists, though, are often criticized for not being scientific enough. Since much of their theory is based on criticizing realism and idealism, some scholars argue that it has not produced a coherent line of inquiry with testable hypotheses. On the other hand, constructivism may contribute greatly to our understanding of new forms of power around the globe and non-state actor authority in the international system. As issues globalize, constructivists seek an understanding of the changing patterns of norms and identities that surround issues and actors. Such an analysis has the potential to bridge the domestic-international divide toward an "intermestic" theory of world politics that examines both international and national political interactions. One such contribution in this area has been human rights scholarship. Scholars, such as Kathryn Sikkink, have linked the change in international and domestic norms on human rights. This has led scholars to rethink dimensions of power and to reexamine the authority of social movements and citizen activism in the international and national arenas.[30]

CRITICAL THEORISTS

The last line of international relations theory we will cover will be **critical theories**. These theories do not all argue the same tenets, but they do have one thing in common: they contend that the previous three main theories misrepresent the true foundations of power in the international system and, according to Marxist scholars, impose ways of thinking that create inequalities in the world. Karl Marx (1818–1883) is the father of Marxist scholarship and posited that the capitalist system and markets would create a division among working classes and owning classes (proletariat and bourgeoisie) that would lead to conflict. From the violence that would erupt from these conflicts, a new socialist system would emerge, leading toward the utopian communist system.

Marxist scholar and communist leader V. I. Lenin (1870–1924) expounded upon Marxist theory to include the concept of capitalist imperialism. Lenin argued that capitalist states would need to expand in order to seek new markets. By doing so, capitalist states would create conflict for new markets and competition. The irony, according to Lenin, is that the people within these states would believe that capitalism was providing them with freedoms guaranteed by their states. However, Lenin said that the working classes around the world would just be trapped within the chains of capitalist production, while the owning classes controlled their interests via that state. For Lenin, the rich essentially controlled state governments to earn more money, while the poor remained laboring without true freedoms.

Today, scholars of world politics view critical theories through various lenses: **feminism**, world systems theory, and dependency theory. Feminists argue that gender is undervalued in the study of world politics and male dominance is another form of imperialism. World systems theorists, most notably Immanuel Wallerstein, view the world through core countries and periphery countries. Core countries are the major industrialized states, while peripheral countries are the developing states. Wallerstein and world systems theorists see the world in a state of peripheral countries providing natural resources to fuel the economies and power the core countries, without much hope of advancement for the periphery. However, Wallerstein has recently argued that the emergence of social movements and citizen activists groups, including the World Social Forum, have created new modes of power in the international system. For Wallerstein, the world is in flux, and he sees the state system on the decline as new forms of global citizen representation emerge. Wallerstein, however, gives no timeline for such changes.[31] He does, however, argue that the 2011 Occupy Wall Street movement may be a sign of the times. He says, "A new and better world-system, a new and better United States, is a task that requires repeated effort by repeated generations. But another world is indeed possible (albeit not inevitable). And we can make a difference. Occupy Wall Street is making a difference, a big difference."[32]

Sometimes students in the United States disregard Marxist scholarship as a remnant of the Cold War. However, it is a valid field of inquiry around the world. Aside from communist regimes, such as China, there are communist parties and citizen groups that subscribe to this line of reasoning. Ironically, Marxists and realists have a lot in common. They view the world as based on power (albeit power resides in states for realists and classes for Marxists). They analyze states, and they see capitalism and economic gain as a source of power. Of course, Marxists view capitalism as the source of conflict in the world, whereas idealists view trade among states as a means of increasing cooperation and, thus, lowering conflict.

Last, feminist scholarship has made an important contribution to our views on world politics over the last fifty years or so, and to giving a voice to women who have been voiceless in the political process. In light of September 11, 2001, feminist scholars reconsidered power in the international system and the role of gender. Some analysts argued

Figure 2.5.   Cynthia Enloe
From globalization to the Iraq and Afghan wars, award-winning feminist scholar
Cynthia Enloe has argued that the politics of women and the poor deserve a voice
among the overwhelming patriarchal arguments of power in the international sys-
tem. In her 2010 book, *Nimo's War, Emma's War: Making Feminist Sense of the Iraq
War* (Berkeley: University of California Press, 2010), Enloe follows the lives of eight
Iraqi and U.S. women through the Iraq war and their experiences as a testament of
ordinary persons and their significance in world politics. Courtesy of Cynthia Enloe.

that the Muslim world attacked the United States for its "occidental" (Western) ways that
included liberated women who worked outside the home. Some said that in response,
the United States needed to show a stronger, masculine-dominated face to the world.[33]
Feminists retorted that gender roles create false identities for men and women, such that
men are associated with conflict and women with peace. Thus, pictures of soldiers saving
women with children displayed images of weakness among women and power for men.
For some feminist scholars, the war in Iraq and conflict in general is an imposition of
masculinity on a global society, or a militarization of world politics. Their scholarship
teases out these gender and power inequalities, and it calls for less division.[34]

4. Specializations and Perspectives within Political Science

As in other branches of scholarship, political scientists become interested in different areas
of the political universe. Let's glance briefly at the principal subfields and even a few "sub-
subfields" in this fascinating and wide-ranging discipline.[35]

SUBFIELDS WITHIN POLITICAL SCIENCE

International Relations

International relations (IR) is the formal study of how countries interact with one another in peace and cooperation, or confrontation and war, or something in-between. A

standard IR course will be part of your immediate future if you decide to major in political science. Within the formal international relations field, individual scholars will focus on some themes to be explored here and in chapter 5: international organizations such as the UN and the European Union,[36] foreign policy and diplomacy, and international law. Defense and security studies, often pursued by military officers, belongs here, as well as peace studies, a field attracting political scientists looking for ways to avoid violent conflict. International political economy is also an IR specialization, borrowing the immense resources of the allied field of economics. Political economists study how political life is driven by economic factors and the deep divisions between rich and poor, a topic we'll explore in chapters 12 and 13.

Comparative Politics

Sometimes titled "comparative government," this is another mandatory way station on your journey to a degree in political science. This wide-ranging area of study considers the ways in which separate countries grapple with similar problems. A normal undergraduate course in the field will look at different governmental structures, party systems, tax structures, educational/health systems, and leadership styles—topics we'll explore briefly in chapter 7. Some comparative government specialists become fascinated by an individual country or closely connected group of countries (such as Latin America or the Arab world). These "area specialists" will typically master the languages commonly spoken in their "patch" of the world and try to explain how their areas function both internally and in relationship to other regions. Some comparative political analysts will develop a "thematic" approach, in which they will conduct transnational studies of some political phenomenon that runs through many countries: religious fundamentalism, health care and disease control, corruption and dictatorial governments are all absorbing themes.

American Politics

In any country, political scientists will be fascinated by their own government, and many scholars in the United States spend their careers trying to understand how the ordering of public affairs takes place at the federal, state, and local level within the United States. The range of sub-specialties here is immense: public administration and public policy experts look at the kinds of programs governments deliver and how these public services are provided. Others will focus on American ideology, trying to work out precisely what Americans and their leaders think ought to be happening in the marketplace of ideas. Some will study electoral politics and political behavior, while others look at specific institutions such as the presidency, the legislature, the judiciary, the media, and interest groups of various kinds.

Political Philosophy and Theory

From Plato to the pundits of cable TV, political philosophers have been trying to put the "ought" into politics, imagining what an ideal society would look like and wondering how desirable political goals such as justice and democracy can best be achieved. Political philosophers will often trawl through history, looking at great political thinkers from Aristotle through Machiavelli to modern thinkers in an effort to establish ethical or moral guidelines for political action. Their thinking is **normative**, which means that they are focusing on how the political world ought to function.

FOCUS AND METHODOLOGY

It will come as no surprise to learn that scholars disagree among themselves about what political phenomenon to study and what methods and procedures they should employ to get results. It is a customary oversimplification to clump political scientists into three rough tendencies: traditionalists, behavioralists, and post-behavioralists (see table 2.2). While these three can sometimes be feuding enemy camps, they are normally merely different approaches, with lots of room for overlap. Whether you are a traditionalist or a behavioralist or something in-between depends to a large extent on the kinds of questions you want to answer and the information available to produce your conclusion. For example, here are a couple of separate political questions.

The Traditionalists

You've just been appointed special advisor on Afghan affairs to the president. Mr. Obama wants to know how the Afghan people really feel about the presence of American troops on their soil. Because of the data at your disposal, this question calls for a traditionalist approach. Why? Well, quantifiable or statistical data is going to be hard to find. Afghanistan has never been a free society, and the endless civil wars and foreign invasions have made it difficult for anyone to organize public opinion polls or reliable voting records. It's too dangerous to roam around Kabul with a questionnaire, asking people what they think.

So where will you look for your answer? A traditionalist will start with the history books, studying other occasions when Afghanistan has been invaded by those whom they perceive to be foreigners. What did they think about the British in the late 1800s?

Table 2.2.   Focus and Methodology in Political Science

Traditionalists:	Behavioralists:
• More Historical and Philosophical Analysis	• More "Scientific" with Interest in Empirical Data and Quantification
• Focus on Law and Structures of Government	• Focus on Society, Social Classes, and Economics
• Greater Interest in Country and Area Studies	• Greater Interest in Transnational Comparisons
• Greater Focus on Problem Solving	• Focus on Methodology
• More Likely to Be "Normative"	• Attempt to Be Dispassionate, Neutral, and Descriptive

Post-behavioralism is a synthesis, accepting the legacy of behavioralism without the intense focus on methodology and quantification, and with more interest in history. Most modern political scientists are reluctant to define themselves rigidly as adherents to any specific school.

How did they react to the Russian invasion in 1979? We'll talk more about languages in chapter 3, but note right now that you won't get far in this quest if all you can read is English. Afghanistan is a disorderly garden of different languages, and words change their core meanings pretty drastically when you translate them from one tongue into another.

The Behavioralists

A little political science fiction takes us forward into the future, specifically to 2016 and another presidential election. Let's say that Hillary Clinton takes a stab again at the Democratic nomination. Behavioralists can study opinion data and polling to determine whether she would be a viable candidate and even what words voters would like to hear in her stump speeches.

Historical data may be less relevant here because there has never been a 2016 before, nor a female president of the United States. But it's a good question for a behavioralist, because these more scientifically inclined scholars are comfortable with computers and mathematics and counting anything that involves hard numbers.

Political behavioralists stress the importance of collecting **empirical data,** often using statistical and mathematical techniques for analysis. Behavioralism is an approach that runs through all the social sciences and is not unique to political science. The essence of the concept is that we need to study what we can **quantify** (measure or count) through direct observation. To quantify in politics is to assign hard numbers to political realities—talking about amounts of income, numbers of voters, and percentages of population growth.

In trying to decide if there will ever be a President Hillary Clinton, a behavioralist political scientist will design a research project calculated to estimate whether the Democrats will gain or lose votes with a ticket composed of a woman. There is a significant amount of data already in existence on past electoral behavior, and you'll need to see first what the polling data tells us. Mr. Obama and Mrs. Clinton ran against each other for the Democratic nomination in 2008; both had considerable support, but are their separate communities of fans going to merge?

Should it make a difference to your analysis whether you personally like Hillary or intend to vote for whomever the Republicans nominate? If you're a good behavioralist, it shouldn't. Some (although not all) behavioralists try to approach their work without making normative or political judgments about the content of political behavior, in the same neutral way that biologists observe the feeding habits of wolves without becoming emotionally involved in the fate of rabbits. When the issues are very personal, however, this can be tough to do.

There is no question that behavioralism, particularly after the invention of the computer, has changed the way we look at politics and operate politically. The basic methodological accomplishments of behavioralism are enormous; it would be hard, for example, to imagine elections without polling and surveys. Government proceeds on the basis of scientifically collected data from **demography**, and statistical information leaps quickly from mainframe to mainstream. The popularity of behavioralism may stem from the fact that sophisticated public-opinion-sampling techniques enable political scientists to tell politicians what they really want to know: how to win elections.

The Post-behavioralists

While few modern political scientists have challenged the basic achievements of behavioralism, many are dubious about the notion that they can deal only with empirical data and must reject anything that cannot be counted or measured. These scholars also bristle under the obligation to remain emotionally uninvolved in what they are studying.[37]

Academics who draw inspiration from both traditionalism and behavioralism are sometimes called post-behavioralists, although most scholars prefer life without labels. They are happy to use the quantified empirical data produced by the behavioralists, but they are also interested in case and area studies, and are prepared to borrow data and insights from sociologists, historians, demographers, and students of the environment.

5. The Wrap: What Have We Learned?

Up until this point, you may have thought that world politics was some amalgam of unorganized policies without road maps or guidelines. While in some cases this may still be true, we have tried to outline the theoretical perspectives of realism, idealism, constructivism, Marxism, and critical theories that surround the global dialog. In fact, you can deconstruct the policies of a state and follow the trend of which perspectives they tend to favor. Certainly, the United States has favored a more realist and idealist foreign policy path, but other countries, such as Cuba, have remained Marxist. Still others, such as Canada, have pursued more constructivist leanings particularly in humanitarian-issue areas. Newer social movements, such as Occupy Wall Street, break the boundaries of state analysis and move us to more radical and constructivist perspectives.

Additionally, we have reviewed the toolbox for all political scientists—that is the traditional, behavioralist, and post-behavioralist ways of analyzing the planet. If you are a behavioralist, you will choose qualitative or quantitative methods of analyzing data that we find in the world (empirical evidence) to seek solutions to a hypothesis. Traditional scholars rely more heavily on philosophical texts, while post-behavioralist use a combination of approaches. The fact of the matter is that political scientists have disciplined methods of investigating issues and proving or disproving world perspectives. Understanding them may help you better understand your own worldview.

Finally, the best way to understand world politics is to go out and try it yourself. If you're interested in serving your country abroad, check out *Careers in International Relations*, 7th ed., edited by Maria Pinto Carland and Michael Trucano and published in 1997 by the School of Foreign Service at Georgetown University in Washington, D.C. *Careers* will give you a sense of what you might need to do to prepare yourself for entry into the State Department or the CIA or one of the many other U.S. government agencies with representatives in the field. It will also give you addresses and contact numbers when it comes time to submit that CV. Also check out Sherry Mueller and Mark Overmann's book *Working World: Careers in International Education, Exchange, and Development* (2008) from Georgetown University as well, which will outline how to get jobs abroad and go on exchange. You might also want to look at Mark Rowh's *Great Jobs for Political Science Majors* published in 1999 by VGM Career Horizons in Chicago. To contemplate a life working abroad, you need good English language skills, competency in at least one relevant foreign language, and familiarity with geography and current events. You also need to be psychologically able to adapt to unfamiliar customs and cultures. Remember that many of these positions require a security clearance, and the process of background investigations takes some time; so apply early to get that process going.

The American Political Science Association (APSA) has a number of excellent resources for career and internship information. In addition, their website lists graduate school opportunities in the discipline. Your career opportunities with a major in political science can span from the corporate world to the governmental and nonprofit sectors. Students who have majored in this area have gone on to work in corporations, international organizations, and various levels of state and national governments. Additionally, those interested in teaching often major in political science. If you're interested in law school or graduate school to work on public policy, this is your major. We encourage you to check out the APSA website and delve into the possibilities, as well as the internship opportunities.

Next stop? We'll look at all the diverse players, languages, and cultures in the game of world politics.

Notes

1. See the American Political Science Association at www.apsanet.org.
2. See the International Studies Association at www.isanet.org.
3. Jean Blondel, *Thinking Politically* (New York: Penguin, 1978), 9.
4. David Easton, *A Framework for Political Analysis* (Englewood Cliffs, N.J.: Prentice Hall, 1965), 50.
5. Harold D. Lasswell, *Who Gets What, When and How* (New York: McGraw Hill, 1938).
6. John Mearsheimer, "Back to the Future: Instability after the Cold War," *International Security* 15, no. 1 (Summer 1990); George Quester, "The Future of Nuclear Deterrence," *Survival* 34, no. 1 (Spring 1992).
7. Andrew Moravcsik, *The Choice for Europe: Social Purpose and State Power from Messina to Maastricht* (Ithaca, N.Y.: Cornell University Press; London: Routledge/UCL Press, 1998).
8. Manuel Castells, *The Rise of the Networks Society* (New York: Blackwell Publishers, 2000); Barry Gills, "Empire vs. Cosmopolis: The Clash of Globalizations," *Globalizations* 2, no. 1 (May 2005); Benjamin Barber, *Consumed: How Markets Corrupt Children, Infantilize Adults, and Swallow Citizens Whole* (New York: W.W. Norton, 2007).
9. Virginia Haufler, *A Public Role for the Private Sector* (Washington, D.C.: Carnegie Endowment for International Peace, 2001).
10. Thomas J. Hall and Rodney Bruce Biersteker, *The Emergence of Private Authority in Global Governance* (Cambridge: Cambridge University Press, 2002).
11. Benjamin Barber, *Consumed: How Markets Corrupt Children, Infantilize Adults, and Swallow Citizens Whole* (New York: W. W. Norton, 2007).
12. David Vogel, *The Market for Virtue: The Potential and Limits of Corporate Social Responsibility* (Washington, D.C.: The Brookings Institution, 2006).
13. Harvey Cox, "The Market as God," *The Atlantic Online*, March 1999, http://www.theatlantic.com/past/docs/issues/99mar/marketgod.htm (accessed July 10, 2011).
14. Alberto Acosta, *Desarrollo Glocal: Con la Amazonia en la Mira* (Quito: Corporación Editora Nacional, 2005).
15. See The Law of the Sea at http://www.un.org/Depts/los/index.htm; the United Nations at www.un.org.
16. See *The World Bank* at http://www.worldbank.org; the *International Monetary Fund* at http://www.imf.org; and *The World Trade Organization* at http://www.wto.org.
17. See the G20 at http://www.g20.org/.

18. See the Patriot Act at http://epic.org/privacy/terrorism/hr3162.html.

19. See British Petroleum at http://www.bp.com/bodycopyarticle.do?categoryId=1&contentId=7052055.

20. See Greenpeace International at http://www.greenpeace.org/usa/ and Amnesty International at http://www.amnesty.org.

21. For more information and the complete text of the convention, please see http://www.un.org/millennium/law/xxvi-22.htm.

22. Kendall W. Stiles, *Case Histories in International Politics*, 4th ed. (New York: Pearson Longman, 2006).

23. Bayless Manning, "The Congress, the Executive and Intermestic Affairs," *Foreign Affairs* 57, no. 1 (1979): 308–24.

24. Thomas Kuhn, *The Structure of Scientific Revolutions*, 3rd ed. (Chicago: University of Chicago Press, 1996).

25. Karen A. Mingst, *Essentials of International Relations*, 4th ed. (New York: W. W. Norton, 2008), 56.

26. Robert Gilpin, *War and Change in World Politics* (Cambridge: Cambridge University Press, 1981); John Mearsheimer, *The Tragedy of Great Power Politics* (New York: W. W. Norton, 2001).

27. Robert Axelrod and Robert O. Keohane, *Achieving Cooperation under Anarchy: Strategies and Institutions, Cooperation under Anarchy*, ed. Kenneth Oye (Princeton: Princeton University Press, 1986); Robert O. Keohane and Joseph S. Nye, *Power and Interdependence*, 3rd ed. (New York: Longman, 2001).

28. Robert Keohane and Joseph S. Nye, "Transnational Relations and World Politics," *International Organization* 25, no. 3 (Summer 1971).

29. Alexander Wendt, "Anarchy Is What States Make of It: The Social Construction of Power Politics," *International Organization* 46, no. 2 (Spring 1992): 395.

30. Margaret E. Keck and Kathryn Sikkink, *Activists beyond Borders: Advocacy Networks in International Politics* (Ithaca, N.Y.: Cornell University Press, 1998); Sanjeev Khagram, James Riker, Kathryn Sikkink, eds., *Restructuring World Politics: Transnational Social Movements, Networks and Norms* (Minneapolis: University of Minnesota Press, 2002); Thomas Risse-Kappen, Stephen C. Ropp, and Kathryn Sikkink, *The Power of Human Rights: International Norms and Domestic Change* (Cambridge: Cambridge University Press, 1999).

31. Immanuel Wallerstein, *The Modern World-System in the Longue Duree* (Boulder, Colo.: Paradigm Publishers, 2004).

32. Immanuel Wallerstein, "The Fantastic Success of Occupy Wall Street," Commentary No. 315, October 15, 2011, http://www.iwallerstein.com/fantastic-success-occupy-wall-street/.

33. Francis Fukuyama, "Women and the Evolution of World Politics," *Foreign Affairs*, September/October 1998.

34. J. Ann Tickner, "Feminist Perspectives on 9/11," *International Studies Perspectives* 3 (2002); Cynthia Enloe, *Globalization and Militarism: Feminists Make the Link* (Lanham, Md.: Rowman and Littlefield, 2007).

35. The classic study of why Americans know so little about politics has been written by Michael X. Delli Carpini and Scott Ketter in their *What Americans Know about Politics and Why It Matters* (New Haven, Conn.: Yale University Press, 1996). For the scholarly feuding within the field, look at Gabriel Almond's classic *A Discipline Divided: Schools and Sects in Political Science* (Newbury Park, Calif.: Sage, 1989). A more recent book covering some of the same ground is Ira Katznelson and Helen V. Milner, eds., *Political Science: The State of the Discipline* (New York: Norton, 2002).

36. See also the European Union at http://europa.eu/index_en.htm.

37. Dr. Jarol B. Manheim has given us the ultimate look at how political science research actually happens in his *Empirical Political Analysis: Research Methods in Political Science* (New York: Addison Wesley Longman, 1998). W. Philip Shively has produced the fifth edition of his readable *The Craft of Political Research* (Upper Saddle River, N.J.: Prentice Hall, 2001). Your library almost certainly has the second edition of Joel Krieger's *The Oxford Companion to Politics of the World* (New York: Oxford University Press, 2001), and it will help you cope with the "terrible terminology" of politics. If you're contemplating writing a term paper or doing some actual scholarship in the field, you might want to consult Diane Schmidt's *Writing in Political Science*, 3rd ed., (New York: Longman, 2004). For a look at how to study the world around you, try Gary King, Robert O. Keohane, and Sidney Verba, *Designing Social Inquiry* (Princeton: Princeton University Press, 1994).

CHAPTER 3

Community and Conflict
A QUICK LOOK AT THE PLANET

During a trial in Wonderland, the king ordered the White Rabbit to "begin at the beginning and go on till you come to the end: then stop."[1] Like most things Lewis Carroll wrote, this is sound advice, but it leaves us with several dilemmas when applied to the study of world politics. Where is the beginning? How will we recognize the end when we come to it?

Most of the havoc that appears in the morning papers involves humans fighting other humans; nothing in the animal kingdom approaches the kind of horrific violence of modern war. Sometimes this human conflict takes place between culturally very similar people, but more frequently, violence occurs between groups that are dissimilar in one or more significant ways. In this chapter, therefore, we will set the groundwork for understanding human conflict by talking about some of the more obvious ways in which groups of people perceive themselves to be different from one another.

- *How many of what sorts of people are there?* As we'll see, both here and in more detail in chapters 13 and 14, a lot of human conflict arises when there are rich people and poor people living in an area where the population outstrips the resources (land, food, fuel, etc.) needed to support it. A great deal of human conflict flows from inequalities in the distribution of wealth both within and among countries; so we'll need to master some basic political science concepts to understand how to measure wealth and what we call rich countries and poor countries. There are even significant political issues flowing from our genders and gender orientations. We all understand that people come in different ages, and this fact also lies at the heart of a very quiet conflict, the rivalry between young and old for scarce economic resources.
- *Capisci soltanto una lingua? Peccato!* If you didn't understand the first five words in this paragraph, it's because they were written in Italian, asking, "Do you understand only one language? Too bad!" As a species, language both defines and separates us, since no other breed of animal communicates with the complexity and elegance that humans have achieved. Language connects us, since we can use the Internet to talk to anyone in the world with whom we share a language. But language can also disconnect us; there is nothing quite so chilling as being in a foreign society where no one speaks your language and you can't speak theirs. Even more dangerous, perhaps, is thinking that you have made yourself understood linguistically, only to find that you have been misunderstood or mistranslated.
- *Is God on your side? Is religion a force for peace, or just one more divisive cultural phenomenon for people to fight about?* Sometimes communities are in conflict with their neighbors over something as clear-cut as land and water, but often they are battling over God or at least dissimilar approaches to the transcendental. Some conflicts are directly about specific religious issues: the American quarrel over abortion is a common example. Sometimes the conflict is actually about something else, but religion is a complicating factor; the apparently endless Israeli-Palestinian conundrum is a case in point.

In order to understand the half-dozen most serious conflicts on this planet, you absolutely need to know the basics about world religions. Who are the Hindus and what do they believe? How is Buddhism different? What is Judaism, really, and what is the difference between Islam's Sunnis and Shi'ites? Without these basics, we're not going to get very far in understanding much of what's happening today.

Yet, many scholars argue that we create our own identities through socialization, networks, and communication with groups. While some women may strongly identify as Palestinian, others may identify more strongly as Muslim, and still others may feel more strongly feminist than the other identities. Such creation and malleability of identity emphasizes the porous nature of nationalism and state sovereignty, meaning one day you may feel "American," but another you may feel like a student, and yet another you may identify more strongly as a female. There are various ways to map the world beyond looking at state boundaries. It's likely that you don't always view yourself through only the lens of your country of origin. In this chapter, we'll take a look at other ways of "seeing" the world—through gender, sexual orientation, race/ethnicity, and language.

1. A World of Diversity

Let's start by counting noses. There is a significant school of thought that holds that a lot of conflict flows from the simple fact that portions of the world are overpopulated, that is, there are more people in certain areas than can be supported by the resources in those areas. Globally speaking, how many folks are we talking about? The U.S. Census Bureau grimly estimates and recalculates the global population on a daily basis, informing us that by November of 2011, the species had reached seven billion.[2] We humans are reproducing at just under 1.2 percent a year, which doesn't sound like much until we crunch the numbers and realize that this represents about seventy-six million more children per year.

How many of us are Americans? There were roughly 313 million Americans in 2012, roughly one out of every twenty-two people in the world. Put another way, Americans are just over 4.5 percent of the human family, a ratio that will drop as time goes by. Much of the U.S. population increase comes from immigration, and Americans have fewer babies than do Africans and Asians, although more than do Europeans. The United States is the third most populous country on the planet, well behind China (over 1.3 billion) and India (just over 1.2 billion), but ahead of Indonesia, Brazil, and Russia. Unless they restrain their impetuous population growth, however, the people of Pakistan will outnumber Americans sometime in the next half century.

THE PLANETARY POPULATION

Whether the planet as a whole is overpopulated is a complicated question we will leave for chapter 13. Clearly, however, a few of the world's seven billion people are quite wealthy, which suggests they control enough resources to make themselves comfortable. A large percentage of humankind lives in varying levels of poverty, a fact that contributes to significant levels of conflict. Since prosperity is a crucial factor in human life, journalists and political scientists have used a variety of sometimes confusing terms to distinguish among rich countries, poorer societies, and populations faced with extremely serious levels of poverty. Even though some of these terms make no particular sense, we need to master them because they are in general use. The United Nations has devised a more rigorously scientific set of terms called the human development index, which we also need to know because it appears throughout this and many other publications.

Table 3.1. Dividing Up the World by Wealth

Very High Human Development (Very High HDI)	14.8% of population but 56.1% of wealth	The "North"	First World	Developed Countries
High Human Development (High HDI)	13.8% of population but 17.4% of wealth		Third World	Developing Countries
Medium Human Development (Medium HDI)	65.7% of population but 25.9% of wealth	The "South"		
Low Human Development (Low HDI)	5.8% of population, but 0.5% of wealth		Fourth World	Less (or Least) Developed Countries (LDCs)

Source: United Nations Development Programme, Human Development Report 2011, http://hdr.undp.org/en/media/HDR_2011_EN_Tables.pdf (accessed November 10,2011).

DIVIDING UP THE WORLD BY WEALTH

Does it have to be as complicated as table 3.1 would suggest? Here's the problem: when talking about rich people and poor people, authors, scholars, and journalists all tend to categorize groups of people differently. We'll deal with this in greater detail in chapter 12, but here is what you need to know to get from here to there. Let's start on the right-hand side of the table.

The term "development" refers to economic prosperity, and economists had long divided humankind roughly into three unequal groups, with the wealthy, industrialized economies of North America and Western Europe classified as the "developed world" and generally poorer economies, such as India and China, classified as "developing." At the very bottom of this economic totem pole were a series of very poor countries, such as Haiti in the Western Hemisphere and the Democratic Republic of Congo (and many other sub-Saharan African countries), and Timor-Lest in the South Pacific, who were usually described as either "less" or "least" developed countries, or sometimes "LDCs."

After World War II, commentators began using the term "First World" to describe the United States and its wealthy and free market allies. The "Second World" was the Soviet Union and its satellites, and the term is still used sporadically to describe the twenty-seven countries that were once either part of the USSR or one of its satellite states. The term **"Third World"** described countries that were poor and often neutral in the struggle between the United States and the USSR. By the 1960s, it was clear that while they were still relatively poor, some Third World countries were actually making economic progress. Another group of mostly African countries, on the other hand, were still locked in devastating poverty, and these poorest-of-the-poor became the **"Fourth World."** Today, it is common to refer to the First, Third, and Fourth worlds, although some commentators confusingly still use the term "Third World" for all poor countries.[3]

"North" and "South" is another vague classification. At least in the Northern Hemisphere, people who live closer to the North Pole are likely to be richer than people who live closer to the equator; so economists have fallen into the habit of talking about the economic "North" and economic "South," generally meaning rich people and poor peo-ple respectively. Things get confusing in the Southern Hemisphere because New Zealand and Australia are both very far to the south and very rich.

If you find all this perplexing, join the party. In fact, scholars have always disagreed on what to call these various groups and argued even more about which country belonged on each list. Until 1990, there was no authoritative classification of countries on the basis of economic success. To bring some mathematical precision into this situation, the UN Development Programme (UNDP) pioneered a behaviorist approach to the comparative evaluation of human societies called the **human development index** (**HDI**), which is annually updated to provide a sort of report card for individual countries. First published in 1990, the human development index has been adopted by scholars and journalists with increasing enthusiasm because it brings some empirical coherence to the business of classifying countries.

THE DEEP END OF THE POOL

The HDI is basically a statistic generated when the UN integrates a country's income with its success in achieving literacy, sending its children to school, and keeping every-body healthy enough to guarantee a decent life expectancy. Based on their performance in creating and using economic resources, the UN then divides countries into very high, high, medium, and low, as suggested in table 3.1. The HDI concept is superior because it is based on mathematics and hard data; terms such as "First World" or "developing countries" have, on the other hand, no definable basis.

Spending a few more minutes on table 3.1, we can see how unequal the distribution of wealth around the world has become. In the UN's very high human development category, just under 15 percent of the human family monopolizes well over half of the total wealth in the world. This group includes all of Western Europe, the United States and Canada, and established Pacific countries such as Japan, South Korea, Australia, and New Zealand.

Just below, there is a "pretty rich" category of countries called "high human develop-ment": this would include many Eastern European countries and some Latin American societies. Almost two-thirds of the human family fit into the medium human develop-ment category and have only about a quarter of the world's cumulative wealth. These are countries that are generally poor but not completely destitute, such as China, Indonesia, Egypt, India, and Pakistan. And—at the very bottom of the pile—we have the low hu-man development countries, who endure a life-threatening level of poverty with about 6 percent of the world's population but only about 0.5 percent of all the dough on the planet. In this text, we will make frequent references to the HDI concept, so make sure you've understood it before going ahead.

HOW FAST ARE WE GROWING?

Humankind is currently increasing at just below 1.2 percent per year. This rate has de-clined a little from frighteningly high rates in the past and will probably drop gradually in the future. But the sheer momentum of growth is still terrific. The world's population has tripled since the beginning of World War II, and it is far from clear how big the human community can or will get, although we'll speculate in chapter 13. How important are these numbers? If we'd managed to colonize a bigger planet, it wouldn't necessarily be a problem that we have big numbers now and can anticipate even bigger numbers in the future. But the earth has limited room and finite resources, which means that societies have increasingly tough decisions to make about the allocation of goods and services.[4]

In the very high human development world, the population growth rate is typically low, and a few European countries (like Russia) have even reached what is absurdly but routinely called "negative population growth," meaning that more people are dying than are being born so that the total population is shrinking. In contrast, low HDI communities are better at increasing their families than their bank accounts; population growth among the very poorest members of humankind is around 3 percent per annum. This rate of growth will double a country's population within a generation, usually destroying any hope of economic growth in the process.

THE CONFUSING GDP AND GNI

In order to estimate prosperity or wealth, the United Nations Development Programme and the World Bank use statistics called the **gross domestic product (GDP)** and the

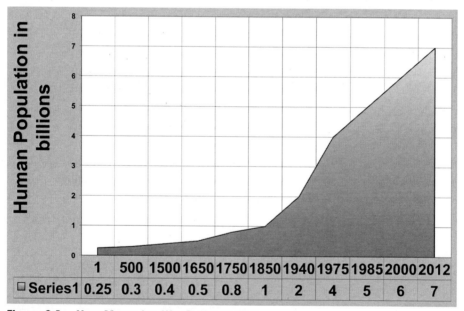

Figure 3.1.   How Many Are We Going to Be?
The eventual size of humankind is the subject of increasingly sharp controversy. Optimists once felt we might level out at a sustainable seven billion, but pessimists seem closer to reality in predicting that we will come close to doubling our present numbers. The UN now believes that we are headed toward a global population figure of about nine billion by 2050. How old will you be in 2050?

Source: Population Division of the Department of Economic and Social Affairs of the United Nations Secretariat, 2009.

gross national income (GNI), which is a newer term for gross national product. We'll talk more about national income in chapter 12, but for the moment you need only remember a couple of key things about GDPs and GNIs. First, GNI is what economists used to call the GNP, a new name for an old statistic. Second, the GNI/GNP is not the same as the gross domestic product, which is calculated differently. So you can't make a direct comparison between a GDP and a GNI.

The GDP is the measure of all goods and services produced within a country—a view of the local, internal economy. The GNI adds the value of goods and services produced outside the country as well, or GDP + flow of goods and services into the country from abroad. In this sense, the GNI is not bound by a country's borders and measures what its citizens earn inside and outside the country. We'll review this in more depth in chapter 12. In this text, we will generally follow the United Nations and the World Bank in describing countries in terms of their gross national income and per capita gross national income (PC/GNI). There will be times, however, when we need, for a variety of complicated reasons, to use the gross domestic product and per capita gross domestic product. Sometimes this will be necessary simply because the GDP is available and the GNI is not. Since you can't switch back and forth between the GNI and the GDP in one context, there will be occasions when we use the GDP to maintain historical consistency with charts that explain the evolution of a phenomenon over time.

Whether we are talking about the GDP or the GNI, we typically adjust these figures to account for differences in the cost of living around the world; a dollar doesn't go very far in New York City, but it can be a lot of purchasing power in central Africa. To signify that we have modified the original number to achieve a more meaningful one, we use the phrase "PPP US$." The "PPP" stands for "purchasing power parity," something we'll explore in greater detail later. For now, just get used to the idea of seeing "per capita gross domestic product" and "per capita gross national income" presented as ways of estimating national wealth after these numbers have been modified to make them comparable to other countries with higher or lower costs of living.

We'll explore the population-and-poverty issue in more depth in part IV. In the meantime, remember that there are seven billion inhabitants on this planet, most of them seriously short of dough. It's hard to be happy when you're broke, and a lot of political conflict flows from this central economic reality.

Thinking about Averages

We need numbers to describe certain political realities, but when looking at statistics like the PC/GNI, remember that these are averages, not real money. Generally speaking, the

Table 3.2.   Average Comparative Per Capita GDP and GNI

Average Very High Human Development	$35,768 PPP US$	$33,352
Average High Human Development	$12,861 PPP US$	$11,579
Average Medium Human Development	$5,077 PPP US$	$5,276
Average Low Human Development	$1,671 PPP US$	$1,585

Note: Figures extrapolated from the United Nations Development Programme, *Human Development Report 2011*, http://hdr.undp.org/en/media/HDR_2011_EN_Tables.pdf.

poorer the country, the greater the gap between rich and poor becomes, so a statistical average can be pretty meaningless in low HDI societies. Here's a pretty hypothetical example: If I earn an annual $990,000 teaching in a university and you bring home $10,000 a year flipping hamburgers, together we have a nifty average income of $500,000 apiece. Do all the arithmetic you want, but in the real world, it's still mostly my money. Yes, I will have fries with that. And no, I'm not leaving you a tip.

GENDER POLITICS

Lying as it does at the heart of every soap opera, the neat division of the human race into male and female may lead us to assume that for every guy there is a gal and love will always find a way. It isn't true in life, and it isn't even remotely true in politics, where political conflict flows from a host of gender-related issues. In poorer societies, the condition of women is so bad that the female population can be unnaturally low, creating an excessive male population. Where women manage to survive to adulthood, they are seldom given equal social, legal, and financial status, and in some countries, they are politically powerless.

The Male-Female Ratio

In the United States and Europe, there are many more women than men, but globally speaking, there are at least sixty million more men than women, giving us a planetary ratio of about 50.4 percent males to 49.6 percent females. The male majority may actually be increasing.[5] What's going on here?

Mother Nature starts off this complicated equation by arranging for the birth of more baby boys than baby girls; males start the race of life with roughly a 5 percent lead in almost every human society. This may be nature's way of compensating for intrinsic male biological weaknesses because males are more susceptible to mortality at every stage of their lives.[6]

In those societies where they are given approximately equal nutrition, equal medical care, and equal protection from danger, women tend to live longer than do men, surviving both the illnesses of childhood and the frailty of old age. In very high HDI societies such as North America and Europe, women outlive their male companions by many years. In human terms, this means that most married women can anticipate becoming widows, a phenomenon compounded by the practice of men marrying somewhat younger women. This is a political and economic problem because women still earn less than men do, and if a husband cannot provide adequately for his wife's old age, she is likely to spend her widowed years in economic distress.

Table 3.3 compares male and female life expectancy in twelve countries. Note how life expectancy in general declines as PC/GNI (or national wealth) drops. Note the very significant gap between male and female life expectancies in high and most medium HDI countries. The extraordinary gap between Russian male and female life expectancies perhaps reflects high rates of alcoholism, criminality, and suicide among Russian men, perhaps stemming from economic instability in Russian society. This gap narrows in very poor countries because the social status of women is so poor, and actually reverses itself in Afghanistan.

Table 3.3.   Comparing Male and Female Longevity
In accordance with the usual statistical practice, the numbers after the decimal represent tenths of a year, not months. In this and all other tables in this book, countries are listed in order of their standing on the most recent edition of the UN HDI index.

Country	PC/GDP (PPP US$)	Male Life Expectancy	Female Life Expectancy	Female Advantage
Very High HDI				
Norway	$56,214	81.1	83.0	+2
USA	$45,989	78.5	80.9	+1.3
UK	$35,155	80.2	82.3	+2.5
High HDI				
Argentina	$14,538	75.9	80.4	+4.7
Mexico	$14,258	77	79.4	+2.7
Russia	$18,932	68.8	73.2	+6
Medium HDI				
Iran	$11,558	73	71.6	–0.3
China	$6,828	73.5	76.9	+3.4
India	$3,296	65.4	70.0	+5.6
Low HDI				
Malawi	$794	55.4	52.5	–1.9
Ethiopia	$934	59.3	58.8	+2.7
Afghanistan	$1,321	48.7	45.3	+0.7

Source: United Nations Development Programme, Human Development Report 2011, http://hdr.undp.org/en/media/HDR_2011_EN_Tables.pdf; United Nations Development Programme, Human Development Report 2010, http://hdr.undp.org/en/media/HDR_2010_EN_Tables_reprint.pdf.

If women outlive men in all but the most desperate countries, why are there more men than women in the world? Here's part of the answer: modest gains in female health have taken place only in recent years and only in countries where there is at least a minimal level of wealth. For much of human history and in the poorest quarters of the globe today, impoverished women have tended to die earlier than men, and contemporary global statistics partly reflect those millions of missing women.[7]

The gender gap, however, actually seems to be getting worse, for reasons we'll address in chapter 13. Part of the explanation is the awful business of female infanticide; in societies where a baby girl represents a financial liability for a family, the infant may be put to death immediately after birth. For similar motives, sex-selection abortion is commonly practiced in India, China, and other parts of Asia, where families resort to prenatal gender-identification tests and then abort unwanted female fetuses. This widespread practice is skewing Asian gender ratios from India to South Korea. The fact that men in Afghanistan actually outlive their womenfolk may be explained partly by the fact that war is more dangerous for women than for men, and partly by the extraordinarily low social and economic status of Afghan women.

Whatever the future, the present shortage of women is not equally spread across the globe. In Latin America generally, the man-woman ratio is about even, but in parts of the Arab world and Asia, there is an increasing shortage of women. In some parts of China, there are 150 men for every 100 women, and in India, the national average is 112 boys to every 100 girls. Libya only has nine women for every ten men. And the ultimate crisis region is the Persian Gulf region, where areas such as the United Arab Emirates have half as many women as men.[8]

There are some general observations to be made on table 3.3. First, there is a general trend for richer countries to have better longevity statistics than do poor countries. Observe, however, that the American longevity rates are nowhere close to being the best in the world. While the reasons are complicated and controversial, Americans who want a long life need to contemplate moving to Oslo. Note the astounding gap between male and female longevity in the Russian Federation. Observers have spoken of epidemics of suicide, alcoholism, and drug abuse among Russian males, factors that may also help explain Russia's declining birthrate.

Power Women

Within every human society, a lot of political conflict surrounds gender issues. Over the course of the twentieth century, many of these quarrels have arisen from the demand for female equality: equal rights under the law, equal pay for equivalent work, and an end to gender-based discrimination at home and in the workplace. The notion that women should enjoy full social and political equality with men has typically been called feminism, a political belief system that continues to support and structure the drive for full gender equality. In general, women in very high HDI societies have made much more social progress than have their sisters in the Third and Fourth worlds. When women serving in the American armed forces deployed to Saudi Arabia in 1990 to prepare for the reconquest of Kuwait, they discovered that their Saudi sisters were not allowed to drive cars, vote, open their own bank accounts, have passports, or go shopping without a veil or a male escort. In 2010, Saudi Arabia remained the only major country in which women were formally denied the right to vote. King Abdullah granted this right in 2011.

On June 17, 2011, however, Saudi women took to the streets to drive their cars in protest of such bans. While many were accompanied by husbands, brothers, and fathers, the action of driving placed increased pressure on the Saudi government to increase women's rights in the country. Saudi police responded to some women by issuing tickets for driv-

Women on Top

Recent years have seen the emergence of a number of remarkable women into significant leadership positions. After a hard-fought election campaign in 2005, Germany's Angela Merkel became the first woman chancellor. Mrs. Ellen Johnson-Sirleaf had been a pro-democracy activist in Liberia most of her life, working as a World Bank economist during periods when her country was a dictatorship, and she was forced into political exile. After a decade of civil war, Liberians turned to this grandmotherly economist in 2005 to lead them out of their protracted misery. In 2011, Mari Kiviniemi was prime minister of Finland, while Julia Gillard took the helm in Australia. Cristina de Kircher was president of Argentina, Dilma Rousseff won the presidential election in Brazil, and Laura Chinchilla Miranda was president of Costa Rica. Rosa Otunbayeva was acting president of embattled Kyrgyzstan in 2010, and in July 2010, Slovakia got Prime Minister Iveta Radicova as leader of a coalition government.

Figure 3.2.   Ms. Ellen Johnson-Sirleaf, President of Liberia, with Nelson Mandela of South Africa. Courtesy of the government of Liberia.

ing without a license, which were promptly uploaded onto Facebook and Twitter. Per our social media discussion in chapter 1, these Saudi female activists coordinated via Facebook and Twitter with each other and with the rest of the globe.[9] Despite many social and political problems in neighboring Iran, women can both vote and hold public office.

Feminists began to demand political equality at the end of the 1800s and had achieved at least theoretical equality in most Western democracies by the end of World War II. While women acquired the same citizenship rights as men (most important, the **franchise**, or the right to vote), genuine female political equality has been slow to develop and is still sometimes explicitly denied.

When women were first given the franchise in Britain after World War I, alarmists fretted that women would use their majority in the population to create political majorities for themselves in parliament, and even a woman prime minister. Ironically, Britain's first female head of government, Margaret Thatcher, won more support among men than among women. In general, however, studies suggest that voters of both genders overwhelmingly vote for male politicians. Traditionally, women tended to vote for conservative and religiously oriented parties, but this pattern is reversing as women become better educated. Why? Some theorists believe that the female experience of politics is different. Mothers may be more interested in safe streets and good schools (typical liberal issues), while their husbands may focus on more-conservative issues such as national pride and power. In the United States, Britain, and most European countries, a female majority votes for the left of center party, while most males tend to favor the right of center party.[10]

One widely used measurement of the intensity of female participation in a political system is the percentage of women in the national legislature. At the beginning of the twenty-first century, the percentage was highest in Scandinavia's social democracies, with

Sweden leading the pack at 45 percent. The United States has an improving, but still lackluster, 17 percent (House of Representatives and Senate combined).[11]

The generally low level of female participation in political life is an obvious reflection of slow-to-change attitudes about gender roles in society as a whole. Men are often perceived as forceful and aggressive, while women are seen as gentle and nurturing. Ironically, many of the women who have achieved dominance in world politics have brought a macho, take-no-prisoners attitude to the job. India's Indira Gandhi, Israel's Golda Meir, Britain's Margaret Thatcher, and Sri Lanka's Chandrika Kumaratunga all led their nations into war.[12]

The Gay Nation

On any list of powerful women, Iceland's prime minister Johanna Sigurdardottir deserves a special mention. She took charge of her financially shaky country in 2009, and formally married her same-sex partner in 2010. The reaction from the Icelandic people? There wasn't one. Ms. Sigurdardottir's future career will depend upon whether or not she can create financial stability in a shattered banking system; her domestic arrangements are, at least in Iceland, her own business. The socialist Bertrand Delanoë (who has never made either an issue or a secret about his gender orientation) has served as the popular mayor of Paris since 2001.

This degree of public indifference to gender orientation is not universal. Political conflict arises not only from gender but also from gender orientation. Homosexuality has been the subject of intense political debate, legislation, and occasional violence in many countries. Homosexuals joined Jews and Gypsies in Hitler's concentration camps and gas chambers during the Nazi era. Suffering the formal disapproval of all major religions, homosexuality has been slow to emerge from the legal shadows.

A few European countries decriminalized same-sex relationships between consenting adults in the 1930s, but the emancipation of homosexual relationships generally did not occur until after World War II. Homosexuality became more or less legal in the United States in 1961, and the U.S. Supreme Court has subsequently struck down some remaining state laws against gay sexuality, bringing American practice more in line with legislation in Europe, Canada, and the democracies of the Pacific such as Japan, Australia, and New Zealand. By the 1970s, the scientific community had generally abandoned the notion that homosexuality was a mental disease, accepting that a small percentage of humans were biologically oriented toward same-sex relationships.

Homosexuality is one of the litmus tests in politics. We'll define concepts such as "liberal" and "conservative" more fully in chapter 6, but liberals tend to regard homosexuality as a private matter and advocate full legal and social rights for gays. Some conservatives view homosexuality as a moral or psychiatric problem and generally do not wish to grant gays the same minority-rights status claimed by ethnic minorities or disabled people. Recognizing an emerging middle-class, politically active community of gay voters, candidate Bill Clinton promised greater governmental sensitivity to alternative lifestyles. After attempting to persuade the Pentagon to accept homosexuals in the military, President Clinton was forced to live with a clumsy "Don't Ask Don't Tell" policy under which homosexuals could still be denied the right to serve in the armed forces. On September 20, 2011, "Don't Ask Don't Tell" was repealed, and gays can now serve openly in the U.S. military.

Should homosexuals be allowed to marry and raise children? In June of 2011, the state of New York decided that they should, but the issue is not a trivial one. When two people set up a household together and create a family, the court system may be required to arbitrate property rights between them should the relationship break down. The safety and protection of any children is also of obvious public concern. In a legally unrecognized same-sex relationship, one partner might be denied the right to visit the other partner in the hospital, look after the partner's biological children, or handle the legal affairs of a disabled partner. On the other hand, most people in most countries continue to regard "marriage" as a religious, social, and legal relationship between two persons of different genders.

Many countries and some U.S. states have attempted to address this political issue by pioneering what is often called "civil union" legislation, which is intended to give life partners some, if not all, of the legal rights of heterosexual partners, while denying them the use of the word "marriage." In five very liberal societies, either legislators or courts have authorized the granting of marriage licenses to same-sex couples who wish to formalize their unions. Belgium, Holland, Spain, South Africa, and Canada have all legitimized gay marriages with varying levels of controversy. This polarizing conflict, involving a mixture of religious, legal, and social issues, seems likely to remain a feature of political debate for decades to come.

THE POLITICS OF AGE: OLD AND YOUNG

What does age have to do with political conflict? As it turns out, a great deal. Older people vote a lot more regularly than young people, and children can't vote in any modern society. A country with a high percentage of older people is likely to be politically stable; a poor country with a large population of unemployed youngsters is ready for revolution. We'll go more deeply into these problems in chapter 13, but for now, let's glance briefly at a couple of age-related problems.

The Graying of the Globe

While most good news contains a touch of bad news, the good news here should cheer us all up. Except in parts of Africa where the AIDS epidemic is cutting life expectancy dramatically, life spans are increasing almost everywhere, even in medium HDI societies. We now have a global life expectancy of about seventy, and some scientists expect that number to rise substantially in the near future.[13]

Money may not buy you happiness, but, generally speaking, it can add a few years to your life span. As table 3.3 illustrates, life expectancy is related to economic success, although the relationship is complex. The Japanese life expectancy at birth is 83.4 years. In war-torn Afghanistan, it is a depressing 49 years.[14] Why do Japanese live about twice as long as Afghans? Clearly, there are many answers, of which "prosperity" is generally the most basic. Public safety is another; Japanese people normally die in bed and without bullet holes in them. Afghanistan has been a brutal battlefield since the 1970s. Japan recently announced that the country had ten thousand centenarians (people over one hundred years old). Although many Japanese men smoke, they also eat a healthy, low-fat diet, exercise regularly, and enjoy universal (but private) medical coverage.

Americans like to assure themselves that they have the best medical system in the world, but the raw statistics don't provide much comfort. In 2011, the life expectancy of often-overweight Americans was 78.5 years, about a year behind the European Union where health care is generally free. Naturally, there are huge internal differences in life expectancy within individual countries; in the United States, white women live approximately twenty years longer than do black men.

How many years does it take to make you a senior citizen? Old age is tough to define, but most sociologists and demographers regard sixty-five as the start of old age. By that standard, about 6 percent of the world's population is elderly, although the number is twice as high in very high HDI countries.

Are you and your grandparents engaged in political conflict? There actually are a variety of ways in which young people compete with their elders for scarce resources. Do we need more day-care centers, or more facilities for senior citizens? There is free medical care for elders in American society in the form of Medicare; should there be an equivalent program for children?

Think, for example, about the American Social Security program into which young people begin to pay as soon as they begin to work. These retirement plans originally assumed many people would have large families, work for many years, enjoy a few years of retirement, and then obligingly die. The trend in recent years, however, has been for people to have fewer babies, retire earlier, and live well into their eighties. This means that fewer workers are supporting more retired people. While a lot of people living a long time is a good problem to have, it's still a problem, and American politicians entertain themselves (and frighten the rest of us) by predicting the exact year in which the U.S. Social Security system will run out of money.

A World of Children

In many respects, it's harder to define childhood than to define old age. Fifteen is about the minimum in most countries for legal sexual relations and marriage, although some Middle Eastern and African countries allow girls to marry a few years younger. Countries following Anglo-Saxon law usually regard twenty-one as the age at which adults can legally sign contracts, run for public office, and drink alcohol. The UN defines childhood as ending on the fifteenth birthday. By this definition, an amazing one-third of the world's population is composed of children, that is more than two billion young people.[15]

Culturally, the meaning of childhood varies substantially from country to country. One could argue that children are those who are still supported by their parents; perhaps we only become adults when we move out and start living on our own paychecks. By this measure, many Western university students in their middle twenties are economic children, while millions of Asian and African youngsters are economic adults, earning all or most of their own living. While the number seems to be edging down, about 190 million children (under age fifteen) are in the workforce, about half of them engaged in hazardous activities.[16] Many are farm laborers, but nearly ten million children are de facto slaves, involuntary prostitutes, beggars, or "mules" who carry narcotics across borders.

No society currently allows children under eighteen to vote, so the interests of politically powerless infants and children in society are often neglected. Despite the fact that the welfare of children is a common theme for politicians on the campaign trail, elected officials can be slow to honor their campaign pledges. In every society, children are more likely to live in economic distress than are adults. The World Health Organization reports that about fifty thousand children are murdered worldwide every year.[17] Even in the generally wealthy United States, about one out of every five children lives in poverty. There are three problem areas in the status of children worldwide: health, education, and legal status.

- Health: There are two commonly used indicators of children's health. The older and more frequently quoted is the **infant mortality rate (IMR)**, defined as the number of children out of every one thousand babies born alive who fail to reach their first birthday. The IMR is often used as a broad but crucial indicator of public health. The U.S. IMR is an almost-respectable 7.8:1000. Arguing that the experience of the first five years of life is a better indicator of health conditions in a society, the United Nations has increasingly shifted to the **under five mortality rate (U5MR)**, which is always going to be slightly higher. Globally speaking, the U5MR is fifty-eight, which means that about one out of twenty children on this planet dies within five years of birth. As we will see in chapter 13, many of these early childhood deaths could be prevented with inexpensive medical treatments.[18]
- Education: The good news about education is that there are now more children attending elementary school than ever before, with about 89 percent of the world's children enrolled in some form of primary education.[19] Problem areas remain, however. In the Middle East, many elementary schools teach almost nothing but the Islamic religion, which leaves their graduates imbued with a narrow view of the world and generally unprepared to earn a living. Globally, many primary and secondary schools are unsafe and underfunded, a particular scandal for well-heeled Europeans and Americans. And there is a gender connection here as well: globally speaking, most children who are not enrolled in any form of schooling are female. As a result, the majority of the world's illiterates are female.[20]
- Legal Status: Globally, about 33 percent of all children are not legally registered when they are born; so, they may not be entitled to the legal benefits of citizenship as they mature. In many parts of the world, children are bought and sold as slaves in all but name, and a thriving sex industry exists in parts of Asia that offers very young children as sex workers. In 1990, the United Nations offered for signature and ratification its landmark **Convention on the Rights of the Child**, a multilateral treaty that defines for the first time what obligations governments and societies have toward children. With the exceptions of the United States and Somalia, the convention has been ratified by every sovereign state on earth, although some are unable or unwilling to fulfill the provisions.[21] Somalia didn't sign because it lacks a functioning government. The United States rejected the convention, partially out of general dislike of the United Nations, and partially because the treaty prohibited the execution of young people for crimes committed before their eighteenth birthday. Since the U.S. Supreme Court has subsequently ruled that child executions are illegal, there is no longer a technical reason the Senate could not consent to the convention, but it would still take sixty-seven senators to pass it.

KINSHIP, "RACE," AND ETHNICITY

After gender and age, the next logical subdivision of humankind is perhaps kinship, often called "race." We leave logic behind, however, when we talk about race, a conceptual minefield that often involves some basic definitional dilemmas. What do we mean when we say "race"? Indeed, do races actually exist in the scientific sense, or should we abandon the whole concept to the Ku Klux Klan?

It's hard to find a scholar who thinks the concept of race is scientifically very useful. The phrase is vaguely used to refer to a group of people who share certain genetically determined physical characteristics such as skin color. A more useful and less emotional term would be "kinship," the sense among a group of people that they are genetically related to one another, having all descended from a common set of ancestors.

We are what we are because of two factors, kinship and culture, and here lies the definitional problem. In the sociological sense of the word, culture refers to the characteristics we acquire after being born, regardless of our kinship. For example, a person of Japanese parentage who lives in Japan, speaks Japanese, practices the Shinto religion, votes in Japanese elections, and cheers for the Japanese team during the Olympics shares both Japanese kinship and Japanese culture. But how do we describe a person who has the same undiluted Japanese genetic ancestry or kinship but was born and raised in Manhattan, speaks only English, goes to an Episcopalian church, and roots for the New York Yankees? Japanese-Americans are still Japanese in the sense of sharing genetic kinship with people who live in Japan, but they are culturally American.

In an effort to combine these two concepts (kinship and culture), scholars often resort to the term "**ethnic** group," which anthropologists use to refer to a group within a larger society that "displays a unique set of cultural traits."[22] African Americans, for example, are often described as an ethnic group because of skin coloration, which is a biological issue, not a cultural one. The African American community is genetically only about 70 percent "pure" African, since many African Americans have some European ancestry. While most of their biological ancestors came from widely separated parts of the African continent, African Americans are culturally American in the sense that they live in the United States, speak English, most practice Christianity, vote in American elections, and self-identify as Americans. Most African Americans would argue reasonably that they participate in a distinctive African American culture or subculture, but whatever their ethnicity, they are far more American than African. The United States, Canada, and Australia are all immigrant societies and each offers many examples of a split between biological kinship and national culture.[23]

Do these imprecise definitions of race, ethnicity, and kinship make sense? No. Are we stuck with them? Apparently yes. For our purposes here, an ethnic group is a community that displays enough similar physical and/or cultural characteristics to distinguish them from neighboring communities.

In a slightly different sense of the word, "ethnic" is often used to describe people of a given cultural/national group who live outside their home country. As we will learn in chapter 11, there are Albanian-speakers who live in Kosovo, which is technically a province of Serbia currently under the jurisdiction of the United Nations and led by a female president, Atifete Jahjaga. To distinguish these Kosovar Albanians from their cousins who live in the nearby Republic of Albania, they are often called "ethnic Albanians."

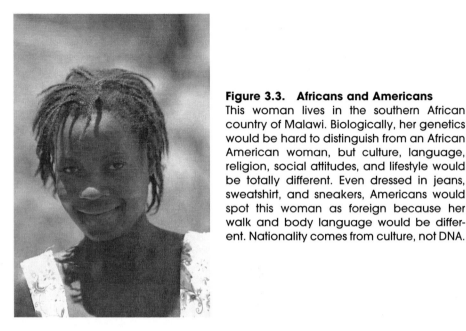

Figure 3.3. Africans and Americans
This woman lives in the southern African country of Malawi. Biologically, her genetics would be hard to distinguish from an African American woman, but culture, language, religion, social attitudes, and lifestyle would be totally different. Even dressed in jeans, sweatshirt, and sneakers, Americans would spot this woman as foreign because her walk and body language would be different. Nationality comes from culture, not DNA.

Some writers have made earnest efforts to demonstrate that race can be correlated with intelligence, but the scholarly community has overwhelmingly rejected this approach.[24] A book called *The Bell Curve* provoked a violent controversy in 1994 by arguing that there were innate differences in intelligence among various "races" or kinship groups. While different ethnic communities perform differently on standardized intelligence tests, most scholars attribute the differences to cultural and economic factors. Notions of racial inferiority/superiority, however, still circulate at the level of popular consciousness. No American reader needs to be informed that racial antagonism is still a potent factor in U.S. politics.

The rapidly evolving science of DNA suggests that we are a single and closely related species. Every human is descended from a small group of people who lived in eastern Africa about 150,000 years ago. About ten thousand generations have passed, but the species has not become very differentiated in physiological terms. Many physical characteristics, like skin coloration, are the result of what Darwin called "natural selection." It is hot and sunny close to the equator, and people with dark skin survive better there because of their greater resistance to skin cancer. Pale skin absorbs vitamin D from sunlight better than does dark skin, so lighter people flourish in northern regions where sunshine is limited. This color adaptation holds true for any species with a planetary distribution. Bunny rabbits and butterflies all become lighter in color the closer they get to the North Pole.[25]

To complicate matters, certain populations first developed these adaptations for survival in specific areas, but then moved (or were moved) to different habitats, so that whites with sensitive skins are now contracting skin cancer in sun-drenched Florida while African Americans catch pneumonia during chilly Alaskan winters. Were everyone disposed to stay home and marry the boy or girl across the street, the world's "races" might display more consistent physical characteristics or "racial purity." Nigerians would forever look like Nigerians, and Swedes like Swedes. As a species, however, we display an increased tendency to move around and—to put it indelicately—sleep around, causing what anthropologists politely call "gene flow."[26] This means that kinship groups do not have very hard edges; traveling from Helsinki to New Delhi involves watching populations blend into one another without sharp and easily definable breaks. Particularly in immigrant societies, the differences among racial groups are slowly breaking down.[27] As the first student of human kinship groups, Carolus Linnaeus, recognized three hundred years ago, we are one species. After a few more centuries of trading genes, we may begin to look more like one species.

2. Dividing Up the World by Language

In terms of fundamental distinctions within the human family, **language** ranks close to gender and kinship groups. The political role played by language diversity is somewhat understudied. Political scientists often don't speak that many foreign languages, and professorial linguists don't always follow world politics very carefully. Traveling with their translators, journalists often miss the linguistic component in world news and social conflict. So we're going to start by cramming Linguistics 101 into a couple of paragraphs, and then look at how the planet's linguistic diversity affects our political and social relationships with one another.

One obstacle to understanding language-based conflict for U.S. students is the fact that Americans tend to view the world from the heart of a monolingual culture. Despite the fact that most U.S. universities still require a few basic courses in some foreign language as part of the core curriculum, Americans seldom master a foreign language. This is regrettable because speaking and reading any foreign language teaches us a lot about the way in which languages work and provides us with a feel for the problems of communicating across language barriers. Let's start with some fundamentals.

SPEECH COMMUNITIES

Linguist David Crystal defines a language as "the systematic, conventional use of sounds, signs, or written symbols in a human society for communication and self-expression,"

Talking Your Way into a Job

Would you like to nail down guaranteed lifetime employment in some profession? Choose one of the less-frequently studied foreign languages and learn it well. After the al-Qaeda attacks in September of 2001, everybody abruptly needed speakers of Arabic. During the 2001–2002 war against the Taliban, the U.S. government scrambled to find translators who could deal with the multiple languages of Afghanistan. If you do the work needed to master Swahili, Portuguese, Tamil, Malay, Chinese, or Arabic, news services, intelligence agencies, multinational corporations, and universities will beat a path to your door with job offers.

Source: James Bamford, *Body of Secrets* (New York: Anchor, 2002), 648.

which sounds obvious enough.[28] If you and I share enough of the same sounds, signs, and written symbols to make communication possible (the technical term is "**mutual intelligibility**"), we're speaking or writing the same language and we share a speech community. At the most elementary level, two people are using two different languages when they encounter overwhelming obstacles to communication. How many languages are there, and what kinds of political problems flow from this fact?

There are about six thousand definably different languages in use today around the world. Clearly, some languages resemble one another quite closely. Anyone who speaks Italian will recognize many words in Spanish, although a serious conversation will be a problem. Other languages bear no resemblance to one another. Knowing French, for example, will be of little use in understanding Hindi (a language widely spoken in India), since there are few similarities between these tongues.

Some linguists believe our most distant human ancestors spoke a common language perhaps about 150,000 years ago that has been completely lost. As humankind grew in numbers and spread around the globe to live in isolated communities, this original language splintered into a series of separate languages that were no longer mutually intelligible. While those protolanguages are also lost, they became the ancestors for several clusters or families of modern languages.

The largest of these is the Indo-European language family, which includes more than half of all the world's existing sublanguages or groups. Subfamilies, such as the Germanic, Slavic, Romance, Persian, and Indian languages are all descendents of an early version of Indo-European. There are a number of other language families that are important to us politically. The Sino-Tibetan language group contains Chinese and Tibetan. The Afro-Asiatic cluster features Arabic, Hebrew, and several North African and Middle Eastern tongues. Many Pacific Ocean islanders speak one of the many Malayo-Polynesian languages. And southern Indians speak a variety of Dravidian tongues such as Tamil. Scholars often disagree about what language belongs in what language family and even about how many distinct language families there are.

What's a **dialect**? From a purely linguistic point of view, the word simply means a variant form of some language. Some linguists use the word very broadly, simply to indicate a different way of speaking a given language, perhaps indicating social class or regional identification. The differences between a dialect and the standard version of a given language, or between two dialects of the same language, will typically involve variations in pronunciation, grammar, and vocabulary. From the political point of view, we might think in terms of "near" dialects (where speakers can understand each other easily) and "far" dialects (where there are enough differences to make communication difficult, but not impossible). If communications problems are so great that the two ways of speaking lack mutual intelligibility, then we are dealing with two separate languages rather than dialects. In real life, the distinction is always going to be problematic. When two people are speaking different dialects of the same language, some will find the difficulty manageable and others will not, which means we can fight about what are merely dialects and what are actually separate languages.

Politics and nationalism can make it difficult to use linguistic terminology in a way that makes political sense. For example, Swedish, Danish, and Norwegian are routinely described as three **cognate** languages of the Germanic family of languages. In fact, the peoples of Sweden, Denmark, and Norway can actually understand each other

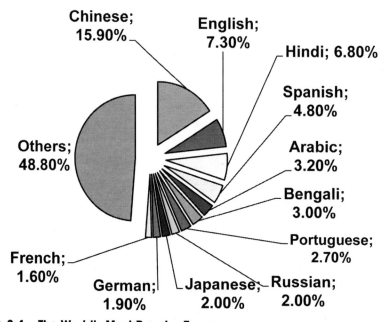

Figure 3.4. The World's Most Popular Tongues
Students of linguistics believe that these eleven languages, spoken by more than one hundred million people, are used by more than half of the human race. There are nine more languages spoken by another 44 percent of humankind. Of these, Punjabi, Bihari, Telugu, Tamil, and Marathi are all South Asian languages. Javanese is widely spoken in Southeast Asia along with Vietnamese. Korean and Italian round out the most popular twenty. Only 4 percent of the human race speaks a language not somewhere on the top-twenty list.

moderately well and read each other's books and newspapers. Someone even once quipped that "Norwegian is Danish spoken in Swedish." Why then don't we describe Swedish, Danish, and Norwegian as three dialects of a single Scandinavian language? Linguistically, it would make sense, but in practice, it would produce howls of patriotic protest in Stockholm, Copenhagen, and Oslo.

Here is another example: Dutch is essentially the same language as Flemish (the language of many Belgians) and Afrikaans (the language spoken by South Africans of Dutch descent). These three mutually intelligible dialects of the same language are usually described as three separate languages, not because they are very different, but because they are spoken in three separate sovereign countries.

The opposite problem occurs when what are really distinct cognate languages are described, for political reasons, as dialects of one language. This practice can convey an impression of national or linguistic unity in cultures where people actually cannot talk to one another. Arabic is one example. From Morocco to Iraq, educated Arabs speak Modern Standard Arabic (a language closely based on the Koran or Qur'an), so a businessperson from Casablanca can communicate with a professor from Basra. But less-educated Arabs will typically speak only one of Arabic's many dialects (sometimes called "vernaculars"), most of which lack mutual intelligibility. This means that farmers from

Oman can't really talk to shepherds from Algeria. Chinese is another good example; while it is usually considered the largest human language, east Asia's 1.2 billion Chinese can't actually all talk to one another.[29]

When countries fall apart, so do languages, and the disintegration of what was once Yugoslavia provides an example. Serbs in Belgrade and Croats in Zagreb were always regarded as speakers of the same **Serbo-Croatian** language, with some minor differences in accent and vocabulary. Now that Croatia is a separate sovereign entity, Croatian linguists are publishing books in what they call the "Croatian" language, a national language with an independent literature and grammar. The Serbians now see Serbian as an independent language, and Bosnians call their language Bosnian, although it is really a cluster of Serbo-Croatian dialects.

A common language can sometimes translate into a political or military alliance. The western front in World War II was essentially a coalition of English-speaking nations. Both wars against Iraq (1991 and 2003) were essentially Anglo-American operations. After the American tragedy of September 11, 2001, the rest of the world sent sympathy cards; Tony Blair's Britain sent troops, battleships, and fighter-bombers to help drive the Afghan **Taliban** out of Kabul. And the popularity of English as a second language has enormous political ramifications. English is used by perhaps two billion people who speak it well enough to conduct at least simple, practical conversations and understand radio and television broadcasts. Some commentators have wondered if this does not allow English-speaking political leaders to impose an essentially Anglo-American point of view on the rest of the planet.

Dialects are almost always regional in the sense that they are spoken in a specific area of a country, in the way that the Sicilian dialect of Italian is found predominantly on the island of Sicily. In any language, dialects frequently are stronger at the bottom of a socio-economic totem pole, so that poorer people in a given community might speak a stronger (or harder to comprehend) version of a given dialect. Speakers of standard English can make themselves understood almost anywhere in the English-speaking world, but you may run into problems understanding what people are saying back to you in a restaurant in Cape Town or a working-class pub in Scotland.[30]

LANGUAGES AND POLITICAL CONFLICT

Sharing a language is no guarantee that people will live in blissful peace. Despite their common language, Americans fought the British in the Revolutionary War and the War of 1812, and then monolingually slaughtered each other in the Civil War. Many central Africans and virtually all Rwandans speak Kinyarwanda, a member of the Bantu family of languages, but this mutual intelligibility did not prevent the genocidal massacre of the Tutsi minority by the Hutu majority in 1994. Conversely, a country where several different languages are spoken is not necessarily a battlefield. In Switzerland, for example, two dialects of German coexist cheerfully with French, standard Italian, and a Latin-based language called Romansch.[31] On the other hand, some political quarrels around the world stem directly from language problems. In other cases, an existing conflict is exacerbated by the presence of two or more languages.

Crossing the Divide

Communicating across a language barrier can be tricky, although some linguistic tangles can be harmless and funny. The people of Warsaw are still chuckling over the time that President Jimmy Carter visited Poland. In his formal remarks, Carter assured his audience that he "liked Polish people," but the president's translator generated a phrase meaning, "I lust after Polish women," which had the audience rolling on the floor.[32]

As President Carter's translator ought to have known, a word in one language has overtones and connotations that may change or disappear when you translate them into a second language, particularly if there are deep cultural differences involved. Here's an example cited by the celebrated Middle Eastern scholar William R. Polk: We routinely read of "terrorist suicide bombers" in places such as Israel/Palestine and in Iraq. Everything linguistic about the phrase "terrorist suicide bomber" expresses our intense disapproval of the practice. Terrorists are bad people, and suicide is the ultimate sin in every revealed religion. To express the same concept in Arabic, however, we start with the basic Arabic root *Sh-H-D*, which conveys the idea of witnessing or giving testimony to one's religious faith. Building upon this Koranic root, we get *ShaHāDa* or martyrdom, and one who actively seeks martyrdom to demonstrate or give witness to his faith is a *muShtaHiD*. This doesn't mean that Muslims automatically approve of suicide bombers; it does mean that the deep meaning of the Arabic word is positive, not negative, whatever we may think of the merits of a given act of self-destructive violence against others.[33] Sometimes everything gets lost in translation.

Word Wars

With a lot of work and goodwill, we can get across a linguistic divide, but crowding two ethnic communities speaking two separate languages (i.e., without mutual intelligibility) into one political space can be a disaster because nobody ever quite understands anybody else.

The troubled island of Cyprus, for example, is home to Greeks and Turks, who utterly refuse to learn one another's languages. The same problem occurs in modern Israel, where resentful Arab employees must learn rudimentary Hebrew to understand their bosses, while Israeli police officers sometimes use an insulting **pidgin** Arabic to shout at West Bank Palestinians.

Some languages are national in the sense that they are spoken almost universally within the borders of one country. Japan and Sweden, for example, are both overwhelmingly mono-lingual; almost everybody in Japan speaks Japanese, and the overwhelming majority of the world's Japanese-speakers live within that country's borders. As a society, Japan has its problems, but at least its people can all understand each other. However, this neat fit between language and country is rare. Many languages, such as English, Spanish, and Arabic, are **transnational**, in that each is the principal language in many countries and often a major second language in many others.

Unfortunately, most of the world's countries are home to two or more speech communities. Individual languages are therefore subnational, only one of several minority tongues. Of Nigeria's 124 million people, about twenty-five million are speakers of the Yoruba language, also spoken by some communities across the border in Benin and Togo, but nowhere is it a majority tongue.[34] The development of black majority rule in South Africa has been inhibited by language difficulties among the ten major Bantu language groups, only some of which are mutually intelligible.

One Language One Country

We'll talk more about nationalism in chapter 4, but for now simply observe that the existence of a language community can create a demand for that community to be granted political independence. About 23 percent of all Canadians speak French as their first (and sometimes only) language, and most of them live in the province of Quebec. Canada is a wealthy and successful society, but it lives with the constant threat that the people of Quebec will someday secede from Canada to create a French-speaking country of their own, a topic we'll consider more fully in chapter 4. In 2010, the Belgian government resigned over that country's eternal language divide. In the prosperous northern part of the country, Belgians speak Flemish, which is basically a dialect of Dutch. In the South, they speak Walloon, which is a dialect of French. Brussels is a linguistically mixed city where Belgians meet to shout at each other in the country's two different languages.

Spain has the same problem in several parts of the country. In the Far North around the city of Bilbao, speakers of the Basque language have always wondered why linguistic independence should not be accompanied by political separation from Madrid. And in Spain's prosperous Catalan region, around the city of Barcelona, speakers of Catalonian have always asserted that they speak a rich and distinctive language of their own, not a mere dialect of Spanish. In the past, the authorities in Madrid responded to these demands for local linguistic rights with brutal repression, but since Spain became a democracy in 1975, the central government has engaged in an endless dialogue with the several speech communities within its national borders, defining and redefining the precise relationship of each with the national government in Madrid.

Even accents can have political importance. People may speak the same dialect of the same language but do it with remarkably diverse accents, pronouncing the same words differently. Here too there is often a class-based difference; in many societies a given accent betrays inferior social status or conversely announces refined breeding. British politics, for example, is rife with controversy over class and accent. The famous Margaret Thatcher was actually born on the line between working class and lower middle class, but when she aspired to national leadership, the Iron Lady took her English upmarket with elocution lessons. To the working class, she sounded "posh," but authentic upper-class people always saw her as a vulgar gate-crasher, and they turned on her with a vengeance the moment she became politically vulnerable.

How Many Languages Can You Speak?

Don't be embarrassed if the answer is only one; comparatively few Americans master a foreign language, even those of immigrant stock who come from households where some ancestral language is spoken. Even American political leaders have seldom learned a foreign language, although the major candidates for the presidency in 2000 and 2004 had a working knowledge of Spanish, perhaps a sign of the growing importance of the U.S. Hispanic community. In Europe, where countries are close together and international travel and trade is very brisk, learning two or more languages is considered normal, and many children are raised bilingual or multilingual. Globally, about two-thirds of the world's population speaks more than one language, since most African and Asian countries have linguistically mixed populations.

THE POLITICS OF WRITING SYSTEMS

Humankind has had written languages for five thousand years, and over the course of that time, a variety of writing systems have evolved. At the risk of gross oversimplification, commentators frequently divide the various scripts or writing systems into three very loose categories.

- Logographic Systems: Each character in Chinese represents either a word or a syllable (i.e., part of a word), but many of these symbols only tell us what the word means, not how it is meant to be pronounced. The Chinese have also adapted a set of phonetic signs to help them write words for which there are no accepted logographs. Politically, the implications are profound: while Americans need only learn the twenty-six letters of the alphabet for basic literacy, Chinese students must master between two and four thousand characters, making it harder to achieve literacy. This arcane writing system acts as a cultural barrier to foreigners who might otherwise learn Chinese. Modern communication systems, such as computers, do not adapt very well to this system of writing. Since a given Chinese character may tell us only what the word means and not how it is meant to be pronounced, people in different parts of China will pronounce the same word differently, contributing to the dialectalization or fragmentation of the language.[35]

Inscrutable Spelling and First Names Last

The Chinese writing system conveys information about the meaning of a word but is not very much help in pronunciation, making it a difficult writing system to transliterate into our roman alphabet. Invented by two British scholars, the Wade-Giles transliteration system was universal until 1958 when the mainland Chinese rejected it in favor of the pinyan or phonetic system. Hence, Peking became Beijing, while Mao's last name mutated from Tse-Tung to Zedung. For the most part, Taiwan continues to use Wade-Giles, however, and people and institutions that became prominent before 1958 are sometimes still known in Western literature by the Wade-Giles version of their names. Hence, the famous Nationalist Chinese leader, Jiang Jieshi, is still more popular in English as Chiang Kai-shek. In reading about China, remember that different authors will make different choices about what to call people and places.

Here is a note on Oriental names: with the exception of Japan, most Asian societies give the family name first, followed by one or more personal names. Should you meet Wen Jiabao, the Chinese prime minister, address him as Mr. Wen, because Jiabao is what his family and friends call him.

Source: David Crystal, *Penguin Dictionary of Language*, 2nd ed. (London: Penguin, 1999), 54–55.

- Syllabic or Consonantal Systems: Ancient Semitic scripts, such as Hebrew, were originally written with only consonants and no vowels, and this script style has spread across from the Middle East to South Asia. Some consonantal systems (such as modern Arabic and modern Hebrew) are still mostly written without vowel signs, which is why we get so many different versions of Arabic words (e.g., Moslem vs. Muslim and Koran vs. Qur'an). **Transliteration** can cause confusion: Americans have decided that Osama bin Laden's organization is "al-Qaeda," but the British press spells it "al-Qaida." Some Indian languages write consonants with diacritical marks to suggest vowels, and a few true syllabic systems have separate signs for every possible consonant-vowel combination. One variant of this system appears in the Japanese writing system, *kana*.
- Alphabetic Systems: The world's most popular system uses both consonants and vowels independently to suggest with some accuracy how to pronounce a given word. English and most other European languages, and many non-European tongues have adopted one of several alphabet scripts. Most Western European languages use the roman alphabet. Most of Eastern Europe was converted to Christianity by Greek missionaries such as St. Cyril, who was partly responsible for the creation of the Cyrillic alphabet, used in the writing of many Slavic languages. The Greek language continues to be written in its own alphabet, and Armenian has a separate and distinctive alphabetic script. There isn't much connection between languages and writing systems, since some oriental languages, such as Vietnamese, are written in modified versions of the roman alphabet.

A lot of politics goes into the clash between roman and Cyrillic alphabets. In ethnically divided Bosnia, for example, Bosnian Serbs write their version of Serbo-Croatian in Cyrillic, while Bosnian Croatians proclaim their allegiance to the West by using the roman alphabet. When Azerbaijan (a new republic on the Caspian Sea) was part of the now-vanished Soviet Union, the Azeris were obliged to write their language (a cognate of Turkish) in Cyrillic. The Azeris have now switched to the roman alphabet as a way of reaching out to their future friends in Europe and the Americas, and rejecting their Russian past.[36]

3. Fighting over Faith: Religions and Conflict

Religion is one of those hard-to-define words, because there are a vast variety of radically different spiritual philosophies all called religions. In general, a religion is a cultural and/or institutional belief system affirming the existence of a supernatural order and providing both an explanation of the meaning of human life as well as a code of conduct. There are two broad categories of conflict that flow from religion, and we will look briefly at both of them in this section, and then see many examples of each as we make our way through the rest of the book.

RELIGION AS NATIONALISM

First, there is the sort of religious conflict that occurs when a faith becomes so closely identified with a given community that it adds religious fervor to nationalism. A classical example of this, to be discussed in more detail in chapter 11, is the antagonism between Catholics and Protestants in Northern Ireland. This nine-hundred-year-old feud isn't basically about the doctrinal differences between Protestantism and Catholicism, although these differences play a minor role. Among other things, it's about nationalism, but mixing religious zeal with national pride creates an explosive combination. Another good example comes to us from South Asia, home to many feuding faiths. As we will see, the country of Pakistan came into existence because some Indian Muslims wanted a **sectarian** state dedicated to the Islamic religion. With a few marginal exceptions, to be Pakistani is to be Muslim.

RELIGION AS IDEOLOGY

The second sort of conflict flows directly and specifically from the content of religion itself and might be called doctrinal conflict since it involves the **doctrine** (or the specific intellectual content of a given religion). In these cases, religious doctrine becomes part of one's ideology, moving out of the realm of religion into the arena of politics. One transnational example is the controversy over abortion, which is about ethics, not ethnicity. Most Catholics, many Protestants, and nearly all Muslims oppose abortion; antiabortion activists do not come from any particular religion. Most pro-life (i.e., antiabortion) activists campaign for their cause entirely within the law in the United States and in Europe. A few have become religious terrorists, assassinating health-care providers who terminate pregnancies.

Osama bin Laden's militant al-Qaeda group practices a violent death-oriented version of Islam that combines these two categories. Al-Qaeda's opposition to the United States and the West in general stems partly from a sense of religious nationalism, since many Muslims see the Islamic world as a spiritual nation fighting enemy nations such as Israel and the United States. At a more specific level, bin-Laden and his senior colleagues are mostly Arabs, who believe that the Arab people must take action to expel the Israelis and Western forces from their corner of the Middle East. In a spiritual sense, however, al-Qaeda sees itself as defending the doctrinal purity of the Islamic faith, regarding the Western world as immoral and the Muslim faith as the repository of insights into the way in which God/Allah wants the world run. We'll talk about al-Qaeda more in chapter 10.

RELIGION, COMMUNITY, AND SELF-IDENTITY

Not all religions assert the existence of a specific personal deity, but they all do involve a core set of ideas about the ultimate meaning of the cosmos with teachings about the transcendental or spiritual aspect to human life. Some religious communities (such as the Roman Catholic Church) are tightly organized or hierarchical, with officers, budgets, and international headquarters. Others (such as the Hindu and Islamic faiths) have little in the way of formal structures and involve folkways and culture as well as religious ideas.

Second, religions normally prescribe a code of conduct or an ethical system of some kind, a set of notions about right and wrong behavior. Since all governments create legislation regulating behavior, there is an inevitable overlap of, and sometimes conflict between, religion and political life.[37] Western religions tend to be monotheistic, based on the assumption that there is one deity ruling over the universe. Polytheistic religions assume multiple divine spirits who are sometimes seen as different manifestations of one universal spirit. The term **animist** is often dismissively applied to the religions of tribal peoples who revere spirits, inanimate objects, djinns, and ghosts.

Faith-Based Communities

Religion in immigrant societies such as the United States and Canada tends to be intellectually separate from citizenship or nationality; there is no Canadian national faith or American religion. People in immigrant societies often change religions as a result of convenience, marriage, or evolving spiritual need. Religion in the West may not be a visible or obvious portion of a person's identity; you may know fellow students or coworkers for years without being aware of their religious affiliation. In most other parts of the world, however, religions are more closely linked to national culture and may even form an essential part of national self-identification. Introductory texts often portray the world as subdivided into large, well-defined religions. As Toby Lester comments, however,

> That's dangerously simplistic. It assumes a stability in the religious landscape that is completely at odds with reality. New religions are born all the time. Old ones transform themselves dramatically. Schism, evolution, death, and rebirth are the norm. . . . The fact is that religion mutates with Darwinian restlessness.[38]

On the other hand, American students are often confused about the identity and general nature of some politically significant religious communities. Trying to understand, for example, the Arab-Israeli conflict without knowing something about Judaism and Islam is going to be tough. Let's start by looking very briefly at three monotheistic religions before focusing briefly on several Eastern polytheistic faiths. All of them have played a central role in specific political conflicts.

- Judaism: Judaism is the oldest of the three major monotheisms, and most of its central concepts, such as the idea of a personal, all-powerful spiritual deity who intervenes in history, have filtered into Christianity and Islam. Judaism sees itself as a covenant between God and a specific kinship group (the Jewish people) in which the welfare of the community depends upon its fidelity to God's commandments.[39] There may be no more than thirteen million Jews worldwide, but Judaism has been at the center of political conflict throughout the last several centuries, as Jews suffered genocidal persecution in Europe, and then created the state of Israel in a troubled corner of the Middle East. At one level, Judaism is a kinship group, since most Jews are biologically related to one another. Within this group, it is also a religious faith, although many Jews do not actually believe in the existence of a Supreme Being. Being Jewish usually also involves participating in a complicated multinational culture with folkways and cuisine and a sense of community. For some citizens of Israel—Judaism is also a political force. Most American Jews regard Judaism as a culture and a religious faith but not the basis for their nationality, since they are generally secure in their self-identification as Americans.

- Christianity: Christianity flows from Judaism generally, and specifically from the assertion that the life of Jesus Christ was the fulfillment of a divine promise to send a Savior to humankind. After the collapse of the Roman Empire, Christians in Western Europe remained under the spiritual authority of the bishops of Rome. In Eastern Europe, which became the Byzantine Empire, Christians tended to identify themselves more on the basis of language and nationality, and developed a number of national Catholic churches such as the Greek Orthodox, Russian Orthodox, and Serbian Orthodox churches. In Christian history, the term "Orthodox" is reserved for those churches that are Catholic in inspiration but do not generally accept the authority of the Roman Catholic pope.

  There is very little doctrinal difference between Roman Catholic and Orthodox Christianity, but the division has been at the heart of many political conflicts. In what was Yugoslavia, for example, Roman Catholic Croatians and Orthodox Serbs were often bitter enemies.[40] In the 1500s, in Western Europe, the Protestant Reformation gave birth to a variety of Christian but non-Catholic religions. Many European wars of the 1500s and 1600s were specifically religious in character. Except in Northern Ireland, there is currently little political conflict between Catholics and Protestants today.

- Islam: Many Americans focused on the Islamic religion for the first time during the first Gulf War (1990–1991), when U.S. troops were stationed in Saudi Arabia, a sternly Islamic society. Islam returned to the American national consciousness after September 11, 2001, when teams of Saudi and Egyptian Muslims attacked the Pentagon and the World Trade Center with hijacked aircraft.

  Islam is a monotheistic religion, a folkway, a political movement, and a philosophy of life tracing its origin to the Prophet Mohammed (570–632 AD). Individual practitioners of Islam are called Muslims (sometimes spelled Moslems). The doctrinal differences between Muslims and Christians are actually less significant than is commonly imagined, since both religions conceive of a spiritual deity, a code of conduct, and an afterlife of some kind. Islamic beliefs allowing multiple marriages and forbidding alcohol distinguish it from European religious practice.

  Many Muslims are Arabic-speakers, but there are non-Arab Islamic populations stretching across Asia from Turkey and Iran to Indonesia. There are two principal branches of the Islamic faith. The overwhelming majority of the world's Muslims are called **Sunni** Muslims, and they live in large communities from Morocco on the Atlantic Coast all the way through Central Asia and into Indonesia, the world's largest Muslim country. The practice of the Islamic religion is fairly standard through all of these Sunni communities, and you will not notice much difference in a Sunni service in a mosque in Atlanta, Georgia, or in Mecca, Saudi Arabia, or Islamabad, Pakistan.

  The minority **Shi'ite** community split away from the mainstream when their leader, Mohammed's son-in-law Ali, was assassinated, and Shi'ites have always believed that leadership in the community should be passed down through Mohammed's direct descendents. About 15 percent of all the world's Muslims are Shi'ites, and they live primarily in the eastern portion of the Arabian Peninsula, Iraq, and overwhelmingly in Iran, with a small community in southern Lebanon. As we will see throughout this book, conflicts within the Islamic world often involve antagonisms between Sunni and Shi'ite Muslims. For example, in the aftermath of the 2003 Iraq War, there has been a lively concern among the occupying powers (Britain and the United States) that Iraq's Shi'ites and Sunnis would be unable to live peacefully with one another.

- Hinduism: The religion followed by most citizens of the Republic of India embodies a set of attitudes about life and society. At the primitive level, Hinduism is polytheistic, preaching the existence of many gods, but to most sophisticated Hindus, this array of deities is merely a human attempt to suggest the characteristics of the one divine spirit.[41] Some Hindus, like some Jews, do not actually believe in a personal deity at all, tending to see the notion of God as a metaphor for nature or the life force that animates the universe.[42] Hindu-based nationalism has become a powerful force in the politics of South Asia.

- Buddhism: Evolving out of Indian Hinduism, Buddhism is based on the teachings of Siddhartha Gautama (Buddha, or the Enlightened One). The Theravada branch of the religion has spread across a great swath of Asia from Sri Lanka to Thailand, Cambodia, Burma, and Laos. The Mahayana variant has had a massive impact on China, Taiwan, Tibet, Nepal, Mongolia, and Vietnam. A variant called Shintoism serves as kind of a state religion for the Japanese. Buddha taught that life is suffering except for those whose level of enlightenment allows them to extinguish desire for earthly things within themselves. While technically polytheistic, Buddhism does not feature the all-powerful spiritual deity central to Western monotheisms.[43]

- Confucianism: Can there be a godless religion? Many Asians describe themselves as followers of Confucius, who lived in China in the sixth century before Christ. Confucianism is essentially an ethical philosophy, a system of behavior and social norms. Although some of his followers have combined his thoughts with Buddhism or Christianity, Confucius did not suggest that the universe came equipped with a deity. Confucianists follow the master's teachings because they feel that society works better that way, not because they anticipate being rewarded or punished in an afterlife. Confucius taught that our goal in life is to find and accept our place in society, be orderly and neat and polite, revere our ancestors, and respect authority. These beliefs (often combined with regular religions such as Christianity and Buddhism) are important in understanding Chinese and Japanese culture today.

Religious Demography

When it comes to religious communities, statistics are generally fallible. The September 11 attacks turned attention to the American Islamic community, but scholars discovered they didn't know to the nearest million how many Muslims lived in the United States and had no obvious way of finding out. The problem is that various religious communities count their members differently.

The Roman Catholic Church, for example, claims about a billion Roman Catholics, but it defines as Catholic all those baptized into the faith, as well as all those born in countries where Catholic baptism is routinely practiced. Hence, Italians are counted as Catholic unless they are specifically Protestants or Jews, despite the fact that relatively few Catholic Italians actually practice their religion.

Another problem in estimating the size (and hence the political importance) of a religious community is the fact that people are often dishonest about this aspect of their lives. During the years when the former USSR preached atheism, affirmation of faith precluded membership in the Communist Party and any hope of a successful career; the situation in today's China is roughly the same. Conversely, it might be socially difficult

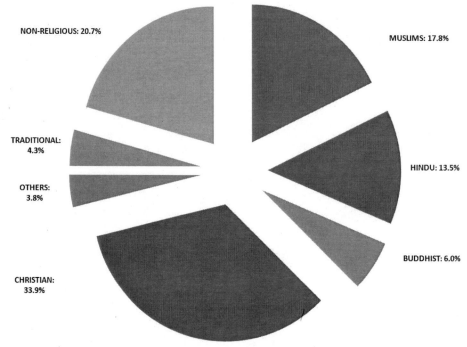

NON-RELIGIOUS: 20.7%

MUSLIMS: 17.8%

TRADITIONAL:
4.3%

OTHERS:
3.8%

HINDU: 13.5%

BUDDHIST: 6.0%

CHRISTIAN:
33.9%

Figure 3.5. Worldwide Religious Affiliation
Many so-called Christian countries have large populations of very secular people
who do not actively believe in or practice their religion. In contrast, most Muslims are
authentically religious at some level.

in intensely religious societies, such as the United States, Ireland, and the Middle East, to
admit to nonbelief; atheism is the ultimate closet.

Is religion becoming more popular or less popular? The issue is complicated. Most
students of the problem argue that mainline Western religions are becoming comparatively less popular (or shrinking as a percentage of the world total). This is partially due
to a basic demographic fact: population growth in Europe and North America is slow. It
may also be due to a process called **secularization**, which is a tendency within some societies for religion to become a less significant factor in people's lives. On the other hand,
Islam, Hinduism, and Buddhism are all booming, thanks in part to brisk population
growth within these communities. Along with Ireland and the Arab world, the United
States continues to be one of the world's most religious societies; 43 percent of Americans
go to church at least twice a month. Contrast this to Great Britain where only 69 percent
of the population say they believe in a supernatural being, and only 16 percent worship
at least six times a year. British religious habits are about average for a Western Europe
that is increasingly indifferent to religion.

Changing world population growth patterns will affect where and how contemporary
religions are practiced. Some scholars estimate that within half a century, two-thirds of
the world's Christians will be in Africa, Latin America, and Asia, while European and

North American communities will remain static or decline in size. In contrast to increasingly secular Europeans, African Christians are more likely to be conservative in their social views, and some have observed that Third-World Christianity is becoming anti-intellectual and fundamentalist.[44]

What is difficult to measure with statistics is the degree of passion or commitment to a given religion. In-depth interviews and surveys suggest that many of those counted as Christian are not practicing or even believing. In contrast, a large percentage of Muslims are fervent about their faith, which may mean that there may really be more practicing Muslims than practicing Christians. The Islamic religion is also booming because of the rapid birthrate among Muslims and the attractiveness of the religion to many Africans and Asians.

The Politics of Belief and Disbelief

If politics and religious belief are interconnected, it is clearly also the case that skepticism in matters of faith has political implications. A number of countries have an "established" religion, that is, one religion that is recognized by the government as the official religion and which may even receive subsidies from public funds. Christian examples include the Church of England (what Americans call the Anglican or Episcopalian Church) and Lutheran churches in Scandinavian countries. Oddly enough, all of these societies are somewhat secular in everyday life, and recognition of a state religion is little more than a historical artifact. In contrast, most Arabic states and some other Muslim countries, such as Pakistan and Iran, regard Islam as their officially sanctioned religion and make little distinction between religious and civil law.

Some political parties represent themselves as the political manifestation of a specific religion. In Germany, the Christian Democratic Union (CDU) represents Protestants (overwhelmingly Lutherans), while the Bavaria-based Christian Social Union (CSU) advances the political interests of Roman Catholics. In India, the Bharatiya Janata Party (BJP) is a specifically Hindu party, although it narrowly lost the 2004 elections and is now the opposition party.

It is always difficult to know what goes on in the hearts and minds of working politicians, but European political leaders tend to downplay their religious beliefs. Religiously inclined voters may cast their ballots for a politician occasionally photographed going into a church, but many of these societies have a rich tradition of anticlericalism (dislike for the hierarchy of a church), and a politician running for office might lose votes if perceived to be too tied to a particular church. Anticlerical sentiments are particularly strong in Roman Catholic Latin America, where the Catholic Church has been perceived to be in league with wealthy, established political classes.

Few politicians, however, would risk the consequences of announcing that they were unbelievers. Labour Party leader Michael Foot was going to lose the 1983 British parliamentary elections anyway, but his self-declared atheism didn't win him many extra votes even in Britain's somewhat secular electorate.

There are a number of countries where a large percentage of the population believes fervently in some revealed religion and where—as a consequence—the political elite treads lightly where religion is concerned. Despite the First Amendment's assertion that religion and politics should be separate, religion permeates American political life. It is difficult to think of a major American politician who has publicly revealed his lack of religious faith, and polls confirm that a majority of Americans would not vote for an atheist as president.[45]

The Irish are even more religiously fervent than are Americans but aren't sure how much political interference they want from the clergy, and issues such as birth control and abortion are bobbing to the surface of Irish politics. Outside of generally Christian Europe and the Americas, religion is undergoing something of a revival. The religion of Islam tends to thrive on political defeat, and Muslims have a way of translating political or military reversals into religious victories. Under the late Saddam Hussein, Iraq was the most secular country in the Arab world; the Anglo-American invasion may coincidentally have had the unintended effect of ushering in an era of Islamic fervor among Iraqis. In most Islamic societies, a public renunciation of faith would be suicidal; the Pakistani legal code, for example, imposes the death penalty for leaving the Islamic religion. We will look at Islamic fundamentalism more closely in chapter 10, but for now we should simply note that the practice of Islam has not historically been associated with the development of democracy.

In Western Europe and North America, many nonreligious people now avoid pejorative terms such as "atheist" or "agnostic," preferring to describe themselves as "humanists." When used in this context, the word "**humanism**" describes a philosophy that focuses with concern and affection on human beings in this world, rather than on the supernatural and the afterlife. Most humanists doubt the existence of a Supreme Being. Humanism suggests instead that we should draw upon human and scientific resources in our struggle for happy lives, and not count on divine intervention. Humanists stress an ethical system based on a sense of community rather than on fear of divine retribution.[46]

CONFLICT AND RELIGION

Most of the world's ethnic conflicts take place between communities with differing religious affiliations. In most cases of what is often called religious conflict, however, the two sides are not actually fighting over doctrinal or theological issues. As mentioned above, the feuding communities in Northern Ireland self-identify or self-define as Roman Catholic and Protestant respectively. While there are some specifically religious issues between them (such as the ever-present dilemma of abortion), the conflict in Northern Ireland has more to do with economics, nationalism, and political power. Seeing it as a religious conflict mostly misses the point. The same is mostly true for the conflict between Hindus and Muslims over the disputed territory of Kashmir and the brawl between Hindus and Buddhists in Sri Lanka. India is primarily Hindu, but about 14 percent of the population is Muslim, and the two communities have sporadically feuded violently. On the Southeast Asian island of Borneo, Muslims have attacked Christian communities for reasons that have more to do with the clash of national identity than with any specifically theological issue.

When there is an unmet political need within a given society, religious leaders can find themselves becoming political activists. The civil rights movement in the United States was largely led by black Protestant pastors such as Martin Luther King. During the early years of the Vietnamese conflict, Buddhist monks protested the authoritarian character of the South Vietnamese government, sometimes by horrifyingly burning themselves alive.

Even if religion usually has little to do with the actual political conflict, political leaders will typically attempt to portray themselves as enjoying divine favor and draw upon the power of religion by identifying it with nationalism. When embarking on any kind of war, national leaders typically surround themselves with priests and pastors and rabbis and mullahs to provide spiritual cover.

Sometimes theological or ethical or doctrinal issues that have little to do with nationalism do lead to heated disputes and even violence. The issue of abortion is a good example, since it is not only a flash point in American politics but also a legal and ethical dilemma in many countries around the world. In the 2004 U.S. presidential election, some Roman Catholic authorities suggested that "pro-choice" Catholic politicians (such as candidate John Kerry) should not be permitted to receive the sacraments. Abortion is illegal in the Republic of Ireland. In February 1992, the parents of a fourteen-year-old rape victim were threatened with imprisonment if they took their pregnant daughter to London to terminate her pregnancy. The Irish Supreme Court fudged the decision, but abortion has been a hot issue in Irish politics ever since.

Abortion has also become a major issue in much of central and Eastern Europe. When these governments were Marxist dominated, abortion was free and available on demand. While they disliked Communism, many Eastern European women saw reproductive choice as a personal issue, not a political one. Opposition to Communism in these countries often emerged from the ranks of practicing Roman Catholics, who disliked both Communism and abortion. The status of abortion in central and Eastern Europe is far from settled and destined to be a hot political issue for decades to come, just as it is in the United States.

In the United States, there is a specifically religious content to disputes over prayer in public schools, government financing for religious schools and "faith-based" charitable organizations, and the question of teaching creationism (the notion that the world was created as a specific event as outlined in Genesis) in public schools as opposed to teaching Darwin's ideas about evolution and natural selection.

Religion has a strong influence on voting behavior in most countries. Studies on the American electorate, for example, have suggested that practicing white Christians have migrated in large numbers to the Republican Party, while more secular/nonpracticing whites are more likely to vote for Democratic candidates, along with African Americans and Hispanics. In the United States, fundamentalist Christians have made a major impact on public policy with spokesmen such as Pat Robertson and the late Jerry Falwell. Their impact has been particularly strong on the Republican Party, whose positions on "family value" issues, such as premarital sex, homosexuality, and abortion, have been influenced by the "religious right." Fundamentalism, however, is a factor in nearly every religious tradition and tends to thrive when people feel threatened by modernity and technology. Losing the safety of a familiar world during times of rapid social change, some fundamentalists return to what they perceive to be the basic tenets of their religion.[47]

4. The Wrap: What Have We Learned?

We have been, quite literally, all over the global block, looking at the raw material of political life and conflict. In this global romp, we may have tripped over some statistical hurtles, so make sure that you understand the United Nations HDI system for dividing humankind into very high, high, medium, and low human development countries. The PC/GNI will be with us for the rest of the book; don't forget that it refers to a rough statistical estimate of an individual's share in national wealth. Note also how wealth and longevity are connected.

Scholars may have concluded that we are a single species, but we have divided ourselves, sometimes artificially, into a large number of groups, many of them mutually antagonistic. We talked a lot about gender politics in this chapter, noting that the cruelty of the world toward girls and women has led them into global minority status. Women are still having difficulty asserting their political power and getting themselves elected to positions of power. Boys and girls may fall in love, but—as genders—they are still going to vote for different political parties. We also focused on the separate but interrelated problems of youth and age. Doting grandparents may cuddle their infant grandchildren, but these widely separated generations have different economic and political interests and compete for the same scarce governmental resources.

We described the whole issue of kinship, race, and ethnicity as a conceptual minefield, distinguishing between those human characteristics we bring with us into the world (kinship) and those we acquire once we're here (culture). Ethnicity is a troublesome word, but we seem to be stuck with it; it refers to a distinctive or distinguishable group within a wider society. We also saw how DNA and human genetics are revising our views of kinship groups, and why "race" and ethnicity are such troublesome concepts.

Sections 2 and 3 of this chapter are quick but focused introductions to elementary political linguistics and comparative religion, but you'll need to know what language has to do with politics and our sense of national self-identification in chapter 4. Religion may or may not save our souls, but it can certainly ruin our lives when spirituality turns to bigotry. In order to have any hope at all of understanding the contemporary world, especially the Eastern Hemisphere, you're going to have to remember all those religions.

Where are we headed next? We may be young or old, Catholic or Hindu, male or female, but we do politics within the context of national political communities. Chapter 4, therefore, will look at how the world is subdivided into self-governing political entities, which we'll learn to call sovereign states. Don't forget what we've learned about kinship groups, religions, and languages, however, because there is often a disconnect between who we are as a cultural or ethnic community and the country that claims us as citizens.

Next stop? We'll look at the states in the world and the nations that form them and cross their borders.

Notes

1. Lewis Carroll, *Alice's Adventures in Wonderland* (Boston: Lee and Shepard, 1869), 182.

2. The U.S. Census Bureau, http://www.census.gov/.

3. John Isbister, *Promises Not Kept: Poverty and the Betrayal of Third World Development*, 6th ed. (Bloomfield: Conn.: Kumarian, 2003),14.

4. Chris Bright, "A History of Our Future," in Worldwatch Institute, *State of the World 2003* (New York: Worldwatch Institute/Norton, 2003), 5.

5. UNIFEM (United Nations Development Fund for Women), *Progress of the World's Women 2000*. UNIFEM Biennial Report (New York: UNIFEM, 2000), 11–12.

6. Edward Dolnick, "Super-Women." *Health*, July/August 1991, 42–48; John R. Weeks, *Population: An Introduction to Concepts and Issues*, 9th ed. (Belmont, Calif.: Wadsworth, 2004), 281–83.

7. Dolnick, "Super-Women," 42.

8. UNIFEM, *Progress of the World's Women 2000* (New York: UNIFEM, 2000),11; Jonathan V. Last, *Wall Street Journal* Book Review, "The War against Girls," June 18, 2011 http://online.wsj.com/article/SB10 001424052702303657404576361691165631366.html (accessed June 24, 2011).

9. NPR News, "A Historical Moment, the Saudi Women Challenging a Government by Driving," June 18, 2011, http://www.npr.org/blogs/thetwo-way/2011/06/19/137271964/a-historical-moment-the -saudi-women-challenging-a-government-by-driving (accessed June 18, 2011).

10. The standard global look at women comes from the United Nations' *World's Women*, published annually in New York. A scholarly and transnational look at gender issues has been produced by V. Spike Peterson and Anne Sisson Runyan in their *Global Gender Issues* (Boulder, Colo.: Westview Press, 1993).

11. United Nations Development Programme, *Human Development Report 2011*, accessed November 10,2011, http://hdr.undp.org/en/media/HDR_2011_EN_Tables.pdf.

12. Harvard's John F. Kennedy School of Government is host to an association of female political leaders; its site is http://www.womenworldleaders.org. The primary American NGO advocating women's rights is the National Organization for Woman (NOW), findable at www.now.org. The United Nations maintains a competent gateway site for women at www.un.org/womenwatch. The Convention on the Elimination of All Forms of Discrimination against Women is the basic global multinational treaty, and the UN monitors women's legal and social progress at www.un.org/womenwatch/daw/cedaw.

13. Susan Raymond, "Foreign Assistance in an Aging World." *Foreign Affairs* 82, no. 2 (2003): 91–106; UNDP (United Nations Development Programme), *Human Development Report 2011*, http://hdr.undp.org/ en/media/HDR_2011_EN_Tables.pdf (accessed November 10,2011), 130.

14. UNDP (United Nations Development Programme), *Human Development Report 2011*, http://hdr .undp.org/en/media/HDR_2011_EN_Tables.pdf (accessed November 10, 2011), 127–30.

15. The United Nation's fundamental publication is the annual *State of the World's Children*, published by UNICEF.

16. ILO (International Labour Organization), *The End of Child Labour: Within Reach*, International Labour Conference, 95th Session 2006, Report I (B) (Geneva: International Labour Office, 2006).

17. WHO (World Health Organization), *World Report on Violence and Health* (Geneva: WHO, 2002).

18. UNDP (United Nations Development Programme), *Human Development Report 2011*, http://hdr .undp.org/en/media/HDR_2011_EN_Tables.pdf, 157–61 (accessed November 10, 2011).

19. The United Nations, "Millennium Development Goals Report 2010," http://www.un.org/millennium goals/pdf/MDG%20Report%202010%20En%20r15%20-low%20res%2020100615%20-.pdf (accessed November 15, 2011), 16.

20. The United Nations, "Millennium Development Goals Report 2010," http://www.un.org/millennium goals/pdf/MDG%20Report%202010%20En%20r15%20-low%20res%2020100615%20-.pdf (accessed November 15, 2011), 18.

21. UNICEF (The United Nations Children's Fund), *The Convention on the Rights of the Child*, http:// www.unicef.org/crc/ (accessed November 14, 2011); Aaron Sachs, "Child Prostitution: The Last Commodity," *World Watch* 7, no. 4 (1994): 25–30.

22. Marvin N. Marger, *Race and Ethnic Relations* (Belmont: Calif.: Wadsworth, 1991), 12.

23. See Jonathon Marks, *Human Biodiversity: Genes, Race, and History; Foundations of Human Behavior* (New York: De Gruyter, 1995) for a good look at the social and genetic implications of race from a well-known evolutionary anthropologist. Linnaeus' 1735 *Systema Naturae* might be heavy going today, but Dr. Lisbet Koerner has given us an updated look at his life in *Linnaeus: Nature and Nation* (Cambridge, Mass.: Harvard University Press, 1999). A new edition of Charles Darwin's 1859 *Origin of the Species* has been edited by Greg Suriano (New York: Grammercy, 1998).

24. Philip L. Stein and Bruce M. Rowe, *Physical Anthropology*, 3rd ed. (New York: McGraw-Hill, 1982), 174.

25. Marvin Harris, *Our Kind: Who We Are. Where We Came From. Where We Are Going* (New York: Harper Perennial, 1989), 113.

26. Philip L. Stein and Bruce M. Rowe, *Physical Anthropology*, 9th ed. (New York: McGraw-Hill, 2005), 150.

27. Frederick S. Hulse, *The Human Species: An Introduction to Physical Anthropology* (New York: Random House, 1971), 353.

28. David Crystal, *The Penguin Dictionary of Language*, 2nd ed. (London: Penguin, 1999), 184.

29. John McWhorter, *The Power of Babel: A Natural History of Language* (New York: Freeman, 2002), 73.

30. Directed by Paul Lewis, Dallas' SIL International maintains the online version of *Ethnologue* (www .ethnologue.com), which contains information on all the languages and dialects of the world.

31. Jonathan Steinberg, *Why Switzerland?* (Cambridge, UK: Cambridge University Press, 1976), 98–128; for a superb and more recent look at Switzerland, see Alexander Trechsel and Hanspeter Kriesi, *The Politics of Switzerland: Continuity and Change in a Consensus Democracy* (Cambridge, UK: Cambridge University Press, 2008).

32. Bill Bryson, *Mother Tongue* (London: Penguin, 1991), 188.

33. William R. Polk, *Understanding Iraq* (London: Taurus, 2005), xvi.

34. David Crystal, *The Penguin Dictionary of Language*, 2nd ed., 371.

35. Henry Rogers, *Writing Systems: A Linguistic Approach* (Oxford: Blackwell, 2005), 20–49.

36. R. L. Trask's *Language: The Basics* (London: Routledge, 2004) is famous and Bernard Comrie, ed., *The World's Major Languages* (New York: Oxford University Press, 1987) is a standard. Daniel Nettle and Suzanne Romaine, *Vanishing Voices: The Extinction of the World's Languages* (Oxford: Oxford University Press, 2000) is a good look at a controversial problem.

37. S. A. Nigosian, *World Faiths* (New York: St. Martins, 1990), 2–6.

38. Toby Lester, "Oh, Gods!" *The Atlantic*, February 2002, 37.

39. Nicholas De Lange, *An Introduction to Judaism* (Cambridge, UK: Cambridge University Press, 2000), 26–44.

40. S. A. Nigosian, *World Faiths*, 153–155.

41. S. A. Nigosian, *World Faiths*, 251.

42. K. M. Sen, *Hinduism* (London: Penguin, 1961).

43. Ian Harris, *Buddhism in Twentieth Century Asia* (London: Cassell, 1999).

44. Philip Jenkins, "The Next Christianity," *The Atlantic Monthly*, October 2002, 55–59.

45. *New York Times*, August 24, 2002, A15.

46. The Association for Religion and Intellectual Life is a New York study group that maintains a gateway site at www.aril.org/World.html. Minnesota State University examines most of the world's most-significant religious communities at www.mnsu.edu/emuseum/cultural/religion. If you want to track down the demographics of world religions, look at www.adherents.com. And if you're feeling secular, check the humanists at www.secularhumanism.org.

47. Karen Armstrong, *The Battle for God: A History of Fundamentalism* (New York: Ballantine, 2001), 309–15; Joseph N. Weatherby, *The Middle East and North Africa: A Political Primer* (New York: Longman, 2001), 177–78.

CHAPTER 4

The Country in Question
SOVEREIGN STATES AND NATIONS

4. The Wrap: What Have We Learned?

Sometimes, the world seems like a real-life version of that surreal croquet game Alice played in Wonderland. Remember how it went? "The players all played at once, without waiting for turns, quarrelling all the while and fighting for the hedgehogs; and in a very short time the Queen was in a furious passion, and went stamping about and shouting 'Off with his head!' or 'Off with her head!' about once a minute."[1]

Today, the players are countries and multinational organizations and even trans-national terrorist groups, and they quarrel with one another most of the time. In Lewis Carroll's fiction, the irritable Red Queen ordered summary executions; in the twenty-first century, it is often the American president who dispatches a battalion of Marines or requires the U.S. Navy to drop by with a carrier group. In fiction and fact, rulers rule and sovereign governments usually get their way, often by imposing violent solutions.

I Want You for the U.S. Army

Sovereign states all claim ultimate rights over the lives and property of their citizens, particularly when national security is believed to be in peril. High-tech developed countries have evolved toward relatively small, highly trained, all-volunteer professional armies, but many developing countries still maintain a universal draft. In the United States, mandatory selective service was suspended after the Vietnamese conflict, but the draft could be reintroduced if Washington decided that the international situation demanded it. At that point, Uncle Sam would, once again, want you.

The fact is that authoritative political decisions in the contemporary world are still made by individual national governments, and we spend our lives obeying their occasionally bizarre orders. In chapter 3, we divided the world into genders, kinship groups, languages, and religious communities, but a language cannot order you off into battle, although people do fight over rival tongues. There are still plenty of countries where you can go to jail for violating a religious law, but usually it is the civil government that locks you up. Feminism is a powerful intellectual force, but empowered women do not yet have their own navy.

- *What does sovereignty really mean?* The U.S. government restored "sovereignty" to the Iraqi people by June 30, 2004; what precisely did Washington give back to Baghdad? In the first section below, we'll look at what it means when we say that a country is sovereign, and talk briefly about some political entities such as states, provinces, regions, colonies, and associated territories that are "sub-sovereign."
- *What is the difference between a "state" and a "nation"?* The two words are often used interchangeably, but political scientists prefer the word "state" or "sovereign state" when focusing on an independent, self-governing country, reserving the word "nation"

for an ethnic group of people who are usually, but not always, organized into a state. In section 2, we'll look at what constitutes a nation and why there are usually problems when two or more nations get crowded into one state.

- *What happens when a state has more, or less, than one nation? Why do problems arise when nations don't manage to acquire a state?* The lack of fit between states and nations gives rise to a substantial percentage of the world's conflict. Sometimes an ethnic or national group sprawls across several separate sovereign states, constituting a majority in all of them. In other cases, we find a national group suffering minority status in one or more countries, a phenomenon that political scientists call a "stateless nation." Students in the United States tend to take Canada for granted, unaware that America's northern neighbor suffers from some of the problems described in this chapter, so we'll close with a look at competitive nationalism north of the border.

- *And are state loyalties, what we call nationalism, something that people have formed over centuries, or are they an allegiance created by state leaders for economic and political gains?* We don't really know our compatriots, but we feel an allegiance to them and some sort of national identity that we hold in common. Is nationalism socially constructed, or is there more to it? As we'll see throughout the chapter, nationalism can be a source of peace, but it has also been used as a source of deadly conflict.[2]

1. Sovereignty and National Independence

In practical politics, real authority over our lives is vested in independent, self-governing countries—what political scientists call **sovereign states**. These sovereign states can send us to prison or to war, tax us into bankruptcy, and marshal our lives with laws and regulations. Professor Chalmers Johnson has cited statistics showing that 170 million people were killed in the course of the twentieth century by their own governments![3] On the positive side, sovereign governments can protect us from natural disasters and provide schools, roads, medical services, and old-age pensions. If politics is what we have called the "ordering of public affairs," then it is clear that sovereign governments do most of that ordering.

Some sovereign states contain one, and only one, significant ethnic or national group (Japan is a good example). Others, such as Switzerland, Russia, and India, are home to many different linguistic and national minorities. After the end of the **Cold War**, the world seemed to explode into ethnic and nationalist strife. In the course of four years of civil strife, for example, the world wondered if Iraqi Shi'ites, Sunnis, and Kurds could ever submerge their separate identities and begin to think of themselves as Iraqi citizens, united under a government of their mutual choice. This chapter investigates, therefore, the complex set of relationships ethnic groups have with the sovereign states that attempt to govern them.

THE QUESTION OF SOVEREIGNTY

We'll start by taking a hard look at the concept of **sovereignty** and at the number of sovereign states in the world. This is important basic material, and we will see that a lot of political conflict flows from the consequences of sovereignty: self-governing states sometimes fight in an effort to impose their sovereignty upon one another. In civil or intrastate wars, sovereign governments battle with rebellious communities within their own borders.

In an effort to clarify a complex subject, we will glance briefly at political entities that may seem to be sovereign but aren't. All countries are divided into sub-sovereign units, such as American states or Canadian provinces, and we'll identify this category for later discussion in chapter 7. Then we'll shift our focus slightly to external possessions of sovereign states, that is, territories that are outside the physical boundaries of a given sovereign state but that are controlled by the sovereign state. These are sometimes called colonies, and we'll see why they are a frequent source of political conflict.

WHO DOES THE ORDERING OF PUBLIC AFFAIRS?

"Sovereign" and "sovereignty" are complex words, hard to spell and even more difficult to define. To be sovereign means to have independent authority over someone or something, and the word is sometimes used to refer to a monarch. For example, King Abdullah II is currently Jordan's sovereign. The word is also used to describe a government that controls a given territory; in this sense, the Canadian government in Ottawa is sovereign (or exercises sovereignty) over all of Canada, a fact that distresses some French-speaking Canadian citizens in Quebec. The American Civil War was fought over the right of the U.S. government to impose its sovereignty over the American South. Finally, a sovereign state is an independent country that rules itself and is not part of, or formally subordinate to, some other country. Sovereign states normally issue their own currency and stamps, fly their own flags, and deploy their own armed forces. In addition, they are typically recognized as sovereign by other sovereign countries, with whom they exchange embassies and diplomats. Most (but not quite all) sovereign states have seats in the UN General Assembly.[4] The United States of America, the Republic of France, the Sultanate of Oman, and the Russian Republic are all sovereign states.

There have been sovereign states in human society ever since Sumerian and Egyptian **empires** arose in the Middle East about 3000 BC. Characteristically, empires are mixtures of kinship groups, political concoctions without linguistic or religious homogeneity, created as the result of wars of conquest. The Roman Empire, for example, involved Italians, Greeks, Germans, eastern Mediterranean speakers of the Semitic family of languages, and a hodgepodge of North Africans. After the fall of the Roman Empire, political power in Western Europe became highly diffused until the gradual rise of what were essentially modern countries in the 1500s and 1600s.

There were still multinational empires after the 1600s, and human institutions don't change overnight, but most political historians use 1648 as a convenient date for the start of the modern state system. **The Treaty of Westphalia**, signed in 1648 to end the Thirty Years War, marked the beginning of a period in which organized sovereign governments ruled populations that were beginning to be more ethnically homogenous in terms of language and religion.[5] Named after the German region where it was negotiated, this treaty destroyed the power of the Holy Roman Empire and created a new Europe with several dozen well-defined sovereign governments, somewhat clearer borders, and countries more frequently organized around ethnic or national groups. French kings in Paris administered a generally French-speaking society, while Spanish monarchs in Madrid collected taxes from Roman Catholics in the Iberian Peninsula, who spoke one of the several dialects of Spanish. People who had previously thought of themselves as subjects of a given feudal nobleman were increasingly likely to regard themselves as French or Spanish or English.

While we're making crucial distinctions about governments, let's mention a kind of international organization that resembles a sovereign government in some ways. We'll talk more in chapter 5 about institutions such as the United Nations or NATO, but for the moment, note that these "**supra-sovereign**" or "supra-national" organizations are clubs of sovereign states but are not themselves sovereign.[6]

NOMINAL SOVEREIGNTY

The concept of sovereignty is clear enough in theory, but real life always gives us problems. When a country is really sovereign, its government makes most important decisions on its own, without undue pressure or influence from other countries. In essence, no one tells it what to do on a daily basis, and it does not function under the threat of invasion or financial sanctions from some more powerful country.[7]

On the other hand, how do we describe a situation when one dominant country can interfere in the decision-making process of a weaker country, in effect, giving a "do-it-or-else" order? Clearly, if this external interference is regular and deals with a wide variety of policy issues, then the subordinate country may be said to have purely **nominal** or "in name only" sovereignty. The subordinate country might have the full range of sovereignty symbols, such as stamps, armed forces, and a seat in the UN General Assembly, but if it doesn't have the ability to make crucial decisions about its own political or economic life, then its sovereignty is nominal. The insulting phrase "Banana Republic" refers to Latin American countries (some of them banana exporters) that are so thoroughly under the influence of the U.S. government or American corporations that their sovereignty can be described as purely nominal. The "or else" can arrive in the form of the U.S. Marine Corps; the United States used military forces to redirect public policy in the Dominican Republic in 1965, Grenada in 1983, Panama in 1989, and Haiti in 1994 and 2004.

During the years of the former Soviet Union's domination over central Europe (roughly 1944–1989), countries such as Poland, Czechoslovakia, Hungary, Bulgaria, Romania, and East Germany were all nominally sovereign; they had their own governments, their own flags, their own currency, and international diplomatic recognition. But what they didn't have was the concrete ability to run their own national affairs because somebody could always call from the Kremlin and say, "do-it-or-else." For Hungarians in 1956 and Czechoslovakians in 1968, the "or else" was an armed invasion by the Soviet Red Army.

To be authentically sovereign, a government should not only be free from external control but ought to be able to get its orders generally obeyed within its national territory. Obviously, this doesn't mean that the police are going to catch every pickpocket in town, or no country in the world would qualify as sovereign. But a sovereign government does need to prevent rebel or criminal groups from establishing their own mini-administrations on portions of the national territory and defying the will of the central government. In chapter 10, for example, we'll look at Latin America's Republic of Colombia, where the Bogotà government has had immense difficulty in enforcing its laws in areas controlled by left-wing guerrilla groups.

A regime that cannot exercise meaningful control over extensive portions of its territory is sometimes called a "**failed state**."[8] Afghanistan's Kabul-based government has seldom influenced the lives of Afghan citizens in Herat or Kandahar, and the American occupation of the country has done little to extend the authority of the central administration over the regional warlords. There is at least one country in the world where the government's penetrating power is almost zero: in the east African country of Somalia genuine government disappeared in 1990 when the long-standing dictator of the nation was overthrown.

On the other hand, world-renowned linguist and scholar, Noam Chomsky, argues that the United States is the world's best example of a failed state.[9] If the term means a state that fails "to provide security for the population, to guarantee rights at home or abroad, or to maintain functioning (not merely formal) democratic institutions," then he argues that the United States qualifies.[10] Chomsky makes a controversial argument; he uses data on the gap between the rich and poor in the United States, as well as the U.S. failure to support international laws, such as the Kyoto Protocol and the International Criminal Court.[11] Even though Chomsky's argument has its flaws, as other scholars have noted, it is still important to include the United States in our analysis of failed states and our discussion of the international system.

HOW MANY SOVEREIGN STATES ARE THERE?

Thanks to decolonization and the decline of imperial structures, such as the British and Soviet empires, the trend since World War II has been for the number of clearly identifiable independent and self-governing states to increase. To be reasonably up-to-date about the status of a given country, you may wish to consult an almanac because the number of sovereign countries is in constant flux. A glance at the *New York Times Almanac* will reveal that the two previously independent Yemens have united and Germany, once divided between East and West, is now a single country. Czechoslovakia has become two different states (the Czech Republic and Slovakia). Yugoslavia has fragmented into seven sovereign entities with **Montenegro** being the most recent state to declare its sovereignty. The former USSR has disintegrated into fifteen separate countries.

Figure 4.1 shows that many of the world's countries aren't much older than the students reading this book. Condescending Europeans enjoy reminding Americans of their historical immaturity, but with more than two centuries of continuous constitutional existence, the United States is actually among the oldest countries in the world.

We think of countries such as Italy and Germany as ancient, but they are actually fairly young sovereign states; both were unified in only the mid-1800s. Most countries are creations of the twentieth century, and the majority of the members of the United Nations achieved national independence only after World War II (1945). This is a world of young countries, and the age of a sovereign state is almost always politically relevant. Youthfulness can mean energy and enthusiasm but can also involve political instability, since new countries are usually former colonies with little practice in administering their own affairs.

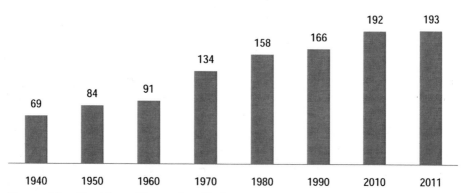

Figure 4.1.   The Rise of Sovereign States
The number on top of each column indicates the number of sovereign states in existence in that year. Different authors produce varying numbers because of disagreements about what constitutes a real sovereign state, but clearly the post–World War II decolonization process produced an explosion in the number of independent states.

How many sovereign states are there right now? The membership list of the United Nations gives us an almost complete list of the world's sovereign states. Under UN guidance, the former Indonesian province of East Timor achieved independence in May of 2002 under the name Timor Leste (East Timor) and asked to join the global club. Having previously abstained from membership in the UN because of a long-standing tradition of total independence, the Swiss voted in March of 2002 to apply for admission. Both countries won uncomplicated acceptance in the autumn of 2002, bringing the total number to 191, and Montenegro made it 192 in 2006. This number rose to 193 in the summer of 2011 when South Sudan won a divorce from its unfriendly parent to the north and achieved independence.[12]

For a variety of reasons, not every actual sovereign state is a UN member. Despite its democratic political institutions and twenty-three million prosperous citizens, Taiwan does not have a seat because of its political problems with mainland China; Taiwan remains the largest and most significant sovereign state outside the world organization for reasons we will discuss below.

Southern Sudan is a newcomer to the international community, having just confirmed a popular **referendum** in February 2011 to separate from Northern Sudan under President Umar al-Bashir. Formal independence took place on July 9, 2011, but is not without turmoil as the war-ravaged South has been battling a border war between northern and southern provinces. Former South African president Thabo Mbeki is leading an **African Union** team of negotiators for peace between the northern and southern border towns. This is another good example of new state formation with the aid of a regional international organization, in this case the African Union.[13]

History is never static, and countries will continue to appear and disappear. Here are some possibilities for the next twenty years: North and South Korea could merge, since the North is close to internal collapse. Scotland the Brave is eligible to become Scotland the

Independent if the Scots so desire, and they stormed into 2012 talking about it a lot and planning a referendum on the topic, to London's intense annoyance. Serbia's Albanian-speaking Muslim population of Kosovo is already self-administering under UN supervision and certainly desires formal sovereign independence.[14] And the process of fragmentation in Russia might not be over yet; look for more changes in Eastern Europe.[15]

THINKING SMALL: THE WORLD'S MINISTATES

A ministate is simply an exceptionally small sovereign state. Some are no larger than a village and can be hard to find on a map. In recent years, a number of remote Pacific islands have become independent despite their tiny populations: Nauru, Tonga, Tuvalu, and the Republic of the Marshall Islands have all achieved international recognition as independent countries. Many ministates are poor, sparsely populated, and obscure, but here are a few of the better-known European examples:

- Andorra: The Principality of Andorra sits high in the Pyrenees Mountains between Spain and France. With a population of seventy thousand mostly Spanish-speaking citizens, Andorra once relied upon multidirectional smuggling for its economic base; nowadays, this diminutive country is inching into modernity with an economy based more on tourism and legal trade.
- The Marshall Islands: Located about two-thirds of the way between Hawaii and Australia and once administered by the United States, the Republic of the Marshall Islands (RMI) is a ministate with nominal sovereignty. Dependent upon the U.S. Treasury for financial stability and still home to a number of U.S. military and NASA installations, these thirty-one atolls were used for decades for the testing of American nuclear weapons. The population suffers generally poor health, although diet and poverty may be more significant factors than is radioactivity. With seventy thousand people spread over only seventy square miles, the RMI is one of the smallest sovereign states on the planet, and its citizens have limited prospects for prosperity and longevity.
- Monaco: The tiny Principality of Monaco is essentially a small town (population: thirty-one thousand) not far from the Italian border but actually located in southern France. Monaco claims sovereignty, enjoys a seat in the United Nations, and is ruled by Prince Albert II and his glamorous and occasionally scandalous family.
- The Vatican: A Rome-based political anomaly is Vatican City, sometimes called the Holy See. Despite the fact that it is the headquarters of the Roman Catholic Church, Vatican City[16] is recognized by most nations as a sovereign state and was confirmed as an independent country by a 1929 treaty with the Italian government. The Vatican is really a walled-in neighborhood on the west bank of the Tiber River, and is home to the pope and his senior officials, a few thousand priests and nuns, and a handful of lay employees. The sovereign and self-governing Vatican has never joined the United Nations because of its parallel status as the headquarters of a world religion. While the political importance of the Vatican is huge, the real estate is small; you can drive completely around it in thirty minutes or less, depending upon the state of Roman traffic.

My Country, T'is of Me

Welcome to Nymark, which sits in the North Sea between Norway and the North Pole. If you're looking for peace of mind, Nymark has no crime, no taxes, no traffic, and no crowds because . . . well, it has no Nymarkians. Having only just emerged from beneath a shrinking polar ice cap, Nymark was discovered and named in 2004 by an English explorer named Alex Hartley in the course of an Arctic expedition investigating global warming. As a joke, Hartley wrote to the United Nations, proposing that Nymark be granted recognition as an independent sovereign state. We will look at international law in more detail in chapter 5, but a sovereign state needs territory, a fixed population, a government, and the capacity to conduct diplomatic relations. Nymark only qualifies on one point: its territory is about the size of a football field, but otherwise Mr. Hartley loses because his little country has no people (he himself lives in London), no government, and no diplomats. The Norwegian government took Hartley's claim seriously enough, however, to counterclaim Nymark on the grounds that Norway owns the rest of the Svalbard island chain to which Nymark belongs.

Almost all of these tiny states survive by being protected by some more powerful state, a protection that sometimes fades into domination and can make their sovereignty fairly nominal.

SUB-SOVEREIGN ENTITIES AND COLONIES

Subordinate to the national government of a sovereign state, there is various lower-echelon governmental structures responsible for the governance of portions of the national territory but lacking full sovereign authority. The state of South Carolina, the city of Moscow, and Ireland's County Cork are all **sub-sovereign** or subnational entities because each is in some measure formally responsive to orders from some higher decision-making authority. Some of these sub-sovereign entities may be located beyond a country's formal borders, such as American Samoa, or Britain's Falkland Islands (in the south Atlantic near Argentina).[17] In some cases, these detached bits have been formally incorporated into the motherland; the Caribbean island of Martinique, for example, is legally as much a part of France as Marseilles or Bordeaux. In other cases, these distant appendages have some special status, such as colony or associated territory. Let's look at this trouble-prone category of real estate.

Provinces, Regions, Counties, and Municipalities

Nearly every country has several layers of government beneath the national level. Americans, for example, have fifty state governments, thousands of counties, and tens of thousands of cities, towns, and village governments. All of them are sub-sovereign in the sense that they have some powers of their own, but are subordinate in a variety of ways to higher echelons of government. For its part, France has twenty-two regions, further subdivided into ninety-five *departements*. Unified Germany has sixteen "Lands" or *Länder*, while Canada is divided into ten provinces and several territories. In some political systems, these sub-sovereign governments can do a substantial amount of the ordering of public affairs, but they are never allowed to behave like sovereign governments. They cannot, for example, issue their own currency or conduct independent foreign policy.

There is typically at least some political conflict within a society over how much power a province or a region should have in its relationship with the central government. As we will see in the Canadian case, there can be even more conflict when a sub-sovereign entity contemplates achieving sovereignty, typically by seceding from the larger state. The American South attempted secession in 1861 and eastern Nigeria tried to walk away in 1967; both attempts at secession were followed by terrible wars. We'll look further at the political implications of these sub-sovereign entities in chapter 7 when we study unitary systems such as France and federal systems such as the United States and Canada.

Colonies, Commonwealths, and Associated Territories

By fair means or foul, many countries have also acquired land that is not part of their national territory but which they claim and control. Over the years, various titles have been generated for this kind of relationship: colony, dependency, dominion, commonwealth, mandate, trust territory, protectorate, and associated territory. By themselves, these designations do not tell us much about the exact relationship between the mother country and the non-sovereign entity. Sometimes the rapport is comfortable, but colonies have often resisted bitterly. Some colonial relationships are voluntary; others enforced by arms of occupation. Let's look at a couple of actual cases to get a sense of the range of situations involved.

A colony, by definition, does not have its own sovereign government, and the term refers to a territory that is in some sense owned by another country without precisely being part of it. In times gone by, a colonial relationship emerged after some aggressive European country militarily seized some weaker territory in Africa, the Americas, or Asia. Great colonial powers such as Britain, France, Germany, Portugal, Belgium, and Italy all colonized Africa over a three-hundred-year period, and they did it with enormous brutality. Sometimes, the colonial power sent its own people to settle the land; the Falkland Islanders, for example, are English, and Dutch settlers became the Afrikaans-speaking Boer population of South Africa. In other cases, the colonial power controlled foreign territory without changing the colony's ethnic composition much; Belgium, for example, controlled the Congo until its independence in 1960, but very few ethnic Belgians ever moved there, and even fewer remained behind to participate in the country's turbulent postcolonial history.

Giant Greenland geographically dwarfs little Denmark, but this cold, underpopulated island in the North Atlantic was once under direct Danish rule.[18] It now has a self-governing status that roughly resembles the relationship between the United States and Puerto Rico. Denmark also owns the Faeroe Islands in the North Atlantic between Scotland and Iceland.

Like most former colonial powers, France still has remnants of its empire. There is French Guiana in South America, which the French claim is actually part of France, despite the presence of the Atlantic Ocean between Cayenne (Guiana's capital) and Paris (the real capital). French Polynesia has been a political issue because of the past French practice of detonating nuclear weapons in the Pacific, where they also control New Caledonia and a variety of other smaller islands. The French also still own St. Pierre and Miquelon off the eastern coast of Canada.

Thanks to the unhappy history involved, the tainted word "colony" is seldom used today to define the legal relationship between possessors and possessed, even if the relationship is still an unequal one. In 1998, for example, Tony Blair's Labour government indulged in some postimperial political correctness by redefining all Britain's possessions abroad as "British Overseas Territories," which the irreverent press immediately christened "BOTs." Whatever you call them, Britain still has lots of BOTs. Having voluntarily surrendered her most important colony, Hong Kong, in 1997, the queen still reigns over just under two hundred thousand subjects on Atlantic islands such as Bermuda, St. Helena, and the Falkland Islands; some sun-drenched tourist destinations in the Caribbean such as Anguilla, the British Virgins, and Montserrat; a few desolate Pacific atolls such as Pitcairn Island; and some mostly uninhabited frozen rocks near Antarctica such as South Georgia.[19]

The relationships between these far-flung outposts and London are varied. Bermuda, for example, enjoys considerable local autonomy and almost total control over its domestic political affairs. The island could have independence by asking for it, but in a 1995 referendum on the subject, the islanders decided two-to-one to retain the association with the United Kingdom. Other BOTS are small and weak and poor and very distant. It's hard to imagine what would happen to isolated Pitcairn Island if London didn't look after this tiny and sparsely populated island in the most distant corner of the South Pacific.

THE COMMONWEALTH OF NATIONS

Once upon a time, Britain conquered and settled Canada, Australia, New Zealand, most of Africa, a lot of South Asia, and a cluster of Caribbean islands. Most of these countries have long since become completely independent and sovereign, but maintain ceremonial ties with the old colonial power for political and sentimental reasons. Canada, Australia, and New Zealand are all totally self-governing sovereign countries today, but they continue to regard Queen Elizabeth II as their ceremonial chief of state. The Bahamas, Barbados, Grenada, Jamaica, Mauritius, Papua New Guinea, Saint Kitts and Nevis, Saint Lucia, Saint Vincent and the Grenadines, Solomon Islands, and Tuvalu all fall into the same category.

It was once called the British Commonwealth, but the community dropped the "British" to avoid the suggestion that the London government has political power of any sort over these sovereign states. In fact, neither British prime minister David Cameron nor Queen Elizabeth II could fix a parking ticket in Ottawa, Canberra, or Wellington. The **Commonwealth of Nations** is essentially a club of sovereign nations, many of which still like to see the queen's image on their coins and postage stamps. Canadians and the "Kiwis" (New Zealanders) seem happy with this arrangement, but Australians keep talking about breaking the royal connection. Don't mix it up with the Commonwealth of Independent States (CIS), which is a loose affiliation of twelve of the fifteen "socialist republics" that used to be the USSR.[20]

Freedom-loving Americans would shun the word "colony" when talking about American overseas possessions, although Washington does control some offshore territories. Hawaii and Alaska, obviously, have now achieved statehood, but the four million Spanish-speaking Puerto Ricans have a complicated relationship with their gringo neighbors to the north. The United States first conquered Puerto Rico during the 1898 Spanish-American War. After a period of direct government from Washington, the island became a "commonwealth" in 1952, which roughly means that the elected administration in San Juan can make and enforce any domestic legislation that is consistent with the U.S. Constitution.[21] If a consistent majority of Puerto Ricans really wanted independence, the United States would not use force to prevent it. While there is a small separatist movement, Puerto Ricans are about equally divided between advocates of full statehood and those who prefer the status quo. Almost everyone recognizes that an independent Puerto Rico would be a very poor island, since the commonwealth's economy depends overwhelmingly on largess from the mainland.

In addition to some minor ocean islands with military importance, the United States has a scattering of other populated territories and commonwealths in the Caribbean and the Pacific: the Virgin Islands, American Samoa, Guam, and the Northern Mariana Islands, all of which are substantively self-governing.

Ownership of colonies by larger powers has always been a source of conflict. Sometimes the colony is prepared to fight long, ghastly wars for independence; the way the Kenyans did against the British and the Algerians against the French until both countries became independent in the early 1960s. Sometimes two powers will quarrel over a given colony. The Falkland Islands have been a British possession for nearly two hundred years, but Argentina has always regarded them as rightfully theirs. In a tragic miscalculation, the Argentines attacked the Falklands in 1982, and sustained a terrible military defeat at the hands of the capable British military. Tensions flared between these two in early 2012 over the islands, so stay tuned for more here.

Map 4.1. Britain's Falkland Islands
A long way from London, the Falkland Islands were conquered by Britain in the early 1800s. While this distant and thinly populated colony lacked much economic and strategic importance, the UK went to war in 1982 when a military junta in Argentina illegally seized what the Argentines call *Las Malvinas*.
Map by R. O. Collin.

2. States and Nations

Thus far, we have generally used the term "country" when speaking about self-governing and independent political entities such as the United States, France, and Japan. While "country" is a perfectly good word, students of politics prefer the more precise term "state" to indicate a sovereign or self-ruling political entity. This can be initially confusing for Americans; since the thirteen original states were briefly independent entities, Americans use the term "states" to describe the fifty provinces or sub-sovereign regions that constitute the United States of America. Australians and Indians also call their principal sub-sovereign entities "states."

But we need to adjust to the terminology that is common in the social sciences, and from now on, we will refer to independent countries such as Saudi Arabia, Norway, and Israel as "states" or (to distinguish them from the American states) "sovereign states." In this sense of the word, a sovereign state is a territory administered authoritatively by an independent government.

STATES, NATIONS, AND NATION-STATES

The phrase "sovereign state," however, tells us nothing about the people who live on that territory, and here begin some interesting complications. In addition to being made up of nearly two hundred sovereign states, the world is clearly also divided up into many thousands of ethnic or national communities. The word "**nation**" is often used as a simple synonym for country, but when students of politics and history use the term, they reserve for it the special meaning of a group of people who are related to one another in a variety of ways. Let's look first at what constitutes a nation and then try to understand why and how political grief can flow from a situation in which a given state has more than one nation within its borders. We'll then proceed to try to define nation-states and see why conflict so frequently develops within multinational states. We can begin by focusing on what we mean by "nation."

The Six Ingredients of Nationhood

A nation is an ethnic community that typically shares all or most of the following six characteristics. It should be noted that immigrant countries such as the United States, Australia, and Canada are melting-pot societies where members of different national groups have blended their national identities; immigrant societies may have only four or five of the six core characteristics of a nation. In general, however, a tightly integrated national group such as the Japanese, the Italians, and the Bangladeshi will share all six of these attributes.

- Language: members of a given nation or national group typically share a common language. As we learned in chapter 3, not everyone agrees on what constitutes a real national language and what should be relegated to the status of a dialect; certainly a lot of conflict can flow out of that disagreement. What is clear, however, is that a real nation typically has its own language. It is difficult to imagine a nation whose members cannot communicate with one another with one common tongue, although they may use a variety of nonstandard (or dialectical) approaches to that language.

Obviously, some languages are transnational in the sense that several different nations may share the same language while retaining their separateness as different peoples. Austrians generally believe they are a different national group from the Germans, but Austrians and Germans and some Swiss all speak German. Peruvians and Spaniards belong to different nations, but both groups speak Spanish, albeit with slightly different accents.

- Kinship: the members of most nations normally see themselves as biologically linked to one another as a kind of extended family. The cousin relationships connecting all (for example) Greeks may be fairly distant, but all members of the Greek nation would regard themselves as having at least a common biological ancestry. An Athenian and a Cretan, for example, would see themselves as distant cousins; a Greek would view a Turk or a Bulgarian as a member of a different family altogether.

The Core Nation

In immigrant societies, a sense of biological or kinship connection is typically weak among the bulk of the population. In the United States and Canada, for example, there are families who have only been residents for a few generations, while others have been established much longer and may therefore feel themselves to be more American or more Canadian than the newcomers. African Americans, for example, have lived in the Western Hemisphere since the days of the earliest settlers, and Jewish people arrived during colonial times. Yet organizations like the Ku Klux Klan and the Aryan Nation view themselves as members of a kind of core nation of "authentic" Americans, charged by history with defending the purity of the Caucasian, Protestant, Anglo-Saxon national soul.

The United States is not alone in this phenomenon. France, Germany, Austria, and Italy all have groups who regard themselves as protectors of core racial purity. Australia and New Zealand both have fringe groups who resent what they view as non-Australians, such as the Aborigines, and non–New Zealanders such as the Maori people. See chapter 10 to learn what happens when the core nation buys a few assault rifles.

This sense of kinship can be confused or absent in immigrant countries. Second- and third-generation Americans, Canadians, and Australians are more closely connected biologically to people in their countries of origin than they are to their fellow citizens in "the new country." If your grandparents were immigrants, then your closest biological kinfolk in terms of DNA might live in England's Lincolnshire, Ireland's County Cork, Italy's Calabrian Peninsula, Poland's Warsaw, or Eritrea's Asmara.

Kinship should not be confused with **citizenship**, although some countries don't make a clear distinction. If you were born in the United States or have been naturalized, then you enjoy a legal relationship with the U.S. government that is called citizenship. In immigrant societies, citizenship is unconnected with ethnicity or national origin. Immigrants into the United States become Americans the moment they complete the nationalization process and swear allegiance, and—except for the fact that they cannot become president or vice president—they are legally no different from citizens whose ancestors arrived on the *Mayflower*. But many countries, particularly in Asia, have difficulty separating kinship from citizenship. To be a Japanese citizen, for example, it is generally necessary to be biologically Japanese.

- National Culture, Customs, and Traditions: **Culture** is the whole range of acquired characteristics and behavioral traits that are typical of an ethnic or national group. Americans eat turkey at Thanksgiving, throw rice at brides, and wear baseball caps almost everywhere. In Saudi Arabia, the men wear thobes (long garments that look like dresses), cover their heads with scarves, and sensibly avoid baseball caps except when playing baseball. The difference between the two is national culture, and cultures help to distinguish one nation from another.

  National culture includes fairly obvious factors such as dress, music, architecture, and diet. It also extends to more subtle behavioral characteristics such as what is called "body space," the distance you need to maintain between yourself and someone else to feel comfortable. Here's a hint for your next multinational cocktail party: people from northern European societies need a lot of room between themselves and anybody else; folks from the Mediterranean and Africa feel uncomfortable standing so far apart and like to get a little closer.

  Within any dominant culture, sociologists and ethnologists will often attempt to identify subcultures. The word "subculture" might suggest an inferior sort of ethnicity, but all it really means is a cultural variant within a dominant national culture. The Spanish, for example, all share Spanish culture, but the people of Galicia in northwestern Spain speak their own dialect of Spanish, enjoy rather different food, and listen to distinctive native music. East across the Tyrrhenian Sea lies the Italian island of Sardinia, where there is a flourishing Sardinian subculture with linguistic, culinary, artistic, and other cultural variations. It makes life interesting.

- Religion: In most parts of the world, all or nearly all members of a given nation will share a national religion or religious heritage. As we discovered in chapter 3, religion for some nations can be the defining characteristic; to be Greek is to some extent to be a member of the Greek Orthodox Church. To be authentically Israeli is to be Jewish, although the complications of Middle Eastern history have created a minority of non-Jewish Israelis who are generally unenthusiastic about their involuntary status as Israeli citizens. Even in an immigrant nation such as the United States, some Americans suffer from unusually high levels of **ethnocentricity**, seeing a kind of generic Protestant Christianity as the only American religion, with Islam and even Judaism sometimes viewed as foreign faiths.

- Territoriality: Most people identify with their national territory in a very special and emotional way. Can you picture the United States without Maine or Florida? Probably not. Are you prepared to die to defend American Samoa? Probably not. Would you take up arms if the Canadians invaded Maine or Mexico tried to reconquer Texas? Probably. People can become very passionate about their national homelands. In World War II, the Italian armed forces performed lethargically when Mussolini tried to conquer Greece and Egypt, creating the myth that Italians were timid warriors. But when Germany turned against its former ally in 1943 and occupied the Italian peninsula, Italian **partisans** fought and died heroically in defense of *la bella Italia*. As we'll see below, troubles start when this sense of **territoriality** is challenged in some way, either by a foreign invasion or the perception that part of "your" national territory has been stolen by some other country.

- National Self-Identification: This concept is less complicated than it might seem. National self-identification is a personal and emotional conviction that you are a member of a given nation. Most of us grow up with a clear sense of nationhood. Frenchmen feel French, and Italians jubilantly assert their *italianità*. Americans belt out their unsingable "Star-Spangled Banner" with more gusto than melodic accuracy, and the English hum along when the band plays "God Save the Queen." To be a member of a real nation is to be consciously aware of participating in its national culture in a clear, uncomplicated, and spontaneous fashion.

  Imagine yourself sitting in a bistro in Paris. A young person at the next table smiles and says, "Hi, I'm a Canadian. What are you?" Your answer will probably be quick and automatic. At least at this stage of the acquaintanceship, you will not volunteer that you are a Lutheran, a North Carolinian, a Republican, a heterosexual, or an avid golfer. Your new Canadian friend clearly wants to know what national group you belong to, and if you're American, Bolivian, or Bulgarian, you'll say so immediately without thinking too much about the implications.

  And yet there are implications. Assuming you're an American, what makes you all that different from the friendly Canadian who wants to have a conversation? Sometimes essentially very similar people come to feel very strongly that they are members of different nations, despite very strong cultural affiliations. If you look at the first five characteristics listed above and think about Canadians and U.S. citizens, for example, it is difficult to make the case that a tourist from Toronto is profoundly different from a wandering Buffalonian. Most Americans who travel to Canada do not have the sense that they are in a foreign country or a distinctively different culture, except in the French-speaking province of Quebec. Canadians, on the other hand, perceive important differences between themselves and Americans, regarding their educational and health-care systems as kinder, and their national culture as more sensitive.[22] Canadian political life is really quite different, as we will see below. Are the differences enough to justify the claim to separate nationalism? They are if you think they are. With their strong sense of national self-identification, Canadians are pretty insistent upon NOT being part of that crass giant to the south!

Confused National Identity

In some troubled portions of the world, many people have difficulty in responding directly to that simple question, "What are you?" Roman Catholics from the British province of Ulster, for example, usually self-identify as Irish, even though the Republic of Ireland is really a completely separate country to the south. Church of Ireland Anglicans of English descent will normally describe themselves as British, but Presbyterians whose ancestors came originally from Scotland usually prefer to call themselves Ulstermen. If you meet members of Spain's Basque minority in Spain, they will self-identify as Basques. Meet the same Basques at Tokyo International Airport, and they will claim to be Spanish. Confused? A land where people are not yet sure of their own identity is likely to be an unhappy place, and both Northern Ireland and Spain have seen their share of ethnic tumult in recent years.

Not all national groups will have all six characteristics, and as we move from country to country, there are boundless complications. But it will help enormously as we move through the material to follow if you can remember that when social scientists talk about a sovereign state, they are focusing on the political entity, its sovereign territory and its independent government. When social scientists talk about a nation, they are discussing an ethnic group that may or may not be organized into a sovereign state but shares all or most of the characteristics discussed above: language, sense of kinship, national culture, religion, emotional identification with a given territory, and a sense of national self-identification.

The Nation-State Phenomenon

In many cases, nations (i.e., ethnic communities) have been able to organize themselves into states (i.e., sovereign political entities). The result is a **nation-state**, a sovereign political entity populated by one dominant ethnic or national group without significant representation from any other ethnic or national group.

If you have a group of people with their own government, speaking the same language, practicing the same religion, and living on their ancestral turf, they are a nation-state unless they have to share that real estate with a significant number of people from some other ethnic or national group. The scholarly American leader Woodrow Wilson saw the nation-state as the obvious and natural unit of government. The League of Nations and the United Nations got their names precisely from a conviction that human political evolution would eventually bring us to a situation in which all ethnic and national groups were able to form their own ethnically consistent governments.

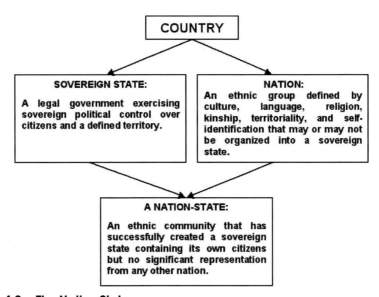

Figure 4.2. The Nation-State
As suggested in this chart, scholars tend to use the phrase "sovereign state" to focus on a country's legal status, while the term "nation" describes an ethnic community. When a nation succeeds in creating its own government and controlling its own national territory, we call the result a nation-state.

Clear-cut, uncontroversial examples of nation-states include Bangladesh, Cambodia, the Czech Republic, Denmark, Germany, Greece, Iceland, Ireland, Italy, Japan, the Kingdom of the Netherlands (Holland), Norway, Poland, and Portugal.[23]

MULTINATIONAL STATES

In cases where a sovereign state has two or more large and coherent resident groups within its borders who differ in all or most of the six characteristics of nationhood, we are clearly dealing with a **multinational state**. There are a number of straightforward examples for us to study.

Many Nations and One Government

Here are four good examples of what are called multinational states:

- Belgium: Belgium is home to two very distinct population groups. Just over half of the Belgians are called Flemings and speak a variant of Dutch called Flemish that is very close to the standard Dutch spoken in the Netherlands. The remainder of the Belgian population lives in the southeast and speaks the Walloon dialect of French.
- South Africa: South Africa, with Caucasians of Dutch and British descent as well as many major subdivisions of Bantu-speaking peoples, is another clear case of a multinational state.
- The United Kingdom: Tourist brochures for merry old England evoke stereotypical images of Buckingham Palace and London Bridge and people taking tea with scones, but an actual visit to Great Britain reveals more people eating Indian curry or Chinese takeout than Yorkshire pudding. In addition to its majority population of ethnic English, the UK contains significant numbers of nationally conscious Scots, Irish, and Welsh, along with Indians, Pakistanis, Caribbean peoples, an assortment of Africans, and others from the now-vanished British Empire. Despite the fact that about four-fifths of the population self-identify as English, the United Kingdom has more than enough non-English residents to qualify as a multinational state.[24]
- The Republic of India: One of the most cosmopolitan countries on earth, the Republic of India contains within its borders perhaps fifteen major national groups and several hundred smaller ethnic communities. There is no single national language that is understood by all Indians, which is a major problem in governing this immensely varied society.

Many very large countries are multinational states. The Russian Federation contains a large number of undigested national minorities along with the ethnic Russian population, so we are correct in regarding it as a multinational state. Nearly every big African state south of the Sahara is multinational: Nigeria and the Congo are good examples. In multinational Rwanda, the genocidal civil war in 1994 was based on hostility between that country's Hutu and Tutsi populations.

Some unhappy societies are so fragmented nationally that there is no one clear dominant group, and the result can be a continuing breakdown of constitutional government.

The Pacific's Solomon Islands, for example, is a nineteenth century colonial cocktail with a thousand islands populated by more than seventy linguistic and cultural communities. Members of these tribal groupings tend to self-identify in terms of clan or family affiliation rather than as citizens of the Solomons and typically ignore instructions from what they regard as an artificial government.

The various nations in an ethnically diverse state are often intensely hostile to one another, but multinationalism doesn't have to be unfriendly. Humankind's most successful example of a multinational state is Switzerland, whose citizens have decided that all four of their ethnic communities are significant. Swiss-Germans make up about 65 percent of the total population, but a solid 18 percent of the Swiss are of French extraction and speak French. Another 12 percent are Italians whose families have lived in Switzerland for many centuries. Romansch is a Romance language and the Romansch people have lived in Switzerland since Roman times. German, French, and Italian are official languages and Romansch has a special protected status. To complicate matters, Swiss Germans actually use a dialect of German called Schwyzerdütsch in casual conversation among themselves, reverting to conventional German for more serious discussions about law, scholarship, and politics. Standard German and Schwyzerdütsch are at the outside limits of mutual intelligibility, making Schwyzerdütsch a sort of subnational language for Swiss Germans.[25] Switzerland considers itself, and is considered by everyone else, to be the classic example of a multinational state with one sovereign government ruling over four ethnic groups or nations that have learned to accept one another. Naturally, human relationships are a little easier in a prosperous state, and Switzerland came in eleventh on the UN's 2011 human development index with one of the highest PC/GDP figures in Europe.[26]

When Are Minorities Significant?

Defining a state as multinational isn't a problem when it contains two or more very large and very distinct national groups, like Belgium. But how big does a minority have to be before it becomes significant enough to make a nation-state into a multinational state?

The key word here is clearly "significant." Denmark is a good example of a nation-state. There are just over five million Danish-speakers living in a part of Europe they have occupied for many centuries. Nearly all Danes share a rich and consistent national culture, speak the same Danish language, practice (or ignore) the same Lutheran religion, self-identify in an uncomplicated way as Danes, and regard themselves as connected to one another in a biological kinship group. Thanks to the Greenland connection, a few **Inuit** (or Eskimo) people have settled in Denmark, and in recent years, a handful of Arab Palestinians have sought refuge there along with a colony of ethnic Chinese and Indians who run restaurants and other service industries. Along the southern border, there is a small community of German-speakers. But the total number of Danish citizens who are not ethnic Danes is miniscule, and no one believes that a few Chinese cooks constitute a significant cultural subgroup. Lacking a significant non-Danish minority, Denmark is uncontroversially a nation-state.

How about France? For most of the last few centuries, France would have been considered a classical example of a nation-state, although there were long-standing minority groups such as the people of the Breton Peninsula, who speak a Celtic language, and the occasionally violent Corsicans, whose language is closer to Italian than to French.[27] In the 1800s, however, France conquered huge portions of Saharan and sub-Saharan Africa, and after World War II, large numbers of Moroccans, Algerians, and other North Africans came to live in France, most of them as legal immigrants. While many non-French residents are actually French citizens who were born in France, they continue to dress and speak in ways that identify them as foreign in the eyes of the French. About nine million people (or some 16 percent of the population) fall into this category; about half of them are Muslims.[28]

Is this a significant minority? Significance lies in the eye of the beholder. This large community of dark-skinned Muslims has upset many Caucasian French Catholics, who have reacted by voting for extremist political parties and sometimes carrying out acts of violence against the foreigners in their midst. Running in the 2002 French presidential elections as the leader of the anti-immigrant National Front, the openly racist Jean-Marie Le Pen stunned France by placing second with 17 percent of the popular vote. Le Pen's strong showing suggests that one out of seven French voters found the non-French population of France both irritating and politically significant. You'll need to crank up your French, but if you want to learn more, look at the National Front website.[29] You'll find that a *Le Pen* is still in charge of the National Front, but it's Marine Le Pen, charismatic daughter of Jean-Marie, who ran for office. Mademoiselle Le Pen is even more popular than her father, and won 18 percent of the first round in the 2012 French presidential elections, finishing in third place behind Socialist president François Hollande.

Many European states that once considered themselves to be nation-states are now reacting with concern to the growth in their immigrant populations, and chauvinist anti-immigrant parties in Italy, Austria, and Holland have been getting more votes in recent years.

Scholars and social scientists are in some disagreement over the question of how big a minority ethnic group has to be before a nation-state becomes a multinational state. This scholarly controversy is liable to go on indefinitely, but we are probably safe in sticking with our key word "significant." If the dominant group within a sovereign state generally feels that a minority population within its borders is big enough to be significant, then we can assume that we are dealing with a multinational state. Language will be our most important clue: if the government prints official documents in two or more mutually unintelligible languages, it is explicitly acknowledging the existence of more than one politically significant national community within its borders.

The existence of minority ethnic communities doesn't have to be a problem; remember Switzerland. But the cohabitation of two nations under one sovereign government can often create political difficulties, as it has in Belgium, Canada, and South Africa. In severe cases, there can be sporadic fighting among the several ethnicities, as in Nigeria, India, and Indonesia. And in the worst cases, ethnic conflicts can be a short cut to civil war and genocide; we'll look at some unhappy specimens in chapter 11.[30]

IS THE UNITED STATES A NATION-STATE OR A MULTINATIONAL STATE?

There isn't a clear-cut, yes-or-no answer. American culture involves American-accented English, a set of shared attitudes about politics, an informal national "personality," and a population that overwhelmingly self-identifies as Christian. Race is a vibrant political issue, but no one thinks there's a separate African American nation in the United States. American blacks are culturally American, no matter where that complicated DNA originally hailed from.

Americans self-identifying as Hispanic, on the other hand, are about 14 percent of the U.S. population, which suggests that they are a significant ethnic community. Hispanics are defined more by language than by kinship: some are Caucasians whose biological connection to Spain is relatively clear, while others are actually Spanish-speaking Americans of Inca or Aztec origin. A significant number of Hispanics are at least partly descended from African slaves. Overwhelmingly, Hispanics celebrate a rich combination of genetic bloodlines, reflecting the turbulent history of the New World.

The problem is deciding how many Hispanics would qualify as members of a separate national group. Many of those who self-identify as Hispanic are actually only honoring a family heritage; about 85 percent of American Hispanics actually speak English as their primary language and think of themselves as Americans. On the other hand, American states such as Florida, California, and Texas are home to significant populations of Spanish-speakers who find English difficult and might self-identify as "hyphenated" Cuban-Americans or Mexican-Americans.

In the United States, the debate about multiculturalism has ramifications for that hard-to-answer question of whether the United States is a nation-state or a multinational state. Some American nationalists feel that the United States can only maintain its status as "one nation indivisible" if Americans focus their attention and educational system on the greatness of core American culture and the standard American version of the English language.[31] They argue, for example, that the recognition of Spanish as an alternate national language would convert the country into a multinational state and open the door to divisiveness and disunity. Texas, California, and Florida have all gone through angry debates over whether instruction should be offered in English, Spanish, or one of the various foreign tongues of recent immigrants. Dedication to the maintenance of a "core culture" or national identity is more usually associated with political conservatives. American liberals, on the other hand, tend to embrace multiculturalism and are more open to the idea of a multinational America in which Spanish is already the country's unofficial second language. Advocates of multiculturalism argue that the blending of ethnicities and nationalities will produce a broad and richly diverse culture.

Tough Choices: Nations and Tribes in Nigeria

The west African country of Nigeria exemplifies many of the points we have made about the complex interplay between sovereign statehood and multiple nationalisms. With over 125 million people, the Federal Republic of Nigeria is the most heavily populated country in west Africa and the largest black society in the world. It has the largest petroleum reserves in Africa south of the Sahara and has become a dominant player in African political life. It is also one of the most profoundly multinational states in the world, with three huge and divergent ethnic communities: the largely Islamic Fulani-Hausa peoples in the North, the

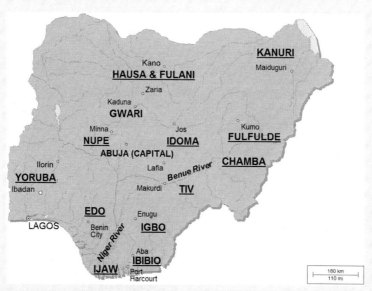

Map 4.2.   Ethnic Divisions in Nigeria
All maps simplify reality. The Islamic Hausa-Fulani communities tend to live in Nigeria's northern states, while the Yoruba people dominate the western border, and the Ibos (sometimes called "Igbos") live in the South. These three population groups actually mingle with one another and with Nigeria's many other minority ethnicities. In fact, the country is an ethnic stew.
Source: The Central Intelligence Agency.

mostly Christian Yoruba nation in the West (and in neighboring Benin), the Igbo or Ibo people of the Southeast, and dozens of smaller groups.

Like many other African countries, Nigeria is a purely colonial artifact, stitched together from parts of earlier countries. The name "Nigeria" came from the Niger River, not from any perceived ethnic unity among the peoples who lived along its banks. A thousand years ago, much of west-central Africa was dominated by a powerful Kanem-Bornu empire, already largely Islamic and encompassing much of what is today northern Nigeria. By the 1500s to the southwest, an artistically advanced Benin society dominated much of western Nigeria as well as the modern Republic of Benin while the Yoruba created a series of independent societies. Further to the east along Nigeria's Atlantic coast were several other smaller, linguistically and culturally divergent communities.

In the 1500s, European slave traders established a flourishing commerce in humans-for-sale along the coast, with the city of Lagos and other ports becoming major commercial centers under predominantly English influence. Even after ending the slave trade in 1807, the British continued to have an economic interest in the area and brought the interior of the country under their control. By 1900, the area had been organized by London into three separate protectorates, although London continued its standard colonial policy of ruling wherever possible through existing tribal structures.

Nigerian independence from Britain in 1960 allowed long simmering regional and tribal antagonisms to explode as the southern Igbos and Yorubas, and the northern Islamic peoples all vied for power. In 1967, the Igbo-dominated eastern region of the country seceded under the title of Republic of Biafra, leading to a brutal three-year civil war with perhaps a million fatalities from combat wounds or war-related starvation.

Conflict flowing from ethnic or national strife in Nigeria has made it extremely difficult for the sovereign state to function as a democracy. The blame for this ethnic dissent is often focused on what is called "tribalism." Commonly employed to describe primitive or aboriginal groups, some would argue that "tribe" is an inherently racist word, but we seem to be stuck with it.

Whatever we call the various national/tribal groups in Nigeria, it is clear that plural ethnicity lies at the core of the country's problems. The mostly Islamic Hausa-Fulani people spill over the border into Niger and Chad and have become increasingly fundamentalist or Islamist in their approach to religion and society. The Hausa language is related to a number of other northern Africa desert languages such as Berber, but is unrelated to most of the tongues used in the Nigerian South. The predominantly Christian Yoruba people live in the Southwest and are concentrated in Nigeria's largest city, Lagos. Because they are the largest and most assertive of Nigeria's minorities, other national-ethnic groups tend to mistrust them. The Igbo (or Ibo) people are the most Westernized of Nigeria's ethnicities, but they are still regarded with suspicion because of the Biafran War. Although English is one of Nigeria's official languages, not everybody can speak it, and the great mass of poorer Nigerians communicate in tribal languages that are not mutually intelligible.

While suspicion and mistrust continue to exist between the Igbo and Yoruba communities, the principal axis of violent hostility today is between the Islamized Hausa-speaking North and the Christian South. Throughout this decade there has been widespread rioting, and street fighting broke out between Hausa and Yoruba men with hundreds of fatalities. A scholarly journalist named Karl Maier has remarked, "Nigerians from all walks of life are openly questioning whether their country should remain as one entity or break apart into several separate states."[32]

Diverse ethnic groups can normally find ways to live together if there is enough money to go around. Nigeria is the world's seventh-largest exporter of crude oil, and 80 percent of the government's revenues come from petroleum sales. Regrettably, oil has a way of distorting a developing economy, since most of the money tends to wind up in a few deep pockets, foreign oil corporations get involved in local politics, and corruption becomes endemic.

Does Nigeria have to remain a single, unified sovereign state? Nigeria's most celebrated writer is Chinua Achebe, an Igbo who writes in English. His most famous book, *Things Fall Apart*,[33] described Nigeria in the last years of the end of the colonial period, but the title serves as a stark warning to Nigerians. History conveys no money-back guarantee that this artificial creation of British imperial whim must always remain a single country. If some form of national unity cannot be created and sustained, things can fall apart in the future as they have in the past.

3. The Complexities of Nationalism

We've talked about nation-states and multinational states, but the complexities of the state-nation relationship don't end there. Sometimes a national group constitutes a majority in several different sovereign states, leading some political scientists to devise the concept of the **multi-state nation** (or multi-state nationality). This is a concept worth thinking about because it helps us understand some of the intricacies of the Middle East.

Furthermore, history has been unkind to some smaller nations, denying them the opportunity to create their own sovereign governments. They exist as national minorities in one or more sovereign states, but are never numerous enough to constitute a majority. They are typically called **stateless nations**, and they are almost always a past or present source of political conflict.

The business of describing our feelings about nations and states has developed a vocabulary of its own, so we'll pause to examine some of the language of nationalism below. And finally, we'll look at the mechanics of multinationalism as they have played out in the sovereign state just north of the U.S. border with a special investigation of the politics of language and nationality in Canada.

MULTI-STATE NATIONS AND STATELESS NATIONS

Sometimes history hands us a very large nation that has been artificially divided into several smaller sovereign states, a phenomenon called the multi-state nation. In other cases, nations are minorities, sometimes within just one sovereign state or, in other cases, fragmented among several different sovereign states. We'll also look at these "stateless nations" below.

When Nations Are Bigger Than States

In describing multi-state nations, remember that we are using the word "state" in the sense of a sovereign state, not an American sub-sovereign state. The United States may or may not be a multinational state, but it is not a multi-state nation. Historically, multi-state nations have almost always been the result of war, and they are normally afflicted with political instability and conflict.

Many scholars would regard the Arab people as a prime example of a multi-state nation. Remember that friendly Canadian at the bistro in Paris asking his neighbors who they were? If he were to say, "Hi. I'm Canadian. What are you?" to a Moroccan or an Iraqi or a Saudi Arabian, what answer would he get?

Depending upon a variety of factors, the simple response might be, "I'm an Arab." And yet there is no single Arab sovereign state; in fact, there are at least twenty-one separate independent countries containing a clear majority of people who would self-identify as Arabs. So why might a Saudi say, "Arab," instead of naming the country of which he is technically a citizen?

The answer is historical and religious. In the years after Mohammed's death in 632 AD, Arabic-speaking Muslims transmitted their culture and some of their DNA to nearly all parts of the Middle East, and for three centuries there was a unified Arabian Empire governing a vast and successful nation-state from Morocco to Iraq. Today, the Arabian Empire is long gone, shattered by war, internal dissent, external invasions, and colonialism. What was once one sovereign state has now been replaced by many different Arab states, all practicing Islam, sharing an Arab culture, speaking the Arabic language, and feeling a sense of biological kinship with other Arabs, but governed by separate and often mutually antagonistic sovereign governments.

So when our Saudi friend responds, "Arab," instead of "Saudi Arabian," he is making a clear and crucial political statement, saying that participation in Arabic nationhood is more important to him than whatever Arabian **successor state** is stamped on his passport. In an even deeper sense, he may be questioning the **legitimacy** of these Arab successor states, suggesting that the only real Arab state would be one that reunifies the Arab people under a single government.[34]

Another clear example of a multi-state nation is Korea. After a half century of Japanese colonialism, the Korean peninsula emerged from World War II to find that the Russians had occupied the northern half of their country, while the Americans had seized the South. Thanks to the Cold War, two mutually hostile successor states emerged. In the South, an American-dominated Republic of Korea evolved slowly into a prosperous democracy, while the North's Democratic People's Republic of Korea (DPRK) has remained one of the world's most repressive regimes.[35] Despite the political division between North and South, the Koreans remain one consistent ethnic community, although some minor cultural differences have grown because of the near-total lack of contact between the two ends of the peninsula.

Is there a Hispanic nation? Thanks to a vigorous program of colonization in the New World, Spanish-speaking Roman Catholics inhabit most parts of Central and South America. Over the course of time, Mexicans and Argentineans have developed distinctive national cultures, but are they foreigners to one another in the way that Bulgarians are foreign in Botswana? Or is there an inchoate Spanish multi-state nation?

Stateless Nations

The multi-state nations described above had at least the advantage of being the majority or dominant nation in some or all of the states they inhabited. The phrase "stateless nation" is used to describe a situation in which a national or ethnic group is deprived by history of any sovereign status at all and lives as a minority population in one or more sovereign states. Depending upon your precise definition of statelessness, there are a fair number of examples.

- Basques: The Basques live in northern Spain and just over the border in France, and speak a language that is totally different from all other European languages.[36] Their unhappiness with their stateless status has led some Basques into an ongoing terrorist conflict with the Spanish government.[37]
- Baluchi: Speaking a cognate of the Iranian subfamily of languages, the Baluchi people find themselves divided between southern Iran and western Pakistan.
- Native Americans: In this same category are the Native Americans of North, Central, and South America, since many Indian peoples continue to practice coherent and distinct cultures, and yet there is no sovereign Native American/Indian state anywhere.

- The Berbers: North Africa's Berber people are divided between two sovereign states in northwest Africa, Morocco, and Algeria. Morocco and Algeria are dominated by Islamic and Arabic-speaking populations, self-identifying as part of the Arab world. In both Morocco and Algeria, however, there is a minority national group of Berber people, the descendents of the original inhabitants of North Africa, who self-identify as Berbers, and speak a language that is totally unrelated to Arabic.
- Palestinians: The Palestinian people suffer from a tragic but complicated situation. Some Palestinians live in exile, either in the Arab world or in the Western world. Others live in the Israeli-controlled territories of the West Bank and the Gaza Strip, where they have an extremely limited form of self-government in the form of the Palestinian National Authority. And others are citizens of Israel, able to vote in Israeli elections, without having much impact on the outcome. Most scholars believe that Palestinian statelessness is an important factor in the violence between Arabs and Jews in Israel/Palestine.
- Gypsies: The Gypsy people are often stereotyped as cheerful migratory fortune-tellers, beggars, and petty thieves, ready to burst into a song or a brawl at a moment's notice. Inevitably, the reality is rather more complicated. While the term "gypsy" is often used to describe a rootless, wandering person, the authentic Gypsy people are a well-defined ethnic group linked by a specific language, a culture, and kinship. The Gypsy people call themselves Roma, and they are an ancient people who drifted westward from India, establishing themselves in Europe by the 1500s. They brought with them a language called Romany, which is clearly an Indian language.[38] Until recently, little has been written in Romany, and many Roma are illiterate in their own language.

  There may be twelve million Roma in the world, most of them in central Europe, and they have had difficulty in adapting to life in modern society. Some continue to be migratory, but many have now settled into life on the margins of larger cities. Commonly regarded as dishonest and predatory, they are generally disliked in Europe, and some European countries have denied them full citizenship rights. During World War II, Gypsies found themselves classed along with Jews, Marxists, and homosexuals as enemies of the Third Reich, and as many as one-half million may have died in Nazi death camps.[39]

  What distinguishes the Roma from other stateless peoples is their lack of an authentic homeland, since the ancient cultural connection to India has long since been broken. While individual Roma have achieved success in the arts and commerce, they are generally educationally and economically marginal.

At a practical level, it isn't going to be economically or politically feasible to carve out independent sovereign states for each and every one of the world's thousands of nations. If the stateless nation in question lives in one specific part of the national territory, one partial solution to the problem can be the creation of a sub-sovereign entity specifically for that national group, something the Canadian government has done north of Hudson Bay. Long before either British or French explorers landed on Canada's chilly beaches, there were Native Americans (called "First Nation" people in Canada) and Eskimos (whose word for themselves is "Inuit") living close to the Arctic Circle. In order to give these native nations as much local autonomy as possible, the Canadian government carved out a hunk of the Northwest Territory in 1999, renamed it "Nunavut," and established its capital at the Baffin Island city of Iqaluit. Inuit living in Greenland have also been given local self-government.[40] (See map 4.5.)

Figure 4.3.   A Roma Child Begging
The Gypsy stereotype suggests that Europe's Roma are all beggars or con artists.
In fact, Gypsies (who prefer to be called Roma) are a complicated and interesting
stateless people who work in all walks of life, although they do face discrimination
in nearly every society and some do force their children onto the streets as beggars.

Tough Choices: Should the Kurdish Nation Become a Nation-State?

The 2003 Anglo-American assault on Saddam Hussein's Iraqi regime focused international attention on the Kurdish people, who are both a stateless nation and key players in the future of this multinational state. The Kurdish people are a political abnormality, a very large national group with a strong territorial attachment to "Kurdistan," a mountain homeland in the Middle East. Thus far, however, the Kurds have been unable to translate Kurdistan's nationhood into statehood, and commentators often describe them as the world's largest non-sovereign national group, numbering perhaps twenty-five million people.

As you can see from map 4.3, most Kurds live uncomfortably in eastern Turkey, while others make their home across the border in the northern portion of Iraq. There are smaller numbers in Syria and Iran. The Kurds are largely a pastoral mountain people trying to survive in terrain as savage as the political life in this corner of the Middle East.

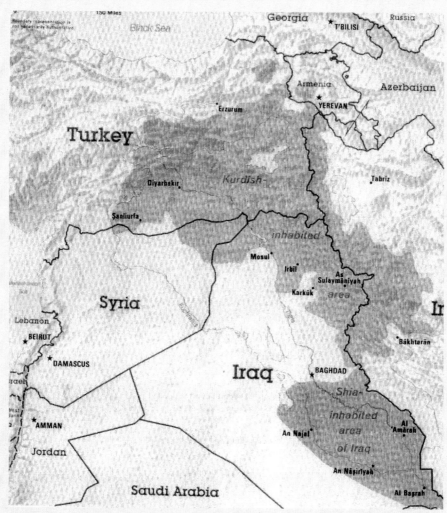

Map 4.3. Kurdistan
A classic example of a stateless nation, there are Kurds living in Turkey, Iran, Syria, and Iraq, the only country where they have established self-government although not formal autonomy.
Courtesy of Professor Joyce Blau, Kurdish Institute of Paris.

Kurdish is actually one of the cognates in the Iranian subfamily of languages, and most Kurds are Sunni Muslims. When the Ottoman Empire came unglued after World War I, the victorious allies neglected to carve out a national homeland for the Kurds, despite Woodrow Wilson's passion for national self-determination. Since then, the Kurds have been the perennial pawns of the Middle East, manipulated by rival regional governments and the CIA, sometimes abandoned, and usually persecuted. In 1988, Saddam Hussein actually used poison gas against the Kurdish village of Halabja, killing thousands of Kurds. After the Persian Gulf War in 1990–1991, the United States and the United Kingdom prevented the Iraqi military from operating in the Kurdish districts in Iraq. Under this umbrella, Iraq's Kurds established a semiautonomous sub-sovereign political entity and made some limited progress toward ending their internal squabbles.

Across the border in Turkey, a very large group of Turkish separatists fought a long battle with repressive Turkish authorities, although an uneasy truce prevailed at the start of the new century. The American government regards Turkey as an important regional ally and has taken no role in defending Kurdish rights on Turkish soil.[41]

The 2003 Iraq War ended with the Anglo-American coalition trying to arrange a new Iraqi government that would control all of the territory formerly governed by Saddam Hussein, including the Kurdish provinces of the North. The Kurds however, still mistrust Sunni and Shi'ite Iraqis and are reluctant to surrender any of their current self-government. Many of them still yearn for independence.

Congratulations on your appointment as deputy undersecretary of state for Kurdish affairs. You represent a government that believes in freedom and self-determination for people, and the United States has sponsored independence for many much smaller groups in other parts of the world. The world has generally supported the right of the Jewish people to have a state of their own in the Middle East, and in recent years, it has become European and American policy that there should also be a Palestinian state. While there are more Kurds than Israelis and Palestinians put together, there is no corresponding global outcry for the creation of a Kurdistan.

On the other hand, supporting independence for the Kurds would mean infuriating America's Turkish allies and perhaps provoking a free-for-all in an already unstable Iraq. You need to advise the president tomorrow. What exactly are you going to say when you get to the Oval Office?[42]

THE POLITICS OF NATIONALISM

Earlier we talked about the concept of territoriality as one of the elements of nationhood, the sense that you are connected with a specific bit of real estate somewhere in the world. In our heads, we all have a mental map of our countries. Humming "This Land Is My Land," Americans see shining superhighways and shopping malls running from Maine to California, while Frenchmen envision a France that extends from the Rhine to the Mediterranean Sea and across to the Atlantic. If, however, part of the territory on your mental map of your nation isn't actually controlled by the appropriate government, you may be seriously unhappy, a topic to be discussed below. In many parts of the world, people become so intensely focused on the greatness or uniqueness of their nations that they frighten their neighbors. We'll talk about hypernationalism as well, along with some of the terminology we use to describe these emotions.

Irredentism and Separatism

When a territory you regard as belonging rightfully to your nation winds up in somebody else's sovereign state, you will probably react with anger and even violence. Depending upon your geographic perspective, this unhappiness is called either **irredentism** or **separatism**.

When the Irish think about the Emerald Isle, for example, many of them frown at the knowledge that about a quarter of it is still governed from London rather than from Ireland's national capital in Dublin. If they are living in the Republic of Ireland, their feelings about Northern Ireland are called irredentism, the notion that part of your national territory has been stolen and needs somehow to be recovered. The expression comes from a Latin word meaning, "that which must be redeemed."

The belief of the Chinese government in Beijing that the island of Taiwan legitimately belongs to mainland China and must someday be restored to Beijing's control is another prime example of irredentism. Almost all border disputes are irredentist in character, occurring when one country believes that a neighbor has stolen some of its territory. Peru and Ecuador battled each other periodically over irredentist claims to the same territory on their common border, but the two Latin American neighbors settled the feud with a compromise in 1998.

Portions of the city of Jerusalem are likely to be the object of Palestinian irredentism for the foreseeable future (see chapter 11 for the details). When the Israelis took military control of the West Bank of the Jordan River in 1967, they formally integrated a massively enlarged version of the city of Jerusalem into their national territory, including neighborhoods in east Jerusalem that are almost exclusively inhabited by Palestinian Arabs.[43]

Change places on the map and you change irredentism into separatism. People who live in a lost territory are likely to call themselves separatists, believing that their territory should be separated from the foreigners who govern it, either to become independent or to be rejoined to its natural homeland. To return to the case of Ireland, Catholic Irishmen who live in Belfast are separatists if they believe that **Ulster**/Northern Ireland should be separated from Great Britain and joined to the Republic of Ireland. Some Corsicans feel that their Mediterranean island should secede from France and become independent. Some Scots would like a divorce from England. Muslims in Kashmir are separatists in wanting out of Hindu-dominated India.

Tough Choices: The Two-China Dilemma

Here's a hypothetical question. Imagine that country A is a harshly authoritarian dictatorship that once waged war against the United States and has been sporadically hostile ever since. Country B is a prosperous democracy with which the United States has always enjoyed good relations. In a crunch, which one should the U.S. government support? We should perhaps mention that country A is fifty-seven times bigger than country B and equipped with nuclear weapons, which means that the dilemma could become deadly serious for U.S. foreign policy makers at almost any time.

When the Chinese civil war ended in 1949, what was once the Nationalist government of China found itself ruling only the island of Taiwan (previously called "Formosa"). The People's Republic of China claimed that Taiwan was part of its national territory, and in 1971, the world resolved its diplomatic dilemma by giving China's UN seat to mainland China while continuing to trade briskly with the generally unrecognized Taiwan.

Map 4.4.   Taiwan and the Republic of China
History is messy, and when mainland China and Taiwan finished their war in 1949, the island of Quemoy remained in Taiwanese hands despite the fact that it is indefensibly close to the mainland. In 2005, the Chinese Parliament passed legislation requiring their government to take military action should Taiwan ever attempt to achieve formal (as opposed to actual) independence.
Source: Map by R. O. Collin.

For a long time, the islanders preferred not to raise the independence issue, since the mere mention of Taiwanese sovereignty provokes strong irredentist feelings on the mainland, only one hundred miles away. As the Nationalist Party became a more democratic political force in the 1980s, it continued to hope for eventual unification with the People's Republic of China on terms that would be favorable to Taiwan. But some Taiwanese began wondering out loud whether unification was inevitable and whether it was in the best interests of Taiwan. Here is the gist of their argument: While historically identified with China, Taiwan was conquered by Japan in 1895 and ruled from Tokyo until Japan's defeat in World War II. After a short, tumultuous period of union with China, Taiwan became the refuge for the defeated Nationalist army after 1949, and has been functionally self-governing ever since.[44] Hence, for virtually all of the twentieth century, Taiwan was not really part of China. Furthermore, mainland China continues to be a dictatorship, while Taiwan has evolved into an authentic democracy. In its 2012 ratings, Freedom House awarded Taiwan a laudatory rating of 1.1 (Free), while communist China received a failing score of 7 (Unfree).[45]

If Taiwan should someday declare formal independence, should the United States support Taiwan or China, or remain neutral? Mainland China has a population of 1.3 billion potential customers (as opposed to Taiwan's twenty-two million), so an accommodation with Beijing makes better business sense. Furthermore, the mainland would certainly be willing to go to war over Taiwan; should the United States risk a military confrontation (or actual war) with China over the issue? On the other hand, the United States has always proclaimed its support for democracy and the rights of peoples to choose their own government, and Taiwan has traditionally enjoyed American support.

After completing your political science doctorate with a dissertation on Chinese foreign policy, you've taken a position as Asian affairs advisor to the Senate Foreign Relations Committee. The senators want to know what to do. Start earning your salary and tell them.

NATIONALISM

There are a number of confusing words about how we feel about nations and kinship groups. In the least complicated sense of the word, **nationalism** is merely the belief that members of a given ethnic group should be governed by their own kind rather than by foreigners who come from a different culture and speak a different language. For many decades, Lithuanians, Latvians, and Estonians wondered why they needed to obey the orders of ethnic Russians in faraway Moscow. When they demanded (and got) freedom in 1991, their feelings of nationalism gained widespread sympathy around the world.

At the next level up, nationalism is perhaps a synonym for patriotism, which—as Samuel Johnson once reminded us—"is the last refuge of a scoundrel," suggesting that we look closely at this emotionally charged word and at those who use it. In normal usage, patriotism merely denotes a reasonable affection for one's country and a willingness to make personal sacrifices in the national interest. At a more complicated level, it describes a kind of passion in which people rank their country's perceived short-term interests well ahead of other plausible values (religion, humanity, common sense, etc.) At various times in history, Germans, Japanese, Englishmen, and Americans have surrendered to powerful nationalistic feelings, believing that their country's interests should prevail uncompromisingly over other countries and other interests.

"Chauvinism" is a **pejorative** or derogatory term describing people who are arrogant about their country's culture and accomplishments. Love of a country or a culture can easily spill over to exaggerated feelings about the presumed superiority of an ethnic community. When members of a national community begin to overvalue a presumed biological kinship, we stumble into **racism**, which assumes a hierarchy of quality among human communities with certain kinship groups possessing greater intelligence or courage or creativity.

In a multinational state, members of the dominant national group may come to see themselves as biologically superior to the allegedly inferior foreigners living on their territory. South Africa is a good example of a multinational state, and white Europeans began settling there in 1652, coming eventually to dominate the southern tip of Africa. This settler population always denied rights to nonwhites in their midst, but after the victory of the Nationalist Party in 1948, this racial segregation was formally established in a policy known as **apartheid**, which means "separateness" in the Afrikaans dialect of Dutch. Apartheid was based on openly racist attitudes toward blacks, Asians, and people of mixed biological inheritance, sentiments even supported by some academics and churchmen.

Whether it is a nation-state or a multinational state, every country will have minority groups of some sort, and, inevitably, there are political problems in establishing the ground rules between dominant communities and smaller ethnic groups. Polite people have always tried to be respectful in dealing with members of other kinship, religious, social, or gender communities, allowing them to define themselves and their relationship to society. As the descendants of African slaves have acquired civil and economic rights in the United States, for example, they self-defined successively as "colored people," "blacks," and "African Americans," eventually coming almost full circle with the phrase, "persons of color." The notion that we should cherish diversity in society by studying our differences in gender, religion, or national/ethnic origin is sometimes called **multiculturalism,** but some conservatives believe that the United States is ignoring core American culture in favor of minority cultures.

COMPLICATED CANADIAN NATIONALISMS

Let's look at some of these ideas and conflicts in the context of an actual multinational state. Canada is an uncontroversial example of a multinational state because it contains two large and well-defined national groups within its borders, as well as the Inuit and Native Americans mentioned above. A statistical majority of Canadians speak English and trace their ancestry to the United Kingdom. They are a mixture of Catholics and Protestants, although Protestants are a majority among Canadians of British descent.

Centered mostly in the province of Quebec, the smaller nation is an overwhelmingly Roman Catholic and French-speaking community, whose forefathers hail from France. People of French origin who live in Quebec are called *Québécois* in French and Quebecers in English.[46] Québécois license plates bear the nostalgic phrase "Je me souviens" ("I remember"), a nationalist evocation of an era before the British conquered this corner of the French Empire in 1759.[47] There has been some level of hostility between these two population groups ever since 1759, and in recent years, there has even been a movement to break Canada into two or more separate countries. Could multinational Canada come unglued? Although it is an extremely polite crisis with little present potential for violence, for much of the last three decades, the stunning answer was "probably not, but possibly yes."

The Canadian Success Story

The modern problem is the consequence of some old history. Canada was discovered by both French and British explorers at the end of the 1400s and the start of the 1500s. While the French established their language, their Roman Catholic religion, and their culture between Quebec City and Montreal, the British eventually took the east coast, the center of the country, and the Far West. During the 1756–1763 Seven Years War (the North American side of which is called the French and Indian War), Britain conquered all of Canada to the irritation of former French subjects in Quebec. For a long time, Canada was merely a collection of separate British colonies, but the British North America Act of 1867 created the basis for the modern Canadian state, and by the twentieth century, the country moved peacefully and gradually toward national independence.[48]

Map 4.5. Canada

Get your Canadian geography under control. U.S. citizens are notorious (at least in Canada) for their ignorance of Canadian affairs. The Canadians have recently divided the Northwest Territory into two separately governed territories. Nunavut in the East will be a homeland for the Inuit (or Eskimos); the Northwest and Yukon territories contain a mix of Native America/Indian peoples, white settlers, and a few Inuit.

Source: U.S. Department of State.

Canada is a federal system with ten provinces that correspond roughly to American states. In the West are a series of generally English-speaking provinces such as British Columbia, Alberta, Saskatchewan, and Manitoba. Ontario (with the national capital at Ottawa) is cosmopolitan and wealthy. Quebec, extending from the U.S. border to the Arctic, actually separates central and western Canada from the Maritime Provinces, which are Prince Edward Island, Nova Scotia, New Brunswick, and the recently renamed province of Newfoundland and Labrador. In the far North lie the underpopulated Yukon and Northwestern territories, which have limited self-government, and the newly created Nunavut Territory for the Eskimo/Inuit people.[49]

Canada's ten provinces are led by politically powerful premiers (similar to U.S. state governors but with more authority), who cannot be easily bullied by Canada's federal government in Ottawa. As a member of the Commonwealth of Nations, Canada still technically regards the queen of England as its head of state, although Elizabeth II is represented in Ottawa by a governor general. This official is actually selected by the Canadian government to carry out in Canada the same largely ceremonial functions the queen performs in the United Kingdom.

We will describe parliamentary systems more fully in chapter 7, but the Canadian federal government resembles the British system in that the prime minister—the actual political leader of the country—is actually chosen by parliament, and is typically the leader of the largest party in parliament. Hence, the Canadian leader is indirectly elected.

In many respects, Canada is one of the most successful societies in the world. Remember the human development index, that report card issued every year by the UN? Over the past decade, Canada has persistently been among the top-ten countries in the world; it scored fourth place in 2009 and has ranked first on several occasions. Despite a population of only thirty million and a chilly climate, Canada can boast a **per capita gross domestic product (PC/GDP)** of US$37,808 per year.[50] The educational system is regarded as outstanding, and the Canadian health-care system keeps its citizens alive an average of one and one-half years longer than U.S. citizens. Canadians claim that their society is kinder and gentler than America's and even the murder rate is dramatically lower. Statisticians report homicides based on the number of people unlawfully killed per 100,000 per year. Canada can boast a life affirming 2:100,000 record against a bloodthirsty American 9:100,000.

The Problem of Quebec

So why should there be a problem? First, the Québécois stumbled through the twentieth century still feeling that they had been railroaded into Canada without their consent and were not sharing fully in the Canadian success story. In their view, most of the money and power lay in the hands of English-speaking Canadians. Constituting about one-quarter of the population, the resentful French-speaking minority was jealously protective of its culture, language, and religion, and overwhelmingly reluctant to see itself absorbed culturally into Anglo-Saxon society. Nationalist antagonisms ran in both directions. English-speaking Canadians are quietly pleased with their country's accomplishments and resent Quebec's ambivalence about membership in one of the world's most successful democracies.

In the 1960s, some Québécois began to contemplate actual independence and the assertion of Quebec's sovereignty as a separate state. Pro-independence Parti Québécois (PQ) was established in 1968 and became the dominant party in Quebec in 1976. There was even a tiny terrorist movement receiving support from Cuba, which used a limited amount of violence to punctuate its demand for Quebec's independence. Leading Canada throughout much of this period was the charismatic Liberal Party chieftain Pierre Elliott Trudeau (prime minister 1968–1979; 1980–1984). Himself a bilingual Quebecer, Trudeau outmaneuvered the separatists by unilaterally granting equal status for French as one of Canada's two official languages.

The constitutional dilemma began in 1982, when Trudeau repatriated (or brought home from London) the Canadian Constitution in what was meant to be a purely formal and final assertion of Canadian independence from Great Britain. All of Canada's ten provinces needed to assent to the constitution, but Quebec worried that the document did not guarantee them enough of a special status and refused its assent, a situation that has never changed.

When Prime Minister Brian Mulroney (in office 1984–1993) offered Quebec the special status they sought, several of Canada's provincial parliaments refused to agree, leaving Canada in a continuing constitutional muddle.[51] By 1995, the secessionist Parti

Québécois (PQ) had organized a referendum asking the people of Quebec to consent to independence unless the Canadian government acquiesced to a series of demands. When 49.4 percent of the province's voters supported the referendum, it became clear that the breakup of the Canadian federal system was a real possibility.[52]

The Rise and Fall of the Liberal Party

For much of the past century, a center-left political movement called the Liberal Party has dominated Canada's federal government. During the 1980s, Canadian voters turned to the right, just as American and British voters did, but in 1993, the Liberal Party staged a historic comeback under the leadership of Jean Chrétien. Chrétien won a second time in 1997 and completed the "**hat trick**" with a third victory in November of 2000, serving until his voluntary retirement in 2003.[53]

Like Trudeau, Jean Chrétien came from the troubled province of Quebec, and his popularity was partially based on his management of the economy and partly on his skill in dealing with those seven million French-speaking Canadians, who continued to wonder if they wanted an independent country of their own. Chrétien's last big victory in 2000 gave him an **absolute majority** in parliament and left him in a strong position to deal with a recalcitrant Quebec. With the economy booming and money flowing into Quebec, Chrétien's Liberal Party mounted a major campaign in the 2003 provincial elections to take the province away from the Parti Québécois.[54] In a hotly contested election, pro-unity Liberal candidates for Quebec's provincial legislature outpolled the separatists, and took control of the Quebec legislature. With Liberals in charge of the federal government in Ottawa and the Quebec parliament, the issue of independence seemed to have been moved firmly to the back burner.

As the new century began, few Canadians could imagine that their country would break apart, although political and business circles worried that there was no basic constitutional consensus holding the country together. The Liberal Party seemed to have the knack for keeping Canada in one piece. The problems began when the Liberal Party began to lose its hold on power.

After a decade in office, Jean Chrétien retired in December 2003, leaving behind a buoyant economy and a federal union less likely to be dissolved than at any time in forty years. He also left behind a significant breach in Canadian-American relations. For most of the postwar period, Canada and the United States were close military allies, but the Canadians overwhelmingly disapproved of the 2003 Anglo-American war against Iraq and refused to provide either troops or political support. While the two countries remained each other's top trading partner, the Bush administration responded with distinct coolness toward Ottawa.

Jean Chrétien's replacement, Prime Minister Paul Martin, tried to continue most of Chrétien's policies, but was plagued by persistent financial scandals within the ranks of his Liberal Party. Polling data does not automatically translate into votes, but if an independence referendum were held today, Quebec might very well vote for national independence.[55]

Then, in January 2006, an electoral explosion took place as Canada's revived Conservative Party roared into the parliamentary elections with a newly unified party and took a "relative majority" of the seats, that is, more parliamentary seats than anyone else.

To Secede or Not to Secede?

Since the secessionist movement began in earnest in the 1960s, there has been a hard core of young and relatively well-educated Québécois who want to break up the Canadian federal union (labeled "PRO" here). In 1995, during a formal referendum on the subject, the Pro-Independence or secessionist movement came within a hair of equaling the "CON" forces who prefer to remain within Canada. Since that time, the secessionist cause has dwindled somewhat, but it has remained in excess of 40 percent of Quebec's voting public for the past two decades. More-recent polling data suggests that as of 2006, the "PRO" (Independence) vote would still be close to 50 percent.

Led by a west-of-Canada Conservative named Stephen Harper, the Conservatives even took some votes away from the Parti Québécois. Harper won a majority of the seats in the legislature in the 2011 election. Conservative westerners are generally less sensitive to complaints from left-leaning Quebecers, and would probably wave good-bye if Quebec were to make another serious stab at secession.

Could Canada as we know it actually come to an end as a unified sovereign state? The answer ought to be no, but Quebec keeps asking the question and the next time the question gets asked, the answer could just be "*oui*."

4. The Wrap: What Have We Learned?

You need to understand the concept of sovereignty and be able to distinguish between a sovereign state and an American state such as California. Why is the Treaty of Westphalia relevant, and what does it mean when a state's sovereignty is nominal? Do you understand the distinction between a sovereign state and those international organizations sometimes called supra-sovereign? What are sub-sovereign entities? How many sovereign states are there, and is the number likely to rise or fall?

In normal speech, nation is just another word for country, but it's crucial to remember that in political science, the word means a group of people who share all or most of those important six characteristics mentioned above. Do you understand precisely what constitutes a nation-state? Why are some sovereign states classified as multinational states?

Sometimes nations and states don't match each other, so remember the concept of the multi-state nation as well as the problems stateless nations pose for themselves and their neighbors. Learn what you can about the Kurdish people; they're never out of the news for long. Irredentism and separatism are two words for most of the world's political problems, so ensure that you have both concepts under your belt. And finally, look at how rival nationalisms have troubled Canadian politics, despite Canada's brilliant success in most other areas of its national life.

We've taken our first look at individual countries, and there's a lot more of comparative politics business to come, but first we need to stop and sample international relations. How do the nearly two hundred sovereign states on the planet interact through diplomacy, international law, and the United Nations?

Notes

1. Lewis Carroll, *Alice's Adventures in Wonderland* (Boston: Lee and Shepard, 1869), 122.

2. For more on this subject, see Benedict Anderson, *Imagined Communities: Reflections on the Origin and Spread of Nationalism* (New York: Verso, 1991).

3. Chalmers Johnson, *Blowback: The Costs and Consequences of American Empire* (New York: Holt, 2000), 67.

4. The United Nations General Assembly, http://www.un.org/ga.

5. The Treaty of Westphalia, http://avalon.law.yale.edu/17th_century/westphal.asp.

6. The United Nations, http://www.un.org; the North Atlantic Treaty Organization (NATO), http://www.nato.int.

7. Ellen Grigsby, *Analyzing Politics: An Introduction to Political Science* (Belmont, Calif.: Wadsworth, 1999), 61–62.

8. Robert I. Rotberg "Failed States in a World of Terror," *Foreign Affairs* 81, no. 3 (2002): 127–40.

9. Watch Professor Chomsky on Amy Goodman's *Democracy Now!* at http://www.youtube.com/watch?v=xVGZSH3X45s.

10. Noam Chomsky, *The Failed States: The Abuses of Power and the Assault on Democracy* (New York: Metropolitan Books, 2006).

11. The Kyoto Protocol, http://unfccc.int/resource/docs/convkp/kpeng.pdf; the International Criminal Court, http://www.icc-cpi.int/.

12. The United Nations' listing of its membership is at www.un.org/members. The U.S. Department of State site at www.state.gov is a great place to start when doing research on anything international.

13. William Davison, *Bloomberg News*. http://www.bloomberg.com/news/2011–06–28/north-south-sudan-to-negotiate-cease-fire-in-border-states-mbeki-says.html, June 28, 2011.

14. The Kosovo Compromise, http://www.kosovocompromise.com/cms/item/analysis/en.html?view=story&id=873&sectionId=2; the United Nations Office of the Special Envoy to Kosovo, http://www.unosek.org/.

15. For more on this subject, see Thomas M. Poulsen's *States and Nations: A Geographic Background to World Affairs* (Englewood Cliffs: Prentice-Hall, 1995). Daniel Philpott's *Revolutions in Sovereignty: How Ideas Shaped Modern International Relations* (Princeton: Princeton University Press, 2001) looks at the issue from Westphalia today. Stephen D. Krasner has edited *Problematic Sovereignty: Contested Rules and Political Possibilities* (New York: Columbia University Press, 2001), a look at the complications of sovereignty in places like Taiwan, Tibet, Bosnia, and Palestine.

16. The Vatican, http://www.vatican.va/.

17. The government of the Falkland Islands, http://www.falklands.gov.fk/.

18. The government of Greenland, http://uk.nanoq.gl/.

19. The Bermuda government is an example of such an island state at http://www.gov.bm/.

20. No longer "British" but still the Commonwealth of Nations, the website for this club of ex-colonies can be found at www.thecommonwealth.org.

21. The government of Puerto Rico, http://www.topuertorico.org/government.shtml.

22. Stephen Brooks, *Canadian Democracy: An Introduction*, 3rd ed. (New York: Oxford University Press, 2000), 59.

23. Ernest Gellner's *Nations and Nationalism* (Ithaca: Cornell University Press, 1983) is probably the best theoretical study of modern nationalism. Another well-known author in the field is Anthony D. Smith, whose recent *Myths and Memories of the Nation* (New York: Oxford University Press, 2000) argues that nationalism will remain an omnipresent force in our lives. Donald L. Horowitz covers nationalist conflict in the Third World in his *Ethnic Groups in Conflict*, updated ed. (Berkeley: University of California Press, 2000). The best known authority on minority nationalism is the University of Maryland's Ted Robert Gurr, who wrote *Peoples versus States: Minorities at Risk in the New Century* (Washington, D.C.: U.S. Institute of Peace, 2000).

24. Philip Norton, *The British Polity*, 3rd ed. (New York: Longman, 1994), 6–7.

25. Jonathan Steinberg, *Why Switzerland?* (Cambridge, UK: Cambridge University Press, 1976), 47.

26. The United Nations Development Programme, *Human Development Report 2011* Statistical Annex, http://hdr.undp.org/en/media/HDR_2011_EN_Tables.pdf.

27. Frank L. Wilson, *European Politics Today: The Democratic Experience*, (3rd ed. (Upper Saddle River, N.J.: Prentice Hall, 1999), 109–10.

28. Michael G. Roskin, *Countries and Concepts: An Introduction to Comparative Politics*, 8th ed. (Englewood Cliffs, N.J.: Prentice Hall, 2004), 174–75.

29. The National Front, http://www.frontnational.com/.

30. For more information on multinationalism, see Robert H. Wiebe, *Who We Are: A History of Popular Nationalism* (Princeton: Princeton University Press, 2001); and Jacob T. Levy, *The Multiculturalism of Fear* (New York: Oxford University Press, 2000). Christian Joppke's *Immigration and the Nation-State: The United States, Germany, and Great Britain* (New York: Oxford University Press, 2000) looks at how governments of nation-states are tested as their populations become multinational. For the language component of nationalism, you'll want to consult Peter Trudgill's fascinating *Sociolinguistics: An Introduction to Language and Society* (London: Penguin, 1995). Ethnic conflict is brilliantly analyzed by Raymond C. Taras and Rajat Ganguy in their *Understanding Ethnic Conflict: The International Dimension*, 2nd ed. (New York: Longman, 2002).

31. Samuel P. Huntington "The Hispanic Challenge," *Foreign Policy*, March/April 2004, http://cyber.law.harvard.edu/blogs/gems/culturalagency1/SamuelHuntingtonTheHispanicC.pdf.

32. Karl Maier, *This House Has Fallen: Midnight in Nigeria* (Boulder, Colo.: Public Affairs, 2000); also see Eghosa Osaghae's *Crippled Giant: Nigeria since Independence* (Bloomington: Indiana University Press, 1998); Professor Toyin Falola has given us two excellent books: *The History of Nigeria* (Westport, Conn.: Greenwood Publishing Group, 2008) and *Violence in Nigeria: The Crisis of Religious Politics and Secular Ideologies* (Rochester, N.Y.: University of Rochester Press, 1998). Rotimi T. Suberu has studied Nigeria's various experiments in sub-sovereign political organization in his *Federalism and Ethnic Conflict in Nigeria* (Washington, D.C.: U.S. Institute of Peace, 2001). See also John N. Paden's *Faith and Politics in Nigeria* (Washington, D.C.: Institute of Peace, 2008).

33. Chinua Achebe, *Things Fall Apart* (New York: Heinemann, 1958).

34. James A. Bill and Robert Springborg, *Politics in the Middle East*, 5th ed. (New York: Longman, 2000), 27–32.

35. For more information on South Korea, see http://www.korea.net/index.do; for more information on the DPRK, see http://www.korea-dpr.com/.

36. Roger Collins, *The Basques* (Oxford: Blackwell, 1986), 8–9.

37. For the Basques' regional government in Spain, hit www.euskadi.net; there's an American perspective at the University of Nevada's Center for Basque Studies at http://basque.unr.edu.

38. For more information on the Romani, see http://www.romani.org/; the European Roma Rights Center has a big site at www.errc.org; See also Thomas Acton and Gary Mundy, *Romani Culture and Gypsy Identity* (Hatfield, UK: University of Hertfordshire Press, 1999); and Isabel Fonseca's journalistic *Bury Me Standing: The Gypsies and Their Journey* (New York: Knopf, 1996).

39. Thomas Acton, and Gary Mundy, *Romani Culture & Gypsy Identity* (Hatfield, UK: University of Hertfordshire Press, 1999).

40. For more on the Inuit government, see http://www.gov.nu.ca/english/.

41. Johnson, *Blowback: The Costs and Consequences of American Empire*, 15–16.

42. For the Kurds, look at Quil Lawrence's *Invisible Nation: How the Kurds' Quest for Statehood Is Shaping Iraq and the Middle East* (New York: Walker Books, 2009); Ed Kashi's dramatically photographed *When the Borders Bleed: The Struggle of the Kurds* (New York: Pantheon, 1994) is excellent. Note also *New York Times* correspondent Jonathan C. Randal's emotional *After Such Knowledge What Forgiveness? My Encounters with Kurdistan* (Boulder, Colo.: Westview, 1998); www.kurdistan.org is a site maintained by the Kurdish American Information Network, a mainline organization of Kurds resident in the United States.

43. Ian J. Bickerton and Carla L. Klausner, *A Concise History of the Arab-Israeli Conflict*, 4th ed. (Upper Saddle River, N.J.: Prentice Hall, 2002), 161.

44. Jonathon I. Chamey and J. R. V. Prescott, "Resolving Cross-Strait Relations between China and Taiwan," *American Journal of International Law* 94, no. 3 (2000): 453–78.

45. Freedom House, Freedom in the World 2011, http://freedomhouse.org/template.cfm?page=363&year=2011 (accessed November 21, 2011).

46. For more on the province of Quebec, see http://www.gouv.qc.ca/portail/quebec/pgs/commun/?lang=en.

47. Stephen Brooks, *Canadian Democracy: An Introduction*, 3rd ed. (New York: Oxford University Press, 2000), 33–35.

48. Raymond C. Taras and Rajat Ganguly, *Understanding Ethnic Conflict: The International Dimension*, 2nd ed. (New York: Longman, 2002), 157–61. See also Fred Anderson's *Crucible of War: The Seven Years' War and the Fate of Empire in British North America, 1754–1766* (New York: Knopf, 2000). The following three Oxford published books are also recommended: Stephen Brooks' *Canadian Democracy: An Introduction* (2000) is a reliable and readable standard. In Will Kymlicka's *Finding Our Way: Rethinking Ethnocultural Relations in Canada* (Toronto: Oxford University Press, 1998), the author examines Canada's multinational character. David M. Thomas asks some uncomfortable questions about the possible breakup of the country in his *Whistling Past the Graveyard: Constitutional Abeyances, Quebec, and the Future of Canada* (New York: Oxford University Press, 1997); a topic updated by David Carment et al. in *The International Politics of Quebec Secession* (Westport, Conn.: Praeger, 2001).

49. For the exciting new appearance of Nunavut, see Quinn Duffy's *The Road to Nunavut: The Progress of the Eastern Arctic Inuit since the Second World War* (Toronto: McGill-Queens University Press, 1988).

50. United Nations Development Programme, *Human Development Report 2011,* 162.

51. Brooks, *Canadian Democracy: An Introduction*, 3rd ed., 105–8.

52. Taras and Ganguly, *Understanding Ethnic Conflict: The International Dimension*, 2nd ed., 164–72.

53. The Canadian government website at www.gc.ca, available in English or French, leads the visitor to every branch of the Canadian government. Quebec's point of view is available at www.premier.gouv.qc.ca; while www.cbc.ca will take you to the website of the Canadian Broadcasting Corporation, where you can read stories online or listen to a variety of Canadian radio stations.

54. The Liberal Party explains itself at www.liberal.ca.

55. The online version of Canada's leading newspaper can be found at www.theglobeandmail.com. And Canada has political scientists too. Find them at www.cpsa-acsp.ca, home page for the Canadian Political Science Association.

Part II

HOW THE WORLD FUNCTIONS
FREEDOM AND POLITICAL CONFLICT

/

CHAPTER 5

Containing Conflict

THE INTERNATIONAL COMMUNITY

5. **The Wrap: What Have We Learned?**

Is world peace possible? And if it really is impossible, could we make it possible by believing in it anyway? Lewis Carroll's Alice thought not.

> "There's no use trying," she said: "one can't believe impossible things."
> "I daresay you haven't had much practice," said the Queen. "When I was your age, I always did it for half-an-hour a day. Why sometimes, I've believed as many as six impossible things before breakfast."[1]

On this side of the looking glass, unfortunately, believing in impossible things (like world peace) can be tough to do. After all, the twenty-first century began with a major terrorist attack on American soil, the threat of nuclear war between Pakistan and India, civil wars throughout the Middle East and northern Africa, and U.S. military campaigns in Afghanistan and Iraq. Is there any reason for optimism in a world where sovereign states quarrel militarily most of the time and prepare for the next war all of the time? On the other hand, the White Queen warned us it would take practice, so perhaps we should suspend disbelief long enough to look at some optimistic and controversial ideas about world peace and organizations designed to defuse conflict and prevent war. We have thus far talked a lot about reasons why conflict and sometimes violence seem hardwired into the human condition. Can we avoid or moderate violent conflict by thinking less about sovereign states and more about international institutions? Here are some questions we need to ask.

- *When sovereign states are trying to avoid war, end a conflict, or improve relations among themselves, how do they accomplish it?* In short, how do sovereign states interact with one another at the formal level? This whole subfield within political science is called international relations (IR), the study of the interaction of sovereign states and other players in world politics. Specialists in international relations often describe the international political scene at any point in history in terms of a series of poles, or centers of power, and we'll glance at these theories in a very preliminary way.
- *And what is international law?* During the 2003 attack on Iraq and the subsequent Anglo-American occupation of the country, we all heard a lot about international law, generally in the form of U.S. accusations that the Iraqis were breaking it and in the form of complaints by some international legal experts that Americans were ignoring it completely. We'll summarize the principal elements of international law, a set of commonly agreed upon rules designed to make peace possible (or at least war less awful). Then we'll look at the central role treaties and executive agreements have in establishing international law and engaging sovereign states in a common commitment to obey it.

- *Is the United Nations the last best hope for humankind or an expensive and pointless bureaucracy that does little to ensure peace and a lot to drain the U.S. Treasury?* Americans disagree vehemently on this issue, and without attempting to make your mind up for you, we will look at the world's only truly global political organization, created with the fundamental goals of structuring diplomacy, enforcing international law, and moderating international political conflict.
- *If the world as a whole cannot manage to avoid conflict, would it be possible for one specific region to ban violence from its corner of the planet?* There is a wide variety of regional international organizations, and they enjoy varying levels of success. The European Union (EU) is widely regarded as the most successful. Since its creation after World War II, Western Europe has known—for the first time in history—complete internal peace as well as democracy. Until 2011, we might have added prosperity to this list of accomplishments, but the EU has joined the rest of the planet in having money troubles. But nobody imagines that a European war is likely in the foreseeable future, so if we're looking for ways to broker and channel conflict, we need to spend a few minutes thinking about how Europe has managed it for hundreds of millions of people.

1. How Sovereign States Interact

If you major in political science, you will spend a lot of time thinking about war-and-peace issues or what we generally call international relations. Often called "IR" on university campuses, international relations is the formal, scientific study of the interaction among sovereign states, international organizations, and a variety of other nongovernmental entities that operate at the transnational level. It is a broad field, but **diplomacy** (the principal formal means by which sovereign states interact with one another) lies at the heart of this important discipline. In the section that follows, we'll see how diplomacy fits into the political science subfield of international relations and then look at what diplomats actually do. The section concludes with a glance at how well things can go when diplomacy actually works, and how badly they can turn out when diplomats don't (or are not allowed) to do their jobs properly.

INTERNATIONAL RELATIONS

In chapter 2 of this book, we observed that the discipline of political science is divided into a couple of very large subfields. Chapters 4 and 7 fall roughly into the category of comparative politics, the study of how sovereign states order their internal affairs. This chapter introduces another major subfield, the increasingly important topic of international relations, which is the study of how sovereign states and certain other international entities interact or relate to one another. For the rest of the book, we will be oscillating back and forth between these two major subdivisions of political science and illustrating ideas with a series of case studies.[2]

Although they are typically introduced in separate university courses, there is really no hard-and-fast dividing line between comparative politics and international relations.

The European Union, for example, is a multinational supra-sovereign institution and is therefore usually studied as an international relations topic.[3] But it is also a political creation of the domestic politics of its member states. To understand it well, we would also need to know something about—for example—French political attitudes toward agriculture, German feelings about the Hitlerian experience, Italian fears of governmental instability, and British notions about parliamentary sovereignty, all areas of comparative politics. The attempt to compartmentalize knowledge often blinds us to the fact that no one field or subfield has all the answers, or even all the relevant questions.

Specialists in IR sometimes see their field as the study of everything, since most political and social phenomena are transnational in some way. Certainly, it is a rapidly changing field. For most of the past half century, students of international relations focused almost obsessively on a sharply divided world in which America and its allies confronted the USSR and its satellites. Thanks to the dramatic events of the 1990s, scholars are now struggling to understand a far more complicated planet, dominated militarily by the United States but perhaps more anarchic than ever in political terms.

Civil Society and Non-state Actors

In their landmark 1965 study called *The Civic Culture*, political scientists Gabriel Almond and Sidney Verba observed that not all governing is done by governments.[4] In fact, there is evidence that individual citizens are no longer confident that politicians and governmental bureaucracies can deal competently with their problems. This loss of faith may have contributed to the decline in voting; in most Western democracies, fewer people voted in the 1990s than in the 1950s.[5] A German opinion poll discovered that more people trusted the environmental watchdog Greenpeace to tell the truth than trusted the German government. In the United Kingdom, Greenpeace has more paid-up members than does the Labour Party.[6]

As a result, many citizens of developed societies seem to be turning toward voluntary public but nongovernmental organizations to get things done. This public "space" is sometimes called **civil society**, and it includes everything bigger than a family and smaller than a sovereign government. Democracies have a very large space for civil societies—all the way from bowling leagues to international aid agencies—and these organizations provide ways for people to interact without being organized by a sovereign government. Less-free societies tend to have a very small public space for civil society because authoritarian governments mistrust anything not directly under their control. One of the big problems Iraqis have faced in reorganizing their country after the ouster of Saddam Hussein is the comparative absence of an Iraqi civil society. Prior to the invasion, there were individual families, and there was the Ba'athist government, but not much in-between. The Iraqi public has never had much experience at being a public.

Organizing an effective civil society group in a traditional society can call for a combination of courage and cunning. Many parts of Africa and the Middle East have a horrific practice of what is usually called female genital mutilation (FGM). FGM typically involves the removal, by a village midwife or female relative, of a young girl's clitoris, a procedure that is fundamentally intended to reduce a woman's sexual drive as well as reduce the possibility that she will offend the moral code of her community or betray her future husband. Estimates vary because the practice is typically carried out by nonmedical personnel without any official record, but some estimates suggest that about 150 million living women have been scarred in this fashion. Now aware of the terrible emotional, physical, and psychological consequences of FGM, a group of Senegalese women joined together to pledge to not subject their daughters to FGM, successfully recruiting teachers and Islamic religious leaders to support their cause. This Senegalese civil society endeavor involves only a few villages at the moment but may well flourish and help abolish a barbaric practice.[7]

Individual groups within civil society are typically called **non-state actors,** that is, the assortment of entities that play significant political roles but are not themselves sovereign states.[8] This category would include anything that isn't a government or part of a government but plays a role in politics: for example, multinational corporations such as Exxon, religious organizations such as the Church of England, and transnational terrorist/guerrilla organizations such as al-Qaeda.[9]

While the distinction is sometimes hard to make in the real world, an **interest group** is a specific kind of non-state actor that represents a financial or other social interest. Many of these groups are successful and famous. In the United States, the National Rifle Association's primary goal is to advance the interests of gun owners and manufacturers. In Britain, the Royal College of Nursing promotes the welfare of British nurses (and their patients) by talking to members of parliament and issuing public statements on medicine and hospitals. The Japanese Keidanren (Federation of Economic Organizations) represents most of Japan's major corporations in their collective effort to extract assistance from the government without submitting to bureaucratic controls. In Canada, the environmentalist Pollution Probe attacks corporate polluters while Canada's Business Council on National Issues defends business interests; both interest groups try to make lawmakers and the general public accept their contrasting points of view.[10]

An interest group will typically attempt to articulate and advance the moral, political, or economic interests of a specific group of citizens or businesses. A professional organization will purchase advertising time, issue press releases, and dispatch experts to appear on radio and television programs. In a less public way, an interest group will often try to influence the behavior of public officials by employing a **lobbyist,** who will attempt to convert legislators to its point of view, and even help lawmakers prepare bills by providing draft texts and technical expertise.[11]

Another kind of non-state actor is typically called a **nongovernmental organization (NGO).** Once again, the distinction is hazy, but we tend to use the term "NGO" to describe an activist organization of some sort, a group of people driven by an idealistic agenda. Virtually any voluntary and noncommercial group of activists who are prepared to contribute time and money in the pursuit of some public cause they perceive to be in the public interest could fairly be described as an NGO. Examples would include cause-oriented organizations such as the human-rights group Amnesty International.[12] In this same category belong the environmental activists of Greenpeace, and the antipoverty charity, Oxfam. While agencies such as the UN Children's Fund (UNICEF) are actually subordinate elements of international organizations, they are also routinely called "NGOs."

Some NGOs began essentially as charities and have now become policy advocacy groups as well. One of the more successful groups is the Oxford-based Oxfam, which

Table 5.1. Civil Society: Some Prominent NGOs

Service and Advocacy	Public Policy	Lobbies and Professional
Oxfam	Greenpeace	International Chamber of
Médecins sans Frontières	Amnesty International	Commerce
Save the Children	Free Burma Coalition	National Rifle Association
Red Cross	International Campaign	American Association of
Care	to Ban Land Mines	Retired People (AARP)
International Planned	Freedom House	British Medical Association
Parenthood Association	"Think-Tanks" such	
	as Cato Institute,	
	Brookings, and	
	Heritage	

Some organizations such as UNICEF are technically subordinate agencies of the United Nations, or intergovernmental organizations (IGOs), but behave functionally like NGOs.

started collecting funds to redress poverty in the underdeveloped world, but has now become a major critic of governmental policy toward poor countries.[13]

What is irreverently called a "**think tank**" belongs somewhere in this category. Some think tanks are organizations dedicated to the study of some public policy problem such as the environment or the welfare of children. They typically receive their funding from public donations and typically advocate more public attention to their cause and increased governmental spending in a given area. Some "think tanks" are funded by corporations or wealthy individuals, and they promote a given point of view. The American Enterprise Institute, for example, is a conservative, business-oriented "think tank" that advocates free market solutions to public policy conundrums.[14] Freedom House, discussed in greater detail in the following chapter, is a think tank dedicated to the study and quantification of human freedom across the world. Often cited in these pages, The Worldwatch Institute in Washington tries to provide the interface between politics and environmental concerns.[15]

The State System and Pole Theory

The discipline of international relations (IR) is a subfield of political science, but IR itself contains a number of its own sub-subfields, each examining some specific component of international politics. Realist scholars, as examined in chapter 2, focus on the changing state system, examining the number of poles or centers of power that exist in the world at any given time. These scholars argue, for example, that until World War II, international politics flowed from a multipolar world in which a relatively small number of sovereign states dominated international discourse. They see this as changing after World War II, when global politics were shaped by the bipolar standoff between democratic free-market economies led by the United States and authoritarian Marxist societies dominated by the USSR. Some of these same analysts then began to wonder if the state system is now headed toward a **unipolar** world dominated by the United States (the dominant power is called the hegemon—all powerful), or some form of a multipolar world dominated by the United States, Russia, China, the EU, and some emerging market states such as Brazil. On the other hand, scholars such as Fareed Zakaria, think that the balance of power has

Table 5.2.   The World's Evolving Pole System

A Multipolar World: Prior to World War II, several major poles of approximately equal power were flanked by a galaxy of weaker powers.

Britain	Russia
United States	Austrian Empire
France	Ottoman Empire
Germany	Japan

The Outer Fringe: Canada, Brazil, Italy, China, Australia, etc.

A Bipolar World: Between the end of World War II and the dissolution of the Soviet Union in 1991, the world was perceived as divided between two extraordinarily important poles, one led by the United States and the other by the Soviet Union.

American Alliance:	Soviet Alliance:
NATO	The Warsaw Pact
Britain	East Germany
France	Poland
Italy	Bulgaria
Saudi Arabia	Czechoslovakia
Israel	Hungary
Taiwan	Cuba
Canada	China
Most of Latin America	North Vietnam

Unipolarity Fading to Multipolarity: After the collapse of the Soviet Union, the United States is briefly perceived as possessing uncontested military and economic power but is increasingly challenged by secondary powers like France and Iran, international organizations like the UN, and insurgent groups like al-Qaeda and the Afghan Taliban. NATO emerges as an important instrument of European-American military force. Most observers forecast a gradual return to multipolarity despite the economic woes of the European Union and the ruse of India, Brazil, China, and Japan.

tipped to a new form: the "uni-multipolar" world in which the United States is dominant but in which other states challenge this dominance in certain areas, such as China does with its large economic influence.

Others, such as Oxford's late Headley Bull, have suggested a slide toward a complex world in which sovereign governments will share their diminished powers with increasingly assertive sub-sovereign governments, a variety of non-state actors, and international supra-sovereign organizations such as the United Nations. Jan Aart Scholte also observes the slippage of state sovereignty, but calls it **global governance** in which states interact with non-state actors in a complex network of agreements and interactions.[16]

Since there is thus far no global organization that has been successful at restraining the aggressive impulses of sovereign states, there are lots of wars, and there are lots of IR specialists studying war and creating specialties such as national security policy and conflict resolution. The desire for a strong international peacekeeping mechanism has led other students of IR to focus on world organizations such as the United Nations, to be discussed later in this chapter.

One important branch of international relations is the investigation of how sovereign states interact with one another and with international organizations such as the United Nations. From the perspective of one individual country looking out, this is sometimes called foreign policy, but from the perspective of a student looking at the entire world, it is perhaps better described as diplomacy, and it's our first stop on this quick tour of international relations.

DIPLOMACY

There's an old joke about how soldiers die for their countries, while diplomats lie for theirs. Like most snappy one-liners, it's only sometimes true; in politically unstable parts of the world, embassy life can be as dangerous as soldiering. And while diplomats do lie occasionally, they aren't practicing very good diplomacy when they do. The reality is more complicated and more interesting.[17]

The Origins of Diplomacy

While the nature of diplomacy has changed over time, diplomats and embassies have been a feature of world politics as long as there have been sovereign states with organized central governments. Thirty-seven hundred years ago, a Babylonian prince named Hammurabi established a kingdom in the Tigris-Euphrates river basin, approximately where Iraq is today. Modern-day Mesopotamians seem to be less skilled at diplomacy, but Hammurabi took time away from giving the world its first known law code to dispatch diplomats and establish embassies in the capitals of neighboring countries.

Hammurabi's example was followed by all the great civilizations of the Mediterranean; in fact, the fundamentally weak Byzantine Empire may have owed its extended life span (roughly 476 AD to 1453 AD) to the cunning of its diplomats. By the 1500s, the Italian city-states were exchanging ambassadors, and in early modern France, Cardinal Richelieu (in power between 1624 and 1642) created the world's first foreign ministry, a governmental department charged exclusively with the conduct of diplomacy. At that time, diplomacy was mostly **bilateral**, in the sense that it involved only two countries at a time, a home country sending an emissary to a host country. The French revolutionary period (1789–1815), however, created such a complex international situation that the world reacted with **multilateral** diplomacy, holding the first **summit** meeting in Vienna in 1815.

Throughout the 1800s, diplomacy was typically conducted behind closed doors and in secret. At the end of World War I, however, President Woodrow Wilson tried to raise the curtains and let the world watch what deals were being done. The results of the 1919 Treaty of Versailles that brought World War I to a close were mixed, but diplomacy has been partly public and partly private ever since.

The Conduct of Foreign Affairs

Following Cardinal Richelieu's example, every modern government has a major department dedicated principally to foreign affairs. In the United States, this is the Department of State, headed by the secretary of state, who is the senior member of the president's cabinet, although the secretary of defense's budget is one hundred times greater.[18] The United Kingdom has the secretary for foreign and commonwealth affairs, and most other countries have a cabinet-level official called the minister or secretary for foreign affairs. In most countries, the foreign minister also controls the country's intelligence-gathering apparatus; the United States is an exception because the CIA reports directly to the president, while the National Security Agency (NSA) and the Defense Intelligence Agency (DIA) are both principally responsible to the secretary of defense.[19]

Over the course of the twentieth century, some American secretaries of state have been famous and powerful figures, while others have been relatively obscure. As political scientist James Q. Wilson has observed, some presidents have deliberately appointed secretaries of state they could dominate.[20] Franklin Delano Roosevelt had the quiet Cordell Hull (1933–1944), while Richard Nixon was initially served by the self-effacing William P. Rogers (1969–1973). Other presidents have lived with dynamic, powerful secretaries of state, such as Dean Acheson who served Harry Truman (1949–1953), or Eisenhower's indomitable John Foster Dulles (1953–1959). Likewise, Gerald Ford inherited the aggressive Henry Kissinger along with the presidency in 1974. For his second term in office, Mr. Clinton appointed the first woman secretary of state, Dr. Madeleine Albright. President George W. Bush, with less background in foreign affairs, turned first to a foreign-policy heavyweight, Colin Powell, to run the State Department. In selecting the less independent Condoleezza Rice as secretary of state for his second administration, Bush may have been displaying his own growing self-confidence in foreign affairs. President Obama, following George Bush, appointed a heavyweight to the office when he selected his former rival, Hillary Clinton, to serve as his secretary of state.

Working for the foreign secretary or foreign minister, every major sovereign state also has a cadre of professional diplomats. Some will serve in the home country's national capital doing analysis and advising their own political leaders; others will represent the home country in host countries abroad. A few very small countries allow larger neighbors to do their diplomacy for them, since maintaining a string of embassies is expensive. For example, tiny Liechtenstein is represented abroad by the Swiss Foreign Service. Young diplomats are recruited by competitive examination and young Foreign Service officers undertake prestigious and well-paid careers. Since French used to be the language of diplomacy, diplomats still have the letters "CD" (*corps diplomatique*) on their cars, by which diplomats announce their claim to **diplomatic immunity**. While there are lots of exceptions, diplomats may not normally be arrested by the host government of the country in which they are serving.

A modern embassy will be a very large office building in or near the national capital of the host country. A modern embassy is administered by the diplomatic service, but it is also home to many representatives of other agencies: intelligence personnel, commercial, scientific, and cultural officers, and defense attachés. The French word "attaché" suggests an officer from another governmental agency who is attached to the ambassador's staff without being part of the diplomatic corps.

Embassies are supposed to look after the interests of home-country citizens and will normally maintain offices known as **consulates**, which typically handle immigration, commercial and other personal matters on behalf of citizens of the home and host countries. There will typically be one consulate attached to the main embassy in the host country's capital, with other consulates located in major provincial cities.

Embassies can represent their home countries in more ways than they would sometimes wish. In recent years, for example, embassies have served as targets for opposition groups wishing to attack the political policies of the home country. U.S. embassies in Africa and the Middle East have often taken the brunt of anti-American fury. In 1998, Americans were stunned by homicidal bombing attacks on U.S. embassies in Nairobi (the capital of the east African state of Kenya) and Dar es-Salaam, further to the south in Tanzania, attributed to the al-Qaeda network then led by the late Osama bin Laden.

Tough Choices: Ambassadorships for Sale

Most political problems are transnational; if something is a dilemma in the United States, it's probably bugging people who live in Botswana, Bolivia, and Bulgaria. The practice of retailing ambassadorships, on the other hand, is a specifically American issue, since nobody else selects their ambassadors in the same bizarre way. Let's look at the issue and see what we think needs to be done.

In theory, politics stops at the water's edge, and the conduct of foreign affairs is meant to be independent of domestic electoral politics. In fact, the two are fatally interconnected, in part because every American president since Andrew Jackson has "sold" ambassadorships.

At the moment, professional, career State Department personnel constitute only about 70 percent of American ambassadors serving abroad. The remaining 30 percent are political appointees who are nominated by the president from outside the ranks of the Foreign Service. These non–Foreign Service ambassadors fall into two pretty clearly distinguishable categories, only one of which is a problem.

What we are not talking about here is the reasonable presidential practice of nominating "hired guns" or "technicians" from outside the State Department. These are senior figures from the political, military, or business world with some expertise that the president needs in his dealings with a specific country. For example, former president Clinton set a very high value on his relations with Great Britain, particularly after the election of Tony Blair to Ten Downing Street. During his eight-year presidency, Clinton sent two "technician" ambassadors to London. The first was retired admiral William Crowe, former chair of the Joint Chiefs of Staff. The second was former White House deputy chief of staff Phil Lader. Neither man was a career diplomat, but both were capable, well-known, senior figures with demonstrated leadership ability and extensive governmental experience. Both men were known to have good personal relationships with Clinton himself, and the two appointments were Clinton's way of communicating the importance of his relationship with Great Britain. These two ambassadorships were not "sold" because neither Crowe nor Lader had made significant contributions to Clinton's campaign fund.

There isn't a generally accepted generic name for the second category, so let's call them the "pure politicals," because they are men and women who have no observable diplomatic qualifications beyond a willingness to contribute heavily to political campaign funds. This practice is bipartisan: presidents from both political parties do it enthusiastically and energetically. Most of the high-profile ambassadorial jobs in famous European cities are reserved for campaign contributors, few of whom bring any credentials to the appointment or achieve even minimal competence at their jobs. The Republic of Italy, for example, has become a major player in global politics, with one of the largest economies in the world and an impressive defense establishment. With a few honorable exceptions, however, American presidents of both parties have sent ambassadors to Rome who had no qualifications beyond being major contributors to presidential campaign funds. Few of them spoke Italian properly or had any knowledge of modern Italian society, and some American ambassadors of Italian descent were openly contemptuous of "the old country" that their grandparents had left behind.

Paris and Dublin are also usually retailed to faithful party contributors. Critics of this system have wondered what the United States is symbolically saying to the French or Irish people when Washington dispatches a diplomatic representative with no discernible knowledge of the country or its people, problems, or politics. According to the Constitution, the Senate must confirm all ambassadorial appointments, and this process typically begins with hearings by the Senate Foreign Relations Committee. One would-be ambassador to Sri Lanka was rejected by the committee when he failed to find his country on a map, and a proposed ambassador to Botswana lost by revealing that his only qualification for this strategic post was a lifelong commitment to the Boy Scouts. Generally, however, the Senate doesn't ask too many tough questions, and the president usually gets his nominee approved.

Why is the ambassadorship-for-sale a problem? At a minimum, it is a misuse of taxpayers' money. Mr. Reagan once dispatched a pleasant Texas socialite to London, who did no particular harm but drew an impressive salary for giving some lovely parties while the real diplomats did all the actual work. At worst, the pure political appointees can hurt good relations between two friendly countries. Mr. Nixon once sent a Massachusetts businessman to Rome, who irritated the Italians by appearing on television and giving them stern instructions on how to vote in elections. Furthermore, it destroys morale among career State Department personnel, who do all the heavy lifting, knowing that the really glamorous jobs can never be theirs.

Furthermore, it's an insult to the host country. President George W. Bush sent a South Carolina moneymaker named David Wilkins as the ambassador to Ottawa; Mr. Wilkins raised more than $200,000 for the presidential reelection campaign, and his previous interest in Canadian affairs had only involved a solitary day trip to Niagara Falls back in the 1960s. A millionaire California car dealer named Robert Tuttle went to London as the U.S. envoy there, and thirty other fat cats began their diplomatic careers after contributing a minimum of $100,000 to the presidential campaign fund.

President Obama promised to keep the number of "pure politicals" to a minimum, but a few have been chosen. The new U.S. ambassador to Austria is well qualified but contributed $500,000 to the Obama campaign fund. The American ambassador to Japan has no visible qualifications beyond his checkbook. The embassies in Britain and France also went to financial supporters. President Obama has dispatched quite a few "hired guns" to difficult positions, many of whom supported him politically in his campaign for the presidency. The new U.S. ambassador to New Zealand is an openly gay attorney and a liberal activist who has spent a lifetime studying the politics of the Pacific region but does not seem to have contributed to the campaign fund.

Should the practice of selling ambassadorships be outlawed? Technically, it already is, thanks to a 1980 law that presidents have been quietly ignoring on a bipartisan basis ever since. Theoretically, the ambassador is the personal representative of the president; an argument can be made that the U.S. president should be free to make his own selection. In practice, however, ambassadors represent the American people, and State Department professionals argue that the practice of selling ambassadorships is a waste of money, occasionally a diplomatic embarrassment, and a gratuitous insult to the host country. Since both American political parties reap dividends from the sale of ambassadorships, this age-old practice is going to be hard to terminate.

Let's create a Committee for the Reform of American Diplomacy and make you the chair. What forces could you mobilize to end this corrupt practice? What arguments could you formulate? Would it be better to lobby the executive branch, where the appointments are made, or the Senate, where they are confirmed? How much public support could you garner, and how might you solicit it?

WHAT DIPLOMATS DO

In a foreign posting, the leader of the diplomatic team is the ambassador, who is theoretically in charge of all personnel, military and civilian, who are stationed in the host country. Reporting to the ambassador will be a group of professional diplomats, whose responsibilities range from attending cocktail parties to dealing with terrorist threats and angry mobs. In addition to sipping Chardonnay and dodging bullets, there are three crucial sets of responsibilities all successful diplomats need to perform.

- Observation and Analysis: Diplomats stationed in a foreign country are well placed to observe what's going on in that society by reading the local press, listening to radio and television, building up a network of contacts and informants, and traveling widely to make a visual inspection of the country. After achieving some level of expertise (and perhaps even learning the language), the diplomat should then be able to interpret the host country's behavior to the home government and vice versa.

  It is crucial for the resolution of conflict that sovereign states understand each other at some level of sophistication. Some societies become so hostile to the outside world that they send very few diplomats out and permit very few in. Since they do not provide the rest of the world with a diplomatic platform for observation, they find it difficult to establish normal relationships with the remainder of the planet. In the past, China and Albania have both gone through periods when they deliberately limited their interaction with the rest of the world. Today, North Korea largely shuns normal relations with the rest of the world.

- Communication: Diplomats are not the only avenue that one nation has for learning about another nation. Countries routinely monitor each other's media for information, and intelligence agencies provide their sporadically accurate insights. But diplomacy is an official, formal way for one nation to transmit information to another government or to the citizens of another country. Sometimes this communication is devastatingly serious. On December 6, 1941, the Japanese government sent an extremely long cable to its ambassador in Washington, which he was to deliver to the U.S. State Department by 1:00 p.m. on December 7. Because of delays in decipherment, the ambassador did not arrive for his appointment until after 2:00 p.m., by which time everybody at the U.S. naval base at Pearl Harbor knew what the ambassador had to say: Japan and the United States were finally at war.

Diplomats or Spies?

What's the real connection between diplomacy and intelligence gathering? When serving abroad, diplomats are supposed to keep their eyes and ears open for information about the host country, but this doesn't usually amount to espionage. Most real intelligence collection is neither covert nor illegal, and you can learn most of what you want to know about a country by reading the morning papers and asking your host-country friends to explain anything you don't understand. Furthermore, the not-very-precise expression "spying" implies a violation of host-country legislation. Genuine diplomats are nervous about breaking laws or engaging in trickery or subterfuge in their pursuit of information, preferring to leave classical espionage to the professionals. Embassies will normally provide cover for intelligence officers who sometimes pose as commercial, legal, or defense attachés.

Ordinarily, official communications between sovereign states are less dramatic than declarations of war. On a daily basis countries need to tell each other about ships wishing to put into ports for repairs, military maneuvers near each other's borders, and the implications of future UN General Assembly votes. Often, an important message is passed twice. The government of Pakistan, for example, has nuclear weapons and has occasionally threatened to use them against India. Desiring to moderate Pakistan's rhetoric, the U.S. secretary of state in Washington might summon the Pakistani ambassador for a calmative chat while simultaneously instructing the American ambassador in Islamabad (capital of Pakistan) to seek an audience with the Pakistani president to urge thermonuclear restraint. And there are less-official channels as well. If an irritated Pakistani leader wishes to tell the United States to mind its own business, an officially sanctioned leak to the *Pakistan Observer* might generate an editorial for the U.S. ambassador in Islamabad to read over breakfast. In response, the U.S. State Department might send one of its South Asia experts to appear on CNN to warn everybody against reckless saber rattling, knowing that the Cable News Network will be closely monitored in foreign ministries around the world.

- Negotiation and Friendship Building: At the least-complicated but still crucially important level, a diplomat's job is to increase the level of cordiality between the host and the home country. This involves giving parties and turning up for host-country parades and public celebrations. Any two modern countries are going to have many kinds of relationships with one another, any of which can generate conflict: for example, trade, aircraft overflights, extradition of criminal defendants, tourism, tariffs, and commercial exchanges. Host- and home-country diplomats can quietly negotiate most of these potential flash points. When the American and Russian presidents sign an arms-reduction treaty, for example, the text of the deal will have been worked out by professional diplomats on both sides, preparing a final document for their respective leaders to approve and sign (and take credit for!).

When Diplomacy Works

Sometimes diplomats have understood important realities in ways that changed history. During his World War II tour of duty at the U.S. embassy in Moscow, George F. Kennan arrived at a set of conclusions about the future rapport between the United States and the USSR. At a time when most people looked forward to good U.S.-Soviet relations after the war, diplomat Kennan predicted that the two powers were destined to be hostile to one another. He further suggested that the United States could do no more than contain the USSR, that is, prevent the Soviets from expanding beyond their own borders and hold the line until Soviet Marxism collapsed of its own deadweight.

Kennan published his views in an influential *Foreign Affairs* magazine article entitled "The Sources of Soviet Conduct," anonymously signing the article "X" because he was still a State Department official at the time.[21] As an operating theory, **containment** became the essence of U.S. foreign policy toward the Soviet Union until the collapse (which Kennan foresaw) of the USSR in 1991.

Negotiation can only be effective if it is both sincere and supported at the highest level. American diplomats have always wanted to make some progress in resolving the contentious Arab-Israeli conflict, but the only real American-sponsored success occurred when President Jimmy Carter committed his own power and prestige to the undertaking. Leading a talented U.S. diplomatic team, Carter invited Egyptian president Anwar Sadat and Israeli prime minister Menachem Begin to Maryland's Camp David presidential retreat for two weeks in October of 1978. The resulting Camp David Accords had many flaws and did not bring ultimate peace to the Middle East. The agreement is monumentally significant, however, because Carter's initiative has thus far prevented another general war between Israel and its Arab neighbors. Camp David created a peace treaty between Israel and Egypt, thus laying the groundwork for later progress if the parties wish to build on the Camp David Accords. As unrest gathered in the Arab world in 2011, there were well-founded fears that Carter's great achievement might be unraveling.

When Diplomacy Fails

American comedian Will Rogers once defined diplomacy as the art of saying "Nice Doggie" to an aggressive mutt while urgently looking for a large rock. Sometimes diplomats are under orders to keep talking while the warriors lock and load, but diplomacy doesn't work very well when it isn't actually intended to work. Bilaterally insincere negotiations between the United States and the government of North Vietnam, for example, deluded the world into thinking that a negotiated solution to the Vietnam War was possible; the

Figure 5.1.   Sadat and Carter at Camp David
On the left, President Anwar Sadat of Egypt talks peace with President Jimmy Carter. While the Camp David Accords left much that has never been accomplished, the 1978–1979 round of negotiations remains one of the few successful diplomatic achievements in the morass of the Middle East. It was essentially a peace agreement between Egypt and Israel, and—whatever else has gone wrong—these two countries have not subsequently gone to war. Courtesy of the U.S. Department of State.

negotiations may actually have prolonged the conflict. The diplomats on either side had very limited authority to negotiate realistically because the United States still wanted to win (i.e., to keep South Vietnam as a separate pro-Western, pro-capitalist sovereign state), while the North Vietnamese government always intended to fight until it could reunify Vietnam under its own Hanoi-based Marxist government. Under the circumstances, peace had to wait until the United States decided unilaterally in 1971 to throw in the towel, withdrawing in 1973 and leaving the ruined country to its own devices. The Marxist North Vietnam conquered the whole country in 1975.

Contemporary North Korea offers an ongoing example of spectacularly inept diplomacy. At the start of the twenty-first century, for example, officials of the P'Yongyang government were talking to very few foreign diplomats. This lack of dialogue makes it difficult for Koreans to predict how the world will react to some of their bizarre foreign policy initiatives and for the rest of the world to understand what the North Koreans are thinking. What North Korea needs from the rest of the planet is food aid, since millions of its citizens are malnourished. In August of 1998, however, the North Koreans gratuitously fired a multistage missile over Japanese sovereign territory. It is unclear what their leadership thought this ballistic diplomacy would accomplish, but their belligerence irritated potential donor countries with agricultural surpluses. By 2006, multiparty talks had broken down completely, and the North Korean government had disclosed publicly for the first time its possession of nuclear weapons, raising the diplomatic standoff to a whole new level, where it has remained, roughly, to the present.

2. International Law: Rules of the Global Road

International law is a set of rules, customs, treaties, judicial rulings, and understandings that regulate the interaction among sovereign states. This important subfield within international relations began to be codified about four hundred years ago. While there is no aspect of international law that is entirely free from controversy, we enter the twenty-first century with a far more extensive, detailed, and authoritative body of international law than ever before. The United States has enforceable treaty obligations with almost all of the world's nearly two hundred sovereign states. There are international courts around the world, passing judgment on governments and individuals, and imposing fines and sentences. The creation of the world's first International Criminal Court has provoked reactions ranging from enthusiasm to hysteria.[22] Let's try to understand what international law is, what areas of human life it covers, why it can be controversial, and how and when it can be enforced. Since treaties and executive agreements are fundamental building blocks of international law, we'll focus on them before studying the landmark Breard case that illustrates complicated American attitudes toward international law.

WHAT IS INTERNATIONAL LAW?

Modern international law flows from many sources, but the generally acknowledged founding father was a Dutch lawyer named Huig de Groot, who wrote under the Latin version of his name, Hugo Grotius. His first important book *Mare Liberum* (or *The Freedom of the Sea*, published in 1609) established the still-honored principle that ships may venture anywhere on the high seas. *De Jure Belli et Pacis* (On the Law of War and Peace) followed in 1625, in which Grotius tried to establish when and why countries could legally go to war and argued strongly against aggressive warfare. In his writings,

Figure 5.2. Hugo Grotius
Seen here in an austere 1631 portrait by Michiel J. van Mierevelt, the Dutch jurist named Huig de Groot or Hugo Grotius is universally regarded as the father of modern international law. Courtesy of Museum Het Prinsenhog in Delft, Netherlands.

Grotius both codified international law as it was understood in his own time and proposed new directions in which what he called the "law of nations" should venture in the future. Let's look briefly at the sources of international law. As Grotius defined it in the 1600s and as we know it today, international law comes from perhaps four principal sources.[23]

- Tradition and Custom: Over the centuries, sovereign states evolved certain traditional or customary habits of behavior in their dealings with one another. One example is the extraterritoriality of embassies, the practice of regarding an embassy in a host country as sacrosanct and sovereign territory of the home country rather than of the host country. This means a crime committed within the walls of the Saudi Arabian embassy in Washington would normally be punished according to Saudi or Islamic law rather than according to the relevant American **statute**. Again, under normal circumstances, U.S. law enforcement officers could not even enter the Saudi embassy to arrest a suspect. Because traditions lack precision, there has been a tendency over time for the custom-based elements of international law to be converted into multilateral treaties or conventions. For example, it was part of traditional international law for ships on the high sea to display a specific pattern of red, green, and white lights at night; the U.S. Supreme Court in 1872 ruled that what had been merely custom was now enforceable international law.[24]
- Scholarship and Expertise: Over the years, students of international law and jurists have written learned books and articles about how governments ought to treat one another if they wish to preserve peace, resolve conflict, and accomplish common goals. For example, scholarship on past problems involving the extradition of suspected criminals is leading to the creation of a standardized Europe-wide arrest-and-extradition system. A professor hunched over a word processor cannot actually create international law, but the United Nations and the World Court often turn to committees of scholars to explain what international law is in a given case.
- Judicial Precedents: Both international and national courts have ruled on certain international legal issues, and these legal opinions have become an important element in international law. For example, the World Court settled a lawsuit between Britain and Albania with its 1949 Corfu Channel decision, establishing that sovereign states have an international legal responsibility to ensure that their own territorial waters are safe for navigation.
- Treaties and Conventions: Today, the bulk of enforceable international law comes from specific legal contracts undertaken by sovereign states and international organizations such as the UN. Perhaps the most fertile source of modern international law is a body of UN-sponsored multilateral treaties (more about this below). The UN reserves phrases such as "conventions" and "covenants" for treaties that are meant to be signed by as many countries as possible and form part of international law.

Prospects and Problems of International Law

Since Grotius wrote his first pioneering books on the subject, international law has expanded into many new areas and evolved into a distinct legal and academic specialty.

While there are many others, here are five of the prime areas of contemporary concern for international legal scholars and jurists.

- Diplomacy: State-to-state relations, diplomacy, and consular affairs (the immunity of diplomats from arrest, the extraterritoriality of embassies, etc.) were probably the first issues to be covered by international law. The making of treaties between or among sovereign states has always been a major focus of attention within international law.
- War and Peace: Historically, violent conflict was another crucial area of concern to international jurists who wanted to define precisely when war was legitimate and work to take some of the cruelty out of military conflict. In recent years, international law activists have been trying to persuade sovereign states to eliminate land mines from their arsenals and sign the 1997 Ottawa Mine Treaty, arguing that this weapon provokes unacceptable casualties among civilians. In 2002–2003, the international legal community focused on the vexed question of an Anglo-American attack on Iraq without UN Security Council approval. In 2002, the American and Russian governments negotiated a treaty to reduce the number of nuclear weapons in their respective arsenals, an effort repeated in 2010 under Presidents Obama and Medvedev.
- Criminality: One of the more successful areas of international law addresses the question of international criminal behavior, defining air and sea piracy as well as questions involving the extradition of terrorists and ordinary criminals. International law has been effective, for example, in creating a standardized approach to the phenomenon of aircraft hijacking. The International Criminal Court (ICC) has now been established to deal with major criminal violations of human rights law, although—as we will see below—this court has been bitterly opposed by the United States.
- Environment: Environmental concerns are now of enormous importance within the field of international law. The United Nations held its famous 1992 Earth Summit (actually titled the UN Conference on Environment and Development [UNCED]) in Rio de Janeiro, creating some substantive areas of agreement. In December 1997, concern for global warming and climate change brought the world together again in Japan's Kyoto for a major conference, and the U.S. refusal to ratify the resulting Kyoto Protocol has been the source of continuing international political conflict. The Copenhagen Conference in 2009 failed to bring the parties any closer to an agreement. In December 2010's United Nations Framework Convention on Climate Change (UNFCCC), parties agreed to a $100 billion environmental mega-fund for the developing world to support sustainable adaptation and mitigation projects to reduce greenhouse gas emissions.
- Human Rights: Ensuring essential human freedoms is a relatively recent branch of international law and the United Nations has fostered a series of human rights covenants or conventions, some relating to specific groups: women, children, ethnic minorities, refugees, and prisoners of war.

Not everybody agrees that international law is a good thing, or even that it actually exists. Some American conservatives view the sovereignty of the United States as absolute and dismiss international law since it suggests limitations to that independence. This nationalist attitude is more typical of large and powerful countries (such as the United

States, Russia, and China), while smaller and weaker nations usually regard international law as a valuable safeguard. Since the 1980s, American political culture has tended to devalue international law in general and treaties in particular. Presidents are less anxious to negotiate treaties and the Senate is often reluctant to advise and consent. We'll talk more about conservatives and liberals in chapter 6, but for now, note that American liberals generally place more confidence in international law and wish their government would obey it more consistently.

Countries that violate articles of international law are seldom punished as consistently and automatically as drivers who get caught exceeding the speed limit. When large and powerful sovereign states with nuclear weapons choose to ignore the provisions of international law, it can be difficult for the world community to discipline them, although they may lose reputation, international sympathy/goodwill, and moral standing. Smaller countries and individuals, on the other hand, can feel the impact of international law more directly. In 2001, former Serbian strongman Slobodan Milošević was arrested and delivered in handcuffs to the International Criminal Tribunal for the former Yugoslavian to stand trial in Holland for human rights violations during his tenure as president of Yugoslavia. It was a long trial; Milošević was still doggedly defending himself when he died in March 2006.

Figure 5.3.
International law was challenged in Europe when the first genocidal slaughter of innocent civilians was carried out between 1992 and 1995, primarily by Serbian forces, in what is now the Republic of Bosnia. Some estimates place the number of murdered people, most of them Muslim Bosnians, at over one hundred thousand. In a cemetery near Srebrenica, some of these victims await justice. Thus far three principals have been arrested: Slobodan Milošević was being tried before an international court in Holland when he died of a heart attack. Army commander Ratko Mladić and political leader Radovan Karadžić are both currently being tried. Photograph courtesy of Michael Büker.

International Courts

Individual governments have always created systems of courts and judges to arbitrate disputes among their citizens. For most of human history, these courts have been national in the sense that they have been established by sovereign governments and generally have **jurisdiction** only over the sovereign territory of a given country. When quarrels between sovereign states broke out, they were either settled by diplomats or soldiers, at least until the League of Nations took action in 1920 to establish the Permanent Court of International Justice or PCIJ to arbitrate disputes among member states. The "permanent" court lasted no longer than the League of Nations did, but when the world community reorganized itself into the United Nations after World War II, the UN restored the institution and rebaptized it the International Court of Justice.

With its fifteen-member bank of judges, the UN's International Court of Justice (almost always called the "ICJ" or "World Court") sits in a city in Holland called The Hague, and decides on cases that are presented to it by UN member states. It is also sometimes asked to make advisory rulings on the application of international law to specific cases. The World Court has jurisdiction in cases when the states in dispute agree in advance to accept the court's decision or when the states in conflict have disputed treaty obligations. Despite the high hopes surrounding its creation, the World Court has dealt successfully with only a few high-profile cases; powerful nations such as the United States have been reluctant to allow international judges restrict their freedom of action.

Although truly global courts have thus far fallen short of expectations, some regional courts have nevertheless turned out to be crucial political institutions. The best two examples are both in Europe; although they have different responsibilities, they are easy to confuse.

- The European Court of Human Justice (ECHJ): The ECHJ is located in the French city of Strasbourg. After World War II, a group of European countries established an organization called the Council of Europe, which has now expanded to include almost every European country from Russia to Portugal. The Council of Europe created the European Court of Human Justice to rule on civil rights issues, and it has established very broad and advanced stands on many aspects of human freedom. The ECHJ, for example, is largely responsible for the elimination of the death penalty in Europe.
- The European Court of Justice: Don't confuse the European Court of Human Justice with the EU's European Court of Justice, located in Luxembourg, which resolves conflicts among European Union member states. We'll talk more below about the European Union, but for now, note that the European Court of Justice now does for Europe much of what the U.S. Supreme Court does for the American legal system.

It is important to distinguish between the courts described above and a variety of temporary international criminal tribunals. The first tribunals to try individuals accused of crimes against international law were set up after World War II to punish German and Japanese officials who had committed war crimes; the Nuremberg Trials were the most famous. Reacting to **genocide** in the Balkans, the UN Security Council set up the above-mentioned International Criminal Tribunal, based on the model of the Nuremberg Trials, for the former Yugoslavia (ICTY), which has been dealing with cases flowing from the breakdown of the former Yugoslavia, and particularly the 1992–1996 war in Bosnia. A similar court was created by the UN to deal with cases emerging from the civil war in Rwanda, during which the Hutu ethnic majority in the country fell upon the Tutsi minority in 1994, slaughtering perhaps a half-million people. While many high-ranking culprits in both situations remain at large, other murderers have been delivered to the appropriate court to receive sentences up to life imprisonment. The UN does not impose the death penalty.

Standing Alone: The United States and International Agreements

The United States was uneasy about the International Criminal Court from the outset, worried that politically motivated indictments could lead to foreign trials of American soldiers or political leaders. As the ICC came closer to becoming an international reality, the U.S. government became increasingly insistent that it would not submit to the jurisdiction of the court.

Critics of American foreign policy sometimes accuse the United States of what is called "**exceptionalism**," the unstated but persistent idea that the United States is so unlike other countries that its national uniqueness frees it from the need to obey the same rules that bind other countries. This sense of national separateness appeared early in the twentieth century when the American Senate declined to ratify the Versailles Treaty ending World War I and refused to allow U.S. participation in the League of Nations. The concern that American sovereignty was challenged by multinational conventions became strong again in the 1980s and 1990s and became a major feature of President George W. Bush's approach to foreign affairs.

In recent years, the United States has refused to join some global treaties that were otherwise widely ratified. The 1990 Convention on the Rights of the Child, mentioned in chapter 3, was signed by President Clinton but never submitted to the Senate. Because of objections from the Pentagon and some conservative thinkers, the United States accepted neither the Comprehensive Test Ban Treaty (which would have eliminated nuclear testing worldwide) nor the Landmine Convention (calling for the elimination of antipersonnel land mines). On the environmental front, the United States has refused to endorse the Kyoto Protocol, which would obligate the United States to join other industrialized states in reducing greenhouse gas emissions.

The persistence of seriously bad behavior on the world scene convinced many internationalists that the world needed a permanent criminal tribunal to deal with those very serious violations of human rights that sovereign governments could not, or would not, punish. In 1992, the United Nations General Assembly decided to begin work on what came to be called the International Criminal Court or ICC. Having established its headquarters in Holland's The Hague, the ICC became a reality in the summer of 2002 when a sufficient number of sovereign states had ratified the treaty authorizing its existence.

Despite the fact that the United States opposed the creation of the ICC, the court burst into activity from the moment of its creation. By 2011, prosecutors for the court had issued indictments against President Bashir of Sudan, and Libya's now-deceased Muammar al-Gaddafi for crimes against international law.

TREATIES AND EXECUTIVE AGREEMENTS

International law has many sources, but for practical purposes, international legality is primarily established by agreements made between or among sovereign states. Different countries define the word "**treaty**" differently, and international law simply regards a treaty as an agreement between two or more countries that all parties regard as binding. Furthermore, countries vary widely in their methods of creating and approving treaties domestically. Let's spend just a minute summarizing some of these problems.

Treaty Ratification

Important treaties with global reach are normally negotiated by the United Nations. Treaties by two or three countries over a matter of common concern are negotiated by the diplomatic personnel of those countries most interested in seeing the treaty succeed. In either case, the final text of the treaty will be presented to national leaders for signing. Their signatures legally commit the executive branch of the government to act in accordance with the treaty while attempting to secure formal approval of the treaty by whatever legal measures are specified by that country's constitution. In some parliamentary systems, the treaty-making process may conclude when the prime minister signs the document, but more frequently, the executive may be required to send the treaty to the legislature for approval. For example, in the United States, Article II, Section 2 of the Constitution states that

> the President . . . shall have Power, by and with the Advice and Consent of the
> Senate, to make Treaties, provided two-thirds of the Senators present concur.

In either case, the entire procedure ends with "**ratification**," which is the act of informing all interested parties (the public, the United Nations, and other signatories to the treaty) that the ratifying country has completed its legal process and now considers itself bound by the treaty.

In U.S. practice, the State Department will normally negotiate a treaty and send it to the president for his signature. For a variety of reasons, the president may not wish to invest any political capital in persuading the Senate to pass it. He may sign it and leave it on his desk, or refrain from signing it; in either case, it remains in legal limbo. Or the treaty may go to the Senators, who may decide not to vote on it—another route to the same legal cemetery. If the treaty is approved by two-thirds of Senators voting, it is returned to the president, who typically ratifies it by notifying the other signatories and the United Nations Treaty Office that the United States is prepared to commit itself to the terms of the treaty; at which point, it becomes American law.

Unlike most other countries, the United States has a sort of second-class treaty called an **executive agreement**. Sometimes the matter at issue is transitory or not important enough for a formal treaty. Sometimes it is important, but unlikely to make it past Senate scrutiny. In either case, American presidents can try to circumvent the whole issue of Senatorial advice-and-consent by signing an executive agreement, a deal with a foreign government in which the president commits only those resources that are normally under the control of the executive branch (for example, the armed forces). A permanent military alliance with another country, for example, will typically be the subject of a formal treaty; a short-term deployment of American troops to another country would be more likely to be covered by an executive agreement. Anything that requires secrecy will be an executive agreement rather than a public treaty. The president must inform Congress within sixty days of any executive agreements he makes. About 90 percent of all legally binding agreements the United States has with other countries are executive agreements, often relating to relatively minor matters. The remaining 10 percent are full-fledged treaties.

Tough Choices: The United States and the VCCR

Is the United States obliged to obey the provisions of treaties it has ratified, even when it doesn't wish to? Let's look at one tough choice made just a few years ago that is still causing ripples of controversy around the world.

In 1963, President Kennedy helped negotiate the Vienna Convention on Consular Relations (VCCR), a generally uncontroversial nuts-and-bolts treaty, which—among many other provisions—stipulates that when citizens of one country are arrested by the authorities of another country, the imprisoned foreigners have the right to consult with consular officials from their own country and need to be informed that they have this right. Here's an example of how it's supposed to work. During a skiing holiday in British Columbia, you are driving under the influence of alcohol when you accidentally kill a pedestrian. After your arrest and imprisonment in Vancouver, the Canadian authorities are obliged to ask if you want the American embassy in Ottawa to be notified. If you do, a U.S. State Department official would visit you in prison, arrange for a lawyer, notify your family, and generally track your progress through the Canadian justice system. The VCCR was confirmed by the Senate and ratified by President Johnson. According to Article VI of the Constitution, treaties join federal statutes in forming part of the "supreme law of the land."[25]

The United States, of course, is a federal system, and at the state law-enforcement level, American authorities are often unaware that the VCCR exists or sometimes choose to ignore it. Here's the background to the Breard case: in 1985, an emotionally troubled and dim-witted alcoholic named Angel Francisco Breard emigrated from Paraguay to Virginia. When Angel murdered a Virginia woman in 1992, the police found overwhelming material evidence against him. Given Breard's broken English, marginal mental health, and limited intellectual competence, the Virginia state prosecutor and Breard's competent public defender negotiated a plea-bargained life sentence in exchange for an admission of guilt from the defendant. Paradoxically, Breard defied his legal team and insisted upon pleading not guilty, explaining that he had slaughtered his victim under the influence of the devil.

Unimpressed, the Virginia court found Breard guilty and sentenced him to death. When the Paraguayan government learned that Breard had never been informed of his right to consult with the Paraguayan consulate, both Paraguay and

Breard sued the state of Virginia, fighting the case through state and federal district courts and losing every step of the way.

Rebuffed by American tribunals, an outraged Paraguayan government took its complaint to the World Court in Holland, arguing that a Latin American lawyer could have explained to Breard in his own language why an American court would not accept a defense based on satanic influences. Since an international treaty was involved, the World Court asserted that it had jurisdiction over the case, and ordered the United States to delay Breard's execution pending an investigation. Concerned about preserving the rights of American citizens who might find themselves in foreign jails, then secretary of state Madeleine Albright also appealed to the governor of Virginia for a stay of execution. The State Department argued that Breard's execution would be considered "as a denial by the United States of the significance of international law . . . and thereby limit our ability to insure that Americans are protected when living or traveling abroad."

Ultimately, the key decision in the Breard case was not made by an international court, but by the U.S. Supreme Court. In a complicated six-to-three decision, the Supreme Court decided that—while the State of Virginia had clearly broken the provisions of the Vienna Convention on Consular Relations—the outcome of the case had not been materially affected—the so-called harmless fault doctrine. Ignoring a standing appeal from the ICJ, the Supreme Court returned the matter to the state of Virginia. The death penalty is politically popular in Virginia, and Governor James Gilmore refused to grant a stay of execution; Angel Francisco Breard was put to death on April 14, 1998.

His first name notwithstanding, Angel Breard was not an angelic personality, and he committed a brutal crime. On the other hand, the state of Virginia did not fully carry out its legal responsibilities toward him. Had you been the governor of Virginia, what would you have done? Breard's case brought the VCCR to the attention of defense attorneys around the United States, but state law enforcement authorities are still paying very little attention to the treaty in their treatment of foreign defendants, arguing that the issue is complicated and their responsibilities are unclear. In 2003, Mexico brought a World Court case against the United States, arguing that the United States had ignored its VCCR obligations for dozens of Mexican citizens on death row; in 2004, the World Court agreed with Mexico, and ordered the United States to stop executing foreigners whose VCCR rights had been violated. The United States has a long history of ignoring the World Court, but the issue is not going to go away. Should the U.S. federal government intervene to force the states to respect the provisions of the VCCR? Or should the United States abrogate the treaty altogether? What effect would this step have upon Americans traveling abroad?

3. The United Nations

A long time ago, the poet Dante Alighieri (1265–1321) wrote a tract entitled *De Monarchia* (*On Monarchy*) speculating that only a world government could end war. People have been contemplating the same idea ever since, but it seems less likely than ever that the world's nearly two hundred independent countries will be ready to surrender their sovereignty to some global authority.

As World War II ground to its conclusion, representatives from China, the USSR, the United Kingdom, and the American government met in Washington to plan for the future United Nations; by 1945, nearly all the then-existing sovereign states in the world had signed the founding documents. They had no intention of creating Dante's world government, but the UN has clearly become something more than just a big club for countries. While its ultimate goals and functions are still being debated, the UN is active today in an unbelievable range of fields.

HOW THE UNITED NATIONS IS ORGANIZED

The United Nations is organizationally complex, so, it might help to think in terms of the following core elements.[26]

The Secretariat

The secretary general, currently South Korea's Ban Ki-moon, is the world's senior civil servant and oversees the activities of UN staffers at the New York headquarters and elsewhere in the world. The secretary general has immense influence but relatively little actual power, since all major initiatives have to be directed either by the Security Council or—less frequently—by the General Assembly. Candidates are nominated by the Security Council before formal approval by the General Assembly. Since the Security Council's nomination must be unanimous, there is a tendency for a lowest-common-denominator candidate to emerge. Since the Security Council places only one nomination before the General Assembly, the Security Council effectively makes the choice. Each new general secretary serves a five-year term and may be reelected.

Kofi Annan took office on January 1, 1997, and was reelected for a second five-year term running from 2002 to the last day of 2006. In October of 2006, the Security Council nominated Korean foreign minister Ban Ki-Moon as his successor, to assume the office of general secretary on January 1, 2007. He too was reelected to this position, on June 21, 2011. Mr. Ki-Moon is a political scientist; he studied international relations at the University of Seoul and earned a masters in public administration at Harvard University's Kennedy School of Government.

The General Assembly (UNGA)

The UNGA vaguely resembles a world parliament, although it cannot make enforceable laws for its member states. Every sovereign state with full membership in the

United Nations has one seat and one vote in the General Assembly. In 2011, Sudan divided in two, and the new South Sudan became the 193rd member of the United Nations, which is nearly four times as many members as there were back in 1945.

Under a charter designed by the United States and its allies after World War II, the General Assembly has a lot of influence but surprisingly limited actual power. Unless there is an emergency, the assembly meets only in the autumn, providing a public forum for the discussion of the world's most contentious issues but little decision-making authority. Like most national legislatures, the General Assembly has a series of standing committees to consider issues such as arms control, the budget, and legal problems. The General Assembly exercises oversight authority over some of those UN agencies that are oriented toward providing direct help to very poor countries. Some of the UN's "nuts-and-bolts" or functionalist agencies are under the supervision of an intermediate body called the Economic and Social Council. The assembly also approves the UN's budget and designs multilateral treaties and conventions for the world's consideration.

Perhaps UNGA's most important function is to act as a global chat room, and many of the smaller countries of the world conduct a substantial amount of bargain-basement diplomacy through the UN. Mongolia and Paraguay, for example, do not have embassies in Ulan Bator and Asunción respectively, but they both have diplomatic legations at the United Nations and can do business with one another at UN headquarters in New York, saving both countries the cost of another embassy.

With more moral authority than legal clout, the General Assembly uses its position as an exponent of world opinion by passing resolutions on pressing issues. Ever since the UN-mandated creation of Israel in 1948, for example, the United Nations has invested a substantial amount of diplomatic energy in trying to bring peace to this tension-wracked part of the world.

The Security Council (UNSC)

The UNSC is the real powerhouse of the UN. When the world organization was created after World War II, the leaders of the victorious coalition intended to maintain leverage over their allies as well as their defeated enemies in the postwar period. For issues involving war and peace, the United Nations Charter gives most real authority to the Security Council, which acts as a kind of cabinet for the global organization. Imagine a situation in which the members of the American president's cabinet (the secretaries of defense and state, etc.) could choose U.S. presidents and then tell them what to do, and you have an idea of the relationship between the Security Council and the UN secretary general.

Of the fifteen members of the Security Council, ten are elected by the General Assembly to two-year terms and the other five are permanent. To pass, a measure must have nine votes and the five permanent members must all consent (or at least abstain) when voting takes place. The "Big Five" are France, the United Kingdom, Russia (which inherited the position when the USSR dissolved), the People's Republic of China (which in 1971 was given the "China seat" in place of Taiwan), and the United States. The choice of the five permanent members reflects the world's power structure as perceived in 1945. The United States and the Soviet Union (now the Russian Federation) stood supreme over the ashes of Europe and Japan. The corrupt but pro-Western government of China had been an important if disappointing ally in World War II. In 1945, no one foresaw that China would soon be dominated by a Marxist government or that Communists would eventually inherit China's UNSC seat. Britain was there because the United Kingdom was still a globally dominant military power in 1945, and war-ravaged France became the fifth permanent Security Council member because the British insisted.

As the UN moves past its sixty-fifth birthday, many have wondered if the U.S./UK/Russia/France/China five-power system still makes sense. Japan and Germany have recovered economically from World War II, and both are now model democracies. India is a nuclear-armed but free society and the second most populous nation on the planet. Huge and sprawling, Brazil dominates Latin America. Should one of these emerging regional powers be awarded a permanent seat? Or perhaps seats should be distributed regionally, with the Arabs getting one, and sub-Saharan Africa another, while Latin American takes a collective seat for people who speak Spanish and Portuguese?

Predictably, the five permanent members are uninterested in redesigning the Security Council. But critics wonder how long the rest of the world will endure a situation that gives Britain (with fifty-one million people and a gross domestic product of $1.2 trillion) a permanent voice on the UNSC but denies a seat to India's billion-plus people and their $1.5 trillion GDP. When the UNSC failed to either endorse or block American plans to attack Iraq in 2003, complaints about the Security Council became intense. The UN commissioned a study, completed in December 2004, that recommended an expansion of the Security Council but left veto power securely in the hands of the original five permanent members.

Tough Choices: Should Palestine Become a Member of the United Nations?

When it comes to admitting new members to the United Nations, the Security Council nominates new members, and the General Assembly votes yes or no on a majority basis. All things being equal (which they seldom are in world politics), membership in the United Nations implies worldwide acceptance as a legitimate sovereign state.

By autumn of 2011, the leaders of the Palestinian National Authority had come to believe that Israel was not negotiating in good faith as it continued to build settlements on West Bank land the Palestinians wanted for their eventual state. With a surprising amount of global support, the Palestinians formally requested UN recognition and membership. Israel and the United States objected, pointing out that the Palestinians actually had two separate and mutually hostile "governments," the Palestinian National Authority (based in Ramallah), and HAMAS (located in the Gaza Strip). The United States urged the Palestinians to drop what the Obama administration saw as a complication in the "peace process," since even UN recognition would not withdraw one Jewish settler or one Israeli soldier from the West Bank.

President Obama is worried that he might not be getting the right advice on this issue and wants your help. If the United States vetoes the nomination, full

Palestinian UN membership will be blocked but at the cost of making the United States even less popular in the Arab world. There is a powerful U.S. coalition of Jewish voters and Christian conservatives that both support Israel and intend to vote in the 2012 election. A pro-Palestinian choice would perhaps risk making Mr. Obama a one-term president.

Ah, don't mean to hurry you, but the White House is on the line asking for your learned opinion. What do we tell them?

PEACEKEEPING OPERATIONS

The world organization is not supposed to meddle in the internal affairs of individual countries, and in general the UN may not intervene in the domestic concerns of a member state unless invited to do so or unless a local situation becomes so wildly out of control that global public opinion demands UN intervention.

Security Council Powers

When the decision to intervene has been made and that sometimes-elusive nine-member UNSC majority is achieved and all the permanent members are in agreement, the Security Council has most of the horsepower in the system. These are the four fundamental options available to the UNSC when trouble breaks out.

- Diplomacy and Political Pressure: The first step is normally a UNSC resolution that demands that one or both quarreling sides refrain from breaking the peace and instructs the secretary general to dispatch a diplomatic mission. This party of senior United Nations diplomats will try to determine the basic facts in dispute and urge both sides to mediate or accept arbitration. A diplomatic mission will not by itself stop a war when two or more parties are determined to fight, but it can assist the international community in understanding the dispute and give its senior people some experience in the area. And it may persuade two contentious parties to back away from armed conflict if the source of irritation is not too profound.
- Economic Sanctions: Sometimes hitting international lawbreakers in the wallet can be effective. Economic sanctions helped persuade South Africa's "Whites Only" government to abandon its policy of apartheid. The United Nations voted an assortment of sanctions against Iraq after its 1990 invasion of Kuwait, which substantially weakened the country and forced it to destroy much of its heavy weaponry. In recent years, the Security Council has imposed economic sanctions on Iran in the hope of persuading it to not develop nuclear weapons. In 2011, the United Nations voted a series of sanctions against Syria for its violent repression of popular unrest.

  Sanctions are controversial. Unilateral U.S. sanctions against Cuba have been in place since the Kennedy administration, and the Havana government is still in control of the island. Some scholars have tried to show that economic sanctions hurt the average citizen of a country without doing much to change the political behavior of their leaders.

- Collective Security Military Operations: On two occasions, the UNSC has authorized member states to employ military force to correct a situation it found unacceptable. This happened for the first time in 1950, when North Korea invaded South Korea, and again in 1990–1991, when Iraq conquered Kuwait. In the later case, the UNSC asked those nations supporting Kuwait to "take all necessary means" to restore Kuwaiti sovereignty, and the United States assembled a coalition of nearly thirty countries. The United States and the UK supplied most of the combat troops, although other countries supplied money and support. It was this type of "all necessary means" resolution that the United States and Britain sought, but failed to get, from the Security Council in the spring of 2003 to legitimatize the subsequent invasion of Iraq.

Blue-Helmet Peacekeeping Missions

When actual violence threatens, the UNSC can ask member countries to contribute armed forces to form a UN-controlled military force to observe or prevent violence. The UN's soldiers-for-peace wear distinctive blue berets in public and blue helmets in the field, from which they get the name (in French) of *Casque blu*, or Blue Helmet troops. These peacekeeping forces are volunteered by member countries, who are partially reimbursed by the UN for the expenses involved. Once in the field, the Blue Helmets are neither intended nor equipped for heavy combat, although they sometimes find themselves caught in the middle of real shooting wars and may defend themselves if attacked. Acting under the direction of the UN secretary general, these gun-toting diplomats are supposed to scrutinize the behavior of both sides to a quarrel, rescue civilians, and sometimes interpose themselves between two potentially violent forces, a practice that is sometimes called "armed passivity."

The UN cannot force individual countries to provide soldiers for peacekeeping missions, although some countries regarded it as a worthwhile exercise. The United States seldom contributes troops to these operations since there is domestic political sensitivity to having American soldiers serving under foreign command.

Peacekeeping missions were dispatched rarely during the years of the Cold War. Between 1948 and 1988, there were only ten missions, and they went to places like Kashmir, the Suez Canal, and Cyprus. As the Cold War wound down, the UNSC was able to be more active, sending out missions to thirty different areas between 1988 and 1998. This increase stems from two factors. First, Russia and the United States are no longer in automatic disagreement over every issue, making it easier to get Security Council consent for a mission. Second, the end of the Cold War has permitted some smoldering ethnic conflicts to burst into flames, since the United States and Russia no longer obsessively control their respective client states. Hence, some long-suppressed regional conflicts have been free to break out destructively.

In evaluating the success or failure of a UN peacekeeping mission, it's wise to remember that the UN is to diplomacy what emergency rooms are to hospitals: nobody ever brings an easy problem to the United Nations, and the Security Council doesn't dispatch Blue Helmets unless the situation is already pretty dire. Therefore, the UN's success rate will be limited, and the quality of success, when it happens, will always be conditional. While some Blue Helmet missions have been disappointing, others have been successful. We'll look at the complications of Sierra Leone in chapter 9, but it was a combined effort

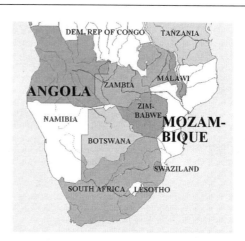

Map 5.1.   Southern Africa
Map by R. O. Collin.

by the British Army and UN Blue Helmet troops that finally brought that decade-long humanitarian disaster to an end.

At the moment, the UN has peace operations going on all over the globe. Some of the more-prominent missions are located in the western Sahara (brokering disputed territory), India and Pakistan (observing conditions in the troubled province of Jammu and Kashmir), Liberia (helping to resolve difficulties left over from the recent civil war), and many parts of the Middle East, where they are working on problems emerging from the endless Arab-Israeli conflict.

The political evolution of two former Portuguese colonies in southern Africa provides a good example of the varying levels of success that UN missions and peacekeeping operations can achieve. Mozambique and Angola were abruptly freed from Portuguese colonial control in 1975. Both countries quickly lapsed into bitter Cold War–related civil conflicts. After several false starts in Mozambique, the UN successfully established a cease-fire in 1992, enforced by seventy-five hundred Blue Helmet troops. Multiparty elections followed in 1994. While poor and subject to many natural disasters, Mozambique is now internally stable and slowly recovering. (See map 5.1.)

With diamond mines and substantial offshore oil reserves, Angola had infinitely greater natural resources than did Mozambique, which ironically was part of the problem because there was more to fight over. When Angola achieved independence in 1975, there were already several rival rebel armies in the field. By 1976, the national capital at Luanda was seized by a Marxist group supported by the USSR and protected militarily by Cuban troops. This government was able to finance itself through the sales of offshore oil resources. In time, the late Jonas Savimbi and his UNITA (National Union for the Total Independence of Angola) guerrilla army emerged as the principal antagonist to the left-leaning Luanda government. Savimbi drew support from South Africa and perhaps U.S. intelligence and paid the bills for weapons and supplies by selling diamonds on the international gem market.

When the Cold War ended, the UN sponsored free elections and arrived with a peacekeeping mission in 1992. When Savimbi's movement lost the elections, UNITA refused to accept the verdict of the ballot box and stormed back into civil war conflict. With appalling loss of civilian life and the devastation of the Angolan economy, the conflict raged through the 1990s. The UN gradually suspended its in-country operations because its own personnel increasingly became the targets of guerrilla attacks. Conflict ended in early 2002, but only because Jonas Savimbi himself was killed in battle.

Comparing the two countries, the UN's role was successful in Mozambique because the contending parties were grudgingly ready to make peace and because foreign sponsors to the two sides withdrew their support after the end of the Cold War. In Angola, with far more wealth at stake, the two sides were able to finance a fight to the death, and the UN was unable to impose the will of a not-very-interested world community.

FUNCTIONS AND CONTROVERSIES

There has always been a body of opinion that suggests that the United Nations cannot always deal with the big war-and-peace issues but should be able to handle the routine "nuts-and-bolts" operations of everyday international life. First, we'll review how **functionalism** works at the UN level, and then we'll conclude by glancing at the troubled relationship between the global organization and the United States.

Functionalism: Global Nuts and Bolts

The theory of functionalism holds that the United Nations should concentrate on handling humankind's nuts-and-bolts problems. In fact, sheltering under the aegis of the United Nations are many so-called functionalist agencies that do quiet but crucial jobs. Some are quite famous; the World Health Organization (WHO) won the world's gratitude by mounting a successful campaign to eradicate the smallpox disease.[27] Others are important but obscure; for example, anyone flying safely from New York to Athens is doing so courtesy of the International Civil Aviation Organization (ICAO), which organizes air-traffic control for the entire planet. Below are three clusters of key UN functionalist agencies.

- Antipoverty and Development Efforts: Famous for publishing the annual *Human Development Report* referenced throughout this book, the UN Development Programme (UNDP) works to encourage sustainable development and to publicize the plight of peoples in underdeveloped countries.[28] In the same area, the **United Nations Children's Fund (UNICEF)** focuses specifically on children, while the UN Population Fund (UNFPA) works on the problem of overpopulation. Based in Rome, the **Food and Agriculture Organization (FAO)** funds efforts to raise nutritional levels around the world. The **UN High Commission for Refugees (UNHCR)** has been active in helping displaced persons who have been driven from their homes by the wars in the former Yugoslavia.
- International Cooperation Agencies: Ever wonder how a postcard actually gets from New Zealand to Russia? Coordination of international mail is all handled quietly by the UN's Universal Postal Union (UPU). Similarly, the UN agency that manages radio, television, and international telephone systems is the International Telecommunications Union (ITU). Although they are primarily charged with regulating the

peaceful uses of atomic energy, scientists from the International Atomic Energy Agency (IAEA) have been active in both the Iraqi, Iranian, and North Korean crises. Sometimes criticized for wasting money and being anti-American and anti-European, the **UN Educational Scientific and Cultural Organization (UNESCO)** has its offices in Paris, and it attempts to protect endangered cultures and languages while encouraging artistic and scientific exchanges.

The United Nations and the United States

If you're having difficulty deciding whether you're a Republican or a Democrat, you can use the United Nations as a kind of ideological litmus test. American liberals (most of whom wind up in the Democratic Party) have always hoped that the UN would survive and prosper. Conservatives in the Republican Party have always worried that the UN represents a drain on the treasury and a threat to American sovereignty. It was the Republican majority in Congress after World War I that forbade U.S. participation in the first global organization, the League of Nations; three-quarters of a century later, Republican-controlled legislatures have periodically refused to pay some of America's dues to the UN.

In the immediate aftermath of World War II, some U.S. policy makers saw the UN as a potentially obedient instrument of U.S. foreign policy. When the Cold War began producing endless Soviet UNSC vetoes and the General Assembly filled up with anti-American Third World countries, many Americans wondered if it was worth the money or the effort. Dissatisfaction with the UN perhaps reached its height during the presidency of Ronald Reagan. Although Presidents George H. W. Bush, Bill Clinton, and Barack Obama have looked more favorably on the world institution, the younger President Bush seemed impatient with the UN, especially when it failed to cooperate with his Middle Eastern policy regarding Iraq.

On the other hand, Mr. Bush found it difficult to bypass the UN in an emergency. When the December 26, 2004, Indian Ocean tsunami devastated Sri Lanka, southern India, Thailand, Indonesia, and other parts of the Indian Ocean, Mr. Bush's first instinct was to channel U.S. aid through an improvised coalition of wealthy countries. When the rest of the world turned to the United Nations as the central coordinating agency for dealing with the disaster, the Bush administration reluctantly worked with the United Nations.

And how much does the UN cost? Not as much as you would expect, but the precise figures can be hard to calculate. The UN has one central administrative budget that remains relatively fixed and has been running roughly at $1.25 billion annually for the past few years. A second budget pays for peacekeeping operations, and this fluctuates fairly substantially from year to year, as crisis operations come and go. In recent years, peacekeeping has run about $3.5 billion a year. The combined total for the core budget and peacekeeping expenses amounts therefore to something approaching 0.3 percent of the U.S. federal government's annual budget and less than the cost of one aircraft carrier for the U.S. Navy. There is a third budget called "Direct Contributions," which is very large but hard to calculate; this represents the budgets of those UN agencies (such as UNICEF) that get some of their money directly from member countries or as donations from individuals. Altruistic groups and individuals contribute funds for UN activities. In 1997, American billionaire Ted Turner pumped a cool billion of his own money into UN-sponsored activities.

Is the United States paying too much? Many conservative Americans are convinced that the United States has been contributing too heavily to the UN and getting too little in return. At the end of 2000, the United States negotiated an arrangement with the United Nations, dropping the U.S. contribution to the general budget from 25 percent to 22 percent, and to the peacekeeping budget from 30 percent to 27 percent.

Almost everybody, however, agrees that the United Nations is here to stay, mostly because of its success in regulating the functionalist affairs of humankind. Whether the UN increases its role as global peacekeeper depends a lot on what kinds of support it gets from its members, how successful it is at reorganizing the Security Council, and how successfully it meets the challenges of the new century.

4. Europe's Un-Common Market

The United Nations is the world's general-purpose organization, but various regions of the world have attempted to create mini UNs to handle regional problems. Much of the Western Hemisphere has signed up for the Organization of American States (OAS), and Africa has just created the African Union (AU) to replace its moribund Organization of African Unity. Southeast Asia has an increasingly active ASEAN or Association of Southeast Asian Nations. The European Union (EU), however, is overwhelmingly the most influential and most powerful of these regional organizations. Let's see where it came from and how it functions today.[29]

THE EUROPEAN UNION

The European Union has undergone several changes in name. It began as the European Economic Community or EEC, before shrinking to merely the European Community or EC. In 1994, the name officially changed to the European Union or EU, but what we have always called the "Common Market" still sometimes refers to itself as the "European Communities." In 2012, the EU had twenty-seven member states, and despite a recent wave of financial problems, the European Union is unquestionably the most successful consensual international organization in history. Let's give it a closer look.[30]

Table 5.3.

Businesspeople	Looking across the Atlantic at the economically successful United States, many Europeans wondered if reducing import tax and tariff barriers would not create a prosperous European market. These were not idealistic dreamers but hardheaded and conservative capitalists.
Peacekeepers	Europe had gone to war with itself twice in the twentieth century. Some of the early parents of the European Union wanted to pull Western Europe together politically to make it less likely that Germany would ever again fight the British and the French.
Society Builders	Europe is rich in "social democrats" (like Britain's Labour Party and France's Parti Socialiste) who wanted to steer a middle course between what they saw as the harshness of American-style capitalism and the repressive character of Soviet Marxism. They saw in a unified Europe the possibility of creating the structures of a just and human society that would provide medical and educational benefits to the citizenry while caring for the poor, the sick, and the disadvantaged.

The European Union has always been a coalition of three overlapping groups want-ing closer contacts among European peoples, albeit for three overlapping sets of reasons. European businesspeople had long looked enviously across the Atlantic Ocean at the United States, where merchants in the fifty states could trade with one another in a single currency, crossing state borders without paying duties or tariffs, and operating in a continent-wide single market for goods and services. We will look more closely at the merits of free trade in chapter 12, but these early pan-European visionaries imagined a Europe in which produce and manufactured goods could be sold from Sicily to Helsinki under one common set of trade regulations.

In an impoverished and war-torn continent, money was important to Europeans, but it wasn't their only concern. In the first half of the twentieth century, antagonisms between Germany and her neighbors had twice brought death and destruction to all of Europe, and the post-1945 generation of leaders wanted desperately to avoid round three. Frenchmen, Germans, and Englishmen needed to stop thinking so exclusively in nation-alist terms, they argued, and start regarding themselves as Europeans, at least where war and peace are concerned.

And finally, the new Europe would offer the chance to build a new kind of society. Some of Europe's founding fathers and mothers were keen-eyed commercialists, interested in maximizing profits, but others were social activists. We'll talk about social democratic parties and governments in chapter 6, but the concept of social democracy springs from a desire to create societies in which the extremes of wealth and poverty are diminished and where the government intervenes in the economy to procure the greater social good.

Despite some areas of consensus, these three groups weren't always the same people, and there have always been lots of disagreements. Some Europeans from smaller and weaker states wanted a robust sovereign federal institution that would protect them from the bigger European states. France envisioned what amounted to a club of sovereign states, and Britain wasn't sure it wanted anything that would interfere with either the Commonwealth of Nations or the British "Special Relationship" with the United States. For its part, the United States was solidly supportive of European integration, believing that a strong Europe would be an important ally against the USSR.

The Creation

The first efforts were modest. In 1950–1951, France and Germany created the European Coal and Steel Community (ECSC), and by 1952, an organization known initially as "The Six" had come into being, uniting France, Germany, Italy, Belgium, the Netherlands, and Luxembourg. Britain opted out, but The Six went on to sign the 1957 Treaty of Rome, which created what was formally called the European Economic Community (EEC).

Expansion of this mini-market came in fits and starts. After much hesitation, the United Kingdom joined in 1973, together with Ireland and Denmark. Greece, Spain, and Portugal were all obvious early candidates, but their entry was delayed until the 1980s when all three had dispensed with their dictators and were clearly democratic in governmental structure. In 1995, Finland, Austria, and Sweden joined the bandwagon.

As the membership grew, the Common Market increased in power and responsibil-ity. The Europeans decided as early as 1964 to harmonize their farming industry, creating the Common Agricultural Policy or CAP, which involves price supports and subsidies for European farmers. By 1968, Europe had eliminated the last of its internal tariffs and had erected a common external tariff barrier against goods coming into Europe from the outside. To give the organization a steady income, the community passed the value added tax (VAT), which works like a sales tax, with the proceeds going directly to the EU operating budget.

In 1992, European activists signed the Maastricht Treaty (after the Dutch city where it was negotiated), which was meant to move Europe closer to a confederal system, with substantial hunks of sovereignty passing from national governments to the EU headquarters in Belgium's Brussels. Maastricht also called for a common European currency, a common foreign policy (which has been slow to emerge), and a unified program of domestic programs, the so-called Social Chapter.

Growth

In 2004, Europe moved into a new expansionary phase by taking aboard ten new countries. The collapse of the USSR had left a series of central and Eastern European states that had historically been part of Europe and were now anxious to consolidate themselves as free-market democracies. The three Baltic states of Estonia, Latvia, and Lithuania had been the first out of the Soviet Union when it came unglued, and all three had moved swiftly to Westernize their economic and political systems. Poland, the Czech Republic, Slovakia, and Hungary followed quickly, making rapid progress toward achieving the kinds of societies that would adapt well to the EU system. Of all the new countries to come out of the collapsed Yugoslavia, only Slovenia is modern and prosperous enough to be a reasonable candidate. The island state of Malta had been on the fringes of the European Union for a long time, but it was now seen as wealthy and stable enough to be a reasonable member. Cyprus has struggled with its division between its Turkish-dominated North and its Greek-administered South, but the Republic of Cyprus (i.e., the Greek section) limped into the EU in 2004.

HOW THE EU WORKS

We find it easier to conceive of governments, even supranational ones such as the European Union, as having executive, legislative, and judicial powers, so let's think in terms of this very unequal trinity of European authority.[31]

- Executive Branch: Still anxious to hang onto some measure of their individual sovereignties, the twenty-seven EU members have a European Council as their ultimate governing authority. This council contains one cabinet-level representative from each member country and makes all ultimate decisions regarding the administration of the European Union. The actual day-to-day work is done by a twenty-seven-member European Commission, which acts as a kind of cabinet, with each European commissioner being responsible for some aspect of pan-European governance. To coordinate the work of the European Commission and the legion of bureaucrats beneath it, the European Council designates a senior international bureaucrat to serve as both president of the European Commission and the symbolic "President of Europe."[32]

- Legislative Branch: The founders of the European Union were nervous about the potential power of an all-Europe legislature, so the European Parliament (EP) was given very little actual responsibility. Meeting in Strasbourg, the EP resembles the UN's General Assembly in being more of a talking shop than a real legislature. Interestingly, the members of the European Parliament (or MEPs) are directly elected by EU constituencies within the twenty-seven countries, but French MEPs do not necessarily sit and work with other French MEPs when they get to Strasbourg. Instead, they have formed themselves into European super-parties. Socialists and British Labourites and social democrats sit together as the Party of European Socialists. Greens and Liberals from various countries sit together in the middle of the assembly, while German Christian Democratic Unionists, French Gaullists and other center-right parties are the European People's Party when they get to Strasbourg. French and Italian Communists have joined with a number of other Marxist parties into a grouping simply but accurately called the "Far Left."[33]
- Judicial Branch: In order to sort out legal disputes, the European Union has established a fifteen-member European Court of Justice, which holds sessions in Luxembourg. The European Court of Justice enjoys the prerogative of judicial review; it can rule that national law is inconsistent with European law and overrule acts of the European Union executive itself. The European Court of Justice has become one of the busiest courts in the world.[34]

The Euro

That 1992 Maastricht Treaty foresaw the creation of an Economic and Monetary Union (EMU), consisting of those EU states prepared to abolish their own national currencies in favor of European money. In the past, trade and travel in Europe was inhibited by the need to exchange national currencies every time you crossed a national border, since you lost a small but significant percentage of your capital with every currency conversion. Perhaps more important, it was difficult for Europeans to do business with one another, or to create joint enterprises, when their currencies floated freely against one another.

Citizens of seventeen European Union states actually began using European paper money and coinage in the spring of 2002. The surrender of Spanish pesos, Italian lire, German Deutschmarks, and French francs was emotionally wrenching and technically complex, but the whole process was completed with remarkably little difficulty. Within a few months, most of a continent had changed its money, and Europeans had quietly created the world's second-largest currency. The European currency has climbed substantially against the dollar, and one Euro is now worth roughly US$1.25. This expensive Euro is making European goods harder to export.

With the creation of the Euro, you can now hold a single currency that is valid in most EU countries and convertible around the world. For the business community, it means that products could be bought and sold all over Europe with one single and stable currency, just the way American companies do business from Maine to California with one single and reliable currency, the American dollar.

The Problematic Future

Commentators had always regarded the creation of the European Euro as irreversible, but in 2011, Greece went spectacularly broke, and Spain, Portugal, and Italy all teetered on the edge of bankruptcy.[35] The December 2011 EU conference that was supposed to mend all the problems didn't reach its goal, especially after the British government vetoed any new treaty involving closer financial integration in Europe. As we move through 2012, most observers are confident that the EU's leaders will find a way through this fiscal minefield, but no one is quite sure how (or if) it can be managed.[36]

Those who foresaw a quick transition from squabbling petty nation-states to a strong and sovereign Europe will need to be patient, because a truly unified Europe is still a long way off. The British still have difficulty in committing fully to the idea; Norway and Switzerland remain stubbornly outside the fold. The Common Agricultural Policy keeps Europe's farmers happy, but consumers are less cheerful about artificially high prices for meats and vegetables. Despite Maastricht's goal of creating a common European Union foreign policy, EU members tend to go their own ways whenever a crisis threatens. For example, when Yugoslavia collapsed into civil war and genocide in the early 1990s, no clear and unified European Union policy ever emerged. When the United States went to war against Iraq in 2003, Europe tore itself apart over the issue; the British, Spanish, and Italian governments offered varying levels of support to the war, but the European "street" was overwhelmingly opposed, except in former Soviet bloc countries such as Poland, where the United States is still popular because of its opposition to the USSR.

In 2003 and 2004, EU countries attempted to negotiate a new constitution for the organization, a document that would in some ways strengthen the central EU administration, create a "president of Europe," and try to harmonize foreign policy. Most EU member states held referendums on this new treaty, but Europe's progress toward further integration was halted when the French and Dutch voted resoundingly against it, albeit for unclear and inconsistent reasons. This reversal does not mean that the EU is coming unraveled, but merely that European leaders will need to do a better job of selling further unification to people who are still nationalists at heart. But the European Union remains difficult to define. It started out as a supra-sovereign organization such as the UN, a club of completely sovereign states. The EU's twenty-seven member states, however, have surrendered significant hunks of national sovereignty to the EU headquarters in Brussels. The EU is not quite a sovereign state on its own, and may never become one, but it is functionally looking a lot like a confederacy, a loose union of semi-sovereign states under a semi-sovereign government. This is something new, and new things are hard to define.

The new members from Eastern Europe are entering nervously into a well-established rich-people's club. Like any club nearly a half-century old, the EU has an established culture, and like any restricted circle, it may not automatically be polite to the new members. The Eastern Europeans, furthermore, will have to adjust themselves to the idea of opening borders to the west and closing them to the east.

On the other hand, none of these problems is ultimately unsolvable and those original European unity theorists of the 1940s and 1950s would not be too dissatisfied with their continent today. Those who wanted to make a European war impossible got their wish because there hasn't been a whiff of armed conflict among EU members since 1945,

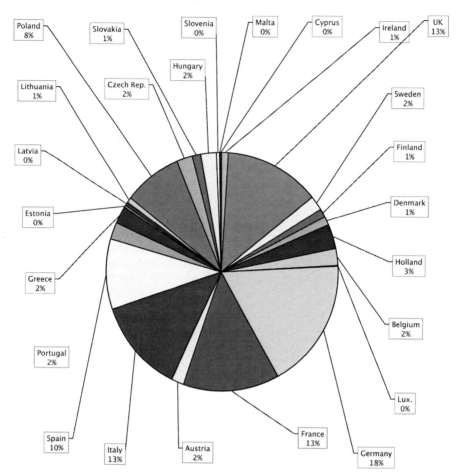

Figure 5.4.   The Population of the European Union
The twenty-seven-member European Union is a collection of big countries and
tiny ones. Figuring out how to satisfy the interests of wealthy and well-established
countries such as France and Germany without neglecting the interests of tiny
places such as Malta and Luxembourg is a challenge for Europe's future. The total
population of this new international organization is just over five hundred million
people. The data here come from UN *Human Development Report, 2009*, 171–74,
as extrapolated by the authors.

and the twenty-seven allied states in the European Union are all thoroughgoing democracies, most of whom have well-established court systems and good human-rights records.
Europeans are legally able to move around their continent and settle wherever they want.
If you come from frosty Riga, and you've always wanted to live on the beach in Barcelona,
all you need to do today is pack a bathing suit and buy a bus ticket.

The Common Market began with an idea about money, and it's a success story
from a commercial point of view. For people and goods, borders are totally open from
Palermo to Helsinki. Business is thriving, and although labor costs are high and products
are expensive, most Europeans have savings and good salaries. As of 2010, the European
Union was generating about 30 percent of planetary gross domestic product, constituting

the largest economic market in the world. The global banking crisis of 2008–2010 hit everybody pretty hard, and Greece needed to be bailed out significantly by its EU partners to avoid defaulting on its debts. By June 2011, the EU was grappling with another Greek default and considering a $17 billion bailout to avoid it.

But those idealistic social democrats haven't done badly. European workers are well paid and well protected by generally moderate trade unions. Most Europeans can get through the winter by looking forward to six-week paid summer vacations, something American employees can only dream about. Since most educational opportunities are provided on a rationed basis by European governments, all Europeans get high quality primary and secondary schooling, and (usually) free university training if they qualify for it. The average American salary is higher than the average European salary, mostly because America's rich people are richer than anybody else's rich people. But the lifestyle of an average European is comparable to an average American, except that Europeans—with their publicly funded health services—live about a year longer than Americans.

5. The Wrap: What Have We Learned?

This chapter has been a brief introduction to several specialties within political science's subfield of international relations. Diplomacy is usually introduced in courses on international relations, along with foreign policy. Both are studied as independent disciplines at the graduate-school level. Similarly, the activities of the United Nations would traditionally form part of an international relations course, and some universities have advanced courses dedicated solely to international organizations. International law is sometimes presented at the undergraduate level and sometimes as part of doctoral programs in political science. After a long period of neglect in law schools, international law is now becoming more popular because of the increased legal interconnectedness of the globe.

If you see yourself someday as a Foreign Service officer representing your country in some romantic location, you should know that they send the new guys to places such as Burkina Faso, and they won't even send you there unless you can find it on a map. You also need to know the principal stages through which diplomacy has passed historically and how it works these days in the United States and elsewhere. Do you remember what diplomats actually do, and can you describe some important instances of success and failure?

You'll need to remember where international law comes from both in terms of historical origins and sources (traditions, scholarship, etc.). What areas of human international life are affected by international law? Have you established in your own mind how important you think international law ought to be in the political life of your country, and can you defend this position with facts? Should, for example, the United States join the International Criminal Court? Also, ensure that you understand the distinction between treaties and executive agreements. How does the Breard case illustrate the complex American relationship with international law?

Don't walk away from this chapter without a clear understanding of the structure of the United Nations and the interplay among the secretary general, the UNSC, and the UNGA. Those functionalist agencies are the alphabet soup of international life, but you'll need to know at least the following just to read the *New York Times*: WHO, UNDP,

UNICEF, UNFPA, FAO, IMF, WTO, IAEA, and UNESCO. Contemplate the whole controversial issue of armed peacekeeping missions, and decide on the basis of the facts whether you think that your country should support them. Can you think of ways in which the United Nations affects your own life in some material way? Does the United States pay more than its fair share of the dues, and how should Americans feel about this international organization?

In these five introductory chapters we've sketched out some of the ingredients of conflict and thought about some international approaches to defusing it. In chapters 6, 7, and 8 of this book, we'll look at how different kinds of governments react to conflict by creating governmental structures and institutions that are meant to moderate or contain conflict within their societies.

Notes

1. Lewis Carroll, *Through the Looking Glass: And What Alice Found There* (New York: Macmillan & Co., 1875), 100.

2. For a really good introduction to IR, see Walter C. Clemons Jr., *Dynamics of International Relations: Conflict and Mutual Gain in an Era of Global Interdependence*, 2nd ed. (Boulder, Colo.: Rowman & Littlefield, 2004).

3. Entry to the massive European Union website can be found at http://europa.eu/index_en.htm.

4. Gabriel Abraham Almond and Sidney Verba, *The Civic Culture: Political Attitudes and Democracy in Five Nations* (San Francisco: Sage, 1963). Almond and Verba's *Civic Culture* is a must-read for political scientists, one of the most persuasive books ever written on culture-bound political attitudes.

5. Shaun Bowler and Todd Andrew Donovan have considered a wide range of issues connected with voting in their *Demanding Choices: Opinion, Voting, and Direct Democracy* (Ann Arbor, Mich.: University of Michigan Press, 2000).

6. Some have three cheers for Greenpeace: see Rex Weyler's *Greenpeace: How a Group of Ecologists, Journalists, and Visionaries Changed the World* (New York: Rodale, 2004). For a two-cheer account of the same organization, see Dr. Patrick Albert Moore, *Confessions of a Greenpeace Dropout: The Making of a Sensible Environmentalist* (Vancouver, BC, Canada: Beatty Street, 2010). Explore the rebellious environmentalism of Greenpeace at http://www.greenpeace.org/international/en/.

7. In her *Female Genital Mutilation: Legal, Cultural and Medical Issues* (New York: McFarland, 2005), sociologist Rosemaire Skaine reviews this problem sensitively and comprehensively. For the Senegalese experience, see the formidable Celia Dugger, "Senegal Curbs a Bloody Rite for Girls and Women," *New York Times*, October 16, 2011, A13.

8. The standard reference on non-state actors is William Wallace, *Non-state Actors in World Politics* (New York: Palgrave Macmillan, 2002).

9. The world of non-state actors who blow up things (and people) is well considered by Kledja Mulaj, ed., *Violent Non-state Actors in World Politics* (New York: Columbia University Press, 2010).

10. Canada traditionally gets neglected in American politics textbooks. To learn more about what's north of us, check out Stephen Brooks, *Canadian Democracy: An Introduction*, 3rd ed. (New York, Oxford University Press, 2000).

11. A lot has been written about the controversial role played by lobbyists, especially in the United States. Colgate professor Bertram J. Levine explains why interest groups are actually important in a democracy in *The Art of Lobbying: Building Trust and Selling Policy* (Washington, D.C.: CQ Press, 2008). Jeffrey H. Birnbaum is far more negative in his *The Lobbyists: How Influence Peddlers Get Their Way in Washington* (New York: Crown, 1992).

12. Amnesty International is a big, influential player in world politics. Investigate further at www.amnesty.org/.

13. Two Oxfam experts have written an interesting study of how development NGOs function. See Ben Heaven Taylor and Tanja Schuemer-Cross, *The Right to Survive: The Humanitarian Challenge in the Twenty-First Century* (Oxford, UK: Oxfam Publishing, 2009).

14. See Murray L. Weidenbaum, formerly of the conservative American Enterprise Institute, *The Competition of Ideas: The World of the Washington Think Tanks* (Piscataway, N.J.: Transaction Publishers, 2011).

15. Attacking the intersection between the environment and politics, Worldwatch maintains an interesting site at www.worldwatch.org.

16. For the United Nation's huge site, see www.un.org. For Headley Bull's views, go to his *The Anarchical Society: A Study of Order in World Politics* (New York: Columbia University Press, 1995). For Jan Aart Scholte, see his *Globalization: A Critical Introduction*, 2nd ed. (New York: Palgrave, 2005), as well as his *Building Global Democracy? Civil Society and Accountable Global Governance* (Cambridge, UK: Cambridge University Press, 2011).

17. See a new book by John Mearsheimer called *Why Leaders Lie: The Truth about Lying in International Politics* (New York: Oxford University Press, 2011) in which this famous Chicago academic proves that the world's leaders are more likely to lie to their own publics than to one another. G. R. Berridge has produced a second and revised edition of his standard academic treatment in *Diplomacy: Theory and Practice* (New York: Palgrave, 2002) and teamed up with Alan James to track down for you all of diplomacy's ten-dollar words in their *Dictionary of Diplomacy* (New York: Palgrave, 2000).

18. This is a huge and massively informative site. See www.state.gov.

19. Spies are a source of endless fascination for students, so here are the relevant links: For the CIA, go to https://www.cia.gov/. The National Security Agency protects U.S. codes and breaks other people's; they can be found at www.nsa.gov but don't expect to find any secrets. DIA is the Pentagon's foreign intelligence operation; see www.dia.mil/.

20. James Q. Wilson, *American Government: Institutions and Policies*, 5th ed. (Lexington, Mass.: D.C. Heath, 1992), 549.

21. George Kennan was an American diplomat who died in 2005 at the age of 101. Stationed at the American embassy in Moscow during World War II, he wrote a famous "long telegram" which was later published anonymously as "The Sources of Soviet Conduct" in the July 1947 edition of *Foreign Affairs*. Few scholars have seen so perceptively into the future.

22. Coming to a democracy near you (but not to the United States any time soon), the International Criminal Court (ICC) will arrest, try, and imprison those indicted for major crimes against international law, typically involving the mass slaughter of civilians. Find it at www.icc-cpi.int/.

23. You can read Grotius in Latin if you want, but it might be a good idea to start with William R. Slomanson's *Fundamental Perspectives on International Law* (Stamford, Conn.: Wadsworth, 2010), which is a standard introduction to international law, used at both the undergraduate and graduate level. Gerhard von Glahn's definitive *Law among Nations: An Introduction to Public International Law*, 7th ed. (New York: Macmillan, 2009) is definitive but may be the deep end of the pool for beginners; start with the delightful introduction by the late Daniel P. Moynihan: *On the Law of Nations* (Cambridge: Harvard University Press, 1992). Bruce Broomhall provides a solid study in his *International Justice and the International Criminal Court* (New York: Oxford University Press, 2004).

24. A surprising amount of international law gets arbitrated at the Supreme Court level. For American jurisprudence, see www.supremecourt.gov/.

25. William R. Slomanson, *Fundamental Perspectives on International Law,* 4th ed. (Belmont, Calif.: Thomson/West, 2003), 356–58.

26. For a quick summary of the United Nations, you could do worse than look at *The Oxford Handbook on the United Nations*, by Thomas G. Weiss and Sam Daws (New York, Oxford University Press, 2009). For more depth, read Thomas G. Weiss, et al., *The United Nations and Changing World Politics* (Boulder, Colo.: Westview, 2009). New in 2010 is Mark Mazower's *No Enchanted Place: The End of Empire and the Ideological Origins of the United Nations* (Princeton, N.J.: Princeton University Press, 2010). For more historical perspective, see Stanley Meisler's easy-to-read *United Nations: The First Fifty Years* (Boston: Atlantic Monthly, 1997).

27. This agency doesn't make a lot of noise but works quietly on health projects around the world. Visit the WHO at http://www.who.int/en/.

28. The United Nations Development Programme is headquartered in New York but has offices all over the world. They are a wonderful source of statistical information; see www.undp.org. Note the British spelling of "programme," which reflects common UN usage.

29. For a serious look at the EU's progress toward a sort of multi-state sovereignty, look at Karen J. Alter's *Establishing the Supremacy of European Law* (New York: Oxford University Press, 2001). The European Parliament is well covered in Amie Kreppel's *The European Parliament and Supranational Party System* (New York: Cambridge University Press, 2002). In 2001, David M. Wood and Birol A. Yeşilada published the 2nd edition of their *The Emerging European Union* (New York: Longman, 2001). Look also at John Gillingham's *European Integration 1950–2002: Superstate or New Market Economy?* (New York: Cambridge University Press, 2003).

30. Oxford University Press to the rescue for those who haven't a clue. See John Pinder's *The European Union: A Very Short Introduction* (New York: Oxford University Press, 2008).

31. For the nuts and bolts of the EU, see Andreas Staab, *The European Union Explained: Institutions, Actors, Global Impact*, 2nd ed. (Bloomington, Ind.: Indiana University Press, 2011).

32. Jonas Talberg, *Leadership and Negotiation in the European Union* (Cambridge, UK Cambridge University Press, 2006).

33. David Judge et al., *The European Parliament*, 2nd ed. (New York: Palgrave Macmillan, 2008).

34. See Aida Torres Perez, *Conflict of Rights in the European Union: A Theory of Supranational Adjudication* (New York: Oxford University Press, 2009).

35. Walter Laqueur is gloomy about the future of the Euro and the EU, and predicted the present spate of difficulties several years before they began. See his *After the Fall: The End of the European Dream and the Decline of a Continent* (New York: Thomas Dunne, 2012)

36. This crisis is serious and complex. Follow it in the pages of *The Economist*, that weekly British journal previewed in chapter 1.

CHAPTER 6

Freedom and Ideology
IMAGINING AN IDEAL WORLD

In the autumn of 2005, a young English couple named Steve Gough and Melanie Roberts decided to hike the nine hundred miles from Land's End (the southwestern corner of Britain) to John O'Groats (the last bit of Scotland before the North Sea). They took a tent, hats, and hiking boots, but left their clothing behind because—to make the case that the naked human body should be an acceptable sight in public—they intended to ramble the length and breadth of Britain entirely in the nude.

Walking about twenty miles a day along hiking trails, public walkways, and, sometimes, secondary roads, it took them seven months, but some of that time was spent in jail because they were periodically arrested for public indecency. Steve and Melanie never stayed in custody for long nor were they punished very severely because a blasé English public seemed generally unconcerned. Most of the time, this attractive young couple were gawked and giggled at, photographed, ignored, jeered, and sometimes cheered. Occasionally, however, irate British citizens out strolling with their children decided that the unwelcome sight of these two unclothed oddities violated their own right to *not* have to look at naked people in public. Whenever indignant locals did complain, a bemused local constabulary would arrest the couple, confine them briefly on misdemeanor charges, and then turn them loose again to ramble nakedly north.

Welcomed by a flash of photographers, they arrived at the top of Scotland in February of 2006, posed good-naturedly for one last set of pictures, and then hurriedly climbed into some borrowed clothing, because it was cold.

Unfortunately for students of global politics, Steve and Melanie left some basic questions unsettled. Like most countries, Britain has laws against lewd or indecent behavior in public, but the various local government jurisdictions through which the couple trekked did not agree on the central legal issue: does simply wandering around naked constitute public lewdness or indecency?

If nothing else, the episode did suggest that "Cool Britannia" is more tolerant of raw eccentricity than are some other countries. Could a plucky couple stroll starkers from

Boston to San Diego without facing felony charges in Mississippi or doing hard time in Salt Lake City? Trying to meander unclothed from the Persian Gulf to Mecca might get you executed in Saudi Arabia. In England, on the other hand, they did actually manage to walk nine hundred miles without their clothing despite the occasional stay in a local lockup. Does this naked liberty mean that Britain is a freer society than the United States? Or is American society more conscientious when it comes to protecting the freedom of its citizens from "immoral" conduct in public?

The larger question posed by Steve and Melanie is one that every society in history has struggled to answer. How free should we be? How much freedom can we possibly enjoy before we begin to infringe upon the rights of others? Should we be at liberty to engage in public (or private) behavior that violates the core moral principles of our fellow citizens? These questions linger at the very heart of political science because—when we order public affairs—we make authoritative decisions about where your freedom ends and mine begins.

Figure 6.1. Don't Try This at Home
Except for some states with controversial "medical marijuana" laws on the books, the use of cannabis products in the United States is generally illegal and punishable with a prison sentence. In Amsterdam, it is mostly legal, although local ordinances demand that you smoke inside specific "coffee houses" and not on the street. Legality and geography are interconnected in odd ways.

Where and when it exists, freedom comes in a variety of packages, and below we will try to distinguish among political freedoms, personal freedoms, and economic freedoms, artificially disentangling three concepts that are really all parts of the same complex puzzle. In this endeavor, we'll explore our own individual ideologies, that is, the sum total of the ideas, feelings, values, and philosophies we bring to the business of thinking about politics. If you've made up your mind about Steve and Melanie, then your thoughts on public nudity are also part of your ideology. How do you feel about tax thresholds? Wars in the Middle East? American energy policy? Publicly funded health care? Abortion? Don't worry if your collection of political ideas aren't very consistent; we'll discover that there isn't anything very logical about ideology.

We'll also discover that ideologies fall into a series of clusters, and we'll try to identify the principal classic ideologies for you. But don't worry if you and John Stuart Mill (or Jon Stewart or Barack Obama or ex-governor Sarah Palin) aren't in perfect agreement. Our task is not to tell you what to think but to help you identify what you do think, and perhaps even understand why you think that way. Here's a few of the questions we'll try to answer:

- *What do we mean when we talk about human freedom? Can freedom be quantified like births, deaths, and taxes?* We can ask ourselves what our core freedoms are, and where philosophically they come from. Is the world getting freer over time? Why is your freedom sometimes an affront to my civil rights?
- *What do ideologies have to do with economics? How free should we be with our money? Should we be free to get rich? What are the major governmental systems for managing the flow and distribution of wealth through a society?* After looking at liberty, we'll try to understand that economic distribution is usually—although not always—at the heart of our political ideologies. We'll explore the deeper meaning of the word "ideology" and try to understand why words are so wobbly in this corner of political science.
- *What is the essence of the free market system and how do we distinguish between "liberals" and "conservatives"? Where did these ideas come from? How do free marketers disagree among themselves?* In section 3, we will see where, how, and why the free-market system originated historically, and how it has evolved over the years. Almost every major American political leader belongs to this tradition, and yet they disagree profoundly on how the free-market tradition should be applied to modern society, a fact that leads us into a look at how modern liberals differ from modern conservatives.
- *What do we mean by "social democracies," "welfare states," and "mixed economies"? Why does every developed society in the world have free public medicine, while the United States does not? How have some political parties and some governments combined some ideas from capitalism and Marxism?* Countries such as Sweden, Italy, France, and Germany have strong social democratic traditions, which make these societies substantially different from more purely capitalist economies such as the United States. We'll look at how social democrats differ from pure free marketers when it comes to providing welfare and owning significant elements of the national economy.
- *What's left of the hard left? What were the basic ideas of Marxism and did this ideology disappear when the late Soviet Union vanished? What countries continue to proclaim Marxism, and which ones are really still practicing it?* After a quick review of Marxist political thought, we'll look at the largest of the so-called Marxist powers, and see how far

modern China has wandered from Marxist purity. We'll close with a look at socialism with a Latino twist, as exemplified by contemporary Venezuela.

1. Thinking about Human Freedom

It might be easier if we divided the essentially indivisible concept of freedom into three overlapping ways of being free. Freer societies are those in which citizens control their own government, live their lives reasonably unburdened by external control, and are able and allowed to acquire, own, and use property and wealth. Let's glance at these three perspectives in greater detail.

- Political Freedom or Popular Sovereignty: When citizens of a sovereign state have the real capability to control their own government and participate meaningfully in the making of public decisions, they enjoy **popular sovereignty**. In any of the world's freer societies, citizens can "do politics" in a variety of ways: agitate or demonstrate for certain public policies, write letters to newspaper editors, publish books and articles, organize protest groups without fear of governmental reprisal, participate in interest groups, contribute to political causes or candidates, or run for office themselves to participate in actual political leadership roles.

    For most citizens, however, the one core method of intervening in the political process is the casting of meaningful votes in free and fair elections. Since the administration of a modern **democracy** requires the making on a daily basis of millions of complicated decisions, all contemporary democracies have developed ways of delegating most of this decision-making power to elected legislators who make laws, to executive leaders who enforce them, and to judges who decide when these laws have been broken. All modern democracies, therefore, are to some extent, at least, **representative democracies** in which the citizens elect political leaders and entrust them with the making of most key political decisions. In chapter 11, therefore, we will look more closely at the structures of this decision-making apparatus, the mechanisms by which the citizens of freer societies translate their political will into political action.
- Personal Freedom: This concept is sometimes described as "human rights" or "civil rights" and describes a country in which people are generally at liberty to do what they wish as long as their actions do not harm others. As we learned with Steve and Melanie, there is always a clash between my freedoms and yours. The right of the factory next door to emit noxious smoke into the atmosphere might interfere with my right to inhale. As Oxford's famous scholar, Sir Isaiah Berlin, once noted, "Freedom for the pike is death for the minnows."[1]

    It is sometimes very difficult to distinguish between personal freedom and popular sovereignty, but when we talk about popular sovereignty, we are focusing on our ability to "do politics." When we think about personal freedom or civil rights, we are focusing on our right to live our lives without unreasonable interference from the government or from other members of our society. Popular sovereignty is what we have the right to do; civil rights is what we have the right not to have done to us.

- Economic Freedom: Enjoying economic freedom means having the right to acquire, own, and use personal property and money. The essential righteousness of the idea sounds pretty obvious, but the practical implications can be complicated, as we will see later in this chapter.

DICTATORSHIPS AND DEMOCRACIES

Thus far, we have talked about "freer societies" and "less-free societies" in order to get away from the simplistic notion that all the sovereign states on the planet can be dumped uncontroversially into one of two neatly defined categories; democracies and **dictatorships**. During the Cold War, we were sometimes too quick to claim that our friends were all democracies and our enemies were always dictatorships. In fact, a continuum or spectrum flows from some very free societies at the top of the scale all the way down to some very unfree countries at the bottom.

Societies are often freer in certain areas, but coercive in others. Great Britain has legislation prohibiting racist speech in public. Hence, you might be able to walk around without your clothing like Steve and Melanie, but—if you think that black people are dishonest and lazy—you can't say so on radio or television. Indeed, all societies are in a constant state of flux, getting freer in some ways and getting less free in other ways. In political science, we can't escape from words such as democracy and dictatorship, but we need also to use terms such as "freer" and "less free" to remind ourselves that all governments permit certain liberties but also coerce their citizens at some level.

Societies have the most difficulty in being civil about civil rights when they feel a threat to their survival. In both world wars, the usually democratic British government passed the so-called DORA (Defense of the Realm) Acts, suspending most freedoms on the home front until military victory had been achieved abroad. After the September 11, 2001, al-Qaeda attack on the United States, some critics worried that former attorney general John Ashcroft and the U.S. Patriot Act had gone too far in limiting civil liberties traditionally enjoyed by Americans.

In a simple sense, democracies are countries where citizens exercise genuine control over their government, enjoy a wide range of personal freedoms, and possess enough economic freedom to acquire wealth and property and to enjoy it without undue governmental interference. A less-free society (sometimes called a dictatorship) would be a government that has interfered over a long period of time and in unjustified ways with the rights of the people to live their lives as they please, and denied them political power, perhaps by refusing to hold fair and meaningful elections. An unfree society might also violate the right of people to enjoy their property if it arbitrarily confiscates their property.

Freedom and Conflict

It is often assumed that freer societies are able to grant more liberty to their citizens because their elected leaders are nicer or nobler than self-selected dictators. As we explore freer societies in chapter 7 and less-free societies in chapter 8, however, we will see that freedom exists in those societies that have comparatively moderate internal conflicts and have developed mechanisms for brokering or managing their disputes. Less-free societies tend to be those with deeply engrained and endemic conflicts—often relating to nationalist or ideological disagreements—that have proven to be too profound to be settled by elections, courts, and judges.

Are societies with deeply divisive problems therefore condemned to be dictatorships? We would hope for the answer to be no, but the jury is still out in some cases. Saddam Hussein's rule over Iraq was generally regarded as one of the most cruelly oppressive in human history, but Iraq has not made a quick transition to genuine democracy in the nine years since the dictator was overthrown. In fact, the latent disagreements and disputes within Iraqi society abruptly became very obvious, and it is far from clear whether Iraq's future lies in the direction of another dictatorship, the fragmentation of the Iraqi state into several successor states, a failed unitary state with an endless civil war, or a struggling democracy.

Similarly, Nigeria made a determined decision in 1999 to try to become a functioning democracy, but the deep social, religious, and ethnic divisions within Nigerian society have kept it trembling ever since on the brink of civil war. Nigeria has yet to develop these mediating mechanisms that allow for disputes to be settled without violence.

Portraits of the Real World: The Nazi Satanist Club

It needs to be remembered that your personal freedom in a society is partially dependent upon the law and partially upon the practical willingness of your neighbors to permit certain kinds of behavior. Under the American Constitution, for example, we have the legal right to declare an admiration for the late leader of the Third Reich, Adolf Hitler. The Bill of Rights guarantees us the freedom to worship the spiritual entity of our choice, to include—were we so inclined—the Prince of Darkness himself. Shall we test our freedoms? Let's rent an empty store to use as the headquarters of our newly constituted Nazi Satanist Club, with big pictures of the Führer in the window and advertisements for Black Masses on Saturday night. Everybody is invited, and we'll have a devil of a good time.

In theory, we'd be well within our constitutional rights, and in the United States, we are covered by the First Amendment on both religious and free-speech grounds. Practically, what would happen? The landlord would revoke our lease. Local government would find a building code violated by our plumbing or the electrical system, and the cops would shutter the front doors. And if we survived commercial and legal challenges, a large number of outraged citizens would descend upon us by night and run all us sadly persecuted Nazi Satanists out of town. At the most profound and practical level, your rights are limited by what your neighbors will tolerate and how well armed they are. And our neighbors have lots of guns.

Getting Free and Staying Free

For a long time, democracy seemed to be on a roll. In the 1970s, Europe became substantially more democratic with the disappearance of a military **regime** in Greece and a pair of old-fashioned dictatorships in Portugal and Spain. The 1980s and 1990s witnessed the unanticipated but welcome collapse of a Marxist dictatorship when the Soviet Union fell apart, liberating central Europe in the process.

Once achieved, is democracy a permanent thing? A conservative scholar named Francis Fukuyama wrote an influential book called *The End of History* in which he argued that the debate about ideology was over.[2] Repressive regimes, particularly Marxist ones, were headed for the rubbish heap of history, and American-style free-enterprise democracy was the wave of the future. In the sense of a battle between competitive styles of government, history was over and the good guys had won.

Challenging the rosy Fukuyama thesis, the brutally realist political observer Robert D. Kaplan noted that

> the collapse of communism from internal stresses says nothing about the long-term viability of Western democracy. Marxism's natural death in Eastern Europe is no guarantee that subtler tyrannies do not await us, here and abroad. History has demonstrated that there is no final triumph of reason, whether it goes by the name of Christianity . . . or, now, democracy.[3]

It would be comforting to shun Kaplan's pessimism in favor of Fukuyama's optimism. We sometimes assume that human freedom is a permanent status, like having a bachelor's degree, an attribute that—once acquired—can never be lost. There is certainly a slow but certain historical trend toward democratization, and there are no clear and recent examples of firmly established democracies collapsing into repressive regimes. Indeed, the spring 2011 protests in Egypt, Tunisia, Syria, Libya, and other parts of the Middle East have made scholars and policy makers wonder if Fukuyama was not right after all: everyone wants to be free within a democracy. Or is something else happening around the world?

The broad sweep of history suggests that there is nothing inevitable about human liberty. Both Germany and Italy were relatively free societies when World War I ended, and yet both countries became rabidly nationalist dictatorships. It took defeat in World War II to bring these two advanced European countries back into the democratic fold. Some Russia watchers would argue that Russia was actually freer in the late 1980s under Mikhail Gorbachev than it is a quarter century later under Vladimir Putin. In the course of the last century, Latin America saw a number of its countries oscillating back and forth between struggling democracies and authoritarian rule. Democracy in Africa has always been difficult to achieve and maintain, and between 2002 and 2005, the United Nations Development Programme issued four special, focused studies of the Arab world. The last of these was the *Arab Human Development Report*, which concluded that the worst of the Arab states were among the most repressive societies on the planet, and the best of them had a long way to go before becoming free societies.[4]

Some scholars have looked hard at the amount of political and personal freedom in the world and declared that—over the last half of the first decade of the twenty-first century—freedom has been taking some nasty hits. How can we be precise about something as nebulous as liberty?[5]

QUANTIFYING FREEDOM

The most commonly cited effort to index or rate countries on their success or failure in granting human rights has been made by Freedom House, a human rights research-and-advocacy group (what we have called a "think tank"), based in New York and Washington, D.C. and funded by public contributions.[6] To quantify human liberty, Freedom House uses two separate but parallel listings, one based on political freedom (what we have been calling popular sovereignty) and the other based on civil liberties (personal and economic freedom). For each of the two categories, countries are given a score ranging from "1" (very free) to "7" (very unfree). The resulting combined mathematical score is then used to divide the countries of the world into three groups: "Free," "Partially Free," and "Not Free."

Not everybody agrees on what to call countries that are somewhere in the middle, not fully functioning democracies but not completely repressive regimes either. The Freedom House designation of "partly free" is probably reasonable. During the Cold War, any not-very-free society that the United States happened to like was sometimes called a "developing democracy" whether it was developing democratically or not. Other authors have used phrases such as "transitional" or "impaired."

The Freedom House Verdict

Of the major countries studied in 2012, Western Europe in general, the United States and Canada, Australia and New Zealand all got a "1" in each category, indicating the very general availability of popular sovereignty and personal liberty in these societies. Encouragingly, some countries that had been Marxist dictatorships only a generation ago were now also lining up for perfect scores: the Czech Republic, Estonia, Hungary, Lithuania, Poland, Slovakia, and Slovenia are now very free societies. And the sometimes bumpy Latin American road to freedom is now smooth riding for Chile, Costa Rica, and Uruguay, as well as a number of Caribbean democracies.

Are We Getting Freer?

In very recent years, Freedom House was forced to the conclusion that—since about 2005—some very important societies were backsliding rather than marching forward. Russia, Venezuela, Vietnam, and Iran certainly became more repressive, and countries that had been improving (such as Bahrain, Jordan, Kenya, and Kyrgyzstan) suffered reverses.

And the worst of the worst? Freedom House again declared that Burma/Myanmar, Equatorial Guinea, Eritrea, North Korea, Somalia, Sudan, Turkmenistan, and Uzbekistan managed to get "twin sevens," that is, the lowest possible mark from Freedom House, suggesting a near-total absence of human liberty. Some of the Arab countries may advance in standing once the 2011 "Arab Spring" plays out and countries such as Egypt, Libya, and Tunisia become stable.

While the liberal Eleanor Roosevelt was one of Freedom House's founders, the organization's approach today is considered politically somewhat conservative in orientation, focusing more on the existence of specific democratic structures (such as open elections) and less on how, in practice, a government actually treats its people. For example, neither

FREEDOM BY SOVEREIGN STATE

FREEDOM BY POPULATION

Figure 6.2. Most of Us Aren't Free
Extrapolated from the 2011 Freedom House report, the left-hand circle represents the number of sovereign states that are considered free, partly free, and not free. As you can see, a statistical majority of the world states are democratically impaired or less than totally free (combining "partly free" and "not free"). The right-hand circle gives the same information based on the numbers of people around the world. Ironically, it works out about the same; 54 percent of humankind lives in less-than-free societies, and on a per capita basis, more than one-third of us live in "not free" societies.

Cuba nor Burma/Myanmar permits free elections, and both are repressive societies we'll look at in greater detail later. The authorities in Havana provide their citizens with free education, free medical care, and free supplies of basic nutrition. What isn't free is the Cuban population; dissidents are kept under surveillance and sometimes imprisoned, although seldom executed. In contrast, the Burmese military regime dedicates almost no attention to the material welfare of their people, many of whom endure grinding poverty and lack of medical care. A harshly repressive military machine, the government routinely tortures and executes its dissidents. The average Cuban lives seventeen years longer than does the average Burmese. Both countries are firmly classified as "not free" but if we had to choose between life in Burma and life in Cuba, most of us would be healthier and happier in Havana.

If you "do the numbers," you see a rough correlation between prosperity (as measured by per capita gross domestic product) and human liberty (as estimated by Freedom House). The overall connection is undeniable: most wealthy countries are free societies, and most very poor nations are unfree. But there are lots of exceptions, suggesting that liberty does not necessarily have a price tag. With all its economic woes, India remains a functioning democracy; with all those petroleum dollars, Saudi Arabia remains one of the least free societies on the planet.

Freedom House is far from alone in the field of studying human liberty. The U.S. State Department maintains a Bureau of Democracy, Human Rights, and Labor, headed by an assistant secretary of state, which renders an annual report to Congress on the status of civil rights around the world. Called *Country Reports on Human Rights Practices*, the report makes no attempt to rank or quantify civil rights, but does provide a well-researched analysis of the civil liberties situation in every country on the planet.[7] The report does have the annual effect of irritating the rest of the world, since European societies generally regard themselves as freer than the United States and dislike this American critique of their performance. London's Amnesty International is a significant advocacy organization in this field, and the New York–based Human Rights Watch produces an annual narrative summary of the progress of human rights around the world, which is exceptionally balanced and insightful.[8]

Identifying Our Core Rights

Pundits and politicians routinely produce three rousing cheers for freedom, but it is more complicated to say, with precision, what specific freedoms we ought to enjoy. Historically, a number of important attempts have been made to identify our core rights as human beings, and they fall into four rather separate categories.

- Guarantees by Sovereign Governments: Individual governments have written into their constitutions and their law codes specific guarantees of human rights. England's 1215 Magna Carta, for example, enshrined the principle of trial by a jury of one's peers in Anglo-Saxon law. The American Declaration of Independence and the subsequent Bill of Rights (the first ten amendments to the U.S. Constitution) began the process of defining the freedoms to be enjoyed by American citizens. In 1789, French revolutionaries took time away from dethroning (and decapitating) King Louis XVI to pen the Declaration on the Rights of Man and the Citizen.[9]
- Regional Efforts to Protect Human Rights: At various times in recent history, geographical regions have formed organizations to protect civil rights within that geographic area. As we learned in chapter 5, the most influential effort in this category was made by the Council of Europe, which created both the European Convention on Human Rights and a functioning European Court of Human Rights in the French city of Strasbourg to adjudicate abuses of human rights within Europe.[10]
- Global Efforts to Protect Specific Groups: Since the mid-1800s, the international community has created treaties and treaty-based organizations to look after individual groups that required special protection. Two UN conventions are good examples: the 1979 Convention on the Elimination of All Forms of Discrimination against Women (commonly called CEDAW) attempts to defend women from a wide range of abuses. The 1989 Convention on the Rights of the Child tries to protect young people. For complicated reasons, the United States is the only major democracy not to have ratified either treaty. The post–World War II Geneva Conventions endeavored to safeguard service personnel, prisoners of war, and civilians in war zones.
- Attempts to Define Universal Human Rights: The notion that the international community could define certain core rights that everybody on the planet should enjoy was hard to sell to sovereign governments, who felt that they had the primary responsibility for assuring (or denying) civil rights for their own citizens. After World War II, however, the United Nations created a thirty-point Universal Declaration of Human Rights. In 1966, the United Nations attempted to build on this universal declaration by creating two binding international covenants (or multilateral treaties). The first, which the United States never ratified, dealt with economic, social, and cultural rights

(the so-called ESC Covenant), while the second, which the United States did endorse with some reservations, attempted to define our civil and political rights (the CPR Covenant). Taken together, these three major UN efforts to define our core rights as human beings are often called the **International Bill of Human Rights**.[11]

• Expanding Global Responsibility and R2P: Responsibility to Protect (R2P) is the most recent development of human rights norms. The Responsibility to Protect ("RtoP" or "R2P") is an international human rights norm adopted at the UN World Summit in 2005 to prevent and stop genocide, war crimes, ethnic cleansing, and crimes against humanity (often called collectively "mass atrocities").[12] The Responsibility to Protect rests on three pillars:

1. The state carries the primary responsibility for the protection of populations from mass atrocities.
2. The international community has a responsibility to assist states in fulfilling this responsibility.
3. The international community should use appropriate diplomatic, humanitarian, and other peaceful means to protect populations from these crimes. If a state fails to protect its populations or is, in fact, the perpetrator of crimes, the international community must be prepared to take stronger measures, including the collective use of force approved by the UN Security Council.[13]

Where Do Human Rights Come From?

Here's a philosophical conundrum: what human rights you think we ought to have probably depends on where you believe human rights actually come from in the first place. With a concept called **utilitarianism**, the British philosopher Jeremy Bentham (1748–1832) persuaded most secular thinkers that human rights are the creation of the human brain and the result of observations on how community life is best lived. Bentham's fol-

Figure 6.3. Protecting Libyans against the Libyan Government
The R2P norm has most recently been applied to the use of force by the late Muammar Gaddafi against civilian uprisings within his country. On March 17, 2011, the UN Security Council adopted a resolution to create a no-fly zone over Libya to protect civilians. Such implementation of R2P has set a significant precedent for the protection of human lives around the globe. Photograph courtesy of William Murphy.

lowers would argue that human rights legislation—like any other kind of law—needs to be codified, enforced as rigorously as possible, and changed when our perceptions change. For these thinkers—most of them political liberals—the whole area of civil or human rights is the legitimate preserve of national and international law.

Jeremy Bentham and Utilitarian Theory

In 1789, the same year the French overthrew the Bourbon Dynasty and produced their Declaration on the Rights of Man and the Citizen, the English scholar Jeremy Bentham published his *Introduction to the Principles of Morals and Legislation*. Bentham had little use for the idea that human rights came from God or from natural law. For him, the concept of utility meant that whatever produced the greatest happiness for the greatest number of people was right, and laws should flow from an analysis of society rather than a close reading of holy books.

More religious and/or more politically conservative thinkers disagree. **Natural law** enthusiasts, for example, argue that human rights in particular and law in general can be deduced from a philosophical consideration of our essential nature as human beings. In this view, human nature does not change, and neither does natural law, which is seen as universal.

Others believe that human rights are the result of certain divine decrees. As the authors of the American Declaration of Independence proclaimed, "All men are . . . endowed by their Creator with certain unalienable Rights, that among these are Life, Liberty, and the pursuit of Happiness." Those who believe that human rights come specifically from heaven have the unenviable task, however, of interpreting the sacred texts of various revealed religions to determine what precise rights God intended us to enjoy. The Hebrew Testament (Leviticus 20:13), for example, calls for male homosexuals to be executed. St. Paul (Romans 1:26) remarks that male and female gays are headed for hell. The Islamic Qur'an (4:16) recommends an unspecified punishment for homosexuals who fail to repent. Despite clear unanimity among sacred monotheistic texts, every Western democracy regards the practice of homosexuality among consenting adults as a protected right. Does this right come from God or Jeremy Bentham?

To see how controversial this can be in practice, let us glance at a couple of contentious issues: the whole complex issue of women's reproductive rights and the problem of the death penalty.

In 1995, the United Nations held the Fourth World Conference on Women (WCW) in the Chinese capital of Beijing, hoping to create a multilateral treaty or convention that would end rape as a military weapon, establish the principle of equal pay for equal work, forbid child marriages, guarantee female sexual freedom, and ensure that women enjoyed reproductive liberty, that is, the right to birth control and abortion.[14] The WCW made a lot of progress, but it ran into objections by American religious conservatives, the Roman Catholic Church, and the Islamic community generally, all of whom argued that fundamental law came from God and could not be changed by a committee of the United Nations.[15] The United States tends to see abortion as an essentially American issue because of widespread concern that *Roe vs. Wade* (the 1972 Supreme Court decision that essentially legalized abortion) could be overturned by a more conservative Supreme Court. But women all over the planet have unwanted pregnancies, and there is no emerging global consensus on the issue: in most European countries, abortion has been legal for a long time, and looks likely to stay that way. Countries such as South Africa and Switzerland have recently liberalized once-restrictive laws. On the other hand, many American states are tightening up legislation in an effort to protect what are deemed to be fetal rights, and the Russian government is moving in the same direction. In many parts of Latin America, abortion is illegal, and in countries such as El Salvador, the government routinely imprisons women who have had abortions. Is it your right as a woman to have an abortion? Is it your right as a fetus not to be aborted?

The death penalty is another difficult issue. A majority (albeit a declining one) of Americans believes in capital punishment, and the Judeo-Christian tradition generally supports it.[16] Secular Europeans, on the other hand, overwhelmingly regard the death penalty as barbaric. In 1998, the Roman Catholic pope announced his opposition to capital punishment, and every Western European society regards the right not to be executed as a fundamental human freedom.

2. Ideologies: Organizing Our Political Philosophies

So, how much freedom should we have? How should we organize the decision making in our society? How do we allocate resources, deciding who gets rich and who stays poor? Your collected answers to these questions constitute your own personal ideology.[17]

An ideology is a set of ideas inside of an individual human brain, and these ideas can vary enormously from person to person. "Ideology" has both positive and pejorative connotations, and the word "ideologue" is negatively used to criticize a person whose common sense has been overwhelmed by rigid, narrow, and partisan political ideas. Most politicians would claim to be "pragmatists," that is, practical folks looking for real-life solutions to everyday problems without reference to abstract theories.

IDEOLOGIES, FREEDOM, AND ECONOMICS

The importance of economics in an ideology can vary enormously. In any religious tradition, fundamentalists or religious conservatives may be more concerned with eternal salvation than fiscal solvency. A religiously oriented ideology might focus primarily on the enforcement of public morality, maintenance of the sanctity of marriage, and the role of religious values in public life. Similarly, an ideology might revolve around a passionately held opinion on one, and only one, central idea. Inspired by the National Rifle Association, some gun enthusiasts will vote for or against candidates on the sole basis of their position on gun control. Many pro-life/antiabortion militants have the same highly targeted ideology. These "tight-focus" activists are sometimes called "single-issue voters," and they can have enormous clout in democratic societies because politicians will go to great lengths to avoid offending them.

Kinds of Ideologies

People who stay well informed about the world, follow public events closely, and think a lot about political affairs tend to have very detailed, coherent, and interconnected ideologies.

News illiterates who never get past the sports pages in their local paper tend to have fairly crude ideologies, for example, "All politicians are crooks and the little guy never wins." Sometimes these primitive political philosophies are internally inconsistent: you might want the government to lower taxes drastically, balance the budget, bolster defense spending, and provide free health care to everyone. These may be great ideas, but it would take some creative accounting to orchestrate them all because the money needs to come from somewhere.

Some people will have passive ideologies, in the sense that they have political ideas, but seldom express them and make no effort—beyond perhaps voting—to turn their ideologies into practice. Activists will be a minority within any society, but there will always be those prepared to spend time, money, and energy trying to fulfill their ideological goals, perhaps joining political parties, campaigning for candidates, protesting or demonstrating, or writing books and articles articulating a given point of view.

Some ideologies might be regarded as "partial" or "ancillary" in the sense that they address one important aspect of human life, but do not attempt to describe an entire worldview or political system. One prominent example would be the feminist movement, which argues in a very general way for equality between the genders and a greater fairness for women in modern society. While feminism would not mesh well with some philosophies (such as fascism), feminists can integrate their views into most of the political ideologies discussed below.

An ideology is a way of organizing the world intellectually and making political life mentally coherent and intelligible. We tend to choose media that reinforce our ideological perspectives. Liberals find it painful to watch the aggressively conservative Fox News; conservatives don't relax over a copy of the *Nation* (a radical left-wing magazine). For Americans, the years after the September 11, 2001, al-Qaeda attacks were ideologically radicalizing. Some agreed with President George Bush's War on Terror and accepted deficit spending for the military and constraints on allocations for welfare, health, and education. Others were infuriated by these same policies, and a country once known for its consensual politics suddenly found itself troubled by cavernous ideological divisions. Similarly, evidence has emerged that wealth is becoming more distinctly polarized in America, with more of the national pie going to fewer consumers at the top end. Some analysts believe that this has created yet another fault line in American politics, with Republicans moving to the right, and Democrats scrambling to decide where they stand on the issue.[18]

Three Core Ideological Clusters

Building an ideology is a do-it-yourself project. You look at the world, consult your most deeply held values, and decide how we ought to proceed with the ordering of public affairs. However, if you like buying things off the shelf ready-to-go and fully assembled, you'll be glad to know that there are sets of available ideologies that have developed over the centuries that you might like to consider before manufacturing your own.[19]

- The Classical Liberal Family of Ideologies: As is so often the case in political science, the name is confusing, but we seem to be stuck with it. Some people call it "democracy," which is simplistic, and other authors call it "**capitalism**" or "the free enterprise" system, either of which works, although both titles focus a little too much on the economic freedom and not enough on political and personal freedoms. As we will see, there are capitalist dictatorships.

The reason "liberalism" is a confusing title is that—for the last century and a half—we have contrasted "liberals" with "conservatives," an idea we'll explore in section 3 below. In fact, all of today's liberals and conservatives from Barack Obama to Mitt Romney qualify as part of the same classical liberal tradition, although they have edged toward the two modern wings of that tradition. We'll describe it in detail below, but generally speaking, the classical liberal family of ideologies is a set of ideas about political freedom, personal freedom, and economic freedom. All modern ideologies are to some extent elaborations of, or reactions against, classical liberalism.

- Social Democracy: While basically free-market/free-enterprise in fundamental inspiration, many continental European societies are uncomfortable with massive economic inequality and worried about the power of big business. These countries are usually called **social democracies**, or welfare states, or (less frequently) mixed economies. While regarding capitalism as the engine of their economies, social democrats want an activist government to intervene in the marketplace in order to direct commerce toward socially desirable goals and eliminate the worst aspects of economic inequality. They will typically tolerate higher taxes in exchange for a greater range of governmental benefits such as free health care and education. These societies are all democracies, but they permit their governments to take ownership of some profit-making enterprises to accomplish certain social goals. They are also typically progressive in permitting a wide range of personal liberty. In Western European social democracies, young people often live together and have children without getting married. Marijuana use is either legal or openly tolerated. The legal rights and political power of women are often more advanced in social democracies than they are elsewhere. We'll examine this political ideology in greater detail in section 4 below.
- Marxist or "Command" Economy Systems: Based on theories formulated by Karl Marx (1818–1883), **Marxism** turned to central ownership and planning to deal with economic conflict. While Marx envisioned theoretically free societies for the future, actual Marxist governments have historically all been dictatorships, and the five surviving examples are unfree societies that score very poorly on the Freedom House scale. A classical Marxist dictatorship would be one in which the bulk of property and wealth is held by the government for the theoretical benefit of the people, an approach that has turned out in practice to be both inefficient and unpopular.

THE ORIGINS OF CLASSICAL LIBERALISM

Where did classical Western liberalism come from? In late medieval society, reigning monarchs insisted upon imposing their own often incompetent control over the economic life of their kingdoms, believing that commercial activity ought to support dynastic and national security concerns rather than economic growth. In the 1600s and 1700s, the emerging middle class (typically called the **bourgeoisie**) produced coalitions of businessmen and political thinkers who demanded both greater participation in the political system and more freedom to manage their own money. The Latin word for "free" is *liber*, and "liberalism" first emerged as a set of interconnected beliefs: individuals should enjoy certain personal civil rights, have some political control over their governments, and be free to acquire and use wealth generally as they pleased. The French phrase "laissez-faire" means roughly "let them get on with it" and was originally an effort to persuade meddling royal governments to stay out of business and economics, and allow the free market to create wealth. In the 1700s and early 1800s, therefore, the word "liberal" simply meant an advocate of free markets, personal freedom, and popular sovereignty; it was only later in history that the term took on its more complex present set of meanings.

John Locke and Popular Sovereignty

The idea that the people should "own" their governments (what we have been calling "popular sovereignty") seems obvious and straightforward today, but it took a long time to banish the idea that monarchs enjoyed property rights over the countries they ruled, a divine right granted to them by God. During England's "Glorious Revolution," the British philosopher John Locke (1632–1704) provided the theory behind the continuing liberal revolution with his 1690 "Two Treatises of Government," in which Locke first attacked the "Divine Right of Kings" theory and argued that sovereignty belonged to a country's inhabitants, not its rulers. He further speculated that governments were man-made institutions, brought into existence as the result of a "social contract" among people who created these political structures in order to serve very specific communal needs. What people create, they own; and popular sovereignty means just this: people should have ultimate authority over their own governments.

The Liberal Revolutions

Beginning in the 1600s and gathering strength in the 1700s, coalitions of bourgeois intellectuals and activists campaigned to subtract power from royal houses and award some or all of it to themselves. These movements have been generically called "liberal revolutions" (or sometimes "bourgeois revolutions"), and one of the first occurred in Britain between roughly 1640 and 1660, when parliament fought, defeated, and ultimately executed King Charles I over the issue of royal absolutism. This English Revolution was complicated by religious issues, but it ended with a sharing of power between king and parliament. The power of England's classical liberals advanced again at the end of the century with the 1689 "Glorious Revolution," which further limited royal authority.

During the 1700s (in a period often called the "Enlightenment"), political philosophers continued this line of speculation. How free should people be allowed to be? What kind of relationship should exist between the government and the governed? Many of these philosophers were working in France, precisely because France had failed to evolve toward an English-style power-sharing arrangement between monarchy and parliament (it remained an absolute royal dictatorship until 1789).

The Swiss-born French philosopher Jean Jacques Rousseau (1712–1778) achieved fame for arguing in books such as *The Social Contract* (1762) that humankind could dispense with monarchs altogether, imagining a future world of direct democracy with people ruling themselves.[20]

The Enlightenment created the intellectual environment in which liberal revolutions in important countries became common, a process that began with the American Revolution in 1776, gathered momentum with the enormously important French Revolution in

1789, and then roared into the 1800s when most of the remaining reigning monarchs of Europe surrendered their absolute power to the subjects.

The Complications of Capitalism

There is a tendency to exaggerate the role of economic liberalism in all of this process. The early liberals did not make a keen distinction between being free in their churches, in their homes, or in their banks. They wanted limited governments that they could control.

The specifically economic component of classical liberalism was addressed in the last quarter of the 1700s by a Scottish economist named Adam Smith. In his seminal *Inquiry into the Nature and Causes of the Wealth of Nations*, first published in 1776, Smith described a self-regulating economic system that could and should operate independently of government.[21] According to Smith's argument, the fundamental reason governments did not need to regulate the economic affairs of the community is that the invisible hand of the market would do the regulating spontaneously and get it right in ways that governments always got it wrong. For Adam Smith, people inevitably acted in their own economic self-interest. Prices would be controlled by supply and demand, seeking natural levels without bureaucratic interference. A healthy economy could be judged by its ability to create an abundance of goods and services, and the government needed to refrain from interfering in the market's natural tendency toward equilibrium.

While individuals had been buying, manufacturing, and selling products since the beginning of time, Adam Smith was writing at the beginning of the **Industrial Revolution** (roughly 1750–1850 in Britain), when the production of goods shifted from self-employed craftsmen to huge factories powered by coal-fired steam turbines. The factory system demanded the investment of large amounts of money or capital, which needed to be obtained from investors. The concept of using money to make more money is at the heart of modern capitalism, and the notion spread quickly across the English Channel to Western Europe and over the Atlantic Ocean to North America.

Even before Adam Smith issued his *Wealth of Nations*, the action of free markets and increasingly powerful capitalist institutions had put great wealth in the pockets of those who were in a position to make the system work. Early capitalism had also created very substantial poverty, since economic freedom allowed factory owners to pay workers as little as the market would bear, and there was no safety net for those who could not find jobs. By the early years of the 1800s, particularly in Great Britain, it became clear that Adam Smith's invisible hand of the market was providing an abundance of goods and services, but not spreading them around very well.

The Irish Potato Famine (1845–1850) provided a good example of how invisible those market forces could be when people began to starve. British colonial control over the island of Ireland had left only about one-seventh of the arable land under the control of the Irish people, with the best turf in the hands of British landowners. Potatoes will grow even on scrub land, and most of the poorer Irish survived by eating the humble potato. Beginning in 1845, however, Ireland's potato crop was infected by a fungal blight, turning this staple of the Irish diet black and inedible. For the export market, Ireland's agricultural economy was still producing high-quality beef and a wide range of grains and vegetables, but the average Irish person could not afford to buy what was on the market. In reality, Ireland had a shortage of money, not food. Hundreds of thousands starved to death while the British government in London generally refrained from effective intervention. British inaction in the face of this humanitarian tragedy was partially motivated by anti-Irish feeling, but to a large measure, the British did nothing because classical liberalism taught them that governments needed to stay out of economics. There was a temporary imbalance between the potato supply and the Irish demand, and free food for starving people would destroy the self-correcting mechanism inherent in the economy. With full tummies, the Irish would have more children, and the supply-and-demand equation would get even harder to balance. As we will see, precisely the same argument rages today over the question of food aid for famine-ridden countries or welfare for poor people in wealthy societies.

Why do we have "liberals" and "conservatives" today? By the midyears of the 1800s, the classical liberal tradition began to fray. Within the mainstream, some classical liberals described themselves as "conservatives," while others continued to claim the word "liberal." From outside the liberal mainstream, the revolutionary Communist movement that spilled out of the French Revolution was being codified by Marx into a systemic critique of liberal capitalism that claimed that the basic philosophy was inherently flawed and was destined to self-destruct. And the early social democrats were stitching together a few ideas from Marx and a lot of ideas from the Enlightenment, and trying to create an entirely new approach to freedom and inequality.

3. Modern Liberals and Modern Conservatives

An ideology is about every kind of freedom, but Western political thought does tend to revolve to a large extent around the distribution and management of wealth within society. There is nothing too abstract or complicated about this argument, and debates about economic distribution take place within most families. On one side of the table is Uncle Fred, a blue-collar worker who belongs to a labor union and votes for the Democratic Party. He wants to know why kids born on the wrong side of the tracks can't get an equal start in life. Why doesn't the government spend more to eradicate poverty and build better schools? And what would be so wrong with affordable, government-sponsored health care?

Careful, because Aunt Faye is the family lawyer and a staunch Republican, and she fires back immediately, wanting to know why all those shiftless malingerers can't work their way through university the way she did and get off welfare instead of waiting for a government handout. And do we really want socialized medicine? Faye hasn't heard about it working anywhere else. Above all, can't we get the government out of our wallets? Aunt Faye works hard for her money and she absolutely hates seeing so much of it going to support the lame and the lazy.

If this kind of debate has happened around your dining room table, welcome to the heart of contemporary political discourse. In your house, this kind of conflict might reach the level of bruised feelings and then stop, but elsewhere on the planet, quarreling over economic freedom has a way of sliding into war. Peaceful or violent, economic conflict is almost universal. Some of us fight some of the time about ideas, religion, and language, but all of us fight all of the time about money. The Cold War was to some extent about

American nationalism versus Russian nationalism, but at the ideological level, it was a conflict between two sets of ideas about economic distribution: the American notion that business should be left to businessmen and a Marxist idea that the Soviet government needed to control the economy for the benefit of the people.

If ideology started and stopped with economics, life would be simpler, but there are collections of ideas about life and freedom that travel with ideas about economics, and we'll need to know a little history to see why they belong together. When cousin Lizzie got inadvertently pregnant while still in high school, Uncle Fred thought she should be allowed to terminate her pregnancy quietly and get some coaching on how to misbehave more prudently in the future; Aunt Faye believes that abstinence before marriage is the best birth control and doesn't think that escaping the consequences of sexual immorality should be made quite that convenient. And when nephew Donald joined the marines and got sent to Afghanistan, Faye bragged that a member of the family was fighting for democracy; Fred muttered that the kid was going to get himself killed in a crazy war. Once again, Fay and Fred were voicing coherent—albeit contrasting—American ideologies. Fred is a liberal; Faye is a conservative.

LIBERALS AND CONSERVATIVES IN AMERICAN POLITICS

By the midyears of the 1800s, "liberal" classical liberals began to argue that it was in the public interest for the government to interfere at least a little in the operation of the free market. Factories needed a literate workforce, which meant raising taxes to pay for government-sponsored schools. Viruses and bacteria failed to distinguish between rich and poor, so it was in everybody's interest to clean up the water supply. More idealistically, some intellectuals were simply offended at the plight of the poor, asserting that human decency demanded public hospitals and welfare in the form of poor houses, orphanages, and public hospitals. When Marx and his colleagues began to talk about revolution in the midyears of the century, pragmatic business leaders realized that the creation of a more **egalitarian** society (one in which wealth was divided equally) was their best defense against class warfare.

Early British liberals were prepared to change society profoundly, and this impetuous rush to the future upset some more "conservative" classical liberals. Adam Smith's near contemporary was Sir Edmund Burke (1729–1797), who wrote his 1790 *Reflections on the Revolution in France* to suggest that England needed to evolve slowly and cautiously if the English wished to avoid the chaos of contemporary France.[22] According to Burke, liberals were paying too much attention to the interests of the individual and too little to country and community. Since the human race was not an infinitely perfectible species, society would always need a strong government capable of enforcing the law.[23]

By the last years of the 1800s, British politics had assumed the classic two-part structure reflected today in most freer political systems around the world (although the names of individual parties change from country to country). On one side, Britain's Liberal Party wanted utterly free-market capitalism to be moderated at least a little in order to provide some benefits for the poor. British Conservatives, on the other hand, believed that governmental intervention in the economy would destroy the delicate, self-adjusting equilibrium that Adam Smith believed lay at the heart of the system.[24] With a lot of complications and additions, liberals and conservatives in the Western world generally still reflect this central disagreement about the management of economic conflict.

Before going on to examine the distinction elsewhere in the world, let's stay on familiar ground long enough to add some nuance to how the words "liberal" and "conservative" are used within the context of American politics.

Modern American Liberals

Today's liberals generally believe in more government assistance for the poor and an activist federal bureaucracy. In the United States, most liberals affiliate with the Democratic Party. Keep an eye on table 6.1 as we look at the differences between liberals and their ideological adversaries in the conservative movement. The first two categories (welfare and regulation of business) relate specifically to economic conflict: liberals find deep and persistent poverty unacceptable and support the use of public funds to eliminate it, believing that the government sometimes needs to interfere with commerce in order to ensure that business functions in the public interest. Liberals tend to belong to the idealist school, feeling that humankind is capable of improvement and that society can act in concert to improve the human condition.

Idealists are optimists about the human condition. Looking out at the world, therefore, American liberals are internationalists, seeing a potentially friendly community of

Table 6.1.   Left and Right in America

Groups:	Mainline Democrats or Idealists or Moderate Liberals	Mainline Republicans or Realists or Moderate Conservatives
Welfare	Government action to abolish severe poverty; affirmative action programs for minorities	Want poor to learn to be independent; safety-net welfare only; no quotas
Regulation of Business	More governmental regulation of commerce, banking, antitrust laws	Less governmental interference in business
Nationalism	Moderate internationalists, support for UN and foreign aid, international law	Moderate nationalists, critical of foreign aid and UN: support for flag and military; disdain for international law
Law and Order	Eliminate crime through social change; handgun controls; hostile to death penalty	Strict enforcement of law; support for police, prisons, death penalty
Religion	Sometimes secular, sometimes liberal religions (e.g., Episcopalians and Quakers); "pro-choice" on abortion	More attention to religion, "family values"; "pro-life" on abortion; sometimes fundamentalist or evangelical religions
Change	Willing to experiment with social institutions and make dramatic innovations in society.	Prefer to remain with "tried-and-true" policies and procedures. Strong feeling for tradition.

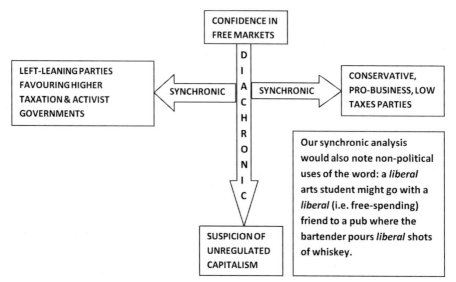

Figure 6.4. Liberals over Time and Space
Political scientists like to talk about synchronic analysis, which is how a word is used at any given time in various parts of the world. A diachronic analysis is a study of how a word's meaning has evolved over time. As you can see from the attached chart, liberals started out trusting free markets and ended up mistrusting them. And the word "liberal" is used in a lot of different senses.

nations and the eventual possibility of world peace. In the hopeful expectation that war will someday be obsolete, they support the United Nations, looking to diplomacy and international law to defuse conflict. On the domestic front, liberals suspect that crime might be better addressed by social engineering than by dungeons and chain gangs. For them, prisons are about rehabilitation rather than punishment, and they generally dislike capital punishment. While many liberals are sincerely religious, they are more likely than conservatives to be secular or nonreligious in their personal thinking about moral issues. This may lead them, for example, to oppose prayer in public schools, take a pro-choice stance on abortion, and support legal rights for gays. Environmentalism is the belief that we need to take infinitely better care of our battered old planet, and nearly every environmentalist will also be a modern liberal.

Word Games and Liberals

There are a couple of factors about the word "liberal" we need to consider:

- The "L" Word: Until the 1970s, "liberal" was a perfectly acceptable word that politicians such as Franklin Delano Roosevelt proudly used to describe themselves. After what some perceived as the unsuccessful presidency of the liberal Jimmy Carter (in office 1977–1981), Ronald Reagan and his fellow conservatives successfully turned "liberal" into a pejorative in the minds of most Americans, suggesting a weak, wishy-washy politician who favors high taxes, wasteful give-away programs for the undeserving poor, a big and intrusive government, and a "blame-America-first" approach to foreign affairs.

As Mr. Reagan moved conservative values into the mainstream, American liberals generally acquiesced in the assassination of their political legacy by dropping the word, and few American politicians will use it today to describe themselves. In the 2004 presidential election, Mr. Bush routinely accused John Kerry of being a liberal, and the junior senator from Massachusetts quietly sidestepped the issue; nor did candidate Barack Obama embrace the label in the 2008 campaign.

- Liberals Abroad: The word "liberal" can change (and even reverse) its meaning outside the United States. In many European societies, opposition to unbridled capitalism is more frequently represented by the social democratic parties and politicians.

Confusingly, some non-U.S. political parties have retained the word "liberal" in their party titles because they hearken back to the original or classical liberalism of the 1800s when "liberal" meant elected governments and free markets, but not high taxes and welfare. Hence Japan's Liberal Democratic Party and Brazil's Partido da Frente Liberal are both conservative parties, notwithstanding their names. Members of Australia's Liberal Party are what we would today call "conservatives," and the party is only liberal in the sense that it flows from the classical liberal tradition.[25]

Canada actually gets its party labels right. Conservatives belong to the ruling Conservative Party, while liberals vote for the Liberal Party. The New Democratic Party is what we will describe below as social democratic.

To augment the confusion, many social democrats outside the United States have taken to using "liberal" or "neo-liberal" in that same 1800s sense to describe someone such as Ronald Reagan or George W. Bush, who believes that Third-World countries should open their markets to "free trade" and sell off state-owned enterprises. This ideology will be explored more fully in chapter 12.

Modern American Conservatives

At least in the United States, conservatives typically find their way into the Republican Party. Remember that the word "republican" fundamentally describes someone who believes in elective (as opposed to monarchical) government; outside the United States, the word often loses its connection to conservative thought; Ulster's Irish Republican Army isn't a conservative organization at all, and a British "republican" is anyone who wants to abolish the monarchy (mostly members of the center-left Labour Party).

In terms of basic philosophy, conservatives usually belong to the realist school, believing that politics involves the ordering of public affairs for a largely imperfect species. Conservatives tend to assume that poverty flows in large measure from human failings: laziness, stupidity, or wickedness. Hence, they are not prepared to impose heavy taxes to provide long-term welfare benefits, preferring a "safety-net" approach that prevents unemployed people from starving until they can be moved back into the workforce. Most conservatives dislike affirmative action programs for minority groups and prefer a color-blind government that treats all citizens as equal, regardless of past injustices. They typically dislike all but the most limited governmental regulation of the economy, fearing that even minimum-wage legislation can unfairly restrict economic activity.

Republicans and Democrats disagree over a lot of issues, but problems such as taxation and government entitlement programs lie at the heart of the debate. In 2012, conservative politicians were demanding that President Obama reduce government spending to balance the budget; liberals wanted him to raise taxes (primarily on rich people and corporations) in order to increase revenue. The debate was acrimonious, but at least conservatives and liberals were staying in character.

In dealing with society's problems, conservatives are the heirs of Edmund Burke in believing that the government needs to be strong enough to deal with both domestic and international challenges; this means big police departments and big armed forces. Domestically, conservatives see crime as more the result of evil choices than of social conditions and think that police and prisons can accomplish more than can sociologists and social workers. As mentioned above, the death penalty is a great ideological litmus test, since conservatives tend to believe in its deterrent effect, while liberals almost universally oppose it.

Word Games and Conservatives

The economic policies associated with former president George W. Bush have led some to wonder if the word "conservative" adequately describes an administration prepared to spend more money than tax revenues produce. Many Republicans are horrified by the idea of deficit spending and would call themselves "**fiscal conservatives**" to suggest that they believe in balancing the books. "**Social conservatives**" or "Christian conservatives" are typically people who are more concerned with morality than with economics; they would like to see a society in which promiscuity was discouraged, sexual abstinence before marriage was promoted, abortion was abolished (except in some extreme cases), and religion was made a more prominent feature of American public life.

The core of the word "conservative" suggests someone who wants to retain the best features of an existing society and who advocates careful thought before altering existing political structures. Complicating this obvious definition, some conservatives actually want to eliminate some time-honored government entitlement programs (such as Social Security and Medicare) that have been standard features of American public policy for many decades.

Many conservative thinkers today would describe themselves as "neo-conservatives" (or "neo-cons"), a tradition that arose in the 1970s when some serious intellectuals who had been liberals decided that they had been "mugged by reality." Many neo-conservatives have been strongly influenced by the work of Leo Strauss (1899–1973), a Chicago University professor of political philosophy. Strauss utterly opposed modern liberalism, believing that it overstressed the freedom of the individual at the expense of virtue and led to a relativistic worldview in which nothing could be seen as absolutely true. He further criticized behavioralism in political science and advised his students instead to read the classics deeply, suggesting that these great works contained esoteric or hidden meanings. His own writing was often difficult to understand, which led some critics to believe that he actually opposed the concept of modern democracy. During his lifetime, Dr. Strauss was well outside the mainstream of contemporary political thought, but some of his students and followers went on to become important political figures in the administration of former president George W. Bush.

When Texas congressman Ron Paul ran for president in the 2012 Republican primary, he popularized the libertarian movement, which travels sometimes uncomfortably with the conservative Republican Party. Libertarianism is focused largely on unlimited economic freedom, a drastic reduction in taxes, and severe restrictions on governmental power, especially at the federal level.

Within conservative ranks, there are a variety of other moods and perspectives. In 2009, a "Tea Party" movement appeared, borrowing rhetoric from the American colonialists who rebelled against the British in 1773. Of the presidential candidates in 2012, Minnesota congresswoman Michele Bachmann quickly emerged as the Tea Party favorite, representing their desire to see lower taxes, a cutting of the national debt, and rigid controls on government spending. The term "populist" is often associated with this movement because it sees itself as a people's movement rather than something guided by intellectuals or conventional leaders. Populists often feel resentment against both big business and big government.

Right-Wingers and Left-Wingers

Why do we call liberals "left-wingers" and conservatives "right wingers"? When the French overthrew the absolutist Bourbon monarchy in 1789, the victorious revolutionaries discovered quickly that they lacked unanimity when thinking about their common future. The French Enlightenment of the 1700s had produced liberal thinkers who wanted a new era in human history and a government capable of delivering a decent life to the poor and downtrodden. More conservative middle-class leaders were anxious to replace royal authority with their own, but less enthusiastic about paying higher taxes for social benefits they themselves were too wealthy to need. In the early meetings of the French Assemblée Nationale, liberals sat to the left of the speaker, while conservatives felt more comfortable on the opposite side of the chamber, to the speaker's right. Given the importance of the French Revolution in political thought, this nomenclature has now become almost universal.

In the modern French legislature and in all other legislatures inspired by the French Revolution, it is still traditional for legislators to seat themselves ideologically from left to right of the presiding officer. In the French case, those deputies who want the most activist government with the maximum redistribution of revenues (France's indefatigable Communist Party) sit on the far left, flanked by the Socialists. Next to them is the left-leaning Green Party. Dominating the assembly is the huge contingent from the Gaullist Party, which keeps changing its name; led by Nicolas Sarkozy, it is currently called the UMP or Union pour un Mouvement Populaire (Union for a Popular Movement).

The language of politics reflects this practice by classifying people and politicians from left to right on the basis of their willingness to accept governmental redistribution of wealth as a solution to economic conflict. Britain's Liberal Democrats and Labourites are further to the left than are most of America's Democrats; Britain's Tories or Conservatives join America's Republicans in being considered right-wingers, although in ideological terms, the British conservatives are not nearly as "conservative" as America's Republicans. In 2010, everyone got confused when the left-leaning Liberal Democrats formed a coalition government with the right-leaning Conservatives, but the fact was that no single party had enough votes to form an administration.

In recent years, American commentators have been describing U.S. states as "red states" if they reliably vote Republican and "blue states" if they prefer the Democratic alternative. This confuses the rest of the world, since everywhere else blue signifies conservative values, while red is the historic color of the left (remember the "red Chinese"?), and a left-winger is often called a "red," while a social democrat might be described irreverently as a "pinko." The language of politics is not consistent and not logical; it might be better to describe ourselves in terms of what we actually believe and avoid facile labels.

FREE MARKETS AND THE MODERN WORLD

As mentioned above, one of the core notions of classical liberalism was economic freedom, something called "capitalism" or "free markets" when divorced from the rest of classical liberal thought. A society can be described as having a free market if individuals and corporations are at liberty to use their money without excessive governmental control, and if the basic economic resources of the society (farms, factories, banks, stores, etc.) are overwhelmingly in nongovernmental hands. People who like free market systems prefer to say "private" hands rather than "nongovernmental" hands, even if it is difficult to think of corporate giants such as Microsoft, General Motors, and Exxon as private. The word "private" merely means that they are owned by individual stockholders rather than by governments. Discussions about the relationship between governments and commercial entities normally involve the term **"public sector"** to describe the financial activities carried out by the government (financing a space program or the military establishment, etc.) and **"private sector"** to describe financial enterprises in nongovernmental hands, such as private individuals, charitable organizations, churches, and commercial corporations.

Free Markets Abroad

Most democratic societies fall into the free-market category, although we must not allow our passion for classification to blur the fact that every political and economic system is unique. In free-market or capitalist societies, the government philosophically accepts the inevitable existence of rich and poor, making only a limited attempt to deal with the worst aspects of poverty. The redistribution of resources is typically done by funding school systems, libraries, police forces, public hospitals, social service departments, and other public services. Welfare tends to be of the safety-net variety, with liberals wanting more aggressive help for the poor and conservatives believing that private charities should carry more of the load and the poor should work harder. On the other hand, these governments will typically foster the creation of wealth by commercial enterprises and represent their major corporations in trade negotiations with other countries.

Within free-market economies, there will typically be parties leaning to the left and others oriented toward more conservative policy positions. Modern liberals worry that capitalism may result in an unacceptably high level of poverty even in wealthy nations, and that it leaves the fundamental resources of society in the greedy hands of a comparatively small number of wealthy individuals, families, and large corporations. Conservative supporters of free-market systems point out that reliance upon market forces has created a large and comfortable middle class in countries such as the United States, the United Kingdom, Canada, South Korea, Thailand, Australia, and Japan, and India is quickly joining the free-enterprise party.

Parallel Lives: India's Amartya Sen and Arundhati Roy

India has one generally liberal movement called the Congress Party and a more-conservative and Hindu-nationalist group called the Bharatiya Janata Party. Two prominent Indian intellectuals, however, have stepped outside the party structure to demand that India work harder to remedy the plight of a large and growing sector of desperately poor Indians who have been left behind as the rest of the country moves toward prosperity.

In recent years, a Nobel Prize–winning economist named Amartya Sen (now teaching at Harvard) has become a voice for political change in his native land. Sen has constantly maintained the liberal notion that it is the responsibility of government to maintain a decent standard of living for its people. He believes, for example, in "judging the goodness of a society by the quality of health of the people."[26]

Where Dr. Sen is dignified and distant, Ms. Arundhati Roy is angry and confrontational. Ms. Roy is an accidental activist who became famous as a novelist when her *The God of Small Things* became a critically acclaimed best-seller in the English-speaking world, winning Britain's prestigious Booker Prize.

While her wealth and beauty might have tempted her into the international jet set, Arundhati Roy stayed home in India and threw herself into social activism. Convinced that India's unrestrained (and somewhat corrupt) Indian capitalism mistreated her country's poor, the novelist has become a permanent thorn in the side of the pro-business government in New Delhi. In her 1999 *The Cost of Living*, Roy slams the Indian government for building a thermonuclear weapon when so many of its citizens were starving. She also bitterly attacks the government's plan to build a gigantic dam in central India, citing mounting evidence that the project will be an environmental disaster and will flood the land of almost half a million already impoverished farmers. *Field Notes on Democracy: Listening to Grasshoppers* is another recent attack on the Indian government.[27]

Plutocracies or Economic Oligarchies

Capitalism and popular sovereignty do not always coexist, and some less-free societies have left the economy in private hands but have denied human freedom in other areas. We will discuss **fascism** more fully in chapter 10, but for now, note that—generally speaking—the political philosophy shared by Mussolini, Hitler, and others was the result of a revolt against almost all of the central concepts of classical liberalism except for the idea that commerce should be in private rather than in public hands. While business was free to flourish in Mussolini's Italy and Nazi Germany, major corporations were expected to cooperate with the government's political ambitions and produce what they were told to produce.

Classical Fascism is gone, but there are still a large number of what may be called capitalist **oligarchies** (rule by a few), in which the government itself does not take control of economic resources but uses coercive instruments, such as the army and the police, to ensure that property remains in the hands of a few friendly families or corporations.

This coercion often involves violence against peasants, trade unionists, and poor people generally. Since most of the wealth sits in the deep pockets of a restricted group of rich people, it is hard or impossible for anyone else to exercise genuine economic freedom. Economic conflict is resolved by making one side the permanent winner and condemning the losers to lose forever. Together with most of the governments of the Persian Gulf region, Saudi Arabia is firmly in favor of capitalism but opposed with equal firmness to Western-style democratic political institutions. Most of the country's enormous oil wealth stays with the extended Saudi royal family. As we will see in section 5 below, China is too complex for simple categories, but in some ways, the Chinese economy may be headed in this same direction.

This kind of government is sometimes called a **plutocracy** (rule by the rich), and El Salvador is another good example. Most of the land in this Central American republic is owned by a handful of agricultural families who enjoy close ties with prominent members of the military and political classes. In the 1960s and 1970s, left-wing political parties and action groups arose to demand a more equitable distribution of the land. The police and military responded with death squads that kidnapped, tortured, and executed left-wing leaders, many of them members of the Farabundo Martí National Liberation Front (or FMLN). By 1981, El Salvador was engulfed in a full-fledged civil war, with the United States simultaneously backing the government and unsuccessfully trying to coax the land-owners into modest reforms.[28]

By the early 1990s, both sides had exhausted their resources without either achieving a clear-cut win. Denied a military victory, the revolutionary left was persuaded to try conventional political activity and contest open elections, and emerged as a left-leaning political party called the FMLN Party. The United Nations brokered a cautious, uneasy truce in 1992 and oversaw a comparatively free election in 1994. But the agrarian-military complex asserted itself in the form of a powerful and well-financed political party called ARENA, which promptly won three successive presidential elections. By 2009, the FMLN had managed to win the presidency, but its revolutionary ambitions had clearly been replaced by modest political goals.[29]

Despite some advances in civil rights, 48 percent of the El Salvadorian population still lives in poverty and the PC/GDP (when adjusted for inflation) is actually lower today than it was before the 1981–1992 Civil War. The new century starts with the landowners still refusing to share economic control over the country or consent to more than a token distribution of farming land. In fact, 1 percent of the landowners still control the best 40 percent of all farming land, and the banking system rests in the hands of wealthy ARENA families. The economic interests of these major landowners invite them to grow export crops, which leaves little land for ordinary food production. For the very poor, there has been little social progress since the 1992 peace accords.

4. The Social Democratic Tradition

Would you rather have a night watchman or a nanny? It's a dramatic oversimplification, but a conservative in a capitalist society sees the ideal government as a kind of

Map 6.1. The Disabled Democracies of Central America
An economic oligarchy qualifies as a less-free society when the government systematically fails or refuses to make it possible for poor to attain some measure of
economic success. Guatemala, San Salvador, Honduras, and Nicaragua have all
experienced periods of intense political violence in which landless peasants formed
left-wing guerrilla armies to fight wealthy families who had traditionally monopolized
ownership of scarce agricultural resources.

night watchman, ready to intervene in emergencies, provide a law enforcement system,
defend the borders from foreign enemies, and otherwise stay out of everyone's hair. In
this section, we're going to look at social democrats, most of them Europeans, who want
a government that more closely resembles an affectionate nanny or nurse. In the "nanny
state," the government frets about the citizenry, tries to educate the children and nurse
the sick, worries about the welfare of the poor, gives everybody advice about a variety of
topics, and interferes (benignly or intrusively, depending on your point of view) in the
lives of everyday people.

What's a social democrat? As noted above, most of the world's democracies possess
what can reasonably be called free-market economies in which the government takes relatively little part in economic conflict, allowing the marketplace to decide who gets rich
and providing a minimal safety net for those who wind up desperately poor. These free-
market governments seldom, if ever, take actual ownership of economic resources such
as stores, factories, and banks, and they regulate commercial activities with a light hand.

There is, however, a handful of significant countries, most of them European,
which do not completely correspond to the classic liberal/capitalist model. Even though
private enterprise remains the principal engine behind their generally prosperous
economies, these social democracies believe that government should take an activist
role in remedying what they perceive to be the negative consequences of capitalism.
And, while a closely scrutinized capitalism gets most of the economy, social democrats
don't want to see everything in private hands. To eradicate poverty and to achieve other
social goals, social democrats are prepared to take actual ownership of some economic
assets such as railroads, airlines, steel plants, and others business that would remain in
private hands in a purely capitalist economy. Let's look at these social democracies and
see what makes them worth categorizing separately from the free-market economies we
have just studied.

THE INGREDIENTS OF SOCIAL DEMOCRACY

Predictably, there is massive disagreement about what to call these social democracies. Some U.S. scholars disapprovingly use the phrase "democratic socialism" to describe this movement; note that "socialism" is a pejorative for most Americans. Since these systems combine private enterprise with some state ownership, other authors call them "mixed economies." A government intensely focused on redressing economic inequalities and providing services to the poor can also be termed a "welfare state." Others have coined the phrase "market socialism," but the most neutral phrase to describe a political party or a government heavily influenced by this ideology is simply "social democracy."

The Origins of the Idea

The idea of social democracy crystallized in the middle years of the 1800s, when capitalism seemed to be making some people so rich and reducing so many others to wretchedness. As Marx began preaching a doctrine of social revolution, a few British thinkers wondered if conventional liberal responses to the challenge would go far enough and fast enough.

As a protégé of Jeremy Bentham, John Stuart Mill (1806–1873) had absorbed utilitarian ideas about the need for society to promote the greatest good for the greatest number of people. In 1848, the same year that Marx published *The Communist Manifesto*, Mill fired back with *The Principles of Political Economy*, perhaps the founding document of social-democratic movements and societies. In his *Principles*, Mill hammered home the point that the free market needed to remain the driving force behind the economy, and governments should—whenever possible—avoid handicapping businessmen with burdensome regulations. However, in the interests of a civilized society, the government did need to levy taxes and spend public money to achieve a variety of common goals. There should be a system of public schools, for example, and the government needed to prevent capitalists from harming their employees by making them work too long or under unsafe conditions. Child labor was to be regulated, and provisions needed to be made for those unable to work.[30]

In the twentieth century, the challenge of the Great Depression acted as a spur to social democratic programs and policies. Faced with widespread unemployment and significant social misery, the Swedish government took the earliest steps toward the development of what was to become the classic social democratic welfare state. In the years after World War II, nearly every European democracy followed suit, creating national health and educational services, taking ownership of public transport, and creating large and important (if sometimes unprofitable) public-sector holdings. Social democratic governments, therefore, intervene in the economy more energetically than capitalist governments do.

Public Sector Ownership of Resources

The essence of a capitalist state is the decision to leave property exclusively in nongovernmental hands. In a social democracy or "mixed economy," some governments have hedged their bets by retaining or taking ownership of limited but important ingredients in the country's economy. In some cases, these government-owned businesses were actually created by the government (such as the British Broadcasting Corporation or BBC), but in other cases, they became public property through the process of **nationalization**, which is the action of a government taking control or buying a previously private industry. How does nationalization benefit a social democratic government? In some cases, it is simply a way of keeping an important company out of bankruptcy court. It can be cheaper to rescue a loss-making company than to pay the social costs connected with mass unemployment. In other cases, a country will decide to retain ownership of a key industry (such as steel) for national-security reasons.

Statism

Some social democratic and some free-market-economy governments also practice what is called "**statism**," which is based on a theory that the government should direct both public and private sectors of the economy. A "statist" government takes an activist role in directing the economy and planning for future economic growth. This typically involves government working to ensure that companies see themselves as national, rather than multinational, and that they operate in the overall general economic interests of the country in question. Some governments that practice "statism" have been very successful: France, Japan, Thailand, and Malaysia are often-cited examples.

Welfare or Wealth Redistribution

While some social democratic systems do still have extremes of wealth and poverty, they find these social cleavages difficult philosophically to accept and sometimes make extensive efforts to redistribute wealth through free education and medical care as well as very extensive welfare services.

Critics of social democracies claim that welfare saps individual initiative. Supporters of social democratic societies like to observe that their societies are compassionate toward the very poor. Some human development indices from Western Europe (longevity, educational attainment, public health, etc.) suggest that some of these social democracies do a good job of caring for their citizens. Some observers have suggested that social democracy may be on the rise because the Cold War has ended; it is now possible to oppose American-style capitalism without being branded an ally of the Soviet Union.[31]

The European countries Italy, Spain, Ireland, Germany, France, Holland, Belgium, and all of the Scandinavian governments are good examples of Western European social democracies. These governments provide medical care free to every citizen and have all achieved substantially better longevity and infant mortality rates than the United States, despite a smaller average income. All European social democracies provide free education from kindergarten to doctorate, although education becomes competitive after the secondary-school level. There are very few private universities in all of Europe, which usually means that you pass the qualifying exams and study for free, or don't go to university at all.

POLITICAL PARTIES AND TAXATION IN SOCIAL DEMOCRATIC SOCIETIES

The axis of American politics is generally to the right of many European and other foreign democracies. In most ways, for example, America's Republican Party is somewhat more "conservative" than some foreign conservative parties. The British Conservatives, the French Gaullists, the German Christian Democrats, and Italy's Forza Italia all believe in a national health system supported by the taxpayer. It would be hard to find an American Republican who would agree. Similarly, social democratic parties abroad tend to be further to the left than the mainstream of the American Democratic Party. Many American democrats supported the war against Iraq, oppose expanded health coverage for poor people, and think that universities should base their tuition on market rates; it would be difficult to find a European social democrat who would agree with any of these ideas.[32]

Social Democratic Word Games

Unfortunately, party labels don't always mean much, and social democratic parties bear many different names. In societies that flow from the British tradition, the term "Labour" (note the British spelling) is often used, and Israel's main left-of-center party is also called "Labour." The term "social democratic" has become a favored term for central European parties that were once called "communist" or "socialist" and are now looking for a more respectable party moniker. At the beginning of the new century, there were social democratic parties running most Scandinavian and Benelux countries.

What happened to social democracy in Britain? Prior to Mrs. Thatcher's election in 1979, the United Kingdom was a model European mixed economy, but the "Iron Lady" emerged from a wing of the Conservative Party that had always loathed social democracy. Winning three successive general elections, Margaret Thatcher worked relentlessly to lower the extent of her government's participation in the economy with a policy of **privatization**, selling to the private sector whatever anybody would buy and closing down loss-making public-sector enterprises if they could not be sold. Under Labour prime ministers Tony Blair and Gordon Brown, the Labour Party became a very centrist grouping, and a lot less social democratic than it once was. In 2010, the Conservatives inched back into power. In 2012, Britain is "social democratic" when compared to the United States, but nowhere near as social democratic as any of the Scandinavian countries.

Table 6.2. Some Social Democratic Parties

Germany Social Democratic Party	Israel Labour Party	Sweden Social Democratic Party	France Socialist Party
Ireland Labour Party	Norway Labour Party	Spain Socialist Workers' Party	Nicaragua Sandinista Party
Brazil Workers' Party	Italy Democratic Party	Denmark Social Democratic Party	Belgium Socialist Party

Thinking about Number One

You can spend a lot of time trying to decide whether you—as an individual—are better off in a social democracy or in a more purely capitalist system. While governments have income from a variety of sources, taxation is the primary method by which a given government gets access to our pockets, and the one feature that liberal capitalist societies and social democracies have in common is a running battle over this issue. How much do we pay, who pays more and who pays less, and what does the government do with the revenue once it has been extracted from our wallets and handbags?

It's tough to calculate what percentage of your income you are paying in taxes, and it is even more difficult to quantify the value of the services that the government provides in return. Taxation is a way of paying for services that a given society has decided it wants the government (rather than private enterprise) to provide. This aspect of taxation is called redistribution, and it involves wealthier citizens paying for services that they themselves may never use. For example, a wealthy couple with no children will pay slightly higher taxes to help support a public school system that benefits a poor couple with six kids.

The United States is a clear example of a free-market system. Canada is a fairly capitalist society, and the Conservative Party won the elections in 2006, but the Canadians have an advanced welfare system (particularly in the area of medical care), making them substantially more social democratic than is the United States, although less social democratic than are many European societies. France, Germany, and Italy are basically social democratic societies despite the fact that their governments are sometimes run by people who describe themselves as conservatives; in exchange for healthy tax thresholds, these governments have all chosen to provide universal health coverage as well as free education from kindergarten to graduate school. In comparison, the United States features substantially lower basic tax rates, but offers partially free medical care only for poor people (Medicaid) and for senior citizens (Medicare). Elementary and secondary schools are free, if desperately underfunded, and even "public" universities are becoming quite expensive.

Are free-market Americans really getting a deal with their low taxes? The math here becomes complicated and changes dramatically from person to person. If Americans add to federal and state taxes the amount they pay for health insurance and university tuition, are they paying more or less than are Swedes? And who has the better standard of living? Economist Paul Krugman attempts a controversial answer:

> Life expectancy in Sweden is about three years higher than that of the U.S. Infant mortality is half the U.S. level. . . . Functional illiteracy is much less common than in the U.S. . . . Though Sweden may have a lower average income than the United States, that's mainly because our rich are so much richer. The median Swedish family has a standard of living roughly comparable with that of the median U.S. family: wages are if anything higher in Sweden, and a higher tax burden is offset by public provision of health care and generally better public services.[33]

Social democrats and liberals in free-enterprise societies want higher taxes to provide for greater social spending by the government. Conservatives in both kinds of societies want a relatively inactive government that leaves more money in people's pockets and allows them to buy health and education if they wish to and can afford to.

5. Marxism and Post-Marxism

Marxism was a reaction to the crisis of classical liberalism and the very real problems of nineteenth-century capitalism. By the midyears of the 1800s, the Industrial Revolution in England and parts of Western Europe had created islands of enormous wealth surrounded by seas of grinding poverty. Concluding that classical liberalism's capitalist system was hopelessly flawed and would eventually self-destruct, Marx asserted that all of society's basic economic resources (factories, farms, banks, etc.) should be taken over by the government and used to level the playing field among the social classes.[34]

At a theoretical level, Marxism contains a number of confusing strains when it comes to personal liberty. Marx himself thought that people could not be genuinely free under capitalism, and some neo-Marxist thinkers have written interesting books suggesting that capitalist advertising reorganizes our brains so thoroughly that we cannot think very clearly about our lives and priorities.

At the practical level, Marxists have tended to see personal freedom as a goal for the future. Overthrowing an entrenched capitalism was not going to be a garden party; Marx foresaw a period when good revolutionaries would have to accept strict discipline in order to impose their will upon the masses. And while the revolution was going to be waged and won in the name of the common people, it would be a long time before the rank and file would have the competence to administer their own affairs, a task that would have to be handled by the Marxist leadership. Marxism is not, therefore, an outgrowth of Western liberal thought or even a liberal heresy; it is a different philosophical tradition altogether. In the 1990s, some previously Marxist regimes became model democracies, but they did it by rejecting Marxism and embracing liberalism or social democracy, not by evolving gently out of Marxism.

The word "**communist**" predates Marx and referred to anyone who believed that social justice demanded a violent overthrow of the government. Marx redefined the word slightly, using it to mean a social activist who foresaw a violent social upheaval followed by an economic structure in which most resources would be publicly owned and managed by the government. During the years of the Cold War, "Marxist" and "communist" were often used interchangeably. It also became fashionable to use the term "command economy" (as opposed to "market economy") to describe a Marxist/communist regime.

In what follows, we'll look at some of the general ideas involved in Marxism before glancing at what's left of the movement today, leaving the special case of Cuba to chapter 10.

MARXIST OR "COMMAND" ECONOMIES

Whatever we decide to call it, here is the theory. From the Marxist perspective, capitalism was a rigged game that denied most people the chance to win. Western Europe emerged from feudalism with society already divided into rich and poor. With no radical redistribution of resources, the already rich would get a lot richer and the poor would be driven into life-threatening poverty. Marx predicted inevitable conflict here, since penniless people could not be expected to starve quietly, and the rich would be reluctant to share their wealth. As we have seen, most Western governments today grapple with economic conflict by doing a certain amount of mandatory redistribution of resources, taxing richer citizens to pay for benefits (free public education, etc.) for poorer citizens. During Marx's lifetime, however, very little redistribution was taking place, and he was unable to foresee that governments in Europe and North America would eventually create the conditions under which most of their citizens would live reasonably prosperous lives.

Marx's Vision of the Future

Marxists believed that after the revolution, a Marxist government would avoid economic conflict by making everybody financially equal. After confiscating all wealth, the government would ration resources equitably to those who needed them, channeling the profits from state-owned enterprises directly to the people in the form of food, housing, educational, and medical benefits.

Marxists first took power in Russia at the end of 1917. Under the leadership of Vladimir Lenin and Joseph Stalin successively, the Soviet government confiscated most productive resources, created a public-sector agricultural system based on huge state farms, and then moved ruthlessly to create an industrial state that attempted to rival the West. Surrounded by hostile regimes and led by the increasingly paranoid Stalin, the USSR became intensely unfree by the 1930s. Despite the cruelty of the Stalin regime, the Communists did generally manage to feed everyone and defend the country's borders, something czarist governments had never consistently accomplished. By the time World War II erupted, Stalin's government contributed massively—perhaps even decisively—to the destruction of Nazi Germany, winning the gratitude of some Russians and Soviet supporters abroad.

The Soviet conquest of much of central Europe in the closing months of World War II brought a number of central and Eastern European governments such as Poland, Czechoslovakia, Romania, Hungary, Bulgaria, and what was then East Germany under Marxist domination. These reluctant satellite states were obliged to create political and economic institutions that resembled to a greater or lesser extent public policy in the Soviet Union itself. Under Chairman Mao, China reinterpreted Marx in a somewhat different way, producing the "Communism-with-a-twist" system described below.

The Crisis of Marxism

Historians still have work to do to explain how and why the USSR fell apart when it did, but clearly the collapse ultimately occurred because Marx's grand vision never worked in practice. First of all, no Marxist state ever became even remotely democratic or permitted its citizens to criticize or influence their government in any meaningful way. Hence, once Marxist bureaucrats had taken control of all that wealth, they tended to use some of the profits from state-owned industries for military projects and the maintenance of huge hierarchies of secret agents; some of it got spent on social benefits for the people, but a lot also got stolen or wasted. And since the governments in question were unaccountable and could never be voted out of office, the people were unable to blow the whistle on their unelected leaders.

An associated structural problem stemmed from the fact that the profits from state-owned business enterprises were seldom very great. Marxist regimes saw competition as uneconomic. Why waste money having two shoe factories competing with one another and conducting advertising campaigns against each other's products? In theory, it would be more efficient to have a committee of experts sit down and decide what kind of shoes people should have, and then order one factory to produce them at controlled prices. Unfortunately, without competition, government-owned companies tended to produce shoes that were expensive to buy and pretty awful to wear. And since workers' salaries were small, nobody had much money to buy shoes anyway.[35]

With the collapse of the Soviet Union, there are only five self-proclaimed Marxist regimes left in the world. In Asia, marginal states such as Vietnam, Laos, and North Korea are still authentically Marxist. Also true to Marx (and a continuing thorn in Washington's side) is Cuba, which we'll study in greater detail in chapter 10. With its 1.3 billion population and booming economy, China is still formally married to Karl Marx while carrying on an open love affair with Adam Smith, making it a good example of a complex ideological situation.

CHINA

For roughly two thousand years, a succession of royal families or dynasties ruled China. European penetration began in the early 1500s, and over the next four hundred years, Europeans fought with the Chinese and with one another to establish spheres of influence and coastal commercial enclaves such as Hong Kong. The imperial government could neither drive out the foreigners nor modernize their country on terms acceptable to the Chinese people.

In 1911, the Nationalist Party (or KMT for Kuomintang, sometimes now spelled "Guomintang") swept away the imperial system, but the resulting government was corrupt and unable to establish its dominion over regional warlords. History never gave the Nationalists much of a chance; by 1927 they were fighting Mao's Red Army, and by 1931, they were unsuccessfully resisting a Japanese invasion.

The Maoist Victory

The Japanese left in 1945, but the battle between Mao's Red Army and the Nationalists continued until 1949, when the Nationalist leader Chiang Kai-shek (sometimes now written as Jiǎng Jièshí) retreated with his defeated forces to Taiwan, forming the basis for the two-China dilemma discussed in chapter 4. Once he had driven the Nationalists from the mainland, Communist leader Mao Zedong created a Marxist government and papered over his differences with the Soviet Union to present a common front to the anticommunist West. Between 1950 and 1953, Chinese and American armed forces fought each other fiercely and directly in the Korean War. The conflict ended in a stalemate but embittered relations between the two countries for a generation.[36]

Mao's government was totalitarian in character, and sometimes appeared to the West to be irrational and unreadable. In an effort to create common ownership of land,

Mao and his colleagues stripped agricultural property from the landlords and tried—not very successfully—to get the peasants to farm it cooperatively and under governmental supervision. Industry was nationalized and run by agencies of the Chinese government. While China remained a very poor country from the 1950s through to 1970s, unable to feed itself adequately or to compete with the rest of the world in industrial production, available goods and services were at least fairly evenly distributed. With its program of "barefoot doctors," the Chinese Communist Party (CCP) did dramatically increase life expectancy and cut back infant mortality rates, especially among the peasantry.

Throughout the Mao era, there was muted internal debate within the Chinese leadership over the question of economic liberty, with Chairman Mao demanding Marxist discipline but others asking for a more pragmatic approach to economic development. By 1958, relations with the Soviet Union had become strained and—now hostile to both superpowers—Mao tried to make China economically self-sufficient. He played only a minimal role on the UN stage, but he tried to develop close bilateral relations with other Third-World powers.

China after Mao

By the time Mao died in 1976, China had publicly moved away from the Soviet Union and opened tentative political contacts with the United States. Within a year or two

Figure 6.5. Chairman Mao Zedong and His Wife, Jiang Qing
A charismatic if brutal leader, Mao helped found the Chinese Communist Party in 1921 and led it into war against the corrupt but pro-Western Nationalist government in 1927. Saving his Red Army during the "Long March" of 1934–1935, he completed his military conquest of mainland China in 1949. After keeping his country in turmoil for most of his reign, Mao turned pragmatically to the West in 1972, meeting with American president Richard M. Nixon and beginning the diplomatic process that eventually led to mutual diplomatic recognition and intensive trade relations. His fourth wife, Jiang Qing, attempted to seize power after her husband's death in 1976 but was arrested and was alleged to have committed suicide. By an unknown photographer, 1946.

of Mao's death, the pragmatic Deng Xiaoping had consolidated his power as party leader, quietly undoing many of his predecessor's policies. The year 1978 was the pivotal year in which Deng began breaking China out of its isolation, albeit without ever formally challenging Marxist theory. First, personal (as opposed to political) freedom was slightly increased, allowing Chinese citizens to travel and trade with the West. The Chinese government dismantled some of the farmers' collectives that had worked so badly and handed title to the land over to local governments, which were empowered to lease the land directly to peasant families. This was a timid half step toward capitalism in the agricultural sector but not quite free enterprise because the government still owned the land and bought the peasant's produce at fixed prices, but it did stimulate agricultural production.

Deng also turned his attention to industry, creating "Special Economic Zones" (or SEZs) where foreign investors could operate freely. At the same time, the government tolerated some informal industrial private enterprise in the cities. The shift in government policy was hard to analyze from the West and far from a whole-hearted conversion to free enterprise, but it worked. China's economy has ripped along with growth rates of over 8 percent per year ever since the 1980s, far better than anything Mao had managed and a lot better than most Western economies.

What did not change much was the government's attitude toward political freedom. When Chinese dissidents stepped over an invisible line in their criticism of the government in 1989, the CCP violently suppressed the demonstrators with a famous bloodbath at Beijing's Tiananmen Square.

Long before his death in 1997, Deng had retired from active leadership of the country, handing over the reins of power to a series of colorless Communist Party bureaucrats. Deng's successors have been more pragmatic than they have been ideological and have established working relations with the United States that range from "fair" to "testy."

But Is It Marxism?

In raw economic terms, China's economic growth has been staggering. From a country that was once one of the poorest in the world, China (in 2011) enjoyed a PC/GDP of just over $7,476 (PPP US$) per year, and it ranked toward the top of the UN's medium human development category. In the years since Deng's quiet revolution in 1978, this represents a gigantic increase, with hundreds of millions of people being lifted out of poverty. Some Chinese, however, are wondering how all this money-making squares with classical Marxism.

China is still administered by the Chinese Communist Party or CCP, although some commentators have wondered if "CCP" might not more realistically stand for "Chinese Capitalist Party." In truth, this surge toward prosperity has been largely driven by Western-style entrepreneurs, not Marxist commissars. The "red capitalists" are a new breed of business executives who have learned to do business with the CCP as well as with European and American firms. While this new alliance of a nominally Communist Party and an ebullient capitalist business elite has brought incredible wealth to some Chinese—the country has over ten thousand men worth more than $10 million each—many of the poorest in society never got their invitations to the party.

China's once vibrant health system, however, has all but collapsed, leaving the poor to pay out of their own pockets for medical care they cannot possibly afford. To a large extent, the once-egalitarian China now struggles with a massive imbalance between the increasing wealthy urban coastal area and the increasingly impoverished rural interior of the country. Despite China's overall economic gains, not everyone believes that a wholesale capitulation to capitalism is Beijing's only option. Political debate in China demonstrates why words such as "conservative" and "liberal" don't travel very well. In 2006, an angry debate erupted between Chinese "conservatives" and Chinese "economic liberals":

- Chinese "conservatives" want to conserve the socialist traditions of the country by focusing on economic equality and continued government control of economic resources. These experts note that riots and demonstrations by rural peasants against the government—once unthinkable—were now becoming common. President Hu may have some sympathy for this position: concern about growing inequality in Chinese society.
- Chinese "economic liberals" want more capitalism and see economic inequality as a temporary but necessary stage through which China needs to pass to construct a modern and globally competitive economy. There is some evidence that the capitalists are winning the debate; a 2006 survey found that 75 percent of the Chinese people think that a free-market economy is the ideal future for their country.

Unhappily, there is only limited support among Chinese leaders for more genuine classical liberalism in the Western sense of the word, that is, more popular sovereignty and more personal freedom. The leaders of the CCP have no desire to follow their Russian colleagues into the dustbin of history, so whatever happens to Marxism, the Communist Party wants to remain firmly in command. In its 2011 ratings, Freedom House (FH) gave China a rock-bottom "7" for political freedom, meaning that the Chinese people have no real ability to affect public policy. A minimally expanded level of personal freedom won China a still-dismal "6" from Freedom House and the combined FH rating of "6.5" puts China near the bottom of freedom's totem pole.[37]

It is commonly predicted that China will be the world's dominant economic power at some point in the coming century. While economic growth has been very rapid since 1978, the gross domestic product is only about one-third of that of the United States, which means they still have a lot of catching up to do. And the future economic progress will depend a lot on securing reliable and affordable access to resources such as oil, and this may be very difficult. If cheap power for the future can't be managed, economic progress may stagnate, and popular unrest may grow.[38]

A country as big and complicated as China is always going to be difficult to categorize. Clearly, we are dealing with a mixed economy in which an ideologically based elite has attempted with considerable measurable success to combine a residual Marxist-style command economy with an 1800s-style buccaneer capitalism, which operates brilliantly but without much reference to any rule book. Unfortunately for students, China doesn't compartmentalize very well in terms of ideology. The Chinese leadership is clearly attempting to split the core concept of classical liberalism, keeping the concept of economic freedom while dumping its natural correlates, personal liberty and popular sovereignty.

Can China create a capitalist oligarchy in which economic freedom is prized and personal/political freedom is denied? On one hand, this unique Chinese experiment has functioned with some success since 1978, but there are no good historical examples of free-market oligarchies being very successful for very long.

THE LATIN AMERICAN BOLIVARIAN REVOLUTION

You've probably seen in the newspapers and on television President Hugo Chávez of Venezuela talking about his quest to create a "Bolivarian Revolution" throughout Latin America. President Chávez was famously quoted in his speech to the UN General Assembly in September 2006 as calling former U.S. president George Bush the "devil" and saying that the United States is trying to spread its "imperialism" around the world to "dominate it."[39] While not completely Marxist in his approach, President Chávez is leading a new leftist movement in Latin America called Bolivarian Socialism. This type of socialism is not founded on the ideas of Karl Marx, but rather on the beliefs of Simón Bolívar, known as the "liberator" of South America.

The Bolivarian Alliance for the Americas (ALBA)

Simón Bolívar led the decolonization movement of northern South American countries against Spain in the early 1800s. Bolivar promoted the concept of pan-South American unification against the domination of global imperialism, which in this case was the Spanish Empire and their history of conquistadores that landed in South America beginning in 1522 in Peru.[40] The current Bolivarian Revolution led by President

Figure 6.6. President Hugo Chavez of the Bolivarian Republic of Venezuela
Courtesy of José Cruz of the Agência Brasil.

Chávez of Venezuela is meant to counter the unification of the Americas under the U.S. free-trade agreement called Free Trade of the Americas. Chávez argues that Latin America needs to counter U.S. imperialism, which he likens to Spanish imperialism of the 1500s–1800s. In that effort, Chávez formed the Bolivarian Alliance for the Americas (ALBA) in 2004 with partner Fidel Castro of Cuba.[41] By 2009, eight countries had joined, including neighbors Ecuador and Bolivia. Rather than trade liberalization (see our discussion of economic liberalism earlier in this chapter), the goal of ALBA countries is economic regional integration based on mutual support and social welfare *without* free-trade agreements with the United States.

Socialism of the Twenty-first Century?

During the summer of 2010, ALBA countries met in Otavalo, Ecuador, to develop their common currency program, called the sucre. While the sucre is not yet widely used among ALBA nations, Ecuador and Venezuela made its first common transaction as a symbol of its potential during the meetings. Meanwhile, indigenous populations from ALBA countries protested outside the meetings against what they called a "false socialism" of the twenty-first century that did nothing to protect the rights of native peoples and the environment. ALBA countries Bolivia, Ecuador, and Venezuela were ranked by Freedom House as "partly free" societies, whereas their neighbors Peru, Brazil, Chile, and Argentina, for example, ranked as "free" societies. Critics of the Bolivarian Revolution argue that it is a new form of dictatorship under the guise of social justice. In each of the ALBA member countries, the presidents changed the constitutions to permit their reelection and have created legislation to nationalize natural resources, such as oil and natural gas. The end result of enhanced democracy and freedom so far remains out of reach for the majority within the Bolivarian socialist nations. Still, the cry from the poor of Latin America for a new type of governance based on social justice and equality remains strong, which places Latin America in a camp of new types of post-Marxist socialism for the twenty-first century.

6. The Wrap: What Have We Learned?

If you've understood this chapter correctly, you should have a historical sense of where capitalism comes from, and why the words we use to describe economic systems are often confused and inconsistent. You should also understand how words such as "liberal" and "conservative" have mutated in meaning over time. Are you clear on how these words are used today by Western Europeans and North Americas? Are you also clear on why—like some wines—ideological terminology doesn't travel very well?

Neither Marxist nor wholeheartedly capitalist in orientation, the governments of many Western European countries are commonly called "social democratic." A social democrat is philosophically uncomfortable with extremes of wealth and poverty, and these governments, most of them European, will collect higher taxes to provide a broad range of social services with the goal of eliminating poverty. In terms of the conflict between rich and poor, they rely upon the rich to provide the resources, but tilt toward the poor in resolving disputes. You should have a basic sense of how these systems have tempered pure capitalism with elaborate welfare systems, government regulation of commercial activity, and some level of public ownership of resources.

It can be argued that Marxist societies never actually functioned the way Marx intended. In theory, they were supposed to side with the poor against the rich. Having seized control of what Marx liked to call the means of production, however, Marxist leaders tended to use this wealth in ways that did not greatly benefit the people in whose behalf the revolution had been staged. There aren't very many of them left, but—thanks to China—Karl Marx is still important for about one-fifth of the world's population. Are you clear on why a very unfree China is Marxism with a capitalist twist?

And just to prove that nothing fits very neatly into political categories, we took a brief look at anti-American, pro-socialist politics in Latin America, symbolized by the controversial figure of Hugo Chavez.

While the world cannot be divided very neatly between democracies and dictatorships, we made the case above that there are some societies with significant levels of personal, political, and economic freedom. Clearly, freedom involves conflict; where does your freedom begin and mine end? If we examine freer societies carefully, we find that they typically manage to sustain freedom because they have developed ways of arbitrating conflict without violence. These techniques go all the way from mental habits (a tendency to see another point of view and compromise) to formal decision-making structures such as courts and police forces and elections. In chapter 7, we will look at a variety of successful political structures that modern democracies have evolved to settle or moderate the kind of conflict that flows out of freedom.

Less-free societies tend to deny human freedom (personal, political, and economic) for a variety of reasons. Sometimes they have areas of conflict so monumental that no system of elections and courts could arbitrate between contending power seekers. Sometimes, they have been unable to evolve or create the governmental and civic structures necessary to sustain a democracy. We'll have a better look at the range of unfree societies in chapter 8.

Notes

1. The key writings of this important thinker have been collected in Isaiah Berlin, *Liberty: Incorporating Four Essays on Liberty*, 2nd ed. (New York: Oxford University Press, 2002). Berlin liked to distinguish between "negative freedom," the immunity from governmental interference in your life, and "positive freedom," the creative ability to have what you want out of life. He worried that the freedom of the powerful sometimes limited the freedom of the weak.

2. Francis Fukuyama, *The End of History and the Last Man* (New York: Free Press, 2006). Fukuyama was originally regarded as a purely neo-conservative political thinker, but his recent work has become increasingly flexible and interestingly hard to categorize.

3. Robert D. Kaplan, "Was Democracy Just a Moment?" *The Atlantic Monthly*, December 1997, 55–80.

4. The United Nations Development Programme, *Arab Human Development Report* (New York: The United Nations, 2009). The United Nations Development Programme (or UNDP) is an active global UN agency that works to assist in economic development, particularly in the poorer portions of the world. It also produces some of the best statistical information available.

5. Many scholars have been influenced by Hannah Arendt's *The Origins of Totalitarianism* (New York: Meridian Books, 1958). Students of the subject have been excited by the thoughtful, if occasionally iconoclastic, views expressed by Michael Ignatieff in his 2001 *Human Rights as Politics and Idolatry* (Princeton: Princeton University Press, 2001). International legal expert Richard A. Falk's *Human Rights Horizons: The Pursuit of Justice in a Globalizing World* (New York: Routledge, 2000) is an excellent resource.

6. While occasionally controversial, Freedom House has become the point-of-reference source for assessments of human liberty around the world, and its annual *Freedom House Annual Report* always receives commentary in the press. You can find them at www.freedomhouse.org.

7. The U.S. State Department can be a source of interesting and usually reliable information. For this interesting and informative set of documents, visit www.state.gov/g/drl/rls/hrrpt/.

8. Amnesty is now opposing the death penalty worldwide and criticizes the United States for American penal policy. Once again, Amnesty International's main site is at www.amnesty.org. More liberal than is Freedom House, Human Rights Watch is an interesting organization with representatives in global trouble spots and in-depth publications on specific issues. Check it out at www.hrw.org/home.

9. Find the text of these documents at http://www.archives.gov/exhibits/featured_documents/.

10. After World War II, Europeans established an organization called The Council of Europe, which in turn created a multilateral treaty called The European Convention on Human Rights (or ECHR), initially signed in 1950, with five "protocols" (or amendments) in the 1960s. The Council of Europe (which is not part of the European Union) contains almost all of Europe's countries from Iceland to Russia, and maintains a very active tribunal in the French city of Strasbourg called the European Court of Human Rights. This treaty and this court have been of enormous importance in defining the forward edge of human-rights thinking, well beyond the shores of Europe. For an idea of the activities carried out by the court under the convention, see www.echr.coe.int/ECHR/homepage_en.

11. The text of this important document can be found at http://www.un.org/en/documents/udhr/index.shtml.

12. In his *The Responsibility to Protect: Ending Mass Atrocity Crimes Once and for All* (Washington, D.C.: Brookings, 2009) Gareth Evans makes a well researched but passionate plea for the protection of helpless civilian populations menaced by repressive governments. A more scholarly defense of the same principle can be found in Alex J. Bellamy, *Responsibility to Protect* (New York: Polity, 2009).

13. For the International Coalition on the Responsibility to Protect, see www.responsibilitytoprotect.org/.

14. The Fourth World Conference on Women, Beijing, China, September 1995 is still controversial. For the background, see www.un.org/womenwatch/daw/beijing/platform/.

15. For the UN's own verdict on this important conference, see United Nations, *From Beijing to Beijing + 5* (New York: United Nations, 2001).

16. See Edward S Greenberg and Benjamin I. Page, *The Struggle for Democracy*, 5th ed. (New York: Longman, 2001), 467.

17. If the word "ideology" means absolutely nothing to you, better start at the beginning with Terry Eagleton, *Ideology: An Introduction* (New York, Verso, 2007).

18. See a fairly technical study by Nolan McCarty, Keith T. Poole, and Howard Rosenthal, *Polarized America: The Dance of Ideology and Unequal Riche* (Cambridge, Mass.: MIT Press, 2008).

19. The easiest way to start is Michael Freeden's *Ideology: A Very Short Introduction* (New York: Oxford University Press, 2003). As a somewhat more general introduction to the beginning student, I like Leon P. Baradat's *Political Ideologies: Their Origin and Impact*, 8th ed. (Upper Saddle River, N.J.: Prentice Hall, 2003). Also worth a look is David Hawkes' *Ideology* (London: Routledge, 2003). For students looking for the deep end of the pool, there is a more advanced book by two formidable scholars called *Political Ideologies and the Democratic Ideal*, 5th ed., by Terence Ball and Richard Dagger (New York: Longman, 2003). Two important 2006 books from New Haven's Yale University Press describe the left and right in American politics; see Francis Fukuyama, *America at the Crossroads: Democracy, Power, and the Neo-conservative Legacy* and then look at Michael Walzer's *Politics and Passion: Toward a More Egalitarian Liberalism* (New Haven, Conn.: Yale University Press, 2006).

20. Jean Jacques Rousseau, *The Social Contract*, trans. G. D. H. Cole (New York: Dover, 1993/1762).

21. Adam Smith, *The Wealth of Nations* (New York: Simon & Brown, 2011).

22. Edmund Burke, *Reflections on the Revolution in France* (New York: Dover, 2006).

23. For an older book that is still very clear, see Charles Funderburk and Robert G. Thobaben, *Political Ideologies: Left, Center, Right* (New York: Harper & Row, 1989), 123–25.

24. To make British politics just a little more confusing, the Labour Party appeared in 1900, assuming a social democratic position to the "left" of the Liberal Party and taking away much of its support. Ironically, the current British government is an uncomfortable Conservative-Liberal coalition bringing these two ancient enemies together, with the Labour Party forming the opposition.

25. In 2012, Australia was led by its Labor Party, which is well within the social democratic tradition. The prime minister is a fiery woman named Julia Gillard. Her opposition comes from a two-party coalition: the Liberal Party is a moderate center-right party, and it is flanked by the National Party, which tends to represent farming interests and is a little further to the ideological right.

26. Stanley Wolpert, *A New History of India*, 6th ed. (New York: Oxford University Press, 2000), 456.

27. Arundhati Roy is a prolific author. After *The God of Small Things* (New York & London: HarperCollins, 1997) made her famous, she churned out a series of angry but well-written books on social policy. *The Cost of Living* (New York: Modern Library, 1989) irritated Indian nationalists. *Field Notes on Democracy: Listening to Grasshoppers* (New York: Haymarket, 2009) and *Walking with the Comrades* (New York: Penguin, 2011) are both recent critical works. Sumit Ganguly and Rahul Mukherji have prepared a superb recent history of their country in *India since 1980* (Cambridge, UK: Cambridge University Press, 2011).

28. Here's a good source for anything dealing with Latin American history: James D. Henderson et al., *A Reference Guide to Latin American History* (Armonk, N.Y.: Sharpe, 2000), 238–44.

29. For a good wrap-up on El Salvador today, see Diana Villiers Negroponte, *Seeking Peace in El Salvador: The Struggle to Reconstruct a Nation at the End of the Cold War* (New York: Palgrave Macmillan, 2012).

30. John Stuart Mill, *Principles of Political Economy with Some of Their Applications to Social Philosophy* (London: J. W. Parker, 1848).

31. Jorge G. Castañeda, "Latin America's Left Turn," *Foreign Affairs* 85, no. 3 (2006): 28–44.

32. Anthony Giddens (advisor to Prime Minister Tony Blair) has written a simple (although somewhat controversial) book called *The Third Way: The Renewal of Social Democracy* (Cambridge, UK: Polity, 1999). Henry Milner's *Sweden: Social Democracy in Practice* (New York: Oxford University Press, 1990) is elderly, but still a pure statement of what it means to be a European social democrat. Alexander M. Hicks has given us *Social Democracy and Welfare Capitalism: A Century of Income Security Politics* (Ithaca: Cornell University Press, 2000), which is a good historical review.

33. Dr. Paul Krugman is a Nobel Prize–winning economist who teaches at Princeton University and writes provocative columns for the *New York Times*. This quotation was taken from his essay "For Richer," which appeared in the *New York Times Magazine,* October 20, 2002, 62–142. While many of his books are intended for an academic audience versed in economics, *The Conscience of a Liberal* (New York: Norton, 2009) and *The Return of Depression Economics and the Crisis of 2008* (New York: Norton, 2009) are both clear and accessible.

34. Princeton's Dr. Peter Singer presents the man and his thought in *Marx: A Very Short Introduction* (New York: Oxford University Press, 2001).

35. University of California historian Peter Kenez has given us a readable review of Soviet history in his *A History of the Soviet Union from the Beginning to the End*, 2nd ed. (Cambridge, UK: Cambridge University Press, 2006).

36. If you want to zip painlessly through five thousand years of Chinese history, start with John Keay's *China: A History* (New York: Basic, 2011).

37. For more on Freedom House, consult www.freedomhouse.org.

38. This capitalist-communist combination is well analyzed by Carl Walter and Fraser Howie in their *Red Capitalism: The Fragile Financial Foundation of China's Extraordinary Rise* (New York: Wiley, 2011). Published online by the Beijing government in occasionally fallible English, *China Daily* (at www.Chinadaily.com.cn.net) is a good guide to events in China and reflects the views of the Communist Party as does the comprehensive *China Today* site at www.chinatoday.com.

39. It is hard to be objective about a polarizing figure such as Hugo Chavez, but professors Javier Corrales and Michael Penfold have done their best in *Dragon in the Tropics: Hugo Chavez and the Political Economy of Revolution in Venezuela* (Washington, D.C.: Brookings, 2010). You can watch President Chavez hugely enjoying himself as he irritated the most powerful man in the world: see www.youtube.com/watch?v=binMjEiS8AY.

40. Benjamin Keen, *Latin American Civilization*, 8th ed. (Boulder Colo.: Westview Press, 2004), 251–64.

41. For this alliance, check out: http://www.alianzabolivariana.org/.

CHAPTER 7

How Democracies Manage Freedom and Conflict

During her visit to Lewis Carroll's Wonderland, Alice spent so much time obeying unreasonable commands issued by a variety of red and white queens that she got into the habit of doing what she was told. "What am I to do?" she asked at one particularly perplexing moment.

"Whatever you like," said a friendly footman, reminding her and us that the essence of democracy is precisely that: the ability to do whatever you like.[1]

On this side of the looking glass, however, doing exactly what you feel like doing can sometimes land you in jail or at the wrong end of a hangman's rope. As we discovered in chapter 6, freedom inevitably creates conflict because your exercise of what you regard as your rights can translate into a limitation on my liberty. In a democratic society, a decision made by 50-plus percent (this can be as little as one vote more than 50 percent) of the population is usually binding on the rest of the population, and this can create unhappiness, lawsuits, and other, more violent forms of conflict.

Successful and established democracies, however, have been able to create structures to moderate or channel or defuse **political conflict** before it becomes violent. In this chapter, we will survey those basic governmental systems that have evolved in freer societies for the preservation of human liberty and the avoidance of violent political conflict over political disagreements. Beginning in chapter 6, we made the case that human freedom has three fundamental aspects, political freedom, personal freedom, and economic freedom. This chapter will focus on the first of these freedoms, investigating the variety of ways in which free citizens in democratic societies order their public affairs.

We should note that this chapter effectively begins our study of what is often called **comparative politics**, one of the principal branches of the field of political science. The result of comparative-politics studies is the structuring or ordering of the internal affairs of individual sovereign states. Comparative politics is normally covered in a course that parallels international relations and follows an introduction to world politics or global studies.[2]

- *How do you divide up the real power in society? By assigning it to local government? Or handing it all over to the national government and letting national leaders delegate authority downward as they see fit?* Every sovereign state in the world has an array of sub-sovereign political entities, what would be called municipalities, counties, and states in the United States. In section 1, we'll see that different societies have made very divergent decisions on this issue, choices with major political ramifications.

- *Why does the United States have a president, while the United Kingdom has a queen and a prime minister, and France has a president and a prime minister?* All three countries are free societies, but each country has made different decisions about the structuring of executive power. In section 2, we'll examine the parliamentary or prime-ministerial system and compare it to the presidential system practiced in the United States and elsewhere. The French have devised their own combination system, and we'll see why it has become increasingly popular on the world scene.

- *How do free societies choose their legislators and decide what is legal and what is not?* The standard way of settling a dispute in a free society is to make a law deciding the issue one way or the other. Depending upon choices made in structuring their executive system, free societies have a range of ancillary choices to make when it comes to electing lawmakers. If the law doesn't resolve the conflict, we need to turn to judges and juries. In section 3, we'll look at how legislatures are chosen, before moving on in section 4 to a preliminary glance at judges, supreme courts, and judicial systems.

- *How do societies combine all these structural ingredients to create a government that works?* Free countries with centuries of constitutional existence have evolved political structures that manage conflict successfully most of the time. More recent history has tumbled some very major societies into existence without much time to prepare; some have coped and others have not. In section 5, we'll look at how India, which became independent only in 1947, mixed and matched from among the available political structures to create a generally successful democratic society against very considerable odds.

1. Unitary and Federal Systems

Here's a simple question: who chooses the sixth-grade math textbook used in your local elementary school?

In France, the choice gets made by a committee of experts working for the Ministry of Education in Paris, and the education minister—a senior political figure who is a member of the French cabinet—can overrule them and make the final call. The advantages are obvious. France saves money by buying textbooks in bulk. Every junior mathematician in France is theoretically on the same page at the same time, which makes comparative evaluation of teachers and schools a lot easier. And French students are all headed for the same national examination, the *baccalaureate* (or *le bac*) which is their ticket to a government-run (and government-financed) university. If they're all going to take the same crucial test, it makes sense for them all to read the same book.

In the United States, picking out sixth-grade textbooks is usually a function of a locally elected school board, advised by a committee of teachers. Knowing their own community, these teachers can select a book that best suits their own local students, and the school board—elected by the parents of those students—can overrule them if there is a conflict. This system may not be very efficient, since algebra doesn't change much at the South Carolina–North Carolina border. The process is very democratic, however, since a community of parents and teachers is making a crucial choice about an issue affecting their own children. How do we know which procedure a given sovereign state is following? The usual starting place is its **constitution**.

CONSTITUTIONS AND POLITICAL STRUCTURES

Most (but not quite all) governments explain their internal functioning in a formal document called a constitution. Some constitutions, such as the American Constitution, are descriptive or functional in the sense that they are detailed and highly structured, providing a reasonable guide to the actual operation of the political system. Others are more normative in the sense that they portray an ideal society toward which the political leadership should strive.[3]

Most countries have a single-document constitution, that is, one hard-to-alter text that has been created in some special way to describe the allocation of power within that society. A few countries, such as Britain and Israel, have multi-document constitutions, which means that there are several different texts that, taken together, function as the country's constitution. The British are fond of proclaiming that their constitution is unwritten, meaning that much of it is based on tradition and custom, but these days even customs and traditions are written down, although not in one single document. Britain's constitution is remarkably fluid, however, and can be changed in some cases by a simple parliamentary decision.[4] Saudi Arabia doesn't actually have a constitution; the king makes decisions, and his government enforces them.[5] Ecuador's constitution is the first in the world that guarantees not only human rights but also rights to nature and a healthy environment as well.[6]

Phony Structures

Whether functional or normative, there is always some gap between what we might call the formal structures of government (what the constitution says ought to happen) and real structures (what actually takes place on a day-by-day basis). A good example comes to us from South America's Republic of Paraguay. In 1954, a military man with the distinctly un-Spanish name of Alfredo Stroessner took power in Asunción, establishing what was, for that time, a standard Latino dictatorship. Under pressure from the United States and international human rights groups, Stroessner gradually emphasized the formal structures of his government until his regime began to look (at least on paper) more and more like a democracy with regular elections, a supreme court, and civil liberties guaranteed by a constitution. Unfortunately, the elections were always fraudulent and all the senior officers of the state were cronies or relatives of the general. Paraguay had the formal structure (or superficial appearance) of a democracy but the real structure of a dictatorship. In 1989, Stroessner finally surrendered power the same way he acquired it: at the point of a gun.[7]

Dictatorships and democracies can both produce flowcharts or diagrams of their governments that look remarkably similar. Saddam Hussein's Iraq had a popularly elected parliament, an "independent" judiciary, and a directly elected president. On paper, it resembled a democratic system. What got left off the organizational chart, of course, were awkward facts like these: there was only one party allowed to run candidates; opposition leaders were tortured to death; and the entire media was controlled by Saddam and his closest colleagues. The real structure of the Iraqi government made it the direst of dictatorships, but the formal structure looked democratic, at least on paper. In order to distinguish between freer and less-free societies, we need to go well beyond what the constitution says, and investigate what actually happens on the ground.[8]

Generally speaking, most established democracies (the United States, Western European countries, Japan, etc.) make an effort to follow their own rules, so there shouldn't be a cavernous gap between their formal and real structures. Nearly all dictatorships and many Third- and Fourth-World countries tend to make up the rules as they play the game of politics, creating a big difference between their published formal structures and real structures in the real world.

National, Regional, and Local Governments

Every political system has a vertical or "up-and-down" way of distributing power. The United States, for example, has a **federal system**; the Washington government has certain assigned responsibilities, and the fifty state governments have other tasks reserved for them by the Constitution.[9] Finally, tens of thousands of local government authorities, such as counties and municipalities, have their own roles to play. Britain has a bewildering local-government system involving counties, unitary authorities, metropolitan districts, and separate systems for Scotland and Northern Ireland.[10] The Russian Federation's sub-sovereign system is even more complex, and every country in the world has some kind of hierarchy of national, regional, and local governments. Look at table 7.1 for clarification of the American system. With some variations from state to state, the three levels of government (federal, state, and local) all resemble one another, at least in having an executive of some kind, a legislature, and a judicial authority.[11]

The debate over where real authority needs to be ranges from great issues to small ones. Should the states have any say at all over foreign-policy decisions that affect them? How much input should state government have in elementary education, or should this be left to the counties? Do we need to get the federal government involved in certifying

Table 7.1.

Federal Executive: the president, cabinet, federal agencies and departments	**Federal Legislative:** U.S. Senate and House of Representatives	**Federal Judicial:** Supreme Court, federal district and appeals courts
↓	↓	↓
State Executive: the governor, cabinet, state agencies and departments, state police, educational system	**State Legislative:** state assemblies and legislatures	**State Judicial:** state supreme court and state circuit courts
↓	↓	↓
Local Executive: county executives, mayors, county and city police, primary- and secondary-school systems	**Local Legislative:** county and municipal councils	**Local Judicial:** county and city magistrate and traffic courts

kindergarten teachers? If the federal government demands that the states pursue some expensive course of action, should the federal government pay for it? Or do we want to try to make all relevant decisions about the conduct of public affairs in the village hall? If the citizens of an individual state really dislike abortion, should the federal government force them to accept it?

Every constitution makes decisions about how to allocate political power vertically, that is, how much authority to give the national leadership, how much to send to the province, region, or American state, and how much to keep downtown in city hall. These decisions are never quite final, and every country has a continuing debate over this division of power. In America, Republicans have traditionally supported giving or retaining power at the state level, while Democrats sometimes want to increase the responsibilities carried out by the federal government. Oddly enough, this debate is generally reversed in Europe, where parties on the left usually favor more local authority, while more conservative parties want to retain power at the national level.

FEDERAL AND UNITARY SYSTEMS IN ACTION

When it comes to organizing power vertically in a democracy, there are two basic styles, as illustrated in figure 7.1. Territorially large countries, such as Brazil, Mexico, and Australia, have usually opted for the federal system, especially if they were originally created out of a number of preexisting states, such as the United States, Canada, India, and Germany, which are also federal systems. Smaller countries, some of whom are nervous about their national cohesiveness, have tended to opt for the **unitary system**. What's the basic difference? At a practical level, citizens empower different echelons of government by voting for it and paying taxes to it.

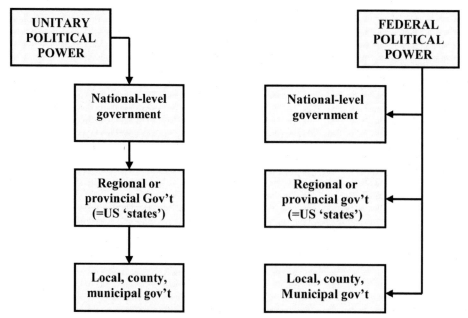

Figure 7.1.   Unitary and Federal Systems Compared

The Federal System

Americans have less difficulty in comprehending federal systems because they live in one of the more familiar examples. Americans pay taxes to the federal government in Washington, D.C., and elect presidents, vice presidents, members of Congress, and senators to represent them at that level. But the founders were nervous about too much power accumulating in Washington, so many responsibilities were reserved in the U.S. Constitution for the state governments, who also elect officials, collect taxes, and regulate most bread-and-butter issues in the United States. Below the state level, are counties and municipalities with their own elected officials and typically more-limited authority to make laws and raise taxes.

Germany is even more federal than is the United States; the German *"Länder"* have more authority in policing, education, and economic growth than American states do.[12] Canada is a very federal system, and so are Australia, India, Malaysia, and Brazil. About one-tenth of the world's sovereign states are federal, although this number includes most of the larger and more significant societies.

What's the Russian Republic? We will review this chaotic situation in chapter 8, but the Russian Republic has many important federal features written into its constitution. In practice, however, Russian leaders seem to have re-created some of the less-democratic features of the old Soviet Union in a highly centralized unitary system. Do you remember our comment about "phony structures"?

The Unitary System

In a unitary system, the central or national government holds most political power. Citizens pay most of their taxes to the national level of government in the country's capital city. This top layer of government will typically manage the police, the educational system, health, public transport, and other essential services. The national government will delegate very little authority to sub-sovereign (provincial, county, or municipal) governments; local leaders carry out national-level decisions, but do not make them.

With the exception of Germany and Switzerland, most European democracies have strong unitary features. During his years (1981–1995) as president of France, François Mitterrand succeeded in giving a little more power to the regions, but the unitary French still pay most of their taxes to the central administration in Paris, and most significant legislation is passed by the National Assembly in Paris.[13] Italy, Spain, Portugal, and the Scandinavian countries all fit roughly the same unitary model, although the Italians are flirting with federalism.

Once upon a time, it was customary to describe the United Kingdom as a classic example of a unitary system, but the Blair-Brown governments (1997–2010) made some interesting changes in the way the four provinces (England, Scotland, Wales, and Northern Ireland) of the UK relate to the center. Prior to Labour's return to power in 1997, the United Kingdom was still a very unitary society, and the four individual provinces had little or no self-government. The British cast their one really significant vote when they elected a member of parliament (MP) to represent their **constituency** (or voting district) in the British House of Commons.[14]

In 1997–1998, the Blair government announced a series of initiatives designed to make the United Kingdom government more federal as far as Northern Ireland, Scotland, and Wales are concerned. These three provinces together make up only about one-fifth of the population of the United Kingdom, so the difference is not as earthshaking as it seems. While there are important differences in the way these three provinces relate to the national government in London, all three of them are beginning to receive the kind of governing power that we would associate with an American state.[15] England itself, by far the largest portion of the United Kingdom, continues to be governed in a very unitary fashion from London, and the popularly elected county, district, and/or "metropolitan" governments have limited independent power.

2. Executive Systems: Presidential, Parliamentary, and Combination

It is crucially important that you understand a few basic concepts before venturing into the rest of this chapter. In every society where the people exercise popular sovereignty or political control over their government, there needs to be a system for organizing the central functions of the government (e.g., executive, legislative, and judicial) at each level of government. To be successful, this system needs to allocate power and responsibility so that the several branches of government will have clearly defined duties. The system must also create a mechanism for electing and/or choosing the principal officers of the state.

Over time, three basic governmental systems have emerged among the world's freer societies. The first is the **parliamentary system**, originally created in England. Second is the **presidential system**, pioneered by the United States and popular in the Western Hemisphere. And finally, we'll glance at France's successful effort to combine the best from the parliamentary and presidential systems into what is often called the **combination system**.

PARLIAMENTS AND PRIME MINISTERS

England gave the world the parliamentary system as part of the legacy of the British Empire. Sometimes called the "Westminster" system, it originated within the Palace of Westminster in London. It is the commonest of the three types, but it is also, in many respects, the most difficult for American students to understand because the fundamental logic of the system is different. The essence of the parliamentary system is an interdependence and mingling of the executive and the legislative.

It is tempting to start by noting how a parliamentary system differs from a U.S.-style presidential system.[16] Imagine a situation in which an indirectly elected U.S. president (or an American constitutional monarch) obediently signed bills (which he could question but not veto), entertained visiting dignitaries, and opened hospitals and bridges, but was normally forbidden to voice his own political views. Meanwhile, over in the House of Representatives, the majority party would select its leader to be the country's actual chief executive, allowing this indirectly elected figure to remain in office indefinitely as long as he or she maintained the support of the majority of Congress.

If this sounds confusing, let's start with the essentials. First, at the top of every parliamentary system there is a figure called the chief or head of state, who has largely ceremonial functions. We'll talk more about chiefs or heads of state below, but remember for the moment that this lofty but usually powerless personage is a constitutional monarch in some political systems (such as the UK and Spain) and an indirectly elected ceremonial president in others (such as Germany and Italy).

In a parliamentary system, actual executive functions are carried out by someone elected by the legislature from within its own ranks. This executive is usually called a prime minister, although the French word *premier* is sometimes used and the Germans call their prime minister the *Bundeskanzler* or chancellor.[17]

The Prime Minister as Chief Executive

How do you get to be prime minister? Before elections to the national legislature, each political party will typically choose a prime-minister designate, usually the party leader, who is preselected to become prime minister if that party wins a majority of the seats in the national legislature. The prime-minister designate is a normal member of parliament who first needs to be elected in his or her local constituency in the same way that congressmen are elected by voters in individual congressional districts. Mr. David Cameron serves simultaneously as prime minister (PM) of the United Kingdom and as the member of parliament (MP) for his home constituency, the city of Whitney in the county of Oxfordshire.[18]

Like other prime ministers in other parliamentary systems, British "PMs" stay in power as long as they command over 50 percent of the votes in Britain's parliament, and they leave Number Ten Downing Street the day they lose the support of the majority of their fellow MPs. In a couple of ways, the prime minister needs to demonstrate that his government commands that majority:

- First, the prime minister needs to survive no-confidence resolutions. At any time, any member of parliament may offer a resolution asserting that "This House has no confidence in Her Majesty's Government." A prime minister who loses a confidence vote must immediately resign.
- At a more practical level, the prime minister must consistently secure majorities for those bills that are major components of his legislative program. These are sometimes called **confidence bills**, and while there is sometimes disagreement over which bills deserve this qualification, any major finance bill is automatically a confidence bill that the prime minister must get through parliament in order to survive.

Because the same political party or **coalition** of parties automatically controls both the legislature and the executive, most bills are produced by the party in power, and most of them will pass; they have to pass, because if the government can't rally the votes it needs to pass its own key bills, then it can't go on being the government. While the American president has far more job security, he may not be able to get any legislation passed if a hostile party controls the legislature. After the November 1994 elections, for example, President Bill Clinton dealt with a Congress controlled by a Republican Party with a different political agenda. President Obama's Democratic Party lost control of the House of Representatives and enjoyed only a thin edge in the Senate. This situation would be impossible in a parliamentary system. If you can't control the legislature, you aren't prime minister any longer.

Anticipated Elections

In presidential systems, elections are normally held at rigidly specified intervals. In parliamentary systems, legislative elections are held when the government in power "calls" them. These are termed **anticipated elections**. Parliamentary systems all have laws requiring the government to renew its mandate periodically by holding an election (usually at least every four or five years, depending on the country). In common parliamentary practice, however, prime ministers are allowed to call elections ahead of the legal time limit in order to achieve certain political goals.[19]

In the British case, prime ministers typically call an election in their fourth year in office, about one year earlier than the law would otherwise demand. Prime ministers have sometimes been forced to call anticipated elections even earlier because they won office on very slender majorities and some of their supporters have died or defected, threatening them with the loss of that magic 50-plus percent (at least one vote more than 50 percent).

If a sitting prime minister can be chucked out of office by a simple act of the legislature, how stable can this system be? Some commentators have alleged that parliamentary systems are inherently less stable than are presidential systems, but the fact is that a political system will reflect the stability or fragility of a given political culture. Politically fragmented Italy has had several dozen governments since the fall of Mussolini, although many were merely cabinet reshuffles that moved the same politicians into different ministerial chairs.[20] During the same period and with roughly the same political system, however, Britain has had about thirteen different governments.

THE CEREMONIAL HEAD OF STATE IN A PARLIAMENTARY SYSTEM

Every political system is headed by a figure called a head of state or chief of state. In presidential systems, the head of state is the president, who combines ceremonial with real executive functions. In parliamentary systems, the head of state is a mostly ceremonial figure who—under normal circumstances—has little or no executive power. Depending upon the political traditions of the country in question, the head of state may be either an indirectly elected ceremonial president, or conversely, a hereditary constitutional monarch. In terms of day-to-day political practice, there isn't actually much difference between the two, at least under normal circumstances.

Constitutional Monarchs

Let's start by focusing on royalty. First of all, we are not talking here about those few monarchs who still exercise real political power, such as Jordan's King Abdullah II or King Abdullah (no relation) of Saudi Arabia. These governments are called **royal executive regimes**, and we'll discuss them in chapter 8. In most European countries and a few Pacific nations, the royals reign but do not rule. Monarchs who have lost their executive power but still have a ceremonial role are called **constitutional monarchs**, and table 7.2 will help

Table 7.2.   The World's Surviving Constitutional Monarchies

Belgium: King Albert II	Japan: Emperor Akihito
Denmark: Queen Margrethe II	Liechtenstein: Prince Hans-Adam II
Luxembourg: Grand Duke Henri	Malaysia: Sultan Mizan Zainal Abidin
Monaco: Prince Albert Grimaldi	Netherlands: Queen Beatrix
Norway: Harald V	Spain: King Juan Carlos
Sweden: King Carl XVI Gustaf	Thailand: King Bhumibol Adulyadej
Tonga: King George Tupou V	United Kingdom: Queen Elizabeth II
Cambodia: Prince Norodom Sihamoni	

Note: Fourteen members of the Commonwealth of Nations continue to regard Queen Elizabeth II as their chief of state, although the queen is represented by a locally appointed figure called the governor general. Malaysia has a kind of rotating constitutional monarchy. Thailand's elderly King Bhumibol Adulyadej was seriously ill in 2012.

you tell who is who. As you can see, there are many sovereign states that still have clear-cut constitutional monarchs; most of these countries are quite stable and democratic.

The continued existence of hereditary nobility in the twenty-first century is a political oddity. Over the course of the last few hundred years, some wise monarchs realized that they could only survive by changing with the times and surrendering real power gracefully. Sovereigns who failed to master the democratic process were normally dismissed by their countries, typically after some historical disappointment. Germany ditched the kaiser after losing World War I, and the Italians divorced the House of Savoy after the disasters of World War II.

Ceremonial Presidents

Countries such as Germany and Italy still wanted a parliamentary system of government, which means having a nonexecutive head of state, so they organized indirect elections for "civilian" ceremonial presidents to perform those largely ceremonial functions. The president in a parliamentary system is a respected senior politician who is prepared to disengage from ordinary political life to accept a lofty but sometimes relatively powerless position as the chief ceremonial officer of the country. These ceremonial presidents are always indirectly elected, sometimes by the parliament and sometimes by a special electoral college.

Chief of State Functions

What do these chiefs/heads of state (constitutional monarchs or indirectly elected ceremonial presidents) actually do? Their functions fall into three broad and overlapping categories: the ceremonial function, the continuity function, and the referee function.

- The Ceremonial Function: As ceremonial figures, heads of state represent the grandeur and dignity of the state, turning up at symbolically important events such as the laying of cornerstones and the opening of schools and bridges. Britain's prime minister has better things to do with his time than snipping red ribbons at new hospitals and supermarkets; this is a job for the "royals" (the queen or some member of her numerous family). The importance of this ceremonial function should not be underestimated. In times of political instability with prime ministers resigning or losing the confidence of the legislature, the public can be reassured by the familiar figure of a well-known and trusted head of state.[21]

- The Continuity Function: A ceremonial head of state can assume serious political power in the event of a breakdown in normal constitutional government. When David Cameron emerged from the 2010 British general elections, his Conservative Party had more votes than did any other party, a **plurality** but not a majority. The Conservatives and the Liberal Democrats were able to assemble a coalition government with more than the needed 50-plus percent of the seats (a majority) in the House of Commons, so the queen was spared making a real decision. Had the parties been unable to agree on a majority government, however, the queen technically would have been able to select someone (probably David Cameron) to lead a minority government until new elections could be called. In other parliamentary systems (Italy is a good example), no single party ever wins a clear majority of the seats in the legislature. If—after a significant period of negotiation—these minority parties are unable to agree on a prime minister, we call the result a "**hung parliament**." Exercising the continuity function, the head of state will usually appoint a nonpartisan figure to serve as prime minister until new elections can be called. In 2011, Italy turned to a respected economist and "technocrat" named Mario Monti to serve as prime minister until the country could be rescued from its financial woes.

- The Referee Function: As referees of the political process, heads of state are supposed to ensure that the elected politicians play by the rules, watching that laws are passed according to constitutional procedures. They have the right to be consulted about important issues and to give whatever advice they see fit.

The Men from F.A.R.T.

While ceremonial chiefs of state normally cannot refuse to sign legislation, they do usually have the right to ask the lawmakers to think again. Just before the breakup of the Czechoslovakian state, for example, then president Václav Havel received for his signature a bill creating a new Czechoslovakian news agency. According to the proposed law, Czechoslovakia's answer to the BBC would be the Federal Association for Radio and Television. As a ceremonial president, Havel used both his knowledge of English and his powers as referee of the Czechoslovakian political system to inform the legislature that in the English-speaking world, Czechoslovakian journalism would be known as F.A.R.T. Gratefully, the lawmakers agreed to rethink their gaseous nomenclature.

Sadly, Havel's personal history as a dissident playwright, a pro-democracy activist during the Soviet era, and a skillful political leader couldn't keep his country united. On January 1, 1993, the Czech Republic and Slovakia became two separate states in a dissolution so friendly it was called the "Velvet Divorce." Although ill, Havel went on to become the ceremonial president of the Czech Republic, which is Czechoslovakia without Slovakia, and in 1999 helped bring this democratic central European country into NATO and the European Union. Retiring from politics, he stepped down in 2003 after an extraordinary career. When he died in 2011, there was a genuine wave of sadness around the world, and leaders from all major countries came to pay their respects at his funeral.

Many former British colonies have retained Britain's parliamentary system. In some of these former colonies, the figure who would normally be a ceremonial president is called the "governor general." Today, these governors general are appointed by the governments of these now-totally-sovereign countries, but to preserve the romance and mystique of what was once the British Empire, the names of perspective governors general are submitted to Queen Elizabeth II in London, who formally "appoints" them as her representatives. In the days of the real British Empire, these governors general were the real representatives of an imperial British government, but nowadays, they are merely ceremonial presidents under a different name, performing all the functions discussed above. Canada, Australia, and New Zealand, for example, are all parliamentary systems where the ceremonial president is called a "governor general."[22]

THE PRESIDENTIAL SYSTEM

For much of human history, the British model of government was the gold standard for emerging democracies. At the end of the 1700s, those insolent colonials in North America not only challenged the might of the British Empire but also designed their own form of government, creating a strong presidency and a dramatic separation of executive and legislative powers. This presidential system became popular in the Americas generally and has spread to countries such as South Africa, Indonesia, and Nigeria.

Every American schoolchild learns how the U.S. government is divided into legislative, executive, and judicial branches, reflecting what are held to be the three primary tasks of all governments: rule creation, rule enforcement, and rule adjudication. In fact, all governments make, enforce, and adjudicate laws, but the division of responsibilities is seldom as clear or as neat as it seems to be in the United States, and the institutions responsible for these several functions are rarely as independent of one another as they are in Washington.

How Presidential Systems Work

In presidential systems, chief executives combine ceremonial and political duties without making a clear distinction between the two. For example, on a given day, the president of

---

Montesquieu's *Spirit of the Laws*

While France itself has never had a purely presidential system, some of the basic thinking behind the concept came from a noble Frenchman, Baron Charles Louis Montesquieu (1689–1755), who lived and wrote under the despotic Bourbon kings in the century before the French Revolution. His 1748 *Spirit of the Laws* (Cambridge, UK: Cambridge University Press, 1989) is an early work of comparative politics in which Montesquieu made the then-revolutionary case that societies would function better and more freely if the executive, legislative, and judicial powers of the government were in separate and independent hands. Montesquieu's thinking was adapted to the American experience by James Madison, who wrote the separation of powers concept into the American Constitution. As a result, what we are here calling the presidential system is labeled by some authors (perhaps more correctly) the "separation-of-powers" system.

Mexico might receive the credentials of the new ambassador from North Africa's Burkina Faso. With a stack of more pressing problems on his desk, El Señor Presidente might have no real business to conduct with the newest member of the Mexico City diplomatic corps. After handshakes and best wishes, a purely ceremonial meeting would conclude with a photo opportunity. Next in the door with credentials to present, however, might be the new diplomatic envoy from Spain, whose government might wish to offer a new level of cultural and economic interaction between the two Spanish-speaking countries. After the ceremonial presentation of letters of introduction, the president and the Spanish ambassador might sit down over coffee to do some serious executive business.

The presidential system predominates in the Western Hemisphere with only a few exceptions. Canada and some of the Caribbean island states follow the parliamentary system. Peru and Haiti both practice modified forms of the combination system to be described below. Otherwise, most of the big countries south of the Rio Grande and many of the little ones have a politically powerful president who is elected separately from the legislature and independent of it.[23]

There are a relatively small number of presidential systems outside the Western Hemisphere, and most former colonies have retained their inherited parliamentary systems. In Africa, however, Nigeria, Sierra Leone, Zimbabwe, Uganda, and South Africa all have fairly standard presidential systems, although only South Africa and Liberia are established democracies. In the Pacific, Indonesia and the Philippine Islands are presidential.

How Executive Presidents Are Elected

The United States may have been largely responsible for creating the presidential system, but the rest of the world has not imitated the antique American Electoral College as a system for choosing the chief executive. All in all, there are two systems:

- Semi-Direct Systems: Alexander Hamilton put little trust in the wisdom of the American people and created this anomaly in the American Constitution to create some distance between the voters and their choice of a chief executive. The idea never did function the way Hamilton envisioned, and no other democracy uses this odd system. The United States is divided into 538 Electoral College districts. When voters in each of these districts choose a presidential candidate, they are actually voting for an elector who has pledged to support that candidate. Within forty-eight of the fifty states, winner-take-all systems give all the state's Electoral College votes to the candidate who got the majority.[24]

  Hamilton's mistrust of the people has spread to a few presidential systems where executive presidents are chosen by parliament. The key difference between using parliament to elect the president and using a special electoral college is that the American Electoral College has no other function and disappears after the election, whereas the parliament remains in existence to carry out its normal legislative functions. South Africa's executive president, for example, is indirectly elected by the South African Parliament. This does ensure that the president and the parliament belong to the same political party, but it doesn't keep them from feuding.[25]
- Direct Elections: For the most part, presidential systems elect their presidents by means of a direct popular vote. Anyone who wants to be president gets nominated by a politi-

cal party, and then faces an initial vote to narrow the field down to the two most popular candidates. If one candidate scores more than 50 percent of the vote, the election is over. If not, the top two finalists face each other in a runoff election so that the victor automatically has a majority. This procedure is called the **double-ballot** system. While the precise procedure varies somewhat from country to country, nearly all presidential systems (outside the United States and South Africa) use some direct one-person, one-vote election system for the presidency.[26]

Brazil offers a good example of a functioning presidential system. In some ways, the Brazilian presidency is stronger than the American model, since the president is empowered in certain cases to hand down emergency decrees that have the force of law. In addition, the constitution grants to its president most of the same powers exercised by the American president: he commands the armed forces, conducts foreign affairs, and formulates general public policy for the country. In both systems, the president is limited to two four-year terms.

Elections to the Brazilian presidency, however, are conducted with a double-ballot system that is almost universal in presidential systems outside the United States. In the first stage, a large number of presidential candidates representing Brazil's many political parties will throw their hats in the ring. When the two top contenders have been identified in the first vote (and assuming nobody got an absolute majority the first time around), there is a second runoff election to choose between the two finalists.[27]

The favorable result of this system is that in the final election, the system forces the electorate to choose between two candidates, and the winner is the one with the largest number of direct popular votes. Every vote counts as much as every other vote.

Change the electoral system and you change the result. In the 2000 American presidential election, Mr. Al Gore won more actual votes (the so-called popular vote) than did Mr. Bush, but lost the presidential election in the Electoral College. This is partly because there were more than two candidates in the election, and Mr. Ralph Nader subtracted just enough votes from Mr. Gore to let Mr. Bush win a few key states such as Florida. Had the 2000 election been run under Brazil's double-ballot system, Mr. Nader would have been eliminated in the first round, after which his supporters would have shifted their support to Mr. Gore, who would have won the election. Election systems can seem boring and complicated, but they make a big difference.

COMBINATION SYSTEMS: THE FRENCH DO IT DIFFERENTLY

If you want to understand what is happening in France, Lebanon, Haiti, Peru, and Russia these days, you need to know that there is one more kind of political system in the world. This increasingly popular French invention is actually a compromise between the presidential and the parliamentary systems discussed above.

In 1958, France's World War II hero, General Charles De Gaulle, returned to power believing that France's parliamentary system was too weak to contend with the challenges the country was then facing. Determined to make a radical change, he wrote a new constitution for what subsequently became the French Fifth Republic. No one has ever managed to invent a universally accepted name for De Gaulle's creation. Some authors call it "semi-presidential" or "premier-presidential" or the equally unimaginative "presidential-parliamentary," or "hybrid." Recognizing the French role in popularizing the system, some refer to it as the "Fifth Republic" system. The French number major changes in their governing system, and De Gaulle's restructuring in 1958 was called the "Fifth Republic." The most commonly used term is "combination system."

How the Combination System Works

Whatever you call it, the essence of the system is simple. As you can see in figure 7.2, France has a directly elected executive president, who serves for one or more five-year terms (reduced in 2002 from seven years). In spring 2007, the French elected Nicholas Sarkozy, and under the DeGaulle constitution, President Sarkozy played the leading role in foreign policy, commanded the armed forces, and presided over meetings of the cabinet. We learned above that most executive presidents around the world are elected with a direct popular vote with the double-ballot system; precisely the same system is used in France and other combination systems. President Sarkozy's five-year term expired in spring 2012 when he lost the presidency to Jacques Hollande, the popular leader of the French Socialist Party.[28]

Subordinate to this powerful president, however, there is a relatively powerful premier or prime minister, who coordinates the work of the cabinet and actually runs the government on a day-to-day basis. The French prime minister needs to have the confidence of the French National Assembly, but is never a member of the legislature.

This combination system is becoming increasingly popular with many of the fledgling democracies of Eastern Europe. The system makes it possible to divide executive

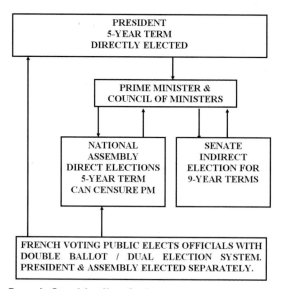

Figure 7.2. The French Combination System
Dividing responsibility between a president and a prime minister works smoothly when the duo are members of the same party and less well when the two senior officers of the French state come from different political traditions.

power between a strong president who expresses the unity of the country and a prime minister who makes the machinery of government work. While the modern Russian government is far from a functioning democracy, it is technically a combination system. At the start of 2012, Dmitry Medvedev was president and Vladimir Putin was his prime minister. Despite ongoing discontent with this semi-dictatorship, the Russians staged a presidential election in 2012, after which Putin returned to the president's office and reappointed Medvedev to his old job in the prime minister's office. The exact power relationship between these two close political allies is a matter for argument, but—at least on paper—it's a Slavic version of the French system.[29]

Belarus, Ukraine, Georgia, and Kazakhstan all have variants of the French system, and several other former Soviet republics are evolving in the same direction. In the Western Hemisphere, Peru and Haiti are the only prominent examples. The Chinese government is technically a parliamentary system, but since the "ceremonial" president is also the powerful general secretary of the Chinese Communist Party, China functions essentially as a combination system, with a dominant president/general secretary figure and a subordinate but still-influential prime minister.

SUMMING UP THE THREE SYSTEMS

We have described three different governmental structures, that is, ways of separating or combining powers in government. Table 7.3 should help identify them. All are popular in freer societies, and each has some specific advantages and disadvantages. Here are some factors to consider.

- The Parliamentary System: This system has been used all over the world for several centuries now, and it is an extremely well-understood system, although Americans sometimes have difficulty in seeing the underlying logic. The constitutional monarch

Table 7.3. Presidential, Parliamentary, and Combination Systems

Presidential (U.S. style)	Parliamentary (UK style)	Combination (French style)
Argentina	Australia	Algeria
Bolivia	Austria	Croatia
Brazil	Bangladesh	Egypt
Chile	Belgium	France
Colombia	Canada	Haiti
El Salvador	Estonia	Kenya
Ecuador	Germany	Lebanon
Indonesia	India	Peru
Mexico	Italy	Portugal
Philippines	Japan	Russia
Sierra Leone	Turkey	Sri Lanka

Oddities: Bosnia and Switzerland have collective presidencies, in both cases to accommodate the multinational character of their societies. The Islamic Republic of Iran is a presidential system on paper, but functions more like a combination system in practice, with the "Supreme Leader" carrying out the duties normally associated with the presidency, while the "president" is really more of a prime minister.

or ceremonial president provides a symbol-of-national-unity figure upon whom popular feelings of loyalty and patriotism can be focused. With ceremonial duties mostly handled by someone else, the prime minister/chief executive can get on with the sometimes squalid business of making political decisions. Citizens who decide they hate their prime minister are not forced emotionally into the uncomfortable position of hating the symbol of national unity. If the head of state is well liked and respected, this ceremonial president or constitutional monarch can provide reassurance during periods of political instability. And, at the simple practical level, it's a time-saver to divide up the chores, since executive presidents have to subtract energy from running their countries to attend banquets and make ceremonial speeches.

- The Presidential (or Separation of Powers) System: This system typically provides stability to a country. If there is a crisis and if the people are united behind the president, this can be a powerful system; think of President Franklin Roosevelt after Pearl Harbor. On the other hand, in a society with a democracy deficit problem, the presidential system can sometimes provide a little too much stability, giving the president so much political horsepower that he becomes a dictator. While they are now gingerly experimenting with democracy, Nigeria's and Indonesia's presidential systems have passed through lengthy periods of authoritarian rule, and many of Africa's presidents are dictators who rig elections and repress dissent ruthlessly.

- The Combination System: This system is the flavor of the decade for countries changing their political structures, and new countries, and old countries with new governments, are experimenting with this flexible hybrid. The combination system allows the president to concentrate on survival issues such as defense and foreign affairs, while the prime minister gets on with the mundane job of collecting taxes and distributing the mail. Maybe the burden of running a modern sovereign state is too big for one person.

  Occasionally a country teetering on the edge of a civil war will try to compromise between two would-be presidents by creating a combination system. Both Kenya and Zimbabwe have attempted this compromise by moving the president's principal rival into office as a prime minister. While civil war has been avoided (for the time being) in both cases, neither country can claim much success from the new system. The combination system works best when it's a real combination, with a strong national leader working in tandem with a skilled technocrat, both of whom come from the same political tradition.

How can you tell these three systems apart? It's not always easy, but here are some clues. If there is a president but no prime minister, then the system is clearly presidential. A constitutional monarch and a prime minister always indicate a parliamentary system, but you need to make sure that monarch is really constitutional. If the king is still giving orders (e.g., Jordan, Morocco, etc.), then the country is neither a true democracy nor a real parliamentary system. We'll discuss these royal executive regimes in the next chapter.

Difficulty arises when you find both a president and a prime minister, since this could be either a parliamentary system with a ceremonial president, or a combination system. One usually reliable way of telling them apart is to look at the election system; ceremonial presidents are almost always indirectly elected, while executive presidents in combination systems are usually the result of direct popular voting. An almanac will contain a brief description of the political life of the country in which you are interested;

if the prime minister seems to be making all the decisions, then you are dealing with a parliamentary system and a ceremonial president. To be sure, you may need to know more about the constitutional structure of the country in question.

Combining Structures

Here's a point that confuses many beginning students of world politics: there is no necessary connection between the vertical dimension (i.e., the federal—unitary distinction) and the horizontal dimension (presidential, parliamentary, or combination). This means that a given government may choose between federal and unitary, and then choose again when it comes to selecting an executive structure. We'll see this more clearly when we look at India, below, but perhaps figure 7.3. will make the concept a little clearer.

3. Legislative Systems

Conflict in society sometimes arises from our objections to the way in which someone is behaving, and one way to resolve this kind of dispute is to enact legislation either legalizing or criminalizing the behavior in question. To accomplish this goal, all democracies have legislatures or lawmaking bodies of some kind. As we will see below, the role this legislature plays in a given political system depends to a large extent on whether we are dealing with a presidential, parliamentary, or combination system.

Furthermore, the system we use to elect delegates to the legislature is also crucial in determining which political parties will prevail in promoting specific public policies. Below we'll look at several election systems, and see why the choice of a system can be so crucial.

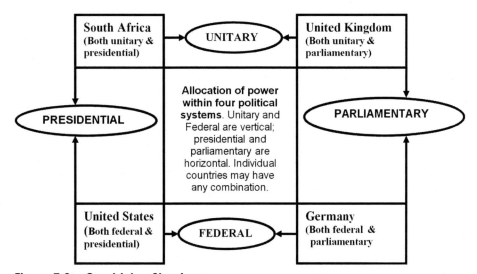

Figure 7.3. Combining Structures
It's a little like ordering by the numbers in a Chinese restaurant. You can build a government by choosing vertical and horizontal structures from separate governmental styles.

LAWMAKERS AND ELECTORAL SYSTEMS

The role a legislature plays in a democratic political system depends largely on the kind of executive branch with which it needs to work. In presidential systems, most laws are formulated by the legislature, and powerful lawmakers can challenge or modify the president's conduct of public affairs. Over time, Americans (perversely or wisely) have tended to elect presidents from one political party and legislators from the other, sometimes compounding the confusion by putting Republicans in charge of the House of Representatives and Democrats in control of the Senate. This practice occasionally results in **gridlock** with the two branches of government effectively blocking each other. In most presidential systems, the chief executive tends to be supreme in defense and foreign policy, while congresses and legislatures control domestic policy and financial affairs.

Parliaments and Power

As we have seen above, the situation is altogether different in a parliamentary system. Prime Minister Stephen Harper (elected 2006) is a member of the Canadian House of Commons and serves as his country's chief executive uniquely because the legislature (in which Harper's Conservative Party commands the most seats) obliged Canada's governor general to appoint him to the post of prime minister. In a parliamentary system, therefore, the legislature is theoretically more important than it is in a presidential system. In actual practice, however, the relationship between the chief executive and the legislature in a parliamentary system can vary depending upon political (rather than constitutional) factors. After the 2000 Canadian elections, the Liberal Party enjoyed a forty-three-seat majority over all the opposition parties put together. With this healthy majority, the Liberal Party leader had a lot of power over his 181 fellow Liberal legislators in the Commons. As we learned in chapter 4, however, the 2006 elections saw a resurgent Conservative Party take more votes than anybody else, although their victory fell well short of giving them an absolute majority. With only 125 of 308 seats in the House of Commons, Prime Minister Stephen Harper needs to be very nice to his Conservative colleagues. He even needs to be tolerably pleasant to the other parties, since—by itself—his own party can't supply him with the 50-plus percent of the votes he needs to get anything done.

Wise prime ministers do not abuse their supporters. During Britain's Thatcher years (1979–1991), the British prime minister enjoyed such huge majorities that she felt able to ignore the feelings of the same Conservative members of parliament who had chosen her. Commentators complained that the Iron Lady brought an imperial style to Ten Downing Street, reducing both her cabinet and the House of Commons to impotence. By 1991, Maggie's authoritarian leadership had irritated so many of her parliamentary supporters that her own party rebelled and selected the more diplomatic John Major as her successor.[30]

Parliaments in French-style combination systems tend to have somewhat less importance and authority. When he was inventing the Fifth Republic system that was to become the model for combination governments around the world, Charles De Gaulle specifically intended to weaken the French legislature. The National Assembly is allowed to sit for only less than half the year. It gets to approve the prime minister but cannot really control him afterward except by the drastic method of censuring him. If the executive so desires, it can punish an uncooperative National Assembly by dissolving it and calling fresh elections. With some variation, this pattern of a relatively weak legislature is standard for other combination systems around the world, Russia being a good example.

Upper and Lower Houses

A few states (Estonia, Israel, Iran, Iraq, Kenya, Vietnam, Peru, Iraq, and New Zealand are examples) have economized by having **unicameral legislatures**, that is, legislative bodies with only one chamber or house, but most legislatures are **bicameral**, in that they are divided into two distinct chambers. Typically, a law may begin in either chamber and end in the other, except for parliaments inspired by the British model (such as the American Congress), where finance bills must always begin in the lower house. In a few cases (Italy is an example), there is no functional difference between the two chambers. The Italian Chamber of Deputies performs approximately the same functions as the Italian *Senato*, leading some Italians to argue that the Senate could well be abolished.

The idea of bicameral legislatures having an "upper" and "lower" house is a verbal fossil. Upper houses were once "upper" because the nobility sat there, but these once-aristocratic chambers have tended to lose power as the nobility has faded from the scene in democratic societies. With the solitary exception of the American Senate, upper houses are now invariably less important than are lower houses and are merely called "upper" for historical reasons.

Most political systems assign specialized functions to the "upper" house. In many cases, the senior chamber represents the various sub-sovereign regions within the country (regions, provinces, etc.), even though these regions may differ in size, population, and importance. In the American model, for example, there are two senators from mighty California whose votes count for no more than those of the two senators from tiny Rhode Island or sparsely populated Montana. Containing representatives from each of Germany's states or lands, the German Bundesrat (upper house) may only legislate on matters relating specifically to the individual German regions, while the **Bundestag** (the lower house) deals with the broad range of national legislation.

How a sovereign people elect their legislature can determine the whole course of political life in society. In a presidential or combination system, the choice of a legislature can make the difference between greatness or gridlock. In parliamentary systems, choosing the legislature and electing the prime minister are the same process. In both cases, these elections are crucial. There are two principal systems or clusters of systems for electing legislators. Let's look at both.

ELECTING LEGISLATURES

When discussing elections systems for the chief executive in a presidential system, the point was made that you can change the result by changing the system. The same is true with elections designed to generate members of the legislature. There are two principal systems, and a variety of interesting compromise and combination approaches.[31]

The Single Member Constituency (SMC) System

Created by the British, the **single member constituency (SMC)** system has been imitated by the United States and most other former British colonies. Some political scientists call it the single member district system, since "constituency" and "district" have about the same meaning. The British use the phrase "first-past-the-post" (or FPTP) system. Some American scholars call it the "single member district plurality" system, emphasizing that the winner needs only to collect more votes than anyone else (a plurality) rather than an absolute majority.

Whatever you call it, the SMC system is straightforward. You divide up the territory of a sovereign state into as many voting districts or constituencies as you want legislators. For the American House of Representatives, there are 435 American congressional districts. Anyone who wishes to represent that district or constituency in the legislature runs for election, and the candidate with the single largest number of votes (a plurality) wins.

So far, simple enough. What's harder to understand is how and why the SMC system can sometimes distort or modify the results of the popular vote. Consider the 2010 British general parliamentary elections, which moved Gordon Brown out of Number Ten Downing Street (the prime minister's residence) and moved David Cameron in. Britain has three major parties: the Labour Party, the Conservative Party, and a smaller third party that is today called the Liberal Democratic Party. Table 7.4 gives us the results of the 2010 election, fought on the basis of SMC. Take a careful look at the contrast between the popular vote and the number of seats won by each party.

See the problems? The Liberal Democrats won 23 percent of the popular votes and felt entitled to something like 141 parliamentary seats (roughly 23 percent of the seats). Instead, they limped away with 57 seats, or less than 10 percent of the House of Commons. How do you get only 8.8 percent of the seats when you got 23 percent of the votes? Remember: in an SMC system, you look at individual constituencies separately, as if they were taking place in isolation. Liberal Democrats tended to get more than one vote in five steadily across the country, but their percentage doesn't vary much from constituency to constituency. The Liberal Democrats attract votes from environmentalists, liberated women, idealists, antiwar activists, and reform-minded centrists, but it is tough to find electoral districts where these demographic groups can combine to manufacture a plurality. Some inner-city districts went big for Labour and the Liberal Democrats came in second. Some prosperous rural constituencies voted for the Conservative Party, while the Liberal Democrats were again number two. But in only fifty-seven constituencies did they actually edge out both of the opposing parties to achieve a plurality.

Table 7.4.   The 2010 British General Election Results

Party	% Popular Vote	Number of MPs Elected	% of Seats per Party
Conservative	36.1%	305	46.9%
Labour	29.0%	258	39.7%
Liberal Democrats	23.0%	57	8.8%
Other Parties	11.9%	30	4.6%

Note: Because of some technical issues, the numbers do not quite add up; math is easy, but political systems are complicated.

So the choice of voting system makes a profound political difference. The Liberal Democrats have long claimed that the system is unfair because it tends to eliminate minority points of view. The flip side of the argument, of course, is that the SMC system gave each voting constituency just what the largest single number of voters wanted. The Liberal Democrats have stayed in business all these years because they are an ancient party (descendents of the nineteenth-century Whigs), and they command a particularly faithful cadre of voters, who support them through thick and (mostly) thin. The same system in the United States produces two big parties and ruthlessly eliminates smaller parties trying to break through.

The bigger problem for the British in 2010 is that no single party won a majority of seats in the House of Commons, and you need 50-plus percent of the seats to form a government. As the leader of the single largest party, David Cameron was invited to try to find that 50-plus percent, which only became possible when he formed a coalition with the Liberal Democrats. Conservatives and Liberal Democrats don't have a great deal in common ideologically, and observers are wondering how long this shotgun marriage can last.

The French have used the single member constituency system since 1958, but in France, SMC is complicated by the existence of so many political parties, the product of France's politically fragmented past. In each of France's 577 parliamentary constituencies, voters first choose the top two contenders, and then hold a runoff election to select the ultimate victor, roughly the same system used for electing the president. In 1997, this second round of voting gave the center-right opposition about 0.4 percent more popular votes than it gave the left wing coalition, but the left actually won forty-three more seats. In districts where the center-right won, however, they tended to pile up more votes than they needed. Where they lost, they often lost by a whisker. The left-wing coalition won the 1997 election because they won in more districts, although sometimes just barely. In 2002 elections for the French Assembly, the center-right managed to rectify the situation, winning both a majority of the popular vote and a comfortable majority of the seats.

We saw above how Britain's Liberal Democrats felt cheated by the single member constituency system. There are a wide variety of alternatives to SMC: one cluster is called **proportional representation**, and another cluster is usually (but inconsistently) referred to as alternative voting (AV).

Proportional Representation (PR) Systems

There are actually a number of slightly different systems all bearing the name "proportional representation" and they are all complicated. All PR systems place less importance on the individual candidate and more upon the political party, ensuring that each political party gets roughly the same proportion of seats in the legislature as its proportion of votes in the actual election.[32]

The world's least complicated version of proportional representation is the system Israel uses for elections to its unicameral parliament, the **Knesset**, which has 120 seats. Israel is an extravagantly multiparty society, and each of the parties wishing to contest an election prepares a 120-name list of its candidates, organized in order of the party's preference, with party leaders at the top of the list and no-hopers at the bottom. Each candidate technically represents the entire country, a so-called national constituency.

Table 7.5. SMC, PR, and AV Compared

Single Member Constituency System (SMC)	Individual elections in separate constituencies produce plurality winners	➜SMC kills small parties ➜SMC creates artificial majorities	Somewhat undemocratic system; favors stable governments
Proportional Representation System (PR)	Party lists in multi-seat districts translate party popularity into legislative strength	➜PR encourages growth of many parties ➜PR favors centrist coalitions	More faithful to will of electorate but can generate instability
Alternative Vote (AV) or Single Transferable Vote System	Voting within individual constituencies, with second votes added to first votes to produce majority winner	➜AV tends to eliminate extremist candidates. ➜AV gives a majority roughly what they want rather than giving a plurality precisely what they want.	Slightly complicated, and generally opposed by big parties, which have the most to lose.

Voters are really casting their ballots for the party, not individual candidates. When the votes are counted, each party gets the same percentage of seats in the Knesset that it had in the popular vote. A party winning 10 percent of the popular vote would then send the first twelve names (10 percent of 120 seats) off to the Knesset.

What's good about the proportional representation system is its inherently democratic nature; even an absolutely tiny minority can get at least one representative of its point of view into the legislature.

Are there disadvantages to PR? Proportional representation can be too democratic for its own good. Whatever its flaws, the SMC system typically produces a clear winner and a loser, and discourages parties from splintering. The proportional representation system can produce elaborate multiparty systems, where no one single party ever gets a clear majority of the seats in the legislature. This means that every government has to be a coalition, and coalition politics can be politically messy. In recent years, societies have tended to drop PR in favor of the SMC system, or one of a series of compromise electoral variations described below.

Alternative Voting Systems

One often discussed cluster of other options is variously called the **single transferable vote (STV)** by political scientists, the "instant runoff" system by Americans and the alternative vote (AV) in Great Britain. Whatever we decide to call it, the system is less complicated than it sounds. Within a given constituency, voters are presented with a list of candidates for—say—a member of parliament. You select the one you really want, typically by putting a "1" after the name. Then you select the candidate you could live with if you can't get your first choice: the alternative or transferable vote. If one of the candidates wins 50-plus percent of the first-choice votes, the election is over. But if nobody wins outright, then the "2" votes are added to the "1" votes until one candidate gets that magic 50-plus percent.

Voting Systems Compared

Imagine an election for a legislature in which there are three candidates: Neal Nazi, a racist with 38 percent of the popular vote, Nigel Nice, a competent antiracist candidate with 32 percent, and Melody Muddle, a reasonable centrist who comes in third with 30 percent of the vote. Under the single member constituency, Mr. Nazi goes to the legislature with a plurality of the votes. Under the alternative voting system, however, Ms. Muddle's supporters would give Mr. Nice their second transferable vote, and vice versa. Add Muddle's 30 percent to Nice's 32 percent, and you get about two-thirds of the electorate who don't like racists, and they send Mr. Nice to parliament.

The German System

The Germans have a widely admired "double whammy" system in which half the seats in the Bundestag (the lower house of the legislature) are elected with the SMC system and half with the proportional representation system, a clever concoction some scholars have called the **mixed member proportional (MMP) system.**

After World War II, Germany wanted the stability that the single member constituency can bring, balanced by the fairness of the proportional representation system. As a federal system, the country is divided into sixteen *Länder* or states, and each state is further divided into a number of single member constituencies based on its population. Every four years, Germans march off to the polls with two votes to cast in what are basically two simultaneous elections. In a straightforward SMC system that resembles elections to the American House of Representatives, Germany elects half of the Bundestag's deputies, one from each district in the country, and these representatives are meant to look after the needs of the local communities they represent.

The other half of the Bundestag is elected on the principle of proportional representation. Each German Länder (or region) is allowed as many seats as that Länder's population warrants. The voters then endorse their preferred political party, and each party sends to the Bundestag a number of deputies that is commensurate with the percentage of the popular vote it received in each Länder. If that seems complicated, try to remember that the essence of the German MMP system is that half the seats are elected under the SMC system, while the other half of the Bundestag's deputies are chosen on the basis of PR. In recent years, the German system has been copied with slight variations by the Japanese, the Mexicans, and the New Zealanders.

What the Germans didn't want was a Bundestag cluttered up with small parties, particularly those with Nazi or Marxist tendencies, so they passed the "5 percent rule." It's complicated in practice, but the rule generally means that a political party that does not score at least 5 percent of the vote nationwide does not get any seats in the national parliament.[33]

Optional Systems

There is no necessary connection between the executive system and the legislature's election system. Brazil is a presidential system, but it uses proportional representation for elections to its legislature. This system facilitates a multiplicity of parties, which means that the president of Brazil usually cannot count on his own party getting a majority in the Brazilian legislature. The United States is a presidential system, and it uses the SMC system for its legislative elections; so does Britain, which is a parliamentary system.

4. Courts and Judicial Systems

Unfortunately, electing executives and passing laws through legislatures doesn't eliminate all conflict in society, and the executive and legislative branches of government cannot always delineate how much freedom we are entitled to have as individuals. In most communities, statute law tells us in a general sense how we are meant to behave, but it takes judges and sometimes juries to decide how a specific dispute should be resolved. Some of these conflicts will be essentially political in character: is the president, for example, obliged to make public the minutes of a White House meeting with a campaign contributor who wants a pardon for a relative? Other antagonisms will be clearly criminal; how long a sentence should be served by a murderer or thief? And many conflicts combine the political and the criminal. How vigorously and intrusively can antiabortion activists picket a clinic providing women's health-care services? Can a loving wife help a chronically ill husband to commit suicide? Almost any court case involving theology or money will have important political ramifications.

JUDICIAL TRADITIONS

Every society on earth has some institutional mechanism for the arbitration of civil disputes and the punishment of lawbreakers in criminal cases. Even dictatorships have courts and judges, but Western democracies feature two principal traditions, and we need to reflect briefly on the differences between them. Authors differ in what they call these two traditions, but we'll follow general practice and title them the Anglo-Saxon Common Law Tradition, and the Roman Civil Law Tradition.[34]

Roman Civil Law

The Roman Civil Law Tradition began with ancient Rome's efforts to write down a universally applicable law for its empire, a set of hard-and-fast rules that could be easily understood and used by Roman judges to resolve any conflict. Roman Law was codified by the Emperor Justinian, strongly influenced by Roman Catholic thought, and modernized by Napoleonic France in the early years of the 1800s. It has now spread to almost all of continental Europe as far east as Russia, most of Latin America, and portions of Africa.

In Roman Civil Law countries, legislators try to create very detailed laws, leaving far less scope for judicial ingenuity. The function of a judge or magistrate in these societies is more simply to determine how the facts of a specific case fit a specific law. The point of reference is always the law itself, rather than some earlier judge's interpretation of the law.

In most Roman Civil Law societies, the judges themselves are part of the criminal justice system. When the police arrest a suspect in France or Italy, the alleged culprit is led before a succession of magistrates who direct the investigation. When the evidence has been assembled, it is a judge, not a policeman or public prosecutor, who sends the case to court. The defendant then appears before a trial judge, who knows that this case has already been investigated by professional colleagues who think there is a case to answer. Clearly, under these circumstances, the presumption of innocence is not very great.

Anglo-Saxon Common Law

Legal systems based on the Anglo-Saxon Common Law Tradition are most frequently found in democratic societies influenced by Britain, including the United States, Canada, Australia, New Zealand, Israel, India, and some former British colonies in Africa. Anglo-Saxon Common Law developed after the Norman invasion of Britain about a thousand years ago, when the king's judges set out to interpret and enforce what they took to be the law commonly understood in England. In Common Law societies, legislators create fairly general statutes and leave to judges the task of applying these principles to specific cases. The decisions reached by individual judges are called **precedents**, which are generally regarded as binding on subsequent jurists dealing with similar cases. The accumulation of legal precedents is sometimes called "judge-made" law and it affects major aspects of public and private life.

Another feature of Anglo-Saxon Common Law is the adversarial relationship between police/prosecuting attorney on one side and the defendant and defense attorney on the other, a drama played out before a neutral judge. Even after arrest on a criminal charge, you are still considered innocent until proven guilty. To make the system work, the judge needs to have considerable institutional independence from the police and district attorney who have brought the charges.

The Sharia or Islamic Legal System

We have focused primarily on two Western legal traditions, both of which make the essential assumption that law is man-made and needs to be changed periodically to suit evolving social attitudes. Much of the Islamic world is dominated by a code of justice called the Sharia. For Muslims, law is an unchangeable divine creation. The function of Sharia judges is to apply these eternal edicts to specific circumstances without modification or reinterpretation. There are some fundamental differences in both theory and practice. In cases involving disputes or personal injury, the Sharia asks the two sides of the quarrel to come to an agreement and grants the injured party a role in determining punishment for crime. For example, the family of a murder victim may be asked to decide on the death penalty for a murderer and can accept money from the murderer's family in satisfaction of their loss. Commentators often remark on the harshness of Koranic punishments (amputation of hands for thieves, stoning for adultery, etc.), but the death penalty is popular in non-Islamic countries such as the United States, Japan, and China.

JUDGING THE JUDICIARY

Judiciaries in presidential systems generally are not directly controlled by the executive nor the legislature, and it is hard to think of a judicial structure with the separateness and independence of the American system of courts and judges. In most parliamentary systems, on the other hand, the judicial system is administered by a member of the cabinet, often a minister for justice, who is a political figure subject to change after every election.

At the lower level, judges are selected in a variety of ways. In countries following the Anglo-Saxon Common Law Tradition, some are elected, such as county court judges in the United States. More frequently, they are appointed, especially at the higher levels. In countries influenced by Roman Civil Law Tradition, judges often choose their careers soon after graduation from university, and they work their way up through a hierarchically structured judicial corps. In almost all countries, high court judges are appointed for life or lengthy terms of office by the executive and subject to approval by the legislature.

The dispute over what is called judicial activism is particularly intense in United States, but the debate is a feature of political life in every country with an independent judiciary. Generally, conservatives believe that judges should interpret the specific text of the constitution and statute law, and leave the solving of social problems to lawmakers and executives. Judicial activists in all societies are judges with a cause, anxious to find the deep meanings in constitutions and apply them to social problems. Activist Italian judges were largely responsible for cleaning up an epically corrupt political establishment in the last two decades of the twentieth century when the Rome political leadership proved unable to reform itself.

Judicial Review

One of America's authentic contributions to the political world is the concept of **judicial review**, which is the power of courts to rule on the constitutionality of official acts. In the American system, Congress could pass a given law with unanimous votes in both houses and send it for signature to an enthusiastic president, only to have the Supreme Court (perhaps with a slender five-to-four majority) find the law in question unconstitutional and therefore unenforceable. Judicial review began in the U.S. legal tradition but has now spread to many other countries.

Take, for example, the relatively rare practice of burning American flags as an act of political dissent. Many states once enforced state-level statutes criminalizing the burning of an American flag. Patriotic legislation is generally popular with Americans and anti-flag-burning laws have been passed by vigorous majorities and signed with pomp and flourish by governors. And yet the American Supreme Court, as an act of judicial review, has repeatedly declared that buying your own flag and then burning it on your own land is an act of symbolic speech and hence protected by the Constitution's First Amendment.

Supreme or constitutional courts not only rule on the constitutionality of laws but can also settle disputes between branches of government, and between governments and citizens. Judicial review is an important factor in the legal traditions of the Scandinavian countries, Australia, Canada, Germany, India, and Japan, where any court can challenge the constitutionality of a law. Other countries, such as Germany, France, Spain, and Italy, have all established specific constitutional courts to deal with judicial-review issues.

The Russian Supreme Court has begun to assert itself in the chaotic world of post-Soviet politics, and courts are often the freest governmental institutions in less-free societies.

High courts with the power of judicial review are clearly the wave of the future, but many parliamentary democracies continue to give the legislature the right to decide what is and what is not constitutional. This is a complex issue, but in some countries following the British system, high courts have the right to say only what the words of a law mean and what the facts of the case are. For example, should the British Parliament pass a law requiring the decapitation of Prince Charles, the British Supreme Court might stipulate precisely how much royal neck goes with the royal head, but they could not declare the law unconstitutional.

5. Case Study: India's Improbable Democracy

Perhaps a case study would allow us to put into context all the constitutional conflict-resolution mechanisms we've studied in this chapter.

Societies with a lot of inherent conflict (perhaps stemming from religious, linguistic, and ethnic differences) have historically encountered difficulty in establishing and maintaining democracies. Born of colonialism and violence, the Republic of India came into existence with every imaginable conflict and problem, and yet the Indians have managed, against the odds, to achieve and maintain the world's largest democratic sovereign state. As Amartya Sen notes:

> In addition to being headed by a Muslim president, the secular Republic of India now has a Sikh prime minister, and a Christian president of the ruling party (not bad for the largest democratic electorate in the world with more than 80 percent Hindu voters).[35]

India's founding fathers were determined to create a free multinational secular society, and they selected political structures that suited the country's needs. Let's look at how India has organized itself to see if we've understood how vertical structures, parliamentary systems, and single member constituencies all fit together.

Breaking with the British tradition, India has opted for a written constitution that provides an extremely explicit diagram of how power flows through the Indian political system, covering areas that would be statute law in other systems. It also has civil rights enshrined in the constitution, although the freedoms enjoyed by women and lower-caste Indians may be dramatically circumscribed in actual practice.

India is a classic example of a multinational state, and the founding fathers of the republic wisely decided to endorse a substantial amount of local autonomy for the country's linguistic minorities. Tamil Nadu state, for example, has its capital at Chennai (once called Madras) and is the home of the Tamil people, who speak a language entirely different from Hindi. Elected Tamil politicians have a lot of clout in Tamil Nadu. The Indian version of the federal system is articulated into twenty-six sub-sovereign states that have only slightly less power with respect to the federal government in New Delhi than American states have in their relationship with Washington. In addition to the states, there are six "union territories" that have limited self-government.

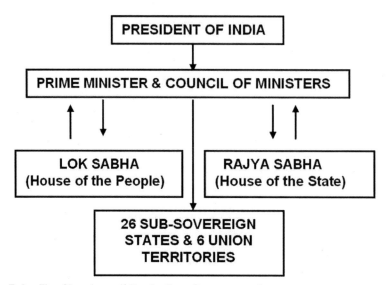

Figure 7.4. The Structure of the Indian Government
The Indian government generally resembles the British system, but the Indians have creatively borrowed features from other societies and invented a few of their own.

Like all parliamentary systems, India has a ceremonial president who is assisted by a ceremonial vice president. This indirectly elected head of state also acts as the referee of the Indian political system and ensures continuity in the event of a hung parliament. The president is elected for a succession of five-year terms by a special electoral college made up of federal and state legislators.

The actual work of governing is done by a prime minister and cabinet (called Council of Ministers in India). The prime minister is elected by (and is a member of) the lower house of the Indian parliament and depends upon the support of at least 50-plus percent of its members. For most of India's postindependence history, the liberal Congress Party provided most of the prime ministers, but in 1996, the more conservative Hindu nationalist Bharatiya Janata Party (BJP or Indian People's Party) won a plurality that it maintained until 2004, when the Congress Party regained power, albeit with a tenuous coalition. All recent Indian governments have been coalitions, because Indian political life is too fragmented for any single party to achieve the magic 50-plus percent on its own. The Congress Party prime minister who took office in 2004 is an economist named Manmohan Singh with a doctorate from Britain's Oxford University.

The parliament is bicameral and—as usual—the lower house is politically supreme. The House of the People (Lok Sabha) has only 545 members for more than a billion people, and each Indian state receives a number of representatives based on the state's population with elections held on the single member constituency system. The upper house is the Rajya Sabha (Council of States), and it resembles the U.S. Senate in that it is intended to look after the interests of the individual Indian states; like the American upper house, members of the Rajya Sabha serve for six-year terms, with one-third of the members coming up for reelection every two years. The Rajya Sabha is elected not by the general public but by the legislators of the state legislatures on the single transferable vote/alternative vote system discussed above. In addition to the 233 elected members of the Rajya Sabha, there are twelve appointed members who have distinguished themselves in the arts or sciences.

India's legal system is headed by a supreme court, whose members are appointed by the prime minister to serve until their sixty-fifth birthday. The judicial system is based on Anglo-Saxon Common Law, but the Indian Supreme Court enjoys the prerogative of judicial review, which it uses assertively and frequently.

Popular sovereignty means that people have some level of at least potential control over their governments, a power usually exercised through votes for elected officials. No two democracies on the planet are precisely the same, but they operate by making choices from roughly the same menu of governmental options. As we have seen, most democratic societies are relatively prosperous, but India proves that a significant level of democracy is possible even in a society with high levels of economic deprivation; ethnic, religious, and communal strife; hostile relations with some of its neighbors; and a fairly low level of engagement with major powers such as the United States. If India can do it, it might be argued that countries such as China, Russia, and Nigeria should be able to do it.[36]

6. The Wrap: What Have We Learned?

Look carefully at federal and unitary vertical structures, since a lot of public policy rides on this issue. Could the American president tell your professor what textbook to use for this course? No. Suppose you were a student in France; could the prime minister or his minister of education make the choice? *Oui!*

If you understand how the British government works, you'll comprehend how half the governments on the planet work, since the British model is popular. Remember how executive responsibility is divided between head-of-state ceremonial presidents/constitutional monarchs and chief executive prime ministers, and why anticipated elections sometimes get called. Can you distinguish between constitutional monarchs and royal executives? It'll be important in the next chapter.

American readers are probably okay on the presidential system, but you should review what you've learned about that French combination, since it might be the wave of the future. And when you've got all three systems in your head, ask yourself some questions about the merits and demerits of each. This chapter of the book explains the two big voting systems, SMC and PR, and then explores the subtleties of STV and that diabolically complex German system that a lot of democracies are copying.

We have tried to describe in this chapter the mechanisms with which societies channel or moderate normal human conflict. When these procedures don't work, the result is often violence, the emergence of a less-free society, or both. The next chapter is a look at how dictatorships and authoritarian societies organize themselves, and how they grapple with the challenge of dissent.

Notes

1. Lewis Carroll, *Alice's Adventures in Wonderland* (Boston: Lee and Shepard, 1869), 80.
2. Two fine texts have been written by teams headed by the late Gabriel A. Almond and published in New York by Longman: *Comparative Politics: A Theoretical Framework* (4th ed.) in 2004 and the large and

definitive 2004 *Comparative Politics Today: A World View* (8th edition). Michael Roskin's *Countries and Concepts: Politics, Geography, Culture* (8th ed.) (Upper Saddle River: Prentice Hall, 2004) is a frequently used undergraduate text.

3. Cass R. Sunstein meditates on the role played by constitutions in *Designing Democracy: What Constitutions Do* (New York: Oxford University Press, 2001).

4. Anthony King writes convincingly on the British Constitution in his *The British Constitution* (Oxford, UK: Oxford University Press, 2011). The classic book on the subject is by Vernon Bogdanor, *The New British Constitution* (Oxford, UK: Hart, 2009).

5. Robert Lacey knows a lot about how government works in Saudi Arabia. See *Inside the Kingdom: Kings, Clerics, Modernists, Terrorists, and the Struggle for Saudi Arabia* (New York: Viking, 2009).

6. If you are able to *habla español*, you can read the Ecuadorean Constitution at http://www.asambleana cional.gov.ec/documentos/constitucion_de_bolsillo.pdf.

7. Paraguay's president today is actually a former Roman Catholic priest who was instrumental in ending the dictatorship. Hugh O'Shaughnessy's *The Priest of Paraguay: Fernando Lugo and the Making of a Nation* (London: Zed, 2009) is an exciting although distinctly partisan story.

8. The nuts and bolts of Saddam's rule are well covered in Joseph Sassoon, *Saddam Hussein's Ba'ath Party: Inside an Authoritarian Regime* (Cambridge, UK: Cambridge University Press, 2011).

9. See Anthony J. Bellia, *Federalism* (New York: Aspen, 2010).

10. J. A. Chandler has published *Explaining Local Government* (Manchester, UK: University of Manchester Press, 2008).

11. For a competent study of federal systems around the world, take a look at Michael Burgess, *Comparative Federalism: Theory and Practice* (London: Routledge, 2006).

12. Arthur Gunlicks takes us through the German federal system in his comprehensive *The Lander and German Federalism* (Manchester, UK: Manchester University Press, 2003).

13. See Ronald Tiersky's excellent portrait of government under Mitterrand, *François Mitterrand: A Very French President* (Boulder, Colo.: Rowman & Littlefield, 2002).

14. In their *Ten Years of New Labour* (New York and London: Palgrave Macmillan, 2008), Matt Beech and Simon Lee attempt an assessment of Tony Blair's "New" Labour government.

15. Hugh Atkinson and Stuart Wilks-Heeg, *Local Government from Thatcher to Blair: The Politics of Creative Autonomy* (London: Polity, 2001). See also the more recent book by Terrence Casey, ed., *The Blair Legacy: Politics, Policy, Governance, and Foreign Affairs* (New York: Palgrave Macmillan, 2009).

16. The famous British political scientist, Arend Lijphart, has done it for us. See his *Parliamentary versus Presidential Government* (Oxford, UK: Oxford University Press, 1992).

17. For the British case, start with Peter Hennessy's *The Prime Minister: The Office and its Holders since 1945* (New York: Palgrave, 2001).

18. Almost all governments maintain a website explaining how they are supposed to work, and sometimes the information is even true. The official website of the British legislature (www.parliament.uk) is the gateway to a wealth of information about British politics; alternatively, you can visit the prime minister's office at www .number-10.gov.uk/.

19. David Denver, Christopher Carman, and Robert Johns have studied how the system works in their *Elections and Voters in Britain*, revised 3rd ed. (New York: Palgrave Macmillan, 2012).

20. James L. Newell takes us through the details in his *The Politics of Italy: Governance in a Normal Country* (Cambridge, UK: Cambridge University Press, 2010).

21. See Vernon Bogdanor, *The Monarchy and the Constitution* (Oxford, UK: Oxford University Press, 1998).

22. See Duncan Hall's *The British Commonwealth of Nations* (Toronto, Canada: University of Toronto Press, 2011).

23. See Peter Kingstone and Deborah J. Yashar, eds., *The Routledge Handbook of Latin American Politics* (London: Routledge, 2012).

24. Paul D. Schumaker and Burdett A. Loomis, eds., *Choosing a President: The Electoral College and Beyond* (Washington, D.C.: CQ, 2002).

25. Allister Sparks writes with careful admiration about the emergence of South African democracy in his *Beyond the Miracle: Inside the New South Africa* (Chicago, University of Chicago Press, 2009).

26. Interested in Brazil? Take a look at Albert Fishlow's *Starting Over: Brazil since 1985* (Washington, D.C.: Brookings 2011).

27. Despite many internal problems, Brazil continues to grow as a major democratic presence on the world scene. Leonardo Avritzer's *Participatory Institutions in Democratic Brazil* (Baltimore: Johns Hopkins Press, 2009) is a good scholarly guide to its political institutions.

28. Roy Pierce's *Choosing the Chief: Presidential Elections in France and the United States* (Ann Arbor: University of Michigan Press, 1995) explains the difference in voting systems. Until someone writes something newer and better (and in English), Alistair Cole and Peter Campbell's *French Electoral Systems*, 3rd ed. (Brookfield, Vermont: Gower, 1987) will remain useful.

29. See Eric Shiraev, *Russian Government and Politics* (New York: Palgrave Macmillan, 2010).

30. Anthony Seldon and Daniel Collings manage to remain neutral on the controversial Iron Lady in their *Britain under Thatcher* (New York: Longman, 1999).

31. Arend Lijphart's *Electoral Systems and Party Systems* (New York: Oxford University Press, 1994) surveys voting in twenty-seven modern democracies. A more analytical study is Michael J. Sullivan's *Comparing State Polities: A Framework for Analyzing 100 Governments* (Westport: Greenwood, 1996). An older book by Jean Blondel, *Comparative Legislatures* (Englewood Cliffs, N.J.: Prentice Hall, 1973) is still valuable. Robert Blackburn (*The Electoral System in Britain* (New York: St. Martin's Press, 1995) doesn't like the English system very much, but he explains it well.

32. Steven Hill tells us what's wrong with the SMC system in his *Fixing Elections: The Failure of America's Winner Take All Politics* (New York: Routledge, 2003). Amy J. Douglas agrees in her *Real Choices/New Voices: How Proportional Representation Could Re-vitalize American Democracy* (New York: Columbia University Press, 2002).

33. If we didn't manage to explain the German system, Gerard Braunthal does it better in his *Parties and Politics in Modern Germany* (Boulder, Colo.: Westview Press, 1996). M. A. Shugart and Martin P. Wattenberg detail the MMP system for you in their *Mixed Member Electoral Systems: The Best of Both Worlds* (New York: Oxford University Press, 2001).

34. Covering the American, British, and French court system, Henry Abraham's *The Judicial Process*, 7th ed. (New York: Oxford, 1998) is probably the place to start; but move on to Alan M. Katz, ed., *Legal Traditions and Systems: An International Handbook* (Westport, Conn.: Greenwood, 1986). A recent (2000) book by Alec Stone Sweet looks at Europe's activist judiciary; see *Governing with Judges: Constitutional Politics in Europe* (New York: Oxford University Press, 2000).

35. Amartya Sen, *The Argumentative Indian: Writings on Indian History, Culture, and Identity* (New York: Farrar, Straus, and Giroux, 2006), 46.

36. Not generally well understood by Americans, this interesting and complex country is well explained in Stephen P. Cohen's *India: Emerging Power* (Washington, D.C.: Brookings, 2002). See also Granville Austin, *The Indian Constitution: Cornerstone of a Nation* (New York: Oxford University Press, 2000); and Strobe Talbott, *Engaging India: Diplomacy, Democracy, and the Bomb* (New York: Random House, 2002).

Part III

KINDS OF CONFLICT
THE WORLD WHEN THINGS GO WRONG

CHAPTER 8

Conflict and Less-Free Societies

5. The Wrap: What Have We Learned?

At the end of *Alice's Adventures in Wonderland*, Alice suddenly realizes that the white and red kings and queens who have been perplexing her are really only part of her extended dream. "Why, they're only a pack of cards, after all," she exclaims. "I needn't be afraid of them."[1]

On this side of the looking glass, some dictatorships collapse like the proverbial house of cards, while others seem to go on forever. Despite its lack of any perceptible competence, a Marxist **dynasty** has ruled harshly over North Korea since 1948, and the third member of this strange family has just succeeded his father and grandfather with no end in sight. A tall, angry Bedouin tribal leader named Abdul Aziz ibn Saud began his conquest of Arabia in 1902 and finished it twenty-four years later with the final conquest of what he modestly named "Saudi" Arabia. While the clock is ticking for the Saudi regime, his sons were still running this troubled oil-producing desert in 2012.

On the other hand, some dictatorships can look eternal and turn out to be ephemeral. Modern Iran came into existence in 1925 when Reza Shah Pahlavi consolidated his hold on the country. In 1941, the British forced his abdication in favor of his son, Mohammed, and by the late 1970s, Iranian royal rule seemed indestructible. Pictures of the shah were everywhere, and so were the shah's well-armed soldiers and police officers, and their American advisors. Although the wealth was not trickling down into the huge slums of Tehran or the impoverished rural villages, there was a lot of money around, thanks to the oil industry. While Western observers detected some deep-seated structural problems in Iranian society, it never minimally occurred either to academics or intelligence officers that this beautiful country was ready to self-destruct. By early 1979, however, this royal house of cards had collapsed. The shah was dying in exile, and the Ayatollah Ruhollah Khomeini had seized control, turning an often-brutal royal dictatorship regime into a bloodthirsty **theocracy**.

We tend to blame dictatorships on evil dictators, assuming that innocent societies that could just as easily have been democracies are being ground under the heel of despots driven only by a desire for domination. Clearly, personal ambition has played a role; in the Iranian case, both the shah and the ayatollah were strong-willed men who favored an iron-fisted approach to management. As we'll try to see in this chapter, however, societies are typically unfree because of their inability to grapple confidently with conflict, either internal or external. If a country is stricken by deep divisions among its people, or feels itself menaced by foreign foes, it can either develop democratic mechanisms to broker these disagreements or, alternatively, surrender to a government that will force a settlement. In the worst cases, even an oppressive government cannot moderate conflict, resulting in a dictatorship presiding over varying levels of revolutionary violence.

Popular unrest in the Middle East and North Africa in 2011–2012 has called into question our thoughts on democracy building and the potential for democratic institutions in this part of the world. Following our earlier discussion of Francis Fukuyama and his argument of the inevitable development of liberal democracy for human society, we take a look at some of the more infamous dictatorships around the world and consider whether they are, or ever will be, on the path toward democracy. Alternatively, these states, as some scholars argue, may just be in some new form of flux toward equally unjust societies.

Are there gradations of unfreedom? At various times, political scientists have attempted to make a distinction between **authoritarian** governments and **totalitarian** governments. The use of these two words was often confused when American presidents designated as "authoritarian" any dictatorship they supported and slammed as "totalitarian" any unfree regime (typically Marxist) that the United States opposed. And yet there are different degrees of dictatorship, and we can make a legitimate distinction among them.

- Authoritarian Dictatorships: In this category, freedom is denied in many significant ways. There may be no elections at all, or elections may be completely fraudulent, leaving an non-sovereign people with no effective control over their government. An authoritarian regime may practice substantial brutality toward the people, employing arbitrary arrest and execution. Putting countries into this category is always going to be controversial, but some relatively straightforward examples would be Belarus, Cambodia, China, Kazakhstan, and Saudi Arabia.
- Totalitarian Dictatorships: The word "totalitarian" is, however, a useful way of describing that handful of extremely unfree societies where some ruthless obsession animates an entire political elite or leadership group. These regimes typically invade every part of an individual's life, rule with enormous cruelty, and demand total allegiance from their citizens. In her great work, *The Origins of Totalitarianism* (1951), Hannah Arendt argues that authoritarian dictatorships exploit the citizenry and repress dissent savagely in an effort to extract obedience.[2] In their early study of totalitarian societies (*Totalitarian Dictatorship and Autocracy*), Carl Friedrich and Zbigniew Brzezinski argue that totalitarian regimes had an official, unchallengeable ideology that posed as a philosophy of life; a single, authorized political party with control of mass communications, the military, and the secret police; and a centrally directed economy.[3]

  A totalitarian government demands not only obedience but also intellectual and emotional consent and even a kind of coerced love. In essence, authoritarian regimes mess with your body; totalitarian governments mess with your body and your mind. Historical examples of totalitarian governments certainly include Germany under Hitler (1933–1945), the USSR under Stalin (1928–1953), and China under Mao (1949–1976). Almost all commentators agree that the least-free society on the planet was probably Saddam Hussein's Iraq until its end in 2003. Sudan and North Korea also belong on the totalitarian list, although 2012 began with tentative hopes that Burma/Myanmar might move up a few rungs on the ladder of freedom.

We can also categorize dictatorships by the identity of the dictator and the character of the regime. Some unfree societies are led by the kind of royalty who still make serious public policy decisions. Other countries have been conquered by their own military establishments and are run by a general or a committee of generals. In a few rare but important cases such as Iran, a society's clergy have seized control and rule in the name of God. And finally, there are many societies that are governed by an elite, a group of people who are all members of some specific group, such as an ethnic or ideological community. We'll look at examples of all of these below, endeavoring in the process to answer the following questions.

- *How do we categorize unfree societies?* In *Anna Karenina*, Tolstoy remarks, "All happy families resemble each other, but unhappy ones are different in their own ways."[4] This also seems true with sovereign states. As we saw in the previous chapter, democracies resemble one another in many important ways. Less-free societies, however, tend to be idiosyncratic and less easy to categorize. But political scientists are relentless classifiers, so we'll try to slot them into a couple of major groups: royal executive, military, theocratic, and elite.

- *When the Red Queen orders your decapitation, does somebody really chop off your head? How, when, and where do hereditary monarchs still retain genuine political power?* As we learned in chapter 7, most royal houses have lost any authentic political power, including the right to order decapitations. There are, however, about a dozen countries in the world where hereditary monarchs still have an impressive array of political powers. In Saudi Arabia, this includes the king's right to say, "Off with his head," and get the order carried out very early the following morning. In section 1, we'll look at the whole issue of what are called royal executive regimes, most of them Middle Eastern, where royal rulers still rule.

- *Why do soldiers abruptly storm out of their barracks and seize political control of their countries? What are the short-term and long-term consequences of the classic military coup?* While military dictatorships are somewhat less common than they were a few decades ago, there are still a number of very significant examples. After a brief consideration of the circumstances that produce military coups and a look at a few classic examples, section 2 will examine the military government of Burma/Myanmar. Pakistan's military barely tolerates civilian control, and 2012 began with a fear that the generals would seize power again, as they have done countless times in the past.

- *What's a theocracy, and why do things keep going wrong in Iran? How does it happen that relatively well-educated and prosperous people have not thus far created a freer society for themselves?* As we'll see in section 3, the Islamic Republic of Iran, a good example of a theocracy, has surrendered power to its religious leaders and their disciples, who base their decisions on their own interpretation of God's law.

- *What is an elite dictatorship? What's happened in Russia after Marxism went away?* An elite dictatorship, or **oligarchy**, is a country in which a collective of some kind has established its rule over a country, sometimes led by an authoritarian figure. When the Soviet Union crumbled in 1991, everybody assumed that democracy was the next stop. In Section 4, we'll try to see why it is evolving instead toward an elite-driven oligarchy.

1. Royal Executive Regimes

Before we talk about kings and queens, remember the distinction made in chapter 7 between constitutional monarchs (such as Queen Elizabeth and Japanese Emperor Akihito) and royal executives (such as King Abdullah of Saudi Arabia). Let's look at the concept, and then move on to study two actual royal executive regimes, Jordan and Oman.

Dictatorships and Corruption

Free or less free, all societies are susceptible to corruption, both in the public and private sector. Businesspeople find ways to avoid their taxes. Elected politicians accept "campaign donations" from interest groups. In a free society, however, it's hard to get away with major fraud forever because the press and the police are (or should be) persistent in their efforts to expose it, and opposition parties are always on the hunt for juicy financial scandals, which means that serving officials are under constant scrutiny.

A less-free society, however, will tend to have infinitely higher levels of corruption precisely because government officials will have less to fear because the press will be subservient and the police force may be crooked. There is a close connection between corruption and poverty. Corruption deprives a society of essential operating funds because the government loses tax income to secret offshore accounts. Potential aid donors are reluctant to donate money to poor countries when a wealthy elite steals charity aimed at the poor. And businesses dislike the unpredictable commercial environment created by endemic corruption. Furthermore, corruption tends to perpetuate dictatorships because corrupt leaders may need to hang onto power to avoid trials and imprisonment

There is a Berlin-based research organization called Transparency International (or TI), which attempts to quantify the level of corruption within individual governments. On Transparency International's scale, a perfect "10" is a totally graft-free government (Denmark and New Zealand each got a laudable "9.3"). An absolute "0" would suggest a government in which every official took bribes. Somalia scored dead last with a "1.1." Worryingly, Afghanistan was the third most corrupt government on the planet with a "1.4," surpassing even the brutal Myanmar/Burma regime. This is depressing because of the deep investment Europe and the United States have made in redeeming this badly damaged society. Check out the whole system at www.transparency.org and note that the more democratic the society, the less corruption there usually is.

Table 8.1. The Remaining Royal Executive Regimes

Bahrain	Amir Hamad bin Isa al-Kahlifa
Brunei	Sultan Hassanal Bolkiah
Jordan	King Abdullah bin al Hussein
Kuwait	Amir Jaber al-Sabah
Morocco	King Mohammed VI
Oman	Sultan Qabus bin Said
Qatar	Hamad bin Khalifa al Thani
Saudi Arabia	King Abdullah bin Abdulaziz al-Saud
Swaziland	King Mswati III
United Arab Emirates	Sheikh Khalifa Bin Zayed al-Nahyan

Jordan and Oman survived protests in 2011 from citizens demanding more democratic representation. In the future, these regimes may implement more representative legislative systems to quell angry protesters.

WHERE ROYALS STILL RULE

A government is described as royal executive if a hereditary monarch still takes a leading role in establishing and carrying out public policy. There are perhaps nine royal executive regimes in the world, depending upon your definition and assessment of individual governments. A few are marginal, but others are important players in international politics: Jordan, Bahrain, Brunei, Kuwait, Morocco, Oman, Saudi Arabia, and the United Arab Emirates. Almost every Western political thinker accepts that democratic government needs to rest on the consent of the governed, which means that a king who really rules is a political anachronism. Faced with pressures for modern participatory democracy, a royal executive has two choices. The royal family may opt for constitutionality, surrendering power gradually to elected politicians, roughly what happened in Bhutan. Conversely, they may cling to authority, proclaim that democracy is a goal for the (very distant) future, and use police and military repression to consolidate political power, which is the situation in Saudi Arabia and Bahrain. And there are quite a few waypoints in-between. The penalties for getting it wrong can be severe for an unhappy monarch. In 2008, the Nepalese decided that they had had quite enough of their inflexible king, dismissed him from the throne, evicted him from the royal palace, and declared Nepal a republic (i.e., a non-monarchical society).

There are a series of Arab countries along the western shore of the Persian Gulf where Islamic leaders have resisted efforts to transform their oil-rich desert kingdoms into democracies. These royal dictatorships include the Persian Gulf states of Saudi Arabia, Bahrain, and the United Arab Emirates. They are basically tribal structures that have managed to become significant economic powers without having evolved in the direction of popular sovereignty.

Let's look more closely at two countries (Jordan and Oman) that continue to have royal executive governments despite mass protests for democratic reform throughout the Middle East in 2011–2012, and try to see how these two regimes function, how they grapple with internal and external conflict, and why they have survived.

Portraits of the Real World: Adultery and Saudi Arabia

Foreign critics of Saudi society wonder how long this antiquated political system can survive in the twenty-first century and whether it deserves American support. Freedom House gives it a dismal "6.5" rating of "Not Free," and it's a good example of a royal executive regime.[5]

In 1978, the grandniece of the then-monarch, King Khalid, was caught trying to flee the country with a Lebanese lover after she had been ordered to marry an elderly relative. In an execution organized by the Saud family, Princess Masha'il was made to kneel before an audience of relatives and was then shot through the head. Her Lebanese friend had his head hacked off with a sword.

It would be difficult to say if Saudi Arabia has become dramatically more democratic in the intervening decades. Oddly enough, the Saudi system does permit contact between rulers and ruled that would be impossible in a Western democracy, and a Saudi citizen may visit the king with a personal or political problem. Some years ago, for example, Richard Collin's Saudi friend Ahmad was distressed when his wife fled with her lover to another country. A humble chauffeur, Ahmad went to see King Faisal, petitioning that his errant wife be extradited back to Saudi Arabia to be stoned to death under the provisions of the Sharia (or Islamic law).

Gently, King Faisal explained that the death penalty was not always an ideal remedy for a dysfunctional family. Presenting him with a gift copy of the Koran, the Saudi monarch told Ahmad to forgive, forget, and find himself a younger and prettier wife. When comparing political systems, we often assume that new and Western are always better than old and traditional. This assumption is generally well founded, but the next time the love of your life departs without leaving a forwarding address, wander down Pennsylvania Avenue to the White House, and see if anybody in the Oval Office has time to dispense tea and sympathy.

SEMI-DEMOCRACY IN THE HASHEMITE KINGDOM OF JORDAN

Despite its persistent presence in the news, Jordan isn't inherently a very powerful country. The population is under five million people. Territorially, it's about the size of Indiana, but little of the land is arable, and most of the population lives in cities and villages in the West of the country, not far from the Jordan River. The word *Hashemite* in the country's title testifies to the fact that the kings of Jordan belong to the same Meccan family that produced the Prophet Mohammed, a fact that confers a significant amount of legitimacy upon the ruling family.

Modern Jordan is an accidental creation of World War I, but the appearance of Israel after World War II utterly destroyed Jordan's chance of normal development. In 1952, King Hussein (no relation to Iraq's former ruler Saddam Hussein) took control of a deeply divided country, bitterly embroiled in the conflict with Israel and home to millions of angry Palestinian refugees. King Hussein survived coup attempts and insurrections and wars to emerge as an honored and respected force for peace in the Middle East. When he died in 1999, he was succeeded by one of his sons, Abdullah bin Al-Hussein (now called King Abdullah II).

King Abdullah II

Born in 1962 and therefore still comparatively young, Abdullah seems to have been a last-minute choice made on King Hussein's deathbed. After study at America's Georgetown University, Britain's Sandhurst (the English version of West Point), and Oxford University, Abdullah was pursuing a military career in Jordan's elite armed forces when his father died.

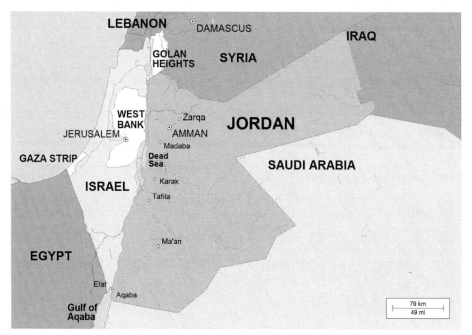

Map 8.1. The Hashemite Kingdom of Jordan

The governmental structure that Abdullah inherited has some potentially demo-cratic elements. At least on paper, it functionally resembles France's combination system with the unelected king exercising roughly the same functions as the elected French president. Helping the king is an appointed prime minister, who is supposed to enjoy the confidence of an elected legislature. Jordan's bicameral legislature doesn't have much real power, however, because all bills must be passed by both chambers and signed by the king. The upper house is completely appointed by the monarch, and these royal supporters would be reluctant to mount a serious challenge to the man who gave them their jobs.

The late King Hussein had slowly and cautiously introduced some democratic fea-tures into his administration, and his son, King Abdullah II, was expected to follow in his father's footsteps by allowing the Jordanian people to exercise as much political freedom as he felt was possible in a fragmented and volatile environment. There are positive signs of his democratic leanings. Abdullah has become famous in his country for circulating in disguise in order to find out what the lives of his people are actually like. He is fonder of free enterprise than his father was and Westernized enough to be comfortable chatting with Larry King on CNN.

On the other hand, for most of his adult life, the king served as a senior officer in the Jordanian armed forces, and he still snaps orders and expects them to be obeyed. When a fiery woman politician named Toujan Faisal accused Abdullah of corruption in 2002, she spent three months in prison before being pardoned.

Figure 8.1. King Abdullah of Jordan
Photo courtesy of NATO.

Internal and External Threats

A second and related problem comes from Islamic fundamentalism or what is often called **Islamism**, the belief that society should be forced to conform to the dictates of Islamic law or the Sharia. In Jordan, the principal Islamist opposition is called the Islamic Action Front, which dislikes Jordan's secular and Western-oriented leadership and demands a return to the purity of Islam. While Islamism will be described in more detail in chapter 10, all Muslim societies are menaced by it to some extent. Not all Islamists are violent, and the government of nearby Turkey has been successfully led by a moderate Islamist party for many years. On the other hand, some Islamists believe in solving political problems with bullets rather than ballots. Osama bin Laden, who was captured in Pakistan and killed on May 2, 2011, was a prime example of an extreme Islamist. Jordanian protesters in 2011–2012 have increasingly demanded that the king open the legislature to more democratic representation. From King Abdullah's perspective, the problem is precisely this: when Arab populations are allowed to vote freely, they tend to elect Islamist politicians, who would become the monarch's instant enemies.

Furthermore, Western-oriented Jordan might move toward a more democratic system, however, if the country were not surrounded by so many violence-prone enemies: Syria seems to be sliding into a civil war. Saudi Arabia is a hostile royal dictatorship. Iraq was a bullying Sunni dictatorship until 2003; since the American invasion, power in Baghdad is mostly in the hands of pro-Iranian Shi'ites, who regard Jordan's Sunni population with mistrust.

After the Arab-Israeli wars of 1948 and 1967, large numbers of Palestinians moved or were driven into exile in Jordan. The two communities have now grown closer through intermarriage and familiarity (Abdullah's wife, Queen Rania, is a Palestinian), but Jordan's Palestinian population drags the kingdom inexorably into every dispute between Palestinians and Israelis on the other side of the Jordan River. And the fighting between Palestinians and Israelis shows no sign of ending soon (we'll see why in chapter 11).[6]

As a result of inside conflict and external danger, Jordan has been unable to make much progress toward re-creating itself as an open, democratic society. Opponents of the king's regime are silenced and occasionally imprisoned, but not executed. The Freedom House evaluation of Jordanian democracy has been dropping pretty steadily, however, falling from a not-very-respectable "4.5" to a dismal "6" in 2011.

Ultimately, Jordan and the other countries in this category can never be truly democratic in the Western sense of the word as long as substantive political power can be inherited rather than elected. On the other hand, this is a country that could be, and would like to be, democratic at some level. At the moment, it is a discouraging fact that an instant infusion of real democracy into the Jordanian political system would almost certainly provoke insurrection and civil war. Progress toward a democratic society will depend in the future, as it has in the past, on the level of conflict that the Amman regime faces and its ability to resolve that conflict peacefully.

Despite all this bad news, a recent UN study concluded that Jordan was actually the least repressive Arab state. Most visitors to Jordan find it to be an extremely pleasant place, beautiful and populated with friendly, generally well-educated people. With a per capita GNI of over $5,000, it is relatively poor but not destitute. If you wanted to live somewhere in the Arab world, you'd have to consider house hunting in Jordan.[7]

The Arab Spring in Amman

Street protests began in January 2011, and as they continued throughout the year, the king responded by twice dismissing his cabinet and bringing in a new team of politicians. The protesters are a mixed bag of trade unionists, students, and Islamists, who have avoided violence against governmental forces. The king's police have been tough but not lethal, containing the crowds generally without the murderous force seen in Egypt and Bahrain, although there have been some street battles fought with stones and batons. As we move into 2012, the protesters are keeping the pressure on the regime while the Abdullah government continues to look for ways to respond without sacrificing ultimate control.[8]

THE DISTANT KINGDOM OF OMAN

Oman nestles between one of the world's most intractable deserts, the so-called Empty Quarter, and the vast Indian Ocean. It's a long way from anywhere, but the sultanate derives strategic importance from a geographic oddity: while most of the country looks

---

Note on Arabic Names

In traditional Arabic society, you are known primarily by your first name. Hence, the new Jordanian King Abdullah bin Hussein is called Abdullah, and he is often called Abdullah II because his great-grandfather was also called Abdullah. The "bin" or "ibn" means "son of," and Hussein was his late father's name. Sometimes the father's name is followed by a tribal name. For example, the full name of the Sultan of Oman is Qaboos bin Said al Said; his name is Qaboos; his father's name is Said (pronounced "Sa-eed"), and he comes from a tribe also called "Said."

Remember that the Arabic script depends mostly upon consonants and omits most vowels. As a consequence, "Abdullah" is sometimes transliterated into the Roman script as "Abdallah" because the vowel is not actually written and needs to be supplied by the mind of the reader. A further complication is the fact that the ailing king of Saudi Arabia (no relation) is also named "Abdullah" or "Abdallah."

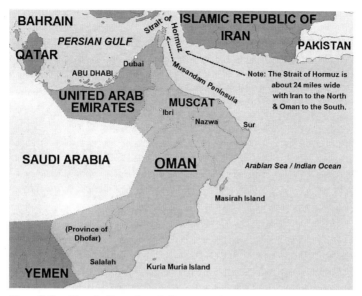

Map 8.2.   The Sultanate of Oman

out on the Arabian Sea/Indian Ocean, one tiny detached finger of land (Oman's version of Alaska) pokes into the strategic Straits of Hormuz. Find the Musandam Peninsula on map 8.2, and note that it controls the southern shore of the maritime route through which about half of the world's oil passes on its way to Europe, Japan, and the United States. The great petroleum-consuming countries of the world have always made it their business to be nice to Oman, because a sometimes unfriendly Iran dominates the northern shore of the straits. In 2012, the Islamic Republic of Iran to the north was threatening to cut off the Straits of Hormuz, and this step would suddenly make the Musandam Peninsula into one of the most important pieces of real estate in the world.

Despite its remoteness, the city of Muscat is more cosmopolitan than most Arab capitals: African laborers, Baluchi oil-field workers from Iran and Pakistan, Philippine maids, Palestinian office workers, and Texan petroleum engineers all meet in Muscat's many Indian restaurants. The population is small, something under three million, but the growth rate has been very brisk in the past and is only now slowly dropping to about 2 percent per year.[9]

Formerly independent, the country came under British control in the 1800s, and Oman's sultans sheltered behind the protection of the British armed forces. Successive rulers kept their people rigidly segregated from the rest of the world, fearing the contamination of Western influence. In order to consolidate their own control, the British helped the Omanese royal family defeat challenges to their leadership, intervening militarily when the Muscat government faced a violent separatist insurrection in Dhofar, a province in the southwest corner of the country.[10]

Sultan Qaboos bin Said

Replacing his very repressive father on the throne in 1970, the young Sultan Qaboos bin Said faced a series of difficult choices. The Omanese people were generally poor and uneducated, but accelerating oil revenues were quickly bringing **foreign exchange** into the

Figure 8.2. Qaboos bin Said, Sultan of Oman
Born in 1940 and educated mostly in Britain, the sultan believes that his people can make only very slow and gradual progress toward meaningful participation in public life, although he himself works hard on their behalf. Qaboos is unmarried and has not named a crown prince or heir apparent. He has several ambitious first cousins, but there is no obvious heir to the throne. Will there be political conflict when he dies? Photo by Sgt. Jerry Morrison, U.S. Department of Defense.

treasury. The Omanese political tradition had always been one of rigid royal rule. Could a royal dictatorship be maintained in an era of expanding democracy? Worried about growing Islamism, and still nervous about national unity after the Dhofar rebellion, Sultan Qaboos bin Said began a cautious program of modernization. Qaboos also encouraged education for both genders from elementary school up to a university in Muscat that he created and modestly named after himself.[11]

The modernization, however, was always tentative where politics was concerned. Qaboos forbade most normal political activity as well as the formation of political parties. While he utterly lacks the brutality of his ancestors, the sultan has always retained the power to rule by decree. Although it may be a little too hard on poor Oman, Freedom House gave the country a failing score of "5.5" on its 2011 report card, unchanged in recent years despite some genuine improvements in the situation. In recent years, the Sultan has begun to lay the groundwork for the eventual conversion of his country into a constitutional democracy, although progress is admittedly slow.[12]

Oman and Democracy

There are already the makings of a bicameral legislature, although it is far from being a real lawmaking body. What might be called the "lower house" is an eighty-four-member elected assembly that has the power to advise the government and recommend legislation. The "upper house" consists of fifty-nine appointed members. There is a significant representation of women in both houses as well as in the cabinet. Labor unions are legal, although forbidden to strike. The franchise is open to women and men. The press is self-censoring where the Sultan is concerned, but is allowed to grumble about public issues.[13]

If Qaboos is a royal dictator, he has the merit of being a hard-working and intelligent one, and his government was recently rated the most efficient Arab state. According to Transparency International, Oman, Qatar, and Bahrain are the three least-corrupt countries in the Arab world.[14]

The Sultan rules through his appointed cabinet and a series of ministries. He himself acts as chief of state for ceremonial purposes, and then puts on another hat to serve as his own prime minister. With still more hats, he reports to himself as defense minister,

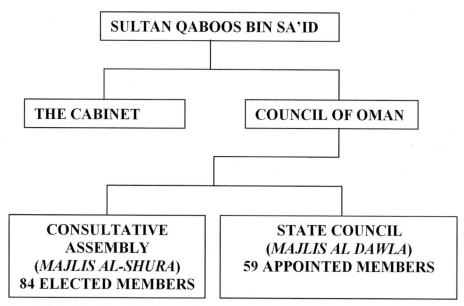

Figure 8.3.   Evolving Structure of the Omanese Government

finance minister, and minister of foreign affairs, although the less-important cabinet posts are actually allocated to other people.

Throughout the spring and summer of 2011, the sultan has experienced some moderate pressure to expand democratic reforms throughout his country. Despite this evolving democracy, there is a financial and human cost to the maintenance of a repressive regime. The primary function of the Omanese armed forces is internal security (since Britain and America defend the strategically important Oman from any foreign enemies). Oman spends about a third of its gross domestic product on security, a lot more than it spends on education and medical care.

Why Is Oman a Dictatorship?

If dictatorships flow from unmanageable conflict, Oman should theoretically be a great deal freer than it is; one could argue that the country has no serious foreign enemies, and the competent and well-liked sultan spends a lot of money on his people. With a PC/GNI at $23,000 a year, there is certainly enough money in circulation. Furthermore, its internal disagreements are modest compared to some other societies.

In the final analysis, however, Oman is democratizing only slowly because the House of Said, which has been running the show in Muscat since 1749, still perceives itself to be facing internal as well as external threats. Sultan Qaboos and his father both endured protracted armed rebellions, and the rising Islamist movement frightens every government in the Middle East. Religiously, most Omanese are Ibadhi, a sect that is sometimes classified as a variant of Shia and sometimes seen as an independent branch of Islam. Sunni societies tend to care about other Sunni societies, and the same goes for Shi'ites; there is no external Ibadhi community to provide support.[15]

Powerful friends notwithstanding, Oman lives in an authentically tough neighborhood. Oman sometimes irritates the United States by maintaining cordial relations with Iran, but Tehran is very close, and Washington is a long way away. Many of the countries that have beachfront property on the Persian Gulf are seriously unstable, starting with Iraq and proceeding down the waterway to Bahrain. To the west is the festering Republic of Yemen, which is currently trembling on the brink of a full-scale civil war. Qaboos allows the unpopular American military free access to bases in his country despite considerable opposition from his own people. In the past, there have been border disputes with Yemen, Saudi Arabia, and the United Arab Emirates.[16]

A serious domestic demand for more freedom has not yet emerged, and the Omanese people are perhaps too isolated from the rest of the world to realize how repressive their benign government is, because they are freer than anybody else in the neighborhood. Sincerely persuaded that his people need his firm guidance, Qaboos is an intelligent and well-meaning ruler who has presided over a rapid improvement in the welfare of his people. When the Arab Spring washed ashore in Oman, even the protesters were restrained and polite, and took the precaution of carrying signs affirming their affection for the sultan when they took to the streets to protest.

Oman could someday be a democracy, but the transition looks like it's going to be slow.

2. Military Dictatorships

Definitions are as difficult here as they are in any area of modern politics, but generally speaking, a military dictatorship is any repressive regime in which unelected soldiers have taken national leadership positions by force while continuing to draw their power from the country's armed forces. The classic military **coup d'état** became extremely common during the Cold War, but the phenomenon is now less frequent. There are only a handful of clear-cut military regimes left today. In this section, we will survey Burma/Myanmar, a land currently suffering under military rule.

Why "Burma/Myanmar"?

You know a country has problems when nobody can be quite sure what to call it. Historically, the country that lives along the banks of the Irrawaddy River has been called "Burma," a practice that continued until 1989 when the ruling military junta decided to change the country's name to "Myanmar." Opponents of the dictatorship objected to the renaming of their country by a gang of unelected generals who, they felt, had no authority. Opponents of the Burmese government (including the U.S. State Department) went on calling the country "Burma." The United Nations gave in and used "Myanmar." Most journalists played it safe and referred to it as "Burma/Myanmar" or "Myanmar/Burma." Write "Myanmar" in pencil; when the opposition eventually resumes power, they will almost certainly return to "Burma" as the country's formal name. Stay tuned: in chapter 11, we'll talk about "Israel/Palestine" and visit the city of "Derry/Londonderry."

POWER TO THE PRAETORIANS

A military dictatorship typically begins with a military coup d'état in which soldiers take political authority away from a civilian government. Given the overwhelming superiority in physical power that the military establishment has over the rest of society, some military coups involve minimal violence. For example, the Portuguese armed forces overthrew a civilian dictatorship in April of 1975 with little or no bloodshed, beginning an orderly transition to democracy. In September of 2006, Thailand's armed forces overthrew the prime minister in a generally nonviolent coup. When the generals permitted the Thai people to vote for a new government, Thailand promptly elected the younger sister of the politician the military had overthrown. Thailand's praetorians decided that they could live with little sister and did not contest the election.

If officials of the civilian government fight back or the armed forces themselves are divided, the coup can become deadly. The Chilean armed forces employed horrific military violence against government buildings and officials when they attacked and killed the legally elected president of Chile in 1973 and installed their commanding officer, the late General Augusto Pinochet, as his replacement.

Why Do Military Coups Happen?

A military coup rarely comes out of the blue, and there are two basic sets of reasons why they take place, with both sometimes operating simultaneously.[17]

- The Failed State Syndrome: Soldiers sometimes leave their barracks because the civilian government has begun to self-destruct, and the military establishment finds that it is the only cohesive institution left. Political scientists often use the phrase "failed state" to describe a government that is no longer functioning well enough to provide basic security or fundamental human services to its people. Pakistan, Nigeria, Sierra Leone, Indonesia, and Somalia have all been described as failed states at various times in the recent past and all have undergone military takeovers.
- Praetorianism: In some military establishments, there is a deeply rooted conviction that soldiers are the ultimate defenders of the nation's destiny. **Praetorianism** convinces military leaders that they have the right and the obligation to intervene when civilian politicians "betray" the people through corruption or unwise public policies. Here are two good historical examples:

1. Egypt's King Farouk had led Egypt to defeat in the first Arab-Israeli war (1948–1949), tolerated British-French control of the Suez Canal, and failed to address his country's endemic poverty. In 1952, a coterie of junior Egyptian army officers staged a relatively nonviolent coup to remove the king and install a Revolutionary Command Council. All the subsequent leaders of Egypt, including Gamel Abdel Nasser himself, came from this core group, although the country's former president, Hosni Mubarek, was the last of an aging generation.

   When the Arab Spring came to Egypt in January 2011, mass protests in Cairo's Tahrir Square ignited political chaos in Egypt. On February 11, 2011, President

Mubarek resigned, but the military establishment remained substantively in control of the country despite free presidential elections in the spring of 2012.

2. In the spring of 1967, a democratic Greece was preparing for parliamentary elections, and conservative soldiers feared that a socialist would become prime minister. On April 21, a mysterious group of colonels took over the country in a desperate attempt to save Greece from a man they regarded as a dangerous radical. Initially tolerated by Washington for Cold War motives, the anticommunist Greek colonels ruled until their incompetence became so blatant that they were driven from power in 1974.

While they do occasionally happen in developed societies, military dictatorships are more typical of poor and primitive societies. Between 1963 and 1987, for example, there were sixty-eight military coups in sub-Saharan Africa; in the years after World War II, nearly every country in Latin America experienced a military coup.

Military Regimes

Whatever the original cause, military regimes seldom work out well in practice. Military officers are supposed to be good at commanding troops in combat, a skill that may not translate well to the management of school systems, taxation, or traffic control. Military men accustomed to obedience can find it difficult to adjust to the give-and-take of practical politics and have occasionally been capable of great cruelty toward the civilian population. In 1976, for example, Argentine generals overthrew an incompetent but democratically elected government in Buenos Aires and established a repressive, anticommunist, antiliberal, superpatriotic government led by a succession of soldiers. To rid Argentina of people regarded as subversives, the military embarked upon what has been called the Dirty War, with so-called death squads kidnapping and murdering tens of thousands of people suspected of left-wing ideologies.[18]

Since free discussion of public issues disappears pretty quickly under these conditions, military leaders can drift foolishly into suicidal public policies. In 1982, that same homicidal Argentine military elite decided to settle a long-standing territorial dispute with Great Britain by invading Britain's Falkland Islands. Intellectually isolated, the generals were unable to predict how the forceful Prime Minister Margaret Thatcher would react to an armed invasion of British territory and were stunned when the British responded with devastating military power. Humiliatingly defeated in their own backyard, the Argentine generals were driven from office in favor of a civilian government. Putting Argentina together again, unfortunately, was more difficult than taking it apart. Argentina is once again a stable and relatively wealthy country, but those praetorian years have left their mark on the nation's consciousness.

BURMA'S MEN ON HORSEBACK

The history of Burma demonstrates how a military elite can react to internal conflict by creating an extremely repressive government. The majority population in Burma is typically called "Burman," an ethnic community with a strong sense of identity, practicing the Buddhist religion and speaking the Burmese language. Thanks to colonial-

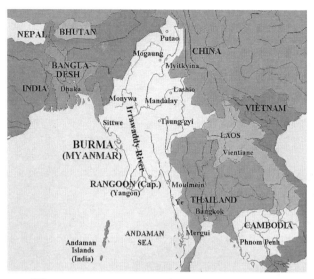

Map 8.3. Burma/Myanmar
Note that Burma shares borders with Bangladesh, India, China, Laos, and Thailand,
making it the center of a very tough neighborhood.

ism, the modern Burmese state also included a hodgepodge of distinctly non-Burman communities such as the Shan, Karen, and other communities with different languages, religions, and alternate senses of self-identification. The core Burman population has always chauvinistically regarded these minority populations as foreigners who have few rights on Burmese soil.[19]

Britain took over Burma in the 1800s, and the territory (about the size of Texas) was a major theater of combat during World War II. In the last months of the war, a charismatic Burmese general named Aung San managed to unify the core Burman population and win the support of the ethnic minorities by convincing his people that they could live happily in a multiethnic society. Aung San became the father of his country by negotiating independence from Britain, but he was assassinated in 1947 by a Burman nationalist fanatic before he could lead Burma into the postwar era. Aung San left behind a two-year-old daughter, however, who was destined to carry his name into the twenty-first century.[20]

The Soldiers' Revolt

The Burmese tried to grapple with Burma's ethnic minorities by creating a federal system, but the military intervened in 1962, replacing the elected government with a soldier's **junta** led by General Ne Win and his Burmese Socialist Program Party. Why? First, Burma's soldiers were anxious about a perceived threat to national unity posed by the country's non-Burman ethnicities. Second, they were Burman nationalists who were obsessed by the fear of economic and cultural penetration from abroad. As a result, they wanted to achieve **autarky** or economic independence from the rest of the world. Third, they wanted a socialist system, which to the generals in Rangoon meant ownership of economic resources by the military, who managed them badly.[21]

By 1988, Burma was involved in genocidal warfare against its minorities, the economy was in ruins, and a new generation of Burmese intellectuals wondered why they needed to live in a **xenophobic** (foreigner-hating) military dictatorship. When students and political activists mounted mass demonstrations, the army resorted to machine-guns, killing tens of thousands of people in 1988–1990. Ne Win stepped down, and the military junta scheduled "free" multiparty elections for 1990, on the assumption that they could fix the vote and perpetuate their own rule.[22]

They were wrong. Aung San's daughter had taken refuge in England, studying at Oxford, doing a history doctorate at the University of London, marrying a British professor, and starting a family. Suu Kyi is her personal name, but for public and political purposes she has added her father's famous name to her own to produce Aung San Suu Kyi (pronounced "Awng Sahn Sue Chee"). A frail, beautiful woman, Suu Kyi visited her turbulent homeland in 1988 because her mother was ill, but was quickly caught up in protests against the junta. When pro-freedom activists organized the National League for Democracy (NLD), they asked Suu Kyi to lead the party in the 1990 elections. To the dismay of the military, the pro-democracy forces of the NLD won an overwhelming 82 percent of the popular vote. Although the election ought to have made her prime minister, Suu Kyi was arrested as the junta consolidated its rule into one of the most repressive societies on earth.[23]

For Burma, the years that followed were a protracted political duel between the military and the pro-democracy movement. For most of the years between 1990 and 2010, Suu Kyi was either in prison or under house arrest.[24] In 2010, the military regime adopted a more conciliatory stance. Aung San Suu Kyi was released from house arrest and used her freedom to organize her National League for Democracy. The newly "civilianized" military government established tentative peace treaties with some of the various ethnic minorities it had fought since the 1940s. In January of 2012, events began to move very rapidly, as the government released political prisoners and the United States reestablished diplomatic ties. While the generals were still firmly in charge, the world finally began to feel some optimism that Myanmar would someday once again become Burma.[25]

Aung San Suu Kyi has been central to this change. Inspired by India's Gandhi and America's Martin Luther King, she has always insisted upon a nonviolent approach to her country's dilemma.

Will Burma Evolve Out of Dictatorship?

The military leaders of Burma's military government have a long criminal record. For decades, they practiced great brutality toward the Burmese people, particularly the non-Burman minorities. Every major international human rights organization as well as the U.S. State Department condemned the regime for arbitrary executions of dissidents, the widespread use of slave/enforced labor, and the systematic denial of ordinary freedoms to citizens of the country. Since there is no independent system of justice, the Burmese military can get away, quite literally, with murder, and they pursued the war against the minorities relentlessly, making systematic use of the mass rape of women and girls. Despite hopes for the future, the Burmese junta flunked the 2011 Freedom House test with a bottom-of-the-scale "7."

Figure 8.4.   Aung San Suu Kyi
Born in 1945, Burmese pro-democracy activist and Nobel Prize–winner Aung San Suu Kyi spent more than a decade confined alone in her house, an experience she survived intellectually by listening to the BBC on a short-wave radio. In 2001, the Irish activist and singer Bono wrote "Walk On" about Aung San Suu Kyi, and his band, U2, dedicated their "Walk On" album to her. Aung San Suu Kyi was released from house arrest by the military authorities in November of 2010 and is now negotiating with the military for an eventual transition to democratic rule. Photograph courtesy of the World Economic Forum.

Apart from political crimes, the Burmese military has involved itself in a lot of pure criminality. Burma continues to be one of the world's largest suppliers of opium, the by-product of the poppy plant used in the manufacture of heroin. Most observers believe that military leaders have made enormous profits from the drug trade. Burma has long been a source of crude oil and natural gas, and major Japanese and Western companies have paid royalties to the junta for the right to search for oil and extract what they find. Environmental activists are concerned about the damage to the environment caused by oil pipelines running through the jungle.

Military regimes tend to be bad money managers. When the Asian economy hit a major bump in the road in the late 1990s, Burma lurched toward fiscal meltdown, with the population suffering badly. With their country ravaged by an out-of-control HIV/AIDS epidemic, the military tranquilly spent millions of oil and drug money on a Russian-made nuclear reactor and a fleet of MIG-29 jet aircraft. In 2008, the country was hit by a devastating cyclone, killing over one hundred thousand people and rendering many more homeless. Xenophobic even in the face of the country's worst natural disaster, the military regime turned down most offers of aid from the international community because accepting the aid would have meant accepting the presence of foreigners on Burmese soil.[26]

Why is liberty so scarce? Part of the answer is rooted in Burman culture, which tends to personalize power, seeing authority as flowing from a given human being rather than the holder of a specific public office. Burmese leaders see themselves as father figures, wiser and stronger than their citizen-children and therefore entitled to rule. Many Burmese find it difficult to master the concept of a loyal opposition. The minorities are a core issue because many Burman nationalists feel threatened by the Aung San family's dream of a multiethnic country in which they would have to share power with other ethnic groups.

Furthermore, some Asian tigers are difficult to dismount, and the regime's senior men have Saddam Hussein's execution and the casual murder of Muammar Gaddafi to remind them of their possible future. Fear of revenge is one of the best reasons why dictators need to stay in power; after breaking a great many laws, the members of the military junta know that a democratic government would put them on trial. Business interests (especially those profiting from narcotics and petroleum) know that a representative government would cost them money. Burmese workers are the most poorly paid in the world, and free labor unions would cut into manufacturers' profits. For the men who kept Suu Kyi under lock and key for two decades, therefore, a dictatorship is at least a short-term solution to all these problems; the transition to democracy will be slow and, for the dictators themselves, exceedingly dangerous.

3. Theocracies

In 1922, the British poet A. E. Housman published an often-quoted poem that began,

> The laws of God, the laws of man,
> He may keep that will and can;
> Not I: let God and man decree
> Laws for themselves and not for me[27]

In distinguishing between divine and human law, Housman was reflecting the common Western notion that there should be two sets of imperatives that sometimes coincide and sometimes differ. Murder is against both the Ten Commandments and the criminal code in every civilized country. Going five miles over the speed limit on an empty highway on a clear day is illegal but perhaps not immoral. Coveting thy neighbor's wife (or husband) may be immoral, but a little quiet coveting is not illegal.

The willingness of North Americans and Europeans to make this state-church distinction is rooted in history. When the Roman Empire collapsed in the 400s AD, the bishop of Rome remained the spiritual leader of the Catholic Church and continued to make moral decisions about what did and did not offend God. At the civil political level, an array of medieval aristocrats decided what was legal and what was not. The king could send you to the gallows, after which the pope could dispatch your soul to hell. There were important sectors of agreement between the two sources of authority, but there was always a significant area of difference that has grown with modernity. Some Catholic politicians, for example, explain that they disapprove morally of abortion, but would not seek to overturn laws giving women the right to choose. Western thinking about free societies depends on making a tolerant distinction between the sacred and the civil.

With a different historical background, Muslims generally have difficulty in seeing how power can be divided between civil and religious authorities. In Islam, spiritual and political authority is essentially unified, and some scholars believe that this concept has made it difficult for Islamic countries to evolve into democracies. Some Islamic countries essentially fudge the issue. The Sharia forbids alcohol, but you can order a beer in a bar in Morocco's famous city of Marrakesh. The Qur'an allows a man to have four wives, but the civil law code of Muslim Tunisia restricts men to one spouse at a time.

In almost every Islamic country, there are secular Muslims who want a more European approach to law, which agrees with Jeremy Bentham's belief that laws are human creations designed to order public policy in a given society. From a secularist point of view, these laws need to be altered when our perception of human needs changes; they must tolerate individual lifestyles, which means generally that you can sin as long as you do it quietly and don't bother your neighbors.[28]

Most Muslim governments make an effort to harmonize their law codes—at least to some extent—with the Sharia. While Islamic countries believe in listening carefully when religious authorities speak, only rarely have Islamic clerics been allowed to take actual control of their societies, creating what we would call a theocracy. In recent times, it has only happened a few times. We will look at Afghanistan more carefully in chapter 10, but for now, note that in 1995, a Kandahar-based cleric named Mullah Omar led a ragtag collection of extreme Islamists in the conquest of about 90 percent of the country. The religious and clerical leaders of the Taliban stayed in control of Afghanistan, giving sanctuary to Osama bin Laden and enforcing a cruel and primitive version of Islam on a suffering people until 2001, when the government was displaced by American forces after the September 11 al-Qaeda attacks. As we will see later, the Taliban did not disappear, and U.S. and NATO forces were still battling with them in 2012. The more important example of a functioning theocracy is the Islamic Republic of Iran, to which we will now turn.

THE IRANIAN CASE

What is today the Islamic Republic of Iran was known for most of its long history as Persia. Despite its ancient greatness, Iran began the twentieth century as a poor and marginal multinational state, independent but weak and menaced by powerful enemies, both foreign and domestic. Territorially, this is a big country, roughly the size of Alaska, with craggy mountains along both the Persian Gulf coast and the northern border near the Caspian Sea. In the South and East, the land is semidesert. What first made Iran fatally attractive to the Western world were its enormous petroleum resources; a century after its discovery, crude oil produces about 90 percent of Iran's total income. Thanks to this resource, Iran is not as poor as some of her neighbors. The PC/GNI is about $10,000, although this oil wealth has never been very equitably divided.

Why Is Iran a Less-Free Society?

Like most other authoritarian states, Iran has never been able to devise democratic solutions to the conflicts built into its own history. Let's look at some of these inherent and enduring problems.

- The Multinational State Problem: Iran is a sprawling and complicated multinational state that could have been either much larger or much smaller than it is, since the country lacks obvious borders. Iran's "core nation" is an ethnic Persian population that practices the Shi'ite variant of Islam and speaks Farsi, a cognate of the Persian language group. Unfortunately, this Persian core constitutes only about 51 percent of the population. Just under 20 percent of Iranian citizens are Azerbaijani (sometimes called Azeris), who speak a cognate of modern Turkish, which comes from a completely different family of languages. A trouble-prone 7 percent of Iran's citizens are Kurds, who live close to the border with Iraq, and there is a variety of other ethnic minorities within the nation's boundaries.[29]
- The Trans-border Minority Problem: Internal ethnic divisions would be complicated enough, but these minority nationalities extend out beyond Iran's borders into

Map 8.4. The Islamic Republic of Iran

neighboring countries that might have been, but did not become, part of Iran. While perhaps twelve million Turkic-speaking Azeris are residents of Iran, for example, another nine million live over the border in Azerbaijan to the north. In the Northeast, Turkoman Iranians (who speak another Turkic cognate) have more in common with their linguistic brethren across the border in Turkmenistan than they do with Tehran's Farsi-speakers. Along the western frontier with Iraq and Turkey, there are Iranian Kurds, Iraqi Kurds, and Turkish Kurds, most of whom would prefer to be citizens of the as yet uncreated state of Kurdistan. Along the southern border with Iraq is a large community of Arabs, who share a language with Iraq's Arabic population. In the Southeast, there are Baluchi tribal peoples on both sides of the border with Pakistan. Iran's arbitrary borders were defined by generals in past wars, not by elections, and they do not reflect local ethnic or national divisions.

- The Hostile World Outside: Iran's past and potential adversaries include some neighborhood enemies and some global antagonists. Iranians and Arab Iraqis have never defined precisely where the border between them lies; Iranians thought it should be the Tigris River, while Iraqis preferred the Zagros Mountains, which run from the Persian Gulf to Turkey. Imperial Russia pressured her northern border until 1917 when the czars were replaced by Marxist commissars, who perpetuated the same policy of meddling in Iranian affairs. Once oil was discovered along Iran's western coast, British petroleum companies began invading the country commercially, bringing British imperial power intrusively into the heart of Iranian politics. As the British Empire subsided, the role of squeezing Iran was taken over by the Americans. In the Far East of the country, Iran's borders with Afghanistan and Pakistan are poorly defined; nomadic tribal peoples move back and forth, and South Asia's political unrest has repeatedly penetrated the Islamic Republic.

- The Sunni-Shi'ite Antagonism: Perhaps the most important problem has been religion. Worldwide, about 85 percent of Muslims belong to the Sunni or Orthodox branch of

Islam. The Shi'ite people are primarily clustered around the Persian Gulf, and over 90 percent of Iran's population belongs to this Islamic sect. Non-Muslims often underestimate the bitterness between these two Islamic communities, which is far worse than any contemporary antagonism between Roman Catholics and Protestants.

When the Prophet Mohammed died in 632 AD, he left behind a son-in-law named Ali, who did not become leader of the Islamic community until 656 AD when a civil war erupted over the succession. Ali was murdered in 661 AD, and his son, Hussein, perished in 680 AD. Those Muslims who revered Ali and Hussein created a spiritual and political movement that has become quite different from conventional Sunni Islam. By the early 1500s, Shia had become the established religion in Iran, and most Iraqis had become Shi'ites.

It is easy to indulge in stereotypes when describing Shia, and the observable differences between Shi'ites and Sunnis are more mood than doctrine. Shi'ites feel isolated and endangered in a world they perceive to be hostile to them. Speaking of Shia's "divine discontent," the celebrated British scholar Karen Armstrong notes that

> Sunnis were basically optimistic about Muslim history, where the Shia vision was more tragic: the fate of the descendants of the Prophet Mohammed had become a symbol of a cosmic struggle between good and evil, justice and tyranny in which the wicked always seem to get the upper hand.[30]

The Shi'ite Clerical Establishment

The early Shi'ites believed that Ali and his sons began a series of twelve imams or prophetic figures, whose moral authority could never be challenged. To some degree, the ayatollahs of both modern Iran and Iraq have assumed that same mantle of infallible authority, leading pious Shi'ites to demand a government that is not only run in accordance with the dictates of religion but also actually administered by clerical figures.

In Shi'ite society (especially in Iraq and Iran), there is a clearer hierarchy of religious leaders than is commonly found in Sunni Islam. Iran has a major theological seminary in the city of Qom and smaller training institutions scattered around the country. In Iran, the **mullah** occupies a spiritual and social position resembling an Irish or Italian parish priest in a small rural community. Iranian mullahs settle disputes and problems, look after the poor, and sometimes preside over the normal civil administration of the town. Those who have studied longer and harder attain the superior rank of *mujtahid* (or jurist) and are permitted to interpret Islamic law. Above the jurists are the *hujjat al-Islam*, who often occupy senior government offices; at the top of the hierarchy are a handful of ayatollahs and grand ayatollahs. This hierarchy of clergymen had always provided Iran with an alternative or shadow government, providing services to the common people that the "real" government often neglected.

When the Islamic world emerged into the bright technological lights of the modern world, however, some Muslims observed that they had fallen far behind a Christian West that they had once challenged. These modernizers demanded that Islamic leaders confine themselves to spirituality, allowing scientists, scholars, and secular political leaders to take positions of leadership in societies trying to catch up quickly with Europe and North

Table 8.2.   An Iranian Time Line

1935: Persia changes its name to Iran	1989: Ayatollah Khomeini dies; Seyed Ali Khamenei becomes spiritual leader.
1941: Britain occupies Iran and crowns Mohammed Shah Pahlevi	1997: Moderate Mohammed Khatami elected president; reelected 2001
1942: U.S. troops help garrison Iran	2004: Islamist Conservatives rig legislative elections to consolidate power
1951: Prime Minister Mossadegh seizes British oil resources; shah temporarily in exile.	2005: Islamist President Mahmoud Ahmadinejad elected.
1953: U.S./UK-inspired coup returns shah to power	2009: Green Movement arises after Ahmadinejad reelected in controversial vote.
1967: Shah achieves absolute rule over Iran	2010: UN Security Council deepens sanctions against Iran for nuclear policy.
1978: Anti-Shah violence begins	
1979: Ayatollah Khomeini takes power; US embassy seized	2012: Iran reaches "brink of war" levels with United States and Israel over alleged nuclear ambitions. Straits of Hormuz closure threatened
1980: US fails to rescue hostages; Iraq attacks Iran	
1988: US ship downs Iranian airliner; Iran-Iraq war ends	

America. This movement created a conflict in every Islamic society between secular modernizers and traditionalists or Islamists. The argument between the two camps was always more strident in the Shi'ite camp than in the Sunni world.

Iran's Quarrel with History

As Iran lurched into the twentieth century, the country was governed by an inefficient and corrupt Qajar dynasty, which grappled unsuccessfully with the country's built-in conflicts.[31]

In 1906, Iranians demanded and got a **majlis** or legislative assembly, although foreign interference mounted because of British interest in Iranian oil and the strategic demands of World War I. In 1921, a modernizing military leader named Pahlevi took power, proclaiming himself shah of Iran. A firm secularist and a modernizing dictator, Reza Shah Pahlevi believed that Islam was retarding the development of his country, and he worked to decrease the influence of the Muslim clergy. While he had little serious interest in democracy, he did encourage women's rights, making it illegal, for example, to wear the veil in public.[32]

In 1941, British and Russian forces occupied Iran for strategic reasons. When Reza Shah Pahlevi objected, the British replaced him with his eighteen-year-old son, Mohammed Shah Pahlevi. The United States joined the war in 1941, and thirty thousand U.S. troops were dispatched the following year to garrison Iran. Most Americans have long forgotten that armed GIs once patrolled the streets of Tehran, but Iranian memories are long.

After World War II, American forces stayed behind to train Iranian troops as anti-Soviet Cold War allies and to support the young and inexperienced Mohammed Shah Pahlevi. In a relatively free 1951 majlis election, however, Iranians chose a feisty nationalist politician named Mohammed Mossadegh as their prime minister. Backed by clerics, nationalists, and the commercial classes, Mossadegh tried to reduce Western interference in Iranian affairs and establish national control over the country's petroleum industry.

Mossadegh convincingly portrayed the shah as the pawn of Western political and petroleum interests, and in 1951, at the start of what is called the **Mossadegh Crisis**, the unpopular shah was forced to flee his country. At the direction of U.S. president Dwight D. Eisenhower, the young American CIA mounted one of its first covert operations in 1953, fostering a military coup that put Mossadegh in jail and the shah back on his throne and firmly in control.[33] Mossadegh's only serious crime was trying to get more money for Iranian crude oil, but the United States was anxious to ensure that nothing of the sort ever happened again. American help in re-creating a royal executive regime made the United States unpopular among religious leaders as well as Iranian nationalists.

From the 1950s to the end of the 1970s, the shah got massive American support because U.S. policy makers were focused on the strategic threat from the Soviet Union. In this high-stakes global contest, both superpowers took their allies where they could find them, and if the shah was a dictator, he was at least a pro-American one. Uninterested in the Cold War, most pious Iranian Shi'ites saw the Shah as an oppressive tyrant and an insincere Muslim who held their religion in contempt. While Iran existed on the fringes of America's consciousness, the Iranians were bleakly aware that it was the United States that bought the oil that made the shah's family obscenely rich and sold his army the weapons he needed to stay in power. Like his father, the shah believed that Iran needed to modernize at the expense of traditionalist Islamic fundamentalism. When an imprudent clergyman named Ruhollah Musavi Khomeini denounced royal misrule, Mohammed Shah Pahlevi first imprisoned and then exiled the irritating ayatollah.

Although some members of his family were famously dishonest, Mohammed Shah Pahlevi was bright and authentically concerned with the future greatness of his country. Unfortunately, his authoritarian rule alienated many Iranians, and he never won much domestic support outside the military and the Westernized middle classes. At a very pro-found level, he was fascinated by Western weaponry, and after striking an alliance with Richard Nixon in the 1970s, he went on a military spending spree, spending billions of dollars for American-made weapons over the next few years. Despite the fact that the Iranian government permitted SAVAK, the feared internal-security agency, to torture and execute dissenters, Mohammed Shah Pahlevi was always a welcome guest in Washington, where every American president from Truman to Carter praised him as a key U.S. ally. An increasing number of Iranians came to see the United States as the enemy of their religion and their culture.

Oddly enough, the shah ran into political troubles at precisely the time when his country's per capita gross domestic product was soaring. As always, we need to look at this kind of statistic very carefully. Per capita means "average" and the arithmetic often disguises a cavernous gap between rich and poor. In fact, little of Iran's oil wealth was actually reaching the rural peasantry, which suffered badly as inflation drove prices up. But royal executive regimes do not provide a peaceful way for citizens to register their discontent with the government. By this time, poor people, farmers, Iranian nationalists, and the Islamic clergy had come to hate their king, and alienated Iranians took to the streets in 1978 with mass riots and demonstrations. The shah fled his country for the last time in early 1979 and was replaced by the same Ayatollah Khomeini he had sent into exile fifteen years earlier.[34]

THE ISLAMIC REPUBLIC OF IRAN

Prior to Khomeini's stunning coup d'état, neither the Iranian nor the American government had much respect for the Shi'ite clergy. When Khomeini returned to his native land in February 1979, he was passionately welcomed by a wide range of Iranians, many of whom had little in common beyond a shared distaste for the shah and his American sponsors. Khomeini's core support came from Iranian Shi'ite Islamists, fundamentalist Muslims who believed that civil society should be strictly organized according to the dictates of their religion.[35]

Fighting the Great Satan

Ruhollah Khomeini's government strived to combine the appearance of a normal administration with the reality of theocratic control. As far as the formal structures of government were concerned, the 270 members of the majlis, a unicameral legislature, held legislative power. Executive authority was vested in a directly elected president, who could serve for one or two four-year terms. Provisions were made for an independent supreme court and a system of regional courts and justices. On paper, it looked a lot like a democracy, and there were certainly areas for public participation in government that had never existed before.

On the other hand, Khomeini ensured that the Shi'ite clergy remained firmly in control. To consolidate his own position, the ayatollah created the office of *faqih*, a supreme religious leader who would appoint senior judges and military leaders. Like other senior Islamic clergymen, Khomeini had the right to issue authoritative orders or commands (called ***fatwas***) on matters of public policy, a power he used to bypass civilian government. To further reinforce the power of the clergy, he created the Council of Guardians, a body of senior Shi'ite theologians with the power to approve or veto anything done by the civilian government. Furthermore, this Council of Guardians could disapprove candidates for the majlis and the presidency if they lacked strong Islamist credentials. In October of 1979, Khomeini became Iran's first faqih and the Islamic Republic of Iran became the modern era's first major theocracy, or government by an elite group of religious leaders.

Death for Literary Blasphemy

The Iranian government has paid little attention to the civil rights of Iranians and non-Iranians, and the ayatollah's government brutally executed tens of thousands of domestic enemies in the early years of the revolution. In the last year of his life, Khomeini picked a fight with writers all over the world by ordering the assassination/execution of Salman Rushdie, an Indian-born writer of Muslim parentage who had become a British citizen. Rushdie's brilliant but difficult 1988 novel, *Satanic Verses*, might have been read by only committed Rushdie fans had the Ayatollah not proclaimed that the novel contained blasphemous insults to Islam. Looking for ways to demonstrate leadership within the Moslem world, Khomeini issued a fatwa (or holy order) that the author be executed, forcing one of Britain's leading writers into hiding. While the fatwa itself has never been formally revoked, the Iranian government subsequently promised not to attempt to carry it out, and Rushdie now lives (nervously) in New York.

Khomeini's supporters were convinced that a great many of their country's problems had come from foreign, and specifically, American, interference in their lives. In keeping with the Shi'ite view of themselves as a people of God besieged on all sides by agents of the devil, Khomeini focused his rhetoric on the "Great Satan" in Washington. On November 4, 1979, a group of students attacked the U.S. embassy in Tehran and took over fifty prisoners. The Iran hostage crisis that followed was a world-class violation of international law on the part of Khomeini's government.

The United States appealed to the World Court, getting the Iranians condemned by the United Nations and using diplomacy to isolate the Khomeini regime. Khomeini's behavior looked suicidal from abroad, but the hostage crisis actually helped him consolidate power at home. In the past, Iranian leaders had surrendered to foreign foes; this time, Khomeini's Islamists had struck back. It was not until the morning of President Reagan's 1981 Inauguration, 444 days later, that the hostages were released. The reasons for the timing remain controversial: Iran has never formally apologized for the hostage crisis and November 4 remains a national holiday.

Between 1980 and 1988, Khomeini's government consolidated its power by defending Iran against a murderous military attack by Saddam Hussein's Iraq. As mentioned above, there had always been a dispute between Iranians and Iraqis over the exact border between their two countries, and this conflict provided the excuse for Hussein's treachery. Hussein's actual motives were more complex and more serious. The leader of a firmly secularist Sunni government, Hussein had reason to fear that Iraq's Shi'ite Islamists (60 percent of the Iraqi population, although firmly excluded from power) would prefer a Khomeini-style theocracy run by Iraqi Shi'ite clerics. If downtrodden Iraqi Shi'ites were persuaded to self-identify more as Shi'ites than as Iraqis, Hussein could be facing insurrection at home. Perhaps with the quiet encouragement of Western powers, Saddam Hussein ordered his army to cross the border in September of 1980, launching a futile eight-year campaign that may have killed three-quarters of a million people.

Saddam Hussein had calculated that the Khomeini regime was too weak to withstand both American wrath and the Iraqi Army, but in fact Iranian Shi'ites were prepared by their theology to see themselves standing righteously alone against wicked enemies. Khomeini's Iranian army defended the country with sometimes-suicidal courage and Khomeini's domestic political foes were effectively silenced.

In the last stages of the Iraq-Iran War, the West became concerned with the free passage of oil tankers through the Persian Gulf, and the United States deployed naval forces to protect U.S. interests in the area. On July 3, 1988, the captain of the USS *Vincennes* decided that a blip on his radar screen represented an attacking Iranian fighter. He shot first, and when the time came to ask questions, the world learned that the U.S. Navy had just blown up a regularly scheduled Iranian Airlines airbus on a routine flight over the Persian Gulf. All 290 Iranian passengers were killed. Khomeini had routinely called the United States the "Great Satan," and the airbus disaster confirmed for many Iranians that their Ayatollah had been right all along.

The Contemporary Government of Iran

The Ayatollah Khomeini died in 1989 and was replaced as spiritual leader by a less-charismatic but equally intolerant follower with a confusingly similar name, the Ayatollah Ali

Khamenei. By the mid-1990s, revolutionary fervor had begun to wane among Iranians. Interested in Western music and fashions, and impatient with restraints on their behavior, a younger generation viewed this theocratic society with declining enthusiasm.

Western hopes that Iran would evolve into a democracy were bolstered in 1997 when a very moderate reformer named Mohammed Khatami was elected president. Moving slowly and cautiously to avoid upsetting the clerical conservatives, President Khatami attempted to open doors to modernity and to the outside world. Without exactly apologizing, Khatami said that he was sorry that American feelings were hurt over the hostage crisis. Khatami granted a famous interview with CNN's Christiane Amanpour (a woman of Iranian heritage), in which he presented himself as a reasonable and likable moderate.

Khatami's overtures to the West were generally ignored by the United States as President Clinton battled through the Lewinsky scandal. When George W. Bush became U.S. president in 2001, the White House began to talk openly about overthrowing the Iranian government, undercutting Khatami's position. Americans believed that the Iranian government was supporting Palestinian resistance groups such as HAMAS and Islamic Jihad, organizations regarded as terrorist in both Washington and Jerusalem. When President Bush added Iran to his "Axis of Evil" trilogy in 2002, Iranians were furious.[36]

When the United States attacked Iran's neighbor Iraq in 2003, the Iranian leadership watched with mixed emotions as its two worst enemies went to war with one another. As much as they disliked Saddam Hussein's regime, they absolutely hated the idea of an American military presence just over their border. They were also grimly aware that the United States had military bases in Afghanistan, to their east, in Turkmenistan, to the north, as well as in Qatar and Oman, just across the narrow Persian Gulf. On the other hand, there was little the Iranians could do to affect U.S. determination. The Tehran leadership protested the war against Iraq but otherwise stayed out of the way.

The Nuclear Turn for the Worse

By the end of his presidency in 2005, Mohammad Khatami had made comparatively little progress in his campaign to bring openness to Iranian society, and Freedom House assigned the country a censorious "6," meaning that civil liberties were few and far between, and noted that adults were still being executed for consensual sexual relations outside of marriage. The dictatorship was erratic, since laws were sometimes enforced brutally and sometimes ignored. Conservative judges and police officers continued to throw liberal activists into prison, however, and continued to close down newspapers that offended the religious establishment.

In the parliamentary elections of 2004, the clerical establishment boldly asserted its real control over the political process by disqualifying over three thousand secularist candidates for election to the majlis, ensuring that the legislature would reflect the theocratic views of the Council of Guardians.

The real meltdown occurred during the June 24 presidential elections, as a previously obscure hard-line Islamist emerged to score an unexpected and overwhelming win in the double-ballot presidential election. Unlike the earlier presidents of the country, Ahmadinejad was not a cleric, although he had been an enthusiastic follower of the Ayatollah Khomeini and was politically very close to the new spiritual leader, Ali Khamenei. Having served the Islamic Revolution in a variety of capacities, Ahmadinejad held a doctorate in traffic management from Tehran University and had been serving as mayor of Tehran. Ahmadinejad's appeal was complex; he ran not only as a dedicated Islamist but also as a reformer who wanted to shake the massive corruption out of the Iranian government.

Taking office, he began systematically offending the West, threatening Israel and indulging in **Holocaust denial**, suggesting that the Jews had invented the story of Nazi death camps for political advantage. For its part, the Bush administration voiced anxiety over the possibility that the Iranian government might be pursuing the development of nuclear weaponry. Iran insisted that nuclear fuel refinement was intended to provide peaceful electrical power. Cynics and scientists observed wryly that an oil-rich country such as Iran hardly needed to worry about power resources and alleged that the country was trying to create an atomic weapon.

President Ahmadinejad ran into his first serious domestic opposition when he stood for reelection in 2009. Almost all observers reported that the vote was fraudulent, and the streets of Tehran erupted in protest. A "Green Movement" appeared, demanding honesty and democracy in public life. The Iranian government struck back brutally, imprisoning, torturing, and executing demonstrators and revealing the stark brutality of the regime. In February 2011, following Arab Spring protests, Iranian opposition protesters filled the streets of Tehran, but the Iranian regime again responded brutally by jailing protesters and using live ammunition to control the crowds.[37]

The possibility of a nuclear Iran has the United States, Western Europe, and Israel distinctly worried, because there are no particularly good options if Ahmadinejad and Khamenei develop a deployable nuclear weapon. The press has reported discussions in the White House and in Jerusalem about a preemptive strike against Iranian nuclear facilities, but it is not clear that there is a meaningful military option. In the meanwhile, Iranian nuclear scientists have been assassinated, apparently by Israeli intelligence operatives. The Iranians have counterthreatened to close the Straits of Hormuz, through which pass much of the world's oil supplies. It is considered likely that an American or Israeli military attack would generate support for the country's theocracy, just as Saddam Hussein's aggression did in 1980. By 2012, rhetoric became increasingly inflamed in both Washington and Jerusalem, and the crisis struck many observers as lacking any reasonable or obvious solution.[38]

4. Elite Dictatorships or Oligarchies: The Russian Case

Some less-free regimes do not fit very comfortably into neat categories, but many of them can be generally categorized as "**elite dictatorships**," that is, countries that are governed by small groups who are not democratically elected. This style of government is sometimes called an oligarchy and they develop in a variety of ways:

- Elite regimes sometimes evolve in the aftermath of a military coup d'état, with the elite being created by former soldiers. The generals trade in their uniforms for well-tailored civilian suits, hire technical experts to administer the complicated machinery of repressive government, and even stage fake elections to legitimize their rule. After General Pinochet overthrew the democratically elected government of Chile in 1973, he became President Pinochet and won a series of carefully orchestrated elections until he was eased out of power in 1989.

- Other elite regimes have emerged from political parties that have gained power through a civil war, a coup, or even an election, but they subsequently declined to share it with anyone. Until it came to a messy end in 2000, the government of what was then Yugoslavia rested on a tainted electoral victory by Slobodan Milošević and his cronies in the Serbian Socialist Party.

- An elite regime may even emerge from an extended family and its business associates and friends, such as the Somoza dynasty that ruled Nicaragua between 1933 and 1979.

- Some elite regimes come from ethnic minorities within a given society. Syria is a generally Sunni Arab society, but the Shi'ite Alawite tribe (only 12 percent of the population) has provided the country with Alawite dictators for several decades. During the Arab Spring of 2011, Syria's Sunni majority mounted such serious protests against the Damascus regime that the country is now threatened with full-fledged civil war.

- Other elites may evolve from the ranks of a victorious revolutionary group. In Africa, Robert Mugabe's Zimbabwean government is still dominated by the now-corrupt ZANU guerrillas who presided over the country's move to black majority rule in 1980. If these revolutionaries are motivated by an ideology, the elite may be the top ranks of a political movement. In this sense, Marxist governments also qualify as elite dictatorships. The Cuban Communist Party evolved from the revolutionaries who followed Fidel Castro to victory in 1959. The Vietnamese Communist Party is generally led by veterans of the 1965–1975 war against the United States. The Soviet Union certainly once qualified as an ideological dictatorship, since it was run by top ranks of the Communist Party. As we will see below, Russia now seems to have become an elite dictatorship led by veterans of the Soviet-era KGB.

Should there be a separate category for one-man dictatorships? At any time, there seem to be a few dictatorships in which one man (this is not sexism; they do always seem to be men) so dominates a society that we are tempted to think in terms of a personal dictatorship. Some authors have made the one-man dictatorship into a category all its own, but if we look carefully at what seems to be a personal dictatorship, we find that the supreme ruler is really only the "first-among-unequals," that is, the leader of what is often a small elite group of backers. No dictator could rule without the support of an elite, and when the support vanishes, so does the dictator. Nazi Germany's Hitler certainly belonged in this category in the sense that Hitler was supported by a coterie of powerful and ambitious Nazis, many of whom had been with him since the beginning of his surge toward power. Saddam Hussein's Iraq was an elite dictatorship dominated by one very powerful strongman who was supported by both a tribal network and a party structure.

LIFE AFTER MARX: RUSSIA RE-CREATES ITSELF

For most of the past century, any discussion of Marxism inevitably focused on the land where Marxism first became a system of government, the Soviet Union, which sponsored a political philosophy that rivaled Western ideas of free markets and democracy. When the Soviet Union abruptly dissolved at the end of 1991, the global Marxist movement was left without a leader, and what became the Russian Federation lost its ideological anchor. What's happening to Russia without Marxism?

Back to the USSR

The USSR (Union of Soviet Socialist Republics) was born of the Bolshevik Revolution in 1917, becoming a sovereign state with fifteen sub-sovereign entities called "union republics," each republic theoretically corresponding roughly to an American state or a Canadian province. The formal structure of the USSR was that of a federal parliamentary system, and on paper it looked something like the government of Australia or Germany. The USSR operated under a succession of constitutions, all of which described it as a federal state, but the actual Soviet government was a tightly centralized unitary system with the Communist Party acting as the Kremlin's policy-enforcement mechanism.

Since real power resided in the Communist Party, the party's secretary general was the acknowledged leader of the USSR. After Stalin, these party chieftains often awarded themselves Russia's ceremonial presidency as well, to give themselves protocol rank at international meetings, very much as Chinese secretaries general do today.

This Marxist system achieved a measure of legitimacy by defending the Soviet Union from Hitler's Germany in World War II and from what it perceived to be an aggressive America during the Cold War. Unlike the czars, the Marxists managed to feed most Russians most of the time and provided a modest level of social services, such as free education and medical care. Although most of their research and development was military, the Soviets challenged the West with technological advances such as the 1957 launch of Sputnik, the world's first earth-orbiting satellite.

Ultimately, however, the USSR's failures outweighed its successes. After Stalin's death in 1953, Russia managed the transition from a totalitarian to an authoritarian regime but never achieved democracy. Nor did the economy fulfill rising expectations. In the minds of most Russians, state-of-the-art military technology was no substitute for the color televisions, high-quality automobiles, and affordable private housing enjoyed

Table 8.3. A Russian Time Line

1917	Russian Revolution ends Czarist rule; Lenin in power
1924	Lenin dies; Bolshevik power struggle ensues
1928	Stalin emerges as absolute leader of USSR
1941	Nazi Germany attacks USSR
1944–1945	Red Army conquers Eastern Europe
1953	Stalin dies; Khrushchev assumes leadership
1964	Khrushchev removed; Brezhnev becomes leader
1985	Mikhail Gorbachev becomes USSR president
1991	USSR dissolves
1992–1999	Boris Yeltsin is president of Russia
2000	Vladimir Putin becomes president of Russia
2008	Dmitry Medvedev becomes president of Russia Vladimir Putin becomes prime minister
2012	Presidential elections and pro-democracy protests

in the West and unobtainable in the USSR. When the Soviet Union stopped reporting detailed demographic statistics, such as infant mortality rates and average life expectancy, in 1974, no one noticed, but alarm bells ought to have been ringing. The Moscow bureaucracy was reluctant to admit that Russians were living shorter lives than ever because of the breakdown of the social and medical system. Inheriting the top party position in 1985, Soviet leader Mikhail Gorbachev moved the USSR toward real **détente** with the West, but his own Communist Party was resistant to reform and sabotaged his efforts to achieve democracy. After a sustained period of political and economic stress, the USSR legally dissolved itself on the last day of 1991.[39]

We should use the term "Soviet Union," therefore, only to refer to the political institution that existed between November 7, 1917, and December 31, 1991. After the USSR dissolved, the fifteen constituent republics all declared themselves to be separate and equally sovereign states, although the largest of these, the Russian Federation, inherited the USSR's seat in the UN Security Council and all its nuclear weapons. Twelve of the fifteen former Soviet socialist republics subsequently joined an international club called the Commonwealth of Independent States or CIS, but this Russia-dominated organization never became much of a player in politics.

Boris Yeltsin's Russia (1992–1999)

As far as the Russian Federation was concerned, the rest of the 1990s belonged to Boris Yeltsin who—like his former mentor Mikhail Gorbachev—was originally a product of the Communist Party. When Russia became independent, the initially popular President Yeltsin imitated the French Fifth Republic's combination system, becoming an executive president himself and appointing a series of prime ministers who could be fired whenever the economy took a turn for the worst.

Yeltsin began his tenure as president of Russia amid high hopes and excitement. He quickly established good relations with America's Bill Clinton, and Western economists persuaded him to push Russia into a rapid transition (sometimes called "**shock therapy**") from Marxism to a free-enterprise system.

Russian political life under Yeltsin contained a mixture of democratic and authoritarian elements: when he found himself challenged by Communist delegates in the Duma, Yeltsin brought in the army and shelled the legislature into submission. In 1993, he dictated Russia's present constitution and got it passed by referendum but without significant public debate. Predictably, the new constitution grants most political horsepower to the president and limits the authority of the legislature.

It was immediately clear that there would be enduring problems. On Russia's southern border with Georgia is a province called Chechnya, occupied by Muslims who speak a non-Slavic Caucasian language and have always demanded independence from Moscow. In 1994, Yeltsin ordered the Russian Army to discipline the rebellious province, but the tough, wily Chechnyan separatists fought the once-mighty Red Army to a standstill.

The Russian economy was no more manageable than the Chechnyans. For the seventy years of the Marxist experiment, free-market competition had been anathema; under Yeltsin, Russians were being asked to play a complicated new economic game under unfamiliar and rapidly changing rules. In the course of the 1990s, the Russian economy crashed, losing more than half its value.[40] Yeltsin put much of Russia's state-owned enter-

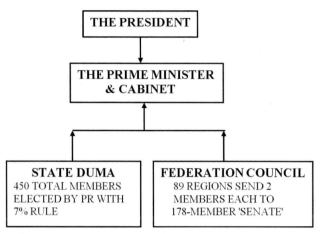

Figure 8.5. The Structure of the Russian Government
Essentially modeled on the French combination system, Boris Yeltsin's 1993 constitution gives the president most of the power. As is traditional in bicameral legislatures, the lower house, or Duma, is where most of the activity takes place. Under Putin, the voting system for the Duma was changed from partial to total proportional representation, which strengthened his own party and eliminated most independents. The 7 percent rule means that a party must garner at least 7 percent of the vote countrywide before getting any seats at all in the Duma. The Federation Council's principal job is to protect the interests of Russia's eighty-nine sub-sovereign regions. Together, the Duma and the Federation Council must approve the president's choice of the prime minister and the cabinet.

prises up for sale, but there were few buyers for inefficient industries unable to manufacture attractive goods or meet their payrolls. The so-called oligarchs who did buy up parts of the state sector often behaved like robber barons, stripping key Russian industries of their assets, siphoning off the profits into foreign banks, and leaving bankrupt companies behind as they themselves slipped into comfortable exile. Shock therapy devastated the lives of many working-class Russians.[41] Commenting on the Yeltsin years, the economist Joseph Stiglitz remarked trenchantly,

> For the majority of those living in the former Soviet Union, economic life under capitalism has been even worse than the old communist leaders said that it would be. Prospects for the future are bleak. The middle class has been devastated; a system of crony capitalism has been created, and the one achievement, the creation of a democracy . . . appears fragile.[42]

With an economy in free fall, an unsuccessful war against Chechnya, and political opposition from a resentful communist opposition, Yeltsin's first term was tumultuous. Although suffering from heart disease, sometimes drunk and confused in public, and increasingly unpopular, Yeltsin won a second term as president in 1996. President Clinton may have been right in believing that "Yeltsin drunk was better than most of the alternatives sober," but during Yeltsin's last years in office, it was often difficult to say who, if anyone, was actually in charge.

THE PUTIN ERA (1999–?)

In 1999, Yeltsin invited Vladimir Vladimirovich Putin, an obscure ex-intelligence officer from the Soviet-era KGB, to serve as his prime minister. Who is Vladimir Putin?

Born in 1952 into a middle-class family, Putin graduated from law school in 1975 and joined the KGB, the legendary Soviet intelligence agency. After extensive service in what was then East Germany, Putin retired from the intelligence service when the Soviet Union collapsed. He returned to his native St. Petersburg where he plunged into local politics. He was deputy mayor of St. Petersburg in 1996 when Yeltsin brought him to Moscow as a Kremlin staffer. With his former KGB colleagues rallying around him, he stepped up in 1998 to become chief of the rebaptized KGB, now known as the Federal Security Bureau or FSB.

In August of 1999, he became Prime Minister, and sent a much more robust Russian military force back into Chechnya. Putin's reconquest of the breakaway province was not gentle. The Chechnyan capital city of Grozny was reduced to rubble and nearly a half-million people became refugees. Russian troops practiced unspeakable brutality with summary executions and mass rapes of Chechnyan women. But the average Russian dislikes Chechnyans too much to worry about human rights; Putin had had begun the process of reversing a national humiliation and military victory made him popular.[43]

On December 31, 1999, Boris Yeltsin said a sudden, final goodbye and abruptly disappeared into retirement, leaving Putin as acting president. Riding high on his victories in Chechnya, Vladimir Putin ran a ruthlessly efficient election campaign, and won a full four-year term in March of 2000.[44] Was it a real election? The voting gave the impression of being preordained with the Communists putting up only token opposition and working quickly to assure Putin that they would cooperate with him in the Duma.

The Creation of an Oligarchy

By the end of the first decade of the twenty-first century, it was clear that Russia was being driven toward a far-less democratic system, perhaps not as bad as the worst years under Stalin but not as free as the best years under Mikhail Gorbachev. Most commentators believe that Putin wants to create an elite authoritarian state that would resemble in some ways the old Soviet Union but without the discredited and moribund Communist Party. The new Putin elite seems to have been constructed from a variety of sources: technocrats from the old Soviet bureaucracy, "red capitalists" from the business community who are prepared to support Putin's rule, and the United Russia political party, which acts as a vehicle for his political ambitions. Furthermore, Putin has given more power to his former KGB colleagues, now reorganized as the Federal Security Bureau or FSB.[45]

After serving two terms as president, Vladimir Putin was unable under the constitution to run for a third consecutive term. Instead, he orchestrated the election of a political ally, Dmitry Medvedev, who became president in 2008, while Mr. Putin retreated somewhat into the background as Medvedev's prime minister. In March 2012, Medvedev stood down as president, and Putin ran successfully for his old job. There is considerable evidence that Putin has lost much of his old popularity. The Duma elections of 2011 seem to have been accompanied by more than the usual vote-rigging, and in December of that year, crowds protested vehemently in Moscow against the crookedness of the election system.

How ideological is the Putin elite? Some would claim that today's Kremlin leadership stands for very little beyond its own perpetuation in power. On the other hand, Putin's circle does seem anxious to reverse the decline of their country, strengthen the power of the state, improve the economy, and reassert Russia's right to take its place among the great nations of the world.[46] To accomplish these goals, they have embarked upon several fundamental "reform" programs:

- Effective Conversion from a Federal to a Unitary System: First of all, Putin has concentrated a great deal of power in Moscow, transforming what was—at least on paper—a federal system into an actual unitary government. In order to bring the sometimes rebellious sub-sovereign governments into line, Putin created seven supra-regions each led by a supra-regional governor appointed by the Kremlin. Taking advantage of a series of terrorist outrages by Chechnyan separatists in the autumn of 2004, Putin then deftly removed the last vestiges of regional authority: henceforth, leaders of the country's eighty-nine sub-sovereign administrative units would be appointed by the Moscow government rather than democratically elected.
- Control of the Legislature: In the combination system designed by DeGaulle, the legislature is already weak in comparison to lawmaking bodies in presidential or parliamentary systems, but Putin was determined to ensure that his power could never be challenged by the legislative branch. First, he dropped the German-style mixed member proportionality system (half SMC and half PR), and arranged for all 450 members of the Duma to be elected by proportional representation. As discussed in chapter 7, there is a lot to be said for proportional representation when there are several genuinely independent parties challenging one another, but in a system with one overwhelmingly powerful party (Putin's United Russia), the PR system made it possible for the Kremlin to preselect all the candidates from their dominant party, eliminating potentially troublesome local candidates who could infiltrate the SMC part of the list because they were popular in their own districts.
- Control of the Media: The free press and television system flowered under Mikhail Gorbachev, grew feeble under Yeltsin, and has virtually disappeared under Mr. Putin. The Kremlin generally didn't bother imprisoning reporters and journalists; they went after media owners instead, making it clear that the price of staying in business was conformity to the Kremlin's point of view. The Internet is still uncensored, but fewer than 10 percent of the Russians are online, and newspapers are too expensive for ordinary citizens. Almost every television or newspaper is now controlled either by the government or by forces sympathetic to the Putin administration, and while the mass media are freer today than they were prior to Gorbachev, they are not free in the Western sense of the word.
- Control of the Economy: After becoming president in 2000, Putin faced early opposition from the buccaneer capitalists, who had made obscene fortunes under Yeltsin. He quickly intimidated them, sending Russia's richest man, Mikhail Khodorkovsky, to a

bleak Siberian prison on charges of tax fraud. Some Russian millionaires moved their money out of the country and went into exile; those who choose to stay in business and in Russia are now careful to comply with the wishes of the Kremlin elite. Some large businesses (such as the Yukos power company) have been effectively renationalized; the rising price of crude oil has helped Putin stabilize the economy, because Russia is a major exporter of oil and natural gas. In fact, while still troubled and massively unequal, the Russian economy is improving at the rate of about 5 percent a year. Russia is servicing its foreign debt and administering its own economy without a lot of interference from American or International Monetary Fund experts.

Why Isn't Russia Democratizing?

At the beginning of the second decade of the twenty-first century, describing Russian politics and economic organization succinctly is a little difficult. Russia has formally abandoned Marxism and embraced the private-enterprise system. There are now functioning and individually owned businesses within the borders of the Russian Federation as well as huge state-owned conglomerates that behave like private companies. Mr. Putin has tamed the oligarchs without quite putting them out of business, and some corporations still enjoy cozy and illegal relationships with corrupt government officials.[47]

Crime and corruption are still pervasive. Smaller companies struggle to pay bribes, and one author estimated that seven out of ten encounters with the police end in the payment of a bribe. As far as the private sector is concerned, there is nothing quite so private as a criminal organization, and evidence abounds that crime syndicates now control an enormous portion of the Russian economy. What the Russians call the "*mafiya*" has made Russia a dangerous place to live and work, and political leaders and journalists who oppose the mob have been assassinated.

Not all Russians are very good at playing capitalism, and the gulf between rich and poor has grown very large, a phenomenon we find in almost all countries. On paper, Russia is an advanced welfare state, offering a wide range of state benefits to orphans, disabled persons, war veterans, and poor people. Because of financial chaos, however, these benefits are seldom actually paid. Doctors and teachers demand bribes to perform their jobs, a moral compromise justified by the government's inability to pay their salaries. Unemployment is impossible to track because out-of-work laborers do not bother to register for unemployment benefits that are never going to be paid.[48]

While life has improved marginally under Putin and Medvedev, about forty million Russians are believed to be living below the meager Russian definition of poverty. Because of poverty and other, rather more complex, reasons, Russia is also suffering from what is technically called "excessive mortality," which means that people are dying at rates higher than those predicted by demographers, a sad topic we will explore further in chapter 13. The early death syndrome affects mostly males, and the life expectancy of a Russian man at the end of the century was sixty, which means that the average Russian worker, if he is lucky enough to have a job, cannot expect to live long enough to retire.

When the Soviet Union came to an end, there was a naïve belief among many Americans and some Russians that Russia could move swiftly and successfully to a Western-style market economy while building a functioning democracy. More than two decades into the experiment, it is clear that these dreams were far too optimistic.

In its 2011 listing, Transparency International gave Russia a dismal "2.4" (out of a possible 10.0), classifying Russia as the most corrupt society in Europe. In its 2011 study of human rights, Freedom House found that Russia was actually less democratic than it had been in the late 1990s and assigned it a desolate composite score of "5.5" and slamming it with a "Not Free" rating.[49]

Ultimately, why has Russia failed to democratize? The reasons are multiple:

- Fear of the Outside World: In modern times, Russia was attacked once by France under Napoleon, twice by Germany, and then menaced (from the Russian perspective) by the United States and NATO for the long years of the Cold War. China remains an ever-present threat. From the perspective of the average Russian, it may be that protecting Russia from a hostile world is more important than the creation of a democratic society.
- Elite Fear of the People: From the czars to the commissars, Russian governments have always eyed their own domestic population with worry and concern, establishing elaborate secret-police structures and ruthlessly eliminating independent voices. There is very little space in Russian life for civil society since independent organizations are viewed with suspicion. In short, the Putin government has not led the Russians into the garden of democracy because they are frightened of a political situation they would be unable to control, or even survive. When the last czar lost power, the Bolsheviks executed him and his entire family; nobody worries more about revolution than former revolutionaries.
- Popular Fear of the Elites: Driven by their own insecurity, Russian governments have always been ruthless in their dealings with the populace. Tens of millions of people died under Stalin's rule, and the Gulag Archipelago described by Aleksandr Solzhenitsyn is not that many years in the past. Faced with a harsh public environment, many Russians prefer to seek personal accommodations with government officials and criminal gangs rather than risk their lives striving for a perhaps-unachievable democracy. These feelings may be associated with the decline in Russia's population, an issue we will study further in chapter 13.
- Russian Fear of Non-Russians: About 20 percent of the population of the Russian Federation isn't actually Russian, and the centrifugal forces that broke up the old Soviet Union may still be running. The Caucasus region is particularly restless, and the Kremlin-imposed leadership of rebellious Chechnya could be temporary. Vladimir Putin is known to regret the disappearance of the USSR, but his empire may see more disintegration in the future.

5. The Wrap: What Have We Learned?

We have surveyed four of the most common types of less-free societies, starting with a consideration of royal executive regimes such as Jordan and Oman, and then moving on to look at some military dictatorships such as Burma/Myanmar, trying to understand why men on horseback keep riding into the presidential palace. Then we tackled the elusive business of religious dictatorships (or theocracies) such as Iran. For our fourth style of dictatorship we looked at Russia's elite dictatorship. There were plenty of awful elite dictatorships we might have studied, but the accelerating Russian slide toward authoritarian rule is the most interesting and—given Russia's storehouse of nuclear weapons—the most important.

What we found in all cases was that these less-free societies faced endemic and apparently unsolvable conflicts, some internal and some external. In all cases, these societies had been unable to evolve reliable political and social structures to mediate these conflicts. There are only a few ways to resolve conflict: We can compromise or submit to arbitration of some sort (such as going to court). We can get out our guns and fight, expecting that the victor will impose a solution. Or somebody can be eternally in charge with the power to resolve conflicts, even if their methods are undemocratic.

Politicians sometimes portray a cartoon world of good guys running democracies and bad guys administering dictatorships, but the issue demands critical thinking, and we've seen that less-free societies are unable to attain democracy for an interconnected array of reasons. A society with deep-seated ethnic, religious, linguistic, or economic conflicts might not find or create political structures powerful enough to broker these splits, or it might not have the self-confidence to try. It should be clear by now that passions about language, kinship, and religion can be powerful sources of conflict in a society. Freer societies manage most of the time to channel and broker conflict so that it does not become violent. Less-free societies deal with conflict by using the political apparatus of the state to insure the victory of one side over the other.

Conflict can be either internal (or domestic) or external (or international) or—most commonly—some complicated combination of the two. In chapter 9, we will continue our discussion of conflict by looking at some situations in which disagreement becomes violent.

Notes

1. Lewis Carroll, *Alice's Adventures in Wonderland* (Boston: Lee and Shepard, 1869), 116.

2. Hannah Arendt, *The Origins of Totalitarianism* (New York: Meridian Books, 1958).

3. Carl J. Friedrich and Zbigniew Brzezinski, *Totalitarian Dictatorship and Autocracy* (Cambridge: Mass.: Harvard University Press, 1956).

4. Leo Tolstoy, *Anna Karenina* (New York: Thomas Y. Crowell & Co., 1899), 1.

5. The biggest of the royal executive regimes is Saudi Arabia, for which, see John R. Bradley's *Saudi Arabia Exposed: Inside a Kingdom in Crisis* (New York: Palgrave Macmillan, 2005).

6. Jordan sponsors a searchable website for official information about the country at www.nic.gov.jo and www.jordanembassyus.org is the Jordanian embassy in Washington. The *Jordan Times* at http://www.jordan times.com is a good English-language newspaper.

7. Dr. Beverley Milton-Edwards and Peter Hinchcliffe have given us a solidly researched *Jordan: A Hashemite Legacy* (London: Brunner-Routledge, 2001). A more critical approach appears in George Alan's *Jordan: Living in the Crossfire* (London: Zed, 2005).

8. Frances Susan Hasso provides a critical feminist look at the Jordanian government in her *Resistance, Repression, and Gender Politics in Occupied Palestine and Jordan* (Syracuse, N.Y.: Syracuse University Press, 2005). Luisa Gandolfo gives us an insight into the Palestinian component of the Jordanian population in her *Palestinians in Jordan: The Politics of Identity* (London: I. B. Tauris, 2012)

9. As has been the case generally throughout this book, statistics of this kind have been taken from *The United Nations Human Development Report, 2011* (New York: UN Development Programme, 2010). Data on population changes are included in table 10, which begins on page 162. The entire report is available online at http://hdr.undp.org/en/reports/global/hdr2011/download/.

10. Calvin H. Allen, Jr. and W. Lynn Rigsbee II. *Oman under Qaboos: From Coup to Constitution* (London: Cass, 2000, 15–27).

11. For a competent history of this period, see Francis Owtram, *A Modern History of Oman: Formation of the State since 1920* (London: I. B. Tauris, 2004).

12. For the 2011 Freedom House discussion on Oman, see http://www.freedomhouse.org/template.cfm?page=22&year=2011&country=8107.

13. The Omanese government maintains an informative site at www.omanet.com. A Germany-based research group called the Oman Studies Center maintains what is perhaps the best site in English at www.oman.org. Published in Muscat, the *Oman Daily Observer* (www.omanobserver.com) comments carefully and respectfully on events in the Sultanate of Oman.

14. Transparency International (TI) is a Berlin-based think tank that studies dishonesty in public life around the world, important information for investors looking to put their money somewhere safe. TI generates the Corruption Perception Index or CPI, ranking countries from the most honest (New Zealand) to the most endemically dishonest (Somalia). You can find the whole index at http://cpi.transparency.org/cpi2011/results/.

15. Marc Valeri provides a good analysis of Omanese society in his *Oman: Politics and Society in the Qaboos State* (New York: Columbia University Press, 2009).

16. See Majid Al-Khalili, *Oman's Foreign Policy: Foundation and Practice* (New York: Praeger, 2009) which notes the uneasy relationship between Oman and the United States.

17. Amos Perlmutter's now-elderly classic *The Military and Politics in Modern Times* (New Haven: Yale University Press, 1977) is the standard study of military coups and governments and still worth a look. Craig L. Arceneaux has given us a study of military coups and governments in Latin America in his *Bounded Missions: Military Regimes and Democratization in the Southern Cone and Brazil* (University Park: Pennsylvania State Press, 2001).

18. For this sad period in Argentine life, see Klaus Friedrich Veigel, *Dictatorship, Democracy, and Globalization: Argentina and the Cost of Paralysis 1973–2001* (University Park, Pa.: Penn State University, 2009). Also see Mark J. Osiel, *Mass Atrocity, Ordinary Evil, and Hannah Arendt: Criminal Consciousness in Argentina's Dirty War* (New Haven, Conn.: Yale University Press, 2002).

19. See a detailed study by N. Ganesan and Kyaw Yin Hlaing, *Myanmar: State, Society, and Ethnicity* (Singapore: Institute of Southeast Asian Studies, 2007).

20. A lot has been written about Burma/Myanmar: see Peter Carey's *Burma: The Challenge of Change in a Divided Society* (New York: St. Martins, 1997) as well as David I. Steinberg's *Burma: The State of Myanmar* (Baltimore: Georgetown University Press, 2001). Burma's tragic Aung San Suu Kyi tells her own story in *Letters from Burma* (New York: Penguin, 1998) and Myint-U Thant gives us the history in his *The Making of Modern Burma* (Cambridge: Cambridge University Press, 2001).

21. Peter Carey, *Burma: The Challenge of Change in a Divided Society* (New York: St. Martin's, 1997).

22. Steinberg, *Burma: The State of Myanmar*, 1–9.

23. In 2012, director Luc Besson released a major film celebrating the life of Aung San Suu Kyi. Staring Michele Yeoh, it is entitled *The Lady* (what Aung San Suu Kyi is called by the Burmese) and has been widely praised by critics.

24. A long-standing leader of the pro-democracy movement in Burma, Professor David Steinberg of Georgetown University has produced a passionate book entitled *Burma/Myanmar: What Everyone Needs to Know* (New York and Oxford: Oxford University Press, 2009).

25. Take a look at the Free Burma site maintained by the University of California [www.ibiblio.org/freeburma/] and then contrast it with *The New Light of Myanmar* at www.myanmar.com, the government of Myanmar's own propaganda effort. The Burma Fund is a Washington-based advocacy group working for a return to democracy and maintaining a site at www.burmafund.org.

26. See Michael W. Charney, *A History of Modern Burma* (Cambridge, UK: Cambridge University Press, 2009).

27. A. E. Housman, *The Collected Poems of A. E. Housman* (London: Wordsworth, 1994), 234.

28. McGill University's Professor Wael B. Hallaq explains the Sharia well in his *An Introduction to Islamic Law* (Cambridge, UK: Cambridge University Press, 2009).

29. If you are going to read only one book on Iran, make it William R. Polk's *Understanding Iran* (New York: Palgrave Macmillan, 2011). A couple of older but still readable books on Iran have been written by scholarly journalists: see Sandra Mackey's lively *The Iranians: Persia, Islam, and the Soul of a Nation* (New

York: Penguin, 1998); and Robin Wright's *The Last Great Revolution: Turmoil and Transformation in Iran* (New York: Knopf, 2000).

30. Karen Armstrong, *Islam: A Short History* (New York: Random House, 2002) 45–50. Ms. Armstrong is a celebrated English writer on religion and politics. A former nun, she has written an impressive series of readable books such as *Muhammad* (London: Phoenix, 2001) and *A History of God: The 4000-Year Quest of Judaism, Christianity* (New York: Ballantine Books, 1994). While written for the general reader, Armstrong's books provide insights for the professional.

31. An A to Z review of the country and its political life has been done by Patrick Clawson and Michael Rubin in their *Eternal Iran: Continuity and Chaos* (New York: Palgrave, 2006).

32. See Said Amir Arjomand, *The Turban for the Crown: The Islamic Revolution in Iran* (New York: Oxford University Press, 1988) 60–68.

33. Read the inside story of that 1953 CIA-managed Iranian coup d'etat in the words of the spy who toppled Mossadegh in Kermit Roosevelt's *Countercoup: The Struggle for the Control of Iran* (New York: McGraw, 1979). With considerably more balance, Stephen Kinzer has retold the same tale in his *All the Shah's Men: An American Coup and the Roots of Middle Eastern Terror* (London: John Wiley, 2003).

34. While it is now an elderly book, there is not much that beats Gary Sick's *All Fall Down: America's Tragic Encounter with Iran* (New York: Random House, 1985). The contemporary U.S.-Iranian relationship is well treated in Ali Ansari's *Confronting Iran* (New York: Basic, 2006). *Democracy in Iran* (New York: Oxford University Press, 2006) by Ali Gheissari and Vali Nasr is an unusually optimistic treatment of this complicated country.

35. Mr. Baqer Moin's *Khomeini: Life of the Ayatollah* (New York: St. Martin's, 2000) introduces the Iranian leader and Wilfried Buchta's *Who Rules Iran? The Structure of Power in the Islamic Republic* (Washington, D.C.: Institute for Near East Policy, 2000) provides a political scientist's perspective on the Ayatollah's life.

36. Ghoncheh Tazmini's *Khatami's Iran: The Islamic Republic and the Turbulent Path to Reform* (London: I. B. Tauris, 2012) offers insights into why it has been so difficult for Iran to evolve democratically.

37. For more in-depth reading on the spring 2011 protests and what they mean for the Middle East, see Robin Wright, *Dreams and Shadows: The Future of the Middle East* (New York: Penguin Publishers, 2011).

38. Critical of U.S. policy toward Iran, Ray Takeyh of the Council on Foreign Relations has written *Hidden Iran: Paradox and Power in the Islamic Republic* (New York: Holt, 2007). To get the news from an Iranian perspective, go directly to the Islamic Republic of Iran Broadcasting Online News Network at http://news .irib.com and click on "English" if that's your language. You can even view a little Iranian television online by going to www.irna.com/tv/ch1.ram, which is the Islamic Republic News Agency. Even in Farsi, it will give you a sense of the people and the culture. See also the news in English at www.iran-daily.com.

39. For a wrap-up of the entire Soviet experience, see Peter Kenez, *A History of the Soviet Union from the Beginning to the End*, 2nd ed. (Cambridge, UK: Cambridge University Press, 2006). Oxford University's Archie Brown has produced a magisterial treatment of the USSR's last leader, *The Gorbachev Factor* (Oxford: Oxford University Press, 1996).

40. Joseph Stiglitz, *Globalization and its Discontents* (London: Norton, 2002), 142.

41. Two good books detail Yeltsin's conversion to free markets: see Joseph R. Blasi et al., *Kremlin Capitalism: Privatizing the Russian Economy* (Ithaca, N.Y.: Cornell University Press, 1999); *Financial Times* journalist Chrystia Freeland describes Russia's abrupt conversion to free markets in her *Sale of the Century: Russia's Wild Ride from Communism to Capitalism* (New York: Crown, 2000). Clinton's top Russia expert was a former journalist named Strobe Talbott, who described the 1992–2000 period in his frank *The Russia Hand: A Memoir of Presidential Diplomacy* (New York: Random, 2002). The Yeltsin experience is also captured in David Remnick's *Resurrection: The Struggle for a New Russia* (London: Picador, 1998).

42. Stiglitz, *Globalization and its Discontents*, 133.

43. Anna Politkovskaya, *A Small Corner of Hell: Dispatches from Chechnya* (Chicago: University of Chicago Press, 2007). Ms. Politkovskaya was murdered after the publication of this book, presumably by forces within the Russian government who were offended by her ruthless honesty. Also see her critical *Putin's Russia: Life in a Failing Democracy* (New York: Metropolitan Books, 2005). Robert W. Schaefer has done a more recent and more comprehensive review of the Chechnyan struggle in his *The Insurgency in Chechnya and the North Caucasus* (New York: Praeger, 2011).

44. Vladimir Putin's *First Person: An Astonishingly Frank Self-Portrait by Russia's President* (New York: Public Affairs, 2000) is less astonishing than the title suggests, but does contain insights from interviews and contributions by family members.

45. Brian D. Taylor, *State Building in Putin's Russia: Policing and Coercion after Communism* (Cambridge, UK: Cambridge University Press, 2011).

46. For the details, see Marshall Goldman, *Petrostate: Putin, Power, and the New Russia* (New York: Oxford University Press, 2010).

47. See a new book by Gilles Favarel-Garrigues, *Policing Economic Crime in Russia: From Soviet Planned Economy to Privatization* (New York: Columbia University Press, 2011).

48. See www.russianembassy.org for the Russian embassy in Washington; www.russiatoday.com is a good commercial portal site for information about the Russian Federation. Read the news about Russia in English with the *St. Petersburg Times* online at www.sptimesrussia.com. *Pravda* survived the fall of the USSR and is still Moscow's morning paper, available in English at http://english.pravda.ru.

49. You can find the Transparency International ratings at http://www.transparency.org/. Freedom House has generated a global freedom assessment at http://freedomhouse.org/images/File/fiw/FIW_2011_Booklet.pdf.

CHAPTER 9

Conflict, Violence, War, and Mayhem

7. The Wrap: What Have We Learned?

Legend has it that an American diplomat once presided over negotiations between some Jewish Israelis and some Muslim Arab Palestinians. When the Middle Easterners persisted in feuding, the exasperated American mediator exclaimed, "Why can't we all be good Christians about this?"

Not funny? The Middle East has never been a bundle of laughs, but the story illustrates both the unreal quality that other people's hatreds have and our own tendency to project our own cultural assumptions onto those who do not share them. Contemplate the appalling savagery of the **Balkan Peninsula** in the 1990s, the eternal antagonism between Russians and Chechens, the genocidal barbarism in Africa's Rwanda in 1994, the sudden brawl in 2010 in Kyrgyzstan when the majority Kyrgyz population began to slaughter ethnic Uzbeks, and the murderous duel between Syrian security forces and protesters in 2011–2012. When communities decide to murder one another, it can sometimes be difficult for the rest of the world to see what's at stake, or why these old grievances can't be settled peacefully.

We might find it helpful to think of conflict as falling into four overlapping levels of intensity, illustrated in table 9.1 below and described in sections 2–5. As table 9.1 makes clear, some conflict remains happily at level one, with normal social mechanisms available to broker conflict long before it escalates into violence. Chapter 5 illustrated how diplomacy, international law, and international organizations can sometimes prevent outbreaks of international war. Chapter 7 was largely dedicated to a survey of how democratic societies have developed structural mechanisms for defusing internal or domestic conflict short of violence. Since a given conflict can rise and fall on this scale (such as the conflict in Iraq discussed in section 6 below), it is important to have a clear sense of the various levels of intensity possible when a conflict cannot be resolved by political mechanisms. Here are some of the questions we're going to try to answer.

- *Why does conflict happen in human society? What kinds of different conflict are there? How can we distinguish between nationalist and ideological conflict? Why does religion complicate our efforts to categorize conflict, and why is "resource conflict" sometimes hard to identify?* We'll start where political scientists typically start: we'll put phenomena into categories, and then go on to explain why this standardized classification system tends to break down in the real world of angry people. It will help, however, if we begin by restating that fundamental distinction between ideological and nationalist conflict before explaining why religion and resources make the equation more complex.

- *How and why do some social conflicts remain nonviolent?* In functioning democracies, the political system has generated institutions for settling disputes nonviolently. In some cases, however, citizens are unhappy with the decisions reached by courts and elections, and move into what we will call nonviolent adversarial conflict. In this context, we'll glance at how civil disobedience without violence has been used to make dramatic changes in society.
- *What is "low-intensity conflict" and how does it translate into mob violence, terrorism, and/or guerrilla war?* Low-intensity conflict (LIC) describes a level of violence involving some deaths and destruction of property that remains short of full-scale war. We'll look at these LIC-level conflicts and ask why the phenomenon of terrorism is so hard to define scientifically.
- *What is the role of war (or high-intensity conflict) in modern society?* In section 4, we'll summarize how war changed over the course of the twentieth century in terms of weaponry, victims, and lethality.
- *Could anything be worse than war?* As it happens, there is an infrequent but horrific stage of violence where conflict becomes the leading cause of mortality in a society. The term "societal mayhem" is reserved for those comparatively rare but devastatingly serious periods when a society implodes into mass murder.
- *What's really happening in Iraq?* Rarely does a foreign-policy initiative raised such animosity as did the invasion of Iraq by American and British armies in 2003. It has been difficult to get accurate information about why the war happened and Iraq's uncertain progress toward democracy. We will summarize what little is known for sure in our examination of a crisis that has skidded up and down the scale from low-intensity conflict to societal mayhem and back to low-intensity conflict again.

1. Classifying Conflict

In this first section, we will look at conflict analytically, first breaking it into manageable categories, and then apologetically explaining why our neatly organized classifications don't always work in the real world. We'll start by examining the motivations for conflict, distinguishing between ideological conflict and national conflict. This will prepare us for chapter 10, where we'll take a closer look at some specific instances of ongoing ideological and religious conflict: Marxist revolutionaries, neo-Nazism, and God-crazed murderers. In chapter 11, we will look at a series of nationalist, ethnic, or sectarian conflicts in greater detail.

Table 9.1. Levels of Conflict

Level One: Nonviolent Conflict: Elections, lawsuits, labor disputes, civil disobedience, pickets, peaceful demonstrations, etc.

Level Two: Low-Intensity Conflict: Mob violence, terrorism, guerrilla warfare, assassinations, etc.

Level Three: High-Intensity Conflict: Conventional warfare between armies, may be interstate/international (i.e., between countries), intrastate/civil (i.e., within a country), or some complicated combination of the two.

Level Four: Societal Mayhem: Generalized multilateral mass violence, genocide, nuclear war.

NATIONALISM OR IDEOLOGY?

Traditionally, political scientists have thought in terms of two clusters of basic reasons why people engage in political conflict. The first category deals with ideology or ideas about public policy, all those "isms" we've dreamed up to complicate our lives: Marxism, Western liberalism, and Islamism. In chapter 10, we call this the "war of the mind." The second category involves the "war of the heart" or nationalist quarrels in which linguistic, territorial, religious, racial, or ethnic groups oppose one another—our topic for chapter 11. To get started, let's introduce Colombia as an example of an ideological conflict and Chechnya as a classic case of nationalist conflict.[1]

- Colombia: We'll talk more about the Republic of Colombia in chapter 10, but for now, let's glance at this Latin American society just long enough to see the difference between nationalist and ideological conflict. Quite apart from the tensions caused by powerful and ruthless narcotics traffickers, Colombian society is divided between two large Marxist guerrilla/terrorist forces on one side and the Bogotá government on the other. The fighting is *not* about whether Colombia should be ruled by whites, blacks, Catholics, Muslims, Spanish-speakers, or Russians. The conflict is ideological with the guerrillas demanding a Marxist or communist solution to Colombia's political problems while the Colombian government prefers a fairly conservative capitalist economic system.
- Chechnya: In chapter 8, we looked briefly at the savage conflict between Russia and the breakaway republic of Chechnya, a clear-cut example of a nationalist quarrel. Representing the Russian government in this war are ethnic Russians, who speak a Slavic language and come from a religious tradition of Russian Orthodoxy, although many of them today are post-Christian atheists. Their opponents, in the sub-sovereign region of Chechnya, speak Chechen, which comes from a completely different family of languages and totally lacks mutual intelligibility with Russian. The conflict has very little to do with ideas about public policy, that is, whether society should be organized around capitalist or socialist principles; the Chechens fought bitterly against the Russian czars, and then hated the Soviet commissars after 1917. The people of Grozny (the capital of Chechnya) don't like Putin's Muscovites any better now that they are would-be capitalists. This nationalist fighting centered on Chechnya's traditional demand to be allowed to organize itself as a separate and sovereign state under Chechen (rather than Russian) leaders.

Hence, in the newspapers, a conflict is normally presented as stemming from either an ideological dispute (e.g., how government is to be run, or left-wingers against right-wingers) or a nationalist quarrel (i.e., which ethnic community shall control a sovereign state). The guerrilla warfare in Colombia, for example, is ostensibly ideological, featuring communists versus capitalists; the never-ending Israeli-Palestinian brawl is clearly about nationalism: two distinct ethnic communities fighting to exercise sovereignty over the same land. Beneath the surface, however, we find that religion and/or resources can sometimes be important factors. Muslims and Christians are fighting in Nigeria, partly because each believes the other religion to be wrong, and partly because Muslim and Christian tribes both claim some of the same land for grazing and farming. And the war in Colombia also hinges to a large extent over valuable resources, the drug market and crude oil.

Political scientists have often observed that the end of the Cold War permitted the eruption of many ethnic or nationalist conflicts around the world. In most of these nationalist conflicts, there is typically a marker (or cultural clue) of some kind that allows observers to tell the contestants apart. These markers are sometimes superficial and often deeply misleading, but they serve at a primitive level to distinguish the two sides. The following "markers" appear commonly in nationalist disputes:

- biological kinship or "race," as was once the case in South Africa when all political power rested in the hands of the white minority;
- language and culture, as continues to be an issue in Canada, which is divided between English-speakers of generally Protestant, British descent and Roman Catholic French-speakers (most of them in Quebec) whose ancestors came from France; and
- economic status (if it coincides with ethnicity), a situation that occurs when one ethnic community is generally very poor and another is significantly richer, as in the Northern Ireland conflict to be reviewed below, where Irish Catholics were traditionally poorer than pro-British Protestants.

FIGHTING ABOUT RELIGIONS AND RESOURCES

We should all have an "Oversimplification!" bell in our brains, and it should be ringing right now. If you've been following the news, you can probably think of a dozen conflicts that do not fit neatly into this nationalism-versus-ideology dichotomy. After we look at the complicating role of religion in conflict, we will shift our focus to the more humdrum human business of fighting over resources such as precious metals, minerals, oil, and water.

Religious Conflicts

When we factor religion into the equation, our neat distinction between ideology and nationalism begins to fray. As suggested by figure 9.1, we can think in terms of "religion-as-ideology" and "religion-as-nationalism." Here's the basic distinction.

- Religion as Ideology: Sometimes, religions create rules about public policy that are essentially ideological in character. The conflict in America and Europe over abortion, for example, concerns issues of morality and law and does not involve nationalism. Pro-life and pro-choice protesters are not members of different ethnic groups. Within individual countries, they all speak (or sometimes shout) the same language. They even come from a mixed variety of religious traditions; there are Roman Catholics, for example, on both sides of the controversy. The fight is not over whether or not Baptists or Unitarians should run the United States, but whether or not the law should permit abortion and under what circumstances the procedure should be permitted. Abortion-clinic bombings in the United States are a violent escalation of this essentially ideological conflict. Religion-as-ideology conflicts evolve when religious ideas overlap ideological ones.[2] In the Muslim-dominated North of Nigeria, the Islamist Boko Haram ("Western education is forbidden" in the Hausa language) organization emerged in 2002, using violence to end Christian influence and install the Sharia as the fundamental law of the country. Boko Haram has punctuated its demands with a series of shooting and bombing attacks on the Christian community, a good example of a conflict in which religion has become central to the conflict.[3]

- Religion as Nationalism: As discussed in chapter 3, it often happens that two national groups in conflict over nonreligious issues practice different religions. To be reviewed in chapter 11, the Catholics-versus-Protestants feud in Northern Ireland is the classic example. The actual intellectual or spiritual content of the two or more religions may not be particularly relevant to the conflict.

- Combination Groups: If only real life could be as cut-and-dried as examples in textbooks! Regrettably, some conflicts belong in both of the categories described above. An example might be Palestine's HAMAS, the victor in the 2006 Palestinian elections and the ruling power in the Gaza Strip. Animated by a profound and visceral dislike of Israel, HAMAS talks in fervent nationalist terms about the need to eradicate the Jewish presence from a restored Arab Palestine (i.e., all of present-day Israel, plus the West Bank, plus Gaza). HAMAS wants more than just an Arab Palestine free of Judaism, however, it demands a severely Islamist Palestine, governed by a strict interpretation of the Sharia. HAMAS recently established rules prohibiting male hairdressers from cutting women's hair because a hairdresser's salon permits unacceptable familiarity between unmarried people of different genders.[4]

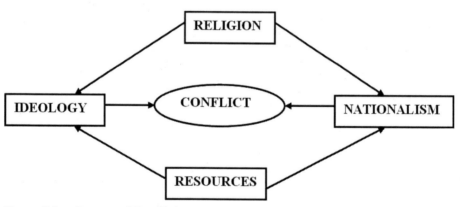

Figure 9.1. Causes of Conflict

Table 9.2. Religion as Ideology, Nationalism, or Both

Religion as Ideology	→	Political groups demanding that civil law reflect religious law. Example: Afghanistan's Taliban.
Religion as Nationalism	→	National or ethnic group self-defining in terms of religion. Example: Catholics and Protestants in Northern Ireland
Combination Groups	→	Group defined by religion demanding both national sovereignty and change in public policy. Example: Palestine's HAMAS.

Resource Conflicts

A further complication stems from the fact that a lot of conflict, both nonviolent and violent, flows from efforts of two separate groups to take control of the same natural resources. At heart, the conflict isn't about ideas, religious or secular. Sometimes the conflict is between two ethnic communities, but in many significant cases, there is no nationalism involved. So what are they fighting about?

Resource wars are typically waged for control of economic wealth in the form of mineral resources, water supplies, or arable land. Sometimes resource wars have a fig leaf of ideological or nationalist justification, but many are pure smash-and-grab operations. The recent conflicts in the eastern portion of the Democratic Republic of Congo and Sierra Leone were mostly about control over mineral resources such as diamonds and metals. In Burma/Myanmar and the Latin American country of Colombia, a lot of the fighting is inspired by the desire to control and profit from the flow of illegal narcotics and crude oil. As we will see, life gets even more complicated when there is a distinct combination of nationalism and resources. Israelis and Palestinians have plenty of reasons to dislike one another, and control over freshwater supplies from the Jordan River is just one more divisive element in a complex conflict situation.[5]

Be prepared for the possibility that major wars can have obscure and controversial motives rather than one clear-cut cause. Societies go to war with one another for a medley of motives, some of them honestly expressed and some covert.

2. Nonviolent Political Conflict

At the individual level, there is hardly a day without conflict of some sort, ranging from a dispute over how dark the breakfast toast should be, all the way to an argument with a traffic cop over your precise speed at that last intersection.

Most of the time in most societies, we solve our differences without violence. Sometimes we make a deal, or we split the difference, or we agree to disagree. Sometimes, we need lawyers, clergymen, marriage counselors, or policemen to keep us from hurting each other. How does this play out in the real world of politics?

NONVIOLENT ADVERSARIAL CONFLICT

In the normal life of a functioning democracy, courts, political parties, and electoral campaigns are ordinary mechanisms for making political decisions and settling political disputes without bloodshed. Most of the governmental machinery discussed in chapter 7 exists for the purpose of making routine decisions and settling everyday conflict. Let's pause for a moment to look at the range of nonviolent (or at least nonlethal) forms of political conflict.

The bill for the 2012 American presidential campaign will run over a billion dollars, demanding the voters' sometimes reluctant attention for more than a year and involving innumerable violations of ethical and esthetic standards. On the other hand, it didn't actually get anyone killed. Even the narrow and bitterly contested presidential

Figure 9.2. Ms. Camila Vallejo of the University of Chile in Santiago
Photo courtesy of Wilson Dias.

election of 2000 did not directly result in a clear-cut assault-and-battery charge, much less a murder conviction.

Sometimes you don't get all (or any) of what you want at the polling booth. At a slightly more intense level, therefore, groups engaging in political conflict may go to court, write angry letters to the editor, picket each other's offices, go on strike, or even stage protest marches. In advanced democratic societies, conflict can be very intense and still remain nonviolent. At the international level, embassies routinely smooth out disagreements and disputes among sovereign states, ranging from minor rectification of borders to trade problems and extradition of criminals. The UN and its subordinate agencies exist for the precise purpose of facilitating this kind of problem solving.

Are You the Next Leader of the Revolution?

Dramatic leadership sometimes comes from the top, but one young geography major at Santiago's University of Chile has demonstrated that leadership can come from the back row in a classroom. Traditionally, higher education in Chile involved expensive private universities for the elite and a few badly underfunded universities for the general public. As leader of the University of Chile's Student Union, Camila Vallejo spent most of 2011 leading left-wing protests against a relatively conservative government, managing to keep her movement almost completely within the law. Her preferred tactic was the *cacerolazo*, nothing more violent than a parade of noisy students banging pots and pans together. When the police responded with baton charges and tear gas, the government found itself on the defensive for its heavy-handed tactics. By the end of 2011, Vallejo had successfully forced the government to drop the interest on student loans by two-thirds. In the public mind, the utopian idea of totally free university education was now a political possibility, and *Time Magazine* named Vallejo one of the "People Who Mattered in 2011." In the midst of it all, the twenty-three year-old Vallejo managed to write and publish her first book, modestly entitled *Podemos cambiar el mundo* (*We Can Change the World*).[6]

CIVIL DISOBEDIENCE

By definition, **civil disobedience** is against the law, but it is still nonviolent. In some cases, the law being broken might be stupid or immoral, but an act of civil disturbance can involve an encounter with the police, a trip to court, and even a stay in a penitentiary. On December 1, 1955, for example, an African American woman named Rosa Parks boarded a city bus in Montgomery, Alabama, taking a seat reserved for white passengers. When a Caucasian man demanded her seat, she broke the law by refusing to yield it. Nobody today (and not very many people in 1955) would defend this ungallant relic of segregation, but it was the law in Alabama at the time, and the late Mrs. Parks paid a $14. fine for the twin privileges of keeping her seat and helping to bring segregation to an end.[7]

Mrs. Parks' action was an example of nonviolent civil disobedience, which occurs when a group in conflict with a government avoids violence but engages in symbolic criminality. In many cases, the "crime" committed is deliberate and propagandistic in character. By inviting the government to bring women and elderly people to trial, the movement gains publicity for its cause and may make the government look foolish or dictatorial.

India's Gandhi and America's Martin Luther King both adopted techniques of nonviolent civil disobedience, encouraging their followers to break what they regarded as unjust laws in entirely peaceful, nonviolent fashions.[8] Both men were brilliant at engineering protests in ways that tempted the "legal" government to put itself in an unfavorable light through illegal behavior. As observed in chapter 8, Burma's Nobel Prize–winning pro-democracy activist Aung San Suu Kyi has employed many of the same tactics against her country's military dictators.

Parallel Lives: Bishop Tutu and the Dalai Lama

Throughout recorded history, religious teachings have been abused by angry prophets to drive us toward war, while gentler souls searched their spirituality for ways to bring us peace. In recent years, the Nobel Peace Prize has been awarded to a Christian cleric, Desmond Tutu, who helped guide his country to democracy with a bare minimum of violence, and to a Buddhist monk (the Dalai Lama), who struggles to free his people without bloodshed.

The history of South Africa is long and complicated, but in the years after World War II, the ruling Nationalist Party formalized in law the long-standing practice of racial segregation. With the full legal implementation of apartheid (or "separateness"), South Africa's black majority was completely disenfranchised. Many black leaders could see no alternative to violent revolution.

Born in South Africa in 1931 of a humble black African family, Desmond Tutu became a priest in the South African wing of the Church of England (called Anglican or Episcopalian in the United States), eventually becoming archbishop of Cape Town. Throughout his career, Tutu insisted upon an ethical stance that won him few friends on either side of the racial divide. On one hand, he denounced the "whites only" government as immoral and incapable of redemption. On the other hand, Tutu demanded that the fight against political immorality be conducted nonviolently.

Winning the Nobel Peace Prize in 1984, he used his influence to persuade many of his black compatriots that civil disobedience was a better tactic than was

Figure 9.3. Archbishop Desmond Tutu
When apartheid came to an end in South Africa in the early 1990s, there was enough guilt to go around. Bishop Tutu strongly felt that reconciliation was more important for South Africans than was justice. His Truth and Reconciliation Commission heard testimony and, in most cases, offered legal immunity to those on both sides of the conflict who told the truth about the violent years that were now ending. Photo by Dale Frost, courtesy of the Port of San Diego.

terrorism. By the 1990s, economic sanctions and an international boycott had forced the apartheid regime to face the reality that a compromise was inevitable. When black-majority rule finally came to South Africa, Archbishop Tutu led South Africa's Truth and Reconciliation Commission. An unusual concept but one that has been copied in other divided societies, this commission was designed to establish the historical facts of South Africa's crisis, persuade those guilty of crimes to confess, and encourage society to move forward without becoming too involved in trials or punishments.[9]

The Tibetan people have not been as fortunate. Tibet began as an independent country, achieving national unity in the 500s A.D. under native Tibetan chieftains. By the 1300s, the mountainous country had become a theocracy administered by Buddhist monks under the leadership of a supreme leader called the Dalai Lama.

There had always been Chinese interference in Tibetan affairs. In the early years of the twentieth century, Tibet was functionally independent, but the Chinese brutally conquered the country in 1950. The fourteenth Dalai Lama, Tenzin Gyatso, attempted to coexist with the Chinese until a Tibetan uprising in 1959 resulted in his flight to India, where he established a government in exile.[10]

The Chinese government in Beijing is adamant that the strategically important Tibet rightfully belongs to them, and most of the territory inhabited by the three million Tibetans is now the Xizang Autonomous Region (XAR). Tibet, or Xizang, is only autonomous in name; in actual political practice, Beijing administers the highlands between the Himalayan and the Trans-Himalayan ranges with an iron fist, importing ethnic Chinese immigrants to consolidate Chinese control over the frontier and discouraging the Buddhist religion.

Figure 9.4. Tenzin Gyatso, the Fourteenth Dalai Lama
By Tenzin Choejor, Office of His Holiness the Dalai Lama.

While previous Buddhist leaders were far from democratic, the Dalai Lama has proposed a convincingly democratic constitution for a future Tibet, a government in which a popularly elected president and legislature will exercise power, with the Dalai Lama and his successors becoming spiritual rather than political leaders. Convinced that nonviolent resistance to Chinese power is the only practical and moral path to nationhood, the Dalai Lama continues to circle the globe, patiently making the case for Tibetan independence and cultivating support from pop stars and politicians. In recent years, the Dalai Lama has retreated from demanding absolute independence and now asks that Tibet be granted self-governing status within China.

There is no question that the Dalai Lama enjoys the overwhelming support of his people. Can he convert immense moral standing and global popularity into genuine political progress for Tibet? At the beginning of the new century, the prospects seemed dubious. To some extent, white South Africans dumped apartheid because the world had generally dumped the white South Africans. The Chinese government, on the other hand, is a much more formidable power, and the international community finds it difficult to bully Beijing. The Dalai Lama is a popular and much-admired figure around the world, but no major power has thus far extended diplomatic recognition to his government-in-exile.[11]

3. Low-Intensity Conflict

The phrase, **low-intensity conflict (LIC)** has become a Pentagon cliché in recent years as a way of describing a range of violent and lethal conflicts that are serious enough to get people killed but fall short of full-scale war (or **high-intensity conflict**). Although the phrase is somewhat imprecise, all low-intensity conflicts involve serious violence, damage to property, and some loss of life. At the lower end of the spectrum, this may mean relatively brief episodes of rioting or violent demonstrations with widespread property destruction and some fatalities. At the more serious end of the scale, an LIC can involve widespread disorders involving some combination of terrorist violence, intermittent guerrilla attacks, frequent and high-profile assassinations, or mob violence involving significant loss of life. A low-intensity conflict can last an afternoon or a lifetime, depending on the circumstances. Furthermore, some forms of low-intensity conflict (such as terrorism) can become components in even more serious forms of violence. For example, terrorism is a frequent feature in war and other forms of extreme mass violence.

We can assume that low-intensity conflict has begun when people are dying with some regularity because of an ongoing political or armed conflict. While the figure is purely arbitrary, some political scientists have suggested that one thousand violent fatalities a year constitute an upper limit to low-intensity conflict. Once the death total reaches a thousand per annum, we begin to talk about high-intensity conflict or war.

RIOTING AND CIVIL DISORDERS

A fairly common form of political violence is the riot or civil disorder, in which a large group of people defy the police, take to the streets, break windows, set fire to cars, and generally disrupt normal life, the sort of behavior that came to characterize Greece in 2011.[12] Some people commit acts of violence coldheartedly, with a clear head and a conscious intention to achieve certain well-defined objectives. In many cases, however, violence can be categorized as **anomic**. A word borrowed from sociology and psychology, "anomic" refers to a conflict situation where there are no rules and little rationality. An anomic riot, for example, might be irrational or even lack clear-cut causality, sometimes the result of what is called "free-floating hostility." In the summer of 2011, inner-city kids in Britain rioted, sacking stores and setting fire to police vehicles. In the aftermath, sociologists and pundits tried to work out what had caused this outburst of rage and found that individual rioters had their own unique medley of emotions and motives. There was no one overwhelming cause, and in some cases, there was no cause at all.

Civil disorders are anomic if there is no logical connection between the violence and the solution to the problem. Poor people who live in ugly and dehumanizing urban conditions might react to an instance of police brutality by setting fire to their own neighborhoods, effectively worsening their own economic situation. We understand their rage, although their behavior makes no sense. Hitting a wall with your fist because you're having a bad day won't improve the quality of your day and might bruise your knuckles. So why do we do it? We hit walls and sometimes other people because there are times when our frustration and anger makes us anomic and irrational.

Anomic or rational, civil disorders can include rioting, looting, stone throwing, vandalism, random attacks on the police or members of enemy ethnic or political groups, widespread resistance to authorities, and refusal to obey laws. A riot can make a bad situation worse, but sometimes it can force a government into changing an objectionable piece of public policy. Recent French experience has provided us with examples of both. In December of 2005, Muslim Arabs, some of them immigrants and some the children of immigrants, rioted violently in France to protest their status at the bottom of French society. This bout of rioting was classically anomic in that it did little to improve the lives of French Arabs but may have strengthened the anti-immigrant forces in French society.

As the French police were recovering, the Paris government proposed new legislation aimed at making it easier to fire employees. In April 2006, students and workers took their objections to the streets with more rioting, and this time, the French government, to avoid further confrontation, prudently withdrew the legislation.

A breakdown in the food supply system will quickly produce civil disorders, and Russia's famous 1917 March Revolution began with riots over the failure of the bread supply. In the early days of the American interventions in Haiti in 1994 and 2009, the breakdown of the food supply prompted hungry mobs to storm food storage facilities and expropriate food before it could be systematically distributed. And, famously, the citizens of Baghdad erupted into an orgy of anomic looting and pillaging when U.S. forces destroyed the Saddam Hussein regime.

TERRORISM

The word "terrorist" has been in circulation since the French Revolution, when it was used to describe Jacobin radicals who used violence to consolidate their 1789 victory over the aristocracy. Throughout the 1800s, European and American political leaders were targeted by people called "terrorists," many of whom were violent anarchists attempting to create the basis for revolution by disseminating terror.

The topic of **terrorism** returned to the front pages after World War II, when it was seen as a tactic available to militarily weak colonies fighting sophisticated European armies for national independence. The Kenyan Mau Mau movement and the Algerian Front Liberation National (FLN) were two obvious examples, since both Kenya and Algeria achieved independence partly because of terror campaigns. A number of separatist organizations have waged violent but unsuccessful campaigns: Kurds continue to fight against the Turkish government, and the Provisional IRA targeted Her Majesty's rule in London in an effort to drive the British from Ireland, a campaign that came to an end in the 1990s.[13]

Americans tend to see terrorism as morally indefensible violence carried out against legitimate governments. There are many Latin American examples, however, of American-funded groups using terror techniques against established governments that had not found favor in Washington. In the 1980s, for example, the American-sponsored "Contras"—with the open support of the Reagan administration—carried out a combination guerrilla/terrorist campaign against a leftist government in Nicaragua.[14]

Portraits of the Real World:
Antonio Savasta in the Paliano Jail

In the course of some research into Italian terrorism a few years ago, Richard Collin visited Antonio Savasta in Italy's Paliano Prison, not far from Naples. The last military leader of Italy's Red Brigades, Savasta was a policeman's son with a photographic memory who grew up in a Roman slum. Like many teenagers, he played guitar in a rock-and-roll band during his secondary school years, but he dedicated most of his free time to community politics, mingling with revolutionary groups well to the left of the official Communist Party. After secondary school, Savasta attended the University of Rome just long enough to be recruited into the Red Brigades and play a role in the 1978 kidnapping and execution of former prime minister Aldo Moro. He then became a full-time Red Brigades activist, rising rapidly in the hierarchy of rebellion and leading his colleagues into their final 1980–1981 campaign, which involved the kidnapping of an American general. Along with his closest collaborators, he was arrested when the police discovered where the general was being held. Savasta broke under brutal questioning, turned state's evidence, and put his encyclopedic memory at the service of the Italian police in exchange for leniency in sentencing.[15]

During the conversation with this thoughtful but largely unrepentant revolutionary, Richard asked how—with Ronald Reagan in the White House and Margaret Thatcher at Ten Downing Street—he had persuaded himself that the world was trembling on the brink of Marxist revolution. Savasta explained that he had been influenced by the apparent collapse of American hegemony in the 1970s. After the disaster in Vietnam, the Soviets had defied the United States by invading Afghanistan. Nicaraguan revolutionaries had deposed an American puppet government in Managua, and Iranian students had closed down the U.S. legation in Tehran, making hostages of its diplomats. With a world in chaos and oil prices soaring, American-dominated world capitalism was apparently sliding into its final decline. When asked what sources of information had been important to him and his colleagues, Savasta said that they had come to mistrust the mainstream press and preferred the classics of Marxism (such as Lenin's *State and Revolution*) as well as the writings of a few revolutionary university professors, a classic case of self-induced cognitive isolation.

"At a certain point, reality came unglued," he confessed, admitting that he and his colleagues had misread the portents in their "gamble with history."[16] But Savasta insisted that Marx's vision of history could not be denied; the armed struggle would begin again and someday it would be successful. While sorry that so many people had died pointlessly during the Red Brigades rampage, he was essentially apologizing for an error in scheduling. It had been bad timing, nothing more.

A charismatic and strangely likable man, Savasta had roughly the attitude of a young military officer, regretting the consequences of violence but feeling that he had been authorized by a legal authority (in his case the Red Brigades) to carry it out. Despite his involvement in twenty-seven homicides, Savasta negotiated an arrangement with the Italian judicial authorities that got him paroled from prison after a decade's confinement. He has now disappeared into the Italian version of the Witness Protection Program and now works—under another name—as a computer programmer.

Defining the Indefinable

The problem with the concept of terrorism has always been definitional, since it is hard to get everybody (or anybody) to agree on precisely what the word means. In common usage, the word "terrorism" describes how we feel about a given episode of political violence, conveying our judgment that the event in question was morally wrong or unjustified. Although sovereign governments occasionally engage in acts of violence that can be difficult to defend, there is a tendency to use the term only to describe violence committed by non-state actors, or private groups, acting against a government. In some cases, terrorist acts may be carried out by secret agents of a government, although the responsible government will typically disguise or deny its involvement.[17]

We typically have no difficulty in accepting as terrorist an act that harms innocent people who have no apparent connection to the conflict in question. On December 21, 1988, terrorists placed an explosive device aboard Pan-American Flight 103, blowing the plane out of the sky over Lockerbie, Scotland, and killing all 259 passengers on board and eleven bystanders on the ground below. In some cases, the targets are innocent but serve as symbolic enemies. Office workers in the World Trade Center on September 11, 2001, were—in the minds of al-Qaeda hijackers—representatives of American economic power when they perished, even the people who swept the floor and made the coffee.[18] In the contemporary Middle East and South Asia, the suicide bomber has become a stunning new reality, as thousands of people, men, women, and children have strapped explosives to their bodies and gone to their deaths to pursue some political goal.[19]

In other cases, terrorism can punish a country in a successful effort to get its government to change some aspect of public policy. In the spring of 2004, for example, the Spanish were preparing to vote themselves another installment of government by the conservative Popular Party. On March 11, three days before the election, terrorists linked with al-Qaeda detonated a series of bombs at the Madrid train station, killing several hundred Spaniards in an effort to persuade the Madrid government to withdraw its troops from Iraq. Participation in this war had been generally unpopular among Spaniards, and when they saw their country becoming a target of terrorist attacks, many of them switched their votes, bringing in the Spanish Socialist Party that had always opposed the American assault on Iraq. The new socialist prime minister promptly withdrew Spanish troops from the coalition in Iraq.

As is the case in every other form of political violence, the urge to commit acts of terrorist violence can flow from deeply felt nationalist passions, or from the ideological desire to alter public policy in some dramatic way. The contrast between Spain's nationalist ETA (*Euskadi Ta Askatasuna*) movement and Germany's ideological Red Army Faction illustrates this point.

• The Basques: In the North of Spain near the industrial city of Bilbao lives a non-Spanish ethnic-national group, described in chapter 4 as a stateless nation. Culturally, the Basques are quite distinct from the Spanish: their language is unrelated to any other known tongue, and the Basques have always nurtured a proud sense of ethnic self-identity. Suffering terribly under the centralizing dictatorship of Francisco Franco (1939–1974), some Basques lashed out in the 1960s with an armed movement called ETA, or *Euskadi Ta Askatasuna*, which means "Homeland and Freedom" in the Basque language. Spain is now a modern democracy with membership in the European Union and NATO. Although many were doubtful that peace could or should be achieved, the Spanish government and the ETA high command have in recent years inched cautiously toward a permanent settlement.

    ETA is not an ideological organization in the sense of being communist or capitalist. Its aims are ethnic or nationalist, and the word "separatist" is applicable here because ETA demands that the Basque country be separated from Spain and allowed to emerge as a separate state.[20]

Figure 9.5.   Spanish Antagonism to ETA Violence
This sign was being waved in an anti-ETA (Movement against Intolerance) demonstration in Madrid, making the case that ETA/Basque operatives are murderers rather than heroes. Why not just give the Basques their own sovereign state? Most prosperous Basques don't actually want to break away from an advanced European democracy, which Spain is, and no Spanish government is ever likely to acquiesce in a breakup of the country.

- The Red Army Faction or Baader-Meinhof Gang: Let's compare this to the much more specifically ideological German case. The year 1968 was tumultuous almost everywhere, with student activists protesting against the war in Vietnam and challenging the status quo on campuses from Berkeley to the Sorbonne. In what was then West Germany, a small group of intellectuals and writers convinced themselves that a worldwide Marxist revolution was at hand, using much of the same narrow reasoning that had persuaded Antonio Savasta that world revolution was imminent. They believed this revolt would begin in the Third World with organizations such as the Palestinian Popular Front for the Liberation of Palestine (PFLP), an Arab Marxist group opposed to Israel. Deciding that they needed to prepare for Germany's participation in this apocalyptic upheaval, these activists created the Red Army Faction, sometimes called the Baader-Meinhof Gang, after two of its most celebrated leaders. Throughout most of the 1970s, the Red Army Faction carried out robberies and assassinations of commercial, political, and military leaders, often in partnership with Palestinian groups. While they never came remotely close to challenging Germany's stability, they did take part in the infamous 1972 attack on Israeli athletes at the Munich Olympic Games.[21]
- The Red Army Faction (*Rote Armee Fraktion* in German) failed, and its leaders are now dead, in prison, or on the run, but they remain one of the best examples in recent history of a purely ideological terrorist movement. Unlike the nationalist Basques, who wanted to change the ethnicity of their leaders, Andreas Baader and Ulrike Meinhof wanted German Marxists, not German capitalists, to be in charge of Germany.

Tough Choices: The Irish Baron's Daughter and Mussolini's Nose

It can be more difficult to use the word "terrorism" when we feel sympathy for the cause behind the political violence in question. Consider this case. Violet Gibson was the wealthy and socially prominent daughter of Lord Ashbourne, an Anglo-Irish Victorian statesman and cabinet minister. During her travels to Italy, Ms. Gibson became convinced that Benito Mussolini was a cruel and ruthless dictator. A deeply religious woman, she felt that she had been commanded by God to kill him.

Mussolini had actually become prime minister of Italy as the result of a disorderly but essentially legal process. When World War I ended, Italy was bankrupt and ready for revolution. The Marxist left was fatally excited by the success of the 1917 Bolshevik Revolution in Russia and openly proclaimed its dedication to the violent overthrow of Italy's shaky democratic government. An ex-socialist journalist who had served in the Italian Army, Mussolini created the fascist movement to exalt Italy's victory in the war, establish a strong, disciplined government, make Italy a presence on the world scene, and destroy Marxism. By 1920, Mussolini's fascist militia was battling the Marxists all over northern Italy with savage and often lethal brutality, breaking the power of the labor unions, assassinating left-wing politicians, and intimidating the police.[22] By October 1922, it seemed that no one else could restore order, and Mussolini was invited by the king to serve as the country's prime

Figure 9.6.   Violet Gibson
Courtesy of Lord Ashbourne.

minister. Accepting, he received the formal assent of the democratically elected Italian Parliament and the best wishes of political leaders all around the world.

Even with Mussolini in office, the fascist rampage continued, with several high-profile assassinations of priests and high-ranking opposition politicians. When Violet Gibson arrived in Italy in 1924, Mussolini was two years into what would be a twenty-three year rule and still very popular at home and abroad despite the blood on his hands. On April 7, 1926, she stood in the front row of a cheering crowd in Rome as Il Duce emerged from a meeting. Violet had a gun in her purse. She expected and accepted the martyrdom she foresaw for herself.

Shall we test our disapproval of terrorism? We have read the history books and know that if he survives this moment, Benito Mussolini will install a ruthless dictatorship over Italy, wage war on his neighbors, and commit genocide against Africans in Ethiopia. In 1940, he will deftly choose the wrong side in World War II, getting millions of people killed and helping Hitler perpetrate the Holocaust against the Jews. While the cheering crowds around her fail to realize it, Violet is perfectly correct in seeing Mussolini as a foolish, evil man whose premature death in 1926 might save the world two decades of wickedness.

On the other hand, we disapprove of terrorism, and if the popular and legally elected prime minister of Italy is to be removed, surely there needs to be a democratic political process with elections and courts, and not an assassin's bullet. Is that what we believe? Are we quite sure?

If we could fly back three-quarters of a century to join Violet Gibson that day in Rome, what would we say to her as she raises the pistol? Might we inform her that terrorism is always wrong, no matter what the circumstances? Or, as we see Mussolini's scowling granite features, we might whisper, "Death to tyrants, Violet. Kill him!"

Without the benefit of our advice, Violet took her best shot but only managed to nick Mussolini's nose, a wound that healed with a tiny scar. Granted nineteen more years in which to ruin his country, Mussolini was ultimately executed in April 1945 by Italian partisans who were better shots than Violet but otherwise shared her views. For her effort to hustle history, Violet Gibson was rewarded with life in an insane asylum. She died, forgotten by everyone, in 1956.[23]

There are tough choices here. Was she a heroine or a terrorist? Can you devise a definition of terrorism that includes Timothy McVeigh and Osama bin Laden but excludes Violet Gibson?

GUERRILLA WARFARE

The twentieth century was the great age of **guerrilla warfare**, a form of conflict in which lightly armed insurgent groups use hit-and-run combat to challenge an established government. These insurgents will typically choose unconventional tactics because they are too weak, at least at the start of the revolutionary struggle, to create and field a regular army with uniforms and heavy weaponry. Guerrillas will therefore be irregular forces, often volunteers and sometimes without a formal rank structure.

What particularly distinguishes guerrilla warriors from conventional soldiers is their use of unexpected attacks (sometimes combined with terrorism) to wear down government troops and destroy the morale of the regular army. At least at the beginning of a guerrilla campaign, guerrillas resist the temptation to try to hold and defend territory, retreating whenever the government concentrates its forces against them. They fight where and when they are strong, and retreat when it suits them, trying to exhaust the enemy.

Twentieth-century theoreticians of guerrilla war first saw it as a form of combat best suited for the countryside, where irregulars could conceal themselves in mountains, jungles, or forests. Guerrillas can fight, however, anywhere they can hide, and this includes the slums and shantytowns of big cities. Clearly, this style of combat is not suited for war against a conventional army in open or level territory, particularly when the conventional army has tanks and control of the air over the battlefield.

In the early years of his struggle against the Nationalist government of China, Mao Zedong used guerrilla tactics, since his forces were not yet strong enough to engage in conventional combat. During World War II, partisan, or guerrilla, forces tormented German and Italian armies of occupation. The campaign fought by Yugoslav communist forces under Josif Broz Tito is a classic example, although the lesser known battle waged by Italian *partigiani* (partisans) against the German Army was equally heroic.

If the terrain is sufficiently rough and there is enough popular support, guerrilla forces can destroy the morale of a much larger and stronger adversary. The Vietnamese under Ho Chi Min fought the Japanese from 1940 to 1945, the French from 1945 to 1954, and the Americans from (roughly) 1959 until the withdrawal of U.S. troops in 1973, scoring three consecutive victories against stronger occupying forces. When the Soviet Union invaded Afghanistan on Christmas Day of 1979, a ragtag coalition of Afghan *mujahideen* took the field against the mighty Red Army and won by the simple expedient of not losing. By 1989, the last Russian soldier had retreated back over the border.[24]

4. War or High-Intensity Conflict

Americans sing an old spiritual called "I ain't gonna study war no more," lyrics that express a forlorn hope that we can someday avoid those protracted, expensive, and deadly armed engagements called high-intensity conflicts (HICs). In this section we will look briefly at the whole phenomenon of war, seeing what makes it different from the low-intensity conflicts we have just studied.[25] While wars are seldom formally declared, we'll see that they have become very frequent and are incredibly destructive of lives and property. In its detailed study of violence, the World Health Organization concluded that a third of a million people died in 2000 (the year of the study) as a direct result of war.[26] While we classically think of war as a blood sport between opposing groups of young soldiers, the casualties are increasingly civilians, especially women and children.[27]

Is war ever justifiable? Many philosophers have written about the prerequisites for what is often called a "just war." In almost every country, attitudes on war, or the institutionalized use of violence, range from absolute pacifism at one end to a belief that military force is simply another political tool to be used whenever the national interest warrants it. Most people endorse military violence if it can be seen as a defense of their homeland. Others would sanction humanitarian operations, such as the NATO offensive against genocidal behavior in Kosovo (see chapter 11 for the details). There were arguments in Europe and the United States when Libyans rebelled against their government in the spring of 2011 and the Qaddafi government resorted to threats of genocide. Britain, France, and the United States mounted an air support operation to give the rebels a chance to survive; when they triumphed, Qaddafi was the most prominent casualty of the war.

When countries have very far-flung economic and strategic interests, self-defense becomes more difficult to define, and critics of American foreign policy have wondered if U.S. attacks on Vietnam, Cuba, Panama, Grenada, and other small countries can be justified as defensive.

American and European soldiers fight with very high-tech weapons systems, and in recent years, they have hoped to achieve military objectives without taking many casualties. These technologically sophisticated countries often fight against primitive or traditional societies who defend themselves with low-tech weapons and sometimes terrorism, accepting high levels of casualties. In the usual Pentagon jargon, this is called "**asymmetrical warfare**," a situation in which the two sides to a violent conflict use highly contrasting tactics and weaponry.

Bring Back the Draft?

One change in modern warfare that has a certain relevance to university students is what is variously called "selective service," "conscription," or "the draft." Faced with very large wars or endemic defense problems, many countries obligate young men (and occasionally young women) to present themselves involuntarily for military service. As the United States discovered during the Vietnamese experience, conscription makes it technically possible to field a very large army, but politically difficult to keep it in the field for very long if casualties run high and the war is unpopular. After Vietnam, the United States joined those European societies that had already moved to all-volunteer, professional armies. During the prolonged occupation of Iraq (2003–2011), the U.S. Army found it difficult to maintain force levels in the field and was forced to keep reservists on active duty for extended tours of duty. Some U.S. politicians have called for the restoration of the draft. The selective service bureaucracy remains in place, and young American males are still obliged to register for the draft at age seventeen. How do you feel about American military operations in the Middle East? Would your feelings change if you personally could be obligated to serve in a combat unit in Iraq or Afghanistan? What, ultimately, is fairer: a draft in which everyone theoretically serves, or a professional military in which the enlisted personnel are overwhelmingly drawn from the ranks of the poor?

THE PHENOMENON OF WAR

On a bad day, the distinction can be hard to make, but high-intensity conflict is substantively different from low-intensity conflict in the following three key ways:

- Fatalities: War involves levels of conflict so high that daily fatalities will number in the dozens or hundreds, and the annual death toll will typically exceed 1,000. In major wars, fatalities can run into millions.
- Combatants: War typically features (on at least one side) conventional military units (i.e., air forces, armies, and navies) who are supported, equipped, and commanded by senior government officals.
- Weaponry: War will typically be fought with heavy, military-style weaponry, ranging from ordinary battlefield weapons, such as rifles and mortars, up to very destructive weapons systems, such as tanks, fighter aircraft, and aircraft carriers. These are usually called "**conventional weapons**" to distinguish them from nuclear weapons, which thus far have been used only by the United States against Japan in the closing days of World War II. The imprecise phrase "**weapons of mass destruction**" is more political than it is military, but it is often used to describe nuclear, chemical, or biological armaments in the hands of an enemy.

Preparing for war is costly and waging it is extraordinarily expensive. During the decade of the 1990s, global expenditures on military affairs ran just under a trillion dollars per year. Many very poor states actually spent more on their armies than they did on their school systems and medical establishments.

Military spending declined briefly and slightly after the end of the Cold War but then climbed again after the terrorist attacks on September 11, 2001, and the beginning of the War on Terror. A careful study done by the Stockholm International Peace Research Institute (SIPRI) in June 2009 suggests that the United States accounted for at least 47 percent of the world's global expenditure on soldiers and weapons. See figure 9.7 for the top ten military spenders in the world. U.S. defense expenditures have about doubled between 2001 and 2009. At $63 billion annually, the United States spends about 25 percent more than do the next nine military powers.

The Era of Endless War

Wars have been a feature of human society since the beginning of recorded history, and the earliest human settlements excavated by archaeologists were fortified against enemy attacks. Various historians have tried to calculate how much of our history as a species we have spent fighting one another, and the results are consistently depressing: on most days in recorded history, there has been a war going on somewhere.

In the years since World War II, it has become more difficult to make the distinction between wartime and peacetime. Traditionally, wars were formally declared, fought more or less continually for a period, and then ended with a truce or a victory for one side and a defeat for the other. World War I, for example, began in August of 1914 after a protracted period of European peace and concluded with the formal surrender of the Central Powers and the Versailles negotiations in 1918–1919.

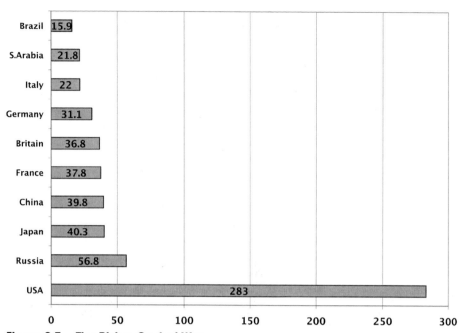

Figure 9.7. The Rising Cost of War
This chart is based on data from the authoritative Stockholm International Peace Research Institute (SIPRI), Yearbook 2010, table 5A.1 (Stockholm: SIPRI). It shows, in billions of dollars, expenditures on military preparedness, which are notoriously difficult to calculate. Countries are secretive and sometimes deceptive, burying money for weaponry in other budgets.

Today's wars are often stop-and-start affairs, evolving out of a series of armed incidents, oscillating between low and high intensity, and continuing for extended periods of time. Furthermore, modern wars are seldom formally declared. Despite the fact that the world has experienced almost ceaseless combat since Pearl Harbor, few major sovereign states have formally declared war on other sovereign states because political leaders are wary of the political implications and concerned that formal declarations of war limit their options for ending the fighting. Many countries have constitutions in which the legislature needs to consent to a formal declaration of war, and lawmakers have been reluctant to shoulder this responsibility. As a result, wars these days are—almost without exception—undeclared.

These days, most LICs and HICs are **civil wars**, that is, they are fought within the boundaries of a given sovereign state by residents of that state. These wars are sometimes called "intrastate" or "domestic." Less frequently, although often more serious, violent conflict can spill over legal national boundaries, with soldiers of one country shooting at soldiers of another country. For example, Iraq attacked and conquered neighboring Kuwait in August of 1990, only to be defeated by a U.S.-led coalition the following year. The impoverished east African countries of Eritrea and Ethiopia fought fatuously in 1998–2000, while NATO attacked what was left of Yugoslavia in 1999, driving the Serbian Army out of the province of Kosovo. In the winter of 2001–2002, the United States decapitated the government of Afghanistan in partnership with anti-Taliban forces already in the country, although they were still in Afghanistan and still fighting the Taliban in 2012. In the spring of 2003, an Anglo-American coalition invaded the Republic of Iraq with the last U.S. combat forces withdrawing only in December of 2011.

The Brutalized Continent

The notion that violent conflict is related to poverty, overpopulation, and human misery seems confirmed by the fact that an enormous proportion of contemporary warfare takes place in sub-Saharan Africa, which is also the poorest portion of the planet. This continent has endured both low- and high-intensity conflict from the end of the twentieth century into the start of the present century, wars that have devastated African society without attracting much attention from the Western media.

Many African conflicts have little to do with political ideas and often qualify as what we have described above as resource wars. In extraordinarily poor societies, young men with guns will sometimes begin to steal food and other resources, often forming ragtag armies with impressive names to legitimize what is basically armed robbery. Increasingly, very young boys, and sometimes girls, are recruited into these armies and forced into battle when they are still prepubescent children. Drugs and alcohol are often part of the mix, and—in the absence of restraining authority—these young males often rape and abuse women.

- The Sudanese Case: Almost certainly, the worst human-rights disasters in recent years have taken place in the artificial African state of Sudan, located up the Nile River just below Egypt, with a long, rocky coastline on the Red Sea. In every important respect, Sudan is several separate societies capriciously forced into one country by British imperialism. About two-thirds of Sudan's thirty-six million people live in the North around the capital at Khartoum. They are Arabic-speaking Muslims who have developed a distinct taste for fundamentalist Islam. In the Darfur region near the border with Chad are black African tribes who have generally become Muslims, although they do not speak Arabic as their mother tongue. The southern portion of the country was inhabited by black African peoples who practice either traditional African religions or Christianity. After decades of civil war, South Sudan emerged as an independent sovereign state in 2011.[28]

  As peace came slowly and uncertainly between the North and the South of Sudan, the Khartoum government quickly turned its aggressive energies against about five million Islamic (but not Arabized) African tribal peoples in the western province of Darfur. The trouble began when Arab nomadic peoples began to drift into the region from the north because their traditional watering grounds had dried up, in what may be a consequence of global climate change. This created hostility between them and the settled African farming population. When several African tribes rebelled, the Khartoum regime began arming and encouraging the Arab pastoralists (the so-called *Janjaweed*), resulting in a genocidal assault on the African population. Nearly three hundred thousand people, mostly children, seem to have died, and perhaps 2.5 million have been driven from their homes and are either internally displaced persons or in exile in neighboring Chad. The crimes against humanity by President Bashir in Sudan have been so heinous that the International Criminal Court (ICC) in July 2010 issued a warrant for his arrest for the crime of genocide, referring to the mass killings of civilians in Darfur. Mr. Bashir was still defying this warrant in 2012.[29]

- The Congo Catastrophe: Southwest of Sudan lies the Congo, a country that has recently suffered from both civil and international war. Let's clear up the nomenclature issue first. When it was a colony of Belgium, this area was called the Belgian Congo. Confusingly, just north of the Congo River lies a former French colony also called Congo, and to distinguish between the two separate sovereign states, journalists sometimes link the two countries with the names of their capital cities: hence Congo-Brazzaville is the smaller northern society, while Congo-Kinshasa is the large state that dominates the heart of central Africa. Congo-Kinshasa achieved independence in 1960, but fell quickly into a confused civil war that ended in military dictatorship by Mobutu Sese Seko, who changed the country's name to Zaire. When Mobutu was driven from power after thirty-two years of corrupt dictatorship, the country was rebaptized the Democratic Republic of the Congo. Since it has yet to become either a real democracy or an elective republic, some people have reverted to the habit of saying Congo-Kinshasa.

  The Democratic Republic of Congo (Kinshasa) has gold and diamonds, oil and uranium, and lots of freshwater, making it a potentially prosperous country despite its present poverty. After Mobutu was ousted in 1997, the armed forces of neighboring Uganda and Rwanda invaded the eastern Congo under a variety of pretexts, fighting the Congolese and each other. Lured by the mineral resources, several of the Congo's other neighbors (such as Angola, Namibia, and Zimbabwe) piled in to protect their interests and secure their share of the treasure. The resulting war has been enormously destructive of life and property, and it has been fought in the jungles and rain forests of the eastern Congo, an area too insecure for most journalists and human rights organizations to visit. As a consequence, news about what some have called "Africa's First World War" has been sparse although some aid agencies have claimed that the death toll over a four-year period may exceed 2.5 million people. At its worst moments, the Congolese situation slides up the scale into what we will describe below as societal mayhem.[30]

THE INCREASED LETHALITY OF WAR

Since the early years of the twentieth century, wars have proven exceedingly deadly. World War II directly or indirectly killed about fifty-two million people, just over 2 percent of the entire human race.[31] While most people lived longer and healthier lives between 1900 and 2000, over one hundred million people died prematurely because of war. According to the International Institute for Strategic Studies, combat claimed over one hundred thousand people in 1998 alone.

Not only have wars become increasingly lethal, the who-gets-killed factor has altered profoundly. Traditional war was primarily dangerous for young men in uniform. Prior to the end of World War I (1918), war was seen mostly as the business of conquering an enemy's territory and destroying its armed forces. Killing civilians not only violated a soldier's code of chivalry, but it was also a pointless diversion of resources.

With the creation of bombers, long-range artillery, and missiles, however, it became possible to win a war by destroying an enemy's infrastructure (bridges and highways, water supplies, factories, electricity grids, communications, etc.). A military establishment with high-technology weapons might even try to undermine the enemy's will to resist by targeting cities and towns, both to destroy the morale of the civilian population and to put the entire enemy society under political and economic stress. Driven by the available technology, the use of air power (such as pilotless "drone aircraft") and long-range missiles (such as the famous American cruise missile) saves lives in a First-World military establishment, but escalates the death toll in a Third-World society.

A Swedish study estimated that 15 percent of all the people killed in World War I were noncombatants or innocent bystanders or civilians. By the time of World War II, this figure had soared to 65 percent of the total death toll. In some recent wars, civilian fatalities may be as high as 84 percent of the total casualties. An independent study published in *Civilians in Wars* reaches similar conclusions, declaring that in the wars of the 1990s, civilian deaths sometimes reached 90 percent of the total. As the martyred war correspondent Marie Colvin (profiled in chapter 1) once commented,

> Despite all the videos you see from the Ministry of Defence or the Pentagon, and all the sanitised language describing smart bombs and pinpoint strikes, the scene on the ground has remained remarkably the same for hundreds of years. Craters. Burned houses. Mutilated bodies. Women weeping for children and husbands. Men for their wives, mothers, and children.[32]

Women and Children Last

There is even considerable evidence that these civilian victims of war are disproportionately women and children. When war disrupts a society and people are forced to flee from their homes, women are often more vulnerable than men are because they typically remain with their children and take risks to find food and shelter for their families. In the Bosnian War (1994–1996) Serbian snipers hidden in the hills around Sarajevo deliberately shot at Bosnian Muslim women fetching water in order to damage the morale of their husbands who were off fighting in the Bosnian Army. For much of the war, it was actually safer to be a soldier at the front than to be a soldier's wife at home. When a "stateless nation" gets caught up in a war, the consequences can be particularly tragic. As a result of harsh military campaigns by both Turkey and Iraq, many Kurdish children have been orphaned and live in bleak refugee camps.

For obvious reasons, children are particularly at risk, and in many cases, the harm comes after the guns have fallen silent. Land mines are routinely left behind, particularly by defeated forces, lurking beneath the soil to injure children playing or working in the fields.[33] With electricity no longer flowing to homes and hospitals, water supplies contaminated, and food resources disrupted, women (especially those who have been widowed by the conflict) may find it impossible to find enough medicine and nutrition to keep their children alive.

Rape as a Military Weapon

Organized sexual violence against women is beginning to be a common feature of modern warfare. Women have been raped during wars since the beginning of time because combat promotes chaos and lawlessness, fighting brutalizes some men, and refugees fleeing from battlefields are uniquely vulnerable. Until recently, however, the practice was strategically irrelevant and regarded as criminal behavior by all parties to the conflict.

When Bangladesh asserted its independence from Pakistan in 1971, however, units of the retreating Pakistani Army carried out the systematic rape of Bengali women as a way of hurling a final insult at a victorious enemy.

In a less clear-cut fashion, rape was used as a tactic during conflicts in Algeria, Kashmir, Liberia, Rwanda, and Uganda, but these episodes lingered at the periphery of the world's consciousness until the 1990s. Perhaps Europeans and Americans comforted themselves with the notion that savage things will happen in savage parts of the world. When Yugoslavia came unglued in 1992, however, mass rape occurred in the heart of Europe, carried out by Serbian Bosnian forces trying to drive Muslim Bosnians out of what they hoped would become their territory; as many as sixty thousand women may have been violated. The Serbian military used the same tactic again in 1999 in an attempt to drive Muslim ethnic Albanians out of Kosovo. The whole complex Yugoslav situation will be reviewed later, but for now note that the motivation for this mass rape was straightforward and may have enjoyed temporary success. In both Bosnia and Kosovo, Muslim men had taken to the field to oppose the Serbians, leaving their wives at home. When these women began to be sexually violated on a large scale, the morale of the fighting troops was depressed, and men may have been tempted to leave their units to protect their women.

The epidemic of rape reached its zenith during the central African wars described above. A study by *Foreign Affairs* magazine suggests that in one two-year period (2006 and 2007), as many as four hundred thousand Congolese women were raped by members of armies and militias.[34]

Nuclear Weapons

In an effort to hasten the surrender of Japan, the United States dropped two nuclear weapons on the Japanese cities of Hiroshima and Nagasaki in August of 1945. The Hiroshima weapon killed eighty thousand people, the largest number of causalities caused by a single weapon in the history of warfare.[35] Aware that it was vastly outnumbered by its potential enemies, the United States led the way into the nuclear era by proposing to utilize nuclear weapons if either Russia or China became militarily aggressive.

In the aftermath of World War II, both the Soviet Union and the Anglo-American alliance quickly produced enormous numbers of these weapons, deploying them in aircraft, submarines, and intercontinental ballistic missiles. By the end of the Cold War, there may have been seventy-seven thousand individual nuclear warheads in the world. The United States, the USSR (and later Russia), China, Britain, and France were all self-declared nuclear states, and Israel's possession of a nuclear capability was an open secret. In the late 1990s, both Pakistan and India (locked into an endless conflict over Kashmir) joined this exclusive club by test-detonating nuclear weapons of their own. After years of speculation, North Korea announced in October 2006 that it had tested a deliverable nuclear weapon, and the world grudgingly acknowledged that the exclusive club of nuclear nations had just acquired an unreliable new member. Meanwhile, Europeans were still hoping to talk the Iranians out of the atomic option while the United States was making threatening noises about Tehran's alleged nuclear ambitions.[36]

For a time, American military and political leaders reacted to Soviet and Chinese nuclear weapons by increasing and refining the U.S. nuclear arsenal. Reacting to the loss of its "first strike" capability, American defense policy began to think of nuclear weapons in a "mutual assured destruction" (MAD) role; since no country could defend itself against an incoming missile, MAD held that nuclear weapons were successfully preventing the Cold War from turning hot. Certainly, by the start of the 1980s, Westerners were skeptical that nuclear weapons were useful for anything except ultimate deterrence. Some scholars produced doomsday or "Nuclear Winter" scenarios suggesting that any significant use of nuclear weapons would terminate human life on the planet. Public pressure for disarmament led to a series of treaties, mostly between the United States and the Soviet Union/Russia, that either discouraged further growth of nuclear arsenals or actually diminished the respective stockpiles.[37]

In April 2010, President Obama changed the course of nuclear policy for the United States and the world, a course that had been in place since the beginning of the Cold War. He announced that the ultimate goal of this revised "nuclear posture" would be no new development of nuclear weapons. In direct opposition to the previous Bush administration, President Obama also declared that the United States would not use nuclear weapons against nonnuclear states, even if the United States was attacked by a nonnuclear state. He declared that the United States might use nuclear weapons if biological or chemical attacks endangered U.S. security, but that nuclear weapons were a last resort. The president said that the country would "make sure that our conventional weapons capability is an effective deterrent in all but the most extreme circumstances." Following these statements, President Obama met with nearly four dozen leaders from around the world to review the Nuclear Non-proliferation Treaty (NPT), which began in 1970, and devise a nuclear strategy that better aligns with the realities of nuclear security in the twenty-first century.[38]

5. Societal Mayhem and Genocide

What could be worse than high-intensity conflict? It can be difficult to imagine anything more horrific than war. Since World War II, however, several societies have imploded, crashing into a state of generalized, multilateral violence so extensive and protracted that more people die of violence or the effects of violence than from natural causes. Not all authors make a distinction between high-intensity conflicts and this very intense form of violence, but it might be worth carving out a separate category called "**societal mayhem**."

In this section, we'll look at several specific cases where a community's defense mechanisms have disintegrated, resulting in an extraordinarily high death toll from military weapons, genocide, terrorism, mob violence, starvation caused by war, and mounting health problems occasioned by the conflict.

WHAT'S WORSE THAN WAR?

Societal mayhem can be said to be taking place when some or all of the following five factors exist:

- Death by Violence and Starvation: Fighting becomes so generalized that war wounds and war-induced starvation become the leading causes of mortality among the civilian population. In many cases, efforts will be made to deny food supplies to "enemy" populations in order to induce starvation deliberately.

- Breakdown of Essential Public Services: Governmental and ordinary commercial services fail, forcing people to use violence to secure food supplies. Schools and hospitals close. Police forces may become essentially criminal gangs, preying on the civilian population. The government cannot or will not pay salaries. The national army may fragment or suffer high desertion rates. This civil breakdown will cause famine even when there are adequate stocks of food in the country.

- Multilateral Conflict: Characteristically, the players in the conflict multiply, with ethnic groups, political factions, criminal gangs, and paramilitary units all fighting one another. Alliances and coalitions tend to shift quickly and mysteriously. Private groups and vigilante gangs control increasingly small territories. Killing may become clearly genocidal in an effort to eliminate or drive whole population groups into exile.[39]

- Anomic Violence: At least from the perspective of outside observers, violence becomes anomic and irrational. The motivation for killing becomes difficult to understand or blatantly senseless, often with very young adolescents becoming involved.

- Refugees: A large portion of the population is uprooted and is forced to flee, seeking sanctuary from the fighting, access to food supplies, or both. Sometimes violence is deliberately intended to create an out-migration of refugees.

In recent years, several societies have gone through a period during which all the usual structures of life crumble. Sometimes these periods have passed within a few weeks or months; in other cases, populations have endured genocidal civil strife for many years. Here are three recent examples of societal mayhem:

- Somalia 1991–present: After twenty-one years of personal rule and a disastrous 1977–1978 border war with Ethiopia, the dictator of Somalia, Mohamed Siad Barre, fled the country in January of 1991, leaving behind him a degenerating situation complicated by worsening drought, widespread starvation, and the complete collapse of governing institutions. Somalia collapsed quickly into societal mayhem with regional and tribal leaders fighting for control and looting food supplies contributed by the international community. President George H. W. Bush dispatched American armed forces to Somalia in December of 1992 in an attempt to control the situation. After eighteen American servicemen were killed in an attempt to capture one of Somalia's warlords, President Clinton withdrew the U.S. military presence, allowing Somalia to slip back into carnage.[40] More than a decade later, no unified government has emerged, fighting continues, and Somalia is often described as a "failed state."[41]

- Bosnia-Herzegovina 1991–1995: As one of the six member-republics of the original Yugoslav confederation, Bosnia-Herzegovina was home to Orthodox Christian Serbs, Bosnian Muslims, and Roman Catholic Croatians. When Yugoslavia began to collapse in 1991, Bosnia's well-armed Serbian minority implemented a program of **ethnic cleansing** to drive the Croatians and Muslims out of territory they wished to consolidate as part of a greater Serbia. In two years of complicated, confused, but terribly lethal fighting, crimes were committed on all sides. Out of an estimated population of 3.8 million, about one-quarter million people were killed and a million wounded. While the essential conflict remains unsolved, the actual fighting was ended when NATO forces physically occupied the country in 1995–1996 under the terms of the Dayton Accords.[42]

• Rwanda (1994–1996): Rwanda perhaps qualifies as the best recent example of societal mayhem/genocide. The majority population in Rwanda was always a large tribal grouping of Hutu people. Under 10 percent of the population were Tutsi, who were regarded as foreigners despite the fact that there are only vague ethnic differences between the two population groups and they share a common language. Long-standing tensions between the two communities exploded in 1994, and some members of the Hutu majority fell upon the Tutsi minority with a clear-cut intention of eradicating them as a people. The total death count will never be known, but never have so many people been killed so quickly and with such primitive weapons, mostly machetes and axes. As many as six hundred thousand people may have been slaughtered before a Tutsi-led army took control of the country and stopped the massacre. By August of 1994, a quarter of the entire population of Rwanda was either dead or in refugee status outside of Rwanda.[43]

SOCIETAL MAYHEM IN SIERRA LEONE

The grotesque, mind-numbing violence that shattered Sierra Leonean society between 1991 and 2002 is a good example of societal mayhem.

A former British colony, Sierra Leone became independent in 1961. Like most ex-colonies, the new country was a multinational state and experienced some friction along ethnic lines. Furthermore, the country was traumatized by a series of military coups d'état that put soldiers in charge of the country between 1968 and 1992. By the end of this period, Sierra Leone had plummeted to the bottom of the United Nations Development Programme's human development index listing. Life expectancy in 1991 was forty-two years and falling. The adult literacy rate was only 13 percent, and the public school system was shattered.[44]

Then things got worse. In 1991, a former army corporal named Foday Sankoh obtained the sponsorship of a warlord named Charles Taylor from neighboring Liberia, created a ragtag army called the Revolutionary United Front (RUF), and invaded Sierra Leone's diamond-rich eastern district. The economics of this devastating, decade-long insurgency were always clear: Sankoh's men smuggled the diamonds across the border to Liberia, where President Charles Taylor fenced them on the world market, using the proceeds to buy weaponry for himself and the RUF.

In 1996, Sierra Leone managed to stage a democratic election, voting a moderate, cautious, and sometimes indecisive politician named Ahmed Tejan Kabbah into the presidency. Reacting to the election, the RUF conquered more and more of the country, using their signature terror tactic of chopping off the forearms of civilians to send a blunt message: hands used to cast ballots will be hacked off.[45]

Appalled at pictures of children with severed limbs, the United Nations fielded a Blue Helmet peacekeeping force, which was joined by British troops. By 2001, the UN had 12,500 Blue Helmet troops in the country and world pressure had forced the Liberians to halt the illegal diamond trade, cutting off the RUF's money supply. In May of 2002, President Kabbah and his allies were reelected massively, and the RUF was destroyed as a political force.[46]

How did things get this bad in Sierra Leone? There is no question that this episode qualifies as societal mayhem. Calculating the death toll from ten years of fighting is difficult, but some estimates suggest that 10 percent of the population died directly as a result of war wounds; ten thousand people have survived with missing arms and hands. Since no one was keeping records, it is even more difficult to say how many people died of starvation generated by the war or disease spread by military operations, but Sierra Leone still has one of the world's lowest life expectancies, estimated in 2011 to be just over forty-seven years.[47]

At a primitive level, some of the violence made a certain raw sense. The RUF wanted to be undisturbed in their operation of the diamond mines, so they used the systematic amputation of hands and arms to send people flying whenever an RUF unit moved into the area. On the other hand, much of the awfulness seemed clearly anomic in character, that is, brutality without a conscious or identifiable purpose. The use of psychotropic drugs and alcohol was common. Having known nothing but savagery since infancy, some of the illiterate RUF soldiers may have been psychiatrically impaired by an insane life.

Throughout this appalling tragedy, very young boys were serving in the RUF and other militia movements. Even before reaching puberty, some of these children had been kidnapped, trained as soldiers, forced to execute other children, given drugs, encouraged to drink the blood of their executed enemies, and sometimes forced to participate in ritual cannibalism. Having been exposed for most of their lives to acts of senseless barbarism, they had come to regard rape and torture as normal behavior. UNICEF now has a program in place to try to rehabilitate these short and shattered lives.[48]

6. The Anglo-American Occupation of Iraq

As a case study, Iraq is an ideal way to summarize this chapter because Iraqi conflicts have been both intrastate and interstate (i.e., both civil and international), and these conflicts have skidded up from nonviolent political conflict to societal mayhem before slowly declining to its present status of low-intensity conflict.

Thanks to its colonial origins, the modern Iraqi state contains three major ethnic and religious communities who dislike each other with considerable intensity. In the country's mountainous North, the mostly Sunni Kurdish people speak a cognate of the Iranian family of languages and have always desired their own sovereign government; "Kurdistan" would include most of northern Iraq, bits of Iran, and a significant hunk of southeastern Turkey.

In the South, Arab Shi'ites resent the historically autocratic control of their Sunni cousins, and their religion tugs them toward their brother Shi'ites in Iran. Iraq's Sunni Arab Muslims live in the center of the country and have—until now—always monopolized political and economic power despite the fact that they are probably less than 20 percent of the population.[49]

Despite its ancient Sumerian and Babylonian origins, the modern Republic of Iraq was created out of the ashes of World War I and assigned fairly arbitrary borders to unify what had once been three disparate provinces of the defunct Ottoman Empire (a Kurdish Mosul, a Sunni Baghdad, and a Shi'ite Basra, respectively).

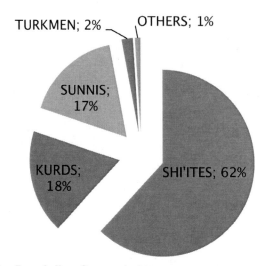

Figure 9.8. Major Population Groups in Iraq
Compiled from a variety of scholarly sources, these figures are very approximate.
The Ba'athist government never took an accurate census because it did not wish to
reveal how small the Sunni population was. Since 2003, no accurate head count has
been possible.

Initially a British mandate, Iraq achieved formal independence in 1932 as a Western-
oriented constitutional monarchy. When political life in the Arabic world became radicalized during the Cold War, the government disappeared in a bloody 1958 uprising. After
a decade of military coups and power struggles, the Ba'ath Party seized control in 1968,
advocating Arab unity and socialist economics. The regime was always somewhat hostile
to fundamentalist Islam; Ba'athist leaders were prepared to see Islam as a state religion but
not prepared to allow religious leaders to intrude into political policy.[50]

BA'ATHIST IRAQ

Born in 1937, the young Saddam Hussein joined the Ba'ath Party as an eighteen-year-
old, climbing rapidly in the ranks of the party hierarchy and building a personal following
based on friends and relatives from his hometown of Tikrit (just north of Baghdad). A
year after the Ba'athist revolution of 1968, Saddam Hussein emerged as vice president of
Iraq at the youthful age of thirty-two. In the years that followed, he ruthlessly consolidated his own power and became the country's undisputed leader in 1979.

The first problem on President Saddam Hussein's desk was the revolutionary new
government in Shi'ite-dominated Iran, then in its most violent phase with the Ayatollah
Khomeini attracting the loyalty of many Shi'ite Muslims, Arabs, and non-Arabs alike.
Given the fact that Shi'ites are a restless 60 percent of Iraq's population, Saddam had
every reason to worry that his own downtrodden Shi'ite population would be infected
by this revived religious radicalism. Taking advantage of a long-standing dispute over the
Shatt al-Arab waterway, which forms part of the border between Iraq and Iran, Saddam
Hussein tried to destroy the ayatollah's government with a long (1980–1988) war. What

Table 9.3.   An Iraqi Time Line

1920–1932	Iraq under British mandate
1922–1958	An unstable Arab monarchy
1958–1968	Military coups and power struggles
1968	Ba'ath Party takes control
1979	Hussein emerges as leader
1980–1988	The Iran-Iraq War
1990–1991	The Persian Gulf War
1991–2002	Protracted confrontation with the United States and UK
March/April 2003	Iraq War and U.S./UK; occupation; coalition; provisional authority in charge
May 2004	Ayad Allawi's interim government in formal control and Iraqi "sovereignty" restored
January 2005	Elections leading to transitional government under Prime Minister Ibrahim al-Jaafari
December 2005	Parliamentary elections for "permanent" government
May 2006	Formation of four-year government under Prime Minister Nuri al-Maliki
Autumn 2006	"Battle of Baghdad" as sectarian fighting verges on full-scale civil war
March 2010 to present	Inconclusive parliamentary elections, continuation of al-Maliki government, and low-level insurgency

historians have dubbed the "Iran-Iraq War" cost the lives of about three-quarters of a million soldiers and perhaps fifty thousand civilians who lived near the front. During this period, Baghdad enjoyed the behind-the-scenes support of the United States, since the Iraqis were perceived by the Reagan administration as acting in the American national interest by protecting the oil fields on the Arab side of the Persian Gulf. In the last year of the fighting, Saddam Hussein turned on his own rebellious Iraqi Kurds with poison gas, killing five thousand civilians in the Halabja township on the Iranian border.

By 1988, the Iran-Iraq War had ended in a draw. Iraq felt that the Arab world owed it a debt of gratitude for having stopped the westward spread of Shi'ite Islamist influence from Iran. When an ungrateful Kuwait refused its cooperation, Saddam Hussein raised a long-standing Iraqi claim to sovereignty over oil-rich Kuwait, and sparked the Persian Gulf War by storming into the country in 1990, inexplicably catching Western intelligence agencies off guard. In what was called "Desert Storm," Anglo-American forces counterattacked in the spring of 1991, driving the shattered Iraqi army out of Kuwait.

There followed a period of protracted hostility between the Iraqi government and the American-British consortium that had defeated Saddam Hussein. The UN sent in a team of weapons inspectors who—we now know—were generally successful in disarming the Iraqi military before the Iraqis forced them out in 1997.[51]

THE ANGLO-AMERICAN ATTACK OF 2003

Iraq was hardly mentioned in the 2000 American presidential campaign, which focused mostly on domestic issues. After taking power in 2001, the Bush administration asserted that Iraq was rebuilding its weapons program. Shortly after the September 11, 2001, al-Qaeda attack on the United States, the U.S. government alleged a connection between the Iraqi regime and al-Qaeda, and sought backing for an armed attack on the country. In September 2002, Congress passed a War Powers Resolution, giving Mr. Bush domestic legal authority for a war.

By the winter of 2002–2003, there was intense political activity within the United States, at the United Nations, and internationally, over the merits of a U.S.-led war against the Iraqi regime.

Motives for the War

The question goes to the heart of the difficulty of establishing why any country voluntarily enters a war. We tend to look for one overwhelming "official" motive, but the public, the press, the military establishment, and various decision makers at the top may have radically different motives for supporting an armed conflict. A major war is an expensive piece of public policy. In the absence of an obvious Pearl Harbor–style attack on the homeland, a national leadership needs to convince a variety of constituencies with different (and perhaps inconsistent) arguments. In the case of the 2003 attack on Iraq, some combination of the following six motives may have been important.

- Control of Crude Oil Resources: While little was said publicly about the issue, some leaders may have privately focused on the long-term security of oil supplies upon which the United States and its allies depend. Saudi Arabia controls the world's largest reserves of crude oil, but many analysts worried that Arabia was headed into a protracted political crisis that might generate an Arabian government hostile to the Western world. Iraq has the second-largest reserves on the planet, and by installing a friendly government there, Europe, Japan, and the United States would theoretically assure themselves of continuing supplies, no matter what happened to Saudi Arabia.
- American Electoral Politics: Many observers believe that George W. Bush's behavior as president was conditioned by a desire to not commit what some conservatives regarded as the political mistakes that had cost his father reelection in 1992. When the first President Bush fought Iraq in 1991, he defined his mission narrowly as the rescue of Kuwait and made no attempt to conquer the Iraqi heartland. As a result, Saddam Hussein survived for another decade's misrule, an "unfinished job" from the perspective of many conservatives. Furthermore, the successful defeat of an evil dictator would bring political capital to the victorious president, and the Pentagon leadership believed the invasion of Iraq could be accomplished easily and relatively inexpensively.
- Protection of Israel: In 2003, Iraq posed no significant short-term threat to a nuclear-armed Israel, but the Iraqi regime had always been the most violently anti-Israeli state in the Middle East, and Iraqi forces had taken part in each of the Arab-Israeli wars. Saddam Hussein had been public in his financial support for the families of Palestinian suicide bombers, and a defeat for his regime would be seen as a victory for Israel in political terms. Militarily, the elimination of Hussein's government certainly made Israelis feel safer.
- Anti-Islamic/Anti-Arab Hostility: Especially after 9/11, many Westerners regarded Arabs, Muslims, and Middle Easterners in general with mistrust and dislike. Arab groups

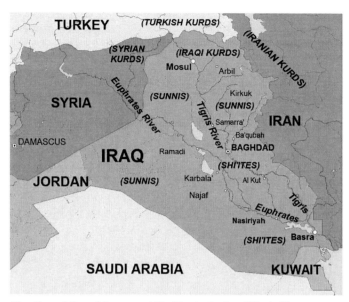

Map 9.1.   The Republic of Iraq and Its Meandering Ethnicities
Astride the Tigris-Euphrates river valleys, Iraq was the home of humankind's most ancient civilizations. The borders of the modern country were established capriciously after World War I, leaving some of the Kurdish people inside its modern borders, while most live in Turkey and Iran, with a few in Syria and elsewhere. To the south, Sunni and Shi'ite Muslims coexist uncomfortably in many of the same communities. The whole Iraq crisis can be understood only by studying the history, religion, and—especially—the geography of the place.

had carried out terrorist operations (mostly against Israel, but often against U.S. and Western interests) for decades, and Arabs were often portrayed as sinister and evil in motion pictures. Americans still resented the 1979–1981 imprisonment of American diplomats, and—despite the fact that Iranians are not Arabs—many Americans confused Iraq with Iran. Some supporters of the war were perhaps reacting to an anomic hostility to Middle Easterners in general.

• The Humanitarian Mission: From liberal to conservative, virtually all observers felt that Iraq's Ba'athist regime was one of the worst governments in the world. The Bush administration argued that the world community had a humanitarian obligation to free the Iraqi people from a cruel and oppressive government. A group of neo-conservative theorists in the Bush administration also felt that the bold use of American military force in Iraq and the stunning victory that would result would lead to the establishment of democratic governments throughout the Middle East. The humanitarian impulse was emphasized more forcefully after the war than before it, but it was the motive that appealed most to those moderate liberals in Britain and the United States who supported the war.

• National Security: While all the arguments listed above were advanced at various times to make the case for war, American national security was the rhetorical cornerstone of the Bush administration's argument, and senior administration officials asserted that Saddam Hussein had "weapons of mass destruction" (WMD) that could threaten his neighbors as well as the United States. After the trauma of September 11, 2001, many

Americans were sufficiently nervous to support a war against a hostile Arab power, even though no connection was ever demonstrated between Iraq and al-Qaeda and no WMD were ever found.

We discussed the phenomenon of cognitive isolation in chapter 1, and it seems to have played a bilateral role in thinking about this war. For their part, American leaders were persuaded that they would be enthusiastically greeted as liberators, showered with flowers, and then be able to depart promptly as the Iraqis quickly created their own pro-Western democracy. If leaders such as Bush and Blair were cognitively isolated, Saddam Hussein is now known to have deluded himself into believing that the Americans would never actually attack and would be defeated if they did. As British and American armies assembled on his southern border, Saddam Hussein was primarily focused on preventing a coup against him from his own army.[52]

The War

Opposition to the war was immense in Europe, but fairly muffled within the United States. Opponents of the war argued that bin Laden and Saddam Hussein had always been enemies, and there was no serious evidence of collusion between them. Any weapons in Iraqi hands that violated UN resolutions could be dealt with by the Security Council, and no proof ever emerged that the Iraqis had possessed weaponry that could have threatened the United States or Great Britain. Furthermore, they argued that an unprovoked attack on a sovereign state would violate the United Nations Charter, which allows countries to fight only in immediate self-defense, unless they secure the approval of the UN Security Council. Most critics of the war felt that the war was being fought partly for political reasons and partly to take control of Iraqi oil resources.

Led by U.S. Secretary of State Colin Powell and Prime Minister Tony Blair, the British-American alliance made the case for war to the UN Security Council in February and early March of 2003, but the U.S.-UK pro-war resolution was withdrawn when it became clear that it would be vetoed at least by the French and the Russians, and would not in any case achieve the necessary nine-vote majority. When diplomacy failed, the Anglo-American alliance acted unilaterally, despite the fact that Iraq's larger neighbors (such as Turkey and Saudi Arabia) denied the use of their territory for land and air operations.

After an intensive psychological warfare campaign desired to convince the Iraqi military not to resist, combat operations began on March 19 with a massive "shock and awe" bombing campaign against Baghdad in an attempt to kill Saddam Hussein and leadership elite. Baghdad was bombed daily with precision-guided weapons until the United States actually took control of the city. The next day, the British (who supplied about one-third of the fighting forces) attacked north from their bases in Kuwait and began the siege of Basra. Simultaneously, powerful U.S. armored units swept about two hundred miles north without meeting much resistance until about March 26, when the weather deteriorated and irregular forces called the Saddam Fedayeen began launching suicidal attacks against them. After a brief pause for rest and resupply, coalition armed forces advanced on Baghdad, fighting and winning several serious battles with the Iraqi elite Republican Guard. Most of the ordinary Iraqi Army evaporated or surrendered, and the United States approached the Baghdad Airport on April 3 and entered the Iraqi capital two days later.

By April 9, 2003, U.S. troops seized the Baghdad city center, and the Ba'athist regime was clearly defeated. By April 15, the cities of the North had surrendered or been captured, and major combat operations were declared over on May 1, 2003.[53]

Catastrophic Success

For the victorious allies, however, winning the conventional war was easier than securing the peace, a fact that led some commentators to characterize the Anglo-American accomplishment as "catastrophic success." Generalized lawlessness made it difficult to restore normal services such as electricity, water, and hospitals. The Islamist Shi'ite clergy moved quickly into the power vacuum, attempting to cement their authority over southern Iraq. The Kurds in the Far North of the country were quiet, but Sunni resistance to the coalition's hegemony over Iraq continued and intensified in the following months, and American soldiers were still being killed on a daily basis. By December 2003, the United States had captured Saddam Hussein and other senior Ba'athist leaders, but the Sunnis in central Iraq continued a violent and sustained insurrection against the American presence, using roadside bombs, sniper attacks, kidnapping, and other forms of armed resistance to the American presence. The U.S. situation was further compromised by the devastating "Abu Ghraib" scandal involving the mistreatment of Iraqi prisoners.[54]

THE RE-CREATION OF THE IRAQI GOVERNMENT

From a political perspective, the postwar period can be divided into four separate phases: direct rule by the Coalition Provisional Authority, April 2003 to the end of May 2004; the Iraqi interim government of Prime Minister Ayad Allawi, from June 2004 to April 2005; the transitional government under Ibrahim al-Jaafari, who took office in May 2005 and stepped down in May of 2006; and the "permanent" government, which limped into existence in May 2006 under Nuri Kamal al-Maliki, survived a national election in 2010, and remains in power in 2012.

American-Appointed Iraqi Administrations

When the purely military phase of the invasion ended in May of 2003, control of the conquered country passed from the U.S. Defense Department to a "Coalition Provisional Authority" or CPA, ultimately led by American diplomat Paul Bremer. Anxious to involve the Iraqis in the running of their shattered country, the Anglo-American coalition created a twenty-five-member "Iraqi Governing Council" with limited power and legitimacy, but the Iraqi Governing Council—appointed in July 2003—did create at least the skeleton of a civil administration and moved a group of anti-Ba'athist politicians into the public eye.[55]

On May 28, 2004, Ambassador Bremer formally dissolved the CPA and returned theoretical "sovereignty" to the Iraqi people, appointing a ceremonial president and an executive prime minister and cabinet. Taking the helm of the first post-Saddam Iraqi government was a moderate secular Shi'ite politician named Ayad Allawi, a physician who had spent many years in exile, working with both British and American intelligence.

Resistance to the coalition armed forces intensified. While the Kurdish region in the North was generally quiet, Shi'ite resentment in the South and in Baghdad's Sadr City occasionally burst forth. In Sunni areas in the center and West of the country, however, resistance to American forces took the form of a frenzied campaign of kidnappings, televised executions, assassinations, suicide bombings, and improvised explosive devices. President Bush's reelection in November of 2004 signaled the American intention to prosecute the war militarily, and U.S. forces shot their way into rebel strongholds such as Fallujah and Ramadi.[56]

In the autumn of 2004, the Iraqi interim government created a provisional constitution that envisioned a ceremonial president and two vice presidents who would be elected by a unicameral National Assembly by at least a two-thirds vote. The president and his deputies would then negotiate with the National Assembly over the choice of a prime minister and cabinet.

On paper, the future Iraqi government looked like a classic parliamentary system, except that it was "unicameral" (without a Senate-style upper house or chamber). Second, elections to the National Assembly were managed on the proportional representation system, which rewards political groups able to get out the vote and punishes communities (such as the Iraqis Sunnis) who cannot or will not go to the polls to vote.

The Iraqi Transitional Government

With mounting civil violence, very few Sunnis participated in the January 30, 2005, election for a "transitional" parliament. A coalition of Shi'ite and Kurdish parties won control of the National Assembly, but Iraqi politicians, suspicious of one another and unused to democracy, found it difficult to make compromises. By April, the new Iraqi Assembly had elected a respected Kurdish leader named Jalal Talibani as the ceremonial president of the country, and had nominated a Shi'ite Islamist physician named Dr. Ibrahim al-Jaafari as executive prime minister. Al-Jaafari experienced difficulty in forming a cabinet and did not formally take office until May 3, 2005, only to be greeted by a furious rise in insurgent violence.

The First Permanent Iraqi Government

Dr. Al-Jaafari did not have an easy year as prime minister, and the insurgency raged on. On December 15 of 2005, Iraqis returned to the polls, and this time Shi'ites and Kurds were joined by significant numbers of Sunnis, who had discovered that not voting in a proportional representational system had left them without much representation. In this ballot, two Sunni-based parties significantly increased their share of the vote, but power remained inevitably with the Shi'ite parties, who chose a previously obscure Dawa politician named Dr. Nuri al-Maliki as prime minister in May of 2006. As of 2012, Al-Maliki continues to occupy this post, although he is disliked outside of his own Shi'ite community.

By 2006, however, Iraqis began to see the beginnings of a genocidal civil war between hard-liners in both the Shiite and Sunni communities, who were battling for control of Iraq's capital city. In the spring of 2007, American forces were struggling to control the

Baghdad city center and President Bush ordered a "surge" of perhaps thirty thousand additional troops to stabilize the situation.

The 2010 Parliamentary Elections and the Permanent Government

Although it had accomplished little, the first permanent government managed to survive the full four years of its mandate, and elections for a second "permanent" government were held in March of 2010. The United States also created the "Awakening" movement, a plan to fund and support the angry Sunni communities in the hope that they would focus their energies on fighting al-Qaeda in Iraq rather than the Baghdad government.

As they had done in 2005, Iraqis voted overwhelmingly for sectarian parties, that is, parties that represented them as secular or Islamist, Sunni or Shi'ite, Arab or Kurds. The problem for Iraqis is that no one actually "won" the 2010 election. Tough, Western-oriented Ayad Allawi emerged with the largest single number of seats, two more than al-Maliki's State of Law Coalition. With 22 percent of the seats in the parliament, the Islamist and pro-Iranian Iraqi National Alliance would be unlikely to support the secularists and Sunnis in the Iraqi National Movement, leaving no alternative to a pro-Iranian and anti-American coalition government with Nuri al-Maliki's State of Law Coalition. By summer 2011, however, the deal still remained to be struck. Claiming that he commanded the most votes in the parliament, Nuri al-Maliki clung to power as his critics complained that his government was using undemocratic tactics to retain the control.

Among American politicians, a controversy raged over the question of the future American military role in Iraq, but the al-Maliki government refused to sign an acceptable status-of-forces agreement with the Obama administration. The last U.S. combat troops left the country in December of 2011.

THE FUTURE FOR IRAQ

Great uncertainty hangs over Iraq. From a political point of view, the three communities making up the modern state of Iraq do not generally seem to have self-identified to any real extent as Iraqis and have contrasting expectations of the future. Furthermore, we need to avoid the temptation to assume that these three communities are monolithic in perspective.

The Sunni people are badly divided between secularists and Islamists; there are those who want to experiment with the political process, those who prefer to continue with the insurgency, and those who are covertly doing both. After several centuries of brutality toward their Shi'ite neighbors, they have every reason to fear that triumphant Shi'ites will continue to take revenge. It is hard to measure the strength and staying power of the Sunni insurgency, but a movement that produced volunteer suicide bombers at the rate of three or four a day for several years clearly has too much momentum to vanish quickly.[57]

Nor is the Shi'ite community internally cohesive. There are still important fissure lines between the two principal Shi'ite parties, each with their own independent militias. A minority of Shi'ites are quite secular, but a large number would wish to see a firmly Islamist state, although perhaps not an Iranian-style theocracy.

CHAPTER 9

The Kurdish population is another pivotal issue, since the Kurds have been fundamentally self-governing since the 1991 Gulf War and want virtual independence from
Baghdad as well as control over both the city of Kirkuk and the oil resources in the region.

The good news? Saddam Hussein, arguably one of the worst dictators in the world,
is gone, having been executed by the Iraqi government. But the bad news is pretty bad.
Prime Minister Nuri al-Maliki's administration has thus far failed to bring stability to
the country, assert its authority over militias and renegade elements within the police
and Iraqi Army, and provide essential services such as water and electricity. Iraq was still
producing less electrical power and less crude oil than it had under Saddam Hussein, and
the material quality of life had degenerated significantly.

The military phase of the 2003 Iraq War seemed to demonstrate that the American
military enjoyed unchallengeable technical superiority over almost any enemy, although it
seemed clear that the U.S. Defense Department was less interested in reconstruction or "na-
tion-building," and consequently less competent at the reshaping of conquered territories.
Furthermore, the intensity of the global anti-American protests before, during, and after
the war suggests that the United States enjoys limited international popularity. European
and Middle Eastern public opinion questions the altruism of American motives in military
operations and believes that the United States prefers unilateral projections of American
power to multilateral cooperation. It also seems clear that many of the problems inherent in
a multinational postcolonial Iraq have survived the fall of the Ba'athist dictatorship. While
no one doubts that the U.S.-led invasion of Iraq has changed the equation permanently and
profoundly, it was not clear if military victory could be translated into a sustained political
victory that would generate a peaceful, stable, democratic, and pro-Western Iraq.

7. The Wrap: What Have We Learned?

In the first section of this chapter, we looked at how conflicts can be, in a very general
way, divided into nationalist quarrels involving differences over ethnic identity, and
ideological fights, where people from the same national community disagree over public
policy. When we look beneath the surface, however, we find that real-life conflict can
sometimes be difficult to slot into these two classic categories. Some conflicts present
themselves superficially as either nationalist or ideological, but beneath the surface, they
can be really more concerned with access to resources such as land, water, and minerals.
Classifying religion can be particularly difficult: sometimes a religion defines a nationality; elsewhere, it can amount to an ideology; and sometimes it does both.

In chapter 7, we learned that successful societies have developed mechanisms for
brokering or defusing conflict. In this and the following chapters, we spend a lot of time
looking at violence, but this concentration should not blind us to the fact that most of
the time in most parts of the world, we manage to get through the day without maiming
anyone. Even in a successful society, however, tensions can lead to a technical breaking of
the law, something that is often called civil disobedience, and in section 2 of this chapter,
we looked at the whole concept of using peaceful means to change society, with special
attention to Desmond Tutu of South Africa and Tibet's Dalai Lama, two lives that suggest the merits of using peaceful means of dissent before locking and loading.

When the two sides of a violent conflict are asymmetrical in power, the weaker side will typically resort to terrorism or guerrilla warfare, while the stronger side will try to use conventional armed forces. With no universally accepted definition of the word, terrorism is to political science what the black hole is to astronomy—a puzzle and a problem. Many terrorist incidents strike us as irrational or anomic, and we sometimes have difficulty making the logical connection between actions and consequences.

The twentieth century sustained two major global conflicts and an unending series of smaller wars that have continued into the first decade of the twenty-first century. In section 4 of this chapter, we learned that war continues to evolve in tactics and weaponry, becoming less formal but more endemic, harming more civilians (particularly women and children) and fewer soldiers. We noted that Africa has endured a particularly tragic concentration of warfare, with complicated multidimensional conflicts ending millions of lives in places such as Sudan and the Congo. The most controversial war in recent years has been the attack by British and American troops against Saddam Hussein's Iraq, and we examined the complicated debate over the causes and justification for this war, a classic example of asymmetrical warfare, the final result of which is still in some doubt. Iraq is also a case study on how difficult it can sometimes be to assign a set of hard-and-fast reasons why a given war takes places. The Iraqi conflict also demonstrates how hard it is for the international community to restrain major military powers who are determined to fight.

Section 5 of this chapter examined those rare but serious cases when political violence becomes the leading cause of mortality in a society, and we looked at instances of societal mayhem in several countries. We focused in some detail on Sierra Leone, where much of the violence was anomic, in the sense that it did not seem to accomplish any perceivable goal. In section 6, we focused on the multilevel conflict that surrounded the Anglo-American decision to invade and occupy Iraq in 2003.

What can we make of this carnage? How to avoid violent conflict has been one of the central dilemmas since political scientists first began studying the human condition in fifth-century Athens. Clearly, when conflicts are deep and intractable, we need powerful civil society institutions and governmental structures to broker them or violence will occur. When sovereign states come into conflict, they can sometimes be dissuaded from fighting by international organizations such as the United Nations, or world opinion, but sometimes—as we learned in the Iraq War—war happens if national leaderships want it badly enough.

We also learned that nothing about the Iraq war was clear-cut. To some extent, it could be described as a resource war with Iraq's abundant oil as the prize. The conflict has been both international and domestic (interstate and intrastate). In many respects, it was also a religious war with Western Christians against Arab Muslims, and Iraqi Shi'ites against Iraqi Sunnis. No one can be totally sure why it happened at all, nor whether or not it will prove to have been successful at any level.

In the next two chapters, we will look at a series of case studies to apply what we learned in this chapter. In chapter 10, we'll survey violence occasioned by Marxist movements. Then we'll listen to the thunder from the right, and study right-wing and neo-fascist groups before settling down to look at the sort of religious fury that animates contemporary Islamist movements such as al-Qaeda.

Notes

1. Interest in ethnic conflict was generated by Daniel P. Moynihan's *Pandaemonium: Ethnicity in International Politics* (New York: Oxford University Press, 1993). America's senior specialist in this field is Ted Robert Gurr whose *People versus States: Minorities at Risk in the New Century* (Washington, D.C.: Institute of Peace, 2000) draws upon a lifetime of study.

2. Jessica Stern's secular viewpoint caused a controversy when her *Terror in the Name of God: Why Religious Militants Kill* (New York: Ecco, 2003) first emerged, but the book still reads well. A similar book with a similar name is Mark Juergensmeyer, *Terror in the Mind of God: The Global Rise of Religious Violence*, 3rd ed. (Berkeley, Calif.: University of California Press, 2003).

3. For the background, see John N. Paden, *Faith and Politics in Nigeria* (Washington, D.C.: U.S. Institute of Peace, 2008).

4. Hamas is complicated. Azzam Tamimi, *Hamas: A History from Within* (London: Oliver Branch Press, 2011) is a scholarly but essentially sympathetic look at Gaza's political leadership. Beverley Milton-Edwards and Stephen Farrell have written the best scholarly treatment in their *Hamas: The Islamic Resistance Movement* (London: Polity, 2010). And finally, Matthew Levitt has given us a firmly negative assessment in his *Hamas: Politics, Charity, and Terrorism in the Service of Jihad* (New Haven: Yale University Press, 2006). Take your pick.

5. The resource-conflict concept is explored in the writings of Michael T. Klare, whose *Resource Wars: The New Landscape of Global Conflict* (New York: Holt, 2001) is fundamental. Klare's book *Rising Powers, Shrinking Planet: The New Geopolitics of Energy* (New York: Metropolitan, 2008) pursues the same themes with a greater focus on the conflict over energy resources, such as oil.

6. In the English-language press, Britain's *Guardian* has done the best reporting. See Jonathan Franklin, "Chile's Commander Camila, the Student Who Can Shut Down a City," *The Guardian,* August 24, 2011, available at www.guardian.co.uk/world/2011/aug/24/chile-student-leader-camila-vallejo.

7. As explained by Rice University Professor Douglas Brinkley in *Rosa Parks: A Life* (New York: Penguin, 2005), the 1955 bus-segregation case was only one moment in a life dedicated to civil disobedience.

8. Mahatma Gandhi, *Non-violent Resistance: Satyagrah* (New York: Schocken, 1972) is a compilation of Gandhi's specific thoughts on what Hindus call *Satyagraha* and Westerners call civil disobedience. Martin Luther King wrote specifically about nonviolence as a strategy in a little-remembered 1967 book entitled *Where Do We Go from Here? Chaos or Community?* (New York: HarperCollins, 1967).

9. Archbishop Desmond Tutu starts the story in his *The Rainbow People of God* (New York: Doubleday, 1994) and completes it in greater detail in his *No Future Without Forgiveness* (New York: Doubleday, 1999). Dorothy Shea has given us a useful study of Tutu's work in her *The South African Truth Commission: The Politics of Reconciliation* (Washington, D.C.: U.S. Institute of Peace, 2000).

10. See the Dalai Lama's *My Land and People* (New York: Warner, 1997).

11. In his *Tibet: A History* (New Haven, Conn.: Yale University Press, 2011), British scholar Sam van Schaik tells the story of this embattled people.

12. Donald L. Horowitz's *The Deadly Ethnic Riot* (Berkeley, Calif.: University of California Press, 2003) is a fascinating study of 150 civil-disturbance riots in fifty different countries. Written mostly from a police point of view, Loren Christensen gives us an insider's look at the modern urban riot in *Riot: A Behind-the-Barricades Tour of Mobs, Riot Cops, and the Chaos of Crowd Violence.* (New York: Paladin, 2008).

13. Some older writing by Walter Laqueur has set the framework for debate in this area. See his *A History of Terrorism* (Piscataway, N.J.: Transaction, 2001) and his *Guerrilla Warfare: A Historical and Critical Study* (Piscataway, N.J.: Transaction, 1988).

14. For a quick update on anything the U.S. State Department thinks might be terrorism, go look at their www.state.gov/www/global/terrorism/. For the British government's perspective, see the Home Office Links Page at www.homeoffice.gov.uk/atoz/terrorists.htm. Israel's International Policy Institute for Counter-Terrorism at http://www.ict.org.il obviously reflects national attitudes but provides accurate data for the world beyond Israel's borders.

15. For the whole story, see Richard Oliver Collin and Gordon L Freedman, *Winter of Fire: The Abduction of General Dozier and the Downfall of the Red Brigades* (New York: Dutton/Penguin, 1990).

16. Richard Oliver Collin, "When Reality Came Unglued: Antonio Savasta and the Red Brigades," originally published in *Violence Aggression Terrorism* 3 no. 4 (1989): 269–96, Reprinted in Bernard Schechterman and Martin Slann, *Annual Editions: Violence and Terrorism 91/92* (Washington, D.C.: Dushkin, 1991).

17. The U.S. Department of State issues an annual *Patterns of Global Terrorism*, which contains a lot of raw data and a great deal of political spin. Graham Allison scares us a little with his *Nuclear Terrorism: The Ultimate Preventable Catastrophe* (New York: Time Books, 2004). The dean of America's "terrorism experts" is the Rand Corporation's Bruce Hoffman, whose *Inside Terrorism*, revised ed. (New York: Columbia University Press, 2006) represents conventional wisdom on the subject.

18. The National Commission on Terrorist Attacks' *The 9/11 Commission Report: Final Report of the National Commission on Terrorist Attacks upon the United States* (New York: Norton, 2004) is unlikely to be "final," despite the name, but it provides a wealth of information.

19. For a hard look at a phenomenon that's hard to look at, see Robert Pope's *Dying to Win: The Strategic Logic of Suicide Terrorism* (New York: Random House, 2005).

20. Written for a popular audience by Mark Kurlansky, *The Basque History of the World* (New York and London: Penguin, 2001), provides an easy-to-read look at the Basque people.

21. A classic early study of the Baader-Meinhof/Red Army Faction was done by Julian Becker in his famous *Hitler's Children: The Story of the Baader-Meinhof Terrorist Gang* (London: Michael Joseph, 1977). Stefan Aust knew many of Germany's top terrorists personally and he has given us a nuanced study in his *Baader-Meinhof: The Inside Story of the R.A.F* (Oxford, UK: Oxford University Press, 2009).

22. Richard Oliver Collin, "Breaking the Police: Mussolini's Use of Terrorism," *Violence Aggression Terrorism* 1, no. 1 (1987): 1–13.

23. Richard Oliver Collin, *La Donna Che Sparò a Mussolini* (Milan: Rusconi, 1988).

24. Here are two books to give you a divergent point of view. Start with Ernesto "Che" Guevara's book on the subject: *Guerrilla Warfare* (Lincoln, Nebr.: University of Nebraska Press, 1983). Then move on to David Petraeus, *US Army/Marine Corps Counterinsurgency Field Manual* (Chicago: University of Chicago Press, 2007). The *Field Manual* was based on the thinking and experience of General David Petraeus, now head of the CIA. If "Che" was good at starting guerrilla wars, General Petraeus is believed to be an expert in bringing them to a (sometimes messy) conclusion.

25. NATO's principal site at http://www.nato.int keeps tabs on Europe's problem children. The War, Peace, and Security Guide at http://www.cfcsc.dnd.ca/links/index.html is maintained by the Resource Center of the Canadian Armed Forces College, an unrivaled site for accuracy and completeness. Known mostly by the initials SIPRI, the Stockholm International Peace Research Institute keeps track of global weapons sales at http://sipri.se. The U.S. State Department stays abreast of disarmament efforts past and present at www.state.gov/www/globul/arms/index/html. You should also glance at the Arms Control Association's site at www.armscontrol.org.

26. See WHO (World Health Organization), *World Report on Violence and Health* (Geneva: WHO, 2002), 10.

27. See Simon Chesterman, ed., *Civilians in War* (Boulder, Colo.: Lynn Rienner, 2001), which examines the vulnerability of women and children in modern conflict.

28. Not much has as yet been published about South Sudan, but the first book out is *South Sudan: Challenges and Opportunities for Africa's New Nation* (New York: Nova, 2012), edited by Paul Hartley and Ronald Bland.

29. A lot has been written about the Darfur conflict. A scholarly journalist named Richard Cockett has given us a good overview in his *Sudan: Darfur and the Failure of an African State* (New Haven: Yale University Press). Another good introduction has been written by two authors who have spent a lot of time on the dangerous ground in the Sudan: Julie Flint and Alex de Waal, *Darfur: A Short History of a Long War* (London, Zed, 2008). Andrew S. Natsios, the former head of the U.S. Agency for International Development, has written an excellent study of the whole Sudanese situation in his *Sudan, South Sudan, and Darfur: What Everyone Needs to Know* (New York: Oxford University Press, 2012).

30. A courageous young author named Jason Stearns has made himself an expert on the Democratic Republic of Congo. His new book, *Dancing in the Glory of Monsters: The Collapse of the Congo and the Great War of Africa* (New York: Public Affairs, 2011), is probably the first stop on understanding this appalling situation.

A well-known Africa-watcher named Gerard Prunier has written a superb book called *Africa's World War: Congo, the Rwandan Genocide, and the Making of a Continental Catastrophe* (New York: Oxford University Press, 2011).

31. Michael Renner, "Ending Violent Conflict," Worldwatch Paper No. 146 (Washington, D.C.: World-watch Institute, 1999) 13.

32. *Guardian*, "Marie Colvin," February 23, 2012, 18. See also international legal expert Simon Chesterman, ed., *Civilians in War* (Boulder, Colo.: Lynn Rienner, 2001).

33. See Kenneth R. Rutherford, *Disarming States: The International Movement to Ban Landmines* (New York: Praeger, 2010).

34. Amber Peterman, Dara Kay Cohen, and Tia Palermo, "Rape Reporting during War," *Foreign Affairs*, August 1, 2011, www.foreignaffairs.com/articles/68008/amber-peterman-dara-kay-cohen-tia-palermo-and -amelia-hoover-gree/rape-reporting-during-war (accessed January 20, 2012). For violence against women during armed conflict, see Amnesty International's powerful 2004 report "Lives Blown Apart: Crimes against Women in Times of Conflict" at http://web.amnesty.org/library/Index/ENGACT770752004.

35. B. H. Liddell Hart, *History of the Second World War* (London: Pan, 1970), 276.

36. For a clear overview, see Michael T. Brown et al., *Going Nuclear: Nuclear Proliferation and International Security in the 21ˢᵗ Century* (Cambridge, Mass.: MIT Press, 2010).

37. John Deutsch, "A Nuclear Posture for Today," *Foreign Affairs* 84, no. 1 (2005): 49–60.

38. David E. Sanger and Peter Baker, "Obama Limits When U.S. Would Use Nuclear Arms," *New York Times*, April 5, 2010, A1.

39. The very best introduction to the horrific business of modern genocide is Samantha Power's Pulitzer Prize–winning *A Problem from Hell: America and the Age of Genocide* (New York: Basic, 2002). Born in Ireland but educated in the United States, Samantha Power divides her time between Harvard, where she lectures, and the White House, where she is director of multilateral affairs for the National Security Council.

40. This incident was the inspiration for director Ridley Scott's motion picture *Black Hawk Down*, released in 2002.

41. Somalia's tragic story is well told in John Drysdale's *Whatever Happened to Somalia? A Tale of Tragic Blunders* (London: Haan, 2002). Diplomats John L. Hirsch and Robert B. Oakley have given us *Somalia and Operation Restore Hope* (Washington, D.C.: U.S. Institute of Peace Press, 1995).

42. Gerard Yoal and Carl T. Dahlman have produced *Bosnia Remade: Ethnic Cleansing and Its Reversal* (New York: Oxford University Press, 2011). In *Rape Warfare: The Hidden Genocide in Bosnia-Herzegovina and Croatia* (Minneapolis, Minn.: University of Minnesota Press, 1996), Beverly Allen studies the systematic use of sexual violence as a mechanism for ethnic cleansing. The late Richard Holbrooke negotiated an end to the war in 1995, and his *To End a War* (New York: Random House, 1998) is a good summary of the effort to halt societal mayhem.

43. Mahmood Mamdani has done a thorough study of the Rwandan genocide in his *When Victims Become Killers* (Princeton, N.J.: Princeton University Press, 2000). Phillip Gourevitch's famous *We Wish to Inform You That Tomorrow We Will Be Killed with Our Families* (New York: Farrar, Straus, and Giroux, 1998) is journalism at its best.

44. United Nations Development Programme, *Human Development Report 1991* (New York: United Nations, 1991), 121.

45. Ambassador John L. Hirsch described the situation well in his *Sierra Leone: Diamonds and the Struggle for Democracy* (Boulder, Colo.: Lynn Reiner, 2000).

46. Larry J. Woods, *Military Interventions in Sierra Leone: Lessons from a Failed State* (Fort Leavenworth, Kans.: Combat Studies Institute, 2011). Anybody interested in following Sierra Leone's recovery from societal mayhem should click on www.sierra-leone.org, maintained by the Freetown government, but lively and reliable. The Campaign for Good Governance tracks Sierra Leone's restored democracy at www.slcgg.org/home.htm.

47. United Nations Development Programme, *Human Development Report* (New York: United Nations, 2010), 129.

48. For a study of this phenomenon, see Myriam Denov's *Child Soldiers: Sierra Leone's Revolutionary United Front* (Cambridge, UK: Cambridge University Press, 2010). A former young fighter named Ishmael Beah has written movingly of his experiences in *A Long Way Gone: Memories of a Boy Soldier* (New York: Farrar, Straus and Giroux, 2007).

49. For the best overview of Iraqi history, see William R. Polk, *Understanding Iraq* (London: Tauris, 2005). For the language situation, see Richard Oliver Collin, "Words of War: The Iraqi Tower of Babel," *International Studies Perspectives* 10, no. 3 (2009): 245–64.

50. The literature on Iraq is enormous. For the pre-2003 period, Samir al-Khalil, *Republic of Fear* (Berkeley: University of California Press, 1989) is still a standard. Marion Farouk-Sluglett and Peter Sluglett have generated a comprehensive study in *Iraq since 1958: From Revolution to Dictatorship* (London: Tauris, 2001). For the history, see Charles Tripp's *A History of Iraq* (New York: Cambridge University Press, 2000). Phoebe Marr has updated her classic *The Modern History of Iraq* with a 3rd edition that takes the reader well beyond the 2003 invasion (Boulder, Colo.: Westview, 2011).

51. This is very well-known history. For more depth, note that Phoebe Marr has updated her classic *The Modern History of Iraq* with a 3rd edition that takes the reader well beyond the 2003 invasion.

52. *Washington Post* correspondent Thomas E. Ricks has written two important books on the war: *Fiasco*, 6th ed. (New York, Penguin, 2006); the sequel focuses on U.S. attempts to stabilize Iraq after the successful conquest of the country and is called *The Gamble: General David Petraeus and the American Military Adventure in Iraq, 2006–2008* (New York: Penguin, 2009). Both books adopt a critical approach to U.S. policy.

53. Britain's celebrated military historian John Keegan has a pronounced political bias, but no one explains the military aspects of a war as well; see *The Iraqi War: The 21-Day Conflict and Its Aftermath* (London: Pamlico, 2005). James Fallows has written an impressive critique of the war in his *Blind into Baghdad: America's War in Iraq* (New York: Vintage, 2006).

54. A variety of books have been written about the Abu Ghraib affair. Mark Danner's *Torture and Truth: America, Abu Ghraib, and the War on Terror* (New York: New York Review of Books, 2004) is massive and thorough.

55. See L. Paul Bremer's *My Year in Iraq: The Struggle to Build a Future of Hope* (New York: Simon & Schuster, 2006).

56. Ali A. Allawi, *The Occupation of Iraq: Winning the War: Losing the Peace* (New Haven, Conn.: Yale University Press, 2008). An Arab-American scholar named Ahmed Hashim has produced a well-received study of the anti-American opposition in his *Insurgency and Counter-Insurgency in Iraq* (Ithaca: Cornell University Press, 2006). A liberal journalist who supported the war, George Packer, has given us *Assassin's Gate: American in Iraq* (New York: Farrar, Straus & Giroux, 2005). Arabic-speaking Anthony Shadid won the Pulitzer Prize for his *Night Draws Near: Iraq's People in the Shadows of America's War* (New York: Holt, 2005).

57. The gruesome topic of Iraqi "martyrdom missions" is explored by Mohammed M. Hafez in *Suicide Bombers in Iraq* (Washington, D.C.: Institute of Peace, 2007).

CHAPTER 10

The War of the Mind
VIOLENT IDEOLOGICAL CONFLICT

In chapter 9, we looked at the varieties and levels of political violence. This necessarily brief analysis may have left us with the impression that some of the deadly conflicts troubling the planet are being fought over essentially trivial arguments, perhaps by morally and psychiatrically impaired people.

Historically, Americans have overwhelmingly agreed on a large number of core issues. While various groups disagree over religious ideas, the United States does not have large and mutually antagonistic religious communities who self-identify with their faith rather their nationality; there is no immediate danger of Southern Baptists going to war with Lutherans, although—in the 2012 presidential election campaign—Mitt Romney's Mormon faith was an issue for many Protestant evangelicals. From a global perspective, American political disagreements are relatively minimal compared to the issues that can divide some badly fragmented foreign societies.

This can make it difficult for Americans to comprehend why people in the outside world are prepared to die for a Marxist cause or commit murder/suicide to advance their version of Islam. While some episodes of violence are anomic, or at least hard to understand, most forms of violent conflict have an explanation that is reasonable at some level, although the rationale may not filter through on the six-thirty news. Young people do not typically decide on a whim some sunny day to get themselves killed by trying to overthrow their government. A movement involving thousands of like-minded revolutionaries cannot be dismissed with the careless assertion that the combatants are collectively insane.

As we learned in chapter 9, people usually resort to violence for two very general sets of reasons: either they don't like the way society is run (ideological conflict), or they resent the fact that it is being run by people they regard as foreign (nationalist conflict). While the real-life distinction is often blurred, we'll try in this chapter to look at several varieties of ideological conflict, reserving more clearly nationalist violence for chapter 11. Here are some of the questions we'll try to answer.

- *Why won't Marx go away? In an era intellectually dominated by free-market thinking, why are there still communist armies in the field?* A fair amount of the world's recent and current ideological conflicts originates on that "left-to-right" continuum described in chapter 6. Conflict can emerge in a capitalist or even social democratic society when a group of determined Marxists decides to reverse the verdict of history and fight for a communist ideal. If a revolution is successful, a Marxist government surrounded by non-Marxist governments can be a source of international conflict, as we'll see when we examine the case of Fidel Castro's Cuba (now being run by his brother, Raúl Castro) and the five decades of animosity between Havana and Washington.

- *If the West won World War II, why is the extreme right still festering in Europe and even in North America?* Not all of the enemies of the open society are on the far left. While right-wing, neo-fascist, or supernationalist movements are less coherent and harder to categorize, there has always been a variety of hard-right movements in the United States, Europe, and elsewhere, and some of these groups have gathered steam in recent years. Mussolini and Hitler are now long in their respective graves, but intolerant neo-fascism lives on, as we will see below.

- *What did Osama bin Laden really want? Why does the West feel so dramatically threatened by Islamic fundamentalism?* While fundamentalism appears in virtually every religious tradition, we will focus in section 3 primarily on Islamism, or violent Islamic fundamentalism, since the new century began with a spectacular display of Islamist fervor in the September 11, 2001, al-Qaeda attacks on the United States. In this context, we'll look at the rise and fall of the Islamist regime in Afghanistan, and the career of the late Osama bin Laden and his al-Qaeda organization.

1. Lenin's Children: Revolutionary Marxist Movements

In chapter 6, we glanced briefly at the theories put forward by Karl Marx, discovering his belief that history operated like a machine, progressing through certain stages in a specific order with communism as the inevitable result of this process. Most of his conventional nineteenth-century followers expected to see revolutions happening only after societies had reached an advanced stage of capitalism and industrialization.

By the early twentieth century, Marxists such as Russia's Vladimir Lenin were prepared to hustle history, making the revolution happen more quickly than Marx had envisioned. In this section, let us look at the evolving Marxist-Leninist legacy, and see how it has played out in a variety of terrorist movements—in the South American state of Colombia and in the rebellious island of Cuba.

THE MARXIST-LENINIST LEGACY

As the leader of what would eventually become the Soviet Communist Party, Russian leader Vladimir Lenin believed that a small, tightly organized, highly disciplined band of revolutionaries could make a revolution occur wherever and whenever a decadent regime was sufficiently weak and vulnerable. At least in Russia, he proved himself correct by taking power in November of 1917 in a coup d'état that served as model for twentieth-century dissidents who were often called **Leninists**. Lenin's 1918 book *State and Revolution* was still an inspiration to wanna-be revolutionaries for many decades after his death in 1924;[1] Italian terrorists were still reverently quoting it in the 1980s.[2]

While there were conspiratorial communist parties in most countries around the world by 1921, a genuine Marxist society existed only in the Soviet Union until after World War II. In the aftermath of this war, China became "Red China" as the result of a successful guerrilla insurgency led by Mao while indigenous Marxist movements took control in Yugoslavia and Albania. Otherwise, Marxist leaders achieved power with a little help from their friends in the Soviet Army; Eastern European countries such as Poland, the former Czechoslovakia, Bulgaria, Romania, and the former East Germany were very reluctant converts to the cause.[3]

By the 1950s, however, Marxism's momentum had stalled, and the United States had created a series of defensive alliances such as NATO to contain communist ideas behind what Churchill called the "Iron Curtain." In the West, some Marxist parties took the legal road, constituting themselves as law-abiding political parties and trying (albeit without much success) to win power through the electoral process. Many European countries (such as Italy and France) had significant communist parties in the postwar era, although most of them were really social democrats who imitated Italy's leftists by dropping the word "communist" from their party titles when the Soviet Union disappeared.[4]

Revolutionaries on the Left

Where Marxists would not or could not evolve into legal political parties, they sometimes translated themselves into guerrilla movements; the Vietnamese Communist Party was one of the few successful examples. Where they lacked the strength to mount a guerrilla campaign, communists sometimes became terrorists, although they preferred euphemisms such as "urban guerrillas."

In the years following World War II, these insurrectionary groups flourished over a wide range, from very poor countries run by economic oligarchies to advanced and prosperous democracies where voters had clearly rejected communism. Other than their common desire to change society radically, they varied widely in inspiration. A few saw the Soviet Union as a direct and obvious model and may have enjoyed covert Soviet sponsorship. Others are called "**Maoist**" because they emulate Chairman Mao's tactics in China, basing themselves on the rural peasantry and attacking urban centers. And a few, such as Nicaragua's communists, joined broadly based opposition movements such as the Sandinistas, fighting alongside liberals and social democrats.[5]

During much of the postwar period, many Latin American societies were right-wing elite dictatorships (or what we have described as economic oligarchies) in which a handful of wealthy landowners oppressed huge peasant populations, providing fertile soil for Leninist revolutionary movements. Reviewed below, the Cuban movement was one of the few to rebel successfully. Uruguay's Tupamaros seemed poised for a time to achieve victory with Robin Hood tactics and popular appeal, but instead provoked the right-wing military into establishing a despotic military regime. Argentina's rebels suffered a similar fate when the army took power in 1976 and launched what was called the "Dirty War" in which tens of thousands of leftists were killed. Peru is the unhappy host to two declining groups, the Tupac Amaru Revolutionary Movement (MRTA), which seized the Japanese embassy in 1997, and a Maoist-oriented Shining Path movement. In Nicaragua and El Salvador, Marxists joined forces with other left-of-center groups to fight guerrilla wars; today, Nicaragua's Sandinistas and El Salvador's Farabundo are both legal political parties. Colombia's revolutionary groups, however, are even larger and have been distinctly more threatening, and we'll glance at them below.[6]

During the 1960s and 1970s, Europe and the United States went through a period when the notion of urban guerrilla warfare became attractive to many young people. In the United States, the Vietnam War and the persistence of poverty and racial inequality produced a variety of groups that toyed with revolutionary themes; the Weather Underground was perhaps the most famous. Italy endured a trying decade (called the "Years of Lead") because of the efforts of the Italian Red Brigades to transform Italy's somewhat corrupt capitalism into a Marxist-Leninist state.[7] We have already encountered the German Red Army Faction (also known as the Baader-Meinhof Gang) that joined forces with the Marxist Popular Front for the Liberation of Palestine to carry out a series of spectacular operations in the 1970s.

Map 10.1. Insurgency and Instability in Northwestern South America
After experimenting with a military coup, Venezuelan president Hugo Chavez was democratically elected in 1998, surviving a coup d'etat against his government while becoming the most vocal anti-American leader in South America. Colombia has a history of persistent ideological conflict, a firmly rooted narcotics industry, right-wing death squads, and the world's largest Marxist guerrilla armies. Ecuador had experienced epic instability until the 2006 election of President Rafael Correa, defaulting on its international debt while extralegally deposing several of its presidents. With most of its basic economic problems unsolved, Peru continues to be politically restless, although the Shining Path movement has been less active since the capture of its charismatic leader, Abimael Guzmán. And Bolivia went through general strikes, massive public unrest, and a series of unstable governments until the radical Evo Morales was elected to the presidency in January of 2006. Reelected in 2009, he is now well into his second term.

COLOMBIA'S COMMUNISTS

The area that is now Colombia was conquered by Spain in the early 1500s, but won its independence in the early years of the 1800s. There are countries that seem condemned by nature and history to be poor, but Colombia isn't one of them. There are large reserves of crude oil (most of it now flowing to the United States) and other important minerals, vast virgin forestlands, and an important agricultural sector. With a per capita GNI of over $8,000, Colombia is categorized by the UN as a high human development country, with the basic resources to become economically comfortable, if not wealthy. And it has a big population; only Mexico has more Spanish-speakers.[8]

Like most developing societies, Colombia suffers from both poverty and a dramatically unequal distribution of existing economic resources. Almost 23 percent of the population lives on less than $2 a day, and there is a cavernous gap between rich and poor. There'll be more on the issue of economic inequality in chapter 12, but, for now, we can roughly estimate how equal or unequal a society is economically by calculating the ratio between the wealth of the poorest 10 percent of the population and the wealthiest 10 percent. Colombia's wealthiest 10 percent of the population controls about 60 percent

Figure 10.1. Social Protest in American Cities
While groups like this Los Angeles community association are neither Marxist nor
revolutionary, they share the same basic dissatisfaction with poverty and social
marginalization. In the United States and Canada, these sentiments tend to funnel
themselves into street protests. In Europe, these same notions are upheld by social
democratic or sometimes communist parties. In Latin America, popular protest of
this sort has often been met with savage government repression, evolving into Marxist guerrilla movements. In 2011, the "Occupy New York" movement spread around
the world, giving voice to protests against what some regard as a predatory form
of capitalism.

of the wealth in the country; its poorest 10 percent have only 0.8 percent of national wealth.[9] This ratio is awful, even for Latin America. The correlation between economic inequality and violence can be complicated and controversial, but there tends to be criminal or political violence in any society that permits this sort of extreme division between wealth and poverty.

Impoverished farmers will grow what they can sell, and few crops rival narcotics for profitability. Colombia had always been a significant source of marijuana, but by the end of the 1970s, this corner of South America began to produce significant quantities of the coca plant, from which cocaine is manufactured, and the poppy, which gives us morphine and heroin. By the 1990s, Colombia began to dominate the drug trade, producing—according to some estimates—about half of all the cocaine in the world.[10] Much of the drug production and trafficking is located in the South and West of the country, with important centers of criminality at Medellín (northwest of Bogotá) and Cali (southwest of the capital).[11]

While a large but hard-to-compute amount of drug money flows into Colombia, not much of this uncountable cash filters into the general economy, and it doesn't do much to alleviate the country's poverty. The money does buy arms and pay salaries for the guerrilla armies that protect the flow of narcotics. As we will see below, some of these are right-wing vigilante groups, and others are Leninist revolutionaries. What they have in common is a willingness to use violence and accept drug money in exchange for protecting the narcotics trade.

The Rebellion of the Colombian Left

Throughout much of its history, Colombia was tormented by intense rivalry between liberals and conservatives, a hatred that exploded six times into civil war. Called *La Violencia*, the worst episode raged between 1946 and 1965 and killed close to a quarter million Colombians. This intense phase of left-right hostility only slackened when liberals and conservatives agreed to share power with one another and exclude other potential rivals.[12]

But the Violencia never really went away. Two Leninist guerrilla groups emerged during the turbulent sixties and took advantage of Colombia's weak central government to seize control of about 40 percent of Colombia's national territory. The smaller is the National Liberation Army (*Ejército de liberación nacional* or ELN). Numbering about five thousand active service troops, the ELN is concentrated in the northern portion of Columbia where it often does battle with right-wing paramilitaries.

With eighteen thousand active-duty troops, the *Fuerzas Armadas Revolucionarias de Colombia* (or FARC) is the largest and oldest revolutionary group in Latin America, fighting continuously since 1966. The FARC is broadly left wing in ideology, although it is focused on very practical issues: controlling territory, raising funds, and ultimately overthrowing the government of Colombia. If nothing else, FARC was most brilliant at making money. After raising the kidnapping business to the level of an art form, FARC's dedicated soldiers have used their military strength to protect the narcotics industry in the South and West of Colombia, and to levy taxes on landowners and businesspeople still operating in their territory. Specialists have estimated their annual take at about $1 billion. With a robust bank account, the FARC can afford to pay their troops well; the average guerrilla earns three times as much as a Colombian soldier.[13]

Increasingly horrified and threatened by guerrilla armies that taxed them, kidnapped them, and threatened their dominion over society, Colombia's wealthy landowners quietly financed a loosely knit **paramilitary** organization to fight the Marxist-Leninist guerrillas. The umbrella organization coordinating the paramilitaries was called the *Autodefensas Unidas de Colombia* (AUC or Self-Defense Units of Colombia). The AUC was a mixed bag: some were essentially security guards; others were motivated by genuine ideological hatred of the Marxist left. The AUC grew to about twelve thousand full-time armed troops and seemed to have been responsible for flagrant human rights violations. Some observers have alleged that the paramilitaries once enjoyed the quiet protection of the Colombian Army; it is clear that they terrorized the peasantry, fought against the guerrillas, and extorted protection money from drug traffickers in the areas under their control. At its worst, the fighting has killed three hundred thousand Colombians, well above that arbitrary lethal threshold of a thousand deaths per year needed to qualify violence as high-intensity conflict. Indeed, there were even elements of societal mayhem here, since the violence was multilateral (paramilitaries, rogue army units, Marxist revolutionaries, and a very high level of homicidal criminality). Much of the violence was also anomic in the sense that it sometimes seemed to have no clear purpose. In 2002, the World Health Organization concluded that Colombia led the world in numbers of murders, but Colombia has become significantly safer over the course of the past decade.

The Bogotá Response

The most remarkable thing about Colombia is that it is still a free-market economy and a democracy. In terms of governmental structure, the country is a presidential system, with its chief executive elected to a maximum of two four-year terms and with a separate vote for a bicameral legislature. Constitutional reforms of 1991 provided for a constitutional court to safeguard civil institutions. While we have traditionally associated Colombia with violence, it has also always boasted a well-educated urban population, a deep attachment for democratic institutions, and a lively cultural life.

Many Colombians were convinced that their weak central government and its underfunded army would never achieve the strength to dominate its enemies on the left and the right. In the May of 2002 elections, Colombians overwhelmingly elected

Figure 10.2.   Ingrid Betancourt
Former Colombian presidential candidate and anticorruption activist, Ingrid Betancourt was held in captivity by the FARC for six and a half years. Upon her release in 2008, she published a memoir entitled *Even Silence Has an End: My Six Years of Captivity in a Colombian Jungle* (New York: Penguin Press, 2010). Photo courtesy of Fabio Gismondi.

a youthful independent candidate named Alvaro Uribe. Abandoning negotiation, President Uribe promised to defeat the insurgents militarily, seeking to strengthen the Colombian Army, tame the power of the paramilitaries, and bring the country under central governmental control by force.

As he came to the end of his second and final term of office in 2010, Uribe had changed his country dramatically. The two major terrorist groups have been badly hurt by governmental attacks and have shrunk dramatically in numbers and influence. Bogotá has evolved from being one of the most dangerous cities on the planet into being a tourist destination. While a long way from total victory, Uribe was rewarded with a second four-year term in 2006 and was followed in 2010 by a tough-minded political disciple, Juan Manuel Santos. Life for most Colombians got dramatically better in the first decade of the twenty-first century, as the security situation improved.

Although reduced in numbers, these Marxist-Leninist guerrillas remain defiantly in the field, however, and significant portions of Colombia are under their sole control. In many ways, the persistence of FARC and ELN into the twenty-first century is a political oddity, since Marxism is in retreat everywhere else on the planet. Most observers puzzle over the hybrid nature of both ELN and FARC. At a theoretical level, both are conventional revolutionary armies, but at a practical, day-to-day basis, they behave like criminal gangs, organizing kidnappings for ransom, bank robberies, and collection tribute from narcotics traffickers. The leaders of FARC and ELN have spent most of their lives as revolutionaries, operating in remote portions of Latin America. While they are smart people, they suffer from cognitive isolation, knowing little about modern urban Colombia or the greater world beyond Colombia's borders. Their goal is to replace Colombia's free-market politics with Marxism, despite the inevitability that this government would be dominated by drug traffickers. In a world that has turned decisively away from Marxism and disapproves of drugs, this sort of government would be met by fierce global hostility.

Tough Choices: Should the United States Stay Involved?

Congratulations on your appointment as undersecretary of state for Latin American affairs! In formulating U.S. policy toward this troubled Andean nation, the State Department needs to answer one complicated question: to what extent should the United States continue to send men and money to support the Colombian government of President Santos? Over the past fifteen years, the American government has contributed about $5 billion to Colombia to help fight drug traffickers, a decision that made Colombia the third-most-significant recipient of U.S. foreign aid after Israel and Egypt. Critics of what is called Plan Colombia worried that the money would either be wasted or find its way into the pockets of right-wing paramilitaries. Others were concerned that this was a billion-dollar escalation in U.S. involvement in Colombia's intractable civil war, which some saw as a Latin American version of Vietnam. Advocates of increased aid to Colombia point to the endless supply of hard drugs filtering through Colombia and the dangers of Marxist instability in a key Western Hemisphere democracy. Former president Bush argued that the United States needed to offer Colombia broad support, training its soldiers, sharing U.S. satellite intelligence, and helping to finance a unified war against drug dealers as well as ideological enemies. President Barack Obama seems indisposed to change this policy.

It will be easy to make a coherent argument for using American money and military expertise to help the Colombians. The FARC is still the most formidable Marxist revolutionary movement anywhere in the world. Doesn't it make sense to eliminate them before they spread the contagion to other Latin American countries? Does the Western Hemisphere need another Cuba? Furthermore, illegal narcotics are corrosive ingredients in American society, and Colombia produces 80 percent of all the cocaine used in North America and Europe, as well as huge quantities of heroin.

Before you write your report, however, here are a few troubling counterarguments. U.S. money might be welcome in Latin America, but the left already perceives American advisors in Colombia as gringo imperialists.[14] The gradual deployment of American military advisors to Colombia has been low key and mostly secret, but American personnel are already involved in providing technical training to units of the Colombian Army. If they are attacked or taken prisoner, there will be strong pressure on the U.S. government to send more troops. If and when that happens, everyone will remember that the Vietnamese experience began when the Kennedy administration sent advisors to train the South Vietnamese Army, leading to a ten-year war and ultimate humiliation for the United States.

Furthermore, the argument about Colombia blends into an ongoing domestic dispute in the United States about drug abuse. Almost all U.S. presidents have echoed calls for a "War on Drugs" that focuses on **interdiction**, that is, keeping narcotics from reaching the domestic American market. Since the beginning of the Nixon administration in 1969, the U.S. government has made heavy commitments in manpower and materiel to keep hard drugs out of the United States, although success has been difficult to measure.

Critics of this policy suggest that money spent on interdiction should be redirected toward what is often called "demand reduction." Theoretically, the market for drugs could be cut through decriminalization of drug use, rehabilitation and medical treatment of drug addicts, and the elimination of inner-city social problems such as poverty and violence that seem to contribute to the consumption of illegal narcotics.

As undersecretary of state for Latin American affairs, you need to propose a solution even though this problem does not seem to have a quick fix. Does the U.S. government send money and advice? Or troops? Or does America try harder to eliminate the drug problem at home? Will it be interdiction or demand reduction? Welcome to the Colombian-American connection where there are no easy answers.[15]

THE CUBAN-AMERICAN CONFLICT

One of the longest continually running international political feuds has been the brawl between a powerful free-market American democracy and a defiantly authoritarian Marxist government in Havana. From the perspective of the United States, the conflict is seen primarily as ideological, a clear-cut case of free market society on one side and a communist dictatorship on the other. In terms of the left-right dimension, the United States asserts the righteousness of its capitalist economic system, while Cuba is predominantly Marxist, with some free-enterprise features emerging after the fall of the USSR, and even more emerging over the course of the past few years.

Cubans, on the other hand, tend to see the conflict as starkly nationalist. From the perspective of "Castro's Children," Cuba has struggled for a century and a half to be free from foreign control, at first seeking deliverance from Spanish dominion, and then battling to deliver itself from Yankee interference. Cuban Marxism is more than a set of ideological choices about structuring a government and an economy; it is a way of proclaiming Cuba's independence from the United States. American capitalism had once controlled Cuba; from Havana's perspective, Marxism may have its flaws, but the system at least gets them more authentic sovereignty over their own resources.

Misunderstanding Cuba

The results of this misunderstanding have been mostly unhappy for both sides. Some Cubans claim that this is Cuba's unofficial motto: "Poor Cuba! Too far from God. Too close to the United States of America." Travel brochures and calypso melodies give the impression of a Caribbean archipelago filled with carefree dark-skinned people, but this

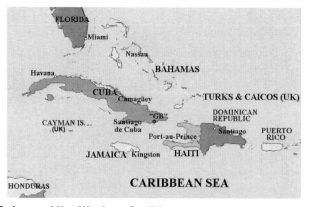

Map 10.2. Cuba and the Western Caribbean
Note the distance between Cuba's capital, Havana, and America's Key West, a scant seventy miles. And take a moment to get your Western Caribbean geography under control, because this is a complicated part of the world. Note that Haiti and the Dominican Republic actually share the island of Hispaniola. Britain still has some colonies here in the Turks and Caicos Islands and the Cayman Islands. Jamaica is now independent, although a member of the Commonwealth of Nations. And Puerto Rico, of course, is a "commonwealth" or associated territory of the United States.

cheerfully racist stereotype misses the mark most of the time and doesn't tell us much at all about Cuba. Let's take a closer look.[16]

On the positive side, Spanish-speaking Cuba has far greater ultimate economic potential than do most of its impoverished Caribbean neighbors. About a quarter of the land is arable (an unusually high percentage), and the soil is suitable for citrus fruits, sugar cane, tobacco, and coffee. Beneath the surface lie deposits of cobalt, nickel, iron ore, and copper. The climate is warm, but the steady trade winds from the northeast keep the temperature from becoming oppressive. The population density is moderate; only about eleven million people occupy this large and lovely island, and the population increase rate is low.

Historically, however, Cubans have found it difficult to translate their potential island paradise into genuine human happiness. After its discovery by Columbus, Cuba became the jewel of Spain's colonial empire in the New World. Cuba's original native Indian population was eliminated by war and disease, and the Spanish repopulated the island with African slaves. Cuban demography today is a reflection of this cruel history. The island is multiracial, but Cubans of relatively unmixed Spanish heritage tend to form the social and political elite. There is a sizable population of people of mixed genetic inheritance and a small number of purely black people, who are usually fairly poor. The Roman Catholic Church has always provided a cultural matrix for the island, but after fifty years of official Marxist atheism, only about a third of the Cuban people still practice any religion.[17]

The Conflict with America

In 1895, inspired by the writings and leadership of José Martí, Cuba rose up in rebellion against the Spanish government. When the USS *Maine* triggered the Spanish-American War by exploding mysteriously in Havana Harbor in 1898, Cuba became the unhappy object of Yankee attention as Americans conquered the island.[18]

Cuba's twentieth-century history falls roughly into thirds: from the 1898 U.S. takeover to 1934, Cuba was essentially an American protectorate, a colony in all but

Table 10.1. A Cuban Time Line

1492:	Discovery by Columbus
1511:	First Spanish settlements
1886:	Abolition of slavery
1895:	Cuban rebellion against Spain
1898:	Spanish-American War: U.S. conquers Cuba
1902:	Formal independence under U.S. supervision
1903:	Guantánamo Bay established as permanent U.S. base
1956:	Castro's revolutionary war begins
1959:	Castro's conquest of power
1961:	Bay of Pigs landing
1962:	Cuban Missile Crisis
1992:	Loss of Soviet support
2006:	Castro falls ill
2008:	Raúl Castro becomes Cuban president

name, and Yankee economic interests took control of important sectors of a largely agricultural economy. In 1901, the United States casually assigned itself a military base at Guantánamo Bay where—more than a century later—the U.S. Marine Corps is still a thorn in Cuba's side. Thanks to Franklin Delano Roosevelt's "Good Neighbor Policy," Cuba achieved greater independence after 1934, but the island quickly slid into a series of corrupt dictatorships, as Havana became famous for gambling casinos, brothels, abortion clinics, and Mafia front organizations. Americans invested heavily there, buying hotels, sugar-cane farms, and cigar factories, but the average Cuban drew little benefit from the U.S. presence.[19]

The third period in Cuban history began in 1959 with Fidel Castro's victory over an American-sponsored dictator named Fulgencio Batista. Born in 1926, Fidel Castro came from a prosperous farming family and earned a law degree from Havana University. After a failed 1953 revolutionary attempt, a short spell in prison, and a period of exile, Castro returned secretly to Cuba in 1956 with his brother, Raúl Castro, Che Guevara, and a handful of other supporters. After building a rebel army in the mountains, Fidel's forces attacked in 1958, and swept Batista from power on New Year's Day of 1959.[20]

At the time of his victory, Castro was a generic leftist, who had never joined Cuba's Communist Party. Believing that American economic power in Cuba was imperialist and exploitative, however, his new government began a wide-ranging program of nationalization, converting about 70 percent of all Cuba's arable land into state-owned farms, although small plots of land remained in private hands. The new Havana government also took control and ownership of industrial and commercial corporations. Since much of this property was American-owned, U.S. enthusiasm for the Cuban revolution cooled quickly. Washington angrily responded with a trade embargo and the interruption of diplomatic relations. In the first two years of the new government, about a million wealthier Cubans fled into exile in the United States, many of them settling in Florida. This refugee community quickly became the focus of opposition to the Castro regime and a powerful anti-Castro voice in the U.S. foreign policy establishment.

President Dwight Eisenhower (1953–1961) habitually countered Latin American challenges to American hegemony with CIA covert operations, and he responded to the Castro gambit by authorizing the U.S. spy agency to train an army of Cuban exiles in nearby Nicaragua. When John F. Kennedy took the oath of office in January of 1961, the young "New Frontier" president learned that his government was preparing to invade Cuba by proxy.

Eisenhower was an experienced military leader and might have deployed enough naval and air support to ensure that the invasion was a success. Kennedy, on the other hand, was deeply ambivalent about the operation. When the invading Cuban exiles waded ashore at Cuba's Bay of Pigs on April 15, 1961, they faced a competent and loyal Cuban Army without the promised help from U.S. Navy gunboats and U.S. Air Force fighters. Many were killed, and the thousands who were taken prisoner later needed to be ransomed by a humiliated American government.[21]

Quite naturally, Castro worried that the humiliated Kennedy administration might redeem its Bay of Pigs disaster with a formal invasion of the island. He may also have been aware of CIA attempts to arrange for his assassination. Looking for protection, Fidel quickly moved closer to the Cuban Communist Party and to the Soviet Union. Under the leadership of Nikita Khrushchev, the USSR secretly began to locate medium-range

Figure 10.3.   Ernesto "Che" Guevara (1928–1967)
A romantic, charismatic 1960s figure, Guevara was an Argentine physician who
helped the Castro brothers achieve power in Cuba, then used the island as his base
while he tried to export revolution to Africa and Latin America.

nuclear missiles in Cuba, both to advance the USSR's strategic interests and to deter an
American invasion. In October of 1962, President Kennedy quarantined the island until
the Soviets withdrew their weapons, a nervous standoff that historians call the Cuban
Missile Crisis. At the time, the Cuban Missile Crisis seemed an undiluted American victory, although it was later revealed that the United States had agreed as a quid pro quo to
remove similar nuclear weapons from Turkey.[22]

With diplomatic relations suspended, the two countries settled into the pattern of
mutual recrimination that has endured until the present day. The CIA made repetitive
attempts on Castro's life, and Cubans maintain that U.S.-sponsored terrorists have sabotaged Cuba's sugar-cane industry. And the United States maintained its Guantánamo
Bay base despite Cuban objections. In revenge, Cuban forces took the anti-American side
in every quarrel around the world, sending well-trained soldiers to fight in Ethiopia and
Angola, and encouraging Marxist rebellions throughout Latin America.

Most important, the American government maintained an economic embargo against Cuba, refusing to trade with Havana, and taking reprisals against other countries and foreign firms that wanted to pursue trade relations with the island. Americans were generally forbidden to visit Cuba, and Cubans who escaped or emigrated were usually given political asylum, a status normally denied to economic refugees from other impoverished Caribbean states.[23]

Marxism Cuban-Style

Despite the animosity of the United States, the Havana government forged ahead with an impressive campaign of social reforms. Free and obligatory public education brought the Cuban literacy rate up to European levels. While they are far from being centers of intellectual freedom, Cuban universities offer excellent technical and professional education, and Cuba has produced engineers and physicians in great quantities. Free medical care, with an emphasis on health maintenance, has nurtured an extraordinarily healthy population. Cuba's per capita gross domestic product is about one-eighth of the American level, and yet Cubans live almost as long as Americans do, and enjoy slightly better infant mortality rates. Food is subsidized and rationed, and while the Cuban diet is Spartan, no one goes hungry.[24]

Once Fidel took the plunge into conventional Soviet-style communism, the economy became rigidly Marxist. Every major economic enterprise was state-owned and managed, and most Cubans in one way or another worked for their government. Salaries are low, even for professionals; a trained physician in Cuba might earn US$25 per month, although this is only about double what an unskilled laborer takes home. In the United States, by comparison, a young general practitioner could expect to earn about eight times the salary of an unskilled laborer.

While it is routinely denounced by American politicians as totalitarian, Cuba gives the impression of being a relatively benign but firmly authoritarian dictatorship. While the regime seldom feels the need to use violence against its people, it continues to be a repressive, party-dominated, undemocratic regime that legitimizes its authority with carefully managed elections. All political activity takes place within the context of the Cuban Communist Party, the only legal political organization.

Cuba first feels like a serious dictatorship when the visitor looks for a bookstore or tries to find some news on the radio or television. In fact, the regime publishes its own newspapers and transmits two television and a number of FM radio stations; this is the totality of the informational input available to the average citizen. No unauthorized books or magazines can be sold on the island. It is illegal to erect antennas or satellite dishes in an attempt to bring in foreign stations. Cubans cannot freely access the World Wide Web. The only unbiased source of world news is short-wave radio, but they are expensive and generally unavailable. The Cuban government puts a lot of effort into jamming the BBC and succeeds at least in making it hard to hear.

Neither Fidel nor Raúl Castro ever demanded cult-of-the-personality status. Pictures of Castro are rarely displayed in public. Most Cubans refer to him as "Fidel," and he seems to be regarded with some affection, even by those who look forward restlessly to a post-Castro era.

Thanks in part to the Cuban exile community in the United States, the authoritarian character of this government is criticized more harshly in the United States than elsewhere. Western European governments have taken a gentler view of Castro's experiment, and the leaders of Venezuela and Bolivia regard Fidel with frank admiration. While critical of Cuba's human rights abuses, most European powers have normal diplomatic relations with Cuba and permit their citizens to visit the island as tourists.

Always short of voluntary friends, the late Soviet Union had nurtured its ties with Cuba, bought most of the island's sugar crop, and bailed out Castro's shaky economy. With the abrupt demise of the Soviet experiment in 1991–1992, Cuba went into a period of sustained economic crisis. Since Castro (born in 1926) slid into his seventies during what Cubans call the "Special Period" of economic distress, observers foresaw the end of his regime.

Their predictions may have been premature. Despite his advancing years, Castro maneuvered ably, permitting some peripheral capitalist features (such as privately owned restaurants) in the economy. Tourism is now being encouraged, and Havana now boasts a little of that alluring sinfulness that gave spice to the city when Ernest Hemingway lived there in the 1950s. Cuban exiles who live in the United States regard the Havana regime with great hostility, American politicians denounce both Fidel and Raúl Castro regularly, and there continues to be no formal diplomatic relations between the two countries.

Tough Choices: What Happens When Fidel and Raúl Castro Die?

The short answer is that nobody knows for sure, although everybody in Havana has an opinion. Those who want to avoid an abrupt break with the past argue that the day after the funerals the island will still be firmly under the control of the Cuban Communist Party, the police, and the army, all institutions that will wish to avoid any quick and dramatic changes. Many average Cubans also have a stake in socialist continuity since they live in public housing or administer state-owned companies that were once the property of Cubans now living in Miami. Poorer and older Cubans remember the pre-Castro era of poverty and repression that was tolerated by the United States. Generally speaking, educated middle-class Cubans seem to want to move from Cuba's authoritarian dictatorship to a Scandinavian-style social democratic system, opening the economy up to some private enterprise but maintaining Cuban advances in health and education. While looking forward to improved relations with Washington, they would also want to keep the United States at arm's length. As one Cuban official said, "One Puerto Rico in the Caribbean is enough."

On the other hand, many Cubans who left the island in the 1960s and now live in the United States regard the 1959 revolution as illegal and deny that property nationalized or confiscated by the Castro regime legitimately belongs to the Havana government. When the Castro brothers disappear, many of them will want to return to the island of their ancestors, reclaim their property, and reassert what they regard as their rightful position in Cuban society. They will demand the assistance of the American government in achieving these goals, and Florida's importance in the Electoral College may give them considerable clout.

What ultimately happens will to some extent depend upon the surviving leadership in Havana and the attitude taken by the authorities in Washington. Since *la revolución* of 1959, Cuba has never been as prosperous as it could be, partly because of Marxist mismanagement of the economy and partly because of the American trade embargo. To be successful, a post-Castro Cuban government would need to convince the Americans to relax trade barriers, persuade the Miami Cuban émigré community that some of its claims will be satisfied, and maintain the existing educational and health benefits of Cuban socialism.[25]

When the day comes, what should the United States do? Given the potential for violent conflict, should we land troops to secure our interests and maintain stability? Or should we stand back, restrain the passions of the Miami émigré community, and allow Cuba to organize its own future?

2. Mussolini's Children: The Extreme Right

At a global level, there is a great deal of violence coming from what is often called the extreme right, but the phenomenon is harder to define and categorize than is left-wing ideological conflict. Once again, it is easier to make the distinction between ideological and nationalist violence in a university classroom than it is in a street fight. While violent rightists are often extreme nationalists or "superpatriots," they are also fundamentally ideological in the sense that they are making a series of imprecise but emphatic statements about the way society needs to be organized. To bring some sense into a generally senseless aspect of political conflict, we'll talk first about European fascist movements and more modern successors groups who continue to revere the memories of Hitler and Mussolini. Then we'll move on to examine a scattering of groups in America and elsewhere (such as the Ku Klux Klan and an assortment of survivalist and racist groups) that have imitated, sometimes unconsciously, that same violent European tradition.

ROOTS OF THE RADICAL RIGHT

We will go on to talk about fascist and Nazi movements in a moment, but let us pause and see if we can identify the essence of the confrontational right. Groups belonging to the extreme right typically (and historically) have two basic ideological themes or factors running through their thought, as follows:

• Hatred of the Left: Go back and look at chapter 6 if you aren't clear on the basic left-right or liberals-versus-conservatives dimension in politics. Focus on this simple point: while they differ in important ways, liberals and socialists and communists all demand economic redistribution from the government, so wealthier citizens will pay higher taxes to provide services for poorer citizens. All functioning societies do this to some extent, but if a society redistributes too energetically, rich people may fear economic or even physical elimination. In an agricultural society where arable land represents the principle source of revenue, landowners may face demands from peasant farmers for a redistribution of land.

- Nationalism or Allegiance to the "Core" Nation: Extreme rightists are distinctly not internationalists, but instead are preoccupied with the danger to national or ethnic purity represented by those they regard as foreigners living legally or illegally on the national territory. Review chapter 4 if you need to refresh your memory here, but there is often disagreement about who belongs to a given nation. In nearly every ethnically fragmented society, some will regard themselves as belonging to the core population and see themselves as more authentically members of that nation than are recent immigrants or members of ethnic or minority communities. For example, some Caucasian, Protestant Americans of undiluted Anglo-Saxon descent see themselves as "real Americans," unlike Orthodox Jews from New York City or Roman Catholics from New Orleans, or black Americans from anywhere. Americans sometimes joke about being a "WASP" or white Anglo-Saxon Protestant.

Here's an important proviso when contemplating these two factors. Not everybody who resents minority groups and dislikes liberals is necessarily a member of the extreme right. Some upper-middle-class Americans and Western Europeans feel that their taxes are too high because of welfare payments to ethnic minorities, and hold liberals or left-wingers responsible for this situation. Typically, these emotions translate into votes for legal and nonviolent but conservative political parties. A smaller group of people who have seriously angry emotions about left-wingers and ethnic minorities will join far right but legal political parties that sponsor these points of view. France's National Front, would be a good example. In this section, however, we are talking specifically about those groups who have crossed the red line into illegality and violence.

After World War I, an Italian journalist and politician named Benito Mussolini (1883–1945) created the world's first successful fascist party, leading it to power in 1922. While Hitler's impact upon history was arguably greater, Mussolini gets the credit (or the blame) for amalgamating the mixed set of ideas that he called "fascism."

Adolf's Enemies

Are you on the list? The extreme right has been consistent in its enemies, hating the same people today whom Hitler and Mussolini despised a half century ago:

- liberals, socialists, communists, trade unionists, and social workers;
- foreigners, ethnic minorities, and dark-skinned and indigenous peoples;
- religious minorities, almost always Jews, sometimes Catholics, and others;
- homosexuals, emancipated women, and feminists;
- dissident intellectuals and avant-garde artists; and
- the government itself, if perceived as weak or dominated by the left.

Although a gifted orator, Mussolini was not a profound thinker, and his fascism was a concoction of ideas and emotions looted from other ideologies. The common elements for all fascist movements were extreme nationalism and/or racism mixed with a populist political rhetoric appealing to the common man. Fascists were proud of being male chauvinists and glorified "manly" violence and war. Fascism was grounded in the apprehension aroused in Western Europe by the successful Bolshevik Revolution in Russia. Oddly enough, many early fascists had begun on the left of the political spectrum and retained some leftist elements in their rhetoric, even after they turned to smashing labor unions in defense of wealthy capitalists. Fascists had little use for democracy, preferring rule by the strong. The ideology was essentially anti-intellectual, and fascists portrayed themselves as employing willpower and force to achieve objectives rather than intellectuality and debate.[26]

Fascism became famous initially as the ruling ideology in Italy (1922–1945) and later spread to Germany (1933–1945), where essentially the same philosophy was called Nazism. By the end of the 1930s, virtually every developed society had a fascist movement of some sort. One of the major groups supporting the dictatorship of General Francisco Franco (1892–1975) was the Falange, a group that survives down to the present day. England's Oswald Mosley led the British Union of Fascists until during World War II and the movement resurfaced, rebaptized as the British National Party (BNP) after the war. Fascism spread because it seemed to supply an energetic response to the problems of the Great Depression. Before World War II, Romania, France, Belgium, and Hungary all had significant fascist movements.[27]

NEO-FASCIST AND RACIST MOVEMENTS

Mussolini and Hitler both perished in 1945, but their ideas didn't quite die with them, and postwar Europe inherited a potpourri of what are generically called **neo-fascist** groups, some of which spread to the United States. There is no significant difference between neo-fascists and **neo-Nazis** beyond the fact that neo-Nazis maintain a particular reverence for the personality of Adolf Hitler and the accomplishments of the German Army in the early stages of World War II.

European Hard-Right Groups

Most fascist movements survived World War II in some diminished fashion. Italy and Germany outlawed the Fascist and Nazi parties, respectively, but the two movements changed their names and attempted with varying levels of success to become political players in the postwar world. In postwar Argentina, Juan Perón employed fascist themes and rhetoric during his nine years (1946–1955) in office.

Neo-fascist sentiments became more popular in the 1980s, thanks to the perception on the part of Europeans that their countries were filling up with African and Middle Eastern immigrants. Today, there is an anti-immigrant, antiblack, anti-Muslim political force in nearly every European country, although these parties seldom self-identify as neo-fascist. France's famous National Front, Austria's Freedom Party, Russia's oddly named Liberal Democratic Party, Great Britain's British National Party, and Germany's Republikaner Partei ("Republicans") all offer a political home for racists and anti-immigrants.[28] These parties all campaign on **populist** themes and attract votes from people who resent the European

Union. In the 2002 French presidential elections, National Front leader Jean Marie le Pen shocked France and the world by winning 17 percent of the vote with an anti-immigrant and anti-EU campaign. Inheriting the *Front National* from her elderly father in 2011, Marine Le Pen became the leader of what is probably the largest anti-immigrant hard-right party in Europe. Mademoiselle Le Pen is a much more skillful politician than was her father and has avoided his harsh rhetoric when making the case that France is the homeland of Caucasian, French-speaking Catholics, whose national heritage is diluted by the presence of so many dark-skinned Muslims of African origin.[29] Some political scientists have suggested that these parties play a useful role in channeling angry emotions into legal (if sometimes unruly) political protest and may actually defuse violence.

On the fringes of these legal political parties, however, there are violent antiforeigner gangs of neo-fascists, and by the turn of the new century, these groups were increasing in size and commitment to violence. Some European neo-fascists are skinheads and members of Hell's Angels–style motorcycle packs. With black leather jackets and shaved skulls, they sabotage synagogues, desecrate Jewish cemeteries, paint Nazi emblems on walls, attack and sometimes kill members of racial minorities, such as Turkish migrant workers, Gypsies (Roma), and people of African descent. Because of Germany's Nazi past, these episodes attract a lot of attention when they occur in Germany, but neo-fascist groups have spread throughout northern Europe, even affecting placid social democratic societies such as Denmark, Sweden, and Norway. The world was stunned in 2011 when Anders Behring Breivik, an anti-immigrant fanatic, went on a killing spree that costs the lives of ninety-three Norwegians.

American White Supremacist or Militia Movements

The grandfather of North American extreme right groups is the Ku Klux Klan, founded in 1865. The KKK recruited from among generally poor whites who feared that they would be marginalized if newly liberated blacks claimed their economic and political rights. One hundred and thirty-five years later, the Klan is still in business. The Southern Poverty Law Center in Alabama estimates that there are 163 chapters of the organization still active.[30]

Figure 10.4. The South Will Rise Again
A century and a half after the end of the American Civil War, the Ku Klux Klan is still in business. This 1992 Klan rally in South Carolina drew a surprisingly large crowd.

While the membership of modern American extreme right organizations tends to be fluid, with individuals belonging to several groups at once or passing frequently from one to another, Mussolini's American children are disturbingly numerous. Most of them share most or all of the following four intellectual ingredients.

- Religion: While a few hate groups have tried to revive paganism, nearly all hard-right groups practicing violence claim a primitive and fundamentalist strain of Protestant Christianity as their legitimizing theology, and some cult-like communities such as the Illinois-based World Church of the Creator sponsor specifically racist views. Another branch of the movement has concentrated on creating a violent response to abortion clinics, killing gynecologists who carry out legal terminations of pregnancies.
- Racism: Some scholars have used the term "neo-confederate" to describe the racial thinking of some of these groups, that is, those that advocate white or Caucasian racial superiority and see themselves as America's core nation. The KKK belongs in this category, as do groups such as the Aryan Nation.
- Subversive Nationalism: While these groups are intensely patriotic about the greatness of the American people, almost all regard the bureaucratic apparatus of the U.S. government as having fallen under the control of Jews, minority groups, homosexuals, communists, the United Nations, or some other arcane force. Many have collected arsenals to defend themselves against a government they now view as hostile. The American Nazi Party combines many of these themes and resembles similar European organizations.
- Militarism: Since they view the government as hostile, many right-wing extremists have collected arsenals to defend themselves and display an unusual dedication to weapons. Some of these groups are called "survivalists" because they have accumulated food and guns in the hope of surviving nuclear war or other apocalyptic disasters. Perhaps influenced by the enjoyment of military paraphernalia, others created informal militias, preparing themselves to defend their community against foreign enemies or an aggressive American government. Timothy McVeigh and his colleagues in the 1995 bombing of the Oklahoma City Federal Building came from a cultural matrix of militia-survivalist groups.[31]

These groups produce hate propaganda, stage marches, maintain websites, and publish books and music. Individual members have periodically gone on shooting or bombing sprees, killing Asians, blacks, Jews, and prominent civil rights activists.

Death Squads

The "death squad" varies from other right-wing violent groups only because it is typically staffed by police or military officers acting either on their own or with the connivance of the government. These death squads, popular in both Latin America and the Middle East, arrest, torture, and sometimes execute people whom they regard as enemies of the regime. The element of racism is not as strong in the death squads, although some of them have targeted indigenous peoples in Latin America.

By definition, these groups are acting illegally, but their operations usually enjoy at least the implicit consent of the governing regime, and there may even be active collaboration. Death squads' operations are traditionally efforts either to frighten the opposition into silence or to physically eliminate opponents of the government or an economic oligarchy. These enemies can include guerrilla sympathizers, left-leaning professors or intellectuals, clergymen who practice liberation theology, labor union organizers, or liberal political leaders.

At various times in the past, police and army officers have imposed their own versions of law and order on many societies. Pakistan, Indonesia, Iraq, Syria, Libya, the Philippines, and the now-extinct apartheid government of South Africa have all been accused of tolerating death squads. But the phenomenon has been most characteristic of Latin American society. Honduras and Peru have both gone through death squad phases, as have Nicaragua, Brazil, Chile, Guatemala, Colombia, and El Salvador.[32]

3. Bin Laden's Children: Violent Islam

A majority of the men who attacked the United States on September 11, 2001, were Saudi Arabian Muslims, and since that awful day the media have focused relentlessly on the Islamic religion. Is Islam inherently more violent or less tolerant than other religions? Most Muslims are kind, generous, warm-hearted, and tolerant people; you are probably physically safer in most Arab cities than in Washington, D.C. or Los Angeles. Nevertheless, the level of religiously motivated violence emanating from the Islamic world is undeniably intense. Pakistani Muslims have been killing Christians in Karachi for the crime of practicing Christianity. Algerian fundamentalists have brutally murdered tens of thousands of their fellow citizens. The Islamic government of Sudan has massacred hundreds of thousands of black Africans. Indonesian Muslims have burned down nightclubs on the Hindu island of Bali, and Chechnyan Muslims have slaughtered Russians in Moscow theaters. Iraqi fanatics have been beheading hostages on television, and suicide bombers from Gaza and the West Bank have brought their own special brand of awfulness to the Israel-Palestinian conflict.

Some historians have argued that most religions were intolerant until civil society forced restraint upon them. Did Christians stop burning heretics and witches at the stake because they came to regard it as a bad idea, or because increasingly secular governments obliged them to stop? Many scholars have argued that the confrontational behavior of some Muslims in recent years is linked to the failure of Islamic states in general to mature into democracies with civil-law codes. Few predominantly Islamic states have mellowed into fully functioning democracies. Turkey has been making important strides toward the establishment of working democratic institutions, but Freedom House still assigns it a "3.0" or "partly free." Indonesia, on the other hand, is becoming progressively freer, having risen into the "free" or "2.5" category in recent years. Until its recent military coup, North Africa's Mali also made the list of "free" societies.[33]

Why have Islamic states experienced difficulty in making the transition to democracy? No one believes that there is anything fundamental about Islam that would make it impossible for a Muslim society to become truly democratic, but history has created some obstacles. While these factors are complicated and controversial, most scholars would regard the following as important:

- The Concept of Unified Authority: There was nothing in Islamic history or culture that encouraged Muslims to make the Western distinction between church and state.

This allows Islamic political leaders to portray distinctly human public policy as divine in inspiration and authority. Muslims believe in a doctrine called *tawhid*, which means the singularity, unity, or "oneness" of God/Allah. At a theological level, this means that God is the source of everything, the "cause of causes" who maintains the world in existence. At a more practical political level, tawhid can be interpreted to mean that there can be only one source of authority or law. It follows, therefore, that humans are not free to create a separate law code that competes or conflicts with the Sharia or divine Islamic law. This concept gives sometimes doctrinaire religious leaders a political importance they would lack in Western society. In contrast, when President George W. Bush decided on war with Iraq in 2002, the Roman Catholic pope announced that it was a bad idea. There was no generalized uproar among American Catholics, many of whom chose to ignore their spiritual leader in favor of their president.[34]

- The Lack of Legitimacy: The legacy of colonialism has created a series of weak postcolonial governments ruling artificial multinational states that came into existence only in comparatively recent history. Thanks to decisions made in London and Paris, these regimes have had their borders drawn to suit European colonial interests and reflect little that is authentically Islamic. Since these governments have often proved to be corrupt and incompetent, they have not gained real political legitimacy over time. Leaders who lack legitimacy cannot safely trust their fates to democratic elections.
- Lack of Global Support for Democracy: While the Islamic world is often criticized for being undemocratic, there has been little authentic external support for democratic movements. Petroleum interests have been prepared to support any regime capable of guaranteeing the safe supply of oil. During the Cold War, the West backed anti-Soviet regimes regardless of their domestic policies. In creating coalitions for two anti-Iraq wars, American-led coalitions took their allies where they could find them, regardless of democratic values. Even after going to war to rescue Kuwait from Iraq, the United States put no pressure Kuwait to democratize its medieval political system. And when the Arab Spring of 2011–2012 occurred, many observers worried that real democracy would produce governments that were dominated by fundamentalists and even more hostile to Israel and American interests in the Middle East. It can be argued, cynically, that dictatorships make more reliable friends than do democracies.

ISLAMISM AND REVOLUTIONARY ISLAM

This chapter has been about ideological conflict, and in this section, we want to try to understand the Islamic objection to Western society and European-American political institutions.[35] Once again, we will find that religion-based conflict does not fit neatly into a specific ideological or nationalist category. For an Osama bin Laden, the Islamic community is a kind of spiritual nation and is in eternal conflict with "crusaders and Jews" (Western society and Israel), perceived as two other hostile nations unified in their hatred of the Islamic nation. In this sense, the conflict can be seen as nationalist, but in another, perhaps more important sense, the quarrel is clearly ideological. How is society to be administered? According to the laws of God, as understood by Muslims? Or according to the laws of humankind, as articulated by the parliaments and legislatures of the world? What is the role of women in society? Are they legally equal to men, a concept enshrined in theory (although not always in practice) by all Western societies? Or are they subordinate to their male relatives, as is customary in the Middle East?

The Politics of Hair

How long you wear your hair, and how much of it is on display, has been a political issue in many societies. In the 1960s, any young man who chose to have long hair was making a countercultural political statement, and U.S. Army barbers made a contrary assertion when they shaved it off. In many parts of the world today, a woman declares her feelings about the role of religion in public life when she reveals or, alternatively, covers her hair. In traditional Islamic societies, a pious woman modestly covered her hair with what Arabs call a *hijab* or headscarf. As the Middle East modernized, increasingly secular governments in countries such as Turkey and Iran actually forbade the public wearing of the hijab, and many modern Arab women joyfully discarded it.

In recent years, however, Islamic fundamentalists and Islamists brought it back into fashion, and by wearing a headscarf in a society where the fashion is optional, a woman is proclaiming her allegiance to a firmly Islamic society. The result has been a hijab war in many countries. Despite its Islamic majority, Turkey tries so hard to be secular that it has banned the hijab, and pious Turkish women are suing for the right to cover their hair in public. In both France and Germany, secular countries with Christian majorities and Islamic minorities, schoolgirls are routinely banned from class if they appear veiled, although in Saudi Arabia, they would be arrested if they failed to cover their heads.

As we learned in chapter 3, Islam was the creation of the Prophet Mohammed, a historical post-Christian figure who was born about 570 AD and died in 632 AD. Seeing his message as a fulfillment and completion of both Judaism and Christianity, Mohammed created a new movement that was fraternal, spiritual, political, military, and even commercial in character. In his own lifetime, Mohammed and his generals brought most of the Arabian Peninsula into the new faith and under centralized political control. Following the doctrine of tawhid discussed above, early Islam made no real distinction between

Figure 10.5. The Hijab
Muslim women wear the hijab or headscarf in a wide variety of moods and circumstances and for an array of different reasons. Women who live in very traditional societies or in very conservative families have very little choice about covering their hair, and the hijab may be simply matter of custom or habit. For others, the occasional use of a hijab may be a way of self-identification in the same way that a Christian woman might wear a necklace with a cross. This multilingual young woman is of Turkish and Iraqi origin, and grew up in Saudi Arabia and in the United States. She is a thoroughly modern and sophisticated professional with several graduate degrees who now lives and works as a senior executive in Dubai. The events of September 11, 2001, drove her to contemplate her own identity as a Muslim, and she has subsequently worn the hijab upon occasions when she wishes to affirm that identity. Courtesy of Ms. Yasemin Saib.

civil and religious authority. Law emanated from the Qur'an (Koran), which contains prayers, history, and laws for the Islamic community. Within a century of the prophet's death, crusading Moslem armies had conquered all of what is today the Middle East and were launching armed attacks into the heart of a terrified Christian Europe. The Arabs saw their empire in both spiritual and political terms. Westerners talk about nations and sovereign states, but Muslims use the Arabic word "Ummah," which does not translate precisely into English, but suggests both a brotherhood of believers and a kind of spiritual nation where the laws of Allah rule supreme.

Arabs and Muslims

Here's a simple but crucial distinction that confuses many people. To be an Arab is to speak the Arabic tongue and trace your ancestry back to the original Arabic conquerors who came from what is today Saudi Arabia. From Morocco on the Atlantic Ocean to Iraq in the Tigris-Euphrates river valley, most Arabs regard themselves as what we learned in chapter 4 to call a multi-state nation, a large ethnic community linked by ties of kinship and culture but divided into separate sovereign states. Overwhelmingly, Arabs are also Muslims, although there are significant minority communities of Christian Arabs in Palestine and Lebanon, and smaller groups elsewhere. Arabs, therefore, self-identify by language, kinship ties, and mostly, but not exclusively, by the Islamic religion. There are scholarly controversies about which countries should be classified as "Arabic," but the Arab League (a regional organization of Arab countries) counts the following twenty-two as members: Algeria, Bahrain, Comoros, Djibouti, Egypt, Iraq, Jordan, Kuwait, Lebanon, Libya, Mauritania, Morocco, Oman, Palestine, Qatar, Saudi Arabia, Somalia, Sudan, Syria, Tunisia, the United Arab Emirates (U.A.E.), and Yemen.

Only a minority of the world's Muslims are Arabs because Islam has spread far beyond its origins in the Arabic community. In the Middle East, Turks and Iranians are Muslims but do not use Arabic as their primary language and generally have no kinship ties with the Arab people. Moving to the east, Pakistanis, Afghans, Bangladeshi, and Indonesians are also non-Arabic Muslims. A very large number of Muslim immigrants (some Arabs and some not) have found a home in Western Europe and the United States, where some African Americans have become converts to the religion.

For nearly three centuries, this triumphant Arabian Empire led the world in arts and sciences. After this period of cultural dominance, however, the Islamic world was hammered by Mongol invaders from the east and Christian crusaders from Europe. Following an era of unrest, Arab North Africa, and the Arab heartland of Syria, Iraq, Palestine, and the Arabian Peninsula itself fell under the control of the Ottoman Empire, which governed the Arabs in the name of Islam. As the Ottoman Empire weakened in the 1800s, European powers such as Britain and France began to enter the area, building canals in Egypt, colonies in Algeria, and spheres of influence in the Persian Gulf. When the Ottoman Empire collapsed after World War I, European control of the Islamic Middle East was nearly complete.[36]

Islam's Crisis of Faith

Pious Muslims found it difficult to understand how this catastrophe had happened. Why had God allowed his people to suffer this humiliation? In trying to answer this crucial question, two divergent tendencies emerged within the Islamic community, with individual Muslims finding a place for themselves along a continuum that runs from secularism to Islamism.

- The Secularist Tendency: Some Muslims believe that Islam needs to be modernized and compartmentalized; Islam should provide answers to spiritual questions, but science and technology need to be borrowed from the West to help Muslims live in the contemporary world. As mentioned above, Muslims have difficulty making a clear intellectual distinction between religious and political authority, but some of these modernizing secularists look forward to European-style democracies, with government by elected politicians and spiritual leadership by clergymen. Not all of them, unfortunately, are dedicated to democracy. King Abdullah II of Jordan, whom we met in chapter 8, is a secularist with very tentative democratic leanings; former president Hosni Mubarek of Egypt was a secularist dictator. The two men have little in common beyond a reluctance to see their societies controlled by religious leaders.
- The Islamist Tendency: Other Muslims disagree, remembering that Islam was stronger when Muslims were pure and strong in their faith. They call for a return to the original vigor of Islam, demanding that the **Sharia** (Islamic law code) be interpreted and enforced sternly, amputating the hands of thieves and stoning adulterous women to death. These fundamentalists are generally hostile to Christian Europe and the United States, and see no reason to imitate Western ideas about the separation of church and state. If certain behavior (drinking alcohol, homosexuality, etc.) is offensive in the eyes of God, how can a human legislature make it legal? Most important, Islamists are prepared to accept the use of revolutionary violence to bring their governments into conformity with their interpretation of the Sharia.

    There are definitional problems in deciding what to call members of this branch of Islam. The popularly used term "fundamentalist" is accurate in the sense that Islamists believe in a firm adherence to the chapter and verse of holy books. Almost all Muslims (and many Christians) would qualify as "fundamentalists" in this sense, but only a minority of them would wish to use revolutionary violence to overthrow the government. Fundamentalism appears in every religious tradition and Christian fundamentalists would generally regard the Bible with the same reverence that Muslims offer the Qur'an. What makes Islamic fundamentalists into Islamists is their willingness to use revolutionary violence to transform their societies.

This division of the Islamic world into secularists and Islamists is, of course, a drastic oversimplification of a complex reality, since there are a thousand doctrinal way stations between the two extremes. There are Muslim communities stretching across the face of the planet. What they all have in common, however, is tension and internal conflict when modernizing secularists confront Islamists. Since these Islamic countries have not generally become established multiparty democracies, Islamists and secularists have not been able to organize themselves into rival political parties and campaign peacefully against one another for votes. Typically, the Islamist movement becomes subversive when secularists are in power, and vice versa.

Tough Choices: Should Sin be Illegal?

Nigeria is a garden of tough choices, but here is a transnational problem threatening any society with a large Islamic population. This specific case is a threatening legal minefield that combines contrasting notions about the origins of law, a troubled society's efforts to avoid conflict, a woman's control over her own sexuality, and a religiously sanctioned death penalty. Nigeria is a multinational state with Islamic tribal groups in the North, who are culturally, linguistically, and religiously distinct from the two major national communities in the South. One standard way of brokering political and ethnic differences within a multinational society is to create a federal system and allow individual communities to create their own law codes. Nigeria presently has thirty-six states, although this number has changed over time. In 1999, Nigerians made a brave attempt to install a domestic democracy and found it difficult to object when a number of Hausa-speaking northern states with overwhelmingly Islamic populations decided to adopt the Sharia (or Islamic law code) as the basis for their civil statute law. This meant judicially sanctioned amputations of right hands for theft and public lashings for minor sexual offenses. The death penalty is permitted under Nigerian law, and Islamic law permits the imposition of the death penalty for adultery when there is irrefutable proof or the testimony of four male witnesses.

In 2001, an extremely poor woman named Amina Lawal bore a child out of wedlock and was accused of having committed adultery. Amina was married, but her husband had deserted her some years before. The man Amina accused of having fathered her baby girl was found innocent because there were no witnesses to the act of conception. Amina, on the other hand, was found guilty of adultery because the birth of her child provided irrefutable proof that she must have had sex with someone. The local court deferred her execution because she was still breast-feeding, but local judicial authorities proposed to stone her to death as soon as the baby was weaned.

When news about the case appeared in the international press, the issue aroused wild controversy. Enthusiasm for the Sharia is high in Nigeria's North, and there was intense pressure to allow the sentence to be carried out. For those who believe that law flows from the divine decrees of Allah, the case was uncomplicated because Muslims find it very difficult to understand how something can offend God and still be legal. The execution of an adulteress is actually comparatively rare in the Islamic world, but it does happen periodically and in conservative Islamist societies, it is as uncontroversial as lethal injections for murderers in Texas. On the other hand, the non-Muslim part of Nigeria operates on the English Common Law Tradition that makes a keen distinction between sin (if that's what Amina committed) and crime.

For Nigeria, the political implications were grave. Interference by the federal government could have led to rebellion in the North or at least the intensification of Christian-Muslim antagonisms. There were (and continue to be) frequent street battles between Christians and Muslims in Nigeria, often leaving dozens dead. On the other hand, letting the decision stand and permitting Amina to die would have made it difficult for the Western-oriented government to convince the rest of the planet that something fundamental had changed in Nigeria. Executing only the woman for an act that must have also involved a man would be a clear violation of the 1979 Convention on the Elimination of All Forms of Discrimination against Women (CEDAW) Convention, which Nigeria (although not the United States) has ratified.

In the end, the Nigerian court system dodged the bullet without disarming the sniper. The case went before a federal appeals judge, who acquitted Amina for insufficient proof, but—significantly—the court did not rule that stoning for adultery was in itself inherently unconstitutional. Islamists promptly located another allegedly sinful woman, sentenced her to death by stoning, and started the whole process over again, determined to demonstrate that Sharia-based law codes could be enforced. In the meanwhile, violent clashes between Muslims and Christians have become a daily feature of life in Nigeria, and the country sometimes seems about to topple into civil war.[37]

If you were the American ambassador in Abuja (the capital of Nigeria) what suggestions would you have for the Nigerian government? How much support should the Nigerians get from the United States if they decide to enforce internationally accepted norms for capital punishment? You will remember, Mr. Ambassador, that Nigeria is an important non–Persian Gulf source for crude oil, and it is distinctly not in the national security interests of the United States to alienate the Nigerians or allow them to drift into a civil war. Using force to rescue a woman accused of adultery could provoke an armed rebellion in the North and get a lot of people killed. Given the fact that ethnic tensions in Nigeria are now very high with Christians and Muslims already slaughtering each other, is it worth the risk? No? Yes?

Islamist Politics

Where fundamentalist Muslims have actually seized the reins of political power, their rule has typically involved high levels of domestic violence and sometimes international conflict. The Taliban government of Afghanistan was a good example until this regime was brought to an end in 2001 by American military intervention. There are still two fairly clear-cut existing examples:

- Iran: As discussed in chapter 8, what is now technically called the Islamic Republic of Iran became an Islamist state after 1979 under the harsh theocratic rule of the Ayatollah Ruhollah Khomeini, a reaction against the secular leadership of the shah of Iran. This sternly Islamic regime in Tehran began the new century locked in an increasingly savage internal conflict over the role of Islam and the Muslim clergy in setting public policy.

- Sudan: In 1989, after years of political instability, General Omar Ahmed al-Bashir seized control of the Sudanese government in Khartoum, instituting a racist and Islamist regime that endures to the present despite Bashir's indictment by the International Criminal Court.[38]

Furthermore, there are Islamist or fundamentalist movements in virtually every other country with a substantial Muslim population. In some of these countries, the leadership elite has responded to the Islamist challenge by making pious concessions to this intensely fervent minority. Outside of Saudi Arabia, the Saudi ruling family is notorious for its decadent lifestyle, but the Saudi princes enforce the Sharia zealously at home. Egypt has reacted to its large and restless Islamist community with repression on one hand and concessions on the other. For example, the Cairo government has halted the enactment of equal-rights-for-women legislation, but arrested members of the Islamist Muslim Brotherhood organization. Pakistan has taken a similar path, using the police against open challenges to the government but permitting its courts generally to enforce the Sharia. In Muslim Indonesia, the Jakarta government has responded only weakly to violent attacks on isolated Christian and Hindu communities.

Where Muslims are a minority, Islamists can step forward to dramatize perceived injustices. The Chechen community in the Russian Federation has some legitimate complaints against Moscow, but their cause is weakened internationally when Chechen Islamists carry out terrorist operations such as the horrific slaughter of schoolchildren in North Osettia's Beslan in 2004.[39]

AFGHANISTAN'S TALIBAN EXPERIMENT

The word "theocracy" should mean "rule by God," but real theocracies are administered by God's self-appointed earthly representatives. Until the end of 2001, modern Afghanistan may have been the best modern example of a theocracy. The population of Afghanistan was estimated at twenty-seven million people, but this is a wild guess and nothing more. On one hand, a great many people died or went into exile during the last two decades of warfare. On the other hand, with Afghan women producing more than seven children apiece, Afghanistan may have the world's fastest population-growth rate.

Figure 10.6. Ethnicity in Afghanistan
The largest community is the Pashtun people, who speak Pashtu and who have always attempted to exert their authority over the smaller national communities in this war-torn multinational state. The Taliban are mostly ethnic Pashtuns from the Kandahar region.

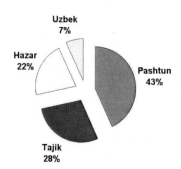

Afghanistan is one of those sovereign states that might more reasonably have been several different countries because the population is divided into several hostile ethnic communities. Pashtuns, Tajiks, and Hazars all speak different and mutually unintelligible cognates of the Indo-Iranian subfamily of languages (i.e., cousin languages of Persian or Farsi). The tiny Uzbek population speaks a cognate of Turkish. About 85 percent of the population is Sunni Muslim, but the Hazari people, who live in the Northeast, are Shi'ites, adding a religious antagonism to a linguistic one.

One of the poorest and most remote societies on the planet, Afghanistan languished on the margins of the world's consciousness until it was caught up in a Cold War competition between Soviet and Western intelligence agencies in the 1970s. A 1978 coup d'état produced a radical Marxist government in Kabul, and Islamist guerrillas or **mujahideen** took to the hills in protest.

Nervous about a war on its southern border, in 1979 the Soviet Union made the catastrophic decision to invade. President Jimmy Carter lashed back with a program to assist the mujahideen, and his successor in the White House, Ronald Reagan, sent enormous quantities of money and supplies to the rebel forces in order to bleed what he saw as the Soviet "evil empire." By 1988, Soviet president Gorbachev threw in the towel and got his troops out early in the following year. Afghanistan had always been one of the UN's low human development societies and part of what others term the Fourth World, and a decade of savage fighting had destroyed urban infrastructure and civic services such as schools and hospitals, brutalizing those Afghans lucky enough to have survived.

When the USSR invaded Afghanistan in 1979, the American government had gone looking for men fanatical enough to die fighting the Russian Army. With the Cold War raging, the CIA and the Saudi Arabians recruited, trained, and armed a generation of mujahideen from all over the Islamic world. Men such as Osama bin Laden first appeared in the Afghan struggle, but when the Russians evacuated Afghanistan, it developed that the mujahideen didn't like Americans any more than they did Russians. No one seriously believes that the CIA fathered Islamism, but U.S. Cold War foreign policy may have given it a critical transfusion.[40]

When the last Soviet soldier left, a furious multilateral civil war broke out as the victorious mujahideen militias fought over ideology, religion, and turf. By the mid-1990s, a new group had emerged from the Islamic theological schools in Kandahar (Qandahar) and quickly began to sweep the country. They were called the Taliban, since "Talib" is Pashto for "student," and many of them were orphans of Afghans killed during the Soviet era and had been raised in orphanages run by Islamic clergymen (called mullahs). By 1996, Taliban tanks had rolled into Kabul. By the end of the century, they had conquered about 90 percent of Afghanistan with only one major militia, called the Northern League, holding out in the Northeast.[41]

Led by a shadowy figure named Mohammed Omar, the Taliban ruled Afghanistan with savage righteousness, and they would almost certainly have remained in charge indefinitely had they not offered hospitality to Osama bin Laden, who used the country as a staging and training area for al-Qaeda. After al-Qaeda's September 11, 2001, attack on the United States, the American military quickly counterattacked with a bombing campaign that began on October 7, 2001. American Special Forces quickly rallied the Northern League, a collection of anti-Taliban forces, destroyed Mohammed Omar's government, and drove his top leadership into hiding. Washington's attention then shifted to Iraq, as the United States mounted its 2003 invasion of that country.

Protected by European and American troops, a new and pro-Western regime was established in Kabul under the leadership of Hamid Karzai. This government legitimized itself with relatively free elections in October of 2004 but then staged notoriously rigged polls in 2009, which confirmed Karzai in power. Corrupt, inefficient, and underfinanced, the Afghan regime actually controls little more than Kabul itself, with warlords, drug smugglers, NATO forces, and the remnants of the Taliban still vying for dominion in the countryside.

By 2007, the Taliban had begun a serious counterattack against American forces, particularly in the southern portion of the country. The West responded with a multinational NATO force, which continues to fight pitched battles against Mohammed Omar's resurgent forces, thought by some military observers to be winning. Taking office in 2009, President Obama dispatched a "surge" of thirty thousand extra troops into the country. At the same time, however, the war was unpopular among Americans and widely considered to be unwinnable. As he entered the 2012 presidential election campaign, President Obama offered a variety of unpalatable policies. He has offered to negotiate with the Taliban, but the Islamists seem uninterested in dealing with the West. He has promised to withdraw most U.S. combat troops by 2014 and focus instead upon training and supporting the Afghan military. Some members of the Afghan military dislike NATO so firmly that they have actually turned their guns on soldiers from Europe and the United States, massacring their "allies."[42]

What is the future for Afghanistan? It can be difficult to assess progress in a guerrilla war. The Taliban has the capacity to mount terrorist operations anywhere in the country, including the capital itself. They do not have the military strength to seize and hold any territory. Knowing that the United States and its NATO allies will be leaving, they have no particular incentive to negotiate seriously. The Karzai government is probably well enough armed to maintain itself in existence, but not to defeat the Islamist insurgency. Mohammed Omar's Taliban troops will certainly continue to challenge the Kabul regime unless the Afghans themselves negotiate a compromise solution of some kind. And a people who have suffered almost continual fighting for forty years seem to be facing more of the same in the immediate future.

OSAMA BIN LADEN AND AL-QAEDA

Thanks to the events of September 11, 2001, the figure of Osama bin Laden and his shadowy but pervasive organization, al-Qaeda, came for many in the West to personify the Islamist challenge to both the physical safety and social values of Europeans and North Americans.[43] There are a great many Islamists in the world, but comparatively few of them would fully endorse the bin Laden approach to the ideal Islamic society or his methods of achieving that goal.

Who was Osama bin Laden? His father came to Saudi Arabia as a Yemeni immigrant and built the Bin Laden Group (still the largest construction company in the Middle East), amassed a huge fortune, sired fifty-two children with an assortment of wives and concubines, and became socially and politically linked with the Saudi royal family. Young Osama was born in Saudi Arabia 1957, but there is little reliable information about his

Why al-Qaeda Hates the United States

1. Political Imperialism: The American military and political presence in the Middle East generally, but particularly in Saudi Arabia, where the holy cities of Mecca and Medina are located; American political support for dictatorial Arab governments such as the Saudi regime in Saudi Arabia, the Mubarek government in Egypt, and other authoritarian administrations.
2. Cultural Imperialism: The projection of secular American values into the Islamic world: rock music, liberated women, "immoral" behavior and dress, and so on.
3. Palestine: U.S. military and financial support for Israeli occupation of the Palestinian West Bank and Gaza Strip .
4. Iraq: American treatment of the Sunni Arab population of Iraq, from economic sanctions to war and occupation.

privileged youth. His father died in 1967, making Osama independently rich, although the extent of his total wealth is disputed. In addition to his father's death, 1967 would also have been a pivotal year for him because of Israel's crushing defeat of the combined armies of the Arabic world in the **Six-Day War**, an event that produced a revival of Islamic fervor. Later, at Jiddah University (near Mecca), he studied public administration and civil engineering, but his intense interest in religion seems to have been stimulated by militant Islamist professors.[44]

As mentioned above, the Soviet Union attacked Afghanistan in December of 1979, stunning and outraging the Muslim world. Immediately, the twenty-two-year-old Osama moved to the Pakistani border city of Peshawar, where he set up what was essentially a logistics base to channel supplies, money, and fighters across the frontier to mount **jihad** against the godless Russians. By 1987, bin Laden had moved from logistics to battle, taking command of a group of "Afghan Arabs" (fellow Arab-speakers who had come from various parts of the Arab world to help defend a Muslim country from the Russians). With his lean, six-foot five-inch frame, bin Laden established a reputation among Arabs and Afghans alike as a fearless and implacable warrior.

When the last Russian soldier left Afghanistan in 1989, Osama bin Laden returned to his native Saudi Arabia, predicting with consummate accuracy that Saddam Hussein posed a military threat to his neighbors. When the Iraqis invaded Kuwait in the summer of 1990, bin Laden offered the services of his Afghan Arabs to lead the counterattack but was outraged when the Saudi monarchy turned instead to an American-led coalition, allowing U.S. soldiers—some of them Jewish and some of them women—onto sacred Arabian soil. At various times, bin Laden had expressed sympathy for the sufferings of the Iraqi people but never relented in his criticism of the secular Saddam Hussein, making it difficult to believe that Iraq and al-Qaeda ever collaborated in any meaningful way.

Uncomfortable in a Saudi Arabia that was beginning to regard him as an internal security threat, Osama returned briefly to Afghanistan, finding the country he had worked so hard to save embroiled in a multisided civil war. Looking for a society that shared his fundamentalist values, he fled in 1992 to Sudan, the only fully Islamist Sunni state then in existence. For a time, he led a double life, apparently building al-Qaeda's infrastructure and worldwide contacts while running a variety of legitimate businesses. By the mid-1990s, however, his name was circulating among intelligence officers as a threat, and the United States prevailed upon a reluctant Sudan in 1996 to expel him.

Osama's return to Afghanistan coincided with the last successful push of the Taliban to take power, creating the total Islamist state that bin Laden had always desired. He quickly established a firm personal relationship with Afghan leader Mohammed Omar and put his money, international expertise, and followers at the service of the Taliban. From 1996 until 2001, he became a public and vocal opponent of the United States and Israel, and during these years, a number of terrorist operations were launched that were either claimed by or commonly attributed to bin Laden's al-Qaeda group. Among these terrorist enterprises were the deadly and nearly simultaneous attacks on U.S. embassies in Kenya's Nairobi and Tanzania's Dar es Salaam in August 1998, killing almost two hundred people and wounding over five thousand.

Under President Clinton, the United States struck back with missile attacks against suspected training camps in Afghanistan, but bin Laden and his followers escaped and are believed to have planned the October 2000 attack on the U.S. Navy destroyer *Cole* while it re-fueled in the Yemeni harbor of Aden. Al-Qaeda then plotted and executed the September 11, 2001, "martyrdom operations" against the World Trade Center and the Pentagon involving four hijacked U.S. commercial passenger aircraft, three of which hit their targets. As noted above, the United States quickly moved to destroy the Taliban government in Kabul, without managing to capture bin Laden himself, who escaped with most of his senior associates and many top Taliban leaders.

Al-Qaeda's war against the West continued. In May 2003, suicide bombers struck against the Russians in Chechnya, foreigners living in Morocco, and American residents of Riyadh, Saudi Arabia, in a coordinated series of attacks that looked like an al-Qaeda operation. When the United States invaded Iraq, an al-Qaeda-sponsored insurgent group took the field against the American occupation and was still actively fighting in the field and mounting suicide missions in 2012. In March 2004, murderous bomb attacks on the Madrid train station killed hundreds, and Spanish police determined that the Arab team responsible had links with al-Qaeda. On July 7, 2005, a quartet of British Muslims detonated bombs on London's transportation system. There is no particular reason to believe that these assaults will cease spontaneously despite the fact that Mr. bin Laden was killed by an American commando raid on his Pakistan hideout on May 1, 2011.[45]

What did bin Laden believe?[46] In terms of a general political vision of the world, bin Laden's beliefs were more intense and more violent but not very different from the views of most Islamists (and even some moderate Muslims) around the world. The Islamic world in general objects to U.S. financial and military support for Israel, to what they regard as U.S. interference in Arab affairs, and to the presence of American military forces on Arab soil. From the Islamist perspective, the United States is always on the anti-Muslim side of every conflict, backing the Russians against the Chechnyans and the Indians against the Pakistanis in Kashmir.

Furthermore, Islamists (like Christian and Jewish fundamentalists) object to the secular character of Western society and what they regard as low moral standards. Saudis such as Osama bin Laden are particularly influenced by a harsh strand of Islamic thought called **Wahhabism**. In the 1700s, an angry Arabian prophet named Muhammad ibn Abd al-Wahhab created this revivalist version of the Muslim religion, linking his theological fortunes to the rising military power of a Bedouin tribe named Saud. After World War I, King Abdulaziz ibn Saud founded modern Saudi Arabia, and Wahhabism became what amounted to the state religion.

Wahhabism is a puritanical, intolerant, somewhat simplistic version of Islam, emphasizing jihad or struggle (in both the spiritual and the military sense). Wahhabis believe that the soul of a soldier who falls in battle against the enemies of Islam soars directly to paradise. Moderate Muslims are quick to point out that this soldierly concept, common in many religions, is a far cry from suicidal "martyrdom operations" in which an airliner is flown into an office building filled with innocent civilians.

4. Considerations on Ideological Violence

Ideological violence typically happens when people reach the passionate conviction that society is not functioning correctly and their government has become unjust. When ideology mingles with religious conviction, the resulting conflicts can be particularly intractable.

It seems wrong, for example, that some people should starve while others enjoy opulence and wealth. While Marxism is quickly fading as a respectable ideology in most parts of the developed world, it continues to sway minds in societies that are deeply unequal in economic distribution with a cavernous gulf between rich and poor. As we will learn in chapter 12, the rich-poor gap is actually increasing in almost all societies, suggesting that redistributionist ideologies of some sort will continue to evolve. The remedy is easier to describe than to translate into public policy. Countries willing to provide welfare for the very poor and restructure the economy to move destitute people out of poverty may avoid the kind of popular discontent that leads to revolution. Ideally, the time to eradicate poverty is before discontented workers and peasants acquire machine guns; eliminating an already well-established insurrectionary group such as Colombia's FARC might be doable, but it is clearly difficult. Similarly, helping Cuba make the transition from a dictatorial welfare state to something that satisfies both the Cubans and the American government will demand more wisdom and more generosity than either Washington or Havana has thus far displayed.

The menace from the hard right is more difficult to summarize, but clearly there are groups that treasure their membership in core nations and dislike immigrants from other "foreign" kinship groups. Some of these same groups are "disloyal patriots" in the sense that they maintain passionate affection for their ethnic community but despise the government and a variety of minority groups. Sometimes they lend their services as militias or paramilitaries to economic interests that employ them as blunt instruments against labor unions or social reformers. In most cases, they find violence fascinating and enjoy military symbolism. Where appropriate, these vigilante or white supremacist groups are a legitimate target for law enforcement. In other cases, they can be tempted into mainstream politics. The Italian neo-fascist movement, for example, was frightening in the 1960s and 1970s, but subsequently amalgamated with other parties of the far right to support conservative government coalitions in the Italian parliament.

Is the current level of hostility between the Christian or post-Christian West and the Islamic world fixable? The British and American governments have pursued a strategy of assuring mainstream Muslims that their culture is not under attack, and they are waging a "war against terrorism" on those movements deemed responsible for violence against Western interests. Ten years after the September 11 attacks, it is frankly difficult to declare this approach either a moderate success or a moderate failure. Others have felt that the West could defuse Islamist anger by lowering the U.S. military profile in the Middle East, and perhaps de-emphasizing U.S. support for Israel. There is no significant political support for this concessionary approach, although many foreign policy analysts believe it would improve the situation.

Clearly, al-Qaeda, and the Islamist movement behind it, is more than Osama bin Laden and will survive bin Laden's death. The organization has been the target of a determined and well-financed crusade by Western intelligence and law enforcement officials for close to a decade now and shows every sign of survival and resistance; Harvard's Jessica Stern credits al-Qaeda's resilience to "the organization's remarkably protean nature. Over its life span, al-Qaeda has constantly evolved and shown a surprising willingness to adapt its mission. This capacity for change has consistently made the group more appealing to recruits, attracted surprising new enemies, and . . . made it harder to detect and destroy."[47]

5. The Wrap: What Have We Learned?

You should have come away from this chapter with a more nuanced view of what the "far left" represents in the modern world. We covered the basic ideas of Marxism in chapter 8, looking at China and North Korea. In this chapter, we've focused on several more movements. You should be familiar with the two persistent guerrilla/terrorist armies in Colombia, the FARC and the ELN. It has always been difficult for Americans to be calm about Cuba, but try to digest the basic facts of Cuban history and the mechanics of the long-standing feud between Washington and Havana.

For young people growing up in the largely secular but generally Christian West, Islamic fundamentalism can be tough to comprehend, and yet—as the events of September 11, 2001, demonstrate—it is crucial that we put some effort into analyzing why a significant portion of the human race dislikes the United States so intensely. Make sure you've understood the basic tenets of Islamism. In this chapter, we've introduced you to what is known about Osama bin Laden, but al-Qaeda is history in the making, and you'll need to stay with the story in the months and years ahead.

We have repeatedly stressed that making a clear-cut distinction between ideological (or public policy oriented) groups and nationalist (or ethnic/linguistic/religious) groups is hard to do. Generally speaking, however, this chapter has surveyed a series of movements that are primarily concerned with how society is to be run. Moving to chapter 11, we will survey a series of conflicts that have nationalist passions at their core. After a quick look at the breakup of Yugoslavia, we'll try to make some sense of the Israeli-Palestinian brawl. Then we'll glance at two long-standing conflicts that might be healing: the Catholic-Protestant standoff in Northern Ireland, and the Tamil-Sinhalese saga in Sri Lanka.

Notes

1. Vladimir Lenin, *State and Revolution* (New York: International Publishers, 1932).

2. For Lenin's impact on Italian revolutionaries, see Richard Oliver Collin, "When Reality Came Unglued: Antonio Savasta and the Red Brigades," originally published in *Violence Aggression Terrorism* 3, no. 4 (1989):

269–96, and reprinted in Bernard Schechterman and Martin Slann, *Annual Editions: Violence and Terrorism 91/92* (Washington: Dushkin, 1991).

3. Sharon L. Wolchik and Jane L. Curry take us through this period in their *Central and East European Politics: From Communism to Democracy*, 2nd ed. (Boulder, Colo.: Rowman & Littlefield, 2010). Richard Pipes explains cogently why he didn't like what happened to Eastern Europe in his *Communism: A Modern History* (New York: Modern Library, 2001).

4. Professors Geoffrey and Nigel Swain explain the collapse of Eastern European communism in their *Eastern Europe since 1945* (New York and London: Palgrave Macmillan, 2009).

5. Florida University professor Ilja A. Luciak has given us a balanced view of Nicaragua's Sandinista revolution in his *The Sandinista Legacy* (Gainesville, Fla.: University of Florida Press, 1995).

6. For two other significant Latin American groups, see Cynthia McClintock's *Revolutionary Movements in Latin America: El Salvador's FMLN and Peru's Shining Path* (Washington, D.C.: U.S. Institute of Peace, 1998). For Peru, the University of Texas has one of the best general sets of links to everything available, both English and Spanish, at http://lanic.utexas.edu/la/peru. Peru's imprisoned Abimael Guzmán has his defenders in an International Emergency Committee that maintains a pro-Maoist site at www.csrp.org/iec.htm.

7. Richard Drake's *The Aldo Moro Murder Case* (Cambridge, Mass.: Harvard University Press, 1995); and a book by Richard Oliver Collin and Gordon L. Freedman, *Winter of Fire: The Abduction of General Dozier and the Downfall of the Red Brigades* (New York: Dutton, 1990) should help unscramble the complexities of political violence in Italy.

8. People who don't speak Spanish, can start researching Colombia with the United Nations website at www.un.int/colombia/english/index.html. The University of Texas site is at www.lanic.utexas.edu/la/colombia, but to get to the Colombia government's own website, point your browser at www.gobiernoenlinea.gov .co. There is a weekly magazine called *Semana* published in Bogotá that provides a lot of its material online at http://semana.terra.com.co/.

9. United Nations Development Programme, *Human Development Report 2011* (New York, United Nations, 2010), 127.

10. For an interesting book by an anthropologist, see Maria Clemencia Ramirez, *Between the Guerrillas and the State: The Cocolero Movement, Citizenship, and Identity in the Colombian Amazon* (Raleigh, N.C.: Duke University Press, 2011).

11. The complexities of Colombian life are well explained in David Bushnell's *The Making of Modern Colombia: A Nation in Spite of Itself* (Berkeley: University of California Press, 1993). Geoff Simons has a new *Colombia: A Brutal History* (New York: Palgrave, 2004).

12. Coastal Carolina University professor James D. Henderson has written some of the best books on this period: see his *Why Colombia Bled: A History of the Violencia in Tolima* (Tuscaloosa, Alabama: University of Alabama Press, 1985), and *Conservative Thought in Twentieth Century Latin America: The Ideas of Laureano Gómez* (Athens, Ohio: Ohio University Press, 1988), as well as his *Modernization in Colombia* (Gainesville: University Press of Florida, 2001). His latest, *Victim of Globalization: How the Illegal Drug Trade Destroyed Colombia's Peace*, is already a best-seller in Spanish and should be forthcoming soon in English.

13. Although he was once a prisoner of the FARC, reporter Gary Leech is not totally unsympathetic to their inspiration in his *The FARC: The Longest Insurgency* (London: Zed, 2011). See also his earlier *Beyond Bogotá: Diary of a Drug War Journalist in Colombia* (Boston, Mass.: Beacon, 2007).

14. Not everybody is equally delighted about the American decision to get involved in Colombia's civil war. The Center for International Policy in Washington site at http://www.ciponline.org/colombia/aid thinks it's a really bad idea. Predictably, the State Department at www.state.gov/www/regions/wha/colombia claims it will be money well spent. Go to www.farc-ep.org to get the FARC's story, but you'll need your Spanish to understand their official website.

15. The American political critic Noam Chomsky and his colleague Doug Stokes explain why they disapprove of Plan Colombia in *America's Other War: Terrorizing Colombia* (London: Zed, 2005). Witness for Peace is an NGO that also opposes Plan Colombia; find them at http://www.witnessforpeace.org/.

16. You should start with Julia E. Sweig's superb *Cuba: What Everybody Needs to Know* (New York: Oxford University Press, 2009).

17. See an excellent book by Adrian H. Hearn, *Cuba: Religion, Social Capital, and Development* (Raleigh, N.C.: Duke University Press, 2008).

18. The best general history of the island is perhaps Louis A. Pérez's *Cuba: Between Reformation and Revolution*, 2nd ed. (New York: Oxford University Press, 1995), but Clifford L. Staten has produced a newer one with his *The History of Cuba* (New York: Palgrave Macmillan, 2005).

19. See T. J. English, *Havana Nocturne: How the Mob Owned Cuba and Then Lost It to the Revolution* (New York: Morrow, 2009); and on the same theme, Peter Moruzzi's delightful *Havana before Castro: When Cuba Was a Tropical Playground* (Layton, Utah: Gibbs Smith, 2008).

20. Sebastian Balfour's *Castro: Profiles in Power*, 2nd ed. (New York: Longman, 1995) gives a good review of the Cuban leader's life. Jorge G. Castañeda has given us a balanced biography of Che Guevara in his *Campañero* (New York: Knopf, 1997).

21. Journalist Jim Rasenberger has reproduced some once-classified data on this event in his *The Brilliant Disaster: JFK, Castro, and America's Doomed Invasion of Cuba's Bay of Pigs* (New York: Scribner, 2011).

22. The Cuban Missile Crisis has generated a lot of books, but the best is perhaps Don Munton and David A. Welch, *The Cuban Missile Crisis: A Concise History* (New York: Oxford University Press, 2006). Anyone wanting to get a sense of the contemporary drama should also look back at Robert F. Kennedy and Arthur Schlesinger Jr., *Thirteen Days: A Memoir of the Cuban Crisis* (New York: Norton, 1999).

23. Nobody's neutral when it comes to Cuba. For the crumbling American embargo against Cuba, check out Patrick Haney and Walt Vanderbush, *The Cuban Embargo: Domestic Politics of American Foreign Policy* (Pittsburgh, University of Pittsburgh Press, 2005). Also worth a look are Peter Schwab's *Cuba: Confronting the U.S. Embargo* (New York: Palgrave Macmillan, 2000); and Joaquín Roy's *Cuba, the United States, and the Helms-Burton Doctrine* (Gainesville, Fla.: University Press of Florida, 2000).

24. Contrasting views of daily life in Cuba can be found in Amelia Rosenberg Weinreb, *Cuba in the Shadow of Change: Daily Life in the Twilight of the Revolution* (Gainesville, Fla.: University Press of Florida, 2010); and Yoani Sanchez, *Havana Real: One Woman Fights to Tell the Truth about Cuba Today* (New York: Melville House, 2011).

25. Here are some dueling websites to visit to get a sense of how mad Cuba can make people. See www.nocastro.com for the Cuban exile perspective, and then visit http://www.cubaonline.com.cu/to see what the Cuban government has to say about itself.

26. See Donald Sassoon, *Mussolini and the Rise of Fascism* (New York: HarperCollins, 2008). Robert O. Paxton's *The Anatomy of Fascism* (New York: Knopf, 2004) is a scholarly introduction to the movement.

27. Michel Mann has studied European fascist movements in his *Fascists* (Cambridge, UK: Cambridge University Press, 2004). Also see Cas Mudde's *The Ideology of the Extreme Right* (Manchester, UK: Manchester University Press, 2003).

28. To get a sense of their preoccupations, visit the British National Party website at http://www.bnp.org.uk/, although you are warned that the information contained there is spectacularly inaccurate.

29. If your French is up to it, you can visit the French *Front National* at http://www.frontnational.com/ where you can see that Marine Le Pen runs an altogether smoother operation than does the British National Party.

30. If you want to track U.S. hate groups of various kinds, visit the Southern Poverty Law Center online at http://www.splcenter.org. The "official" KKK holds forth at www.kkklan.com, but for a "message of love not hate" go to the website of the "Christian" Klan, where you can buy your KKK T-shirt.

31. See Darren Mulloy, *American Extremism: History, Politics and the Militia Movement* (New York: Routledge, 2004). More dueling websites: Are you an extremist? Check out www.americannaziparty.com, which is home base for America's premier right-wing extremist organization and helpfully supplies links to everybody else in this sector of violent politics.

32. In his book *Our Own Backyard: The United States in Central America, 1977–1992* (Durham: University of North Carolina Press, 1998), Professor William M. LeoGrande makes the uncomfortable case that the United States shares some of the blame for the prevalence of Central American death squads. Bruce B. Campbell and Arthur D. Brenner have put together an overview anthology of violent right-wing paramilitaries in their *Death Squads in Global Perspective: Murder with Deniability* (New York: Palgrave, 2000).

33. See *Freedom in the World 2011* at www.freedomhouse.org.

34. Bernard V. Brady, *Essential Catholic Social Thought* (New York: Orbis, 2008), 257–67.

35. A French scholar named Gilles Kepel has written *The War for Muslim Minds: Islam and the West* (Cambridge, Mass.: Harvard University Press, 2004) to argue that Islamic fundamentalism is already a failed movement, kept artificially in existence by Western animosity.

36. The classic history of the Arab people was written by Albert Hourani, *A History of the Arab Peoples*, 2nd ed. (Cambridge, Mass.: Harvard University Press, 1991). Another standard reference is Bernard Lewis, *The Arabs in History* (New York: Oxford University Press, 2002).

37. Rory Carroll, "Nigerian Woman Escapes Death by Stoning," *The Guardian*, September 26, 2003, www.guardian.co.uk/world/2003/sep/26/rorycarroll?INTCMP=SRCH.

38. For Islamism in the Sudan, see Robert O. Collins, *A History of Modern Sudan* (Cambridge, UK: Cambridge University Press, 2008), although South Sudan seceded after this excellent book was written. See Beverley Milton-Edwards, *Islamic Fundamentalism since 1945* (London: Routledge, 2005).

39. See Timothy Phillips, *Beslan: The Tragedy of School No. 1* (London: Granta, 2008).

40. To get a sense of the sweep of Afghanistan's history and people, look at the late Louis Dupree's classic *Afghanistan* (Princeton, N.J.: Princeton University Press, 1978).

41. For the general history from 1978 to the Taliban takeover, see Barnett R. Rubin's massive *The Fragmentation of Afghanistan* (New Haven: Yale University, 1995). A British scholar/activist named Peter Marsden wrote the compelling *The Taliban: War, Religion, and the New Order in Afghanistan* (London: Zed, 1998). Journalist Ahmed Rashid has covered South Asia for twenty years and this expertise shows in his *Taliban: Militant Islam, Oil and Fundamentalism in Central Asia* (New Haven: Yale University Press, 2000).

42. The "basic" book is probably Thomas Barfield's *Afghanistan: A Cultural and Political History* (Princeton, N.J.: Princeton University Press, 2010). Also see Seth G. Jones, *In the Graveyard of Empires: America's War in Afghanistan* (New York: Norton, 2009). Stephen Tanner's *Afghanistan: A Military History from Alexander the Great to the War against the Taliban* (Philadelphia, Pa.: DaCapo/Perseus, 2009) makes for very depressing reading.

43. There have been a large number of books written about 9/11, but we all need to be cautious about accepting some of the more outlandish conspiracy theories that have arisen from the ashes of the twin towers. No established academic specialist believes that the tragic episode was anything other than what it seemed to be, four parallel suicide missions carried out by members of al-Qaeda. Lawrence Wright's *The Looming Tower* (New York: Vintage, 2007) is a thorough and systematic rendition of established facts.

44. Peter L. Bergen's *Holy War: Inside the Secret World of Osama bin Laden* (New York: Free Press, 2001) is generally well researched and reliable. In 2006, Bergen gave us *The Osama bin Laden I Knew: An Oral History of al Qaeda's Leader* (New York: Free Press, 2006).

45. Fawaz A. Gerges takes the view that al-Qaeda was a spent force even before the death of its leader. See his *The Rise and Fall of al-Qaeda* (New York: Oxford University Press, 2011). Peter L. Bergen, however, does not see a final victory over Middle Eastern terrorism as imminent; see his *The Longest War: The Enduring Conflict between America and al-Qaeda* (New York: Free Press, 2011).

46. Former U.S. government official Bruce Riedel's *The Search for al Qaeda: Its Leadership, Ideology, and Future* (Washington, D.C.: Brookings, 2008) is short but competent.

47. Jessica Stern, "The Protean Enemy," *Foreign Affairs* 82, no. 4 (2002): 27–40.

CHAPTER 11

The War of the Heart
VIOLENT NATIONALIST CONFLICT

"Tweedledum and Tweedledee agreed to have a battle," wrote Lewis Carroll, making fun of soldiers, politicians, and their wars.[1] Born after the Napoleonic period and dying just before the Boer War erupted, the author of *Through the Looking Glass* was fortunate to have lived through a period of relatively minor military conflict. Alice and the rabbit hole, however, were a long time ago; today there seem to be more frequent and more savage wars. When the global conflict between the United States and the USSR came to an end, we were left with what the late Daniel Patrick Moynihan called "pandemonium," a world of ethnic or nationalist conflicts, many of them ancient and most apparently unsolvable.[2] Can you personally remember a time of peace? Many of today's university students will be in their late teens or early twenties; the United States has been at war since 2001, half a young person's lifetime.

In this chapter, we'll look at four well-known examples of nationalist conflict, all at different stages: the former Yugoslavia, Israel-Palestine, South Asia (Kashmir and Sri Lanka), and Northern Ireland. Not all scholars use precisely the same terminology to describe feuds such as these: some would say "ethnic" or "nationalist" conflict, while others would stress the role of real estate by calling them "territorial conflicts." This raises a question: does a given ethnic community want a given territory because they believe it is ancestrally theirs? Or because they need its resources for economic well-being? And it is easy to overlook the role played by economic inequality in those nationalist conflicts where one community is significantly richer than another. In this context, it may be worth noting that the Swiss, who enjoy a lofty standard of living, do not have guerrilla warfare among their several distinct national groups.[3] Here are some of the questions about nationalist conflict we'll be trying to answer in the pages that follow:

- *What background information do you need to understand ethnicities at war?* Do you recall, for example, what makes up a nation (as opposed to a sovereign state)? If not, go to chapter 4 and review. Remember at least that members of a given nation will typically (although not always) share a language, a sense of biological kinship, a national culture, a religion or religious heritage, territoriality or a feeling of ownership over a specific area, and a sense of national self-identification. In each of the conflicts under consideration, pay special attention to the roles played by language, religion, and territoriality.
- *Why do multinational states often suffer from internal conflict?* We'll spend the rest of this chapter answering that question, but you will recall that sometimes nations manage to create sovereign governments for themselves, becoming what are called nation-states. In less happy situations, two or more nations are obliged by history to coexist within one sovereign state and under the rule or misrule of one sovereign government, becoming a multinational state. There is normally at least some level of tension within every multinational state, and in the cases discussed in this chapter, competitive nationalisms have created varying levels of violence.
- *Where did Yugoslavia come from, where did it go, and why did so many people die in the process?* The twentieth century was the historical stage on which this Balkan tragedy was performed, from the country's hopeful beginnings after World War I to Yugoslavia's genocidal self-destruction in the 1990s. Today U.S. and NATO troops are still serving as peacekeepers in the former Yugoslavia, and courts in Holland are trying mass murderers. We'll try to unravel the process in section 1.
- *Will the Israelis and Palestinians ever find peace? What makes this particular ethnic dispute so diabolically difficult to solve?* We won't resolve this Middle Eastern conundrum in

section 2, but we'll try to make the history, the geography, the demography, and the politics a little less confusing.

- *How have religion and ethnicity combined in South Asia to create such a bewildering brew of angry conflicts?* We'll glance first at the feud most likely to involve nuclear weapons, the dispute between India and Pakistan over the disputed territory of Kashmir. Then section 3 will take us to the disputes within India itself between its Muslim and Hindu citizens. Finally, we'll look at the Hindus-versus-Buddhists brawl in Sri Lanka, which moved to a new level of horror in 2009–2010.

- *Why do Protestants and Catholics get along everywhere but in Northern Ireland? What are the prospects for peace in this historically troubled corner of the United Kingdom?* Relations between England and Ireland have been rocky for about a thousand years, but a corner of sorts may have been turned in the 1990s, and Northern Ireland is substantively at peace today. In section 4, we'll see why the civil war happened, and how it (mostly) ended.

Languages and Methodology

Of the four conflicts to be considered in this chapter, only the Northern Ireland example can be studied competently by English-only scholars. A scholar can never get very far into a violent conflict without learning the relevant languages at some level of proficiency. The other three conflict areas in this chapter involve a confusing welter of different and difficult languages, few of which are commonly spoken or taught in Europe or North America. South Asia or Middle Eastern professors, journalists, and government officials routinely speak English, but limiting your research interviews to these well-educated intellectuals involves several methodological problems.

Wealthier and more Western-oriented people are more liable to speak English than malnourished farmers or slum dwellers. They are also far less likely to become revolutionaries or suicide bombers, who typically do not speak English and therefore cannot explain to you the motives for their drastic political choices. If you only speak English, you can only talk to representatives of a given social (and sometimes political) class, who may only tell you what they want you to hear or they think you want to hear.

Perhaps more fundamentally, when you let people explain their culture to you in English, you lose an important immediacy of contact with the roots of the culture itself. There are complicated words and phrases in foreign languages that don't always render well in European languages. A language embodies and embraces the culture that generates it; really understanding the people of a foreign society means really knowing the language.

---

1. The Shattering of Yugoslavia

Since the early 1990s, the global community has puzzled over a part of the Balkan Peninsula that seemed unwilling or unable to join Europe's overall march toward peace and prosperity. After World War I, the victorious allies tidied up the real estate in the Balkan Peninsula by creating a political entity that was known for most of its unhappy history as "Yugoslavia."

This country fell apart spectacularly as the Cold War ended, and NATO troops are now stationed in several of the country's successor states. Getting NATO in was tough; extracting NATO is liable to be significantly tougher.[4] Despite the presence of international peacekeeping forces, the antagonisms that had generated the violence have merely been contained, and only minimal real progress has been made toward healing the underlying hatreds.

A SHORT, UNHAPPY HISTORY OF THE SOUTH SLAVS

The geography of the Balkan Peninsula contains great contrasts. The coastal plain is lush and gorgeous, with deep azure waters and tiny islands made for millionaires and their yachts. The interior is craggy and mountainous; in places, the land is so rough that parts of it are only suitable for goats.

The eastern coast of the Adriatic Sea has been an ethnic meeting ground and sectarian battlefield for most of its history. When the area was still the Roman province of Illyria, the Romans divided their empire administratively in 395 AD between East and West, with the new border running right through what later became Yugoslavia. When the Roman Empire collapsed, the West generally fell under the spiritual leadership of the Roman pope, and in the Balkan Peninsula, the people of what is today Croatia and Slovenia became Roman Catholic. At the same time, the Eastern Roman Empire generally became Orthodox Christian, a religious movement that dominated the eastern areas of Macedonia, Serbia, and Montenegro. Caught as always in the middle, Bosnians split their religious identification between the two rival branches of Christianity.[5]

With the collapse of the Roman Empire, Slavic-speaking peoples moved into the area. A member of the Indo-European family of languages, the Slavic language group is a collection of very closely related cousin languages. Russia and Polish are both from the northern branch of this language community, while Slovenian, Serb, and Croat are South Slav tongues. Complicating this language mix was the persistence in the region of several dialects of Albanian, a separate Indo-European language completely unrelated to the Slavic family. Some South Slav languages/dialects had a high degree of mutual intelligibility, and others did not; the ability of South Slavs to communicate with one another was further hampered when Serbians and Montenegrins imitated other Orthodox Christians by using the Cyrillic alphabet, while Croatians and Slovenians adopted the roman script. Thanks to the difference in scripts, people who could talk to one another sometimes could not read each other's alphabets.[6]

It has always been hard for independent sovereign nation-states to survive in central Europe. For much of their history, the Christian Orthodox countries of Serbia, Montenegro, and Macedonia were controlled by the Muslim Ottoman (Turkish) Empire. Slovenia and Croatia were conquered by the Roman Catholic Austro-Hungarian Empire. Life for little Bosnia, on the other hand, became intensely confused. After a short period of independence, Bosnia followed Croatia into the Austro-Hungarian Empire. After the 1389 **Battle of Kosovo** (a heroic defeat for the Serbs), the Ottoman Turks conquered both Serbia and Bosnia. During the long years of subordination to a Turkish and Muslim government, a significant number of Bosnians converted to Islam. For their Christian neighbors, this was more than a religious choice; it was a kind of national betrayal, and both Roman and Orthodox Christians in the region have tended to dislike their Muslim neighbors ever since.[7]

Map 11.1.   The Former Yugoslavia
When it was a unified state, Yugoslavia had six constituent republics: Slovenia, Croatia, Bosnia-Herzegovina, Serbia, Montenegro, and Macedonia. Subordinate to Serbia were the two "autonomous" provinces of Vojvodina and Kosovo. Yugoslavia disintegrated in the early 1990s, with Slovenia, Croatia, Bosnia, and Macedonia all becoming sovereign states with seats in the United Nations. As the name "Yugoslavia" disappeared, Serbia and Montenegro remained linked in a tenuous federal state called simply "Serbia and Montenegro," which dissolved in 2006. The battle-torn province of Kosovo in the South is still technically part of Serbia, but most Kosovars are ethnic Albanians, and the United Nations has administered the province since the 1999 war.

Bosnia was later "rescued" by the Austrians in 1878 and incorporated into the Austro-Hungarian Empire until World War I. With the Turks no longer able to protect their Bosnian Muslims, the Islamic community in Bosnia became isolated.

The twentieth century was tough on empires. World War I began with a quarrel between the Austrians and Serbians over Bosnia, and ended with the extinction of both the Ottoman and Austrian-Hungarian empires. The peacemakers at Versailles in 1918–1919 decided that the communality of language would justify the creation of one sovereign state from the six fragments of two shattered empires.

Slovenia, Croatia, Bosnia, Serbia, Montenegro, and Macedonia were therefore unified under a Serbian monarchy. Eventually adopting the name "Yugoslavia," this artificial little country was occupied by the German and Italian armies in World War II. Led by a charismatic communist named Josef Broz Tito (1892–1980), a partisan movement took the field against the Axis Powers and Tito's Marxists seized control of the country in 1945. The feisty Marshall Tito refused to submit to totalitarian rule from Moscow, however, and Yugoslavia broke with the Soviet Union in 1948. Aware of the explosive power of ethnicity, Tito organized Yugoslavia into a federal system in which each of the six principal sub-sovereign entities was called a "republic."[8]

At first, there seemed a chance that this multinational state could succeed. During its years of unity under Tito, many citizens of Yugoslavia self-identified as "Yugoslavs," and

Table 11.1. A Yugoslav Time Line

1918:	Modern Yugoslavia created at Versailles
1943:	Nazi Germany invades Yugoslavia
1945:	Tito's Communist Party takes power
1948:	Tito breaks with USSR
1980:	Tito dies
1989:	Slobodan Milosevic takes power in Serbia-Montenegro
1991:	Multilateral fighting begins as Slovenia, Croatia, and Macedonia secede
1992:	Bosnia secedes and Bosnian Civil War begins
1995:	Dayton Accords bring end to Bosnian Civil War
1998:	Muslim Kosovar Albanians rebel against Serbia
1999:	NATO halts genocidal Serbian attack on Kosovo
2001:	Slobodan Milosevic delivered to UN tribunal in Holland
2006:	Montenegro secedes from Serbia.

the beginnings of an amalgamated national culture emerged. Croats, Bosnians, Serbians, and Montenegrins could all communicate with minimal difficulty, while Slovenians and Macedonians typically learned Serbo-Croatian as a second language.

This nonaligned country prospered only as long as Marshall Tito controlled it and the USSR frightened it. Tito died in 1980, and the Soviet Union became less menacing after Mikhail Gorbachev took the helm in 1985. Nationalist politicians in the several republics began to convince Slovenians, Croats, Serbs, Macedonians, and Muslim Bosnians that they were all foreigners to one another.

In 1989, the Serbians elected a former communist named Slobodan Milošević to the presidency. Whatever he may privately have believed, Milošević reinvented himself as a fanatical Serbian nationalist, frightening non-Serbian Yugoslavs. In 1991, wealthy, modern Slovenia fought a successful ten-day war for independence, and won its sovereignty. Croatia followed suit, but it took a two-year war before the Zagreb regime was able to claim independence, albeit with the considerable loss of territory. Macedonia also became independent in 1991, leaving only Bosnia and Montenegro as part of the original Yugoslavia.[9]

SOCIETAL MAYHEM IN BOSNIA

Bosnia (or Bosnia-Herzegovina, to give it its full formal title) had always been an ethnic melting pot where Croatian Roman Catholics and Serbian Orthodox Christians and Muslims got along reasonably well. In fact, Bosnians were fairly secular, and religion served more as a national or ethnic marker than anything else. There had always been more intermarriage among Bosnians than there had been elsewhere, and many Bosnians self-identified simply as Yugoslav.

This tolerant, multiethnic Bosnia watched nervously as Yugoslavia fell apart, fearful of being left to the mercies of an increasingly nationalistic Serbian leadership. There was little agreement among Bosnians on what course to take. Croatian-Bosnians generally wanted their portions of Bosnia to join the newly independent Croatia, while Bosnian Serbs proclaimed their allegiance to Serbia. Supported only by native Muslim Bosnians, the country's leadership declared independence in March of 1922. Bosnia's Serb population rebelled instantly, effectively seceding from this secessionist state.[10]

Table 11.2.   Ethnicity in Bosnia

	Croats (17%)	Serbians (31%)	Bosnian Muslims (44%)
Religion	Roman Catholic	Orthodox Christian	Sunni Islam, although secular until recently
Language	Croatian dialect of Serbo-Croatian	Serbian dialect of Serbo-Croatian	Generally the Serbian dialect of Serbo-Croatian
Alphabet	Roman	Cyrillic	Alphabet of dominant local community
Imperial Heritage	Austrian	Ottoman	Confused
Foreign Focus	Western Europe	Central Europe	Middle East, Turkey

There are observable cultural differences among these three population groups, but lots of countries have far greater ethnic variations among their subcultures and still manage not to slaughter one another. About 8 percent of Bosnians are of mixed ethnic heritage or belong to other small ethnic communities.

The civil war began in spring 1992 when Bosnian Serbians moved quickly and ruthlessly to seize as much of the country as possible. Methodically, they forced Bosnian Muslims to flee by carrying out large-scale massacres, the execution of captured combatants, and the systematic rape of Muslim women, a strategy known as "ethnic cleansing."[11] As three-cornered fighting raged, the international community found it difficult to agree upon a coherent response. Perhaps as many as three hundred thousand people, most of them Muslims, died while the world dithered. The role played by the United States during this period was controversial. While the Clinton administration eventually played an active role in bringing this episode of societal mayhem to an end, American intervention was hesitant, with armed forces only arriving after the worst was over.[12]

In 1995, a tough American diplomat named Richard Holbrooke bullied the contending factions into an agreement called the Dayton Accords, after which NATO moved twenty thousand peacekeepers into the country.[13] The Dayton Accords were intended to create a unified Bosnian state, but fifteen years later, the Serbs were still ruling their portion of Bosnia without much reference to Sarajevo, while the rest of the country remained under an uncomfortable joint Croatian-Muslim administration. On the other hand, NATO and the Dayton Accords have halted ethnic cleansing and produced a relatively stable government. Some of those who committed genocide have been brought to trial, and the NATO mission counts as a moderately successful (if belated) humanitarian intervention.[14]

KOSOVO AND THE 1999 NATO WAR

Most politicians gather popularity by winning wars, but Slobodan Milošević seemed to gain influence every time another piece of his country disappeared. In fact, the power of the Yugoslav leader stemmed largely from his ability to portray Serbia as the eternal victim, misunderstood and abused by the outside world and betrayed by its enemies within an ungrateful South Slav community. These rhetorical talents came to the fore again when the Serbian province of Kosovo finally boiled over in 1999.[15]

The importance of Kosovo to Serbia is more emotional than economic; Kosovo is where the Serbs fought and lost an epic battle against the Ottoman Turks in 1389, and the area has some of the same sentimental appeal that the Alamo would have for Americans or Dunkirk for Britain.

Albanian-speakers have lived in the Balkan Peninsula longer than have the Slavs. Most of them were conquered and converted to Islam by the Ottoman Empire in the 1400s, managing by the 1800s to carve out a small and impoverished national state in the present-day Republic of Albania. Other ethnic Albanians, however, continued to live under Serbian rule, predominantly in Kosovo (where they are often called "Kosovars" or "Kosovar Albanians"). Over time, Albanian-speakers became the majority of Kosovo's population. During the Tito years (1945–1980), Albanians enjoyed substantial local self-government, studying, publishing, and broadcasting in their own language. After Tito died, however, Kosovar Albanians began agitating for even greater autonomy or even independence. In 1989, newly elected Serbian president Milošević slammed the Kosovars brutally, removing most local government and many civil rights. A separatist group called the Kosovo Liberation Army struck back, launching guerrilla attacks on Yugoslav army and police units. By 1998, the situation had degenerated into a low-intensity conflict, and the Europeans and Americans were anxious to avoid another Bosnia.[16]

When negotiations failed, the Yugoslav Army and an assortment of Serbian paramilitary forces stepped up their atrocities against the Kosovar Albanians. On March 24, 1999, NATO air forces intervened with a bombing campaign designed to force then president Milošević back to the bargaining table. Instead, the Serbians escalated into societal mayhem, driving about eight hundred thousand Kosovars into exile and murdering close to ten thousand of them. The NATO aerial campaign lasted for seventy-eight punishing days before the Belgrade authorities withdrew their troops from Kosovo. After-action analysis suggests that Milošević retreated only when faced with the real prospect of a NATO ground invasion.

After the effective loss of Kosovo, the Serbs finally turned on Milošević, voted him out of office, and handed him over to The Hague for a trial that was still underway in March 2006 when he died of a heart attack. The United Nations took over the messy business of providing a government for the province in the form of the UN interim administration in Kosovo.[17] The province was left in legal limbo, however, since the Western world was reluctant to allow it to secede formally from Serbia, although there was no practical likelihood that Muslim Kosovars would ever again live willingly under the rule of a people who had tried to exterminate them. Kosovo's legal status is complicated. The UN has largely delegated governance in the territory to the European Union, although NATO forces are still there. Kosovo is internally self-governing, and its parliament has declared a unilateral independence that is recognized by the United States and most European states, but not by Serbia itself. The border between the two countries has yet to be firmly established, and there are residual problems involving Serbs who live in what is fast becoming an independent Albanian-speaking state. There has been no suggestion that Kosovo merge with the Republic of Albania, and the two sets of Albanians speak different dialects of the same language.[18]

At this point, all that was left of Yugoslavia was the two very unequal republics of Serbia (with some six million people) and Montenegro and its six hundred thousand inhabitants, a union that dropped the name "Yugoslavia" in favor of "Serbia and Montenegro."

As mentioned in chapter 4, the Montenegrins voted in May 2006 to divorce the Serbs and become a sovereign country. Montenegro has now been admitted to full membership in the United Nations in its own right.

2. The Israeli-Palestinian Conflict

There is a tendency for journalists to overstress the ancient character of this conflict. Clearly, various tribes and nations have fought over the land of the eastern Mediterranean at many points in human history, but these ancient combatants were not actually the modern **Jews** and the **Arab Palestinians**. At its most intense level, this crisis is really a product of the twentieth century, and it only became a source of international tension after World War II. Apologies to those for whom this is obvious, but it is crucial to get these distinctions right.

In a sense, the bitter tribal feud between Israelis and the Palestinians ought to be internationally less significant than it is. The territory at issue contains no strategic resources and a comparatively small population. The Cold War is two decades behind us, so it is no longer a case of American-sponsored Israelis fighting pro-Soviet Arabs.

When religion and ethnicity enter the fray, however, conflicts that are objectively marginal have a way of becoming emotionally central, and the Israeli-Palestinian feud has become one of the most persistent and most intractable struggles on the planet, poisoning relationships at both a global and a regional level. While successive American governments have been staunch in their defense of (and material support for) Israel, many Europeans are horrified at the unending nature of the quarrel and the passions it generates. Americans typically see Israel as feisty and courageous, and sometimes see Europeans as anti-Semitic. For their part, Europeans sometimes view Zionism as a complicated form of colonialism, and they have lost patience with what they perceive as the endless violation of Palestinian civil liberties. While American political leaders deny a connection between Israel-**Palestine** and issues such as al-Qaeda, Iraq, and Iran, most Middle Easterners see the problem of Israel as the central and defining issue in their modern histories. Let's look briefly at this thorny dilemma.

WHERE THE PAST IS PROLOGUE

Understanding the Israeli-Palestinian conflict would be easier than it is if we could all agree on what to call this unhappy land. The real estate in question was once named Canaan, after the polytheistic **Semitic**-speaking Canaanite peoples who once lived there. A monotheistic tribal people variously called Jews, Hebrews, or Israelites moved into the area about 2000 BC and conquered most of it in a series of wars beginning in the 1200s BC. Around a thousand years before the Christian era, they established a small nation-state on the eastern shore of the Mediterranean, but this first Jewish homeland fissured in 922 BC; over the course of the next thousand years, the Jewish nation was attacked and conquered by a succession of Middle Eastern predators.

When the Romans acquired the territory in the years prior to the birth of Christ, they called it *Palestina,* the origin of the modern word "Palestine." Romans and Jews found each other uncomfortable company, and after one Jewish rebellion too many, the Emperor Hadrian decreed in 135 AD that the Jews had to leave. Many complied, migrating through the Roman Empire into Europe, although a Jewish community of uncertain size must have remained in the region.

In the 600s AD—more than four centuries after most Jews had left Palestine—the Islamic movement arose to the south in the Arabian Peninsula. Arab warriors spread their language, their new religion, and a lot of their DNA across the Middle East, conquering Palestine by 730 AD. At that time, Palestine was mostly populated by Orthodox Christians who spoke Semitic sister languages of Arabic, making it easy for them to learn Arabic, the triumphant language of the Qur'an (sometimes spelled "Koran"). Some of these Orthodox Christians accepted the language of their Arabian conquerors, but rejected the religion; about 15 percent of the Palestinians today are still Christians, although they identify strongly as Palestinian Arabs.

Now Arabic and mostly Islamic, Palestine was no more than a portion of the vast Arabian Empire, but Jerusalem was spiritually important to the Muslims and the Dome of the Rock became one of Islam's most important shrines. When the Arabian Empire disappeared, Palestine became once again a dependency of foreign kingdoms, eventually becoming a patchwork of several different sub-sovereign entities within Turkey's Ottoman Empire. If you're not clear on who's who in Israel-Palestine, take a close look at table 11.3.

Table 11.3. Palestinians and Israelis: National Ethnic Markers

Marker	Israeli Jew	Palestinian Arab
Religion	Orthodox Judaism is their "established" religion, but many Israelis are secular.	Most are Sunni Muslims, but some wealthier families are Orthodox Christians.
Kinship	While many Jews are biologically related, they are physically very different. Some are European in appearance; others are hard to distinguish from Arabs.	Most Palestinians of Arabian stock are not physically much different from Syrians and Jordanians in being moderately short and slender in stature, and in usually having dark hair and eyes and a tan complexion.
Language	With the revival of the ancient biblical language, Hebrew is national tongue, but many Israelis speak English as well as a variety of European mother languages, plus Yiddish and Ladino.	Arabic is their common language, spoken with an accent that is closer to Syrian than it is to Egyptian. English is the preferred second language for Palestinian Arabs.
Wealth	Most Jewish Israelis live comfortably, although recent immigrants can be disadvantaged.	A few are moderately wealthy, especially among West Bank Christian Arabs, but most Palestinians live on less than 10 percent of Israeli income, with malnutrition common among children in Gaza.

In the meantime, the descendents of Palestine's original Jewish population found themselves increasingly unwelcome in central and Eastern Europe, where many of them had lived for hundreds of years. By the last years of the 1800s, a Zionist movement had convinced many Jews that they needed to return to Palestine and re-create the Israel that had disappeared more than two thousand years earlier. The Jewish nationalism movement resembled other nineteenth-century nationalist movements and paralleled an essentially similar movement arising among the Arab people at the same time. These first Jewish pioneers arrived legally, becoming citizens of the Ottoman Empire, buying land, and setting up businesses in a mostly Muslim Arabic society. Initially, their appearance caused no alarm. Indeed, for many centuries, Jews had been living safely as a tolerated minority in Arab lands such as Egypt, Iraq, and Morocco, and those early Jewish settlers in Palestine were welcomed by their Arab neighbors.[19]

World War I (1914–1918) changed everything. The British took Palestine away from the Ottoman Empire in 1917, leading many Jews to hope that Britain might favor a substantial Jewish presence there. Immigration increased steadily in the interwar years

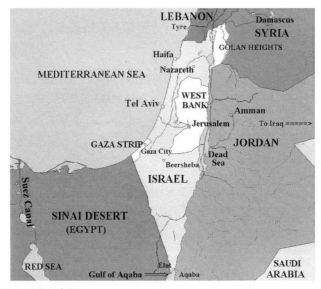

Map 11.2. Israel-Palestine
Israel conquered the Gaza Strip, the West Bank, the Golan Heights, and the center of Jerusalem in the controversial Six-Day War of 1967. Since that time, hundreds of thousands of Israeli settlers have gone to live in the West Bank, establishing settlements that the Israeli government will find difficult to surrender to a future Palestinian state. From the Palestinian point of view, obviously, it will be difficult to constitute a country with several hundred "foreign" settlements in the midst of their territory. Smaller numbers of Israeli settlers also moved into the Gaza Strip; in September of 2005, then prime minister Ariel Sharon removed Israeli settlements and soldiers from Gaza entirely, but kept most of the settlements in the West Bank. This problem clearly will not be solved without a major shift in social attitudes and huge concessions on both sides.

Table 11.4. Israel-Palestine Time Line

1917:	Britain conquers Palestine
1948:	Israel declares independence; most Palestinians driven into exile
1956:	The Suez War
1967:	Six-Day War; Israel conquers West Bank and Gaza
1973:	Yom Kippur/Ramadan War
1978:	Camp David Accords
1993:	Oslo Accords
2000:	The al-Aqsa Intifada begins
2004:	Yasser Arafat dies and is replaced by Mahmoud Abbas
2005:	Israel evacuates Gaza but retains much of West Bank
2006:	HAMAS wins Palestinian elections; second Lebanese Border War
2007:	HAMAS takes control of the Gaza Strip
2008:	Israeli War with HAMAS-controlled Gaza
2009:	Benjamin Netanyahu becomes Israeli prime minister

(1918–1939) particularly after the **anti-Semitic** Adolf Hitler took power in Germany. By the end of World War II, about one-third of Palestine's population was Jewish, including many survivors of the European Holocaust. Alarmed by this massive influx of Jews, Palestinians now felt threatened. A triangular intercommunal low-intensity conflict began with Palestinians and Jews fighting one another as well as the British Army.

Financially drained by World War II, Britain decided in 1947 to surrender the mandate for Palestine, handing over the problem to the United Nations. After studying the issue, the UN Security Council proposed a **Partition Plan** that put Jerusalem under international control and divided the rest of Palestine into six zones, three for the Palestinians and three for the Jews.[20] The Jewish community accepted the plan, but the Arabs rejected it, and the preexisting low-intensity conflict escalated quickly into a serious intercommunal war by November of 1947.[21]

THE SACRED BATTLEGROUND

While outnumbered in terms of overall population, the Jews of Palestine had both military experience and the financial resources to buy weapons. Leaderless and disorganized, the generally impoverished Palestinian community was unable to mount a coherent response to the determined Jewish challenge. On May 15, 1948, **David Ben-Gurion** proclaimed the existence of the Republic of Israel with himself as the country's first prime minister. Infuriated, all the neighboring Arab states declared war, and fighting raged intermittently until the armistice of January of 1949.

We have to use words when we talk about politics, but definitions can be devastating. The slaughter of European Jews during World War II was called *Shoah (catastrophe* in Hebrew). The Israeli war of liberation in 1948 was called *Naqba (catastrophe* in Arabic) by the Palestinians. Sometimes my liberation is your catastrophe.

Whatever your perspective, it was a limited victory; the Israelis failed to secure the Jerusalem city center, and the size and shape of the West Bank left the new country perilously thin in places (see map 1.1). For their part, the Palestinians lost virtually everything. A few families managed to hang onto their homes and form the core of the present Israeli Palestinian population (i.e., Palestinians who are legal citizens of Israel). Most fled from the fighting or were deliberately driven from what became Israeli territory and have never been permitted to return. The crack Jordanian Army crossed the Jordan River and seized most of Jerusalem and what is commonly described as the West Bank, but the Jordanians annexed this territory, rather than handing it over to the Palestinians as a homeland. The Egyptian Army hung onto the narrow coastal region called the Gaza Strip, which effectively became a giant refugee camp.

With less of the Promised Land than it had wanted, Israel got on with the task of nation building, bringing in Jewish refugees and immigrants from all over the world and quickly doubling its population. Independence did not, however, lead to international security. In league with the British and French, Israel fought with Egypt in 1956 (the so-called Suez War), worsening already sour relations with the Arab people. In 1967, Israel waged the famous Six-Day War, seizing the Sinai Desert, some territory between Israel and Syria called the Golan Heights, the Gaza Strip, all of Jerusalem city, and all of the West Bank.[22]

Figure 11.1. Yasser Arafat
Loved by many Palestinians and loathed by most Americans and Israelis, Yasser Arafat was at the center of both war and peace in Israel/Palestine from his university days in the 1940s to his death in 2004. His legacy is controversial, but his lifelong commitment to the Palestinian Liberation Organization was acknowledged to be total. Photo by Remy Steinegger, Courtesy of the World Economic Forum.

Victory without Peace

The Six-Day War created an impossible situation for both Palestinians and Israelis. At first, it was assumed that Israel would trade the conquered land for an Arab peace treaty, an approach demanded by the United Nations.[23] The Arabs demanded the land back before they would talk peace, however, and the Israelis wanted guarantees of peace before they would discuss the issue of land. Frustrated and furious, Palestinians turned increasingly to the late Yasser Arafat and his Palestinian Liberation Organization (PLO). Political terrorism in the form of air piracy and assassination quickly became a feature of Palestinian unrest while Israel responded with repetitive military reprisals.

Desperate to break out of the impasse, Egypt and Syria launched a surprise attack in October of 1973, variously called the Yom Kippur War (after the Jewish holy day) or the Ramadan War (after the Islamic Lent). Since the 1973 war provoked a troubling Arab oil embargo against U.S. interests, President Jimmy Carter brokered the Camp David Accords of 1978–1979. America's only major diplomatic success in the Middle East, Camp David generally took Egypt out of the equation by restoring the Sinai to Cairo's control and creating a "Cold Peace" between Egypt and Israel. But Camp David did nothing for the Palestinians, some of whom were refugees, while others languished under Israeli military control.[24]

Israel made a serious attempt at the physical elimination of the Palestine Liberation Organization in 1982, chasing Arafat's guerrillas through Lebanon all the way to Beirut, but the PLO escaped, leaving Israel bogged down in a Lebanese civil war. In December 1987, Palestinians in the West Bank and Gaza slid into an *intifada,* a low-intensity conflict involving rock throwing, civil disobedience, mob violence, and generalized resistance to Israeli authority.

In the early 1990s, Norwegian diplomats actually made what seemed at the time to be serious progress, organizing secret negotiations between high-level representatives of the Israeli government and the Palestinian Liberation Organization (PLO). By August 20 of 1993, Palestinians and Israelis had reached a set of agreements (called the **Oslo Accords**) that created a Palestinian National Authority with the power to govern many of the Arabs conquered by Israel in the 1967 war.[25] Some scholars believed that the Oslo Accords would establish a framework for eventual peace between Israelis and Palestinians, and the agreement did fundamentally change the way most Palestinians in the West Bank and Gaza Strip live their lives.

As part of the Oslo agreement, Palestinians at last said aloud what many of them had been saying privately all along: Israel would continue to exist as a sovereign state on a substantial portion of what had once been Palestine. For their part, the Israelis recognized that the Palestinian Liberation Organization legitimately represented the Palestinian people, and should be given some not-well-defined role in governing the Arabs who lived in "the territories" (i.e., the West Bank and the Gaza Strip).

The negotiators at Oslo had decided to get agreement where agreement was possible, so they simply put aside issues that were too fraught for compromise. Oslo made no provision for a future Palestinian state, nor did it establish that Arab east Jerusalem would fall under eventual Palestinian rule. It did allow the late Yasser Arafat to head his Palestinian National Authority (PNA), although this not-quite-a-government was soon accused of being corrupt and dictatorial. Only about 19 percent of the West Bank was under the exclusive control of the Palestinian National Authority, although the Palestinians also had the mostly worthless Gaza Strip.

Amos Oz

Sometimes great tragedy generates great literature, and the conflict between Israelis and Palestinians has produced several world-class literary talents. Amos Oz was born of Jewish parents in Jerusalem in 1939 and lived for most of his life on an Israeli kibbutz (or communal farm). Oz served in the Israeli Defense Forces (IDF) and was recalled as a reservist to fight in the 1967 and 1973 wars. As a writer, he became famous for novels like his 1972 *My Michael* (New York: Knopf) and the 1985 *A Perfect Peace* (San Diego: Harcourt Brace Jovanovich), in which he portrayed the Israelis as spiritually and emotionally traumatized by the endless, remorseless conflict with their Palestinian neighbors. In 2011, he released a collection of short stories called *Scenes from Village Life* (New York: Houghton Mifflin Harcourt), which has been praised as his best work.

For the past quarter century, Amos Oz has become a major advocate of reconciliation, helping to found the Peace Now movement in 1977, and continuing to call for the establishment of a Palestinian state in the West Bank and the Gaza Strip. Oz believes that nationalism has become a harmful obsession for humankind. As he said when accepting the 1992 Frankfurt Peace Prize,

> Even as I advocate the partition of one small land between two nations, I am still convinced that this is no more than a measure born out of necessity. . . . I think that upon this crowded, poverty-stricken, and decomposing planet of ours there should exist hundreds of civilizations, thousands of traditions, millions of regional and local communities—but no nation-states. . . . There ought to be ways of fulfilling yearnings for identity and self-definition within a comprehensive commonwealth of all humankind. We ought to be building a polyphonic world, rather than a cacophony of separate, selfish nation-states. . . . Flag-patriotism must give way to humanity-patriotism, earth-patriotism, patriotism of the forests, the water, the air, and the light.

After Oslo

Some conservative Israelis opposed the Oslo Accords, believing that too many concessions had been made to Israel's eternal enemies. Some super-Orthodox Israelis maintained that the entirety of what had once been Palestine was God's gift to the Israeli people and that relinquishing any part of it was blasphemy. Yitzhak Rabin, the prime minister who signed the Oslo Accords for Israel, was murdered by one such Israeli fanatic in November of 1995. Similarly, a lot of Palestinians believed Arafat had signed history's worst real-estate deal. Indeed, groups such as HAMAS felt strongly that the campaign of violence needed to be continued until what they called the "Zionist Entity" was destroyed.

More progress might have been made under Oslo had Rabin lived, but his Labour Party lost power after his death and was replaced by the right-wing Likud Party. The final nail in Oslo's coffin was driven by the controversial Ariel Sharon, known as the "Bulldozer" in Israeli politics. As leader of the nationalist Likud Party, Sharon provoked the Palestinians on September 28 of 2000 by approaching their sacred al-Aqsa Mosque near the Dome of the Rock in central Jerusalem with hundreds of armed police. Infuriated, Palestinians launched a new round of violent protests, often called the "al-Aqsa Intifada," which quickly evolved into suicide bombings and attacks on Jewish settlements in the West Bank. Stunned by the resumption of violence, Israel shifted dramatically to the right and elected Ariel Sharon prime minister in March of 2001.

Sharon's conservative and nationalist government ordered the Israeli Defense Force (IDF) to repress Palestinian violence with massive counterviolence, reoccupying much of the West Bank militarily and sealing off the Palestinian-controlled sections of Gaza. Despite international opposition to the policy, the Israeli government continued to establish and expand Israeli settlements in the West Bank, creating facts on the ground by taking over more of the land the Palestinians hoped to one day see incorporated into a Palestinian republic.

When Yasser Arafat died in November 2004, the PLO passed to the control of a pragmatic PLO veteran named Mahmoud Abbas, who opposed the use of violence by Palestinian militants against Israel.[26]

As a general, Ariel Sharon was famous for ignoring orders he didn't like, and his capacity for bold and controversial strokes stayed with him during his political career. By 2005, Prime Minister Sharon had concluded that negotiations with a fractious Palestinian National Authority were getting Israel nowhere. Instead, he decided, Israel needed to take unilateral decisions about keeping the territory that it wanted and surrendering what it didn't want. Ignoring objections from his own Likud Party, Sharon decided to evacuate the ultimately indefensible Gaza Strip, removing eight thousand angry Israeli settlers and handing the territory over to 1.2 million Palestinians.

Simultaneously, the Israelis began work on deciding what portions of the West Bank they would retain and what would be surrendered to the Palestinians, and then building a security barrier between the two separate portions of Palestine.

When Sharon's own Likud Party rebelled against the surrender of any land to the Palestinians, the prime minister struck back, resigning from his own party and forming a new one (called Kadima or "Forward") to support his new policy of unilateralism. You may recall from chapter 7 that Israel operates on a very simple version of the proportional representation system in which individual politicians can take their "share" of the vote with them when they create new parties. Kadima was an instant success, but Sharon yielded to age and poor health when he suffered a massive stroke in January of 2006 that left him in a coma. As prime minister, he has been followed by a series of figures from the right, or nationalist, side of Israeli politics.

Within the Palestinian National Assembly, there were two major parties, al-Fatah led by President Mahmoud Abbas, and HAMAS. In the January 2006 elections, HAMAS unexpectedly took a clear majority of the seats and nominated a HAMAS stalwart named Ismail Haniya to be prime minister. Since the Palestinian National Authority had never before functioned as a democracy, it was suddenly unclear whether the Palestinian government was really a French-style combination system (which would mean al-Fatah's Mahmoud Abbas would remain in overall charge) or a conventional parliamentary system (in which Ismail Haniya would be Palestine's new executive).

In the summer of 2006, a Shi'ite Lebanese group called Hezbollah (Party of God) kidnapped two Israeli troops near Israel's northern border. Israel unleashed a savage month-long war against Lebanon, briefly occupying the southern portion of the country and conducting bombing raids all over Lebanon. While clearly outgunned, Hezbollah fought back, and when the carnage was finished, neither side could claim to have scored much of a victory. The United Nations offered to send in yet another observer force to police the truce, with French and Italian forces taking the lead in what is liable to be a thankless task.

Isolated from the world and suffering massive poverty, Gaza teetered on the edge of a serious societal meltdown until it was taken over entirely by the HAMAS movement in 2007. There are now two separate and mutually hostile Palestinian governments: the Palestinian National Authority (PNA), which is dominant in the West Bank, and the Islamist and unrecognized HAMAS movement, which is supreme in the Gaza Strip. At the end of 2008, Israel responded to missile attacks from Gaza by launching a controversial month-long attack on the territory.[27]

THE FUTURE

By 2012, the Israeli-Palestinian situation was a stalemate (perhaps the worst since 1948), with no one very optimistic about a peace settlement any time soon. Despite a United Nations Security Council resolution calling for a two-state solution to the problem, the Israeli government was unwilling to commit itself to the establishment of a sovereign Palestinian entity with specific borders and any serious sovereignty. The status of Jerusalem was a completely unresolved issue, since the Palestinians demand that east Jerusalem be set aside as the future capital of a Palestinian state, and the Israelis were creating "facts on the ground" that would make Jerusalem Jewish forever. The creation of a hard-line rejectionist HAMAS government in Gaza offers no immediate prospect of improving the situation. The problem is complicated by the level of stark hatred that exists between the two nations. Hardly any Israelis have Arab friends or even acquaintances, and vice versa.

Figure 11.2. Unfriendly Friends
On May 20, 2011, Israeli prime minister Benjamin Netanyahu met at the White House with President Barack Obama. The two leaders have different and contrasting visions of what needs to happen to make peace in Israel/Palestine; reportedly, their negotiations did not go at all well: Mr. Obama demanded more concessions to the Palestinians than the Israelis wished to contemplate. At the press conference following their negotiations, Netanyahu and Obama put brave faces on their disagreement, but commentators noted their hostile body language with the American president holding onto his chair with one hand and his chin with the other, while Mr. Netanyahu lectured Mr. Obama with a stony face. Photograph courtesy of the White House Press Office.

The status of Israeli settlements and military outposts in the West Bank remains a crucial issue, even for very moderate Palestinians. About three hundred thousand Israelis live in areas conquered by Israel in the 1967 war. Palestinian zones are not contiguous, that is, they do not connect with each other, making it difficult to see how a Palestinian national homeland can be constructed there.

By May 2011, President Obama announced his support for pre-1967 borders as a start to Israeli-Palestinian peace talks. This suggestion was in response to Israeli prime minister Benjamin Netanyahu's strident remarks against the Palestinian application for recognition of statehood within the United Nations. Given the 2011 upheaval in the Middle East, world leaders in Europe and the United States have been keen to foster serious peace negotiations between the two parties.[28]

The demography of Israel-Palestine suggests that the problem—if left unsolved—can only become more difficult. At the moment, there are about ten million people who live between the Jordan River and the Mediterranean. While demographic figures differ, some scholars believe that only about 51 percent of these people are Jewish. The Muslim population is increasing about twice as fast as the Jewish population. At some point in the next decade, this balance will inexorably shift in favor of the Islamic Arab Palestinian population, and Arabs will be a clear majority by 2020. It is very difficult to see how an embattled minority of Jewish Israelis can live peacefully while maintaining control over a hostile majority, and at the same time, preserve both a democracy and the Jewish character of their political system.[29]

Alan Dowty sagely makes the point that the Israel-Palestine conflict has come to be perceived by the participants as a "**zero-sum**" contest, in which anything that is good for one side is automatically regarded as bad for the other side. For the Israelis to win completely, the Palestinians must lose absolutely, and vice versa. Both sides maintain a "you first" negotiating stance, in which the Israelis demand that the Palestinians halt all violence before any discussion of Palestinian independence can begin, while the Palestinians require their own sovereign state before they will agree to peaceful relations with Israel. Dowty predicts that there will be no resolution until both sides move from "zero-sum" thinking to recognition that they are involved in a "mutually hurting stalemate" that demands a negotiated settlement with significant sacrifices on both sides.[30]

Tough Choices: What Should America Do?

Some observers have described U.S. policy in the Middle East as schizophrenic. On one hand, Washington values good relations with oil-rich Arab countries, but the Arab world demands a more pro-Palestinian U.S. policy. While American society needs oil, its elected officials need votes, and most American politicians believe that high levels of political, economic, and military support for Israel will secure the loyalty of Jewish Americans and Christian conservatives. Consequently, Israel continues to be the leading recipient of U.S. foreign assistance and diplomatic support. In fiscal year 2001, the United States gave Israel about $2 billion in military and economic aid, in addition to military and intelligence support that would cost many billions of dollars if the Israelis had to pay for it. During that same fiscal year, U.S. aid to various Palestinian groups amounted to $85 million, none of which went directly to the Palestinian National Authority. Given this minimal level of support for the Palestinian cause, it is difficult for the United States to pose as an "honest broker" between these warring communities.

This central dilemma notwithstanding, U.S. leaders have all worked on the problem, although only President Jimmy Carter, with his Camp David Accords, ever achieved even limited success. After the al-Qaeda attacks on September 11, 2001, however, American attention was diverted by military operations against Afghanistan and then by the 2003 attack on Iraq. In April 2004, President Bush endorsed both Prime Minister Sharon's proposed withdrawal from the Gaza Strip and his decision to retain control over significant portions of the West Bank, irritating some peace-oriented Israelis and virtually all Palestinians. President Obama is said to be less pro-Israeli than was his predecessor, but he has yet to create a clear policy on the situation. By 2012, the Israeli and American governments regarded each other with some level of muffled hostility.

Can the United States play a meaningful role in this intractable problem? Both sides to the conflict demand U.S. involvement, although typically on their own terms. Palestinians often entertain distorted visions of the U.S. role in the world, insisting that America could make Israel behave; in practice, Israel is extraordinarily resistant to external pressure, even when it comes from Washington. The Middle East sometimes seems to be a giant minefield through which Americans are condemned to tiptoe forever.

3. The Gods of War in South Asia: From Kashmir to Sri Lanka

In a recent book, *Identity and Violence*, Amartya Sen reflects that we may self-identify in many different ways and slot ourselves into a variety of different categories.[31] What is most important to you: the language you speak, the religion you practice, the kinship group of which you are a member, or the citizenship written in your passport?

In many ways, these multiple identities are more complicated for South Asians than they are for Westerners. The subcontinent is home to dozens of major languages and thousands of minor ones. Kinship groups are multiple and confused, and citizenship has sometimes been imposed arbitrarily. As a partial consequence, religion can sometimes play a crucial role in self-identification—the business of deciding who you are and who your enemies might be. We'll start this section by remembering what we learned in chapter 3 about religion in South Asia, and see how contrasts and antagonisms among Muslims, Hindus, and Buddhists have fueled feuds between Pakistan and India over Kashmir, within India itself between Hinduism and other faiths, and in neighboring Sri Lanka between the Buddhist majority and the Hindu minority.

Map 11.3.   South Asia
This strategic geographical area is defined in different ways by various scholars, but it clearly includes at least the modern successor states of the former British India, which include Pakistan and Bangladesh, the Himalayan states of Nepal and Bhutan, the island country of Sri Lanka (once called Ceylon), and the Republic of India itself.

QUARRELING OVER KASHMIR

Of the three dominant religious traditions in South Asia, Hinduism is the largest and most ancient. The early history of Hinduism is far from precise, but the ancestors of today's Indian people seem to have settled in South Asia at least by 1500 BC. The religion they brought with them continued to evolve in the centuries that followed and was never strictly codified, coming to represent a wide variety of belief systems and religious practices.[32]

About five centuries before the advent of Christianity, several reformists challenged Hinduism; the most important was Buddha or Siddhartha Gautama (about 563–483 BC), who was impatient with Hinduism's caste system and hierarchy of gods and goddesses. While Buddhism remained a minority faith in India itself, one important variant called Theravada Buddhism spread south and east into Sri Lanka, Thailand, Cambodia, Burma, and Laos. Mahayana Buddhism became dominant in China, Japan, Korea, Tibet, and Nepal. Islam appeared in South Asia as a conquering faith, imposed by foreign military rulers. Islam's power reached its height under the Mughal emperors, who ruled from the late 1500s until the 1700s.

Europeans began the economic and political penetration of India as early as 1498, but the British Empire ultimately won the scramble to control almost the entire subcontinent. By the beginning of the 1800s, the London government dominated most of what is today India, Pakistan, Bangladesh, and Sri Lanka, either ruling directly or through local princes and maharajas. By the twentieth century, a group of intellectuals led by Mohandas K. Gandhi had formed the Congress Party to demand popular sovereignty for their country. The Congress Party proposed an independent, multinational state with many religious communities under a secular government.[33]

As Indian independence approached in 1947, however, fighting broke out between the two communities, forcing a portion of India's Muslims to escape north to what became the Islamic Republic of Pakistan. Initially, Pakistan included what is today the People's Republic of Bangladesh, but the Bengali people won their independence in 1971.

This wrenching apart of British India caused distress, death, and exile for millions on all sides, but nowhere was the tragedy more starkly defined than in a province called Kashmir (technically "Jammu and Kashmir" but usually simply "Kashmir"), for which, see map 11.4. This area is mountainous in the north and south, with a picturesque and potentially prosperous Vale of Kashmir in the center near the capital at Srinagar.

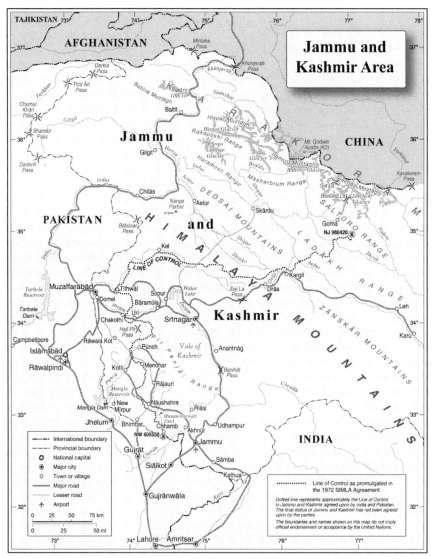

Map 11.4.   Jammu and Kashmir Area
Map No. 3953, rev. 4, December 2011. Courtesy of the United Nations.

Table 11.5.   The Kashmiri Crisis

1947–1949:	First India-Pakistan War divides Kashmir at Line of Control (LoC).
1962:	India loses northeastern Kashmir to China.
1965–1966:	Second India-Pakistan War leaves LoC unchanged.
1971–1972:	Third India-Pakistan War liberates Bangladesh.
1988:	New terrorist/guerrilla campaign against India
1998:	India and Pakistan develop nuclear weapons.
1999:	Bitter mountain fighting at LoC.
2001:	Terrorist attack in Delhi creates military tensions.
2004–2006:	Tentative peace initiatives mixed with intermittent terrorism with no real solution in sight

Under the British, a dynasty of Hindu maharajas reigned over a mostly Muslim Kashmiri population. When independence came to South Asia in 1947, the last of these princely Hindus decided to merge his kingdom with India. When the Pakistanis invaded to claim the territory as their own, Indian troops counterattacked in what became known as the First India-Pakistan War. When the United Nations established a cease-fire in 1949, Kashmir was divided along what came to be called the Line of Control (LoC). The West (Azad or "Free" Kashmir) and the Himalayan North were occupied by the new Islamic state of Pakistan. India grimly hung on to the rest of the South and East and the provincial capital at Srinagar.

The issue of Kashmir quickly became the focal point for the larger dispute between India and Pakistan, illustrating the differing self-images that the two young countries generated for themselves. Under the leadership of Mohandas Gandhi and Prime Minister Jawaharlal Nehru, India saw itself as a secular homeland for people of many faiths, notwithstanding its clear Hindu majority. While many Muslims had fled during the First India-Pakistan War, tens of millions of Muslims had stayed put and were living with their Hindu neighbors, in most cases peacefully. For the Indian leadership, therefore, it was crucial to the inclusive, multireligious character of this new democracy that Kashmir's Muslims find a place for themselves in India. Pakistan, on the other hand, was born of the principle that Muslims had a right to an Islamic government. For the Muslim leadership in Pakistan's capital city of Islamabad, Kashmir constituted a permanent irredentist complaint against their larger neighbor to the south.

Pakistan demanded a **plebiscite**, a national ballot that would allow the Kashmir people to choose by majority vote which country they wished to join, but the Indian authorities rigged local elections and announced that no national vote on the destiny of Kashmir was conceivable while a dictatorial Pakistani government controlled a significant portion of Kashmiri territory. In 1962, a long-standing border dispute with China exploded into high-altitude combat in which India lost control of sparsely populated portions of Himalayan east Kashmir. Two successive wars with Pakistan in 1965 and 1971 both saw heavy fighting in Kashmir, leaving the LoC unchanged but feelings more intense than ever.

From 1949 on, local separatist Muslims carried out armed resistance to the Indian government, assisted periodically by Pakistan irregular forces. India responded repressively, stationing large numbers of police and soldiers in the province, and responding to Islamic terrorism with government-inspired civil rights abuses. In 1988, the situation worsened as pro-Pakistani groups launched a sustained terrorist campaign against

Indian authority. As tension mounted, many Pakistanis and other Islamic fundamental-ists who had been fighting against the Soviet Union in Afghanistan moved south, their battle with the Russians crowned with victory and seeing Kashmir as the next theater for jihad against infidels.

Always prone to overreaction where Kashmir is concerned, India imposed direct rule from New Delhi and flooded the unhappy province (with a population of about seven million) with half a million troops in an attempt to seal off the border. The Pakistani armed forces have always been the dominant political force in Pakistan, and they are obsessed with the goal of "liberating" of Kashmir. With some justification, the Indian government charged that Pakistan was funding and directing the terrorist activities of several thousand mujahideen.[34]

Since 1989, Kashmir has been the scene of a low-intensity conflict on good days, with periodic spikes to high-intensity conflict. There have been periods when there was firing across the border nearly every day and tens of thousands of people have been killed. In 1998–1999, with both India and Pakistan deploying nuclear weapons, there was heavy fighting along the LoC, which ended only when world opinion pressured both sides to back down. In December of 2001, a Muslim suicide team assaulted the Indian Parliament in New Delhi, and although the attack failed, Indian authorities took their country again to the brink of nuclear war. In 2008, a commando team of Pakistani suicide gunmen assaulted several buildings in the center of Mumbai (the new name for Bombay), killing 250 Indians.

Thus far, efforts to resolve the crisis have been unsuccessful. Kashmiri Muslims tend to boycott elections for the state government. The Indian government is accused of forcing Kashmiris to vote at gunpoint and rigging the results to keep pro-Indian Muslims in power.

Since the al-Qaeda attack of September 11, 2001, the Kashmiri conflict has begun to blend in complicated ways with the U.S.-led "War on Terror." Countries such as India with indigenous insurgencies demanded U.S. cooperation in their domestic antiterrorist campaigns as the price for their help in the war against America's enemies, and relations between Washington and New Delhi have generally warmed.

Pakistan has made several important gestures of friendship toward India, but the Kashmiri situation remains substantively unresolved and constitutes one of the world's most dangerous flash points. Although it would kill millions of people, a nuclear exchange between Pakistan and India is far from unthinkable. Popular passions are high on both sides of the border. Any government making substantive concessions to the other side would face furious indignation from its own people. This conflict is going to be tough to solve.[35]

THE SRI LANKAN CONFLICT

While the American press has generally ignored it, one of the world's most savage na-tionalist conflicts exploded in Sri Lanka in 1983, displacing about a million refugees, and killing perhaps sixty-five thousand people. The violent portion of the conflict may have come to an end, or at least a transformation, in 2009. Who are these two "nations" at war? About three-quarters of the Sri Lankan people are Buddhists who speak the **Sinhala** language and are sometimes called Sinhalese. Hindus who speak a Dravidian language called Tamil are the principal minority, and conflict between these two rather distinct cultures and communities had been brewing for decades before it exploded into open war. Let's look at the background.

Sadness in Serendip

Squarely athwart east-west shipping routes, Sri Lanka was touched by a long list of conquerors. Visiting its shores, Arab explorers called it "Serendip" (from an Arabic term meaning a "happy surprise"), giving us the modern English word "serendipity." For most of its history, Sri Lanka was divided among feuding, independent principalities. One of these was a Hindu Tamil-speaking kingdom in the peninsular North of the country, which was culturally separate from the Sinhala-speaking Buddhists in the South: different language, different religion, different sense of ethnic self-identification.

Beginning in the 1500s, Europeans arrived in the form of the Portuguese, the Dutch, and the inevitable British who first landed troops, traders, and missionaries in 1795 and consolidated their power in 1833, making the whole island into the single Crown Colony of Ceylon.

Sri Lanka/Ceylon was one of the jewels of the empire, and the British restructured the economy to grow rubber and tea, importing even more Tamils from India to work on the tea plantations. English became the language of government and politics, although the British allowed local communities to use their own languages (primarily Sinhala and Tamil) freely in education and local civil administration. The xenophobic Sinhalese resented the British, who tended to favor the Tamils with contracts and government jobs.

When the British departed in 1948, they left behind a potentially viable political system. The education system was good, and the impact of the caste system, so crippling in India and Nepal, was minimal in Sri Lanka. Women enjoyed much higher social standing than in India, and a tolerant multiethnic democracy seemed distinctly possible.[36]

Unfortunately, the British also left behind a deeply divided society. About 74 percent of all Sri Lankans think of themselves as Sinhalese. The Sinhalese are passionate about their ancient tongue, and education is conducted uniquely in Sinhala through the university level, putting young Sinhalese at a commercial disadvantage in an English-speaking commercial world. Most Sinhalese are practitioners of Theravada Buddhism and believe that Buddhism should enjoy the status of a state-supported religion.

The vast majority of Tamils are Hindus, cousins to the sixty million Tamils who live in the nearby Indian state of Tamil Nadu. If the Tamils were one sovereign state (an idea that makes India and Sri Lanka both nervous) they would constitute one of the world's twenty largest countries. Wealthier and better educated, most Tamils (both in India and Sri Lanka) are cheerfully bilingual, bouncing back and forth between English and Tamil.

There is also the hint of a racial divide here: the Sinhalese are lighter in skin complexion and see themselves as the descendants of the ancient Aryan peoples who originally came from northern India, while the Dravidian Tamils are darker in skin tone.[37]

The Tigers from the North

Over the years since independence, the Sri Lankan government had evolved into something like the French combination system with an executive president and subordinate prime minister. If Sri Lankans had embraced the multiethnic character of their community, they might have established Sinhala and Tamil as dual official languages, with English serving as the nexus between the two communities and a bridge to the rest of the world.

As the dominant community, however, the Sinhalese controlled the government, enforcing their belief that they were Sri Lanka's "core nation." Hindu Tamil-speakers were essentially foreigners, and if they wanted to stay, they would need to accept permanent minority status. While a federal system might have been a more obvious choice for a multiethnic society like Sri Lanka, the Buddhist Sinhala majority established a highly centralized unitary system, which left Tamils feeling that their lives were controlled in a faraway city where no one spoke their language. To make matters worse, Sinhalese nationalists made Buddhism the state religion with a new constitution in 1974.

Inevitably, a Tamil independence movement was born, and in the 1977 elections, Tamil politicians favoring independence for Tamil Eelam swept the available seats in Tamil districts. "Eelam" means "homeland" in Tamil, and Tamil Eelam was the name for their prospective country. Young Tamils flocked into a paramilitary organization called the Liberation Tigers of Tamil Eelam (LTTE). The Tigers were led by a charismatic but ruthless guerrilla leader whose name was normally transliterated as Velupillai Prabhakaran.

By 1983, intercommunal fighting began in earnest, with both sides resorting to periodic savagery to achieve their military goals. The LTTE divided its energies between guerrilla warfare and blatant terrorism. Their most famous tactic was the use of human bombs: young girls were induced to wear explosives on their bodies and detonate themselves close to their targets. Tamil fighters customarily wore a cyanide capsule around their necks, preferring suicide to captivity. In the years of civil war that followed, nearly a million of Sri Lanka's nineteen million people became refugees, and as many as one hundred thousand were killed.

Inevitably, the giant Republic of India became involved. Tamils from India's Tamil Nadu state contributed money, supplies, and arms to the combatants. In 1987, Indian prime minister Rajiv Gandhi helped broker a cease-fire and then sent Indian troops to help enforce it. But the agreement was a disaster; within a few weeks, Indian army troops found themselves fighting the Tamil Tigers on their own turf while the Sri Lankan government faced a rebellion by Sinhalese hard-liners. The Indian troops withdrew in 1990, but not before the LTTE had sentenced Rajiv Gandhi (husband of the Sonia Gandhi discussed above) to death. A female suicide bomber blew him up in 1991, punctuating the remorseless character of South Asian politics.

When the Indians went home, Sri Lankans seemed to run out of ideas, and the war turned into an endless round of military battles and high-level assassinations. Because of Sri Lankan government censorship, it even became difficult for foreign observers to keep track of what was going on. Negotiations occurred from time to time, but the Tamils claimed much more land than they could ever hope to control militarily, and the Sinhala majority always refused to grant independence to what they regarded as a foreign immigrant community.

The Failure of Peace Initiatives

In December of 2001, the same Norwegian diplomats who had negotiated the Israeli-Palestinian Oslo Accords took up the Sri Lankan challenge. With their quiet, patient style of third-party diplomacy, the Norwegians brought representatives from the two sides together for discreet conversations about what would and would not be possible. The Tamil community had come to realize that it could never militarily achieve independence and that no Sinhalese leader could grant them independence and survive in office. For their part, the Sinhalese finally understood that the LTTE would fight forever unless some of its demands were met. By February of 2002, a cease-fire had been achieved.

Unfortunately, the politicians were unable to move beyond the cease-fire, which crumbled by the winter of 2006–2007 as open and particularly savage warfare began again. Prime Minister Mahinda Rajapakse moved up to become the country's president in 2006, and the island's military began preparations for a complete military victory over the Tamil Tigers. Fighting escalated throughout 2007 and 2008 as the Sri Lankan Army pushed ever more deeply into what had been Tamil-controlled territory. The final defeat of the Tigers in May of 2009 was particularly horrific, with terrified civilians being butchered as a by-product of the fighting. Tamil leader Velupillai Prabhakaran himself died in the fighting, although the precise circumstances are unclear.[38]

As of 2011, most of the North and Northeast of Sri Lanka is under military control, and large numbers of Tamils have been housed in camps under army control. It is as yet unclear whether the victorious Rajapakse government will feel the need or possess the capability of reaching out to the shattered Tamil community to achieve some sort of national reconciliation. By winter 2011–2012, the Colombo government was cracking down on opposition leaders and criticizing the UN report on national reconciliation in Sri Lanka.[39]

4. Sectarian Conflict in Northern Ireland

Throughout most of the twentieth century, an intractable political and terrorist war raged in Northern Ireland; most observers thought that the feud would be as perpetual a feature of European life as the Israel-Palestine crisis is in the Middle East. In the 1990s, however, what had been a serious low-intensity conflict began to mellow into a brisk adversarial conflict, still bitter, but generally nonviolent. There are still occasional corpses on the streets of Belfast, and many Protestants are still furiously antagonistic toward Irish Catholics, but the two communities have begun to solve their differences with ballots rather than bullets while continuing to maintain an enormous social space between them. Let us look more carefully at this fascinating story.

WHEN IRISH EYES STOPPED SMILING

Thanks to a long and turbulent history, the organizational and territorial structure of the UK can be hard to explain, so we need to start with some basics. The formal title of the country is the United Kingdom of Great Britain and Northern Ireland. At the least complicated level, this sovereign state today consists of four provinces. England is the largest, wealthiest, most populous, and politically the most significant. Wales and Scotland have now acquired their own provincial parliaments and are gradually redefining their status as sub-sovereign governments within the United Kingdom. England, Wales, and Scotland share the same island and are collectively called "Great Britain," a more commonly used term than is the slightly awkward "United Kingdom," which today is Great Britain plus Northern Ireland.

For more than seven centuries, Britain dominated the Emerald Isle, but in 1921, the southern and western portion of Ireland began the transition toward complete independence. What is now called the Republic of Ireland shares membership in the European Union with the United Kingdom, but the Republic of Ireland is a completely separate and independent sovereign state with its own seat in the United Nations.

The United Kingdom's fourth province is the northeastern corner of Ireland, and is formally called Northern Ireland (although many Protestants who live there prefer the term "Ulster"). A slight majority of the 1.6 million population is Protestant (mostly Presbyterian). Most want to remain part of the United Kingdom, fearing being submerged in an overwhelmingly Roman Catholic Ireland. They call themselves "unionists" because they desire a continued union with Great Britain, or "loyalists" because of their self-proclaimed loyalty to the British throne. A large minority of Northern Ireland's population is Roman Catholic, and many (but not all) of these Catholics would prefer to see Northern Ireland become part of the southern Republic of Ireland.

An Irish Catholic "Nationalist" is someone who wants unity with the nation of Ireland. A significant number of these Irish Catholic Nationalists have been prepared to use violence to unify Ireland and often call themselves "**Republicans**," which confuses Americans. In European politics, the term "republican" indicates nothing more than a dislike of royal families, in this case Britain's monarchy. In Ireland, a republican is typically a supporter of the Irish Republican Army (IRA), or the IRA's political wing, **Sinn Fein**, a legal political party operating in both the Republic of Ireland and in Northern Ireland.[40]

The Awful History

What actually happened in history is often less important than what people think happened, and Northern Ireland is cursed with two separate and distinct versions of a shared and contested past. Furthermore, Catholic Irish and Ulster Protestant both tend to see themselves as the innocent victims of their separate histories with the other community as the eternally hostile aggressor. How much common history can we establish?

Objectively, it seems to be the case that the original Stone Age occupants of both Great Britain and Ireland were overrun about 500 BC by Celtic-speaking people. Just before the Christian era, the Romans invaded England, but did not penetrate into the Celtic fringe of Ireland, Scotland, and Wales, although Christianity spread throughout the two isles. Ireland's original Celtic tongue evolved into Irish Gaelic in the same way that Latin became Italian.

In the 400s AD, the Roman Empire was pummeled by waves of barbarian invasions that brought German-speaking Anglo-Saxons to England. The Old English of these early Brits evolved after 1066 AD, when French-speaking Normans appeared and the two languages (Anglo-Saxon and French) merged to become Middle English and later modern English. William the Conqueror and his successors created a vigorous sovereign state in England, and in 1169, the Norman kings of England began the conquest of Ireland.

Here's the relevant formula: Nationalism + Religion = Trouble. For reasons that initially had little to do with Ireland, the British monarchy broke its religious ties with the Church of Rome in 1541, profoundly upsetting the fervently Catholic Irish. In order to maintain its hold over an increasingly restless Irish population, the London government began a policy of seizing land from rebellious Gaelic-speaking Catholic Irishmen and handing it out to English noblemen. In the 1600s, the government began moving large numbers of Presbyterian Scots into Northern Ireland as part of a deliberate plan to hold the land by creating a loyal local population. The Irish hated these settlers because they took their land away; religious doctrine had little to do with the quarrel. The people losing their land were Catholic Irish, and the folks seizing it were Protestants from across the water, so religion and national self-identification became fatally mixed.[41]

Between 1688 and 1690, the British staged their "Glorious Revolution" to rid England of the unpopular and pro-Catholic Stuart King James II. His rival was a solid Dutch Protestant named William of Orange. The final iconic battle between the two kings was a brawl along Ireland's Boyne River that William won handily, an event that modern Ulster Protestants celebrate on July 12 every year by wearing Orange sashes and banging loud drums while marching through Catholic neighborhoods; in 2010 and 2011, these "Orange Day" marches produced unusually violent rioting in Belfast.

For the following two centuries, moderate English and Irish leaders looked for a way of combining Ireland's desire for self-government with Britain's colonial ambitions, but Protestant landowners were always able to prevent the British Parliament from making any significant concessions. The Irish Potato Famine of 1845–1847 starved hundreds of thousands of Irish, drove even more to emigrate, and profoundly embittered the Irish people. When Britain failed to enact Home Rule for Ireland on the eve of World War I, Dublin skidded into insurgency with the 1916 Easter Rebellion, triggering a 1919–1921 separatist war that was waged against the British by an armed group called the Irish Republican Army and a political movement called Sinn Fein.[42]

Divided Ireland

The inconclusive rebellion produced a muddled result that pleased no one. In 1921, Britain grudgingly conceded substantive independence to the twenty-six counties in the South and West of Ireland. The six counties that became Northern Ireland, however, had Protestant majority populations and were therefore retained as part of the United Kingdom.

The IRA-Sinn Fein movement refused to accept this settlement, but in Northern Ireland, they were outnumbered and outgunned by a suspicious and repressive Protestant-dominated local government. While the Ulster Protestant majority thrust the Irish Catholic minority aside, monopolizing political and economic power, the British government in London distanced itself from the problem by granting Northern Ireland the power to administer itself internally. This Protestant-dominated regime was called the Stormont government after its headquarters in Belfast's Stormont Castle.

In the years that followed, Northern Ireland's two communities drew even further apart. Irish Catholics in the North believed themselves to be the direct descendents of the ancient Celts. The dominant Presbyterians liked to trace their ancestry back to Scotland or England. Both groups saw the conflict between them as tribal, imagining themselves

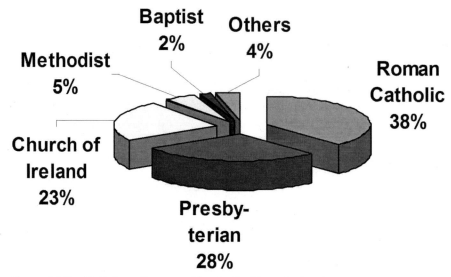

Figure 11.3. Religious Communities in Northern Ireland
Note that Roman Catholics constitute a plurality. The Church of Ireland is simply
the Church of England or Anglican Church in Ireland.

to be wholly different national groups. This "ethnic" divide is somewhat artificial, however. From a biological point of view, there is no real physical difference between "papes"
(Papists or Catholics) and "prods" (Protestants) and DNA analysis suggests one gene pool
rather than two. Until the nineteenth century, Catholics and Protestants had intermarried
(or at least interbred) frequently, particularly in cosmopolitan Belfast.

Roman Catholic and Presbyterian clergy quickly took over the leadership of their respective religious communities, assigning great importance to remaining within the flock
and shunning the rival faith. As hostility between these two artificially created groups
grew, they tended to avoid one another socially and slowly fled for safety to different
neighborhoods.

FROM TERRORISM TO DETENTE

By the 1960s, there was a clear pattern of discrimination against Catholic Irish, who made
up the poorest sector of the UK's poorest province. Gandhi and Martin Luther King
had both achieved much with nonviolent protest, but early efforts at similar civil rights
marches and civil disobedience got nowhere in Northern Ireland. After their unsuccessful
efforts to mount demonstrations, young Irish Catholics turned to violence by the end of
the 1960s, flowing into the ranks of the Irish Republican Army (IRA) as the era of the
"Troubles" began.

The first stages of the conflict took the form of intense intercommunal fighting
between the rival communities, with most of the damage being done to the smaller and
weaker Roman Catholics. The British Army moved into the urban centers, initially to
protect the Irish Catholics against Protestant violence. Inevitably, these mainland troops
quickly sided with the loyalist Protestant community. When the reinvigorated IRA

mounted a terrorist/guerrilla campaign to drive the British out of Ireland, the struggle took on the proportions of a low-intensity conflict, with a lot of violence directed against police officers, British soldiers, and officials of the British government.

The Protestant community joined the fray by generating a variety of "loyalist" paramilitaries such as the Ulster Volunteer Force (UVF) to carry out terrorist operations against the IRA and members of the Irish Catholic community. Unable to coax the Stormont government into making any concessions, the British government disestablished it in 1972 and began the policy of ruling the province directly from London through a secretary of state for Northern Ireland.

The "Troubles"

At its worst, Northern Ireland's LIC was very bad indeed. The center of every major city looked like a prison camp, with police and army blocks at every turn. Between 1969 and 1994, about three thousand people (out of a population of 1.6 million) died in the conflict, including British troops, police officers, members of the various militias, and a few innocent bystanders. Both sides occasionally took revenge on property belonging to their enemies and bombed-out pubs and betting shops became common sights. Large numbers of Irish men found themselves spending significant portions of their lives in jail because of membership in the IRA. In the early 1980s, the IRA leadership challenged the Thatcher government when ten prisoners deliberately starved themselves to death in a dramatic hunger strike. Margaret Thatcher was unmoved, but the IRA scored a public-relations victory with this display of courage. In order to bring the war home to the British people, the IRA conducted massive bombing campaigns against targets on the mainland of Great Britain and even against the British Army in Germany.

By the end of the 1980s, however, the situation had stalemated. The British clearly had the military and economic capacity to remain in possession of Northern Ireland forever, although the British public was sick of the war and its cost in lives and treasure. With backing from sympathizers in Ireland and the United States, the IRA could also continue the battle indefinitely. What neither side had was the ability to defeat the other in any meaningful way.

By the start of the 1990s, some IRA leaders who had begun the battle thirty years earlier now wondered if this unwinable military conflict could not be fought more effectively in the political arena. What had changed? First, the rapid birthrate among Roman Catholics ensured that the Irish Catholic would eventually constitute a majority, and hence would be able to use British democracy to vote themselves whatever they wanted. Second, the material welfare of both Catholics and Protestants had improved. An increasingly assertive Republic of Ireland had pulled itself out of poverty and was now becoming a political and economic powerhouse. The United Kingdom was now headed by more pragmatic men such as the Conservative John Major (1991–1997) and Labour's Tony Blair (elected in 1997). Leadership of the IRA/Sinn Fein movement was a dyad by the 1990s. The able Sinn Fein president Gerry Adams had spent most of his activist career as a political rather than military leader and had wanted all along to wage his struggle politically. His colleague, the more complex Martin McGuinness, is believed to have been the actual military commander (or Army Council chief of staff) of the IRA, but McGuinness was tentatively ready to negotiate.[43] Today, Mr. McGuinness is deputy first minster in the Northern Ireland administration.

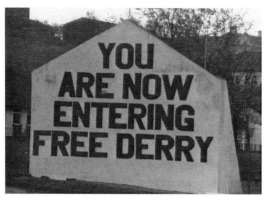

Figure 11.4. Free Derry
During the years of the Irish Republican Army's armed insurgency in the British province of Northern Ireland, portions of the province became effective no-go areas for officials of the British government. Positioned at the edge of Bogside, this sign announced that—as far as the Irish Catholic community was concerned—British sovereignty ended here.

Portraits of the Real World: Romeo and Juliet in (London)Derry

Maybe we've been missing the point all along. Perhaps the whole purpose of a political system is to permit us to love, and politics becomes dysfunctional when it hampers love or destroys it altogether.

Doing some research during the worst years of Northern Ireland's celebrated "Troubles," Richard Collin rented a room in the home of a warm Roman Catholic family in Northern Ireland's second-largest city, which Catholics call Derry and Protestants call Londonderry. His host's house sat on the edge of Derry's Bogside neighborhood, then controlled by the Irish Republican Army. In his youth, the father of the family had been a volunteer for the IRA, what some would call a freedom fighter and others would consider a terrorist. He had a wonderful sense of humor, and told Richard a joke that is only funny in Northern Ireland. A man comes out of a pub and walks down a dark alley. A stranger pops up behind him, and puts a gun to his head, demanding, "Are you Catholic or Protestant?" Unable to decide which answer would best ensure his survival, the hostage claims to be an atheist. "Alright," says the terrorist patiently, "but are you a Catholic atheist or a Protestant atheist?"

Well, you had to be there. The point is that everybody in Northern Ireland who isn't actually from Bangladesh gets labeled Catholic or Protestant no matter what they privately believe or don't believe. And Catholics and Protestants can't really tell each other apart by dress, appearance, or accent, although they do tend to live in separate neighborhoods and go to different schools.

The family was in an uproar during Richard's visit because their daughter Megan had gone off to Queens University in Belfast, where she had met her first Protestant and become fond of him. He was a Presbyterian lad named Garth, also from (London)Derry. The two students had come home for the summer and wanted to pursue their friendship, but Garth lived—with all the other "Prods"—on the east side of the River Foyle. Megan asked her father to make it possible for her and Garth to go on being friends.

For the Catholic head of the household to cross the Foyle River into Protestant territory would have been as suicidal as the Presbyterian Garth trying to walk into Bogside. This Irish Catholic father had limited affection for Protestants, but he loved his daughter, and once a week, he drove to the middle of the bridge spanning the Foyle River, picked Garth up, did an illegal U-turn, and escorted the terrified young man back into Papist territory for a strenuously supervised visit with Megan in the parlor.

While the Catholic family tried to be enlightened about this fragile romance, they really didn't want it to happen. For his part, the "Prod" Garth told his parents he was out drinking with the lads because they'd have locked him in the cellar before approving a friendship with an Irish girl. By the end of the summer, Megan and Garth had drifted apart, realizing they could never really get to know one another, much less fall in love.

Why couldn't Garth and Megan walk hand in hand through the ancient cobbled streets of one of Europe's authentically beautiful spots? Northern Ireland is home to a conflict that raged for centuries between Protestant people who self-identify strongly with British society, and generally Catholic people who see themselves as Irish, descendents of the ancient Celtic or Gaelic civilization that once dominated the island. They live in different neighborhoods; go to different schools, where they study different versions of history; drink different kinds of beer; root for different sports teams; and very seldom fall, successfully, in love with one another.

The Cease-Fire

In 1994, the IRA announced a cease-fire, and while it was broken several times in serious ways, 1994 does effectively mark the end of the low-intensity conflict that had plagued both islands for more than a quarter century. In 1995, Bill Clinton unambiguously used the power of his presidency by offering former senator George Mitchell as a mediator.[44] In 1997, both the Republic of Ireland and the United Kingdom got new prime ministers as Bertie Ahern took over the government in Dublin and Tony Blair achieved power in London. For the first time, the United States, the UK, and the Republic of Ireland were all led by men who knew and trusted one another, and were prepared to spend some political capital on Northern Ireland.

Real negotiations began in 1997 and concluded at Easter of 1998 with what is called the Good Friday Agreement. This arrangement called for the **devolution** of real political power back to Northern Ireland in the form of a 108-seat provincial assembly with real legislative power, led by an indirectly elected "first minister" and a cabinet. This government would have roughly the level of authority enjoyed by a U.S. state or German Länder. Furthermore, a North-South Council was created to create a forum in which officials from the Republic of Ireland could coordinate relations between the two long-separated portions of Ireland. The Republic of Ireland did its part by surrendering its formal claim to the territory of Northern Ireland, removing even the remote possibility of a new war. And—crucially—the IRA agreed to stand down in its war against the British government in return for a guaranteed share in the civil governance of the province.

The Divided Society

Not everyone really wanted a compromise. Some Ulster Protestants found it impossible to overcome a deep-seated mistrust of the IRA, and a scattering of IRA hard-liners rebelled and continued to carry out acts of violence. Most major political forces in Northern Ireland endorsed the idea, however, which was confirmed by a plebiscite in both Northern Ireland and the Republic of Ireland. After elections for the 108-seat Provincial Assembly, the Northern Ireland government was created.

Unfortunately, the mistrust between hard-line Ulster unionists and the recently reformed gunmen of Sinn Fein was profound. Elections for the Northern Ireland Assembly tended to reward hard-line parties instead of politicians who wanted compromise. The Democratic Unionist Party (DUP) represents the mostly Presbyterian community and tends to get the most votes, but never a majority. Sinn Fein, representing the IRA and the nationalist/republican community, has always come in second. This means that two tough-minded political parties are faced with the task of finding enough common ground to administer the province.

While the military violence in Northern Ireland has stopped, political progress continues to be very difficult. Here are some of the underlying reasons:

- The Separated Society: Irish Catholics and Ulster Protestants still live very separate lives, going to school separately, working separately, and marrying almost exclusively within their own communities. There has been a political deal among politicians, but not a social deal among everyday folk, and real peace will not truly happen until this artificially splintered community begins to feel like one kinship group.
- The Violent Fringe: Both Irish Catholic and Ulster Protestant splinter groups remain in the field and have created sporadic incidents of violence. Among the assortment of Protestant paramilitaries, there has been fratricidal violence, and extremists in Protestant neighborhoods are still attacking their neighbors in Catholic districts.
- The Lasting Mistrust: As a result of the continuing hostility, it has proved politically very difficult for Irish Catholics and Ulster Protestants to work together in government for the first time. Many Protestants still believe that the Sinn Fein leadership belongs in jail, although the IRA seems to have decommissioned most of its store of weapons.

On the positive side, the conflict confronting the people and the politicians of Northern Ireland has de-escalated from hate to anger, from terrorism to bitterly confrontational politics. While the people of Belfast continue to live rather separate lives, their city—once the least desirable in Europe—is charming, cosmopolitan, and friendly, with some of the best primary and secondary schools in the United Kingdom and a vibrant artistic and cultural life. There is still some rioting and fighting between Catholic and Protestant communities, but we've come a long way since Good Friday.

5. Common Features in Ethnic or Nationalist Quarrels

The South Slavs of the Balkan Peninsula; Arabs and Israelis in the Middle East; Muslims, Hindus, and Buddhists in South Asia; and combative Christians in Northern Ireland: what do these four trouble spots have in common?

- Religion exacerbates Nationalism: In this chapter, we have looked at four very distinct nationalist conflicts, each with a strong religious element. In none of the four cases does the conflict hinge specifically on a difference in religious doctrine; in each instance, however, religion is a crucial part of national self-identification. When religion and nationalist politics mix, they seem to inflame each other, producing conflicts that are longer and more violent. In the Yugoslav case, there aren't really profound cultural or linguistic differences among Croats, Islamic Bosnians, and Serbians beyond the fact that they are Roman Catholics, Muslims, and Orthodox Christians respectively. The fighting in Kosovo involved both language (Serbian versus Albanian) and religion, but the genocide and mass rape flowed from a Serbian conviction that Islam was an "enemy" religion.

    In the Israeli-Palestinian case, life would be tough enough were it merely a case of two rival communities quarrelling over scarce resources and real estate. Both groups, however, regard themselves as having a special relationship to God, who first "gave" Palestine to the Hebrew people, and then allowed the Prophet Mohammed's Muslims to conquer and settle it in the eighth century. South Asia is a garden of competitive theologies. If Pakistan was designed as a sanctuary for Muslims, why is Muslim Kashmir beyond its borders? If India has some essential connection with Hinduism, why are there so many Muslims in Gujarat? And, from the perspective of the Buddhist Sinhalese in Sri Lanka, why did these Hindus try to control part of Buddhism's special island? In Northern Ireland, Catholic clergy and Protestant ministers have taught their respective flocks that the most important thing about them is that they are Catholics and Protestants, not participants in Anglo-Irish civilization or citizens of an expanding European community.

- Everybody's a Victim: A sense of victimization pervades each of these crisis areas. Historically, Serbia was conquered by the Ottoman Turks, menaced by the Austrians, and generally victimized by the outside world. The people of Belgrade look out at a Europe that has robbed them of national greatness, interfered with their historical development as a people, and stolen their natural territories. Reflecting back on two thousand years of injustice and exile that terminated in the Holocaust, the Jewish people feel they have a clear right to a sanctuary in their original home. Brutalized by colonialism and European ambition, the Palestinians have lost their land and their liberty to invading foreigners, and they too feel the right to a homeland. And everyone has suffered in South Asia from colonialism and a host of ancient wrongs. In Northern Ireland, the Catholics have seen their land stolen from them by Scots and Englishmen from across the water. Protestants see themselves as an endangered minority on an island dominated by belligerent Catholics, and fear that the British will purchase peace by selling them out. Each of the sides to this conflict has a well-ground feeling of injustice. They have all suffered, and it is difficult to get victims to feel much sympathy for other victims.

- Mutual Hatred: History has known conflicts between groups that disagreed violently on issues but did not fundamentally despise each other. Americans and Germans fought two world wars without hating each other as ethnic groups. In the four conflicts we have reviewed in this chapter, however, the communities in question dislike each other with almost physical force. Between 1992 and 1995, Yugoslav paramilitaries displayed implacable hatred when they marched into each other's villages, killed the men and boys, and raped the women and girls.

Jewish Israelis and Palestinians Muslims seem to loathe one another. There are few friendships across Israel's ethnic front line; intermarriage is unthinkable in practice and formally illegal under both Israeli law and the Islamic Sharia. There are hardly any intercommunal friendships. In both the Indian case and the Northern Ireland situation, there are friendships across sectarian lines, but there are also very large communities who do not know each other, lead entirely separate lives, and hate each other emphatically.

In all of these four conflict situations, peace can only come about as a result of very substantial concessions on both sides. The political **socialization** of these societies, however, does not generally favor compromise and negotiation. Socialization is the process of learning how to behave in a given society. Western political socialization stresses cooperation and compromise, but socialization in the Middle East, for example, tends to encourage aggressiveness, physical bravery, and group allegiance. Neither former prime minister Sharon nor the late Yasser Arafat achieved fame by mediating disputes, winning debates, or writing books; both macho Middle Easterners displayed courage in the face of danger and personally killed enemies in combat.

- Internally Divided Power Contenders: Life and conflict would be simpler if the two sides of a given quarrel were internally united and knew as an ethnic community precisely what they wanted, and what it would take to reach an agreement.

In none of the disputes we have studied, however, are the two sides completely unified. There are Serbs who want a democratic and cooperative society that can someday join the European Union; there are others who want to use violence to seize those portions of Bosnia and Kosovo that were historically part of a greater Serbia. In Northern Ireland, there are moderates, mostly in the Alliance Party, who want a more secular society in which religion ceases to be a divisive issue; there are Catholics and Protestants who will only settle for a kind of graveyard peace in which the other side has been completely vanquished. Indians, who are some of the gentlest people on earth, are internally divided about what to do about Kashmir in particular and Pakistan in general. In Sri Lanka, the two principal Sinhalese political parties have been at each other's throats over the issue of concessions to be made, or not made, to the Tamil minority.

In the Israeli-Palestinian case, the internal disunity on either side is near total. A large number of Israelis are still convinced they can impose a settlement that will keep Jerusalem exclusively in their hands, leave Jewish settlements in the West Bank, and prevent millions of Palestinian refugees from returning home. Most Palestinians believe that a portion of east Jerusalem needs to be the capital of the Palestinian republic of the future, and that a sovereign Palestinian state should be free to expel Jewish settlers within its territory and repatriate its Palestinian exiles. A few Israelis still nurture dreams of taking over the entire West Bank and driving out the Arabs altogether. Conversely, some Palestinians still yearn for the destruction of the Israeli state. Only a minority within each community seems prepared to contemplate a deal remotely acceptable to a minority on the other side. The ideological ingredients for peace are simply not yet there.

- Money Talks and Minorities Walk: In every case, there is some level of economic disparity between the two sides. Yugoslavia broke up partly because wealthy Slovenians and Croatians no longer wished to support a Serbian dictatorship in Belgrade. The average Israeli is about ten times wealthier than the average Palestinian, and the Muslim community is now so poor that large numbers of Palestinian children are undernourished. In South Asia, Pakistan and India both crave the lush fields of Kashmir, and in Northern Ireland, Roman Catholics were traditionally at the bottom of the economic totem pole. Progress in resolving the conflict may be related to the fact that the Catholic Irish are no longer quite as poor, although there are economic inequalities in the province that still need to be addressed.

These four case studies, Yugoslavia, Israel-Palestine, South Asia, and Northern Ireland, all suggest that nationalist conflicts can be difficult to resolve. The wars in Bosnia and Kosovo were brought to an end by external force, not internal reconciliation. Serbs are still governing themselves in the portions of Bosnia they control, while the United Nations administers Kosovo without cooperation from Belgrade. The conflict in Israel-Palestine is at its worst stage in the long sad history of the eastern Mediterranean. Despite encouraging noises made by politicians from time to time, the two sides there have never been further from an agreement. In Kashmir, the domestic terror-against-terror campaign between Kashmiri separatists and Indian security forces continues to exacerbate relations between India and Pakistan. In Sri Lanka, a very tentative truce is failing, and the politicians are not very close to a political settlement. Of all four conflicts considered, Ireland is perhaps closest to peace, but no true reconciliation at the street level has occurred.

Each of these problems has both a regional and a global impact. Northern Ireland complicated relations between Great Britain and Ireland for decades. The collapse of Yugoslavia brought NATO into an armed conflict for the first time in its history. The Kashmiri conflict keeps South Asia trembling on the brink of nuclear war. And the Israeli-Palestinian standoff is a central factor in American domestic problems, U.S. relations with Europe, and the politics of petroleum right across the planet.

6. The Wrap: What Have We Learned?

You should come away from this chapter with a rough sense of both the history and the demography of the portion of the Balkan Peninsula we have studied. Religion is important here, so ensure that you can distinguish among Catholic Croatians and Slovenes, Muslim Bosnians and Kosovars, and Christian Orthodox Serbs, and understand why it was religion, rather than language or culture, that divided the former Yugoslavia. Remember also the role played by Slobodan Milošević in the breakup of his country. We took a special look at the conflicts in Bosnia and Kosovo because both of these cases involved foreign intervention involving U.S. troops. Ensure that you understand what was at issue in both cases, and what the contemporary status is in the two areas.

Of the four crises studied in this chapter, the Israeli-Palestinian conflict seemed to have touched bottom by 2012. Once again, this is a conflict involving kinship, language, religion, and culture, so be sure that you understand the ethnicity involved. Israel isn't a very old country, so it isn't that difficult to carry a rough chronology around in your head. Understand why both Arabs and Israelis feel themselves to be victims of history, and why both believe they have a divinely sanctioned right to the same land.

Once again, South Asia is an area where people self-identify partly on the basis of language and partly by religion. We looked at three separate but interrelated conflicts. Do you understand the background to the Indian-Pakistani conflict over Kashmir? The adversaries are both nuclear powers, so a peaceful settlement to this issue is a global priority. Indian democracy is challenged by a conflict between those who think that India should be a secular society and home to many different religious traditions, and those who believe that Hinduism should be the country's primary religion. Do you understand why India's ability to protect and enfranchise its Muslim minority is crucial to its traditional self-image as a multiethnic society? We also reviewed the Sri Lankan conflict between Hindu Tamils and Buddhist Sinhalese; do you understand the demographic and historic basis of the problem?

We ended the chapter on a relatively optimistic note, since Northern Ireland seems to be recovering from the bloodbath of its recent past. Having battled each other for centuries, the Catholic Irish and the Ulster Protestants still live largely separate lives, and the politicians have stopped exchanging bullets but not quite yet started trading votes. Is peace possible? Only time will tell, but the alternative is a return to violence.

What's next? Part IV of this book takes us into another dimension of conflict altogether. In chapters 12, 13, and 14, we'll be looking at the clash between rich and poor societies, the challenge of rapidly growing populations, and environmental issues involving nonrenewable resources and sustainable development.

Notes

1. Lewis Carroll, *Through the Looking Glass: And What Alice Found There* (New York: Macmillan & Co., 1875), 68.

2. While his book is out-of-date in terms of specific factual information, Moynihan's take on international affairs is hard to beat, and the author predicted the collapse of the USSR before anyone else. See Daniel Patrick Moynihan, *Pandaemonium: Ethnicity in International Politics* (New York: Oxford University Press, 1993).

3. The best recent overall study was done by Raymond C. Taras and Rajat Ganguly in their *Understanding Ethnic Conflict: The International Dimension* (New York: Longman, 2002). From Johns Hopkins University Press comes Daniel L. Byman's *Keeping the Peace: Lasting Solutions to Ethnic Conflicts* (Baltimore: Johns Hopkins University Press, 2002). With his special emphasis on smaller ethnic communities, also see Ted Robert Gurr's *Peoples versus States: Minorities at Risk in the New Century* (Washington, D.C.: U.S. Institute for Peace, 2000).

4. For NATO's take on its role, go to www.nato.int/ifor/ifor.htm.

5. Less has been written about Orthodox Christianity than one might expect. For a good introduction, see John Anthony McGuckin's *The Orthodox Church: An Introduction to Its History, Doctrine, and Spiritual Culture* (Hoboken, N.J.: Wiley-Blackwell, 2008).

6. Richard Oliver Collin, "Revolutionary Scripts," in *Culture and Language: Multidisciplinary Case Studies*, ed. Michael Morris (Frankfurt: Peter Lang, 2011), 29–67.

7. No one writes as well about Yugoslav history as Misha Glenny; see his *The Balkans: Nationalism, War, and the Great Powers 1804–1999* (New York: Viking, 2000).

8. Geoffrey Swain gives us a sympathetic portrait of Marshall Tito in his *Tito: A Biography* (London: I. B. Tauris, 2010).

9. The life of the late and generally unlamented Slobodan Milosevic is ably told by Louis Sell in his *Slobodan Milosevic and the Destruction of Yugoslavia* (Raleigh, N.C.: Duke University Press, 2002). Duke University Press has also released Judith Armatta's *Twilight of Impunity: The War Crimes Trial of Slobodan Milosevic* (Raleigh, N.C.: Duke University Press, 2010).

10. For a portrait of Bosnia before and during the disaster, see a splendid volume edited by Jasminka Udovicki and James Ridgeway, *Burn This House: The Making and Unmaking of Bosnia* (Raleigh, N.C.: Duke University Press, 1997).

11. This horrific story is soberly told by Beverly Allen in her *Rape Warfare: The Hidden Genocide in Bosnia-Herzegovina and Croatia* (Minneapolis, Minn.: University of Minnesota Press, 1996).

12. Samantha Power, *A Problem from Hell: America and the Age of Genocide* (New York: Basic, 2002), 247–327.

13. You can find detailed information about the Dayton Accords at www.state.gov/www/regions/eur/bosnia/bosagree.html. Also see Richard Holbrooke's own account of the negotiations that halted the fighting: *To End a War* (New York: Random House, 1998).

14. For a sense of what is happening in Bosnia today, look at www.bosnia.org.uk, maintained by London's Bosnian Institute, an NGO that seeks ethnic reconciliation in the region.

15. You will see references to "Kosova," which is the Albanian spelling of "Kosovo."

16. See Henry H. Perritt, *Kosovo Liberation Army: The Inside Story of an Insurgency* (Champaign, Ill.: University of Illinois Press, 2008).

17. In a harsh critique, Iain King and Whit Mason regard this UN effort as a failure. See *Peace at Any Price: How the World Failed Kosovo* (Cornell, N.Y.: Cornell University Press, 2006).

18. It may be an "instant book," but it will give you the basics; see Tim Judah's *Kosovo: What Everybody Needs to Know* (New York: Oxford University Press, 2008). For the international politics, see James Ker-Lindsay, *Kosovo: The Path to Contested Statehood in the Balkans* (New York: Vintage, 2008).

19. Walter Laqueur tells this story in a gracefully written book: *A History of Zionism: From the French Revolution to the Establishment of the State of Israel* (New York: Random House, 1972).

20. The Partition Plan was far from perfect, but it might have solved the problem at some level. Before making up your mind, see the original at www.yale.edu/lawweb/avalon/un/res181.htm.

21. The eminent historian Martin Gilbert takes us gently through this confusing period in his *Israel: A History* (New York: Morrow, 1998).

22. The 1967 Six-Day War is absolutely pivotal to understanding the current situation, and BBC correspondent Jeremy Bowen tells the story well in his *Six Days: How the 1967 War Shaped the Middle East* (New York: Simon & Schuster, 2003).

23. Scholars like to look at the original documents. To see the text of the famous Resolution 242, go to: http://unispal.un.org/unispal.nsf/0/7D35E1F729DF491C85256EE700686136.

24. See the original text at www.ibiblio.org/sullivan/docs/CampDavidAccords.html.

25. The Israeli government version of Oslo can be found at www.mfa.gov.il/MFA/Peace+Process/Guide+to+the+Peace+Process/Declaration+of+Principles.htm.

26. PLO president Mahmoud Abbas is sometimes known by his Arabic nickname Abu Mazen.

27. The bibliography here is vast and contentious, but a short and easily digested text that is often used as a textbook is Ian J. Bickerton and Carla L. Klausner, *A Concise History of the Arab-Israeli Conflict*, 6th ed. (Upper Saddle River, N.J.: Prentice-Hall, 2009). Covering much of the same ground but in greater detail is *Righteous Victims: A History of the Zionist-Arab Conflict: 1881–2001* (New York: Vintage, 2001) by the famous dissident Israeli historian Benny Morris, who has also reissued his *Birth of the Palestinian Refugee Problem Revisited*, 2nd ed. (Cambridge, UK: Cambridge University Press, 2004).

28. With the famous Ian Black as its Middle Eastern editor, Britain's *Guardian* newspaper is a good source for following the Israel-Palestine conflict from a non-American perspective. In this context, see Chris McGreal, "Barak Obama to Push Israel for Two-State Pledge," *The Guardian*, May 17, 2009,

http://www.guardian.co.uk/world/2009/may/17/barack-obama-israel-palestine?INTCMP=SRCH. See also McGreal's report on Netanyahu's defiant response in "Israeli PM Binyamin Netanyahu," *The Guardian*, May 24, 2011, http://www.guardian.co.uk/world/2011/may/24/binyamin-netanyahu-israel-palestinians -congress?INTCMP=ILCNETTXT3487.

29. See Jimmy Carter's contentious *Palestine: Peace Not Apartheid* (New York: Simon & Schuster, 2006). See also Benny Morris, *One State, Two States: Resolving the Israel/Palestine Conflict* (New Haven, Conn.: Yale University Press, 2010). A good blog ("Informed Comment") is maintained by Juan Cole at www.juancole.com/. If you want to follow the controversy in the Israeli press, try the left-leaning *Haaretz* at http://www.haaretz.com/ or the more conservative *Jerusalem Post* at http://www.jpost.com/. The Al Jazeera news organization has evolved a moderate Arab voice; see them at http://www.jpost.com/. See also Bitter Lemons at www.bitterlemons.net/.

30. Alan Dowty, *Israel/Palestine* (Cambridge, UK: Polity, 2005), 5, 169.

31. Amartya Sen, *Identity and Violence* (New York: Norton, 2006).

32. Oxford University Press has "Very Short Introduction" books that are remarkably good if a short introduction is what you are seeking. See Kim Knott's *Hinduism, A Very Short Introduction* (New York: Oxford University Press, 2000). And while we are being short, glance at Damien Keown's *Buddhism: A Very Short Introduction* (New York: Oxford University Press, 2000) in the same series.

33. Of the many good histories of India, John Keay has given us a concise view in his *India: A History* (Boston, Mass.: Atlantic, 2000). Specifically addressing the split between India and Pakistan is Yasmin Khan's excellent *The Great Partition: The Making of India and Pakistan* (New Haven, Conn.: Yale University Press, 2008).

34. Jessica Stern, "Pakistan's Jihad Culture," *Foreign Affairs* 79, no. 6 (2000): 115–26.

35. For the India-Pakistan quarrel over Kashmir, look at Sumit Ganguly's *Conflict Unending: India-Pakistan Tensions since 1947* (New York: Columbia University Press, 2002). For the specifics of the Kashmiri conflict, see Manoj Joshi's *The Lost Rebellion: Kashmir in the Nineties* (New York, Penguin, 1999). Victoria Schofield has provided an extended history in her *Kashmir in Conflict* (London: Tauris, 2000). Perhaps the best overall summary is Sumantra Bose's *Kashmir: Roots of Conflict, Paths to Peace* (Cambridge, Mass.: Harvard University Press, 2003), but an Indian civil servant named Wajahat Habibullah has written an excellent new *My Kashmir: Conflict and the Prospects of Enduring Peace* (Washington, D.C.: Institute of Peace, 2008).

36. Bowdoin College professor John Clifford is an acknowledged expert on Sri Lanka and Buddhism. He is particularly good on the colonial period, for which, see his *The Sri Lanka Reader: History, Culture, Politics* (Raleigh, N.C.: Duke University Press, 2011).

37. See Sharika Thiranagama's *In my Mother's House: Civil War in Sri Lanka. The Ethnography of Political Violence* (Philadelphia: University of Pennsylvania Press, 2011).

38. International law expert Francis A. Boyle maintains that the Sri Lankan government committed mass slaughters, the view taken in his *The Tamil Genocide by Sri Lanka: The Global Failure to Protect Tamil Rights under International Law* (Atlanta, Ga.: Clarity Press, 2009). Another very dramatic book has been written by former UN official Gordon Weiss, *The Cage: The Fight for Sri Lanka and the Last Days of the Tamil Tigers* (London: Bodley Head, 2011).

39. *The Economist*, "Sri Lanka and War Crimes: Keep Quiet and Carry On," April 11, 2011, http://www .economist.com/node/18561107.

40. This is explained well in Marc Mulholland's *Northern Ireland: A Very Short Introduction* (New York: Oxford University Press, 2003).

41. Jonathan Bardon, *A History of Ulster* (Belfast: Blackstaff, 1992), 75–147.

42. The whole horrible history is detailed in Thomas Bartlett's *Ireland: A History* (Cambridge, UK: Cambridge University Press, 2010), See also *Making Sense of the Troubles: The Story of the Conflict in Northern Ireland* (Chicago: New Amsterdam). An experienced journalist named Jack Holland has given us the excellent *Hope Against History: The Course of the Conflict in Northern Ireland* (New York: Holt, 1999).

43. Richard Oliver Collin, "When Irish Eyes Stop Smiling," *International Counterterrorism*, Winter 1990/1991, 18–26.

44. See Senator George J. Mitchell's own account: *Making Peace* (New York: Knopf, 1999).

Part IV

POPULATION, POVERTY, RESOURCES, AND HUMAN DEVELOPMENT

CHAPTER 12

Economic Development
THE RICH AND THE WRETCHED

4. The Wrap: What Have We Learned?

In Lewis Carroll's *Through the Looking Glass*, the White Queen explains her basic theory of economics. "You couldn't have it if you did want it," she tells the perplexed Alice. "The rule is, jam tomorrow and jam yesterday—but never jam today."[1] Hence, jam may be future or past, but never present, except—one supposes—for the queen herself and the other privileged members of her exalted family. As always, Lewis Carroll was making an acute observation on the economics of his life and ours. In today's world, rulers and governments make most of the real decisions about the distribution of good things to eat and drink. Governments often promise that things will get better soon; there will be jam (or jobs or health insurance or elementary schools) tomorrow. And in the good old days, there was jam for everybody, and it tasted better back then. Some competent governments actually deliver nutrition today, but there are important parts of the world where jam (in the sense of economic security) is always tomorrow, even if people need it, badly, today.

International political economy is complicated stuff, and we'll take it in measured stages. Here's a quick look at what we'll try to learn:

- *How do we measure wealth? Are there more meaningful alternatives to the standard gross domestic product tool? Why does money change in value? What role does government play in circulating wealth through society?* In section 1, we need to do some basic homework on the interaction between politics and money, defining some key terms and discovering how governments intervene in the financial aspects of our lives.
- *Why is there such a gap between the global rich and poor? Can anything be done about the extremes of wealth and poverty?* Since these are burning questions now, and will become more important in the future, we need to spend some time on the rich-people-poor-people conundrum in human society. The UN's very high, high, medium, and low human development index (HDI) measurement tool is based on the important premise that societies have access to differing levels of wealth, and make vastly different choices about the allocation of scarce resources. This will involve a careful look, therefore, at the levels of economic inequality that exist between prosperous and impoverished societies, and between the wealthier and poorer citizens of individual countries. We also need to look at past and present efforts to assist the very poor, and see what works and what doesn't.
- *Will free enterprise and free trade eventually help humankind turn the corner into global prosperity? Is globalization ultimately a good idea or a bad one?* The United States has led the way in proclaiming that classic American economic principles of free enterprise need to be accepted universally, with "free trade" becoming the standard for economic interaction among the world's economies. We need to look at what has been called the "Washington Consensus" and see how it has functioned in real life. And we will close with a final glance at the question of globalization, trying to understand how intercon-

nected and intermestic the world has become. Globalization makes everybody mad, one way or another; get to the bottom of this chapter, and you'll see why. You might even get mad too.

1. Wealth and International Politics

Did you ever try to read an article in *The Wall Street Journal* or Britain's *The Economist*, and fail? Was it because the vocabulary was arcane, and you couldn't make it through all the acronyms? When scholars who investigate wealth and prosperity in international society talk and write, they sometimes do it in a language that only superficially resembles English. Unfortunately, the interface between politics and economics is terrifically important. In this section, we need to do some basic homework and see how we measure money or wealth within individual societies and how we make economic comparisons between countries. We'll look a little at money itself, seeing how and why it oscillates in value. We'll end up by making sure we understand how governments finance themselves and why debt is sometimes a real problem for rich and poor societies alike.

MEASURING MONEY

Throughout this and every other book on world politics, you've seen fearful acronyms like GDP and GNI (also known as GNP), along with similar statistical indicators of wealth and poverty. Let's now look more closely at these magic numbers and see what they can and cannot do to help us understand the economics of our world, and the conflict that flows from economic problems.

The most common way of describing wealth and poverty involves the use of a big number called the gross domestic product (GDP), which is basically an estimate (normally expressed in U.S. dollars) of the total market value of all the goods and services generated by a given economy within a given year. The GDP may be calculated for a sovereign state, a sub-sovereign element within a country (such as an American state), or a region of the world, such as Africa, but we will be dealing here primarily with the GDP figures for sovereign states.

It is important to note that the GDP can only measure the formal, legal, and reported part of a country's economy. If a wealthy female business executive hires a butler, pays him wages, and makes social security contributions for him, his income is part of the GDP. If boss marries butler, the former servant may continue washing the dishes, but the

---

You, Me, and Bill Gates . . .

Please remember that the PC/GDP does not represent personal income or even real money. It is an economist's way of suggesting your theoretical participation in the wealth of your country. You and I and Bill Gates all have precisely the same PC/GDP, but the Microsoft Corporation still belongs mostly to him and not to us.

informal househusband allowance he may receive in place of his salary is not factored into the GDP. Sometimes true love means that the GDP goes down. Other transactions not counted by the GDP range from bartered and informal favor-swapping arrangements (he fixes her car, she tutors his kids) to downright illegalities (she gives him a hundred dollars, he sells her marijuana). Unreported and/or unlawful transactions might range as high as 20 percent of the American economy. In many less-developed societies, corruption and/ or unreported transactions can be so rampant that the actual wealth of the country can be vastly higher than the reported GDP.[2]

A somewhat different unit of measurement is the **gross national income (GNI)** or **gross national product (GNP)**. This book uses the term GNI in line with UNDP and World Bank indicators. For some countries, such as the United States, the difference be-tween GDP and GNP is not numerically very significant. The GNI measurement adds to the GDP all wealth flowing into a country from abroad, such as returns on foreign investments or profit-making companies owned by citizens of the country in question but physically located abroad. Some countries, such as Turkey and Mexico, receive considerable revenue from citizens working abroad and sending money home to support their families, called remittances. This revenue becomes part of the gross national income, but not the GDP. The GNI calculation also subtracts money earned by foreign nationals in the country under consideration and exported back to their countries of origin. The World Bank, a sig-nificant player in international economics, uses the phrase "gross national income" (GNI) in place of "gross national product." Although politicians, journalists, and world bankers occasionally refer to the GNP or GNI, international practice favors the use of the gross domestic product, and we have adopted both terms throughout this book.

Per Capita Measurements

Table 12.1 shows us that we don't learn much just looking at the respective gross do-mestic products of two countries. Switzerland's unadjusted 2010 GDP expressed in U.S. dollars was $522,400,000,000. This is about half the size of India's seemingly robust fig-ure of US$1,430,000,000,000. Are Indians therefore twice as rich as the Swiss? Perhaps they are spiritually, but tiny Switzerland has only about 7.2 million people sharing a third of a trillion bucks, making it a high HDI society. In contrast, there were over a billion Indians in 2010 scrambling to divide $600 billion, which lands India at the low end of the medium HDI scale.[3]

A country with a GDP over half a trillion dollars has impressive economic clout in the world markets, even if the national pie has to be divided into a great many tiny slices. To get a sense of the average wealth of Swiss and Indian citizens, however, we need to divide the GDP by the population, generating a number that suggests the relative indi-vidual wealth enjoyed by members of a given economy. Here's the formula: GDP ÷ popu-lation = PC/GDP. Using unadjusted numbers, we can see in table 12.1 that Switzerland's PC/GDP is some nineteen times higher than India's. But we also see that Switzerland's PC/GDP is higher than its PC/GNI. This is likely due to the myriad of international agencies and corporations, and citizens from other countries located in Switzerland, that send their money outside the country. However, India's case is different. There, we see a higher PC/GNI than PC/GDP. This may be due to the number of remittances (money sent from abroad to a home country) that Indians living outside of India send home.

Table 12.1.   Switzerland vs. India

	Switzerland	India
Population	7.7 million	1,189.2 million (over 1 billion)
GDP	US$475,800,000,000,000	US$1,730,000,000,000,
PC/GDP	US$66,367	US$3,500
GDP (PPP US$)	PPP US$326,000,000,000	PPP US$4,046,000,000,000
PC/GDP (PPP US$)	PPP US$45,224	PPP US$3,296
PC/GNI (PPP US$)	PPP US$39,924	PPP US$3,468

Source: United Nations Development Program (UNDP), Statistical Annex *Human Development Report 2011,* http://hdr.undp.org/en/media/HDR_2011_EN_Tables.pdf (accessed December 26, 2011).

We also use per capita figures to factor out the effect of population increase. If a country's overall GDP grew by 2 percent in a year but its population jumped by 3 percent, the average or per capita GDP actually went down, even though the raw GDP grew slightly.

Adjusting for Cost of Living and Inflation

Is all this math making you hungry? If we zip over to Zurich with $20, we can maybe get a coffee and a donut. Maybe we should go to New Delhi instead, because there for $20 we can eat out for three days. Switzerland is a very expensive country, and there are real bargains in India.

Shouldn't the cost of living be factored in when making this kind of comparison? It should be and it is, albeit in a slightly complex fashion. Consider how we get the basic GDP for a given country. First, we add up all those goods and services and come up with a very large number (the U.S. GDP is over $14 trillion). We then convert this figure into U.S. dollars at the prevalent exchange rate, which is roughly the rate you would get if you walked into a bank with Swiss francs or Indian rupees. This unadjusted GDP is an interesting figure for some purposes, but it doesn't tell you how far your salary will stretch in either country, or how many dollars a loaf of bread is going to cost in Zurich or New Delhi.

Table 12.2.   The Big Mac Index

It isn't very scientific, but students who find the PPP US$ concept too challenging sometimes prefer to compare the price of a Big Mac at a McDonald's restaurant in various parts of the world. These hamburgers are all supposed to be precisely the same, so differences in price give you a sense of the varying cost of living around the world. For $10, you can get four Big Macs in China but only one in Switzerland.

Country	US$ Price
United States	$4.07
Britain	$3.73
China	$2.30
India	$3.22
European Union Area	$4.49
Switzerland	$6.94

Source: *The Economist,* "The Big Mac Index," July 28, 2011, http://www.economist.com/blogs/daily chart/2011/07/big-mac-index.

In order to get a truer picture, economists produce a **purchasing power parity (PPP US$)** version of the GDP and the PC/GDP that takes into account how much a dollar would actually buy in any given country. When a number is adjusted to reflect differences in the cost of living, economists write "PPP US$" after it to indicate that this number has been altered to reflect how much a dollar (or its equivalent in local currency) would actually buy in a given country. Glancing again at table 12.2, note that if spending power is taken into consideration, India wins a much bigger number with its PC/GDP increasing by a factor of five. Because of Switzerland's high cost of living, a PPP US$ conversion actually lowers the Swiss GDP and PC/GDP. By this more refined measure, we see that the average Swiss is only about ten times richer than the average Indian in terms of spending power.

Be warned, therefore: throughout this book, we have used "spending-power-adjusted" figures whenever feasible, with the identifying "PPP US$" notation.

Another complication is the impact of inflation. Let us say that the GDP for a very small and very poor country in 2011 is $100 million. In 2012, economists determine that it has climbed to $102 million, a modest rise of 2 percent. Part of that increase might be due to a growth in the economy, but part is certain to be a product of inflation, the general tendency for prices to rise in an economy. This is an area of some complexity, but most economists deal with this problem by distinguishing between the "nominal" GDP, which is the raw figure, and the "**real GDP**," which is calculated by factoring out the amount caused by inflation. When examining statistics, make sure you know whether you are looking at the nominal GDP or the more meaningful inflation-free real GDP. Inflation is a very significant factor in politics, and we'll consider it in greater detail below. What you need to know for the moment is that GDP and PC/GDP and GNI and PC/GNI figures presented in this book are "real" rather than nominal.

As we'll see below, both good things and bad things can drive up the PC/GDP, but a declining figure is never good. In the decade between 1990 and 2001, the Russian PC/GDP fell an average of 3.5 percent per year, which was distinctly bad news for the Russians. Among high HDI countries, annual increases have been modest over the past decade, averaging between 1 and 3 percent. The United States clocked up a regular 2.1 percent increase during the 1990s. Some medium HDI countries advanced very rapidly during the same period; China hit 8.8 percent per year. Economist Amartya Sen warns us against reading too much into these figures. Moderately poor countries such as China have a lot of room for improvement, a fact reflected by their high growth rates. Some high HDI countries have already done a lot of development, which tends to lower their annual rate of increase. While China was increasing by 8.8 percent, Japan only advanced by 1 percent a year. Would you rather live in China or Japan?

Buying Bad Things with Good Money

The GDP and GNI figures presented in this book, therefore, are adjusted for both the cost of living and inflation. After torturing poor GDP and GNI like this, is it reasonable to start saying bad things about them?

There's nothing objectively wrong with the GDP and GNI as long as we remember that they are value-free measurements of economic activity and not—as is all too often assumed—a general indicator of social well-being. Here's the basic difficulty: the GDP and GNI simply follow the money trail, not distinguishing between expenditures that make us happy and those that don't. We are often reminded that money can't buy happiness, but no one ever mentions that unhappiness can sometimes generate money. For example, when the late and unlamented Timothy McVeigh blew up the Oklahoma City Federal Building in 1995, the act made money circulate through the system: life insurance companies paid off, funeral homes showed a profit, construction crews and police worked overtime pulling charred bodies from the rubble, and journalists booked into local hotels, interviewed sobbing survivors, and padded their expense accounts. If there were a human happiness index for this time period, it would have taken a nosedive.

Second, the GDP and GNI do not take into account unpaid labor such as housekeeping, caring for the sick and elderly, or charitable volunteer work. This tends to undervalue the contribution women make to society, since much of humankind's unpaid domestic work is performed by women and girls. The UK's Office of National Statistics recently calculated that if unpaid workers were actually remunerated for these services, their "salary" would constitute 104 percent of Britain's GDP. As two scholars noted recently,

> The GDP is blind to the social value of economic activity and simply adds up all the recorded expenditures. So the more spent on cleaning up toxic waste, housing prison inmates, or burning gasoline while trapped in traffic, the better. It also ignores all the beneficial activities not captured in the market, such as volunteer work, unpaid childcare, and housework.[4]

Are there alternatives to the PC/GDP and PC/GNI? Unhappy with this focus on the financial, some social and political scientists have attempted to find a new unit of measurement, one that would present a clearer picture of whether or not we were actually "doing okay."

For example, the Redefining Progress research institute has devised a statistical tool called the genuine progress indicator (GPI) that subtracts socially negative elements such as the cost of crime, automobile accidents, commuting, divorces, pollution, loss of natural habitats, and long-term environmental damage. Smashing up your car and landing in an emergency room help boost the GDP; the disaster-related costs are subtracted from the GPI. In the year 2000, the American PC/GDP was $33,497, while the GPI was only $9,550.[5]

Moving beyond the GPI, ecological economist Herman Daly and colleagues have devised the happy planet index.[6] This index, like the *Human Development Report*, takes into account life expectancy and life satisfaction (this is an expanded variable in the 2010 report) but adds impact on the planet (or sustainability levels). It turns out that wealthier countries aren't always the happiest. In fact, Costa Rica ranks number one in the happy planet index. The highest-placed Western nation is the Netherlands—43rd out of 143. The UK still ranks midway down the table—74th, behind Germany, Italy, and France. The United States comes in at 114th place. The creators of this index argue that living in a healthy environment includes not only employment, income, and access to hospitals and schools, but also access to clean air and water.

Classifying countries into categories based on economic status has always been a methodological horror show, since no one can say with precision where the "First World" ends and the "Third World" begins or define with precision the distinction between "developing" and "developed." As we learned in chapter 3, the United Nations Development Programme (or UNDP) has created a mathematically concrete system for dividing the countries of the world into very high, high, medium, and low development based on a very simple quality-of-life statistic called the human development index (HDI). It's easy to get bogged down in the details of the HDI, so focus on the concept. Every country has some income; the UN uses the per capita gross national income expressed in real terms and adjusted for cost-of-living variations with the purchasing power parity system. The UN believes that a sensible society should use as much as possible of that income to purchase the highest possible quality of life for itself, such as investing in health and education. To create the HDI, therefore, the UNDP combines three quality-of-life indicators: education (computed as a combination of the literacy rate and the number of years of schooling), health (drawn from life expectancy figures), and prosperity as measured by the PC/GNI. It also uses the PC/GDP figure to measure poverty. Glance at table 12.3 to get a sense of the range.

The UNDP then crunches the numbers to create a score between 0.00 and 1.00, the higher the better. For the 182 countries on which the UN believed that it had sufficiently accurate data in 2011, it then listed the countries of the world in order of their success in creating wealth and using that income for socially desirable outcomes, such as health and education. Table 12.3 gives us a sampling of countries from the UN's four basic country categories. Because of their effective use in translating good incomes into great health and education, the Scandinavian countries are perennially near the top of the chart.

Because it provides mathematic precision and because it softens the "only money matters" bias of the PC/GDP, the human development index is gradually becoming the standard method of classifying countries. In recent years, the HDI has been adopted by newspapers such as the *New York Times* and is becoming an increasingly common part of our political vocabulary.

WHEN MONEY CHANGES VALUE

An enormous amount of political conflict stems from the fact that money's value, or buying power, can change with bewildering speed and devastating effect. Life would certainly be simpler if, decade after decade, $1 or £0.66 (British pounds) or €0.81 (Euros) or ¥89 (Japanese yen) always bought you a standard loaf of bread. With a fixed-value currency, you could plan eternal budgets, know exactly how much money would be required to send your kids to university, and retire confident that your pension would always meet your needs.

In every society, however, the value of money changes in small ways every day and in very substantial ways over the course of a lifetime. In some unstable parts of the world, the currency upon which you depend for that loaf of bread can lose most of its value abruptly, leaving you with a lot of worthless paper money and nothing to eat. There are two ways this can happen.

A given currency can change its value in relationship to the goods and services it buys within a given economy, a phenomenon called **inflation** or **deflation**. A currency's value can also be altered with respect to other currencies, something called an exchange rate, and we'll talk about this phenomenon below.

Table 12.3.

This table gives us the "top ten" in each of the UN's four categories of society. With a dismal HDI score of 0.286, Democratic Republic of Congo is dead last; Afghanistan is in the bottom fifteen countries.

Rank	Country	Score
Very High Human Development		
1	Norway	0.943
2	Australia	0.929
3	Netherlands	0.910
4	United States	0.910
5	New Zealand	0.908
6	Canada	0.908
7	Ireland	0.908
8	Liechtenstein	0.905
9	Germany	0.905
10	Sweden	0.904
High Human Development		
48	Uruguay	0.783
49	Palau	0.782
50	Romania	0.781
51	Cuba	0.776
52	Seychelles	0.773
53	Bahamas	0.771
54	Montenegro	0.771
55	Bulgaria	0.771
56	Saudi Arabia	0.770
57	Mexico	0.770
Medium Human Development		
95	Jordan	0.698
96	Algeria	0.698
97	Sri Lanka	0.691
98	Dominican Republic	0.689
99	Samoa	0.688
100	Fiji	0.688
101	China	0.687
102	Turkmenistan	0.686
103	Thailand	0.682
104	Suriname	0.680
Low Human Development		
142	Solomon Islands	0.510
143	Kenya	0.509
144	São Tomé and Príncipe	0.509
145	Pakistan	0.504
146	Bangladesh	0.500
147	Timor-Leste	0.495
148	Angola	0.486
149	Myanmar	0.483
150	Cameroon	0.482
151	Madagascar	0.480

Source: United Nations Development Programme (UNDP) Statistical Annex *Human Development Report 2011*, http://hdr.undp.org/en/media/HDR_2011_EN_Tables.pdf (accessed December 26, 2011).

Inflation and the Cost of Living

While there have been extended periods in history when prices have slumped (a trouble-some trend called deflation), prices have generally tended to rise in recent decades, a familiar process called inflation.

Unless it is quickly brought under control, inflation can metastasize into **hyper-inflation** and contribute to widespread criminal or political violence and possibly insurrection and civil war. After the collapse of the Soviet Union, Russians on fixed and meager incomes faced a ruinous 94 percent annual inflation rate, which devastated savings and made pensions meaningless. In Colombia, inflation averaged over 20 percent per year in the 1990s, compared to an American inflationary rate of about 2 percent. A great deal of the popularity of the Uribe government is due to its success in getting the rate of inflation down to about 5 percent in the course of the first decade of this century. The Argentine peso collapsed in January 2002, losing three-quarters of its value and plunging the country into political and economic chaos.[7] In Latin American, African, and sometimes Asian societies, hyperinflation can sometimes become so rapid that products double and triple in price in a matter of weeks. Defined as an increase in prices of over 50 percent per month in the value of money, hyperinflation is politically unsustainable for long. Even if it falls short of the "hyper" category, rapid inflation is always a political issue.

Exchange Rates

The second way that a currency can change its value is when it is used to buy the currency of some other country at a price called the "**exchange rate**." Since the 1970s, currencies have generally floated freely against one another. This means that the relationship between every currency and every other currency changes—sometimes slightly and sometimes dramatically—over time.

Market forces, supply and demand, political crises, and economic factors can drive some currencies up and others down, often to the dismay of international travelers or businesspeople trying to broker international deals. The process of losing value against another currency is called "**devaluation**" or sometimes "depreciation." A currency "appreciates" when it gains value against one or more other currencies.

American tourists traveling to Britain in the summer of 2011, for example, bought British pounds at the approximate rate of US$1.59 = UK£1.00. The dollar-pound relationship is generally stable, but over the last few years, the U.S. dollar has been sinking against most world currencies.

America trades a lot with the rest of the world, so the exchange rate of the dollar has always been crucial. When the dollar is low with respect to other currencies, it takes more of our hard-earned cash to buy a Mitsubishi automobile, Italian *fettuccine*, a package tour of Britain's Lake District, or a barrel of crude oil from Kuwait. On the plus side, a "cheap" dollar means that American-manufactured goods are less costly for foreigners, perhaps meaning more jobs here in the United States. A strong dollar buys a lot of other people's currency, allowing us to travel cheaply, purchasing foreign goods and services at minimal cost to ourselves. Unfortunately, customers abroad need to get their hands on dollars to buy American goods, and if U.S. dollars are expensive, so are U.S. goods.

Why do exchange rates fluctuate? This is a complicated question, but the exchange rate of a given currency can grow or decline for several reasons.

- Confidence: If a country's economic future looks bleak, people will be nervous about holding its currency. And if the political institutions of a society are crumbling, investors will hurry to dump that currency, selling it at a loss to get their wealth into a more stable currency. Public confidence in a country's political and economic future will help steady a currency.
- Market Manipulation: It is possible for currency speculators or governments themselves to manipulate the value of a currency. The Chinese government, for example, has traditionally maintained the Chinese yuan at an artificially low exchange rate, making Chinese products abnormally cheap on the world market. China makes almost half of all the world's microwave ovens, paying its workers $6 a day and selling microwaves retail in the United States for about $100. The U.S. government has been trying to get the Chinese to "float" the yuan, that is, allow it to seek its own natural exchange rate without Beijing's interference. A freely floating yuan might rise about 40 percent, which would make Chinese microwaves cost $140, a price high enough to allow a U.S. manufacturer to compete. This would be good for General Electric, but bad for anybody shopping for a microwave.
- Balance of Payments: The **balance of payments** is the difference between the quantity of money a country spends abroad for imported goods and services on one hand, and the amount of money the same country receives in exchange for its own exported goods and services. This balance of payments becomes unfavorable when one country buys more from the rest of the world than it sells to the rest of the world. The United States has suffered from an unfavorable balance of payments for some years, because of America's endless appetite for Italian fashions and Japanese cars and Chinese gadgets. At the same time, the United States is no longer selling enough merchandise to the rest of the world to bring home those exported dollars. An oversupply of anything tends to drive down the price, and money is a commodity; America's unfavorable balance of payments with its trading partners creates a permanent downward pressure on the dollar, which has been falling in recent years.

Despite its recent weakness, the American dollar is still the world's currency in the sense that most other countries define the value of their currencies in relationship to the dollar and many international transactions are conducted in dollars. As other industrialized countries recovered from World War II, however, the dollar was joined by other "hard currencies" that enjoy easy convertibility in banks all over the world.

Seven top industrialized nations (the United States, Canada, UK, Germany, France, Italy, and Japan) are called the Group of Seven (G-7), and their currencies are sometimes regarded as the world's core "hard" or freely convertible currencies. The leaders of this informal club meet in highly publicized summits to deal with economic policy differences. The Russians have a hugely dysfunctional economy but all their hydrogen bombs still work, so the G-7 issues a courtesy invitation for the Russians to sit in on their meetings. This slightly artificial arrangement is called the Group of Eight (G-8).

In the wake of the 2008–2009 economic crisis and increasing instability in our economic and financial systems, the Group of Twenty, (G-20), the world's twenty largest economies, encompassing developed and developing world states, is the new normal for economic policy making on the global scale. The 2010 G-20 meeting was held in Seoul, South Korea. Including Brazil, China, India, and other traditional G-8 members, these states discussed issues including financial markets and banking sector bailouts, currency exchange, and revised policies for the International Monetary Fund (IMF), an organization that gained renewed momentum as it provided loans to fledgling economies in the post-2008 crisis.

One such example of loans came from a joint European Union and IMF bailout of the Greek economy during the summer 2011, which consisted of $17 billion to simply keep the government from going bankrupt. This economic calamity was accompanied by massive protests in the streets of Greece against austerity measures that included cutting pension funds and increasing the retirement age, among other cost-saving measures. Greece is only one sign of the new times of cost-cutting and budget-tightening measures among many developed states, including the United States.

GOVERNMENTS AND MONEY

The relationship between sovereign governments and money typically begins with the creation of a national currency: Russia has its not-very-stable ruble and the Japan has the ever-reliable yen. The advantage of printing your own national currency is control. A government can fine-tune its economy by altering the money supply, which affects interest rates, which in turn makes the currency more or less valuable for trade purposes.

Some whole regions have seen economic benefits in possessing a common currency. Everyone is justifiably excited about the creation of the Euro, but the European Union didn't invent the idea. In the Caribbean, a collection of small island states has collectively created the East Caribbean dollar (currently worth about thirty-seven U.S. cents). A very large group of former French colonies in West Africa has joined forces in a common currency called the Communauté Financière Africaine (CFA) franc.

Budgets and Expenditures

No matter how economically developed or how poverty-stricken, every government will have a budgetary process that attempts to account for revenue and expenditure. In most free market societies, more than 90 percent of revenue or governmental income comes from tax receipts, although there will also be some non-tax revenues, such as fees, fines, **tariffs**, and profits from state-owned enterprises. This pattern may change in medium or low HDI countries. Iran, for example, gets much more income from its state-owned oil company than from taxes paid by generally poor Iranians. Some extremely underdeveloped societies have almost no tax base because a community based on barter, hunting, and subsistence farming has not yet moved fully into a monetary economy. These low HDI governments will survive on loans and grants from abroad and ownership of a few key industries.

The expenditure of revenue begins with an annual legislative act called a budget, which—as you can see in table 12.4—will reflect the government's ideology. Depending upon national priorities, the budget may focus on social welfare—lifting people out of

Table 12.4. Government Spending as a Percentage of GDP

Country	Education	Health	Military
United States	16.2	16.2	4.8
France	11.7	11.7	2.3
Israel	7.6	7.6	6.5
Oman	3	3	9.6
Iran	5.5	5.5	1.9
Pakistan	2.6	2.6	3.2
Yemen	5.6	5.6	4.4
Chad	7	7	3
Ethiopia	4.3	4.3	1.1

Note how spending priorities shift from country to country. Compared to the United States, France spends significantly more on health and less on its military. With a social democratic background but real security problems, Israel spends a lot in all three categories. Dictatorships such as Oman and Pakistan save on social spending but break the budget when it comes to guns and soldiers. Look at the comparison between two of Africa's poorest countries: Chad's expenditures on military in previous years were at 6.6 percent of GDP, but recently those have changed in favor of health and education. Ethiopia has a more socially responsible budget.

Sources:
United Nations Development Programme (UNDP), Statistical Annex *Human Development Report 2011*, http://hdr.undp.org/en/media/HDR_2011_EN_Tables.pdf (accessed December 26, 2011).
The World Bank Database, *Military Expenditures as Percentage of GDP*, http://data.worldbank.org/indicator/MS.MIL.XPND.GD.ZS (accessed December 26, 2011).

poverty, building schools, hospitals, and endowing public services such as libraries and symphony orchestras. An unpopular and dictatorial government will typically invest in a pervasive internal security apparatus, funding secret police and spies who can detect and defuse rebellion against the regime. A more conservative government will typically maintain lower taxes and generally lower spending, except in the field of national security. In recent U.S. history, Republicans, such as Ronald Reagan and George W. Bush, reversed tradition by engaging in deficit spending in order to finance military operations and simultaneously lowering taxes, even though this increased the size of both the deficit and the national debt. Newer members of the Republican Party have made cuts in social spending their mantra as they seek to cut the national debt.

There are disagreements in every society on which classes of citizens get to pay what levels of tax. All developed societies practice **progressive taxation**, based on the idea that wealthier citizens should pay a greater percentage of their income. In social democratic societies, taxation is steeply progressive, with high earners paying a very substantial amount of their income in taxes. Progressive taxation has been seriously challenged in America, where advocates of the "**flat tax**" argue that we should all pay the same percentage of our income in taxes. In North America and Western Europe, liberals and social democrats argue for fairly steep progressive taxation. Conservatives in both kinds of societies claim that if wealthier taxpayers (or "job creators") are allowed to keep more of their income, they will invest in society, creating jobs and wealth for everyone, a theory called "supply side economics" or sometimes "trickle down" theory, since money is supposed to trickle down from the rich to the poor.[8]

Deficits and National Debts

Revenue and expenditure rarely balance precisely. When a government takes in more money than it spends in a given fiscal year, the happy result is a **surplus**. When a government spends more money than it takes in, the situation is called a **deficit**. A government can deal with a deficit in two ways. A sovereign government can legally print as much currency as it wishes. Unfortunately, in the absence of genuine economic growth, pumping a lot of paper money into the economy will typically stimulate inflation, making a bad situation worse. Money is like any other commodity; an oversupply drives down its value.

Normally, a government with a deficit will cover its revenue gap by borrowing. A very high HDI country will normally borrow the needed money from investors by selling government bonds and other securities. People buying treasury or savings bonds are actually loaning money to the U.S. government; many foreign countries put their reserves into U.S. government securities, effectively loaning money to America. A poorer country may be obliged to seek help from international lending agencies such as the World Bank or the International Monetary Fund (IMF).

It is tempting, but sometimes misleading, to view governmental finance in the same light as household budgets. All things being equal, it is obviously better to have a surplus than to have a deficit at the family level. On the other hand, we might reasonably take out a mortgage to purchase a home, since owning a house contributes to long-term financial security, even if it means an extended period of debt. We might get a student loan to attend a university or graduate school, sensibly calculating that a higher future salary will enable us to repay the debt easily.

In the same manner, a government with good future prospects but a temporarily weak economy might wish to borrow and spend money to build roads, dredge harbors, or create universities, all of which should contribute to future economic growth. On the other hand, if a government is borrowing money for expenditures that don't foster economic development, it may simply be piling up debt for future generations to pay off. With an enemy at the gates, a government may need to invest heavily in armies and weapons, but military expenditures—even if they are unavoidable—may not translate into future prosperity.[9]

The accumulated total of past not-yet-paid-off deficits is called **national debt**. Both deficit and debt are usually calculated as a percentage of the gross domestic product. These days, most governments are running a deficit, and their national debts are growing. Glance at table 12.5 and note in nine sample countries how the pattern plays out. In percentage terms, both deficit and debt tend to increase as we move toward the bottom of the HDI scale. Canada and Germany both have stable and prosperous economies, but Canada has accumulated a significant national debt that is equivalent to almost two-thirds of the value of all the goods and services generated within a year. About one-seventh of the revenue Canadians pay to their government goes to "servicing" this national debt, and is therefore not available for other forms of spending.

In the space of just a few years, the United States and several of its wealthier trading partners have abruptly run up huge deficits and debts. Worryingly, Japan's national debt in 2003 climbed to 250 percent of its annual gross domestic product, putting this Asian superpower into bed with unhappy Sierra Leone. Italy's national debt is more than 100 percent of GDP. Thanks to a weak stock market, the tax cuts introduced by

Table 12.5.   National Debts

It is customary to show both deficits and national debts as a percentage of GDP. As you can see, most countries are spending more money than they have, creating large annual deficits, which contribute to the national debt, which in turn must be serviced. For example, 8 percent of the U.S. federal budget is dedicated strictly to paying off the debt. The recent financial crisis and related stimulus packages that industrialized countries such as the United States have had to implement to prevent extreme economic downturns, have increased the ratio of debt to GDP. Greece, one of the worst-case scenarios of the current financial crisis, now owes more in debt than it is producing annually. Based on the Greek financial crisis, the United States and Europe have pledged to rein in spending and lower budget deficits in the upcoming years.

Russia	9.00
Iran	16.30
China	16.30
Bolivia	38.10
India	50.60
United States	62.90
France	82.40
Greece	142.70
Zimbabwe	233.20
Japan	199.70

Source: The Central Intelligence Agency (CIA), The World Factbook, https://www.cia.gov/library/publi cations/the-world-factbook/rankorder/2186rank.html, estimated figures for 2010.

the Bush administration, and the costs associated with the 2001 al-Qaeda attack and the subsequent wars against Afghanistan and Iraq, the U.S. federal government deficit in 2004 was close to 4 percent of GDP, and the American national debt was nearly 40 percent of the U.S. gross domestic product. By 2010 these U.S. figures had risen to a U.S. government deficit of about 10 percent of GDP, with the national debt rising to nearly 53 percent of gross domestic product.

The size of the U.S. deficit has a complicated relationship with the value of the dollar. The U.S. government finances its deficits largely by selling treasury bonds and other governmental securities to anyone—foreigner or U.S. citizen—who wishes to buy them. Given the traditional power of the American economy, many foreign countries keep a significant portion of their cash reserves in these U.S. Treasury notes. Indeed, the continued ability of the U.S. government to operate at a deficit depends upon the continuing willingness of foreign societies such as China to "loan" the United States large amounts of money in this fashion. In the short term, a "weak" dollar is good for U.S. exporters and bad for Europeans and Chinese who want to sell their products to Americans. If the dollar becomes too weak, however, those same foreign investors and governments may stop buying the treasury bonds with which the United States finances its fiscal self-indulgence.[10]

In section 2, below, we'll look at the grievous impact high debt levels have for very poor countries. How does debt affect richer countries? In 2011, for the first time in American history, there was talk of deliberately defaulting on interest payments, but no one doubts that countries such as Canada, Germany, and the United States can pay off or at least service the interest on their high levels of debt, but there are clusters of problems associated with running big deficits and accumulating a giant-sized national debt.

- Loss of Investment Capital: A large national debt soaks up investment capital, since people will loan their money to the government rather than risk it in business opportunities. Interest rates tend to rise, since the government will have to compete with other borrowers for available funds. This consumption of capital is multigenerational, since the debt will need to be paid or at least serviced by future generations.
- Strain on National Budgets: Servicing a debt (paying at least the interest) can use up a healthy portion of a country's annual budget. As of July 2011, the United States had a total national debt of about 14.5 trillion dollars ($14,490,610,000,000 if you prefer to see all those depressing zeros). In 2009, the U.S. government spent $700 billion "servicing" or paying the interest on the debt, soaking up money that might otherwise have been available for homeland security, education, or health care.[11]
- Loss of National Control: Furthermore, U.S. Treasury notes or British Savings Bonds can be bought by anybody regardless of citizenship, and foreign investors control a large portion of the U.S. national debt. These foreign investors are effectively loaning money to American society, and they can call in these loans at a time when it is convenient for them and not for the U.S. economy.

2. Poor People on a Rich Planet

It has been noted that the rich get richer and the poor get pregnant. As we'll see in chapter 13, the poor continue to get pregnant although not as much as they once did. Some are becoming less poor, while others are getting steadily poorer. Leaving the issue of who gets pregnant to the next chapter, let's turn now to the issue of wealth and poverty, trying to understand the actual dimensions and causes of economic inequality. We'll see what can and is being done to help the poorest people in the world, and why these efforts are only partially successful.

A WORLD OF INEQUALITIES

The most conventional approach is to define wealth and poverty in terms of money; rich people have deep pockets and poor people have empty ones. As we will see, this purely financial analysis can distort a complex reality, but let's start by seeing who has cash to burn and who is broke. Then we'll move on to look at the whole fraught question of how equally wealth is distributed within societies. In chapter 13, we'll look more carefully at the practical implications of poverty and its relationship to population growth.

We have already discovered that money and people are not distributed very evenly around the globe. Geographically, where do you go if you want to rub shoulders with wealthy people? North America, Western and parts of central Europe, and portions of the Pacific Rim (South Korea, Japan, Singapore, Australia, and New Zealand) are all sub-

Figure 12.1.   Malawi Mothers and Children Bathing and Washing Clothes
In very poor societies, there are usually extremes of wealth and poverty, and life at the bottom of the socioeconomic totem pole is often rough. Here at the Mua Mission in Malawi, ranked 171 out of 187 countries in the UN *Human Development Report 2011*, these mothers are bathing their children and washing their clothes in muddy waters—illustrating the lack of clean water available. The average gross national income (GNI) here is $753 per year, compared with $47,000 or so in Norway per year. While the Norwegians can expect to live on average to eighty or so, these women and children can expect to live only until fifty-two or so. It's these inequalities that so starkly divide the rich and the poor on our planet.

stantially wealthy, at least in terms of average statistics. Generally, the Asia/Pacific region has been recovering in recent years, with China steadily rising out of poverty. Portions of Latin America and the Caribbean have been "stalled" in economic terms. Some former satellites of the Soviet Union (such as the Czech Republic and Hungary) have been doing astonishingly well, while some portions of the old USSR are struggling.

According to both World Bank and UN Development Programme calculations, about 1.2 billion people, most (but not all) in low HDI countries, subsist on less than $365 per year. This means that one-fifth of humankind is trying to survive on a dollar a day or less. As always, these are purchasing power parity dollars that have been adjusted to take local spending power into account, but adjusted or not, a buck a day doesn't buy very much in any economy. This dollar-a-day statistic is regarded as rock-bottom, life-threatening poverty by the UN. Economists believe that there are 1.2 billion more people, another fifth of humankind, living on less than US$2 a day.[12]

Indeed, in the poorest portions of the globe, people may live completely marginal economic lives in which they have no actual money at all, surviving by subsistence farming and food gathering, which can range from finding nutrients in forests to eating food discarded by wealthier people as garbage. In the outskirts of Manila, for example, there is a slum ironically called "The Promised Land" where about fifty thousand people live in an extended garbage dump and earn a meager living scavenging for edible leftovers. In 2000, several days of heavy rain in the Philippines caused mountains of refuse to collapse on the ramshackle houses below, killing dozens of people and providing the ultimate ironic comment on life and death at the bottom of the heap: garbage pickers killed by falling garbage.[13]

Mind the Gap

Not only is there enormous inequality between very rich and very poor countries, but the gap between the richest and the poorest is growing dramatically.[14] While the rest of the world made solid advances in economic status, fifty-four countries lost ground between 1990 and 2000: twenty in sub-Saharan Africa, seventeen in Eastern Europe and/or the former Soviet Union, six in Latin America, six in east Asia/Pacific, and five in the Arab world.[15] In 1960, the wealth differential between the twenty poorest and the twenty richest countries in the world was 1:18; by 2000, the ratio had increased to 1:37, more than double.[16]

There is good news, though, in terms of global poverty. Recent studies on the millennium development goals (MDGs), agreed upon by member states of the United Nations, show that the overall poverty rate is expected to drop below 15 percent of the global population, well below the 23 percent target. East Asia reduced poverty the most, while sub-Saharan Africa has made only meager gains. Most significantly, hunger is still an issue on the planet, another goal of the eight MDGs. Sixteen percent of the world population still goes hungry every day.[17]

There are often cavernous internal inequalities within both rich and poor societies. In essence, every wealthy nation contains its own Fourth World, while even desperately poor countries have their millionaires. And when the gap gets too big, there are inevitably social problems such as alienation and high levels of criminality and sometimes even revolutionary violence between the socioeconomic classes.[18] From a methodological viewpoint, there are two generally used measurement tools to estimate the disparity in wealth within a given society.

• The Rich-Poor Ratio: In table 12.6's top four countries, note that the gap between rich and poor is comparatively high in the United States, as denoted by a higher Gini index number. Canada is substantially more "equal," and Japanese income is very evenly divided. Partly because of extreme free-market economics under General Pinochet's 1973–1989 dictatorship, the rich-poor ratio in Chile is very high. The rich-poor ratio generally worsens as we move down the chart; in countries such as Brazil and Russia, a handful of entrepreneurs are beginning to create some serious fortunes, but the poorest 10 percent hasn't yet been invited to the party. Note that allegedly Marxist China is less equal than free-market India. At the bottom, the ratios are generally very high; in troubled Sierra Leone, the richest 10 percent of the population control nearly half of all the country's wealth.

- The Gini Index or Gini Coefficient: Listed in the right-hand column of table 12.6, the **Gini index or Gini coefficient** is the second and more-sophisticated mathematical tool used in political analysis to measure inequality within a given society. The calculus is complicated, but the Gini index is generated by examining how much of the national wealth is controlled by each fifth or quintile of the population from the poorest to the wealthiest. The result is expressed either as a number between 0.00 and 1.00, or more commonly, a number between 0.00 and 100; we have followed the later system in this text. A society in which everybody possessed precisely the same amount of wealth would both bring joy to the ghost of Karl Marx and produce a Gini index of 0. A country in which Uncle Scrooge had all the income and everyone else was destitute would create a Gini index of 100.

As you can see from table 12.6, the wealthier countries of the developed world have relatively low Gini index numbers, reflecting fairly equal societies. This is particularly the case in Scandinavian countries as well as Germany and France, and reflects a rich social-democratic/welfare-state tradition. They tend to have large middle classes, very few paupers, and even fewer billionaires. The more sternly capitalist United States has a large gap between rich and poor, almost as large as Russia. When it gave up Marxism for what some have called "gangster capitalism," Russia's Gini index doubled in just a few years. Latin American and developing societies generally have huge gaps between rich and poor. In poorer societies, the indices are typically very high, with Namibia coming in at 73.4 in 2010.[19]

In recent decades, there has been a general tendency for Gini indices to grow, even in fairly egalitarian societies. Princeton economist Paul Krugman has noted how high the American Gini index has climbed in comparison to otherwise similar societies in Western Europe. He observes, however, that even the Gini index is too crude a tool to understand

Table 12.6.   The Bottom versus the Top

This table compares the amount of national wealth controlled by the poorest and the richest, and establishes the ratio between them. The "Gini index" is a more precise measure of inequality. The larger the number, the more unequal a society is.

Country	Gini Index
United States	40.8
Canada	32.6
Japan	24.9
Chile	52.1
Russia	42.3
Brazil	53.9
China	41.5
India	36.8
Swaziland	50.7
Kenya	47.7
Nigeria	42.9
Sierra Leone	42.5

Source: UNDP, *Human Development Report 2011*, Statistical Annex http://hdr.undp.org/en/media/HDR_2011_EN_Tables.pdf.

what has been happening to U.S. society. Measuring the top 10–20 percent of society, says Krugman, isn't enough, because "Most of the gains in the share of the top 10 percent of taxpayers over the past 30 years were actually gains to the top 1 percent. . . . In turn, 60 percent of the gains of that top 1 percent went to the top 0.1 percent."[20] In essence, Krugman is saying, the United States not only has a widening gap between rich and poor, but a gulf between the merely affluent and the super rich.

The U.S. economy boomed in the 1990s, but so did the economic difference between rich and poor. In real dollars (dollars adjusted for inflation), workers' wages in America have fallen since about 1968, particularly among lower-paid employees. For most of the 1990s, the poorest 20 percent of the American public owned less than 5 percent of the nation's wealth, while the richest 20 percent controlled almost half of U.S. prosperity.[21]

There is some evidence that rising inequality and falling wages can create real social problems ranging from insidious alienation, disaffection, and anomie in some societies to violence and revolution in others. Analyzing the American situation, MIT economist Lester Thurow notes, "These are uncharted waters. . . . America has never experienced falling real wages for a majority of its work force. . . . We are . . . putting a pressure cooker on the stove over a full flame and waiting to see how long it takes to explode."[22]

Portraits of the Real World: The Cost of Happiness

Richard Collin, one of the authors of this book, spent a few weeks of 1975 in a small village of perhaps five hundred people in southern Iran. His hosts had no electricity or telephones. Water had to be carried uphill in plastic containers, a job mostly left to women and little girls. Everybody worked hard growing vegetables in dry fields and raising goats and sheep, some chickens, and a couple of cows. The village's only radio worked when somebody brought a supply of "D" cell batteries in from Kerman, the big city to the north. Social life consisted in going to a kind of general store/restaurant, sitting on the floor, and drinking tea while listening to the broadcast from Tehran. Richard couldn't follow much of the Farsi-language broadcasts, but came for the tea and the company.

Despite their poverty, Richard's Iranian friends didn't seem unhappy, and the only complaining came from the small, seriously overworked donkeys that carried everybody up and down the hill. The children had wonderful, luminous eyes, and laughed all the time. The local mullah (who also acted as mayor and judge) assured Richard it was the best place in the world to live, and suggested that he convert to Islam, learn Farsi, marry a local woman, and become the village schoolmaster. The contentment of his Iranian hosts may have been rooted in their near-total ignorance of the outside world. There was no television to make them aware of how rich people were in Tehran, London, or New York. The village and its land met most of their immediate physical needs. They felt secure and nobody starved because Allah had—at least in recent years—blessed both their fields and their women with fertility.

Before launching into our consideration of global wealth and poverty, it is worth remembering that once our basic nutritional requirements have been satisfied, how poor we are depends a lot on what we think we need. We (the authors of this book) live in pleasant homes in England and America. We "need" everything we have: televisions, cars, thousands of books and CDs, and lots of computers. Were Richard's Iranian friends to visit his home, they would perhaps conclude that professors live like shahs and sultans. They would be wrong, but the error would be understandable. We and our professorial colleagues are better off in every measurable way than those villagers whom Richard met a lifetime ago, but are we actually any happier? A good question.

Actually, some serious research has gone into probing the link between economic prosperity and contentment. While his research is not free from controversy, Holland's Professor Ruut Veenhoven has assembled enough raw data to suggest that there is a demonstrable but complicated relationship between dollars and delight. Generally, the citizens of wealthier societies report themselves to be happier than do the residents of poor countries. Within a given country, happiness seems to rise as growing income translates into material security, that is, shelter, enough to eat, and medical care.[23] In his *Happiness: Lessons from a New Science*, social scientist Richard Layard observes that it doesn't take very much money to produce this basic level of contentment and suggests that we could inexpensively augment humankind's store of happiness by looking for ways to make desperately poor people less desperate. When our wealth increases beyond what we need to organize basic comfort and security for ourselves, however, the "money = happiness" connection becomes less clear. A paddle in a rowboat is likely to cheer us up; a cruise on a yacht might not.[24]

WHY IT'S HARD TO HELP

Deciding how to help the poorer countries in the world depends a lot on our analysis of why these countries have remained economically underdeveloped. It is tempting to answer the question, "Why are poor people poor?" with a series of platitudes and oversimplifications, but the issue is really quite complicated. Clearly, the legacy of colonialism bears some of the blame. Over the course of the past five hundred years, technologically advanced nations in Europe (and later the United States) exercised enormous control over backward areas of the medium and low HDI world. The colonial powers then shaped the economies of these captive countries entirely for their own benefit, pushing them in the direction of one-crop economies and denying them normal economic development.[25]

Radicals, some liberal analysts, and Asian/African intellectuals generally make much of the colonialism argument, but some conservative economists focus on governance, demanding that the world's poor begin to accept some responsibility for their own problems. For many African societies, colonialism ended forty years ago, and yet some sub-Saharan nations are actually poorer today than they were under European rule. In the 1990s, the planet's poorest fifty-four countries actually lost ground economically, declining in wealth while the rest of the world got richer.[26] Most of these developing world hard cases are inefficiently managed by corrupt and/or ideologically rigid dictatorships. Free trade and an honest free-market economy, conservative economists argue, would produce economic growth.

The Bottom Line

To some extent, both arguments must yield to a third and more fundamental factor related to the basic availability of natural resources. The U.S. system of government notwithstanding, America is rich because it is a huge, sparsely populated continent with abundant mineral deposits, great inland waterways, a temperate climate, and fertile soil. Contrast this to North Africa's Burkina Faso, a country with little rain, not much fertile soil, no significant mineral resources, and no way of generating power. While it is clearly the case that resource-poor and landlocked Burkina Faso has been the victim of both French colonialism and epically poor government, changing its history would not change its geography.

As suggested by table 12.7, poor countries are poor because of basic geographical conditions, such as bad soil and lack of water, compounded by social factors, such as poor health, overpopulation, bad educational systems, and bad governments. But the economic status of each country needs to be studied independently. Japan has very limited natural resources, but is a very high HDI country; Nigeria has oil, mineral wealth, and potential agricultural power, but ranks 156th in the UN's 2011 human development index. Generally speaking, poverty in medium HDI countries is the result of distribution and infrastructural problems; the basic potential is there; poverty in many low HDI countries is often more closely related to the absence of any resources from which wealth can be generated, complicated by extremely corrupt government.

From a methodological point of view, political scientists need to be very careful when looking at the relationship between variables. There is always a temptation to assert that a causal connection exists when we repeatedly find two variables together in the same situation. But determining cause and effect can be tricky. Are the people of Sierra Leone poor because they suffer from ill health and bad government? Or do they endure health and political problems because they are poor? Or are they caught up in a self-reinforcing loop in which poverty and bad social conditions contribute to one another?

Table12.7.   Are Some Countries Destined to Be Poor?

The Geography➜	poor soil, water shortages, poor transportation, lack of natural resources, susceptibility to natural disasters
The People➜	malnutrition, high birthrate, poor public health, political instability, poor educational system, bad governance, and corruption

Foreign Aid

Here's the nub of the problem: since scholars and politicians don't really agree on what ultimately causes poverty, they aren't going to agree on what to do about it. Let's look at some of the proposed antipoverty solutions and see where some of the arguments lie. The first and most obvious answer is charity or foreign aid. If the specter of poverty bothers you, why not donate enough money to make poor people less poor? "**Foreign aid**" generally implies gifts of money, low-interest loans, food, pharmaceutical supplies, or other benefits to some impoverished foreign country. There are several different kinds of foreign aid.[27]

- Multilateral Aid: Multilateral aid is typically aid from a sovereign government that is funneled to the poor through an international organization of some kind. For example, the UN's wealthier members contribute money directly or indirectly to UN agencies, such as the Food and Agriculture Organization (FAO) or the UN Children's Fund (UNICEF), with the understanding that their pooled donations will be used for specific purposes. More controversially, the World Bank and the International Monetary Fund both collect contributions from member countries in order to make loans and grants to needy recipients.
- Private Charitable Aid: This type of aid typically comes from individual philanthropic NGOs such as Oxfam, CARE, Médecins sans Frontières, the Red Cross, and Save the Children. The Catholic Church maintains orphanages and hospitals in many parts of the underdeveloped world. The Rotary Club has been working since 1985 to abolish polio. Some wealthy Westerners have contributed very large sums of money to improve life in the less prosperous parts of the world. For example, Microsoft founder Bill Gates has made a significant contribution to malaria research. Private charitable aid is difficult to quantify, but some have estimated that Americans may send as much as $35 billion a year overseas, a figure that is about three and a half times the amount contributed by the federal government.[28]
- Bilateral Aid: Bilateral aid is the direct gift of funds or goods by a richer country to a poorer country at least ostensibly for the purpose of alleviating economic distress. At least on paper, bilateral aid accounts for about 70 percent of all aid, but governments like to inflate their aid budgets to appear generous. For example, instead of scrapping obsolete military equipment, governments will sometimes give it to a poorer military ally. The donor government then awards itself a mammoth financial credit for "aid," although it may actually be cheaper to donate an elderly tank than to dismantle or store it. Furthermore, aid figures for a given country will typically include the bureaucratic costs of running an aid program. For example, the American budget for foreign aid includes the salaries, health insurance, and pension plans of all the officials who administer the U.S. foreign assistance effort and the Peace Corps. While some of these administrative costs are necessary, a significant portion of the aid budget is being spent in the United States on Americans, not needy foreigners.
- Micro-finance as Aid: In 2006, the world turned its attention to a new type of banking in the less-developed world, called micro-credit and micro-finance banking. Founder of the Grameen Bank in Bangladesh, Muhammad Yunus, won the Nobel Peace Prize for his work on creating a new form of "development" for poor people in Bangladesh and

the world. Instead of relying on large development loans from the World Bank or from the traditional banking sector, which are generally guaranteed by collateral (material items you own) or land (which poor people do not generally hold title to), this type of credit and financing does not ask for such guarantees. Rather, it gives smaller loans in the hundreds of dollars or less to individuals and/or communities to develop small businesses that generate income for their families, communities, and for future savings and investment. Yunus and Grameen Bank colleagues found that for every $1 loaned, families invested $2.50 of their own savings in their microenterprises.[29] Recently, however, micro-finance has been criticized, as it risks personal savings of the most vulnerable of society who can least afford to lose such income. It may also create a separate banking sector outside of the formal banking sector, which could threaten economic stability. For an interesting global take on micro-finance, visit the website and mircrofinance plan called Kiva.org.[30] Anyone can go there, choose a borrower, lend as little as $25, and be repaid to lend again. Check it out and see if you think it's a better form of "development" for yourself.

In absolute terms, the three leading donor nations are the United States, Japan, and France, and deciding which one is first depends upon how you do (or cook) the books. As you can see in figure 12.2, the wealthier countries of the world dedicate only a negligible percentage of their income to charity or foreign aid, and in recent years, many donor countries have become even less generous. Between 1985 and 1997, overseas development aid by all major countries declined dramatically. This decline is partly explained by economic problems in Europe and the United States, and partly by "donor fatigue," a perception that rich countries are giving too much for too little reward, or that foreign aid just doesn't work.

WHY AID SOMETIMES DOESN'T HELP

The world's principal donors have contributed tens of billions of dollars per year, but critics complain that even this generosity has not had much impact on world poverty, and some even charge that foreign aid actually makes matters worse.[31] Why hasn't aid made more of a dent in world poverty? There are several factors to be considered.

- Politics: A lot of foreign aid is given for purely political reasons, often to people who are objectively not that poor. An analysis of the American foreign-aid budget, for example, suggests that a lot of money is donated in response to domestic American political objectives rather than humanitarian concerns. Relatively wealthy Israel gets about $550 per person from the U.S. Treasury, while sub-Saharan Africa, arguably the poorest region of the world, receives about $1.40 per person. Why? You can't win an American election by giving money to Chad or Niger, but money for embattled Israel appeals to pro-Israeli American voters. During the Cold War period, there were massive U.S. aid and loan packages to anticommunist dictators in the Philippines, Uruguay, and Ethiopia.[32]
- National Security: A great deal of foreign aid is military. For example, about 37 percent of all U.S. aid is defense related, and while guns for poor people may have other

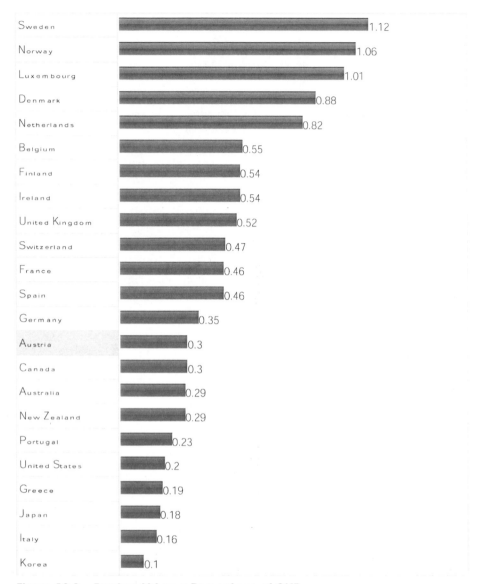

Figure 12.2. Foreign Aid as a Percentage of GNP
Virtually all of the world's foreign aid comes from the richest twenty-four countries that make up the Development Assistance Committee (DAC) of the OECD. The UN calculates foreign aid as a percentage of GNP or GNI and recommends that 0.70 percent of GNP be channeled into foreign aid. Most countries miss that target, and most of them miss it by a great deal. At 0.2 percent of GNP, the United States is close to the bottom of global aid contributors.

Source: Global Issues.org, http://www.globalissues.org/article/35/foreign-aid-development-assistance.

foreign-policy benefits, military technology does little to pull a society out of poverty. Egypt, for example, is one of the neediest societies in Africa. The Cairo government is a major recipient of U.S. bilateral aid, but one-quarter of that aid is military, and all of it depends upon Egyptian willingness to follow American foreign-policy requirements.

- Corruption and Misuse: Furthermore, significant amounts of aid money are stolen, wasted, or misused. While some bilateral aid goes from a donor government to a charity within a target country, most aid is government-to-government, and may wind up in the pockets of the bureaucracy instead of the people who need it. A Commerce Department study revealed that 63 percent of U.S. aid to Haiti during the Duvalier dictatorship was misappropriated.[33] The world's largest recipient of aid is the war-torn Republic of Sudan, where the UN is currently spending about a $1 million a day for food and medical supplies. This influx of aid money permits the Khartoum government to focus on internal conflicts rather than the more prosaic business of feeding its population. While the UN's effort in the Sudan is feeding hundreds of thousands of people who would otherwise starve, it is also—in effect—financing arms purchases for the Sudanese Army. On the other hand, the food is keeping hundreds of thousands of people alive. If we stopped giving food aid to Sudan, we would turn a barely manageable disaster into an epic human welfare catastrophe. When war and hunger occupy the same stage, the play is always going to be a tragedy.[34]

- Economics: Another problem is structural in the sense that aid can distort or damage an already crippled economy. For example, the most dramatic form of assistance is the delivery of emergency food aid to starving populations. Food aid works best when the recipient society is merely going through a bad patch after a war or some natural disaster. On the other hand, if a society's problems are deep and systemic, food aid can create a condition of dependency, creating slum-cities of people who are permanently "hooked" on international charity. Donated food can also damage the existing agricultural industry, since it is difficult for a farmer to sell food when a foreign donor is giving it away for free. On the other hand, in a situation where people are actively starving, it's tough to know what else to do.

- Conditionality: A final problem is what is often called "**conditionality**." Aid or loans are said to be conditional or coercive when the donor demands that the recipient obey instructions from the donor country. In the mildest cases, aid is "tied" in the sense that the recipient must use it to purchase goods or services from the donor. In many cases, the donor country requires that recipients restructure their economy in ways that are economically beneficial to the aid-giving country.[35] For example, the U.S. government, the IMF, and the World Bank all condition aid to poor countries by insisting that the recipient governments open up their economies to foreign (i.e., U.S.) competition, and privatize public services such as water and health, problems discussed in greater detail below. Depending on the individual country, the conditionality may or may not involve good advice, but it effectively imposes a "beggars can't be choosers" limitation on the sovereignty of poor countries.

What's the answer? In recent years, the nations of the underdeveloped world have been asserting that only a massive donation of wealth and technology from the high HDI world would address their problems. The UN has argued that wealthy countries could well afford to donate 0.7 percent of national income, but no large-scale transfer is likely to take place, since there is little donor sentiment for any massive taxpayer-financed charity toward low HDI countries. Aid, promised from developed countries in 2005, reached $128.7 billion in 2010, a record high, but this was still $19 billion short of the commitments. UN reports show that Africa receives the least amount of aid, only $11 billion out of the $25 billion promised in 2005.[36]

There may be ways of getting better results with the aid money already on the table, however. Some experts have noted, for example, that in areas where food production is permanently problematic, donor countries could fund and staff long-term agricultural programs that have education and engineering projects designed to help hungry people grow their own food. Generally speaking, poor educational and health systems hold back development. Workers cannot perform efficiently if they are weak from chronic illnesses or handicapped by low literacy skills. More effort might be put into developing what is often called "human capital," that is, provide health and educational programs to people so that they are better able to provide for themselves.

Loans and Debt Relief

Some analysts have long argued that targeted, low-cost loans would better serve the interests of underdeveloped societies than do grants. All governments borrow money. Most underdeveloped societies turn to international lending agencies such as the World Bank, which lends money for economic development, or the International Monetary Fund, which makes loans to stabilize weak currencies. Sometimes a wealthy industrial state will help one of its corporations make a sale to a poorer customer by orchestrating "credits." In this complicated arrangement, a commercial bank often provides the actual cash with the donor government guaranteeing the loan and perhaps paying a portion of the interest.

In the 1960s, the international financial community began an optimistic policy of loaning money to very poor countries. The prosperous "swinging sixties" generated money to lend along with the confidence that investments in the impoverished underdeveloped world could stimulate real economic growth there. Lending was also seen as a way both of fighting communism and of involving poor countries in the developing global capitalist economy. After the 1973 Arab-Israeli War, the price of crude oil rose astronomically, driving many poorer countries further into debt as they borrowed to pay escalating fuel costs.[37]

By the 1980s, some of these heavily indebted poor countries were borrowing even more money just to pay the interest on earlier loans. In the two decades that followed, the poorest countries in the world saw their total debt triple, partly because of mounting interest payments. By the end of the century, a group of very poor and heavily indebted countries owed far more money than they could ever pay, a collective debt exceeding $2.5 trillion, about half of which is owed to the IMF/World Bank and similar lending institutions.[38]

For many poor countries, complete repayment of this debt will strangle economic recovery. In 1998, Oxfam estimated that the African continent was spending four times as much in debt repayments as it was on health and education for African children. In 2002, the World Bank determined that the twenty-three poorest countries in the world were using most new aid for the purpose of servicing existing debt. The African nation of Zambia, for example, devotes about 30 percent of its national budget to debt repayments and spends only 10 percent on basic social services, and Indonesia has a similar problem.[39]

The lending institutions reacted to the debt crisis with two interrelated approaches: debt forgiveness and austerity/structural adjustment programs. Let's talk about these two approaches separately.

- Debt Forgiveness: In the 1990s, a coalition of NGOs mounted the "Jubilee 2000" campaign to pressure the IMF/World Bank into the creation of the Heavily Indebted Poor Countries (HIPC) Program. First launched in 1996, the HIPC Program attempts to reduce or cancel unsustainable debt for countries such as Bolivia, Guyana, Honduras, Nicaragua, Afghanistan, Pakistan, Cambodia, Myanmar, Vietnam, and most of sub-Saharan Africa. HIPC has now enrolled forty-two countries prepared to restructure their economies according to the desires of Washington policy makers, but relatively limited amounts of debt have actually been canceled. Where the debt has actually been written off, however, the results have sometimes been important, and governments have been able to shift budgetary allocations from debt repayments to more socially useful goals. After seeing $1 billion of its debt disappear, Uganda used the money to double elementary school enrollment. Mozambique has plowed forgiven debt money into hospitals and housing.[40]
- Austerity Programs: In some cases, the IMF/World Bank complex decided that individual debts could be at least partially serviced if the indebted countries put their economic houses in order with what are sometimes called "austerity" or "structural adjustment" programs. This collection of programs is often called "The Washington Consensus," and will be discussed in section 3 below.

Tough Choices: Odious Dictators, Odious Debts

If the Mafia put a pistol to your head and forced you to sign a contract promising to fork over "protection" money, no court in the world would enforce the mob's right to collect if you got brave and decided not to pay. In contract law, free and genuine consent is the absolute requirement for a legally enforceable agreement. Were you to die, could the mob legally collect from your children or grandchildren? Absolutely not. Even if the debt were legal, the money could only be collected from your estate, not your descendants.

Let's go international with our scenario. A corrupt and evil dictator seizes control of a small, impoverished society. He cancels elections, executes the opposition, and maintains himself in office with the brutal use of internal security forces. As head of state, he negotiates loans from a superpower that wants his political support, but most of the borrowed money winds up in the dictator's offshore bank accounts and contributes nothing to the economic development of the downtrodden population. When the inevitable popular revolution comes, the dictator flees with a billion dollars in stolen money. The international banking community now demands that the traumatized and impoverished country repay the ex-dictator's debts. Can they enforce compliance?

Absolutely. Moreover, if the present generation is too bankrupt to pay off the debts, the international banking community can extract the money from their children and grandchildren. Under conventional legal thinking, states bear the responsibility for debts incurred by present and past governments.

Why is international law so different from national legal principles? First, the nations who developed international law were more likely to be lenders than borrowers, and they fashioned laws to suit their business interests. Second, the banking community argued that it could never loan money if debtors could simply walk away after a regime change.

The United States has been historically inconsistent on this issue. On one hand, the United States normally insists that inherited debts need to be repaid. On the other hand, when the United States took over Cuba in 1898, the American government renounced Cuba's foreign debt, arguing that Cubans should not be obliged to pay off money borrowed by the Spanish administration to maintain a repressive colonialist military occupation.[41] After World War I, an international law scholar named Alexander Nahum Sack advocated what is called the "odious debt" doctrine, arguing that people should not be responsible for the repayment of loans incurred against both their will and their best interests. Despite the cogency of Sack's reasoning, the Odious Debt Doctrine has seldom actually worked in international law because of practical complications. Generally, a new government is obliged to pay off the old regime's debts.

The principle that successor governments inherited debts from previous dictatorial regimes would perhaps never have been questioned had it not been for the Anglo-American conquest of Iraq in 2003. The Bush administration wanted to stabilize Iraq as quickly as possible. Arguing that Saddam Hussein had been an illegitimate leader, the Americans suggested that the world needed to forgive Iraq's foreign debt (in excess of $120 billion). Much of the money was owed to the French, the Russians, and several Persian Gulf states, all of whom were predictably unenthusiastic about American generosity with their money.

On the other hand, making Iraq cough up $120 billion as it climbs out of the wreckage of its past is a recipe for disaster. The American economist Joseph Stiglitz has recalled how the victorious allies extracted massive reparations payments from a defeated Germany after World War I, which helped set the stage for the Great Depression and another world war. Noting that individuals can declare personal bankruptcy and corporations can file for protection from their creditors, Stiglitz wondered if there shouldn't be an international bankruptcy court.[42]

Bankruptcy assumes, however, that the debts are legal but can't be paid. If an unwilling society finds itself burdened with a profitless debt, maybe international law should revisit the Odious Debt Doctrine and examine the inherent legality of those original contracts. Perhaps this should be the new principle of international finance: only debts incurred by democratic societies are legal contracts; dirty deals with dictators are unenforceable.

Of course, the practical implications would be staggering. If this fair-contract principle were applied retroactively, all debts incurred by every dictatorship, past and present, would come under scrutiny. Most of the HIPC countries are or were undemocratic regimes, and most of their debts are owed to American banks or American-dominated international lending agencies, which means some of that lost money might be yours. The Odious Debt Doctrine would be an earthquake for the world economic order.

On the other hand, it would be a very democratic earthquake. A bank would think twice before making an unsecured loan to an undemocratic government, and this would make it hard for poor dictatorships to survive. A poor country that needed external finance would be under pressure to become democratic, since no one would make uncollectible loans to an authoritarian ruler. You've just been nominated chair of the U.S. Council of Economic Advisors, and the president wants to know how to handle this particular hot potato. Your advice, please?[43]

The 2008–2011 financial crises impacted not only the developed world banks and investors but also foreign direct investment (FDI) and aid to the poorest countries. Foreign direct investment means the amount of money invested in another country, such as placing a company branch in another country. While the early 2000s witnessed an increase in FDI, 2008 and 2009 recorded major losses in aid and investment for the developed and emerging market economies. Top recipients of global FDI are China, India, Brazil, Mexico, and Turkey. In 2008, companies invested $150 billion in China. By 2009, this dropped to $80 billion.[44] To put it in perspective, the world spent nearly seven times more on bailing out companies during the 2008 financial crisis than it did in thirty-eight years of providing international aid to the poorest in the world.

3. Trade and Globalization

"Trade, Not Aid!" has long been a famous mantra, and poorer societies ask wealthier countries to do mutually profitable business with them rather than hand out charitable donations with lots of strings attached. We have seen that both developmental aid and loans have problems as well as benefits. Is trade the answer to the problems of the poorer corners of the world?

The answer ought to be a simple "yes," but the political and financial relationship between rich and poor is never simple, and the answer turns out to be a complicated "semi-yes." Since the 1980s, major U.S.-dominated financial institutions have reached a rough general agreement, or consensus, on what the global poor should do to address their problems. Since many of the institutions controlling significant amounts of public money are headquartered in Washington, D.C., this shared sense is called the "**Washington Consensus.**" For poorer countries needing foreign aid or debt forgiveness, obedience to the Washington Consensus is no longer a matter of choice. In this section, we will see what Washington is asking these underprivileged countries to do, and ask ourselves if the advice is good or bad.

The efforts of these global money managers to direct the world's economy is part of a larger phenomenon popularly called "globalization," which we will survey in greater detail below. Those who believe that the Washington Consensus is wrong-headed and hypocritical range from distinguished but dissident economists such as Nobel Prize–winning Joseph Stiglitz to the antiglobalization street protesters who rage against the World Bank and the International Monetary Fund. This interesting and crucial controversy may at first seem more complicated than it is. Let's take it step by step and see what the Washington Consensus really is; why globalization means different things to different people; and what can and is being done to bring some relief to the people whom revolutionary writer Frantz Fanon called the "Wretched of the Earth."

TRADE, TARIFFS, AND INTERNATIONAL BUSINESS

For private business finance, London, Tokyo, and New York are the dominant trio of rival global centers. For public financial transactions (such as credits, aid money, and developmental loans), the center of the world is Washington, D.C., home to both the World Bank and the International Monetary Fund, as well as the U.S. Treasury Department, the U.S. Agency for International Development, and the decision-making apparatus of the American government. These organizations are pivotal in making decisions about who gets what, and under what conditions. Let's look, therefore, at Washington's conventional wisdom on economic development, and see how trade and international business factors into it all.[45]

The "Washington Consensus"

By the end of the twentieth century, the World Bank, the IMF, the U.S. Treasury Department, and many senior American political leaders had concluded that high HDI countries should adopt a more aggressive stance toward very poor societies, forcing them to tackle tough issues. According to what came to be called the "Washington Consensus," badly underdeveloped countries needed to deregulate their capital markets to allow the free movement of money in and out of their territories, reduce import tariffs to encourage free trade and international business, and put some discipline into their own internal financial affairs. Sometimes, this would be bitter medicine, but the Washington Consensus had the political and economic clout to make almost anybody swallow almost anything.

The essence of the Washington Consensus is that Marxists, liberals, and social democrats are all utterly wrong in believing that governments should take charge of economies. Adam Smith, on the other hand, was right in maintaining that free markets are self-correcting, and governments need to let the invisible hand of the market operate. The unrestricted operation of global market forces and the laws of supply and demand, as understood by mainstream economists, would eventually boost even the poorest of countries into self-sustaining economic growth.[46] Specifically, there are three ingredients of the Washington Consensus.

- Austerity or Macroeconomic Stability: The first obligation of a poor government is to practice fiscal discipline. The budget needs to be balanced to avoid having deficits that create debt or inflation. Fiscal discipline means keeping a tight lid on public spending for social services such as education and health care, even if this means a temporary increase in poverty and unemployment.

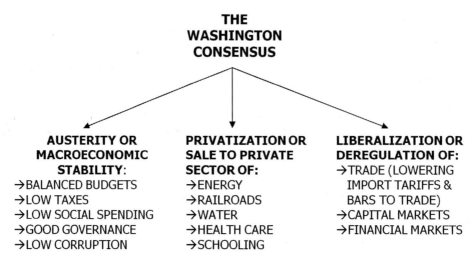

**THE
WASHINGTON
CONSENSUS**

**AUSTERITY OR
MACROECONOMIC
STABILITY:**
→BALANCED BUDGETS
→LOW TAXES
→LOW SOCIAL SPENDING
→GOOD GOVERNANCE
→LOW CORRUPTION

**PRIVATIZATION OR
SALE TO PRIVATE
SECTOR OF:**
→ENERGY
→RAILROADS
→WATER
→HEALTH CARE
→SCHOOLING

**LIBERALIZATION OR
DEREGULATION OF:**
→TRADE (LOWERING
   IMPORT TARIFFS &
   BARS TO TRADE)
→CAPITAL MARKETS
→FINANCIAL MARKETS

Figure 12.3. The Washington Consensus
Key international financial institutions believe that poor countries need to stabilize
their domestic finances, sell off inefficient state services, and open up their markets
to international trade.

Self-discipline and belt tightening sound like good advice, and some poor countries are clearly spending too much on unproductive projects such as jet fighters or
gaudy palaces for their rulers. Governments that waste money through inefficiency or
corruption need to mend their ways. When local political leaders are told to tighten
their belts, however, they often find it easier to tighten the belts of their poor, cutting
health, education, and social-welfare projects. If they fail to adopt these harsh measures,
they can find it difficult to get new loans or have existing debt forgiven. When the
Dominican Republic's economy went seriously sour in 2003, the International Monetary Fund offered a loan that was contingent upon the implementation of an austerity program. With inflation running at 29 percent, the necessities of life were already
becoming prohibitively expensive for poor people. When the Dominican government
displayed reluctance to cut public services any further, the IMF put the loan on ice.
The Dominican Republic already dedicates 40 percent of its annual national budget to
servicing foreign debts.

• Privatization: In every non-Marxist society, the government will perform some tasks
(such as maintenance of armed forces), while other functions will be carried out by private enterprise (running restaurants, driving cabs, etc.). Depending upon choices made
by a given society, some in-between functions can be placed either in the public sector
or the private sector, that is, run by the government or entrusted to profit-making
corporations. The Washington Consensus does not believe that governments are much
good at building roads, providing electricity, administering health care, running school
systems, and operating transportation grids. Privatization means selling these operations to private enterprise on the theory that the profit motive will drive the private
sector to outperform the public sector.[47]

In practice, privatization has merits and demerits. In the 1960s, development
economists told governments to create heavy industries such as steel mills, but indus-

trialization never took off in many poor societies, and these state-owned companies had to be endlessly bailed out with government subsidies. Selling them off to the private sector (or closing them down altogether) made obvious good sense. In other cases, privatization deprived the public of valuable services. Under pressure from the IMF, for example, the Bolivian government sold its state-owned railroad system to a foreign company. The outsiders promptly closed the loss-making line Paz to Cochabamba, the third largest city in Bolivia. This might have been good fiscal policy for a profit-making corporation, but it was bad public policy, because Bolivians needed to move goods, services, and people between the two big cities.[48] Cochabamba has not done well with privatization; when the government sold the municipal waterworks to a private company, the water simply stopped, leading to riots and deaths.

Privatization works better when people have at least a little money to spend. Big water companies, such as Suez, Vivendi, and Saur, have the technical expertise to bring clean water to hard-to-reach places, but no private company is going to show a profit trying to sell water to absolutely destitute people who are used to getting it for free. The central problem with privatization is this: when people are very poor, their government is not likely to do much of a job at providing them with water, electricity, schooling, or medical care. If they are that poor, a commercial firm may not be able to do any better, since there is little prospect of making any money.[49]

When done rapidly and on a massive scale, privatization is sometimes called "shock therapy." When Russia stumbled out of Marxism in 1992, the Washington Consensus announced that a corrupt and inefficient Marxist economy could be made into efficient capitalism virtually overnight. As we saw in chapter 8, the result was more shock than therapy for most Russians. We'll read more about Canadian researcher and activist Naomi Klein later; her book, *The Shock Doctrine*, argues provocatively that modern day capitalism has been enforced upon the globe by a series of shocks on unknowing working-class people. She argues that this radical form of capitalism is akin to psychological, and at times, physical terrorism on the human population. Her documentary on what she defines as "radical capitalism" has been the source of much global attention and debate. Has global capitalism spiraled out of control, or is Naomi Klein really the radical?[50]

- Liberalization: Every government places some restrictions on the movement of money, goods, and services across its borders, and the Washington Consensus maintains that these restrictions should be relaxed or eliminated, a process sometimes called "**liberalization**" or "deregulation." When restrictions on capital are relaxed, foreign investors can buy stocks and bonds in local companies, or put their money directly into the economy by building commercial enterprises. This sort of investment capital tends to go to medium HDI countries such as China, Mexico, and Brazil, where governments are relatively stable and labor costs are very low. Investors are less likely to put their money into politically unstable low HDI societies where the workforce is uneducated and corruption is too deeply engrained. Another problem is the fickleness of foreign investors. What Thomas Friedman calls "The Electronic Herd" consists of investors all over the world who are capable of moving huge amounts of money in or out of a country at the touch of a computer keyboard. If these money managers don't get the profits they expect, they can move their capital somewhere else, quickly bankrupting a poor country.[51]

The Age of (Almost) Free Trade

An important aspect of the Washington Consensus is free trade. While international trade has long been a feature of the global economy, business across borders became particularly brisk in the twentieth century, and international trade increased by about 12 percent a year throughout the 1990s.[52]

The U.S. example is instructive because Americans sometimes find it difficult to adapt to their new global interconnectedness. In 1960, about 9 percent of the U.S. GDP stemmed from foreign trade. At the end of the century, the figure was over 24 percent and rising rapidly. This meant that about a quarter of U.S. national prosperity depended upon relationships with the rest of the world. Over the same period, customs duties or tariffs declined from about 40 percent to a range between 2 and 0 percent.

Regrettably, the growth in global trade tends to leave the less-developed world out of the profitable end of the traffic. As figure 12.4 illustrates, developed countries exchange goods and services briskly with one another. The less-developed countries of the "South" have little to trade among themselves and are frequently reduced to selling raw materials and unprocessed food cheaply to the "North," while they buy comparatively expensive food and manufactured items (computers, vehicles, pharmaceuticals, etc.) in return.

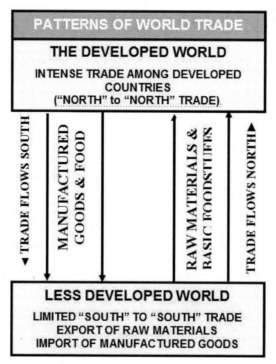

Figure 12.4. Patterns of World Trade
The bottom line? Economically developed or "Northern" countries trade briskly with one another at very low tariff rates. They also sell manufactured goods or finished products to the South, sometimes crowding locally produced merchandise off the shelves. Less-developed countries have little to sell to one another and are forced to compete with each other to sell very inexpensive products to the wealthier world, often paying high tariff rates in the process.

The opposite of free trade is **protectionism**, the belief that a government should use whatever barriers are available to protect domestic industries against the threat of foreign competition. The most common restraint on free trade is a tariff (or customs duty or import tax placed at the border on goods being imported from another country). Why have them? Obviously, a tariff raises easy money for the treasury, but the underlying reason has always been "protectionist" in the sense of guarding a domestic industry against competition from a foreign one. France and Italy, for example, make wonderful wines but even *vin ordinaire* can be pricey, and skilled workers in EU vineyards get European-level salaries and benefits. Algeria makes fair wine, usually red and a little rough, but *vin rouge algérien* is cheap because Third-World Algerians don't take quite so much home on payday. Hence, European winemakers have pressured the European Union to slap a hefty import tax on wine from outside Europe.

Over the course of the twentieth century, tariffs have risen and fallen periodically. After World War II, Western leaders signed a treaty called the General Agreement on Tariff and Trade (GATT), which evolved into an actual organization that campaigned for lower tariffs and expanded trade. In 1995, GATT transformed itself into the more powerful World Trade Organization or WTO, accumulating some 140 member countries worldwide. In late 2011, Russia's accession brought the member total to 156.

The United States, the European Union, and highly developed countries such as Japan are all somewhat fonder of free trade when it involves other countries opening their markets and less fond when parts of the developing world (such as China and India) invade their markets with cheaper products that compete with locally produced goods. In wealthy countries, this sometimes generates pressure on politicians to defend domestic jobs and factories. As Nobel Prize–winning economist Joseph Stiglitz has noted, "Politicians should have faced up to what globalization actually means, been honest about it, and responded by making sure that most Americans, and most Europeans are better off."[53]

Some regions of the world have attempted to foster trade and lower tariff barriers within more narrowly defined global neighborhoods. The European Union (discussed in chapter 5) is the most successful example, and the North American Free Trade Agreement (NAFTA) is the developing commercial trade relationship among Canada, the United States, and Mexico. Trade among high HDI countries is extremely brisk and carried out with very low tariff barriers, and it is believed to be an important factor in the overall prosperity of the developing world. On the other hand, it is very difficult for the poorer countries of the world to trade profitably with the rich. Why?

Are the Rich Trading Fairly with the Poor?

There is a large global community of activists and thinkers who believe that trade and the Washington Consensus have stacked the deck against the interests of the poor. What are the merits to this argument?

Some middle HDI countries have done moderately well with free trade, although the most successful of them took advice from the Washington Consensus slowly and selectively. When rapidly growing countries such as China and South Korea were starting their industrial growth after World War II, they zealously practiced protectionism to give their local industries a chance to thrive before they were exposed to the full blast of international competition. Once these industries were capable of withstanding global competition, tariffs came down and they competed successfully with products from Europe and the United States.[54]

Where free trade and the demands of the Washington Consensus have demonstrably not worked is in the very poorest regions of the world, what we have been calling the low HDI countries: sub-Saharan Africa, some newly independent states of the former Soviet Union, and portions of Central and Latin America. These very poor countries do not have the luxury of picking and choosing from the menu of Washington Consensus suggestions. Burdened with debt and mounting domestic poverty, they need IMF/World Bank support to stagger from one fiscal year to another. In consequence, they are forced to lower domestic tariffs and allow foreign-made goods from the United States and Europe to enter their markets, often destroying fragile young local industries.

In return for opening their markets to U.S., EU, and Japanese products, they would argue, it is only fair that they should be able to sell their products freely in the high HDI world. Quite frequently, however, high HDI countries such as the United States and the European Union preach free trade but practice protectionism. The global poor argue that they are being treated unfairly because of tariffs, subsidies, and unfair prices. Let's review these three problem areas.

Responding to the Global Financial Crisis and Emerging Markets

Throughout the twenty-first century emerging market economies, such as China, India, and Brazil, have been growing and competing with the developed world. Given this new influence, the IMF has responded to pressures to increase the voting rights of the developing and emerging market world. In 2010, the IMF agreed to a set of reforms that will increase the quotas for emerging market economies by 6 percent, which also means that their voting rights (tied to their quota payments) will increase. That means that Europe, Japan, and the United States will now have to listen more intently to their developing and emerging market neighbors.[55]

- Tariffs: The first problem is the high level of tariffs levied by rich countries such as the United States, the EU, and Japan against products from poor countries. The United States buys goods and services from both France and Bangladesh, for example, but the terms of trade are completely different. Americans import relatively expensive items from France (wines, fashions, sports cars, etc.), and the French pay almost nothing in tariffs. The United States imports inexpensive items from Bangladesh (cotton clothing, etc.), but these products have to struggle with 12.3 percent tariffs. Let's think for a moment about the economics of underpants. The U.S. tariff on French silk panties is 1.1 percent, for example, while importers of women's ordinary cotton knickers, made in South Asia, are paying over 16 percent.[56] Why? Favoritism toward France is rooted in the American realization that the French could retaliate effectively were the United States to put high tariffs on French products. The Bengali people lack this retaliatory clout, since they manufacture a range of products that American consumers can find almost anywhere in the Third World.

  Are these import taxes good for American consumers? They may or may not have limited success in protecting jobs for American workers, but protectionism of this sort inflates the prices of things that poor people buy (such as clothing and inexpensive consumable items) and holds down the prices of things that rich people buy (such as Paris fashions and Italian sports cars). The policy is a disaster for the Bengali people, who are forced to throw open their markets to American products, only to pay high import taxes when they try to exploit their comparative advantage of cheap labor and export products to the United States.

The United States is far from being the only sinner, however. During the 1990s, the wealthy OECD community put an average tariff of 3.4 percent on goods coming from the underdeveloped world. In return, the poorer countries were only able to impose a minimal tariff of 0.8 percent on products they imported from the OECD.

• Subsidies: A second and similar problem is the system of **subsidies** (mostly on agricultural products) used by developed societies such as the United States, Japan, and the EU. Subsidies are payments made by a government to a domestic producer, typically a farmer. The ostensible purpose is to help stabilize prices and ensure the continued production of some critical manufactured good or food product. These subsidies are typically paid to the larger and wealthier agricultural companies, and seldom wind up going to small family farms. The more authentic purpose may be political, to secure votes or campaign contributions, but the end result is to enable the product in question to compete more effectively with rival foreign goods.[57]

The United States, the EU, and Japan all subsidize agricultural products heavily. American sugar producers, for example, are heavily subsidized. This hurts foreign sugar producers who could help satisfy America's sweet tooth if they were allowed to compete on a level playing field. It hurts U.S. consumers when they pay more for sugar and U.S. taxpayers, who are funding the whole business. The European Union offers its cattle farmers an average daily subsidy of $2 per cow, which is above the daily income of the poorest 40 percent of the world's population. The United States spends $4 billion a year subsidizing U.S. cotton. This sum is substantially greater than the amount of aid the United States donates to cotton-growing countries, and makes it difficult for them to compete with the North American cotton growers.[58]

• Unfair Prices: This is another thorny issue, because the logic of supply and demand insists that the price of a given commodity is whatever it will fetch on the open market. In pure free-market thinking, there is no such thing as an unfair price, just high prices and low prices.

Here's the problem, however. Primitive economies in very poor countries can usually sell only primary products (raw materials and unprocessed foods). Prices of these commodities tend to be unstable, rising and falling rapidly because of changing consumer tastes or market conditions elsewhere in the world. And many of these products are too abundant, which means the price is depressed by oversupply. Coffee is a good example; the plant is grown in quantity in Africa and Latin America. Some countries have become utterly dependent upon it; for example, coffee accounts for 75 percent of Ethiopia's total exports. Coffee producers in the developed world have structured the market to suit their own economic interests. They can store beans for long periods of time, buying their supplies when and where they are cheapest. They buy "green" beans cheaply from the farmer, and ship them to Europe and North America where they are processed, roasted, and freeze-dried. Coffee-producing countries could earn more for their crop if they could process it themselves, but there are harsh U.S./EU tariffs blocking the import of processed coffee.

The coffee economy is structured so that there is no relationship between the cost of a cup of coffee at your local cafe and the price paid to the farmer who grew the beans. About twenty-five million farmers worldwide depend upon coffee beans for their income, and the price has collapsed so badly in recent years that the cost of one latte at your favorite coffee bar could actually equal a farmer's weekly salary. Most of what you pay goes to the company that created the brand name. The coffee industry is a $60 billion industry, of which less than 9 percent actually goes to the people growing the beans.[59]

GLOBALIZATION: THE INTERCONNECTEDNESS OF THINGS

Like all important and complex political phenomena, globalization is easier to fight about than to define. Harvard's Joseph Nye calls it "networks of interdependence at worldwide distances,"[60] while Thomas Friedman adds that "globalization is everything and its opposite."[61] Words such as "globalization," "interdependence," "globalism," "interconnectedness," and "intermesticity" are used by different authors to signify slightly diverse shades of meaning, but they all refer to the process by which the earth is shrinking into a "global village."

What Is Globalization?

For our purposes in this book, globalization is the ongoing worldwide process of establishing interconnections among disparate population groups as well as the creation of an increasingly Westernized global culture, wider economic and commercial relationships, the rapid global movement of people and information, and the increased influence of the United States through political, economic, and military power. In a globalized world, some non-state actors are gaining power, sometimes at the expense of sovereign governments. This would include multinational corporations, NGOs such as Greenpeace and Amnesty International, and international organizations such as the UN and the EU.[62] Globalization has a number of relatively distinct ingredients that require separate discussion.

- Cultural Globalization: In the years since World War II, American and Western European cultural products have spread throughout the world. This is perhaps the most obvious aspect of globalization. In any corner of the planet, you can see kids in jeans and baseball caps listening to Anglo-American pop music on iPods or portable CD players. These days, you can explore the far corners of your planet without ever getting too far from a McDonald's restaurant, since the company serves twenty million customers a day around the world. And CNN seems to come out of every television set in every hotel room on the planet.

  Many worry that a homogenized and Americanized global culture is destroying local traditions and regional customs. The invasion of Western icons irritates those who regard McDonald's restaurants and Madonna's music as affronts to their culture and religion. When a French farmer knocked down an American fast-food joint a few years ago, he was arrested by the police, but proclaimed a hero in the French press. Political scientist Benjamin R. Barber defined this clash brilliantly in his 1995 best seller *Jihad vs. McWorld*, arguing that cultural globalization would inevitably produce a violent backlash.[63]

- Commercial Globalization: According to some economists, the United States controls about half of the world's financial wealth. This gives the impression that big business is really American business, but most of these companies are really transnational in personnel and penetration. Japanese and European business interests now also control increasingly significant hunks of the domestic American economy, and corporations from wealthy countries have all penetrated one another's markets. Business executives in Berlin and Tokyo close factories and raise prices in the United States, while American CEOs decide who will eat what all over the planet. Increasingly, Chinese firms are taking the lead in the top global corporations. In the 2011 rankings, only three U.S. companies were in the top-ten list, followed by three Chinese companies.[64]

- Communications/Transportation Globalization: The world is undergoing a revolution in communications in at least two distinct senses. In terms of transportation, people are moving physically around the world at an unprecedented rate, crossing borders, living in new countries, bringing with them languages, customs, cultures, and diseases. Perhaps even more important, information is now rocketing through the world through new electronic media such as satellites, the Internet, and cell/mobile phones. The cost of both transportation and communication has gone down enormously. This means that it is possible to locate some kinds of service industries anywhere in the world. Help lines and customer service lines, for example, are increasingly routed to Bombay (Mumbai) because many Indians speak English and are good with computers. Sitting at consoles in South Asia, they do tax returns, check out health insurance claims, sell insurance, and make reservations for airlines. At about $200 a month, they earn a fraction of an American salary, but this is very good money in India, where the average salary is about $3000 a year.[65]

- Political Globalization: At its most primitive level, political globalization means little more than "intermesticity," the notion that the cleavage between domestic and foreign politics has largely disappeared. It also suggests that there are now many more "players" or "actors" in the global political game. Nongovernmental organizations, multinational corporations, and even criminal and terrorist groups now engage briskly in world politics.

The notion of political globalization also suggests the growing preeminence of Western and specifically American power over the rest of the world. When the USSR passed into history at the beginning of the 1990s, it took with it any claim Marxism might have had to be a viable alternative to Western-style free-market economic structures. While European social democracies quietly maintain modified versions of capitalism, triumphant American-style capitalism has taken to presenting itself as the only workable model for development. The Washington Consensus, described above, is essentially a form of political globalization through which powerful international financial institutions demand that all countries, rich and poor, align themselves with U.S. political and economic beliefs and policies. Thomas Friedman calls this "the Golden Straitjacket," which he believes everybody needs to put on, whether it fits perfectly or not.[66]

The United States also dominates the world militarily, thanks to extraordinarily high levels of defense spending. After the September 11 attacks, President Bush bluntly demanded that the world join the United States in a campaign against terrorism, denying that any country could be neutral in a war against "evil-doers." The argument about political globalization blends with the resentment felt in many parts of the world over what seems to be American unilateralism or hegemony over an unwilling world.

The Puzzlements of a Globalized World

Globalization was no sooner a concept than it became a threat to many protesters around the world. In 1999, the World Trade Organization attempted to hold a meeting of global economic leaders in Seattle, Washington; thousands of angry demonstrators disrupted the meeting, setting a pattern that has persisted down to 2010 G-20 meetings in Canada. Ironically, antiglobalization activists typically use globalization's products, such as the Internet and mobile phones, to advance their cause. Who are these demonstrators, and what is their motivation? Antiglobalization sentiments are difficult to analyze because activists object to different aspects of a broad social phenomenon, but they fall roughly into four categories.[67]

- Critics of U.S. Foreign Policy: Since globalization is identified in the minds of many with U.S. economic and military policy, many antiglobalization activists protest what they perceive as a unilateralist and arrogant American foreign policy. They object to military operations such as the 2003 Iraq Gulf War and what they see as ruthless and heavy-handed U.S. treatment of poorer and weaker countries. Clearly, they dislike the Washington Consensus and IMF-World Bank efforts to force poor countries to repay debts.
- Trade Unionists: Industrial workers in the developed world are aware that globalization in high HDI countries often involves the export of their jobs to places where wages are lower, part of a process called "outsourcing." The economics are not complicated. One of the motives behind the 1994 North American Free Trade Agreement (NAFTA) was to allow Canadian and American corporations to take advantage of low wages in Mexico, and then reimport the manufactured products without having to pay tariffs. The resulting goods are cheaper, but the original American and Canadian workers lost their jobs. They are now facing unemployment or have been forced into lower paying positions.

   As tariffs generally have declined, American manufacturing operations have been exported all over the globe, especially to the poorer and less-democratic states of Southeast Asia. In the 1980s, some American companies concentrated on building up an attractive brand and advertising strategy, but actually got out of making their products themselves. It was less complicated to outsource production, which meant licensing companies in the underdeveloped world to manufacture these products to be marketed by the American company. American students who like Tommy Hilfiger fashions, for example, may be surprised to learn that Hilfiger's products are mostly manufactured by other companies before the Hilfiger logo goes on.[68] As a partial result of outsourcing, American salaried employees—particularly those at the bottom of the pay scale—have seen little or no improvement in their standards of living since the beginning of the 1980s.
- Human Rights Activists: Many of the protesters are angry at what they perceive globalization is doing to workers in the poorer corners of the planet. This is a complicated argument, about which there is room for honest disagreements. It is clear that multinational corporations have frequently gone to very poor societies in search of precisely those social conditions that made people poor in the first place: low wages, corrupt governments, harsh laws against labor unions, and limited social concern for environmental factors. Either directly or through outsourced companies, they have established

sweatshop manufacturing facilities that pay low wages, sometimes less than the cost of living, and force their employees to work long hours in inhumane conditions. Manufacturers avoid moral or legal responsibility for labor conditions because they do not generally own the facilities abusing the rights of their workers. If a labor union or a political party tries to improve conditions for workers in a given outsource country, manufacturers simply move production facilities to another, even poorer country and set up shop, a process sometimes called the "race to the bottom."[69]

- Environmentalists: Some antiglobalization protesters are green activists who believe that international business is damaging the environment, and doing it with the permission of governments more concerned about short-term profits than the long-term livability of the planet. When multinationals move into less-developed countries with weak or corrupt governments, they sometimes ignore environmental considerations. Along the Mexican-American border are a long series of the so-called *maquiladoras*, factories famous for emitting pollution and for unsafe labor practices. As Barber comments, "When it comes to acid rain or oil spills or depleted fisheries or tainted groundwater or sexually transmitted diseases, national frontiers are simply irrelevant. Toxins don't stop for customs inspections and microbes don't carry passports."[70]

When antiglobalization protests occur, they inevitably attract anarchists and troublemakers with no serious ideology, but a number of serious intellectuals support the antiglobalization cause. A minority within the antiglobalization movement are die-hard Marxists, who identify globalization with capitalism and have not resigned themselves to the victory of their historic enemy. But most of them are simply unhappy at the way modern commerce seems to be dehumanizing the planet. Calling for "globalization with a human face," Joseph Stiglitz has complained trenchantly that "globalization today is not working for many of the world's poor. It is not working for much of the environment. It is not working for the stability of the global economy."[71]

In response to neo-liberal economic globalization (meaning the spread of free trade and markets), many around the world have complained with Joseph Stiglitz that economic globalization is doing little to improve the quality of life for the majority around the world. As an alter-conference to the World Economic Forum in Davos, Switzerland, where the world's largest economies meet each year, a growing multitude of private citizens, social movements, nongovernmental organizations, and other civil society groups meet at the World Social Forum (WSF) to discuss ideas about their slogan, "another world is possible." What is this other world to which they refer? It includes a global economic system that creates justice and equality of opportunity for all and opposes systems that are solely dominated by capital, meaning money or profit. While the WSF began as one centralized global meeting in Brazil, it has since branched off to regional meetings, including those organized in 2010 in the Brazilian rain forest city of Belem and Detroit, Michigan, and, in 2011, in Dakar, Senegal. Issues at the WSF include not only a more just economy but also one that is sustainable—creating jobs and products without harming the planet. Some scholars and policy makers see the WSF as a future form of global democratization where citizens from around the world can exchange ideas and strategies about how to change their local, national, and global institutions and policies toward a more democratic and just existence. The success of the WSF remains to be seen, but since 2001, its supporters have increased and include well known scholar activists such as Immanuel Wallerstein of Yale University and Noam Chomsky of MIT.

Parallel Lives: Thomas Friedman and Naomi Klein

Having both published famous books in 1999, these are two of the best political writers working today in the English language. They are both brilliant, passionate, and—in their separate ways—immensely likable. There are many people who think Tom Friedman is the best thing that ever happened to the *New York Times*, while others tear open *The Nation* or *The Guardian* to catch the latest Naomi Klein column. Tom and Naomi represent the yang and yin of the debate over globalization.

After taking his master's in Middle Eastern studies at Oxford, Thomas Friedman joined the *New York Times* as a correspondent in Beirut and later Jerusalem before returning to the United States to write columns on diplomacy and global economics. Two Pulitzer Prizes later, he penned *The Lexus and the Olive Tree: Understanding Globalization* (New York: Farrar, Straus and Giroux, 1999), which became the ultimate statement of why globalization is a largely beneficial inevitability. His 2005 book, *The World Is Flat* (New York: Farrar, Straus and Giroux) and the environmentally aware follow-up in 2008 *Hot, Flat, and Crowded* (New York: Farrar, Straus and Giroux) argue that the world is inextricably interconnected in new, horizontal ways—meaning communication among the people, not just diplomats and statesmen. Friedman argues that this new era of globalization that enables regular people to work and talk with one another will usher in more innovation and environmental solutions than there have been in the past. This author travels compulsively, and he likes the smaller world he's come to know since the end of the Cold War, noting that fast modems have largely replaced big missiles as symbols of national strength. He celebrates globalization's role in spreading free trade and liberal democracy.

Figure 12.5. Thomas Friedman
Photo courtesy of Greg Martin of Greg Martin Photo.

Having grown up in Toronto's most radical family, Naomi Klein started both writing and agitating at a youthful age. Her first poke in globalization's eye came in the form of an edgy best-seller called *No Logo: Taking Aim at the Brand Name Bullies*, published in 1999 by New York's Picador. *No Logo* has been called the *Das Kapital* of the antiglobalization movement, and the book savages corporations for exploiting working people all around the world. Ms. Klein notes, for example, that in 1992, Nike paid Michael Jordan more for endorsing its gym shoes than it did all thirty thousand of the Asians who actually manufactured them.[72] Her subsequent book, *Shock Doctrine: The Rise of Disaster Capitalism* (New York: Metropolitan Books, 2007), outlines the "radical capitalism" of our times and calls on people to put humanity before money. When Naomi Klein isn't writing, she's organizing antiglobalization protests, and she has been a prominent member of the activist coalition that has halted meetings of the G-7 and the World Trade Organization, and more recently, she was a member of the Occupy Wall Street movement.

Both *Lexus and the Olive Tree* and *No Logo*, which directly relate to Friedman and Klein's views on globalization, are fair-minded books. Each author looks at somewhat different sets of data from widely contrasting points of view and value systems. Excited about the authentically limitless possibilities of globalization, Friedman has spent a lot of his life in expensive hotels talking to prime ministers and central bankers, and he reflects the privileged insider's point of view. Ms. Klein is far more concerned with the third of humankind being damaged by globalization, and cares more about peasants than plutocrats. If you want to reach an understanding of the contemporary debate over globalization, these very different books and their subsequent writings are the first steps on the ladder.[73]

Figure 12.6. Naomi Klein
Photo by Ed Kashi. Courtesy of naomiklein.org.

Thinking about Globalization

This is a complicated topic, about which there has always been more heat than light, and we have done little more in this chapter than summarize some of the principal issues. No one seriously believes that the main thrust of globalization can be reversed or that we can or should create a world of small autonomous communities living in isolation from one another. For better or worse, we will continue to live on an increasingly interconnected planet. The argument hinges over the extent to which governments and international organizations ought to control the way the global economy functions. For example, is it possible and desirable to limit the social degradation caused by sweatshops? Or should we hope that Adam Smith's invisible hand of the market will make things right over time?

Clearly, globalization has been associated with some significant progress. In recent years, for example, the world's overall wealth has grown enormously, even if most of the benefits have gone to the wealthier members of society. Medium HDI societies such as India and Brazil have made substantial overall progress, and China—while continuing to be a dictatorship—has made an astounding economic leap forward. Advances in communications and transportation offer the possibility of a richer and more authentically global life than we have ever had before. At the political level, interconnectedness should eventually mean greater levels of cooperation among countries and less frequent armed conflicts. Increased communication among countries should ultimately mean that we will eventually get to know and understand each other better than we do today.

In the midst of rising average prosperity, however, there continue to exist very substantial regions where poverty is still a major human problem. According to the United Nations "Millennium Development Goals (MDGs) Report 2011," one in five workers globally are living in extreme poverty, defined as less than $1.25 a day. This is combined with the startling statistic that, although extreme poverty has declined around the globe, the number of undernourished people has not changed at all since 2001; 16 percent of the global population goes hungry each day. In fact, urban migration and clean drinking water access are growing issues in the poorest regions of the world, particularly in sub-Saharan Africa where the slowest progress has been made.[74]

Except for the social democracies of Western Europe, economic inequality is increasing in virtually every society. As the Gini index rises and the gap between rich and poor increases, poor people may feel more deprived and discontent, even if their incomes are increasing in actual monetary terms. The Washington Consensus recognizes that growth will always be uneven, but has always argued that money would eventually distribute itself through society. This is the so-called "trickle down" effect in which richer people spend money that allegedly makes its way to poorer members of society, ultimately contributing to general well-being.

If you are a comfortable middle-class North American, you may ask yourself if global poverty is something you personally should worry about. From a philosophical point of view, this is a hard question to answer because it goes to the heart of our individual value systems. Is there a moral or ethical argument that can be made? As Stephen Radolet commented, "Poverty and inequality around the world simply run counter to the values of many Americans who believe that the widening income gap and high levels of absolute poverty in poor countries are morally unacceptable."[75]

From a practical political perspective, furthermore, it may be that North Americans need to care. As we will see in the final two chapters of this book, political instability, disease, and environmental destruction all spring from this epidemic of poverty, and it may be difficult for people in the developed world to insulate themselves from the contagion. In an earlier and simpler era, it was possible to imagine that the United States, Western Europe, and the richer states of the Pacific Rim could withdraw into their comfortable cocoons, and let the rest of the planet go to hell. This was never true and doesn't even appear plausible today. In an increasingly interconnected world, when Africa contracts pneumonia, the developed world is at least going to get a very bad cold.

4. The Wrap: What Have We Learned?

This has been a tough march through some of the thickest intellectual forests in the world, but to function intelligently in our globalized society, you'll have to remember the basic elements of international political economy. Ensure that you understand how wealth is customarily measured and why these classical GDP-style statistics can sometimes be misleading. Be particularly sure that you understand the UN system of classifying countries as low, medium, and high on the human development index (HDI), since we will continue using this terminology in the two chapters that follow. You can't pick up a paper these days without joining the debate over deficits and national debts, so take the time to review this material carefully.

It ought to be clear by now that poverty is a problem, even for people who aren't themselves particularly poor. From section 2, you need to understand how the world's wealth is divided both among and within individual societies. We also looked at the controversy over the causes of global poverty and some of the debates about what to do about it. The debate over foreign aid is likely to go on forever, and our grandchildren will still be grappling with national debts, their own and other people's, so make sure you have these concepts firmly under control.

Most experts agree that trade is a better way of lifting people out of poverty than are aid or loans, but global commerce has its own dilemmas. In our discussion of the Washington Consensus, we looked at the demands wealthy countries have placed on poor countries for a greater austerity in their domestic financial affairs, privatization of public resources, and liberalization of the economy, that is, opening their internal markets to foreign penetration. We then looked at the debate over free trade versus protectionism, and asked if the developed world was trading fairly with its poorer commercial partners, arguing that the United States, the EU, and Japan have all engaged in covert forms of protectionism. The debate on globalization can only be summarized briefly in a book of this length, but we tried to break the phenomenon into its principal elements, talking about globalization in the realms of culture, commerce, communications, and politics.

In chapter 6, we looked at how economic conflict at the domestic level translates into political ideology. In this chapter, we saw how the decline of Marxism has not meant the end of savage debate over economic distribution.

What's next? Economists such as Amartya Sen keep warning us to pay less attention to statistics and more to how people actually live, and in the next chapter we'll look at the practical consequences of underdevelopment. One of the major factors is population, and chapter 13 studies what happens to population growth rates when income rises, and why poverty typically distorts natural population growth patterns.

Notes

1. Lewis Carroll, *Through the Looking Glass: And What Alice Found There* (New York: Macmillan & Co., 1875), 94.

2. Ed Ayres, "The Expanding Shadow Economy," *World Watch* 9, no. 4 (1996): 11–23.

3. United Nations Development Programme (UNDP), Statistical Annex *Human Development Report 2011*, http://hdr.undp.org/en/media/HDR_2011_EN_Tables.pdf (accessed December 26, 2011).

4. Thomas Prugh and Erik Assadourian, "What Is Sustainability Anyway?" *World Watch* 16, no. 5 (2003): 18.

5. Clifford Cobb et al., *The Genuine Progress Indicator 2000 Update.* (Oakland, Calif.: Redefining Progress, 2001).

6. See the Happy Planet Index 2.0 (2011), http://www.happyplanetindex.org/public-data/files/happy-planet-index-2–0.pdf.

7. Tony Smith, "Peso's Devaluation Gives Argentina Cost Advantages," *New York Times*, October 24, 2002, http://www.nytimes.com/2002/10/24/business/peso-s-devaluation-gives-argentina-cost-advantages.html?pagewanted=all&src=pm.

8. Paul Krugman, "The Tax Cut Con," *New York Times Magazine*, April 14, 2003, 54–62.

9. David Malin Roodman, "Still Waiting for the Jubilee: Pragmatic Solutions for the Third World Debt Crisis," Worldwatch Paper No. 155 (Washington, D.C.: Worldwatch Institute, 2001), 27.

10. National budgets are complicated affairs; take a look at the U.S. version at www.whitehouse.gov/omb, brought to you with a lot of zeros by the Office of Management and the Budget. Redefining Progress Inc. is a Sacramento-based think tank at www.rprogress.org, advocating that Americans focus more on social structures than on the stock market, offering its "Genuine Progress Indicator" as an alternative to the GDP. And if you're thinking of taking your declining dollar on a trip, check first with the foreign exchange converter at www.oanda.com/convert/classic.

11. To get an up-to-the-minute debt account, you can go to the U.S. Treasury at http://www.publicdebt.treas.gov/.

12. Joseph Stiglitz, *Globalization and Its Discontents* (London: Norton, 2002), 25.

13. Christopher Flavin, "Rich Planet, Poor Planet," in Worldwatch Institute, *State of the World 2001* (New York: Worldwatch Institute/Norton, 2001), 6.

14. Paul Kennedy, *Preparing for the Twenty-First Century* (New York: Random House, 1993), 193.

15. United Nations Development Programme (UNDP), *Human Development Report 2003*, http://hdr.undp.org/en/reports/global/hdr2003/, 2.

16. Worldwatch, *State of the World* (New York: Worldwatch Institute/Norton, 2003), 88.

17. Mark Tran, "Global Development: The Millennium Development Goals," *The Guardian*, July 7, 2011, http://www.guardian.co.uk/global-development/2011/jul/07/millennium-development-goals-2011-report.

18. Lester Thurow, "Why Their World Might Crumble," *New York Times Magazine*, November 19, 1995, 78–79.

19. UNDP, *Human Development Report 2011*, http://hdr.undp.org/en/media/HDR_2010_EN_Tables_reprint.pdf.

20. Paul Krugman, "For Richer," *New York Times Magazine,* October 20, 2002, 62–142.

21. John D. Clark, *Worlds Apart: Civil Society and the Battle for Ethical Globalization* (Bloomfield, Conn.: Kumarian, 2003), 58; World Bank, *World Development Report* (New York: Oxford University Press, 2000), 239.

22. Lester Thurow, "Why Their World Might Crumble," 28; also consult David S. Landes' *The Wealth and Poverty of Nations: Why Some Are So Rich and Some So Poor* (New York: W. W. Norton, 1999). In 2002, the conservative Kevin Phillips wrote a surprisingly liberal book called *Wealth and Democracy: How Great Fortunes and Government Created America's Aristocracy* (New York: Broadway Books, 2002).

23. Don Peck and Ross Douthat, "Does Money Buy Happiness?" *The Atlantic Monthly*, January–February 2003, 42–43.

24. Richard Layard, *Happiness: Lessons from a New Science* (London: Penguin, 2005).

25. John Isbister, *Promises Not Kept: Poverty and the Betrayal of Third World Development*, 6th ed. (Bloomfield: Conn.: Kumarian, 2003), 66–101.

26. UNDP, *Human Development Report 2003*, 2.

27. A lively blog on foreign aid is findable at http://aidthoughts.org/.

28. Carol C. Adelman, "The Privatization of Foreign Aid," *Foreign Affairs* 82, no. 6 (2003): 9.

29. Nobel Prize, Muhammad Yunus and Grameen Bank, 2006, http://www.nobelprize.org/nobel_prizes/peace/laureates/2006/yunus.html#; see also The Grameen Bank, http://www.grameen-info.org/.

30. See Kiva at www.kiva.org; for more reading on the subject, explore the small-is-wonderful world of village entrepreneurs in Shadhidur R. Khandker's *Fighting Poverty with Microcredit: Experience in Bangladesh* (New York: Oxford University Press, 2003). Jeffrey D. Sachs of Columbia University is the reigning poverty guru and his *The End of Poverty: Economic Possibilities for Our Time* (New York: Penguin, 2005) is a must-read. For something quirky and basic, see Stephen C. Smith's *Ending Global Poverty: A Guide to What Works* (New York: Palgrave MacMillan, 2005).

31. Michael Maren, *The Road to Hell: The Ravaging Effects of Foreign Aid and International Charity* (New York: Free Press, 1997).

32. William Finnegan, "The Economics of Empire," *Harper's Magazine*, May 2003, 44.

33. Jim Yong Kim et al., *Dying for Growth: Global Inequality and the Health of the Poor* (Monroe, Maine: The Institute for Health and Social Justice/Common Courage Press, 2000), 51, 68–71.

34. Randolph Martin, "Sudan's Perfect War," *Foreign Affairs* 81, no. 2 (2002): 122–23.

35. Stiglitz, *Globalization and Its Discontents*, 9.

36. Tran, "Global Development: The Millennium Development Goals."

37. Roodman, "Still Waiting for the Jubilee: Pragmatic Solutions for the Third World Debt Crisis," 18.

38. Worldwatch, *Vital Signs 2003: The Trends That Are Shaping Our Future* (UK: Earthscan Publications Ltd., 2003), 46.

39. Kim, *Dying for Growth: Global Inequality and the Health of the Poor,* 25; Worldwatch, *Vital Signs 2003,* 46.

40. Carol Lancaster, "Development in Africa: The Good, the Bad, the Ugly," *Current History* 104, no. 682 (2005): 222–27; UNDP, *Human Development Report 2003*, 12, 153.

41. Roodman, *Still Waiting for the Jubilee: Pragmatic Solutions for the Third World Debt Crisis,* 16.

42. Joseph Stiglitz, "Odious Rulers, Odious Debts," *The Atlantic Monthly*, November 2003, 40.

43. Transparency International is a Germany-based NGO at www.transparency.org that attempts to quantify levels of corruption. Probe International is a Toronto-based public interest activist group urging the international banking community to forgive "odious debts," for which, see www.odiousdebts.org.

44. World Bank, *Global Development Finance 2011: External Debt of Developing Countries*, http://issuu.com/world.bank.publications/docs/9780821386736.

45. William Finnegan, "The Economics of Empire," 44; for international financial institutions, see the International Monetary Fund (IMF) at www.imf.org/external/index.htm and the World Bank at www.worldbank.org. The Organization for Economic Cooperation and Development (or OECD) was originally created to deliver Marshall Plan benefits to Europeans but has evolved into a club of more than thirty industrial countries who exchange information and harmonize policy to maximize economic growth; find them at www.oecd.org. The World Trade Organization maintains its gateway at www.wto.org. North Americans will want to know all about the North American Free Trade Agreement, and the U.S. Department of Commerce at www.mac.doc.gov/nafta/nafta2.htm offers a text of the basic treaty, and links to other resources.

46. UNDP, *Human Development Report 2003*, 16.

47. Stiglitz, *Globalization and Its Discontents*, 54.

48. Finnegan, "The Economics of Empire," 46.

49. World Bank, *Report* 2003, 3.

50. Watch for yourself at http://www.naomiklein.org/shock-doctrine/short-film. See also, Naomi Klein, *Shock Doctrine: The Rise of Disaster Capitalism* (New York: Metropolitan Books, 2007).

51. Thomas L. Friedman, *The Lexus and the Olive Tree* (New York: Straus Farrar, Giroux, 1999), 11.

52. Clark, *Worlds Apart*, 22, 28.

53. As quoted by Heather Stewart in "Is this the end of globalisation?" *The Observer*, March 5, 2006, http://www.guardian.co.uk/business/2006/mar/05/money.theobserver. Despite her hyperbolic title, Amy Chua's *World on Fire: How Exporting Free Market Democracy Breeds Ethnic Hatred and Global Instability* (New York: Doubleday, 2003) is a sober study of globalization's pros and cons. The scholarly Nancy Birdsall has written a series of fundamental books; in 2002, she and John Williamson published *Delivering on Debt Relief: From IMF Gold to New Aid Architecture* (Washington, D.C.: Center for Global Development, 2002). Jeffrey Sachs and his colleagues wrote *Implementing Debt Relief for the HIPCs* (Cambridge, Mass.: Harvard University Center for International Development, 1999). Anne O. Krueger explains the World Trade Organization in her *The WTO as an International Organization* (Chicago: University of Chicago Press, 1998).

54. Clark, *Worlds Apart*, 63.

55. International Monetary Forum (IMF), Reform Press Release, November 5, 2010, http://www.imf.org/external/np/sec/pr/2010/pr10418.htm.

56. Edward Gresser, "Toughest on the Poor," *Foreign Affairs* 81, no. 6 (2002): 13.

57. UNDP, *Human Development Report 2003*, 156.

58. UNDP, *Human Development Report 2003*, 156–58.

59. Clark, *Worlds Apart*, 34.

60. Joseph S. Nye, "Globalization's Democracy Deficit," *Foreign Affairs* 80, no. 4 (2001): 2.

61. Friedman, *The Lexius and the Olive Tree*, 321.

62. Robert O. Keohane and Joseph S. Nye, *Power and Interdependence*, 3rd ed. (New York: Longman, 2001), 3.

63. Benjamin Barber, *Jihad vs. McWorld* (New York: Random House, 1995), 24.

64. Clark, *Worlds Apart*, 59; CNN Money/Fortune, *Global 500 List 2011*, http://money.cnn.com/magazines/fortune/global500/2011/full_list/.

65. United Nations, Human Development Index 2011, http://hdr.undp.org/en/statistics/hdi.

66. Friedman, *The Lexus and the Olive Tree*, 84.

67. Nye, "Globalization's Democracy Deficit," 2.

68. Naomi Klein, *No Logo: Taking Aim at the Brand Bullies* (New York: Picador, 1999), 24.

69. Robert J. S. Ross and Anita Chan, "From North-South to South-South." *Foreign Affairs* 81, no. 5(2002): 8–13.

70. Barber, *Jihad vs. McWorld*, 12.

71. Stiglitz, *Globalization and Its Discontents*, 214, 247; see also Jagdish Bhagwati, "Coping with Anti-globalization: A Trilogy of Discontents," *Foreign Affairs* 81, no. 1 (2002): 2–7.

72. Klein, *No Logo*, 376.

73. Thomas Friedman and Michael Mandelbaum released *That Used to Be Us: How American Fell Behind in the World We Created and How We Come Back* (New York: Farrar, Straus, and Giroux, 2011). Naomi Klein has been publishing on capitalism and climate change and is due to release a new book as well.

74. United Nations, "Millennium Development Goals Report 2011," http://unstats.un.org/unsd/mdg/Resources/Static/Products/Progress2011/11–31339%20(E)%20MDG%20Report%202011_Book%20LR.pdf.

75. Steven Radelet, "Bush and Foreign Aid," *Foreign Affairs* 82, no. 5 (2003): 110.

CHAPTER 13

Too Many Plates at the Table

POPULATION AND POLITICAL CONFLICT

3. Demographic Decisions
   Birth Control and Abortion
     Reducing the Problem
     Population, Politics, and Religion
     The U.S. Role in Population Stabilization
     The Status of Women
   The Uncertainty Factor
   Where to Find the Data
4. The Wrap: What Have We Learned?

> "I wish you wouldn't squeeze so," said the Dormouse, who was sitting next to her. "I can hardly breathe."
> "I can't help it," said Alice very meekly: "I'm growing."
> "You've no right to grow here," said the Dormouse.
> "Don't talk nonsense," said Alice more boldly: "you know you're growing too."
> "Yes, but I grow at a reasonable pace," said the Dormouse: "not in that ridiculous fashion."[1]

During her strange visit to Wonderland, Alice periodically experienced spurts of physical growth and shrinkage, seldom managing to be the right size for the odd company she was keeping. In writing this wonderful passage, Lewis Carroll might have been thinking of the extraordinary population growth England experienced during his own lifetime.

For our purposes, Alice might represent the Fourth World, since low HDI countries are increasing their population size at a rate that makes the wealthier world (the Dormouse) decidedly uncomfortable. From a global perspective, we are all growing and shrinking in odd ways. Some countries are losing population; will they eventually disappear? Others are growing too rapidly, squeezing their neighbors the way Alice squeezed the Dormouse at the tea party. The earth is a large place, but there are those who claim that too many guests have already been invited to the festival of existence. Is there room for all the Alices who will be born in the years to come? And enough pots of tea?

The overarching theme of this book has been conflict and cooperation in an increasingly interconnected human society. Many, if not most, conflicts flow from a tension between population and resources, although this factor often goes unrecognized when the conflict explodes. Author James Gasana, for example, has demonstrated how the 1994 Rwandan societal mayhem was rooted in environmental degradation combined with population pressures, two linked factors that translated into ethnic hatreds.[2]

Overpopulation and resource scarcity are reciprocals of one another, and neither can be considered in isolation. You and I meet for lunch in an empty football stadium, but I forget to bring any food, so all we have is your peanut-butter-and-jelly sandwich. The stadium has seats for ten thousand, and the present population is only two, but in nutritional terms our environment is overpopulated because the snack bar is closed and the resources (one sandwich) are inadequate for the lunchtime nutritional needs of the population (us).

Since we're both rich and terribly hungry, we dump your peanut-butter-and-jelly sandwich and head for a fancy restaurant, where we order three-course dinners with side salads, appetizers, and dessert, plus a couple of bottles of nice wine. There are only two of us in the restaurant, but when all that food arrives, the place is underpopulated in the sense that there is enough nutrition there to feed perhaps six or eight people. When we pay the bill and stagger off, we leave thousands of calories behind on the table to be thrown away.

This is complicated, fascinating, and terrifically important political material, and it's going to take us two chapters to tackle both sides of the population vs. resources equation. In this chapter, we'll look at population, and ask ourselves how we got to be quite so numerous and what the prospects are for the future. In the following, and final, chapter, we'll look at the resource factor and think about what we have available in terms of food, land, and water to nurture whatever population we're going to have in the future. Here's a sense of the kind of questions we'll try to answer in this chapter.

- *Why do population explosions occur? More precisely, why, in most human societies, does the population remain constant for a long time, suddenly expand, and then—if all goes well—suddenly level off?* This is not an easy question, but demographers have elaborated a powerful theory to explain the phenomenon. Of equal importance, we need to understand why a given population just keeps on growing.
- *How do politics and population growth interact? Why is Russia losing population? Why are there more baby boys than baby girls in China and India? And what are the political and demographic consequences of HIV/AIDS?* Since politicians are sometimes reluctant to talk about population matters, we may miss the connection between abnormalities in population growth and the world of politics. We'll try to see how human conflict can flow directly and tragically from human fertility.
- *What, if anything, can be done about this mountain of political-demographic problems?* This is an area where almost anything is going to be controversial, but we need to look beyond the political brawls over abortion and foreign aid to see what real remedies there are to reduce the population side of the resources equation.

1. The Politics of Population Growth

In order to understand the connection between conflict and overpopulation, we need to think about the basics of demography, the scientific study of human populations. Among other things, demographers try to estimate how many people we presently have in any given region, how fast this number is increasing, and what the prospects are for the future. Simply knowing how many people exist in a country, however, doesn't tell us everything we need to know. In order to estimate future political stability, we need to understand the shape of the population, how fast it's growing, how many are young, and how many are old.

It will become clear that humankind is currently working its way through a growth spurt of epic proportions, bringing the planetary population higher and higher with every passing year. Scholars have elaborated a theory called **demographic transition** to explain why populations suddenly begin to grow rapidly, and why, sometimes but not always, they slow or even reverse their growth. Demographic transition is to the study of population what natural selection is to biology. To avoid the inevitable conflict that comes from too many people trying to share the same crowded planet, we need to do a condensed version of Demography 101.[3]

POPULATION AND SOCIETY

As suggested by figure 13.1, **Rapid Population Growth (RPG)** is a very recent phenomenon. For most of history, human population increased very slowly, since famine, disease, and limited life expectancy kept the death rate and the birthrate in some kind of bleak harmony. Our species did not reach the one billion mark until the early 1800s. Then, for reasons we will explore below, population growth accelerated throughout the nineteenth century and exploded after World War II. The peak years occurred between 1965 and 1970, when global annual population growth hit a record 2.1 percent.[4] While the percentage rate of growth slowed to a present figure of slightly under 1.2 percent per year, we still grew to seven billion people in 2011.

At present rates of growth, we are crowding about 76 million people per year into our global habitat, a group roughly the size of the current population of the Philippine Islands. In the first years of the new century, this was the result of about 130 million births minus about 54 million deaths or an annual rate of growth of around 1.2 percent. If it continues, this rate of growth will add a billion people to the family every thirteen years.

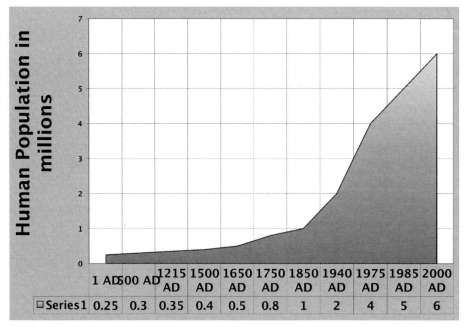

	1 AD	500 AD	1215 AD	1500 AD	1650 AD	1750 AD	1850 AD	1940 AD	1975 AD	1985 AD	2000 AD
□ Series1	0.25	0.3	0.35	0.4	0.5	0.8	1	2	4	5	6

Figure 13.1. The Rise in Human Population
Today's huge human population is a new factor. At the time of Christ, there may have been 250 million people living worldwide. The population doubled in sixteen hundred years. In contrast, it doubled again in only thirty-five years between 1940 and 1975.

Source: United Nations Development Programme (UNDP), *Human Development Report 1998*, 128–130.

The Population Explosion

Population change is most commonly expressed as a percentage. For example, there might be one hundred people in a village at the beginning of the year. During the course of the year, one dies and two babies are born. If no one moved away and no new residents arrived, the end-of-the-year population is 101, having increased by 1 percent over the course of the year. Textbox 13.1 demonstrates that upward-population changes result from an increased number of births and a reduced number of deaths, plus an adjustment for migration. The population-increase percentage peaked between 1965 and 1970 and has since edged downward.

Global population increase is being driven more by the extension of **life expectancy** than by the birthrate. As demographer John R. Weeks commented, "It is not that people breed like rabbits; rather, they no longer die like flies."[5] Global life expectancy now stands at an astonishing sixty-nine years, thanks mostly to advances in nutrition and modern medicine.[6] According to the National Center for Health Statistics, an American baby born in 1900 could look forward to 47.3 years of life. A child born a century later had a projected life expectancy of 77.2 years. Demographers are looking forward to a further extension of life expectancy over the course of the next half century, prophesying that people in the developed world may average 82 years of life by 2050.[7]

In our search for the causes of conflict, however, we need to remember that our present 1.2 percent global population increase does not take place uniformly across the planet. In very high HDI societies, population hovers between slow growth and slow decline. Below we'll discuss the worrisome case of Russia, where the total population is dropping precipitously. Several European countries have achieved what is called **zero population growth**. We will be referring to this situation frequently below, so let's give the "no significant growth" status its habitual acronym of **ZPG**. In recent years, Germany and Italy

---

Calculating Population Change

To see how fast a given society is growing, start with the birthrate (sometimes called the "crude birthrate" [CBR]). Add any immigrants and subtract anybody who has departed through emigration or death. When doing global figures, obviously, we can drop the out-migration factor because nobody leaves the earth except for a few astronauts, and—as far as we know—nobody migrates here.

Calculating Population Change

add	+	birthrate
add	+	in-migration
subtract	−	out-migration
subtract	−	death rate
	=	change

NB: Change is usually expressed as an annual percentage increase or "negative increase" (i.e., shrinkage) of the population.

Table 13.1.   Countries with the Oldest and Youngest Populations, 2011

Those countries with a generally older population tend to be settled and domestically peaceful, although they may have difficulty in funding their old-age pension systems. "Young" countries can be poor, restless, and violent.

	Percentage under 15		Percentage over 65	
Niger	49	Japan	23
Uganda	48	Germany	21
Burkina Faso	45	Italy	20
Dem. Rep. Congo	46	Sweden	18
Zambia	46	Greece	19
Malawi	45	Portugal	18
Afghanistan	44	Bulgaria	18
Chad	45	Austria	18
Somalia	45	Latvia	17
Tanzania	45	Belgium	17

Source: Population Reference Bureau, http://www.prb.org/DataFinder/Topic.aspx.

have both seen their birthrates slip below replacement level, although both countries will probably receive immigrants to keep their population roughly stable. Where population is dropping so seriously that a society is actively declining, demographers refer to **negative population growth (NPG)**.[8]

For reasons we will try to explain, most population growth takes place in the poorer portions of the world. As you can see in table 13.2, growth is substantial in medium HDI countries, although it is expected to fall as we move further into the new century. In the poorest Fourth World or low HDI countries, however, population growth has been brisk in the past, and will continue to be moderately high in the near future. In what is arguably the most wretched corner of the Middle East, the people of the Gaza Strip are producing the highest birthrate in the world, a record fifty-two babies for every one thousand people.

Table13.2.   The Rapidity of Population Growth

High HDI societies are increasing fairly slowly, less than 1 percent per year; a few have dropped past ZPG into negative population growth. Medium HDI countries in the classic Third World are still growing at roughly the world's average. The very poorest of the poor, down in the Fourth World, are still suffering from very rapid growth, and while it's projected to fall over the next fifteen years, it isn't going to fall fast or far enough to avoid the kind of conflict that flows from overpopulation.

HDI Category	1975–2001	2001–2015
High HDI	0.8%	0.5%
Medium HDI	1.7%	1.0%
Low HDI	2.8%	2.3%

Source: United Nations Development Programme (UNDP), *Human Development Report 2003*, 253; United Nations Development Programme (UNDP), *Human Development Report 2011*, http://hdr. undp.org/en/media/HDR_2011_EN_Tables.pdf.

Population growth can be politically very significant when one ethnic community within a society is growing rapidly while other communities are growing slowly or contracting. We have already noted that the rapid rise in the Palestinian population poses a huge strategic question mark for the future of Israel and the Palestinian territories. In the old Soviet Union (and to some extent in modern Russia), ethnic minorities (many of them Muslims) are increasing their numbers while the core Slav population is losing population share. And in Northern Ireland, the minority Roman Catholics are steadily breeding their way toward majority status. As we will note below, Hispanic Americans are producing more children than are U.S. citizens of direct European descent, changing power and population relationships in American society.[9]

Demographic Data

Most of our data on world population change comes from a few important sources. The United Nations Population Division (UNPD) does most of the scholarly work in calculating population growth and change.[10] Try not to mix up the demographers of the UNPD with the social engineers over at the UNDP (UN Development Programme); despite the potential for alphabet-soup confusion, the UNPD and the UNDP are different agencies with different jobs.[11] A sister organization is the United Nations Population Fund, which coordinates international reactions to population problems. Since it was originally called the UN Fund for Population Activities, this branch of the world organization still confusingly goes by the initials UNFPA.[12] For the United States, most official demographic work is done by the Department of Commerce's Census Bureau, and nearly every government maintains a similar organization. Want to know how many passengers are on Spaceship Earth today? Check the World PopClock projection.[13]

There is a lot of population information available on the Web. For the results of the 2010 U.S. Census, your best site is www.census.gov. The Population Reference Bureau at www.prb.org is another good source for detailed statistical information about U.S. and global population figures. For global studies, the ultimate source is www.unfpa.org, the homepage of the United Nations Population Fund. The professional association for demographers and other scholars interested in population matters is the Population Association of America (www.popassoc.org). The International Union for the Scientific Study of Population (IUSSP) promotes scientific studies of demography and population-related issues; see them at www.iussp.org.[14]

Fertility Rates and Doubling Times

While we often talk about population increase as a percentage, it can also be useful to look at the **total fertility rate** (often abbreviated TFR by demographers), which is the predicted number of live births each woman can be expected to produce within the course of her reproductive life. For practical purposes, 2.1 children per woman is regarded as the replacement level. The world TFR is now about 2.3, but it is 4.5 in may developing countries, well above what we need, but it is coming down slowly, as figure 13.2 reveals.[15] While the total fertility rate is universally dropping, it is still highest in the low HDI world, where scholars feel it should be lower. Furthermore, high population growth in the past has given us a very large global population of women of childbearing age and even

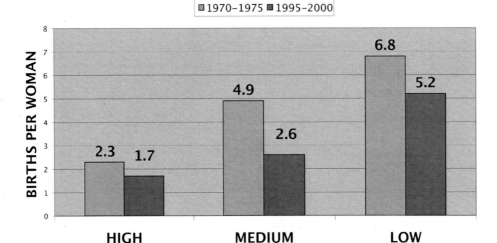

Figure 13.2. Declining Fertility Rates
This chart compares the number of babies women typically bear in the course of their lifetimes in the three sections of the world, and shows that these rates have declined dramatically over the thirty-year period in question. On the negative side, fertility has not significantly decreased in parts of sub-Saharan Africa, where many women are still bearing six or more children.

Sources: United Nations Development Programme, *Human Development Report 2000*, 226; World Bank, *World Development Report 2000* (New York and Oxford: Oxford University Press, 2000), 242–44.

more who will move into a window of maternity over the next decade. These women may be having fewer children, but the avalanche effect of "demographic momentum" is still enormous. In fifty-six developing countries, the poorest fifth of women still average six births, compared to 3.2 in the wealthiest quintile of these same societies. Reproductive health care related to pregnancy and childbirth has been shown to reduce the productivity of women by 20 percent.[16] The consequences of high fertility rates can be dramatic. India's 2.5 total fertility rate means that India will overtake China (where TFR is 1.6) and become the most populous society on earth by the middle of the next century.

It is also very useful to know the number of years it will take for a given population to double in size. How do we determine the **doubling time**? To start, let's assume that the population of the planet continues to increase by its current approximate annual rate of just over 1.1 percent. We hope it isn't going to turn out that way, but to get the doubling time for the whole planet at constant (i.e., present) rates of growth, we divide the number 70 by the annual rate of increase. The result is the number of years in which the population of the planet can be expected to double if current rates remain constant. Hence 70 ÷ 1.1 = 63.6, or sixty-three years and seven months. This is another way of saying that if the present rate of population increase is projected into the future, our present planetary population of about seven billion will double in a little over a half century.

The doubling time concept is of enormous importance in understanding why rapid population growth contributes to conflict. Let's look, for example, at the turbulent

Republic of Pakistan, where population growth is still roaring along at 1.8 percent per annum, which seems insignificant until you crunch the numbers and learn that 176 million generally poor, often angry, and sometimes fanatical Pakistanis will become 304 million in only thirty-eight years, outnumbering the United States a few years after that. This volatile South Asian state is already failing badly at providing basic services to its growing population. In just one generation, Pakistan's doubled population will require 200 percent of everything: twice as many roads, houses, nurses and doctors, schoolrooms, hospital beds, toilet paper rolls, jobs, and television sets, not to mention twice as much food. As you can see from table 13.3, the higher the population growth rate is, the shorter the doubling time is. Some of the highest growth rates and quickest doubling times come from the Arab world. In the southwest corner of the Arabian Peninsula, for example, sits the conflict-ridden and unstable Republic of Yemen, Osama bin Laden's ancestral home and headquarters for one particularly violent wing of al-Qaeda. Yemen's population is increasing by 3 percent per year, which gives us a doubling time of only twenty-three years.

Table 13.3. Population Pressures on Rich and Poor

Country	Population in Millions 2011	Growth Rate 2010–2015	Total Fertility Rate 2010–2015	Doubling Time	PC/ GDP 2010	PC/ GNI 2010
Very High HDI						
France	63.1	0.5	1.9	140 years	39,460	42,390
Japan	126.5	–0.1	1.4	289 years	42,831	41,850
U.S.	317.6	0.9	2.1	77.7 years	47,199	47,390
U.K.	62.4	0.6	1.9	116.6 years	36,144	38,370
High HDI						
Croatia	4.4	0.2	1.5	350 years	13,754	13,870
Mexico	114.8	1.1	2.2	63.6 years	9,123	8,890
Russia	142.8	–0.1	1.5	230 years	10,440	9,900
Turkey	73.6	1.1	2.0	63.6 years	10,094	9,890
Medium HDI						
China	1,347.6	0.4	1.6	115 years	4,428	4,270
Sri Lanka	21	0.8	2.2	98 years	2,375	2,240
Indonesia	242.3	1.0	2.1	69 years	2,946	2,500
Egypt	82.5	1.7	2.6	40 years	2,698	2,420
Low HDI						
Togo	6.2	2.0	3.9	30 years	523	490
Malawi	15.4	3.2	6.0	25 years	343	330
D.R. Congo	67.8	2.2	5.5	26 years	199	2,150
Afghanistan	32.4	3.1	6.0	21 years	501	410

Sources: United Nations Development Programme, Human Development Report 2011, http://hdr.undp.org/en/media/HDR 2011 EN Tables.pdf; The World Bank GNI Per Capita Data, http://data.worldbank.org/indicator/NY.GNP.PCAP.CD; The World Bank GDP Per Capita Data, http://data.worldbank.org/indicator/NY.GDP.PCAP.CD.

Here are a couple more things to note about table 13.3. First, statistics such as the population doubling time assume that the present rate of growth will be perpetuated into the future. In fact, in real life, rates of growth go up and down for a variety of reasons, so every doubling time contains a significant margin of error and simply indicates a trend. Note also that wealthier countries typically have lower population growth and total fertility rates. For reasons we will consider below, a few countries, such as Russia and Hungary, have total fertility rates well below the replacement level and an annual net population loss. Countries such as Nigeria and Sierra Leone have astonishingly high total fertility rates but only moderately high population-increase rates. Why? If you think about the math, this suggests that the two countries are producing a lot of babies, but that life expectancy is unhappily still very short.

Let's pause for one minute and ensure that we have our terminology under control. To isolate and examine different aspects of population change, demographers use two separate statistics, and we have seen them both briefly above. Population change rate is the percentage rate by which a given population is growing or shrinking, with births, deaths, and migration all taken into account. The total fertility rate or TFR is the average number of children an individual woman can be expected to have in the course of her lifetime, with a theoretical "replacement value" of 2.1.

A Note on PC/GDP versus PC/GNI

As we all know, there are many ways to read the numbers and statistics thrown at us in the news every day. While we briefly introduced this in chapter 3, let us remind you of the following as you review table 13.3. Gross national income (GNI) accounts for flows of wealth in *and* out of the country. For many countries, the flows tend to balance out, leaving little difference between GDP and GNI. But not so for Egypt, because outflows of wealth often exceed flows of wealth back into the country. In other words, while Egypt produces $2,698 per inhabitant, GNI shows that less of it stays in the country than GDP might suggest ($2,420). France's GNI rank, in contrast, is a little higher than it is for GDP, reflecting the effect of strong net financial inflows from firms and workers based abroad.

Median Ages and Demographic Profiles

Since we want to know ahead of time where conflict is likely, students of international politics are always anxious to know the **median age** of a given population. The median age of a population is simply the age at which half the population is older and half the population is younger. We use median averages in economics and demography to factor out the mathematical impact of very large numbers at either end of the scale.

The median age of a population will be low if the birthrate is high and life expectancy is short, a condition typical of poorer countries where the median can be under twenty. The median age will be high in societies where the birthrate is relatively low, but people look forward to lengthy lives. Globally, the median age is 29.2 years, which means that about half of the world's population is under 29.2 years of age. The world as a whole is aging; by 2050, the global median age will rise to 36.8 years.

In the high and medium HDI societies, median ages run a lot lower. Egypt and Mexico, for example, have median ages of about 26.6 years and 24.4 years respectively.

Compare this to the American and British median ages of 36.9 and 39.8 years respectively, numbers that will rise as U.S. and UK life expectancy increases. Most European countries are even "older" than the United States is in terms of their median ages, and Japan is the most "elderly" society on earth with a median age of 44.7 years.[17]

How does the median age connect with conflict? The higher the median age, the more likely it is that a country will be politically stable. People in their thirties typically have jobs, mortgages, car payments, and children in school. The last thing they want is war or revolution, and the structure of their lives does not give them the time or the interest to become involved in radical political movements. Contrast this to sub-Saharan Africa, where the median age ranges between sixteen and twenty. These volatile societies contain a large number of unemployed young African men with minimal levels of schooling who are footloose, unmarried, and sometimes a little reckless. If you want a riot, a robbery, or a revolution, a mob of teenagers is more likely to oblige than a bunch of yuppies in the thirty-something generation.

A more graphic way to look at this same concept is by dividing society into three parts: the young who are below fifteen years of age; adults, who are between sixteen and sixty-four years of age; and the elderly, who are arbitrarily defined as those over sixty-five years of age. A wealthy and "elderly" society such as Japan has significantly more senior citizens than it has teenagers, and the United States is headed in the same direction. Poorer countries such as India have huge populations under fifteen years of age. And in a high birthrate African country such as Uganda, half the entire population is under fifteen years of age. If you add those who are under fifteen and those who are over sixty-five, divide the sum by those of working age (between sixteen and sixty-four years of age), and then get rid of the decimal place by multiplying by one hundred, you get a statistic called the "**dependency ratio**," a very crude way of showing how many nonworkers every worker is supporting. For example, table 13.4 shows that the United States has a dependency ratio of roughly 60, which means that every two American workers are supporting a third nonworker, or, more precisely, that every six workers is supporting ten nonworkers. When the number of workers declines in relation to the number of nonworkers, a society will begin to have economic problems and difficulty supporting its children and senior citizens.

As we saw above in our consideration of the median age, a very young society can be extremely volatile socially and politically. When the American baby-boom generation moved through their late teens and early twenties, the United States experienced an extended crime wave. Baby boomers are individually no more vicious than anyone else, but most violent crime tends to be committed by males between fifteen and twenty-nine years of age, and the baby boom had simply produced a lot of young men in that category.

An "oversupply" of young men can contribute to political violence. Iran, for example, went through a long population boom in the 1960s and 1970s, and the rural

Table 13.4. Dependency Ratios in Six Selected Countries and World Average

	Japan	U.S.	India	China	Oman	Uganda	World
15–65 years	54.2	59.2	55.6	39.1	51.5	105.1	54

Source: Data extrapolated from UNDP, Human Development Report 2010, table 11.

peasantry became far too numerous for the land available. Many young people drifted into huge slums around the principal cities, unsuccessfully seeking work and "camping" in shacks and makeshift accommodations. The shah's royal Iranian government did very little for them, and they were assisted only by Islamic mullahs, who preached vigorously against the Tehran regime. When the Ayatollah Khomeini swept back into his homeland in 1978, he found these angry, radicalized, reckless young men were available to become the shock troops for his theocratic revolution.

Tough Choices: Should the United States Welcome More Immigrants?

Let's think for a moment about the whole issue of migration. In the past, migration has served as a demographic safety valve. When population growth in a given area became too intense, people could move to a region where economic opportunities were available. For example, Italy survived a demographic boom in the 1800s because young Italians were able to move to the New World, especially the United States and Argentina.

Over time, governments have differed significantly in their willingness to welcome newcomers to their shores. Japan, for example, regards itself as the exclusive home of the Japanese people and does not generally permit non-Japanese people to reside permanently on its territory, unless the Japanese need some specialized skills. Until recently, some European countries refused to grant citizenship even to those children born there if their parents were from Africa, the Mediterranean, or the Middle East.

One of the liveliest controversies in every EU-member country today is the issue of migration. Right-wing parties typically worry about the ethnic "purity" of their societies, and the French, Germans, Spanish, and Italians are unhappy about the number of undocumented North Africans living and working in their midst. On the other hand, these are countries with very low total fertility rates. Are these immigrants performing the hard, underpaid, and disagreeable jobs at the lower end of the employment scale? Or are they—by working for illegally low wages—taking jobs away from natives of the country?

How about the United States? American political culture has been traditionally open to immigration. In recent years, however, the flood of migrants (both legal and undocumented) has been massive. Many of these new arrivals are from Latin American cultures and tend to have higher levels of fertility than long-term U.S. residents do. About one-third of the annual American population increase comes from in-migration.[18] Census figures released early in 2001 suggest that one-tenth of all America's residents were born outside of the United States, making America more of a multinational country than hitherto realized.

The economic impact of Latino immigration from Mexico has been difficult to summarize. A careful study by two Harvard economists has concluded that competition from low-skilled Mexican labor has lowered the wages of low-skilled

American labor, so U.S.-born high-school dropouts have seen their own wages decline sharply. Among wealthier Americans, the impact is more defused. Food budgets go down because fruits and vegetables are picked by undocumented aliens, but taxes go up when Latino immigrants use public medicine or education. For people rich enough to hire maids and gardeners, illegal immigration is an illegal dream come illegally true.

To complicate matters, population growth in the United States in the 1900s turned out to be faster than anticipated. U.S. fertility is somewhat higher than otherwise similar European countries, and Americans are producing babies at just below the replacement rate, with high levels of immigration keeping the U.S. population percolating along, while the European fertility rate is well below that famous 2.1 replacement level. Long-range population forecasts are always risky, but by 2050, the United States could hit the half-billion mark, almost double the current level. Given this already rapid growth, is it in the interests of the United States to permit even moderate levels of immigration in the future?

In 2004, the celebrated if controversial American political scientist Samuel Huntington wrote *Who Are We? The Challenges to America's National Identity* (New York: Simon and Schuster) in which he suggested that this rising tide of immigration was threatening America's "core nation."[19] In fact, by the 2010 census count in the United States, the Hispanic population was 16 percent of the total citizenry. That is quite a large number of the "core nation." What are the arguments, pro and con?

- CON—Ethnicity: Some see American culture as primarily Christian, Anglo-Saxon, and English speaking. To the extent that new immigrants do not correspond to this model, they will change the ethnic character of the country, making the United States less of a nation-state and more of a multinational state.
- CON—Drain on Public Finances: People coming to the United States from abroad tend to be poorer than the average American, and are therefore more reliant upon public services funded by U.S. taxpayers. Their numerous children need to be educated in state-supported schools.
- CON—Overpopulation: The United States is becoming overpopulated and overcrowded. In the first years of the twenty-first century, the U.S. population grew at over 1 percent. We do not want the U.S. population to soar to over half a billion people by mid-century, because American prosperity and U.S. quality of life depend upon open spaces and ample resources.
- PRO—Cultural Richness: The presence of many cultures and ethnicities within the United States is a source of strength, not weakness. Immigrants have brought international cuisine to U.S. tables, exciting world music to concert halls, foreign expertise to universities, and rich color to monochromatic Anglo-Saxon culture.
- PRO—Economic Importance: In most cases, immigrants are paying taxes and funding medical care provided by Medicaid in public hospitals.
- PRO—Medicare and Social Security. The United States has an established tradition of immigrant groups "making good" after a generation or two, so today's penniless immigrants may be tomorrow's multimillionaires.

- PRO—Human Capital: From seasonal workers in agriculture to foreign doctors in emergency rooms, immigrants are making a solid contribution. Given the rising U.S. dependency ratio and dropping native fertility rate, who is going to support American retirees in the future if the United States doesn't allow energetic and ambitious people in to pick up the slack?

The immigration decision will be made and remade by voters and elected officials over the course of the decades to come. Where do you stand?[20]

DEMOGRAPHIC TRANSITION

It is an established fact that wealthier societies generally have fewer children than do poorer population groups, suggesting that economic change has a lot to do with human fertility. As you can see in table 13.5, many factors change as a society modernizes and gets more prosperous.

The Developmental Cycle

To summarize the complicated process of social modernization, a society will have difficulty becoming wealthy unless its agricultural sector is efficient enough to feed the population easily. Mechanized agriculture frees workers to move off the land into industry, and then later into services such as education and medicine. Education becomes widely available, and—as we will see below—sending young women to school has a profound effect on population growth. Public health tends to improve, partly because people know more about their bodies and partly because society has more money to spend on health care. Better health, as we will see, affects fertility and population growth in a variety of ways.

As people leave farming and turn to offices and factories for employment, they tend to move out of the countryside and into cities and towns, a process called **urbanization**. Demographers have long understood that urbanization tends to make children less useful and more expensive, which discourages parents from having too many of them. Urbanization is projected to continue into the next decade and, eventually, urban populations will exceed rural populations, making mega-cities in the developing world not only a population issue but also an environmental issue. Included in urbanization is the issue of property rights and the lack of them among the poor in many areas of the less-developed world, such as the *favelas*, or slums, outside of Sao Paolo, Brazil.

Employment is another crucial issue. As we will see, those who find salaried jobs in a modernizing society will tend to have fewer children. For a variety of reasons, unemployed people tend to have more children. The UN's **International Labour Organisation (ILO** and note that the UN uses British spelling) estimates that there are about 212 million unemployed adults (i.e., people between fifteen and sixty-five years of age) worldwide, a global record, up thirty-seven million from 2007. In 2008, 633 million workers and their families were living on less than US$1.25 per day, and 215 million additional workers were at risk of falling into poverty in 2009. In 2009, the global unemployment rate rose to 6.6 percent.

Table 13.5. Modernization from Low to High Human Development

Category	Low Human Development	High Human Development
Agriculture	Poor land and primitive farming practices limit yields and cause food shortages and famines.	Efficient and scientific large-scale agriculture on good land creates food surpluses for export.
Industry	Low-tech export of craft items and raw materials, but balance of payments suffers because most manufactured items are imported from abroad.	High-tech, export-oriented industrial sector brings in cash from foreign sales and creates domestic consumer-oriented society.
Education	Low literacy rates, limited free schooling, few public libraries, few Internet connections.	High literacy and developed public school sector creates literate and numerate population.
Health	Environmental problems, poor housing, unavailable or expensive medicine create high maternal mortality and shortened life spans.	Clean water and air, available medical care, affordable hospitals create long lives and low infant mortality rates.
Population Growth	Population usually increases rapidly.	Population roughly static.
Urbanization	Majority of people are rural or have moved to urban slums.	Bulk of population lives in urban or suburban centers.
Employment	30 percent to 70 percent may be unemployed or seasonal workers with no government support.	Generally over 90 percent of workforce in work with unemployment benefits for unemployed.
Political Stability	Frequent and violent regime changes combine with civil wars to inhibit development.	Democratic systems produce predictable government and safe society.
Governance	Corrupt practices pervasive in public and commercial life, with politicians systematically looting public funds and preying on commercial enterprise.	Corrupt practices among some politicians and business leaders, but generally honest government provides stable business environment.

The developed world suffered the most, accounting for 40 percent of the increase in global unemployment. However, Africa's unemployment has remained unchanged, meaning economic growth and employment opportunities are nearly nonexistent. In sub-Saharan Africa, for example, about 30 percent of all adult males are unemployed.[21]

Political stability is also a vital factor. Most low HDI countries suffer from endemic political violence in the form of civil wars, terrorist or guerrilla movements, and frequent unconstitutional changes in government. Business leaders are reluctant to invest in a country where the rules are susceptible to unpredictable changes and where their property could be confiscated in the next coup d'état. A parallel issue is what is commonly called "**governance**," the level of effectiveness and honesty political leaders bring to their work. Governance is different from government because implementation of policies, particularly in the area of population, includes a number of actors—government and nongovernment, such as NGOs—to get things done. Prosperity becomes impossible when crooks take complete control of a government and loot the entire society. Endemic, corrosive, systemic governmental corruption in these societies exacerbates poverty. Since political stability and good governance help grow an economy, we will see a tendency for the birthrate to decline as political leaders become both democratic and skilled at public administration.

Demographers and social scientists have created a widely accepted theory called demographic transition to explain why some populations soar while others go flat. The essence of the theory is that a modernizing and developing society will move through several phases, starting with a traditional phase, when the population is kept roughly static, a medical modernization phase, which produces a rapid population increase, and—if all goes well—a social modernization phase, when the population levels off with few births and long lives. Demographic transition is one of the core concepts in understanding the modern world, so let's look at each of these three phases in greater detail.

Demographic transition is a historical process that happens to different countries at different times in their individual histories. Some countries passed through it very slowly in the past, while other societies are going through it somewhat more quickly today. The very poorest societies in the contemporary world are halfway into demographic transition, and are experiencing difficulties in getting all the way through, a phenomenon—to be explained below—called "incomplete demographic transition."

Historians have observed that populations in Western Europe and North America, for example, grew very slowly until the 1800s, when they went through a rapid expansionary phase. On both sides of the Atlantic, this increase began to slow after World War I and has continued to fall to about 1 percent or below in almost all European and North American societies. In the contemporary world, some poorer societies have had high rates of growth until they became socially and economically modernized, and then saw rapid declines in population growth, effectively completing in a few decades the same process that Europeans had taken a century or more to work through. Whether we are talking about historical demographic transition or contemporary demographic transition, the factors that make it happen seem about the same.

The Traditional Phase

In a traditional or primitive society, the cruelty of nature ensures a rough balance between births and deaths. There is little or no effective medical care. Disease and violence creates high mortality, particularly among the very young and elderly. Parents, and particularly fathers, react to this uncertain world by having as many children as possible, particularly sons, for the following reasons:

- Children as Social Security: The first old-age pension plans were a product of the early twentieth century. Even today, they only function in reasonably developed societies. In a traditional society, a large family takes the place of a retirement plan, since an elderly couple can count on their offspring to feed them when they become too elderly to work. In harsh economic conditions, adult children will make great sacrifices to keep their parents comfortable. The more children parents can produce, the more comfortable they are likely to be in their old age.
- Children as Workers: Since traditional societies are still largely agrarian or pastoral, children are economically useful at a very early age. Even small children can tend goats, sheep, or chickens. Even marginal land responds to intensive cultivation, which is possible in a low-tech agricultural environment if there are many hands to do the work.
- Sons as Protection: In restless, lawless societies without competent governments and adequate police forces, healthy male children provide protection for parents and property.

In a traditional society, the status of women is likely to be extremely low and a woman can best assure her status by providing as many sons as possible for her husband. It makes sound economic sense for a man to take as many wives as possible, since polygamy increases a man's chances of begetting a large number of sons. Daughters are less valuable economically, and in some societies a baby girl is a net loss. In many South Asian societies, a father must provide a dowry to ensure a decent marriage for his daughter, and a series of baby girls can mean bankruptcy. An individual mother might privately object to endless pregnancies, but she lacks the social status to place her personal desires over the perceived welfare of her family.

Medical Modernization

Over the course of the late 1800s in Europe and North America, a minimal level of medical care became generally available. Medical practitioners became aware of the existence of germs, and turned to antiseptics and disinfectants to fight off contagion. The importance of cleanliness in childbirth and surgery was discovered. The supply of drinking water was made safe. A variety of effective medical techniques made childbirth less dangerous for mother and infant, leading to a drop in the infant mortality rate. This phase in demographic transition is sometimes called the "mortality transition."

While the mortality rate fell rapidly, nothing inhibited people from continuing to have as many children as possible, since there were still the above-mentioned economic advantages to large families. A woman who does not practice birth control and has regular sexual relations can expect to become pregnant about sixteen times in her lifetime. Women went on producing very large families for their husbands, sometimes raising a dozen or more children with half again as many spontaneous abortions and miscarriages. In these years, a man might wear out two or three wives in the course of his own lifetime.

The obvious result of a decline in the death rate and a continuing high birthrate is rapid population growth, which is what occurred in Europe and North America in the

1800s and the early years of the 1900s. The larger population was supported by increases in agricultural productivity and the beginnings of industrialization. Some countries only moved into medical modernization in the twentieth century. The Indian population, for example, grew very slowly until after World War I, when the British brought better medical care to the subcontinent. At this point, mortality declined sharply, and the population began to increase rapidly.[22] Both world wars helped bring European health-care practices to some medium and low HDI countries.

Since 1945, the United Nations (and specifically the World Health Organization [WHO]) has scored impressive victories over infectious diseases, even managing to eliminate smallpox. In the 1950s, antibiotics were available at relatively low cost almost everywhere. While it had unhappy consequences for the environment, DDT killed the mosquitoes that had made malaria almost universal in parts of the tropical world. Medical researchers created vaccines against smallpox, measles, whooping cough, polio, and diphtheria. While the public-health situation in the Third and Fourth Worlds is a long way from even minimal levels of acceptability, the death rate has generally declined over the course of the past forty years.

Social Modernization

By the end of World War I, societies in the developed world and some parts of the developing world began to change in ways that made very large families no longer economically advantageous. The following factors were important when the high HDI world went through demographic transition, and they continue to be crucial where demographic transition is happening today:

- Changing Occupational Patterns: Thanks to the advent of mechanized farming, fewer people work on the land, which means that children are less useful as little farm hands. As society modernizes, more and more adult men and some women are engaged in salaried employment in offices and factories, where their children cannot help them. Some of these jobs involve pension plans, and governments in developed societies create national old-age pension schemes such as the U.S. Social Security System, which means that parents are increasingly able to support themselves in their old age without depending upon their children. In this new world, children are no longer economically useful, but they need to be fed, clothed, and educated, making them financial minuses rather than pluses. Some scholars describe this change with the phrase "wealth flow": if wealth or financial advantage runs from children to parents, a society can expect to have RPG. If children become a drain on a poor family's finances, parents find ways to have fewer of them.
- Safer Societies: Defense of home and family become more and more the responsibility of police and armed forces. Even in areas where society is still not particularly safe, no one expects to be able to breed enough sons to defend the farm against soldiers with machine-guns and tanks.
- Progress in Female Emancipation: Schooling for girls makes it possible for women to help support their families through salaried employment, rather than as breeders of sons. From the husband's perspective, an educated wife might be a better economic "deal" when working as a nurse, a schoolteacher or a secretary rather than as a mother.

And a woman with her own paycheck is more empowered to defy a husband who wants more children than she feels comfortable providing. In modern American society, wealthier women defer (sometimes indefinitely) the motherhood experience while they complete university training and begin careers.

- Contraception and Health Care: It was once felt that the availability of contraception was the single most important factor in regulating population growth, and it is now clear that economic factors are more important. When condoms and other contraceptive devices gradually became available and acceptable, however, couples were better able to avoid accidental pregnancies. Indeed, the appearance of some contraceptive devices, such as the birth-control pill and the IUD, allow a woman to take charge of her fecundity without her husband's knowledge or consent.

THE DEEP END OF THE POOL

The venerable (and in some eyes controversial) Planned Parenthood Association believes in disseminating information about family planning techniques.[23] On a worldwide basis, some believe that the only proper way to avoid unwanted pregnancies and sexually transmitted diseases is abstinence before marriage and fidelity within marriage. The British action group Avert considers this issue.[24]

Similarly, better health care for newborn babies actually helps lower the birthrate. At first, this might seem counterintuitive. Why should the survival of more babies cut the fertility rate? In societies with very high infant mortality rates, families have no way of knowing how many of their children will survive to adulthood. If the existence of several adult children is an economic necessity for a family, a woman will be pressured to have as many as possible in order to improve the parents' chances of seeing at least a few survive. On the other hand, improved infant health care and a lower infant mortality rate allows parents to decide in advance how many children they want.[25]

When the role of the supernatural and religion is reduced, individuals sometimes feel empowered to ignore preachers, priests, mullahs, and rabbis, and make personal decisions about crucial issues. Roman Catholicism, some strands of Protestantism, most branches of Islam, and many other faiths regard birth control as a moral evil, and even more religions are critical of abortion. The more secular the society, the more likely it becomes that a couple will make independent judgments about the size of their family.

The theory of demographic transition, therefore, holds that once a society achieves social modernity with a modest level of prosperity, the birthrate will come down rapidly, and some demographers have called this the "fertility transition." Thanks to modern medicine, those who are born can look forward to an extended life expectancy. In a secularized society, couples will make more rational choices about the number of children they will have, and contraceptive technology will allow them to achieve their fertility goals with reasonable accuracy. Rich and modernized societies will therefore have slow population increases, and in some cases, no increase at all.

Figure 13.3 illustrates what a completed demographic transition cycle looks like. The top line is the birthrate, and the bottom line is the death rate. At the beginning in a "state-of-nature" traditional society, both lines are roughly parallel, and the population will be somewhere near ZPG or zero population growth. When the medical modernization

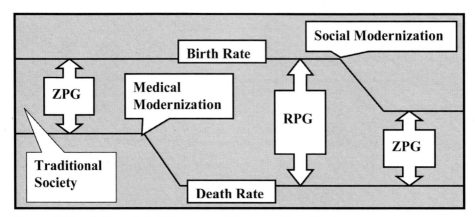

Figure 13.3. A Completed Demographic Transition Cycle
The theory of demographic transition helps explain why prosperous societies such as North America, Japan, and Western Europe have gone through periods of rapid population expansion but have now almost stopped growing.

phase occurs, the death rate will decline rapidly, and the birthrate will remain unchanged because large families still make economic sense. In fact, the total fertility rate might even edge up, since healthier mothers will bring more infants to term. Society then moves into a period of RPG or rapid population growth. When the social modernization phase occurs, children lose their economic importance, and parents begin deliberately having fewer of them. The birthrate declines to somewhere near ZPG again, and the cycle is over, having produced a much larger population.

Incomplete Demographic Transition

For demographic transition to work, however, society must eventually hit that all-important social modernization phase, where governments and employers start offering pension and health plans, children become economically less useful because people work in factories and offices rather than on farms, and society becomes more secular in its approach to family planning.

The world's poorest societies, however, have blundered halfway into demographic transition, going through some level of medical modernization but not managing to achieve social modernization. Aid agencies, NGOs, and sometimes occupying armies have generally managed to get the mortality rate down, but have done little to change the basic economic structure of these wealth-deprived societies. As Joel Cohen noted, "After World War Two, the rich countries of the world exported more health than wealth."[26]

The people of many medium HDI societies and nearly all low HDI countries still work in inefficient forms of primary food production. In low-tech farming, children (particularly males) are still economically important. Industrialization has generally not occurred, and neither business nor government in the underdeveloped world has begun to make pension plans available. As Marvin Harris commented: "Aging parents . . . cannot rely on company pension funds, social security payments, welfare allotments, food stamps, or bank accounts; they can only rely on their children."[27]

While the infant mortality rate has declined almost everywhere in the world, it is still unreasonably high in these very poor societies. As mentioned above, a high infant mortality rate actually contributes to RPG. Knowing that some proportion of their children will die young, parents in very poor societies customarily "overshoot," conceiving more children than they actually want in order to ensure that the minimum number live to adulthood. Another issue is the persistence of the traditional male belief that a man's virility is expressed by the production of many sons.

The consequences should be clear. A primitive society begins in a state of nature, in which deaths and births balance each other out. It is a cruel but stable existence. Along comes a minimal injection of medical care into the society, perhaps in the form of a Western-trained doctor or a chlorinated water supply or a nurse from the World Health Organization dispensing shots against common childhood diseases. The result is a quick and drastic lowering of the death rate. The birthrate remains unaffected, however, because the social causes that produce RPG cannot be changed by a nurse with a hypodermic. The consequence, therefore, is a continuing rapid expansion of the population, which itself hampers economic growth. When people remain poor, they can typically see no rationale for limiting their fertility, and the cycle continues.[28]

Poverty and Population Growth

There is a clear overall contemporary connection between rapid population growth and poverty. The per capita gross domestic product usually rises as population growth rates decline, and vice versa. It would be simplistic, however, to assert a straight causal relationship between rapid population growth and poverty. Clearly poverty and population reinforce one another in complicated ways. It can be difficult to raise the economic status of a society if the problem (i.e., the number of people) keeps getting worse faster than you can fix it. And as we have seen, people in some societies react to poverty by attempting to breed more children. However, there are some clarifications and complications that need to be made.

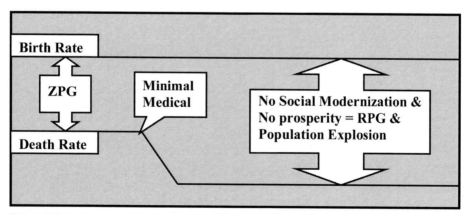

Figure 13.4. Incomplete Demographic Transition
Almost everywhere, minimal medical care is available to help people live somewhat longer. But if society cannot move quickly to a social modernization phase with emancipated women and pension plans, families will go on breeding children for economic motives and RPG will limit the prospects for economic growth.

Exceptions to the Rule

While the poverty-population growth connection is generally true, it isn't universally true. For reasons we'll discuss below, the Russian population is actually declining even though there are dark areas of dire poverty in Russian society. The Sultanate of Oman had one of the highest birthrates in the world throughout the 1990s and early 2000s, but the country is making good economic progress.[29] During the economically ebullient 1990s, the American birthrate went up, not down.[30]

Counting All the Numbers

Another cautionary note: politicians and economists make much of annual increases in the gross domestic product as evidence of growing national wealth. While this is an oversimplification of a complex connection, it is worth remembering that if the rate of population growth outruns the rate of GDP growth, then nobody is really getting any richer. Put more simply, if a country's real GDP rises 3 percent in the same year that the population increases by 3 percent, the two increases effectively cancel each other. In the United States, the population increased by a hair over 1 percent in 2003, and the GDP increased by about 4 percent, suggesting that the economy's actual growth was closer to 3 percent.

People and Resources

We'll look more carefully at this conundrum in the next chapter, but remember that populations can increase without pain if they have sufficient resources to support their growth. Historically, the rapid economic development of the United States and Western Europe took place against a background of steady rapid population growth. Moderate population increase in an environment of unexploited natural resources can contribute to economic growth. However, when a very rapid population increase occurs in an area where exploitable resources are limited, there is a distinct risk that population will overwhelm the "**carrying capacity**" of the environment and contribute to poverty.

2. Demographic Disasters

Having a population soar can produce a lot of problems, but abrupt and selective reverses in growth rates can be painful as well. As we will see when we look at the case of post-Soviet Russia, a declining population can be evidence of a deep societal malaise. A second problem is the gender gap. All things being equal, it would probably be better to have an equal balance between men and women in human society, and there are political implications to the fact that it doesn't work that way. The issue of sex-selection abortion, to be explored below, is both interesting and scary. And finally, we need to pause a moment on the demographic and political implications of HIV/AIDS, and question what impact this frightful disease is likely to have on human population figures.

Very rapid population growth in an environment of limited economic potential does generally seem to be a recipe for social disaster. We'll conclude this section by looking at some consequences of this sort of population increase.

UNHEALTHY DEMOGRAPHICS

The models of demographic transition presented above suggest that population will achieve a rough equivalency between births and deaths so that society achieves something close to zero population growth. This is generally true, but it doesn't always work out that neatly. In fact, ZPG is not hardwired into the equation, and there is no way of predicting precisely where a given population will end up at any given point in the future.

Several Western European countries bear witness to the emerging truth that parenthood is not an inexorable choice in a prosperous and secular society with birth control information easily available. With children no longer even remotely having any economic value, and women increasingly engaged in high-status careers during their childbearing years, a great many couples may elect to pursue pleasure and profession over delivery rooms and diapers. In this case, the total fertility rate will slip below that theoretical replacement level of 2.1 children per woman, and the population will eventually decline, unless there are enough immigrants to take up the slack.

Fertility rates can decline in surprising places. Italy and Spain, for example, were both once poor societies, strongly influenced by the anti-contraception beliefs of the Roman Catholic Church, and were consequently blessed/cursed with high birthrates. In an amazingly rapid political evolution, both Mediterranean countries have become surprisingly prosperous and modern. To the distress of the Vatican, both are now extremely secular, and the total fertility rate has declined to 1.5 in Italy and a rock-bottom 1.5 in Spain, well below replacement levels. Italy, in fact, is now registering an annual net population loss of –0.1 percent, while immigration barely keeps Spain in positive numbers. Both of these democratic and prosperous societies enjoy wonderful life-expectancy rates and seem generally unworried by the prospect of slowly shedding population.

A declining birthrate means an aging population and a long-range problem for social security/old-age pension systems in wealthy societies. Put simply, almost all Western countries have government-operated pension funds into which workers pay a portion of their salaries and from which retirees draw their pensions. All of these old-age pension systems were created in an era in which there were lots of workers, and—thanks to short life expectancies—not that many retirees. In the twenty-first century, on the other hand, a declining birthrate means fewer workers to pay into the fund, while extended life expectancy provides more retirees to draw money out of it. What's the answer? Some governments are toying with pro-fertility policies. Prosperous Singapore, for example, has watched its total fertility rate decline to the point that the government has intervened with a program to convince overworked Singaporeans to take the time to manufacture a few more babies for the next generation. Other governments are relaxing immigration controls, so that workers from poorer countries can finance the golden years of retiring natives.

Russia's Declining Population

What has been happening in Russia, however, is different in both severity and causality. With a total fertility rate lower than either Spain or Italy and a Third-World mortality rate, Russia is actually losing population at a net rate of over 0.5 percent per year, roughly seven hundred thousand people per annum, a trend that demographers expect to accelerate over the next few decades.[31] This population loss seems to have begun in the 1970s, two decades before the Soviet Union self-destructed, although it was not widely understood at the time.

Russia became the primary successor state to the defunct Soviet Union in 1992, and in the ensuing eight years, deaths exceeded births to the tune of 3.3 million. With the population today standing at 142.8 million, the United Nations is forecasting a further 4.5 million drop over the next fifteen years. Some Russian scholars are predicting that Russia will level off at the size it was during the 1917 Russian Revolution. Why? A population decline this drastic can only happen when there is a precipitous change in both fertility rates and human mortality. Check the U.S. Census Bureau take on the situation.[32]

- Fertility Rates: The Russian fertility rate stands at 1.5 percent with a growth rate of −0.1 percent.[33] Russian women are generally well educated and have access to birth control information and resources, as well as the right to abortions if birth control fails. There is ample evidence that Russian women are making a conscious decision not to bring babies into the social and economic reality of post-Marxist Russia. Russian women complain that their present or potential husbands cannot find jobs, earn enough money, or provide homes for families. The economic and political future of the country is uncertain; pessimistic women are hesitant to marry and reluctant to become mothers. The total fertility rate, therefore, has declined sharply.
- Life Expectancy: Ever since the 1970s, the average life expectancy for Russians, particularly Russian males, has been declining, although the downward spiral may have halted in recent years. Normally, it takes an extremely lethal war or a devastating plague to kill as many people as Russia has lost "of natural causes" in recent years. In the years after World War II, Russians enjoyed longevity rates that were approaching those of Western Europe thanks to a national health system that provided free—if sometimes primitive—medical care to the entire nation. As Russia stumbles toward a market economy, health care is becoming informally privatized, and patients need to bribe poorly paid public health physicians to provide theoretically free services. Infectious diseases such as tuberculosis are on the rise, but Moscow has been slow to mount a medical counterattack.[34]
- Self-Destructive Behavior: Self-destructive behavior seems to be part of the Russian mortality problem, perhaps related to a loss of national self-confidence: suicide, drug abuse, sexual promiscuity (producing an epidemic of sexually transmitted diseases), rampant alcoholism, and the results of criminal violence (i.e., gunshot and knife wounds). Life expectancy for Russian men is now about sixty-eight, which is eleven years behind Western European and North American expectations.[35]

How does this affect politics? Americans were delighted when "democracy" came to Russia after seventy-four years of Marxist dictatorship, and U.S. leaders made the assumption that Russians could make a quick, happy leap into capitalism. The stark character of Russian demography, however, suggests that it isn't working at a very basic level. While public-health conditions may have improved slightly in the first years of this century, the real task facing Prime Minister Dmitry Medvedev and President Vladimir Putin may simply be keeping their people alive.

By 2006, then president Vladimir Putin had decided to treat this declining population as a national security issue; Russia has vast and underpopulated areas in Siberia that might someday tempt an overpopulated China. Beginning in January 2007, the Kremlin intends to foment fertility by offering a "baby bonus" of about $10,000 to women who produce a child for mother Russia. So far, in about three years, the negative growth rates have dropped from –0.3 to –0.1 percent. As we'll read here and in chapter 14, not all scientists are enthusiastic about these public policies.

Tough Choices: Should the CIA Count Bombs or Babies?

We always need to look for interconnections, even among factors that don't seem to relate to one another. For example, here's a less-than-obvious tie-in between demographics and strategic intelligence. In 1974, with the Vietnam War in its final phases and the Cold War at its frostiest, the Soviet Union was commonly regarded by U.S. intelligence as a formidable military threat, a strong, vital society that provided an economic model capable of challenging American notions about free enterprise and democracy. In that same year, however, the Soviet Union quietly stopped providing basic demographic data to the United Nations. Guessing that the health system was deteriorating rapidly, the late senator Daniel Patrick Moynihan mused that the Soviet Union would probably self-destruct without American intervention, but no one paid much attention to the prescient scholar statesman.[36] At the time, American intelligence was focused on Soviet missile launchers and troop deployments, and few Western intelligence officers asked themselves why the militarily powerful Soviets were suddenly keeping their life-expectancy and infant-mortality statistics secret.

The collapse of the Soviet Union in 1991 largely caught both the intelligence and academic communities off guard. Had we spent less time counting rocket launchers and paid more attention to maternity wards, however, we might have realized as early as the 1970s that the Soviet experiment was beginning to collapse internally. A landmark 1992 book by Murray Feshback and Alfred Friendly called *Ecocide in the USSR: Health and Nature under Siege* (New York: Basic) finally blew the whistle, revealing that the Soviet health-care system had been disintegrating for decades, bringing premature death to the two most vulnerable categories of citizens, the very young and the very old. The Soviet Union didn't collapse simply because of health problems, but those bad health-care numbers should have told the West that the whole Soviet system was imploding.

Does this style of demographic analysis work for the future? The southern African country of Zimbabwe (once Rhodesia) is languishing under the dictatorial rule of Robert Mugabe, and the past decade has seen a worsening of health statistics similar to what the USSR experienced before it self-destructed. The Zimbabwean infant mortality rate has climbed from fifty-seven in 1994 to sixty-two today. The under five mortality rate (U5MR) has bounded from eighty-one to ninety-six, and maternal mortality has risen steeply. Perhaps a government that cannot keep its people alive will ultimately be unable to maintain itself in power. Stand by for news bulletins announcing riot and revolution in Mugabe's Zimbabwe.

Sex-Selection Abortion

Why, in wealthier societies, do women tend to outnumber men? For poorly understood biological reasons, the mothers of the world deliver between 105 and 106 baby boys for every 100 baby girls, but that is the last break males get in the race for numerical supremacy. After arriving in the maternity ward, males suffer higher levels of mortality at all stages of life. In prosperous societies, therefore, the two genders achieve a rough parity during adulthood and then get out of sync again as the population ages, leaving us with a lot of little old ladies and not quite as many gray-haired gents.

In some very poor societies, however, men outnumber women quite dramatically, and on a planetary basis, males today are a slight majority. Demographers keep track of what they call the **sex ratio** by calculating the number of males for every 100 females; the global sex ratio is roughly 108 males for every 100 females and there are between sixty and ninety million more men in the world than there are women. In the United States, there are 105 males to every 100 females.[37]

If women are inherently the stronger gender in biological terms, then why are there fewer women than men? There are clearly many factors. In extremely poor and violent societies, females are murdered as infants, starved as children, and abused as adults. With global improvements in health and education for women, however, the planet should theoretically be moving toward a female majority everywhere, with profound social and political implications.

A new phenomenon called **sex-selection abortion** (SSA), however, may prevent this from happening. Where demographic transition remains incomplete, and where society has still not hit that social modernization phase, the preference for male offspring continues to be very high. Without adequate government-sponsored social security or corporate pension plans, a Chinese or Indian family must still look to its male children for support in old age. A baby girl will live with her family until she marries, absorbing precious financial resources for food and clothing. In India and some other countries, she needs a dowry to be married at all, and after the wedding, she passes under the control of her husband's family, supporting her in-laws in their old age, but not her own parents. A male child, on the other hand, will inherit the family property, perpetuate the family name, and care for his mother and father in their declining years.[38]

In the past, there was little that an Indian or Chinese parent could do about this roll of the sexual dice except for the horrific business of practicing infanticide when a baby girl was born. The twentieth century, however, provided the world with a variety of medical techniques for determining the gender of a fetus. Because it's inexpensive, ultrasound testing has been the procedure of choice for prospective parents in poor societies. Ultrasound is the noninvasive use of high-frequency sound waves to create a computer-enhanced picture of the fetus.

While sex-selection abortion is technically illegal in China and India, the law is plainly impossible to enforce. And there is growing evidence that couples are using amniocentesis or ultrasound scanning to check the gender of their fetus, and then systematically aborting unwanted females. China, for example, has a sex ratio of 121 males for every 100 females, which is unnaturally unbalanced from the demographic point of view. By contrast, in Hong Kong, which has a different culture but the same biological ethnicity, the sex ratio is 108 males for every 100 females, which is about what scholars would expect. The mainland Chinese sex ratio is likely to get worse.

So what has happened to China's missing females? China has a one-child-per-couple policy, so a couple giving birth at home to a baby girl may simply elect not to register the baby girl with the authorities. Two American scholars have concluded that Chinese families did practice mass infanticide in the past and acknowledge the difficulty in establishing how often this particular awfulness continues to occur. Increasingly, however, they determined that China's gender imbalance is now mostly the result of the widespread use of sex-selection abortion.[39]

In India, the figures are equally striking. In January 2006, Britain's most prestigious medical journal, *The Lancet*, published the results of a huge 1.1 million household survey concluding that sex-selection abortion is massively distorting sex ratios in India.[40] Couples having their first child are producing 114 boys for every 100 girls, for a sex ratio of 114, which is too high to be natural. If the first child is a girl, Indians then generate only 100 girls for every 131 boys when the second baby appears. If the first two children have been girls, the third child ratio drops to 100 girls for every 138 boys. This suggests that India is "losing" about one-half million girls a year, or 2.5 million over a five-year period.[41] In a different study, researchers found that in the rich, agricultural Punjab, about 9 girls are born for every 10 boys and in Delhi only 84.5 girls are reported for every 100 boys, a dramatic worsening of the ratio over the past decade.[42] As is the case in China, the out-of-kilter sex ratio in India is partly the result of infanticide but increasingly the consequence of sex-selection abortion.[43]

Sex-selection abortion is a political, medical, and ethical dilemma. At the human level, the practice is a brutal affront to a woman's health and dignity, since wives are denied the right to bear their own daughters and are forced to become repetitively pregnant until they conceive a male. Furthermore, ultrasound is not very accurate before the fourth month of pregnancy, which means that the subsequent abortion is later than would be medically desirable. And finally, there is already evidence in China that the skewed sex ratio is making it difficult for young men to find wives, and there are reports of Chinese men purchasing girls from impoverished North Korea.[44]

AIDS and Population Change

Will the HIV/AIDS epidemic slow global population growth? In the opening years of this new century, there were fifty-three countries with significant levels of HIV infection, including some very large societies such as China, India, and the United States. Worldwide, about thirty-three million adults seem to be HIV-positive. The disease kills about eight thousand people every day, and 13,700 new infections take place every day. About two-thirds of all AIDS victims are in sub-Saharan Africa, and especially in the southern part of the African continent. Thanks to the AIDS epidemic and nutritional problems, the life expectancy in southern Africa has been declining by about two years a decade, and now rests at a dismal forty-seven years. About 20 percent of the population of countries such as Botswana, Lesotho, Namibia, South Africa, Swaziland, Zambia, and Zimbabwe are HIV-positive. A look at the UN AIDS Global Report 2010 reveals that, unfortunately, these numbers have barely moved since 2001.[45]

Tragically, AIDS and poverty reinforce one another. When women and children are desperately poor, they may trade sex for food or money, exposing themselves to the risk of AIDS contagion. Once infected, they may feel compelled to continue as sex workers (and spread HIV infection) as their only means of short-term survival.[46] Endemic political violence is also a factor. As we learned in chapter 9, Africa is currently the setting for a large number of civil wars and armed conflicts. Poorly disciplined troops have taken to raping women and girls on a massive scale, and many soldiers turn out to be HIV-positive.

For the planet as a whole, most specialists believe that AIDS will slow population growth but not reverse it. The UN lowered its 2050 forecast from 9.3 billion to the current prediction of 8.9 billion partly because of a slackening in the total fertility rate and partly because of the impact of AIDS.[47] For some severely affected individual countries such as South Africa, however, AIDS will actually limit population growth over the course of the next half century.

Most Americans became conscious of AIDS in the early 1980s, when it was naively believed to be a problem uniquely for those male homosexuals who were promiscuous and those drug users who shared unclean needles. AIDS mortality rose in the United States until the mid-1990s, when changes in behavior and powerful (and expensive) new drugs began to bring down the mortality figures, although there is no real cure yet available.

In sub-Saharan Africa, AIDS kills people in the prime of their working years, and leaves their children without financial support and sometimes HIV-positive. Africa south of the Sahara is the poorest portion of the planet, and governments there are not well organized to provide adequate care for the healthy, much less the mortally ill. Nor are political and religious leaders always clear on what needs to be done: South African president Thabo Mbeki has perplexed the charitable world with his past insistence that the HIV microorganism does not actually cause AIDS. Almost all specialists believe that a more widespread use of condoms would slow HIV contagion. To avoid offending religious communities, however, the U.S. government has virtually halted the donation of condoms to most poor countries.[48]

Pharmaceutical products are expensive everywhere, and even wealthy countries have difficulty paying for health care. The 1.2 billion people who subsist on less than a dollar a day cannot possibly afford AIDS treatments that cost an average of $10,000 per year.

HIV/AIDS has generated a powerful international conflict over intellectual property rights. Any country with a modern pharmaceutical industry can produce generic versions of the most popular anti-AIDS medicines that would keep AIDS-infected people alive even in poor countries. The problem is that most sophisticated medicines are produced by pharmaceutical corporations who have invested heavily in research, development, and marketing. These companies hold patents that are protected by international treaties such as the 1995 Trade Related Aspects of Intellectual Property Rights (TRIPS), an international agreement that strengthens the interests of patent holders and makes intellectual property rights enforceable by the World Trade Organization (WTO).[49]

The drug companies argue that they need the profits to fund future research and reward stockholders for past investment. Antipoverty organizations (such as Oxfam) and countries (such as India, Brazil, Thailand, and South Africa) complained that the "pharmas" would rather let poor people die than lower their prices. This is a violent, lacerating dispute where people are not very good at understanding each other's point of view.

In 2001, a partial compromise was reached whereby poor countries could respond to a national health emergency (such as AIDS) by producing generic versions of patented drugs, but only for their own populations. Some countries, such as Brazil and India, are now producing cheap versions of anti-AIDS medicine like AZT, but small and very poor countries that do not have their own domestic pharmaceutical industries are reliant upon special low-price offers from Western pharmaceutical companies, or donated medicines. For some years, India has been selling "copycat" generic HIV/AIDS drugs to Africa and Asia that cost only about $200 per year. The bottom line: despite some substantial progress in getting pills to sick people, most AIDS medications are far too expensive for the people who need them the most. In Africa, less than 1 percent of AIDS sufferers are receiving the standard "cocktail" of drugs that has been available in the developed world since the mid-1990s.[50]

In July 2011, some good news was on the way as Gilead Pharmaceutical Company negotiated rights to Indian pharmaceutical companies (brokered through the United Nations) to reproduce two drugs that have been found to prevent HIV in heterosexual people in clinical studies. This means that there could be hope, if these drugs can be administered effectively, for the 2.6 million people who would otherwise get HIV each year.[51]

AIDS hurts even those who haven't got it, because it absorbs so much public health finance that other illnesses are neglected, the blood supply is contaminated, and talented people are frightened away from careers in medicine. In Africa and South Asia, AIDS has

Figure 13.5. Abstinence against AIDS
Not everyone agrees on the best approach to fighting AIDS, and governments that relied heavily on foreign aid from the Bush administration often stressed chastity before marriage and fidelity within marriage. In highly religious Malawi, President Mutharika appears on billboards all over the country stressing the importance of sexual self-control.

become a female and a heterosexual disease; south of the Sahara, for example, over half of all HIV-positive adults are female. There is evidence that an uninfected woman having sex with an infected man has a substantially greater chance of contracting the infection than an uninfected man would have if he had sex with an infected woman. In societies where women have limited legal rights and low social status, a woman may be unable to insist upon safe sex or demand that her partner wear a condom. Experts believe that dealing with this disease is going to involve more than creating a vaccine; some societies will need to renegotiate gender relationships.[52]

THE CONSEQUENCES OF OVERPOPULATION

The connection between overpopulation and poverty is complex and mutually reinforcing. If you have understood the theory of demographic transition outlined above, you should now understand that poverty is both a cause and a consequence of overpopulation.

The conventional approach to studying poverty is to measure it in terms of money. In some ways, this is an obvious and reasonable first step. If 1.2 billion people living in overpopulated societies struggle for survival on less than $1. (PPP US$) a day and a second 1.2 billion earn less than $2. a day, we don't need a pocket calculator to understand that about 40 percent of humankind is desperately poor.

Dr. Amartya Sen, the famous Indian-born scholar who won the Nobel Prize for Economics in 1998, advises us to spend less time crunching numbers and more time looking at how people actually live.[53] Let's think about three ways in which the overpopulation-poverty connection affects human lives: nutrition, health care, and the impact of poverty on children.

Food and Nutrition

In one sense, not having enough to eat is a fundamental measure of poverty; you die pretty quickly without basic nourishment. As we'll learn in chapter 14, there is not yet a global food shortage. Hungry people are hungry because they lack the funds to buy available food. The United States, for example, produces enormous food surpluses, but the U.S. Agricultural Department estimates that about 14.7 percent of the population, or 17.4 million Americans, worried about their food supplies in 2009. Approximately 6.8 million U.S. families actually experienced hunger because of an inability to buy food.[54] Globally speaking, the UN's Food and Agriculture Organization (FAO) estimates that there are about one billion people who suffer from insufficient food supplies or actual hunger.[55]

"Hunger" is difficult to define and measure. While some students of world food issues use the term "malnutrition" broadly, most prefer to think of "undernutrition" and "malnutrition" as two separate but interrelated variables:

- Undernutrition: Undernutrition means that an individual's consumption of calories (the body's basic fuel) is insufficient to maintain a desired level of activity. A male of average size with a normal lifestyle will usually need between 2,400 and 2,800 calories a day.[56]

When we are short of calories for more than a few hours, we feel hunger, lack energy, and find it difficult to concentrate. Cutting back on calories, voluntarily or not, will result in weight loss. If caloric intake is severely restricted for more than a few days, body systems begin to fail, illness sets in, and—in cases of extreme caloric deprivation—death results fairly quickly, often in a few weeks.

- Malnutrition: Malnutrition, on the other hand, is nutrient deprivation, resulting from a diet lacking in protein, vitamins, minerals, and other essential food elements. The distinction between undernutrition and malnutrition is worth making because pediatricians in wealthy societies routinely treat overweight youngsters on junk food diets who are obese but malnourished because they are not getting enough of what they do need, and take in far more fat than they require. A double cheeseburger with fries can fill your tummy with over a thousand calories (or about half your recommended daily intake) and up to seventy-five grams of fat (or twice the ideal). Various international studies have demonstrated that the global numbers for overweight and underweight people are about the same.

The two major epicenters of food insecurity are South Asia (the Indian subcontinent and the surrounding area), and sub-Saharan Africa. There are localized smaller epicenters in Central and South America, the Caribbean (especially Haiti), and in some Pacific island societies. The good news is that the situation has been gradually improving. In China and Latin America particularly, there have been important strides toward feeding the hungry, and former president "Lula" of Brazil has made it a national priority. The bad news is that only the easier parts of the problem have been solved, leaving us faced with some very serious cases of persistent food deprivation.

Medical Care and Health

There is a complicated but dramatic relationship between public health and economic prosperity. On one hand, people need to be healthy in order to generate wealth because sick people can't work efficiently. Conversely, a prosperous society can provide the ingredients of a healthy life for its citizens: nutrition, medical care, and a clean environment. Life expectancy is the number of years we can expect to live, assuming the continuation of current mortality factors. Life expectancy is the most frequently used yardstick for public health, and the statistical evidence is clear. If you want to live a long time, arrange to be born in a high HDI country and try to choose rich parents. Money may or may not be the root of all evil, but it is certainly the root of most health care. It should come as no surprise to read table 13.6 and learn that wealthy people generally live longer than do poor people.

The statistics in table 13.6, however, should present a puzzlement for American readers. If money buys good health, why aren't U.S. citizens living longer than everybody else? This is a thorny question. First, it is generally true that life expectancies are greater in wealthier societies, but people live the longest in those societies with greater economic equality, that is, low Gini coefficients. Japan, for example, has the longest life expectancy of any industrialized nation. The very significant economic inequality in American society is reflected in lifestyle inequality. In his important study of the impact of prosperity and social status on life expectancy, Dr. Michael Marmot notes that if we "travel from the southeast of downtown Washington to Montgomery County, Maryland, for every mile

Table 13.6. Buying Years with Money

This chart contains much that is predictable: rich people clearly live longer than do poor people, and seriously impoverished folks die very young indeed. Despite their higher incomes, Americans don't live as long as most EU citizens, although the explanation for this fact is controversial. Life expectancy declines substantially for poorer people and plummets dramatically when we consider the very poorest members of the human family. In reporting life-expectancy statistics, the number after the decimal place refers to tenths of a year, not months.

Country	PC/GDP PPP US$	Life Expectancy	Gini Index
Norway	$56,214	81.1	25.8
Japan	$32,418	83.4	N/A
United States	$45,989	78.5	40.8
Mexico	$14,258	77.0	48.1
Russia	$18,932	68.8	43.7
Iran	11,558	73.0	38.3
China	$6,828	73.5	41.5
India	$3,644	65.4	36.8
Zambia	$1,430	49	N/A
Dem. Congo	$319	48.4/	44.4
Afghanistan	$1,321	48.7	N/A

Source: United Nations Development Programme, *Human Development Report 2011*, http://hdr.undp .org/en/media/HDR_2011_EN_Tables.pdf.

traveled, life expectancy rises about a year and a half. There is a twenty-year gap between poor blacks at one end of the journey and rich whites at the other."[57]

A related aspect of the debate revolves around the way in which different countries pay for and provide health care. In virtually all other high HDI countries, the government uses tax revenues to sponsor a universal health-care system of some sort. While it became a controversial issue early in the Obama administration, U.S. public policy has traditionally dictated that health care should be left mostly to the private sector, that is, insurance companies. U.S. society divides itself into people with the health insurance that comes with good jobs and people who are without health insurance because they have marginal jobs or are unemployed. The U.S. Census Bureau has determined that over forty-four million Americans lack any form of health insurance or coverage for prescription medicines, a figure that should decline after the 2010 health-care bill takes full effect.[58] These poorer-than-average and frequently unemployed citizens suffer illness and premature mortality at a higher rate than those with at least minimal coverage, thus bringing the American statistics down.

While there is an obvious overall correlation between prosperity and health, the issue is more complex than the stark numbers would suggest. In poor societies, people are prone to illness for a series of interrelated factors: cost of health care, cultural factors and ignorance, and some environmental factors.

- Cost and Availability of Medical Care: One conventional way of assessing the availability of health care is to look at the number of medical-care workers available to the general population. Predictably, health care is less available in poorer societies.

Another part of the problem is the high cost of prescription drugs. The global pharmaceutical industry is almost entirely located in high HDI countries and funded by private investors. The research and development efforts of these companies are oriented toward the health needs of wealthier patients and often overlook illnesses that affect millions of people in developing societies. The medicines produced by pharmaceutical companies are routinely too expensive for use in poorer societies. Since medical research is profit driven, there is no real relationship between the global damage a disease does and the money spent to cure it. As Anne Platt McGinn notes, the annual death toll from malaria comes close to matching the damage done by HIV/AIDS, but the world is only spending $150,000 annually to counteract a disease that threatens the poorest 40 percent of humankind.[59] The United States alone spends billions of dollars looking for a cure for AIDS.

- Ignorance: We have seen that wealth is a core indicator of how long we live and at what level of health. There is a similar statistical correlation between the number of years we spend in school and the number of years we spend alive.[60] In some very primitive societies, patients may be unaware of basic health information. It may be difficult, for example, to persuade people to clean up drinking water, dress wounds, or accept inoculations when they are still unclear about the existence of invisible bacteria and microorganisms. Because women suffer from low social status, some traditional societies may not provide adequate care for a mother having a difficult pregnancy or postdelivery recovery. Furthermore, the pressure to produce sons may be so strong that a woman will be compelled to become pregnant so often that her health will be jeopardized.

- Environmental Problems: While we'll look at environmental problems in greater detail in chapter 14, we should pause here to note that problems with the delivery of pure water, the removal of sewage, and the degeneration of air quality are all factors promoting the spread of infectious diseases. In what has been called an "epidemic of epidemics," tuberculosis, malaria, sleeping sickness, and other diseases are staging a comeback, principally in the low HDI portion of the world.[61] The growth of urban slums is a related problem. When rural overpopulation and/or unemployment drive people out of the countryside, they often migrate into huge, unhealthy urban slums. A recent United Nations study found that about 940 million people, mostly in Africa, South America, and Asia, were living in these sprawling slum cities. In most cases, their dwellings were primitive, lacking clean water and electricity. Their neighborhoods are chaotic, crime ridden, and lacking services (electricity, sewage, etc.) of any kind. Cities such as Phnom Penh in Cambodia, Nairobi in Kenya, Brazil's Rio de Janeiro, Sri Lanka's Colombo, and Mumbai (Bombay) in India are flanked by slum cities sometimes larger in population than the original city. The statistics indicate that urban populations are projected to increase, further complicating the lives of the poorest in these crowded areas.

When the Big Losers Are Little

You can tell a lot about a society by the way in which it treats its very young children. Infants are frail and require a lot of care and special nutrition. As children move toward puberty, they need education and protection from a dangerous world. There are serious problems, even in the wealthiest societies on the planet; children are sometimes starved, abandoned, abused, and frequently even murdered. The welfare of young people declines dramatically as we scale down through the developing world and into the desperate low HDI societies of the Fourth World.

It might be that the infant mortality rate (the number of babies per one thousand born alive that die before their first birthday) is the ultimate statistic. A society that brings babies into the world but cannot get them even one candle on a birthday cake can perhaps be said to have failed its most important test. As figure 13.6 shows, wealthy countries, such as France, have relatively low (and low is good) infant mortality rates. The U.S. rate (7:1,000 or twenty-second in the world) has always been something of a scandal, however, because high-tech U.S. medicine sometimes doesn't reach far enough into the lives of the poor to raise Americans to European levels.

While the infant mortality rate is the more famous of the two statistical indicators, the **childhood mortality index** (sometimes called the **under five mortality rate [U5MR]**) is used by the United Nations and other agencies and is defined as the number of children per one thousand born that fail to celebrate their fifth birthday. Because our life experience and risk of death changes somewhat between our first and fifth birthdays, both statistics are valuable.[62]

In societies with few children, parents routinely sacrifice themselves for their kids, giving up that new car to make college tuition payments for the next generation. In

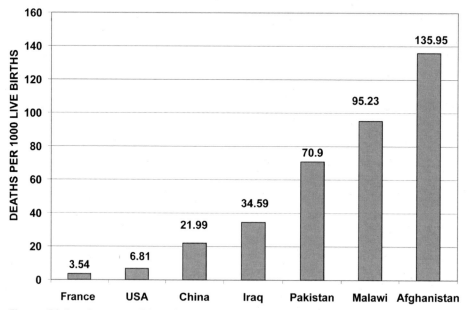

Figure 13.6. Comparative Infant Mortality Rates
The infant mortality rate (IMR) is perhaps the most crucial number a society can produce. The news is getting better. In the past thirty-five years, the global IMR has been cut in half, standing now at forty-four per thousand.[1] This still means, however, that of every twenty-five babies born annually on this planet, one will die before that crucial first birthday, and one woman will be sad forever.

1. UNDP, *Human Development Report 2010,* http://hdr.undp.org/en/media/HDR_2010_EN_Tables_reprint.pdf.

Source: United Nations Population Division, available at: http://esa.un.org/unpd/wpp/Excel-Data/mortality.htm.

Figure 13.7. The Health of Children
The extreme poverty of countries in sub-Saharan Africa takes a terrific toll on the lives of very young children, who often die in infancy or in the first few years of life. Malnutrition, inherited HIV-AIDS infection, and susceptibility to infectious diseases such as malaria all contribute to high childhood mortality rates. Will this Malawian child live to become an adult?

very poor families where there are too many children, the kids are often neglected, often out of necessity, occasionally out of choice. Sometimes parents die young, frequently of AIDS, leaving their orphaned offspring without economic security. About 43 percent of all Indian children under five years old are malnourished. India is home to 25 percent of the world's hungry.[63] In neighboring Bangladesh, UNICEF and the UN World Food Program estimate that 48.6 percent of the country's twenty million children aged six months to five years are chronically malnourished, a problem caused by food shortages and high prices in a country prone to natural disasters. In much of sub-Saharan Africa, about 42 percent of the population survives on barely one meal per day.[64] According to a 2006 UNICEF report, the Chinese government has successfully improved childhood nutrition, while the Indians have done significantly less well. In much of Africa, there has been no progress at all.[65]

Malnutrition, particularly during the first two years of life, has a severe long-term effect on child development, causing irreversible mental and physical harm. Thanks to UN agencies, such as UNICEF, and NGOs, such as Oxfam, there has been some authentic progress in children's health and nutrition.[66] Over the past two decades, childhood malnutrition fell globally, but still three hundred million of the world's two billion children go to bed hungry each night. This, according to UNICEF, is caused by extreme poverty, and it makes them prone to disease.[67] There is also a gender issue here: in societies such as India, where women and girls have a lower social standing, authors Gardner and Halweil have determined that little girls are four times more likely to be "stunted" or undernourished than are little boys.[68] The tragedy is that much of what can go medically wrong in a child's life would be easily reversible if governments had the money and could be persuaded to spend it on children's health.

The United Nations believes that approximately ten million children die each year of diseases that are preventable. Measles, for example, still infects thirty million children a year. It kills about nine hundred thousand and leaves many of its survivors with lingering health problems. Seventeen percent of all children worldwide lack the vaccination for it. The vaccine has been available for thirty years, but fewer than half of all African children have been given the twenty-six-cent inoculation.[69] For Americans, diarrhea is the topic of vulgar TV commercials, but for poor countries, it is still a major killer. Cleaning up the water supply is the first big step, but in 1979, scientists created oral rehydration therapy (ORT), which has saved perhaps sixty million lives in twenty years; it could save many more lives if it were universally available.

When a population outgrows its housing supply, people wind up on the street. The UN estimates that there are about one hundred million children worldwide who do not have homes or families. These orphans often live on the streets or in garbage dumps, and exist by begging and petty theft. Homeless and undernourished girls tend to become pregnant very early in life and produce undernourished babies. Some are forced into child prostitution to survive. In fact, the number of child prostitutes may be increasing because of a belief that sex with a very young child lowers the risk of HIV/AIDS infection. Brazil alone is reputed to have more than one-half million child prostitutes.[70]

Portraits of the Real World: Medicine or Politics

The year that India and Pakistan declared themselves to be nuclear powers, Richard Collin was traveling through India's Tamil Nadu state when the car developed an odd noise in the engine. His driver pulled into a mechanic's shop to have it checked, giving Richard the chance to stroll through the small and very poor village near the mechanic's garage. Not far from the mechanic's shop, he came upon a gaggle of little girls, seven or eight years old, walking home from school with tattered textbooks and little backpacks. They waved to him with the instinctive, friendly dignity of the Tamil people. They were all neatly dressed in school uniforms, but—with a shock—he realized that they were all so underweight that they would have been given medical treatment in the United States.

It struck Richard that things such as medicine and childhood nutrition are really very political. Governments make crucial decisions about the allocation of scarce resources. If a sovereign state chooses to spend its revenue on building hydrogen bombs, it may not have much left over to provide extra nourishment for its children. Given the fact that both India and Pakistan have very high levels of low-birth-weight babies, rampant malnutrition, and sky-high infant mortality rates, South Asia might have launched a regional children's health initiative. Instead, both governments poured scarce funding into building nuclear weapons. As Arundhati Roy grumbled, "It'll go down in history books, provided of course we have history books to go down in."[71] The decision to invest in bombs rather than babies was a decision made by politicians, not pediatricians.

Some scholars believe that an annual expenditure of only $19 billion would eliminate hunger and malnutrition. Ten billion dollars would furnish drinkable water for everyone, and only $1.3 billion would inoculate all the world's children against easily preventable diseases.[72] The decision not to spend these relatively small amounts of money was a political choice made by the elected leaders of the world's wealthiest democracies and, ultimately, by those who elected them. In case you're missing the point, that would be us.

3. Demographic Decisions

Since the relationship between poverty and overpopulation is complex, it is inevitable that our responses to the problem will be multidimensional and sometimes controversial. As we will see, birth control is not in itself the determinant factor in population control, but it does remain terrifically important. Both birth control and abortion, however, are politically controversial, and we need to pause for a moment on the political ramifications of both. Almost all scholars who have addressed the population question have concluded that the status of women is also crucial.

It would be pleasant to end this chapter with some hard-and-fast conclusions about the future demographic direction of humankind, but out of necessity, we need to end where we began, with disagreements and debates. Since we still need to examine the issue of resource availability, we'll save the argument between optimists and pessimists for the next chapter, but we do need to look at the UN's basic range of estimates about the future of population growth.

BIRTH CONTROL AND ABORTION

In the 1950s and 1960s, some Westerners naively believed that controlling the world's population was merely a question of getting birth-control information and techniques to portions of the world where overpopulation was a problem. Once people understood that RPG was "causing" their poverty, they reasoned, they would take the obvious step of controlling their fertility.

If you've understood how demographic transition works, you can see the shallowness of this explanation. From a macroeconomic point of view, it might be in the best interests of a given overpopulated society to control its numbers; from a microeconomic perspective, it may not be in the perceived (or genuine) individual economic interest of any specific father to limit his own family. In 1968, a Stanford University biologist named Garrett Hardin published an essay called "The Tragedy of the Commons," in which he made this essential point: it is better for society in general if parents limit the number of their children, but as long as it continues to be in the narrow interests of parents to have large families, they will continue to have them.[73] The personal trumps the public every time.

This was demonstrated clearly by a famous Harvard study done in the Indian Punjab region. During the 1960s, the rural Punjabi population practiced subsistence farming, and local agricultural practice made children an economic asset to a farming family. Between 1954 and 1960, Harvard University conducted an intense birth-control campaign in the area. A follow-up study in 1969 concluded that the free contraceptive advice and equipment provided to these Punjabi villagers had had no effect at all on fertility, and the population had continued to grow.[74] Farmers in all Punjabi communities were producing children as field hands to suit their short-term financial interests, and the availability of birth control did not change their economic interests. As demographic historian Massimo Livi Bacci has commented, "Contraception is a necessary technical instrument for controlling fertility but its availability—other factors being equal—has little impact on fertility."[75]

Reducing the Problem

Almost every student of the problem now believes that we can only reduce human fertility in poor and overpopulated societies by coaxing them into the "modernization phase" discussed above. With the slogan, "Development is the best contraceptive," most demographers believe we could "fix" overpopulation in low human development societies by making them somewhat less poor.[76]

Unfortunately, as we learned in chapter 12, improving the economic status of the underdeveloped world has proved to be a daunting task; the leaders of wealthy high HDI societies seem little interested in investing significant amounts of capital in the project. Foreign aid is failure prone and doesn't win many votes at election time.

Clearly, in very backward societies where dominant husbands insist upon large families, the availability of birth-control devices will continue to be irrelevant. But there are many areas—particularly in those medium HDI societies, where assertive women are beginning to have some say in their own reproductive lives. In these circumstances, birth-control equipment and education could be crucial, and a change in childbearing behavior among these women could have a significant impact upon future population growth.[77]

Unfortunately, birth control techniques that work reasonably well in the well-educated and prosperous North can be problematic in the South. Men in the developing world can feel that their virility is challenged by condoms and threatened by vasectomies. In many cases they refuse to cooperate with female desires to limit fertility. Women who are illiterate may find it difficult to use some techniques reliably.

Can people be forced to limit their fertility? Garrett Hardin advocated that we all agree to coerce ourselves into family planning in what he called "mutual coercion mutually agreed upon."[78] No Western democracy, however, has even remotely contemplated endorsing Hardin's advice. There have been two major historical efforts to limit family size by law, one a failure, and one a technical success despite the moral and ethical dilemmas it continues to pose.

- For a few years in the mid-1970s, the Indian government of Mrs. Indira Gandhi implemented a heavy-handed, coercive vasectomy program. This affront was just one of the objectionable aspects of the "State of Emergency" declared by the Gandhi government in 1975, and ended with the electoral defeat of Mrs. Gandhi's Congress Party in 1977. When she returned to office in 1980, all talk of enforced birth control had vanished.[79]

• In 1980, China adopted a strenuous One-Child Policy, which restricted families to a single offspring. Chinese couples were encouraged to delay marriage until their mid-twenties, and premarital sex was sternly forbidden. Couples were required to acquire the specific permission of local political authorities before becoming pregnant. Punishment for "illegal" births occasionally included enforced abortion, imprisonment, and loss of job, but was more normally a draconian fine, sometimes amounting to several years combined salary for the unhappy parents.

In concept and implementation, the One-Child Policy is an indefensible violation of human rights, but there is a moral dilemma involved in lecturing the Chinese on civil liberties and reproductive freedom. Without reproductive coercion, China would have three hundred million more people than it has today and many more than it could possibly feed. A hugely increased population would hinder economic growth, make it even more difficult for China to move toward democracy, and perhaps even destabilize this massive country. At the moment, about one-fifth of the human race lives in China, and about one-fourth of humankind is of Chinese extraction. If China accepts the Western model of civil rights, its population will increase even more, and it is not clear that this is in the best interests of world peace.

Population, Politics, and Religion

Part of the problem stems from the attitudes of many religions toward birth control. In the developed world, some Protestant fundamentalists, some Orthodox Jewish communities, some Islamic religious teachers, and virtually all Roman Catholic clergy oppose what they regard as "artificial" methods of controlling fertility. Acting as lobbies and pressure groups, well-organized churches can have a demonstrable effect on public policy. Birth control was illegal in most Catholic countries in southern Europe until the 1970s. The Roman Catholic hierarchy in Central and South America has generally been successful in discouraging regional governments from adopting population-control policies. A recent study found that Latin America has about four million abortions a year, the vast majority of them illegal. Ironically, the percentage of women having abortions in Latin America is greater than the percentage in societies such as Western Europe, where abortion is legal.

The influence of church leaders reaches into international public policy. For example, at the 1992 United Nations Conference on Environment and Development (the so-called Rio Conference or Earth Summit), Ireland, Argentina, and Colombia joined the Vatican in successfully blocking any reference to contraception in the conference's resolutions. A few years later, at the 1994 UN-sponsored Cairo Conference on Population (ICPD), the Vatican and the world's Islamic leaders made an odd alliance in opposing a woman's right to regulate her fertility.[80]

The Qur'an actually contains no particular theological prohibition against birth control, but some fundamentalist Muslims feel that avoiding pregnancy borders on blasphemy, since it implies rejection of a gift (in this case a child) from God. There is wide difference in law within the Islamic world. Many Muslim societies follow Saudi Arabia in criminalizing birth control despite the fact that the Arab birthrate is roughly twice the

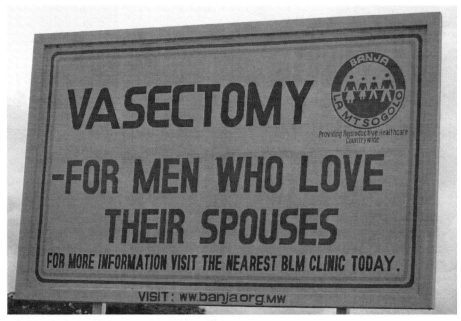

Figure 13.8.   Vasectomy for Birth Control
While the operation frightens some men in both the developed and underdeveloped world, vasectomy is actually safe and almost painless, offering an effective way for male partners to contribute to family planning. Malawi has made it an important part of its population-control campaign.

world average. The Islamic Republic of Iran, however, has recently created one of the more advanced birth-control programs in the Middle East.

Abortion is fiercely condemned by an even wider spectrum of religious leaders. Despite the ethical questions it poses for many people, however, abortion remains a persistently popular form of birth control. Clearly, in an area of such intimacy, statistics are going to be hard to acquire, particularly with reference to illegal abortions. Some authors have suggested that abortion terminates between 20 percent and 35 percent of all pregnancies. In recent decades, the number of abortions among American women has drifted downward, but made a slight increase in 2011—possibly due to the ailing economy. The general decline, though, may be the result of better birth control and effective public campaigns against teenage sex. It is also possible that the declining abortion rate in America is the consequence of a "pro-life" campaign that has discouraged gynecologists from offering therapeutic abortions, making it much more difficult to get an abortion in rural America.[81]

Of the estimated forty-six million abortions carried out annually worldwide, just under half are illegal. When conducted in a hospital by medical personnel, an abortion can be accomplished without much physical risk to the mother, but illegal abortions are often performed by amateurs and under unsanitary conditions. These illegal backstreet operations account for nearly all abortion-related maternal deaths. It is difficult to estimate how frequently this happens. Estimates range from about eighty thousand per year to a high of two hundred thousand annually. In Africa and Latin America, abortion fatalities account for one-half of all maternal deaths.

The moral and political dilemmas posed by these stark statistics are not simple. Nobody regards abortion as a good means of birth control. Even pro-choice activists regard the procedure as an emergency or last-resort measure, and multiple abortions pose significant health risks. The criminalization of abortion satisfies the ethical demands of those who regard it as a form of murder; successful elimination of legal abortions, however, seems to have the practical effect of driving many women toward risky illegal procedures.

The U.S. Role in Population Stabilization

As we have seen, overpopulation and poverty are closely associated with political instability. Given its desire for a stable world free of terrorism, the United States could be expected to have an important stake in lowering fertility in the poorest parts of the world. Terrorists typically come from societies with rapid population growth: Egypt, Saudi Arabia, the Palestinian territories, Iraq, and Pakistan.

While there was always some objection to government sponsorship for birth control from the Roman Catholic hierarchy, the U.S. Agency for International Development (USAID) established a quiet and modest program to supply condoms to poor countries as early as the 1960s.[82] In the 1970s, support for population control abroad began to come under fire from Christian conservatives who were primarily concerned about abortion. During the administrations of Ronald Reagan and George H. W. Bush (1981–1993), there was almost no U.S. funding for population control of any kind. During the 1984 International Conference on Population in Mexico, the Reagan administration enunciated what came to be called the Mexico City Policy, which held that population growth was neutral in economic growth and therefore population control did not need to be pursued energetically. In what was called the "Gag Rule," programs that even featured advice about abortions could not receive U.S. financial support, even if the actual abortions were performed for a different organization and paid for by non-U.S. funds.

After his election in 1992, Bill Clinton was able to persuade Congress to allocate $385 million annually for population-assistance programs, mostly channeled through the UN. When President George W. Bush took office in 2001, however, he reinstituted the Gag Rule and took the United States back to the Mexico City Policy originally formulated by President Reagan, even cutting support for the United Nations Population Fund.[83] Following the wishes of those evangelical Christians who were an important part of Mr. Bush's political base, the administration tied aid funds for both population control and AIDS prevention to the concept of abstinence before marriage and fidelity afterward.[84] In Mr. Bush's second term, the U.S. government attacked the generally pro-choice United Nations, denying that there was any inherent right to abortion abroad, even though the U.S. Supreme Court's 1973 Roe v. Wade decision continues to guarantee that right for American women.[85] In 2009, the Obama administration reestablished the rules that had been in place under former president Clinton.

Critics of the Gag Rule believe that the Mexico City Policy is generally counterproductive. One scholar has estimated that limitations in funding for population-control activities between 1995 and 2002 resulted in three hundred million unintended pregnancies and one million female deaths from unsafe abortions and other maternal complications.[86] The NGOs involved in family planning in low HDI societies typically provide education, counseling, birth-control information, and advice about abortion. Without funding, they are unable to provide basic family planning advice, which results in accidental pregnancies and hence more illegal (and dangerous) abortions.[87]

As we have seen, people will not reduce the size of their families until the economics of their lives make it possible. Once that point has been reached, however, effective birth-control techniques become important, because a certain percentage of pregnancies will be unintended and birth-control technology can reduce that number.

The Status of Women

Almost all demographers have concluded that improving the status of women is the most fundamental step in nudging the birthrate down. Economic development will inhibit population growth, but it sometimes can be difficult to accomplish in societies afflicted with endemic poverty. Birth-control techniques will work if people will adopt them, but they won't if the influence of religion is too strong or if the economics of their lives are still driving a demand for male children.

What seems to work all the time is an upward shift in the status of women, since better educated, more assertive women who are capable of earning their own livings and making their own reproductive choices almost inevitably decide to have fewer children. Here are some of the factors that have been shown to have an impact upon both economic development and reproductive patterns.

- Educated Women: Almost everyone who has studied the issue believes that educating young girls and women is crucial. Most forms of birth control require some level of female competence. Women must know that birth-control techniques exist and how to use them. In the absence of medical support, a woman needs to be able to read written instructions and have some basic familiarity with the functioning of her own reproductive system. One study in Brazil shows that illiterate women bear, on average, 6.5 children over the course of their reproductive lives, while Brazilian high school graduates customarily bring only 2.5 new Brazilians into the world. The trend is replicated among African women, who inevitably produce fewer babies if they have completed the equivalent of high school.
- Working Women: In medium and low HDI societies, a better-educated woman can find salaried employment (typically as a nurse, a factory worker, an elementary school teacher, or as a domestic servant). A paycheck and perhaps a pension plan will change her economic relationship to her family, perhaps making her more valuable as a wage earner than as a producer of male children.
- Assertive Women: A better-educated woman may be more assertive in demanding personal, sexual, and reproductive freedom, even in the face of counterdemands from the men in her life. In this context, it is important for girls to avoid very early marriages. In the United States, women tend to be about two years younger than their husbands; in the Islamic world, the age gap typically runs to about eight years, with the bride often passing from her father's control to her husband's dominion while she herself is still basically an unassertive child. Sending that same girl to school will keep her out of a marriage situation long enough for her to give some educated consideration to questions of marriage and family size. Getting men to wear condoms has both health and fertility implications, and an educated woman is more likely to insist upon at least this form of protection when it is appropriate.[88]

THE UNCERTAINTY FACTOR

In his magisterial *How Many People Can the Earth Support?* Joel Cohen demolishes the notion that demographers can predict the future with any degree of accuracy.[89] In fact, population growth is closely tied to a host of hard-to-predict variables, and most predictions have been wildly high or absurdly low.

In 2003, the United Nations Population Division (UNPD) issued a series of forecasts, using four variables, as suggested in figure 13.9.[90] The "constant variant" assumes the current rate of increase (1.2 percent per year) will continue unchanged. This is unlikely, but if it does happen, we would max out in 2050 with a planet-busting 12.8 billion people, almost double the present number. If fertility declines a little, but not enough, we might hit a pessimistic "high variant" of 10.6 billion, but the UN's best guess will have us facing a "medium variant" figure closer to 8.9 billion, meaning that we will have added "only" 2.5 billion people in forty-four years. The most optimistic figure assumes that birth-control information and technology becomes available to an increasingly prosperous global society, giving us a barely manageable 7.4 billion people in 2050, after which the fertility rate and hence the population might actually begin to decline.

WHERE TO FIND THE DATA

These days, we take to the Internet to argue about public policy, and the population debate is no exception. With a site at www.ippf.org, the London-based International Planned Parenthood Federation (IPPF) is the principal nongovernmental organization attempting to provide birth control and family planning advice and technology to couples around the world. Negative Population Growth maintains a site at www.npg.org to promote its belief

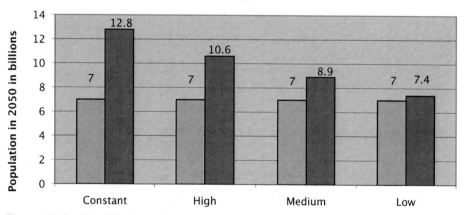

Figure 13.9. The World in 2050
This figure provides estimates for future population growth over the forthcoming forty-four years. The "constant variant" assumes that humankind continues to grow at present rates. The high and low variants are pessimistic and optimistic estimates respectively, while the medium variant of 8.9 billion represents the UN's "best guess" at global population in 2050. Don't be too reassured; the "best guess" still represents half again as many people as we have today, and most of them will be very poor.
Source: UNPD (United Nations Population Division), *World Population Prospects: The 2002 Revision* (New York: United Nations, 2003).

that the world needs to take specific, active measures to reduce global population to achieve a sustainable society. Population Action International (www.populationaction.org) is a Washington-based organization, supported by private contributions, that generates studies on population control/family planning activities and advocates a more energetic U.S. and global policy toward birth control. The Center for Reproductive Law and Policy is a think tank organized to worry about the legal aspects of women's reproductive freedom worldwide. Find them at www.crlp.org. Funded by the Rockefeller Institute and working from a medical and scientific perspective, the Population Council does research on the social and technical aspects of family planning. Visit them at www.popcounciol.org. The opposite side of the argument is represented by the Family Research Council (at www.frc.org), a New York–based think tank/lobby that generally opposes the use of condoms and argues for voluntary restraint as a remedy for AIDS and rapid population growth. The Population Research Institute (www.pri.org) is an antiabortion group with close ties to the Christian conservative movement. The organization once known as "ZPG" (for Zero Population Growth) changed its name in 2002 to Population Connection, but it continues its advocacy of slowing down population growth; find it at www.populationconnection.org. At www. childrensdefense.org, the Children's Defense Fund compiles some of the best statistical information available on the status of young people in the United States.

Whether humankind in the future is a big family or a comparatively small one, all the kids will still need to eat, wear clothing, live in houses, attend schools, get medical attention, find jobs, marry each other, and start the process all over again. Too often we have seen population growth as somehow divorced from our material needs. We consume resources, some of them renewable and generated on a sustainable basis, others nonrenewable and finite. Ascertaining how many people the world can support demands answers to a host of complicated questions. How prosperous do we all expect to be? How long do we want to live? How many of us get to drive SUVs? How much crude oil is there, really, and do we have an alternative technology ready for the day when the last barrel of petroleum is pumped? Are environmental changes, such as the now-famous phenomenon of global warming, going to increase the capacity of the globe or diminish it?

As we will see in the following, and concluding, chapter, the answers to these questions are not simple, and predictions for our ultimate future on the planet are not only fascinating but also complex and controversial.

4. The Wrap: What Have We Learned?

We discovered in section 1 that modern demography comes equipped with a lot of specialized terms to describe population change; we need to be able to distinguish between the percentage rate of growth (or shrinkage), and the total fertility rate (TFR). We also learned that one of the political consequences of a high birthrate is a lowered median age and a heightened dependency ratio, both of which pose social problems. Then we investigated the fundamental theory of demographic transition and saw that when it is complete, demographic transition takes a society from a cruel state-of-nature ZPG to a period of rapid expansion, thanks to lower death rates. When a society becomes modern enough that children are no longer an economic advantage, the birthrate declines, and society can achieve stability, or even a slight decline in population size. We concluded by noting how and why population can continue to increase dramatically if society fails to pass the threshold of social modernization.

In section 2, we looked at an assortment of population problems such as the precipitous fall in Russia's population, the dangers of sex-selection abortion, and the awfulness of the HIV/AIDS epidemic. To get a sense of what life is like in poor and overpopulated societies, we looked at nutrition and health in the unhappier corners of the world, with a special focus on the world's children. Terms such as the infant mortality rate and the under five mortality rate are common in the literature.

We also learned that birth-control techniques and technology are not cures for overpopulation, but become important when social modernization and secularization have allowed a society to turn the demographic corner and reduce the size of its families. In this context, we looked at the moral and religious objections to some forms of population control and tried to understand why the United States in recent decades has been a very minor player in the global effort to stem overpopulation. We ended with some speculation on the total future size of the human race.

It should be clear that population has a lot to do with conflict. When resources become scarce and population is expanding, people fissure into ethnic or ideological communities, and fight over raw materials, land, or water. And politicians and people brawl over phenomena such as abortion and birth control, debating what is ethnically permissible and what is not.

What's next? It should be obvious that the total number of people on the planet is only one-half of humankind's equation. Overpopulation is a function of the resources available to support a given population in a given area. In the final chapter of this book, we need to look carefully at some critical issues. How many people can ultimately live on the planet depends to some extent on how much food is available to feed them. Do we have enough food now? Can we anticipate having enough in the future? And life is more than calories. Do we have enough power, arable land, pure water, and mineral resources? Finally, people make a mess, and a lot of people means a global mess of enormous proportions. Are we polluting the planet to the extent that we won't be able to live on it in the future? What are the politics behind climate change, and how do we as a species avoid contaminating the world we bequeath to our children?

Notes

1. Lewis Carroll, *Alice's Adventures in Wonderland* (Boston: Lee and Shepard, 1869), 169.

2. James Gasana, "Remember Rwanda?," *World Watch* 15, no. 2 (2002): 24–33.

3. For the University of Wisconsin's exploration of demographic transition, and further links to just about everywhere, go to http://www.marathon.uwc.edu/geography/demotrans/demtran.htm.

4. Joel E. Cohen, *How Many People Can the Earth Support?* (New York: Norton, 1995), 13.

5. John R. Weeks, *Population: An Introduction to Concepts and Issues*, 9th ed. (Belmont, Calif.: Wadsworth, 2011), 10.

6. United Nations Development Programme (UNDP), *Human Development Report 2011*, http://hdr .undp.org/en/media/HDR_2011_EN_Tables.pdf.

7. United Nations Development Programme (UNDP), *Human Development Report 2003*, 5; see the National Center for Health Statistics at http://www.cdc.gov/nchs/.

8. Demographers disagree about the virtues of negative population growth, but one organization that believes the U.S. population is already too large can be found at http://www.npg.org/index.html.

9. Check out the grandfather of the field, Thomas Robert Malthus, whose 1799 *Essay on Population* was republished by the Cambridge University Press in 1992.

10. United Nations Population Division, http://www.un.org/esa/population/.

11. United Nations Development Programme, http://www.undp.org.

12. United Nations Fund for Population Activities, http://www.unfpa.org/public/.

13. World PopClock Project, http://www.census.gov/ipc/www/popclockworld.html.

14. The leading U.S. expert in this field is Nancy Birdsall who edited and contributed to *Population Matters: Demographic Change, Economic Growth, and Poverty in the Developing World* (New York: Oxford University Press, 2001). Joseph N. Weatherby et al., *The Other World: Issues and Politics of the Developing World*, 5th ed. (New York: Longman, 2003) is a good study of the impact of poverty in the developing world.

15. United Nations Population Fund, *2011 Report*, http://www.unfpa.org/public/home/factsheets/pid/3856.

16. United Nations Population Fund, *2011 Report*, http://www.unfpa.org/public/home/factsheets/pid/3856

17. United Nations Development Programme, *Human Development Report 2011*, http://hdr.undp.org/en/media/HDR_2011_EN_Tables.pdf.

18. John R. Weeks, *Population: An Introduction to Concepts and Issues*, 9th ed. (Belmont, Calif.: Wadsworth, 2011), 25.

19. Samuel J. Huntington, *Who Are We? The Challenges to America's Identity* (New York: Simon and Schuster, 2005).

20. The United States Census Bureau, 2010 Census Data, http://www.census.gov/prod/cen2010/briefs/c2010br-02.pdf; John R. Weeks, *Population: An Introduction to Concepts and Issues*, 9th ed. (Belmont, Calif.: Wadsworth, 2011); George J. Borjas and Lawrence F. Katz, "The Evolution of the Mexican-Born Workforce in the United States," National Bureau of Economic Research (NBER) Working Paper No. 11281 (2005), www.nber.org/papers/w11281.

21. United Nations Development Programme, *Human Development Report 2000*, 40; International Labor Organization (ILO) Employment Trends 2010: http://www.ilocarib.org.tt/portal/index.php?option=com_content&task=view&id=1330&Itemid=1209; World Bank, *Indicators 2003* (Washington, D.C.: World Bank, 2003), 60.

22. Cohen, *How Many People Can the Earth Support?* 46, 48.

23. Planned Parenthood Association, http://www.plannedparenthood.org/health-topics/birth-control-4211.htm.

24. Avert, http://www.avert.org/abstinence.htm.

25. John Firor and Judith E. Jacobsen, *The Crowded Greenhouse: Population, Climate Change, and Creating a Sustainable World* (New Haven, Conn.: Yale University Press, 2002), 36; Barry Commoner, *Making Peace with the Planet* (New York: Pantheon, 1990), 159.

26. Cohen, *How Many People Can the Earth Support?* 45.

27. Marvin Harris, *Our Kind: Who We Are. Where We Came From. Where We Are Going* (New York: Harper Perennial, 1989), 217.

28. Massimo Livi-Bacci, *A Concise History of World Population*, 3rd ed. (Oxford, UK: Blackwell, 2001), 128–46.

29. The birthrate went down from 6.5 to 2.8 in Oman (UNDP, *Human Development Report 2011*); The Sultanate of Oman, http://www.omanet.om/english/home.asp.

30. Weeks, *Population: An Introduction Concepts and Issues*, 9th ed., 443–63.

31. UNPD, *Human Development Report 2011*, http://hdr.undp.org/en/media/HDR_2011_EN_Tables.pdf.

32. The U.S. Census Bureau, http://www.census.gov/ipc/prod/ib96-2.pdf.

33. UNPD, *Human Development Report 2011*, http://hdr.undp.org/en/media/HDR_2011_EN_Tables.pdf.

34. Livi-Bacci, *A Concise History of World Population*, 104–5, 188.

35. UNPD, *Human Development Report 2011*, http://hdr.undp.org/en/media/HDR_2011_EN_Tables.pdf.

36. Michael Marmot, *Status Syndrome: How Social Standing Directly Affects Your Health and Life Expectancy* (London: Bloomsbury, 2004), 9.

37. UNPD, *Human Development Report 2011*, http://hdr.undp.org/en/media/HDR_2011_EN_Tables.pdf.

38. For the UN take on sex-selection abortion, go to http://www.unfpa.org/gender/case_studies.htm.

39. Ansley Coale and Judith Bannister, "Five Decades of Missing Females in China," *Demography* 32, no. 3 (1994): 459–80.

40. *The Lancet*, http://www.thelancet.com/.

41. Prabhat Jha, Rajesh Kumar, Priya Vasa, Neeraj Dhingra, Deva Thiruchelvam, and Rahim Moineddin, "Low male-to-female sex ratio of children born in India: national survey of 1.1 million households," *The Lancet* 367, no. 9506 (January 21, 2006): 211–19.

42. The United Nations Population Fund (UNFPA), *Missing—Mapping the Adverse Child Sex Ratio in India* (New York: United Nations Population Fund, 2000).

43. Lalitha Sridhar, "India: Killing in the Cradle," *Populi: The UNFPA Magazine* 28, no. 2 (2001): 10–11.

44. For issues surrounding women and how changing their lives can change the planet, read *Half the Sky* by Nicholas Kristof and Sheryl Wudunn, (New York: Knopf, 2009).

45. UN AIDS, *Global Report Score Card 2010*, http://www.unaids.org/globalreport/AIDSScorecards.htm (accessed December 27, 2011); Holly Burkhalter, "The Politics of AIDS," *Foreign Affairs* 83, no. 1 (2004): 8–14.

46. Food and Agriculture Organization (FAO), *The State of Food Insecurity 2003* (Rome, Italy: United Nations Food and Agriculture Organization), 11.

47. Worldwatch Institute, *Vital Signs 2003: The Trends That Are Shaping Our Future* (UK: Earthscan Publications Ltd., 2003), 66.

48. Don Hinrichsen, "Ladies, You Have No Choice," *World Watch* 17, no. 2 (2004): 29.

49. Trade Related Aspects of Intellectual Property Rights, http://www.wto.org/english/tratop_e/trips_e/trips_e.htm.

50. Burkhalter, "The Politics of AIDS," 9.

51. Betsy McKay, Jonathan D. Rockoff, and Mark Schoofs, "AIDS Drugs Can Prevent Infection, Studies Show, *Wall Street Journal*, July 14, 2011, http://online.wsj.com/article/SB10001424052702303678704576442901100190640.html?mod=dist_smartbrief.

52. Danielle Nierenberg, "Correcting Gender Myopia: Gender Equity, Women's Welfare, and the Environment," (Worldwatch Paper #161) (Washington, D.C.: Worldwatch Institute, 2002), 30–31; this epidemic is well treated by Tony Barnett and Alan Whiteside in their *AIDS in the Twenty-First Century: Disease and Globalization* (New York: Palgrave, 2003).

53. Dr. Amartya Sen, http://www.economics.harvard.edu/faculty/sen/cv/CV-Final.June2008.pdf; Amartya Sen, *Development as Freedom* (New York: Random House, 1999).

54. Mark Nord, Alisha Coleman-Jensen, Margaret Andrews, and Steven Carlson, "Household Food Security in the United States" (Washington, D.C., U.S. Department of Agriculture: 2009), http://www.ers.usda.gov/Publications/ERR108/ERR108_ReportSummary.pdf.

55. United Nations Food and Agriculture Organization, *Report 2010*, http://www.fao.org/docrep/012/al390e/al390e00.pdf.

56. Thomas Prugh, and Erik Assadourian, "What is Sustainability Anyway?," *World Watch* 16, no. 5 (2003): 10–21.

57. Marmot, *Status Syndrome: How Social Standing Directly Affects your Health and Life Expectancy*, 2.

58. United States Health Care Bill 2010, http://thomas.loc.gov/cgi-bin/query/z?c111:H.R.4872.

59. Anne Platt McGinn, "Malaria, Mosquitoes, and DDT," *World Watch* 15, no. 3 (2002): 10–17.

60. Robert Sapolsky, "How the Other Half Heals," *Discover*, April 1998, 46–52.

61. Anne Platt, "The Resurgence of Infectious Diseases," *World Watch* 8, no. 4 (1995): 26–32.

62. The former first lady of Mozambique and wife of Nelson Mandela, Graça Machel, has written the passionate *The Impact of War on Children* (New York: Palgrave, 2002).

63. United Nations World Food Programme (UN WFP*)*, *India Overview*, http://www.wfp.org/countries/India/Overview.

64. UN WFP, "Many Bangladesh Children Malnourished News Report," http://www.wfp.org/content/un-many-bangladesh-children-malnourished; UN WFP, "Sub-Saharan Africa's Promise is Growing," http://www.wfp.org/content/guest-column-sub-saharan-africas-promise-growing.

65. UNICEF (United Nations Children's Fund), *Progress for Children: A Report Card on Nutrition* (Number 4) (New York: UNICEF,2006), 8–9; for more information, see UNICEF at www.unicef.org.

66. See Oxfam at www.oxfam.org.

67. UNICEF, *Children Living in Poverty 2011*, http://www.unicef.org/sowc05/english/poverty.html.

68. Gary Gardner and Brian Halweil, "The Overfed and Underfed: Escaping Hunger, Escaping Excess," *World Watch*, 13, no. 4 (2000): 27.

69. UNDP, *Human Development Report 2010*, http://hdr.undp.org/en/media/HDR_2010_EN_Tables_reprint.pdf; World Bank, *Indicators 2003*, 68–72.

70. UNDP, *Human Development Report 2003*, 4; Worldwatch Institute, *State of the World 2006*, (New York: Worldwatch Institute/Norton, 2006), 33.

71. Arundhati Roy, *The Cost of Living* (New York: Modern Library, 1999), 94.

72. Worldwatch Institute, *State of the World 2004*, (New York: Worldwatch Institute/Norton, 2004), 10.

73. Garrett Hardin, "The Tragedy of the Commons," *Science* 162 (1968): 1243–48; also at http://www.garrethardinsociety.org/articles/art_tragedy_of_the_commons.html.

74. Mahmood Mamdani, *The Myth of Population Control* (New York: Monthly Review Press, 1972), 21.

75. Livi-Bacci, *A Concise History of World Population*, 153.

76. Barry Commoner, *Making Peace with the Planet* (New York: Pantheon, 1990), 159.

77. Jodi L. Jacobson, "Improving Women's Reproductive Health," in Worldwatch Institute, *State of the World 1992*, 83–99.

78. Hardin, "The Tragedy of the Commons," 1243–48.

79. Stanley Wolpert, *A New History of India*, 6th ed. (New York: Oxford University Press, 2000).

80. Danielle Nierenberg, *Correcting Gender Myopia: Gender Equity, Women's Welfare, and the Environment*, Worldwatch Paper No. 161 (Washington, D.C.: Worldwatch Institute, 2002).

81. The Guttmacher Institute does periodic surveys of abortion in the United States. See their website at: http://www.guttmacher.org/sections/abortion.php.

82. See USAID at www.usaid.gov; Firor and Jacobsen, *The Crowded Greenhouse: Population, Climate Change, and Creating a Sustainable World*, 30–31.

83. Hinrichsen, "Ladies, You Have No Choice," 24–30.

84. Burkhalter, "The Politics of AIDS," 12–13.

85. See the decision at http://www.law.cornell.edu/supct/html/historics/USSC_CR_0410_0113_ZS.html.

86. Hinrichsen, "Ladies, You Have No Choice," 27.

87. Ann Hwang, "Exportable Righteousness, Expendable Women," *World Watch* 15, no. 1 (2002): 24–31.

88. Firor and Jacobsen, *The Crowded Greenhouse: Population, Climate Change, and Creating a Sustainable World*, 39.

89. Cohen, *How Many People Can the Earth Support*, 14–16.

90. See the UN Population Division at: http://un.org/esa/population/unpop.htm.

CHAPTER 14

The Greening of a Blue Planet

The Environmental Controversy: The Data
Conclusions and Reflections
    What We're Going to Need
    Tough Choices: Your Role in the Future
4. The Wrap: What Have We Learned?

If you've read Lewis Carroll's *Alice's Adventures in Wonderland*, you remember what happened when Alice tried to join the Mad Hatter's tea party: "The table was a large one, but the three were all crowded together at one corner of it. 'No room! No room!' they cried out when they saw Alice coming."[1]

The March Hare, the Mad Hatter, and the Dormouse were doing a reasonable imitation of the United States, the European Union, and Japan in revealing a reluctance to share scarce resources. In Lewis Carroll's imaginary world, there wasn't enough tea to go around. On this side of the looking glass, it is commonly believed that there isn't enough of anything to go around.

In the previous chapter, we established that the number of guests turning up for our global tea party is going to increase massively, although the actual number is difficult to predict. The United Nations believes that we hit the seven billion mark in 2011, and we'll sail on to at least ten billion before stabilization. Will there be enough tea, food, space, physical resources, pure water, and breathable air? Will Europe, Japan, and North America cry, "No room!" and seal their borders against an impoverished developing world?

In the introduction, we mentioned that environmental scientists, demographers, and international organizations have tended to use the year 2050 as a target for making projections and predictions. We also noted that—assuming you refrain from smoking and watch your health—many of today's university students should live at least halfway through the twenty-first century, so the questions asked in this chapter should have some special relevance to most readers of this book.

Environmental politics is a big field, and we will inevitably leave a lot out in this brief consideration of food, forest, power, and climate change. We do need to note, however, how problem areas such as population, nutrition, energy production, global warming, and **biosphere** damage are all intimately linked. Change, both positive and negative, is the complex and combined result of politics, corporate interests, scientific innovation, and public opinion. Political decisions and nondecisions in one arena will inevitably have their impact on all the others. As Garrett Hardin, one of the fathers of modern environmental studies noted wryly, "You can never do merely one thing."[2] Everything we do will have a series of consequences, some of them unforeseen and some of them unwanted. So, while we neatly packaged theories of international relations in chapter 2 into categories of realism, liberal idealism, constructivism, and critical theories, this final chapter will likely lead you to the conclusion that world politics is not easily confined to one theory and, in fact, not even confined to state borders. Air, water, and other resources know no borders.

In this final chapter, therefore, we need to address the other half of the population-resources crunch presented in the previous chapter. Here are some of the issues we need to face:

• *Are we going to have enough food, water, and other material resources to sustain a future population perhaps half again as large as the world's current population? Will there be enough power to give us heat, energy, and mobility in the decades to come?* When we speculate about the future, we often focus exclusively on food, which is an understandable error because food is easy to measure and its importance is hard to miss. But producing food involves the provision of large quantities of freshwater, which in turn depends upon forests and biodiversity. And running a planet calls for a lot of power, most of it currently coming from **fossil fuels** such as coal, natural gas, and derivatives of crude oil. If we continue to use crude oil, there has to be a point at which we burn the last drop. Will it be in 2050? We'll pause to offer some informed speculation on this vexed question.

- *In our efforts to feed ourselves and power our societies, will we destroy the planetary ecosystem upon which we depend?* This is an area of violent and highly politicized controversy, since left and right in the political spectrum have different rhetorical answers to what is essentially a scientific question. When we speculate about the exhaustion of finite energy supplies, however, some would argue that we are asking the wrong question. Many environmental activists believe that the planet's ecosystem cannot survive the environmental damage caused by burning even the fossil fuels (coal, natural gas, and oil) that we already have. They claim that we are destroying the harmony of nature, and that nature will pay us back by altering earth's biosphere. In section 2 below, we'll take a quick look at environmental politics, thinking about the issue of global climate change and the destruction and repair of the ozone layer.

- *Where ultimately are we headed? Can we reach any preliminary conclusions about the population-versus-resources crunch?* Predictably, neither scholars nor political leaders agree on a final answer, although the academic community is in substantially greater harmony on certain of the core issues than is the political world. We'll see how the pessimists in the scholarly world began the whole contemporary debate in the 1960s, and how some optimists see light at the end of our demographic tunnel. And we'll understand why differing views about the adequacy of our resource supply translates into bitter political battles.

1. Resources and Sustainability

Let's get out our crystal ball and look into the future, or at least the next forty years of it. As we learned in the last chapter, the United Nations is currently estimating that our present global population of just over seven billion people will expand to a worldwide total population of something like nine billion people. Almost all of the new arrivals will be born in parts of the world (Africa, South Asia, Central America, Southeast Asia, and the Pacific) that are already food stressed.

Food is both a present and a future challenge. We are accustomed to seeing pictures from famine-stricken regions of Africa of children with distended bellies and old men who look like walking skeletons. Important as food can be, however, there is a dangerous tendency to see the population versus resources dilemma exclusively in terms of nutrition. We need water and raw materials, as well as power. In this first section, let's look at some of the primary resources (such as food, water, and power) we need to survive and prosper.

FOOD TODAY AND FOOD TOMORROW

Is there enough food to feed everybody who needs to eat? The answer is "yes" and "no" and "it depends." Although the future might be another question, most specialists believe that enough food is currently being produced on the planet to feed all of us at our present (albeit unequal) levels of nutrition. In 1999, the UN's Food and Agriculture Organization (FAO) estimated that planetary food availability averaged about 2,800 calories/kilocalories per person per day.[3] Obviously, this abundance is not evenly distributed, but if it were, the world would have enough current food resources. We have many hungry people, some of whom will be actively starving at any given time, but their condition is not the result of a planetwide lack of available food, but rather a regional inability to grow food or to pay for imported food.[4]

The Limits of Food Production

Obviously, even food-surplus societies will have some people who cannot afford to purchase the food available on the shelves of their local supermarkets. This includes the United States, which is both the world's leading food producer and home to several million undernourished people.[5] Even India creates a food surplus, but there are hundreds of millions of Indian citizens without the financial resources to buy food grown in their own backyard. The prices of most commodities have actually declined in real terms over the past quarter century, but even at a discount, the world's food is mostly out of the reach of its poorest inhabitants.

The UN's Food and Agriculture Organization (FAO) has estimated that thirty-six countries are afflicted with serious food emergencies, sometimes because civil wars have destroyed normal supply lines, and sometimes because changing weather patterns have made it difficult for farms to raise enough crops. According to the FAO, this translates into about eight hundred million people who were clinically undernourished at the start of the twenty-first century. Compared to the early 1990s, this figure has actually grown, meaning that the number of hungry people on the planet is increasing rather than diminishing, a figure currently at 925 million people.[6] While poverty seems to be on the decline globally (mostly due to Chinese and Indian economic growth), this millennium development goal (MDG) related to food security has not improved at all. Quantity is, therefore, an important consideration and one crucial difference between high and low on the HDI scale is more than a thousand calories a day of nutrient consumption. This figure will vary from country to country, but wealthy societies generally have more than thirty-five hundred calories available for per capita daily consumption (much of it wasted), while poorer countries make do with daily caloric intakes around two thousand or less.

One problem in analyzing the current food situation is that it has developed so quickly and is changing so fast. Until the twentieth century, the world's agriculture was largely **sustainable** in the sense that farmers used seeds saved from a previous year's harvest, fertilized the soil with plant and animal waste, relied upon rainfall for water, and preserved biodiversity by planting many different crops on a small amount of land. By the twentieth century, however, the technology of farming had changed, becoming unsustainable in the sense that food production involved using resources that could not be renewed.

For example, food production increased in the third quarter of the twentieth century because of the so-called Green Revolution, which involved new kinds of grain seeds that generated exceptionally high crop yields. This sort of agricultural technology, however, is not sustainable in the long run because it requires massive amounts of inorganic nitrogen-based fertilizers and large quantities of water from sources that are being depleted. It also needs more pesticides, with the associated environmental and health risks involved. This highly mechanized style of farming consumes an extravagant amount of energy from irreplaceable fossil fuels.

As a result, the twentieth century produced a great deal of extra food, but only at the cost of increased pressure on the environment and on hard-to-renew resources such as fossil fuels, freshwater, and arable soil. Thanks to those "miracle" grains and extensive use of water and fertilizer, grain production soared after World War II but began to level off and even decline toward the end of the twentieth century. In 1950, the world was producing 247 kilograms of grain per person per year. Massive use of fertilizers, pesticides, water, and new kinds of seed boosted that total to 342 kilograms per person in 1984, the highest in history. By the end of the century, however, the figure had dwindled to a less impressive 308 kilograms per person per year.[7] By 2002, it had further declined to 294 kilograms per person per year.[8] In the 1990s, the world's gross grain production seems to have increased by 9 percent, which is good. Unfortunately, the population of the planet increased by about 12 percent during the same decade, meaning there was less grain, not more, available to each person. Some moderate optimists such as Vaclav Smil argue that the trend is temporary, and related to the collapse of the USSR and the highly regional problems of sub-Saharan Africa. Moderate pessimists such as Lester Brown believe that the decline of grain production is an ominous forecast of hunger to come. While scholars feud about the reasons, the stark fact remains that—if we are going to feed several billion more people in forty years—these numbers need to go up, not down. What are the problems?

Biofuels

As the price of oil rises, biofuels become more enticing forms of substitute energy supplies to power our industrial output. Corn, used in the biofuel ethanol, has had price increases steadily over the past ten years. By March 2011, corn and other grain prices had increased 36 percent year over year. The World Bank estimates that forty-four million people may have been pushed into poverty due to rising grain prices, because 80 percent of the world population feeds itself with grains.[9] The problem is that farmers make more money selling grains now for biofuel use rather than for food. The new demand for these grains has created price inflation and less availability for them as a food source. This also means that the demand for grains such as corn and soy has expanded their production, clearing land that was forested and provided a carbon sink for the planet. One such example is the Amazon, where Brazil has lost nearly 150,000 square kilometers of forest—an area larger than Greece—to grain and cattle production between May 2000 and August 2006.[10]

Nudging the Nitrates

The enormous expansion of agricultural productivity in the twentieth century was largely due to the 1899 discovery of an industrial technique for creating synthetic nitrogen fertilizers. The dramatic increase in grain production after World War II was due in large measure to the fact that miracle strains of grain, rice, and corn respond well to intensive use of nitrogen-based fertilizers. Unfortunately, most farmers are now already using as much nitrate as plants can absorb, so we cannot significantly boost crop yields on currently cultivated land by increasing nitrogen fertilization. Another quantum leap in food production will require another scientific breakthrough as dramatic as the discovery of synthetic nitrogen-based fertilizer, and that hasn't happened yet. Furthermore, our massive reliance on this kind of fertilizer is causing serious environmental problems. Nitrates are polluting water supplies in agricultural regions and killing fish in lakes and rivers. Escaping gas from intensively fertilized soil contributes, as we will see, to the destruction of the ozone layer and to global warming.

Losing Land

Scholars have long recognized that our statistics on the amount of arable (i.e., farmable) land are subject to debate because it can be difficult to distinguish among prime agricultural acreage, pasture land, and fields so dry and degraded that they have become economically marginal or outright desert. Only 10.6 percent of the world's land surface is classified as arable, a percentage that has remained almost unchanged in the past twenty years.[11] The quality of that arable land, however, in terms of its ability to produce food, has generally declined because of dwindling water resources and the loss of topsoil. When water tables fall, farmers often compensate by irrigating with polluted or heavily saline water, which eventually poisons the soil. Thanks to changing weather patterns, a slackening of rainfall can turn farmland into grazing land and grazing land into terrain too dry for any economic use, a process called **desertification**. And topsoil is depleted through erosion and repetitive monocropping (growing the same farm product over and over again on the same land). And the sprawling human population captures land for housing, roads, golf courses, and other nonagricultural human uses.

The areas most likely to be affected by desertification are on the edges of existing deserts in sub-Saharan Africa, China's Gobi Desert, and the American Southwest. In Africa, for example, available land for crops has declined about 8 percent since the 1980s, with another 8 percent forecast in twenty years if the pace of erosion continues.[12] As land is lost because of falling water tables and loss of topsoil, farmers are clearing forests on a massive scale in places such as the Amazon Basin and Southeast Asia. Since forests hold and purify water, this "slash-and-burn" approach invites erosion, flooding, and a decline in water quality. And for environmental reasons we will discuss below, the earth cannot afford to lose any more forest cover.

The loss of farmland can combine with a rapid increase in population to set the stage for violent political conflicts, and Rwanda is a tragic example. Thanks in part to opposition from Rwanda's religious leaders, virtually no effort was ever made to control a rapidly rising population there. Despite the country's scarce resources, Rwanda grew from 1.9 million in 1948 to 7.5 million in 1992, making it the most densely populated country in Africa. The average Rwandan practices subsistence farming on a small plot of not-very-good soil, because much of the best real estate is owned by wealthy people. In order to secure firewood for fuel, Rwandans began chopping down their country's forests. Since forests have the function within an ecosystem of holding and purifying water, deforestation caused erosion to wash away much of the available topsoil, further reducing both the amount of arable land and the supply of freshwater. This caused an uncomfortable decline in the country's food supply. By 1994, Rwandans had access to only nineteen hundred calories per person per day, not enough to sustain heavy work in a hot climate.

As a multinational state, Rwanda has always been home to two mutually antagonistic ethnic groups, Hutus and Tutsis. Hutu political leaders deftly persuaded the majority Hutu population that the problem could be solved by eliminating the Tutsi people, and in 1994, Hutu mobs massacred perhaps eight hundred thousand innocent Tutsis, creating tensions that have yet to be calmed in the heart of Africa.[13]

Scholars have been slow to connect the dots between environmental devastation and armed conflict, but these otherwise inexplicable civil wars breaking out in various poor countries clearly flow from the lack of resources. In 2004, the late professor Wingari Maathai of Kenya won the Nobel Peace Prize for creating the Green Belt Movement, which encouraged African women to plant trees to conserve topsoil and water, in order to keep communities from battling over increasingly scarce land. As the late Dr. Maathai said,

> Unless we properly manage resources like forests, water, land, minerals and oil, we will not win the fight against poverty. And there will not be peace. Old conflicts will rage on and new resource wars will erupt unless we change the path we are on.[14]

The Final Fish Fry

Healthier in a variety of ways than is meat, fish is another important source of protein. Thanks to new technology, ocean and freshwater fishing became a significant source of food in the years after World War II, increasing rapidly until the 1980s, when the demand for fish began to exceed available supplies. In the 1990s, for example, the cod fishing industry collapsed from overfishing in Canada's eastern provinces, putting thirty thousand people out of work. Globally, 25 percent of the most important maritime stocks are depleted or overharvested, while a further 44 percent of ocean stocks are already being fished at their biological limits.[15] We are currently catching and consuming fish at an unsustainable level, that is, we are taking out of oceans and lakes more food than nature is restoring, a situation that cannot be protracted indefinitely.

A 2011 report on the state of our oceans concludes that all coral reefs could disappear by 2050, oysters are "functionally extinct," and all oceans are suffering from acidification and lack of oxygen, further threatening the underwater environment. In fact, nitrates from farming brought via Mississippi River runoff and the 2010 British Petroleum oil spill are creating the largest dead zone in the U.S. Gulf Coast in history (dead zone means loss of biodiversity and disease).[16] The report recommends that the UN Security Council and UN General Assembly create a Global Ocean Compliance Commission (GOCC). The oceans, and animal and plant life that inhabit them, know no boundaries, which makes global politics even more important to their protection.

In deep ocean waters, fish stocks are disappearing because of overfishing, but closer to shore and in lakes and rivers, pollution has become a serious problem. The aquatic "commons" of the Mediterranean Sea, for example, is being poisoned by untreated sewage pumped heedlessly into it by southern Europeans and North Africans alike. Where

Figure 14.1. Traditional Fishing Techniques
In their wooden boat and with their hand-woven nets, these Malawian fishermen are trying to make a living on southern Africa's Lake Malawi, but increased population is both polluting the lake and overfishing it, endangering the livelihood of those who dwell along its shores.

agriculture is carried out with intensive fertilization, nitrate that is not absorbed by plants runs off in streams and filters into lakes and slow-moving rivers where it enriches water in a way that favors the growth of plant life, such as algae, over fish. Called "eutrophication," this process chokes the fish and renders the water useless. In America, the Chesapeake Bay is suffering from nitrate pollution from nearby farms, and the runoff of fertilizers into the Mississippi River was seriously affecting fishing in the Gulf of Mexico until the 2010 BP oil spill became an even greater issue.[17]

We need to keep reminding ourselves why this is all about politics. Sovereign governments have the power to regulate pollution, but it is often cheaper and politically easier to ignore the problem.

Actual individual consumption of fish has flattened statistically, with fish being eaten in much greater quantities by the health-conscious citizens of developed societies, but in smaller quantities by Third and Fourth World populations who find their own offshore waters being emptied by giant commercial fishing fleets from Japan and Europe.

Since there is little hope for a rapid expansion of wild fish catch, we have increasingly turned to raising fish domestically, a practice called **aquaculture** or fish farming, the practice of raising and harvesting fish in artificially constructed tanks or pens rather than catching them from the wild. About one-quarter of all the fish we consume today have been bred under controlled circumstances, specifically for human consumption. Fish farming does involve some significant problems, however. Artificial fish can be higher in toxins and lower in nutrients than are "natural" fish, and the technology of fish farming poses some environmental problems.[18] Most of these problems are fixable, but they haven't, thus far, been fixed.[19]

The bottom line? If we practice careful conservation and cooperate internationally, we could maintain our supply of seafood at something just below our current levels of consumption, but we cannot look to the sea for a solution to our global food problems. There seems to be no short-term way of expanding ocean fishing, although aquaculture could bring us a lot of healthy, high quality, low-cost protein in the future, if the environmental problems associated with fish farming can be solved.

Genetic Modification (GM)

Since GM's appearance about twenty-five years ago, Europeans have been irritated and worried by what they sometimes call "Frankenfood." South Asian farmers are frankly furious, although the business community is intrigued. Except for GM-friendly Argentina, South Americans are badly divided on the issue, but North Americans shrug and wonder what the fuss is all about. What is GM and why is it so intensely controversial?

Genetic modification (or genetic engineering or biotechnology) is the generic term for a battery of DNA-based technologies in which genetic material is borrowed from one species and inserted into the genetic code of another to achieve desired changes in the target species. Since the invention of agriculture, farmers have been trying to improve their crops and domestic animals by selective breeding; until recently, this meant centuries of replanting seeds from the best plants and arranging for superior farm animals to interbreed with one another. GM technology allows these changes to take place dramatically and quickly, although critics would argue that Mother Nature shouldn't be modified too quickly.

GM is commonly used to increase crop productivity. The giant Monsanto Company, for example, has bioengineered a product range of genetically altered (sometimes called "transgenic") plants that are unharmed by Monsanto's own popular weed-killing herbicide. This "Roundup Ready" process allows farmers to plant—for example—Monsanto soybeans and then kill unwanted weeds with Monsanto's herbicide without endangering the soybeans themselves. Soy is overwhelmingly an American product that finds its way into many foods; about half of all U.S. soybeans are produced with this GM process. Other transgenic crops are engineered to produce within themselves a pesticide that wards off natural predators.[20]

It is also possible to genetically modify crops to deliver health benefits to the consumer and economic benefits to poor people. The Swiss, for example, have created a "Golden Rice" in which borrowed genetic information from the carrot allows rice to produce beta carotene. When ingested, this rice produces vitamin A and lowers risk of the vitamin deficiency that is the leading cause of blindness, especially among children in low HDI countries. Another team of researchers has been working on crops that can flourish on the kind of salty, marginal soil found in many parts of the low HDI world.

The Perfect Tomato

Tomatoes have been bioengineered to resist insect predators thanks to an insecticide that has been inserted genetically into the DNA of the plant itself. While some students are concerned about the development of superbugs that may evolve immunity to this and other pesticides, actual environmental damage from GM crops has thus far been difficult to demonstrate. While GM technology does make food last longer and look better, some critics maintain that GM has also created a perfectly tasteless tomato.

Why should any of this be a problem? First of all, recognize that GM is a general term for a whole armory of different genetic techniques, each with different promises and problems. Here are some of the controversies:

- Safety for Humans: Opponents of GM foods are concerned that they have not been tested long enough or widely enough to be regarded as totally safe. Luminaries such as Britain's Prince Charles and singer-songwriter Paul McCartney have joined the anti-GM campaign. Most Europeans simply will not touch the stuff, and the European Union has attempted to prohibit its importation.[21] GM advocates, on the other hand, argue that Americans have been eating GM foods in increasing amounts for the past quarter century without any reported damage to health. The American Food and Drug Administration has cleared some four hundred GM species for general consumption, but there is no one single U.S. federal agency in charge of GM technology, and—in the absence of any specific threat to public health—the pro-business American government has generally taken a hands-off approach to the new technology.
- Safety for the Environment: If we convert any significant portion of our global agricultural economy to genetically modified foods, then the system will need to work without damaging either non-GM crops nor the environment in general. Some skeptics are worried that pesticides and herbicides may encourage the mutation of "superbugs" and "super-weeds" that might devastate future crops. Furthermore, environmentalists are concerned about further insults to the balance of nature. The bugs that once ate farmers' wheat were themselves dinner for animals further up the food chain. Furthermore, no one knows what unintended victims the toxins artificially engineered into plants will have in the future. A related issue is the question of contamination when genetically modified plants interbreed with "natural" plants and spread into agricultural environments where they do not belong.
- Control: While some universities and NGOs have produced GM products designed specifically to help the poor, most genetic engineering is done by a small group of major American companies such as Monsanto, Dupont, and Dow. These companies control the patents on their products, and thanks to the powerful World Trade Organization, they can decide who uses their products and under what contractual arrangements. These will doubtless enable First World farmers to increase both production and profits, but they have little financial incentive to bioengineer anything specifically for very poor countries suffering from food insecurity.

The European Union (EU) has taken a very firm stand against most forms of genetically engineered food, and it has generally prohibited the import from North America of these products. To some extent, this ban is based on safety concerns that are more keenly felt in Europe than in the United States. Europeans often resent the intrusion of American culture, technology, and commercial zeal into their lives, and this boycott is partly fueled by anti-American sentiments. It is also a quiet way of preserving European markets for more expensive European agricultural products. For its part, the United States regards this anti-GM prohibition as a violation of EU commitments to the World Trade Organization (WTO), which obligates member countries to accept one another's products.[22]

Reaction to biotechnology in the poorer portions of the world is mixed. India might actually be able to profit from some aspects of GM technology, but public opinion there is not only hostile but also sometimes even actively violent. In Latin America, where public concerns about environmental issues are somewhat muted, there is more interest and willingness to experiment.

Can GM technology help us feed that 2.6 billion extra people arriving for lunch over the next quarter century? At its present state of marketing and development, GM has limited relevance to the needs of low HDI countries, partly because the really poor cannot afford to buy the technology, and partly because their intellectuals oppose it on ideological grounds. As a result, much of the world's current GM crops are not actually feeding poor people but are feeding cows and other meat animals that will be slaughtered and fed to rich people. But could GM affect the lives of the poor in a positive way? Some African societies lose an important portion of their annual crops to insects and plant infestations of various kinds. Existing GM technology has already produced strands of corn/maize that are not harmed by herbicides or insecticides, allowing farmers to spray their fields to kill weeds and bugs without harming the crops themselves.[23]

Developing countries fear the aggressive tactics employed by major manufacturers of GM products and have an understandable reluctance to allow Monsanto to control their destinies. On the other hand, there are a lot of hungry people in the developing world, and it would make a lot of difference to them if they could grow corn that bugs can't eat but people can. GM technology, which is potentially of enormous importance to very poor societies, has been lost in confused controversies over globalization and anti-Americanism, and opposition to multinational corporations. It remains to be seen if GM technology and GM business techniques can be modified so that people who need more food can grow it themselves.[24]

Parallel Lives: Vandana Shiva and Marina Silva

In recent years, two women of color have been giving ulcers to the powerful white men who want genetic modification to succeed on a global level. India's Dr. Vandana Shiva and Brazil's Marina Silva have been active in defending small farmers, peasants, and indigenous peoples against the pretensions of multinational corporations and sometimes against their own governments.[25] In their respective countries, both women have become controversial and high-visibility critics of GM technology.

The daughter of an intellectual north Indian family, Vandana Shiva studied science at the University of Western Ontario and returned to her native India with a Ph.D. and the determination to become the multinational agro-business' worst nightmare. In books, lectures, and articles, Dr. Shiva accuses the big business practitioners of genetic modification of recolonizing the Third World and claiming enforceable patents over the same crops peasant farmers have grown for generations. As a feminist, Shiva makes the case that—if it works—genetic modification will

Figure 14.2.   Dr. Vandana Shiva
Courtesy of Right Livelihood Award Foundation Archive at www.rightlivelihood.org.

primarily benefit wealthy white men. If it turns out badly, she claims, poor women of color will feel most of the consequences.[26]

Very few world leaders have come from such humble origins as Marina Silva, who was born into an impoverished family of rubber tree tapers in the Acre region of the Amazon. She was illiterate until age sixteen, when an illness brought her to a city where she could learn to read and eventually finish a university degree. True to her origins, however, Marina Silva returned to her forest home, where she joined forces with the legendary Chico Mendes in organizing the forest-dwelling rubber workers into a labor union, fighting to prevent deforestation and environmental destruction.

When Mendes was murdered in 1988 by political opponents, Silva soldiered on alone, becoming Brazil's youngest senator at age thirty-six. When Luis Inacio Lula da Silva (no relation) of the Brazilian Workers' Party swept into the presidency in 2003, he installed Marina Silva as his minister of the environment. Genetic modification is the subject of a brutal controversy even within Lula's own left-leaning government. When Lula declared a "zero hunger" program, vowing to stamp out malnutrition, some of his supporters believed that GM technology was essential to that goal. Ms. Silva is no longer a member of the cabinet, but continues to lead those Brazilians who want no part of this Yankee technology. She won 20 percent of the first round presidential election in 2010 with the Green Party, an environmental party. In July 2011, she left the Green Party, but hinted at another bid for president in 2014. Silva continues her fight to create a better environment and has inspired great interest in environmental politics in Brazil and around the world.

Make Mine a Veggie Burger

One way in which currently available resources could be used to feed substantially more people would be a change in global diet that featured less meat and more fruits and vegetables. High HDI countries eat not only quantitatively more food but also different kinds of food, with a significantly higher percentage of their calories coming from meat and other animal products such as cheese and eggs. North Americans, for example, get about 30 percent of their calories from meat and dairy products; in a typical low HDI society, meat and dairy products account for less than 10 percent of caloric intake.[27] In the last half century, we have globally doubled our individual consumption of meat products, and eating meat, particularly beef, is an inefficient way of trying to feed the planet. The World Health Organization (WHO) predicts that we will have a meat shortage in the coming years if we do not change our dietary needs and planetary growth.[28]

In the developed world, most meat is produced in factory farms, with cattle, sheep, pigs, and poultry bred specifically for human consumption. In a poor, low-tech society, these same species would graze on open land for their food, but traditional pastoralism is too slow for modern meat producers, who feed their livestock on grains specifically raised for this purpose. This means that a great deal of land must be set aside to produce food for livestock, and these fields cannot be used to grow fruits and vegetables. Furthermore, a meat-intensive diet places a much greater strain on already limited water resources. To produce a given amount of protein from meat requires about twenty times as much water as the same quantity of protein in vegetables or grains. Expressed in other terms, to create a two-thousand-calorie daily diet with 20 percent of the calories coming from animal products requires about 560 cubic meters of water a year. To provide the same two-thousand-calorie diet with vegetarian foods requires only 330–350 cubic meters of water a year.[29]

Furthermore, raising meat under modern factory conditions puts a specific strain on the environment. When animals graze uneconomically but happily in open fields, their nitrate-rich dung fertilizes the same fields from which they draw their food. In a high-tech factory-farming environment, animal waste generally becomes a pollutant, too concentrated to be economically useful as fertilizer and a major disposal problem. Unless very carefully treated, these nitrates pollute the water supply.[30]

Quite apart from environmental concerns, a carnivorous diet involves health considerations. When consumed in large quantities, meat and dairy products leave unhealthy fats in our bodies, placing a strain on national health systems when strokes and heart attacks happen. Since many factory farm animals are raised under conditions that keep them permanently sick, they are fed huge amounts of antibiotics that remain in the flesh of the animals when consumed by humans. When we become ill with bacteriological infections, antibiotic medicines intended for humans may be less effective or may not work at all because the bacteria may have developed a partial immunity to them. Certain hormones intended to stimulate growth in animals may also have negative health implications for human consumers.

In essence, we can get healthy protein directly from grains; it is therefore uneconomical to produce grain, feed it to animals, and then eat the animals, no matter how much we may like thick steaks or chicken legs. While interest in vegetarianism was high at the beginning of the twenty-first century, the trend hadn't yet put a detectable statistical dent in humankind's meat craving. Nevertheless, shifting to more (if not exclusively) vegetarian diets would make us healthier and able to nourish ourselves with less land.

WATER AND TREES

About 1.1 billion people (something like one-sixth of the human race) live with chronic water insecurity. In an effort to understand what we're liable to run out of between now and 2050, we need to take a close look at our unsustainable use of freshwater. Since forests and plants have a crucial role to play in many aspects of the biosphere, we should also linger for a moment over our rapidly disappearing woodlands and jungles, as well as the political consequences of destroying species of animals and plants.

Hydrating the Planet

For most of the twentieth century, concerns about increasing population and declining resources may have blinded us to what may be the most significant danger of them all, the present and future scarcity of water. In many parts of the world, there isn't enough freshwater, and there is going to be even less in a more heavily populated future. In many developed societies, water usage is unsustainable, depleting resources much faster than they can be replenished. And finally, what water remains is no longer as pure as it needs to be to sustain human life and agricultural consumption.

There is, of course, a great deal of water on the planet, but most of it is saltwater and is destined to stay that way. Desalinization (the process of removing harmful minerals from seawater to make it drinkable) is expensive and energy intensive. The most common technique is called "reverse osmosis," which involves forcing water through a membrane that filters out salt and other impurities. While some wealthy but thirsty communities continue to explore desalination, it is currently too expensive to serve as a major remedy for the world's water shortage. Barring some technological breakthrough, desalting the oceans will be an option primarily for countries such as Saudi Arabia, who have lots of cheap oil and don't mind adding to global warming by burning it.

Where does freshwater come from? About 70 percent of all existing freshwater is unavailable to us because it is frozen into glaciers or polar ice caps. The water we *can* use comes from a complex ecosystem in which moisture evaporates from the oceans (leaving its salt and mineral content behind) and falls on land as freshwater. Most rainfall filters into streams and rivers, or sinks down to form a water table relatively close to the surface that can be tapped with wells. Aquifers, large reserves of water deep beneath the surface, are another major source of water. Most aquifer water has been trapped underground since the last ice age, but these aquifers can also be very slowly replenished by rainfall seeping down through the earth.

We use most available water for agricultural purposes, a lot for industry, and the rest for personal activities such as drinking, watering our lawns, filling our baths and swimming pools, and flushing the toilet. As the population increases, so does the demand on the world's water, and we are currently consuming more clean, freshwater than the ecosystem is putting back into the supply chain, an unsustainable practice.[31] In the poorer portions of the world, access to water for personal use and waste removal (about

8 percent) is very limited. According to the United Nations, many low HDI societies are supplying sustainable water access to less than half of their population. Fifty-three percent of Ethiopians, for example, have ready access to drinkable water, and 83 percent have a sewage system for carrying human waste away from the home. That's up from 24 percent and 12 percent respectively since 2003—good news. Still, globally about 1.1 billion people lack access to clean water, and another 2.4 billion people do not have sanitation facilities (i.e., toilets and sewage systems).[32] The consequence of human waste penetrating the water supply is an epidemic of water-carried infectious diseases. We associate impure water with the poor and developing world, but studies of the American and European water supplies have revealed an uncomfortably high presence of chemical residues, antibiotics, petroleum products, and other potentially harmful pollutants in the drinking water.[33]

Because modern, fertilizer-intensive agriculture demands more water than is available on or close to the surface, farmers have begun to tap into those hard-to-replenish aquifers, pumping this ancient water in increased quantities. The Ogallala aquifer, for example, extends beneath the surface of the American Midwest. It is already about half depleted, and we are continuing to pump more from it than is being replenished by natural means. We will require even more water in the future than in the past, and there isn't a lot more available anywhere that can be made sustainably available for agricultural, industrial, and direct human use.

Waiting for the Rain

In most parts of Africa and Asia, local agriculture is totally dependent upon natural rainfall. With limited access to groundwater and no resources for irrigation, many farmers can only hope that the rainy season produces enough moisture to give their crops a healthy start. Climate change for many regions close to the equator may make rainfall even more problematic in the future than it has been in the past.

The most exhaustive recent study of global water requirements has been done by the United Nations World Water Assessment Programme and published in New York as the *World Water Development Report* in 2011. The conclusions of the report are shocking: by 2050, about seven billion of the world's anticipated 8.9 billion inhabitants will face water shortages of some severity. The problem is particularly acute in areas where food supplies are already problematic because the successful use of fertilizers depends upon the availability of large amounts of water. As the water crunch intensifies, it will be particularly troubling for portions of Africa and South Asia. One scholar estimates that about nine hundred million people will move into extreme water scarcity over the next two decades.

According to millennium development goal (MDG) data from the United Nations, one billion people lack access to drinking water. The corresponding sanitation target will not be met by 2015. If the 1990–2002 trend continues, it is thought that some 2.4 billion people will be without improved sanitation in 2015—almost as many as are without it today. This lack of sanitation and water supply has caused 3.1 million deaths globally due to diarrheal and malarial diseases.[34]

The politics of water are already tense and will almost certainly deteriorate as the scarcity of water increases. At a domestic level, poor people are already being squeezed off good land and expelled onto dry turf far from a good source of pure water. At an international level, countries that share rivers or aquifers may be driven into armed conflict by their desire to control these resources. Examples of "water wars" are numerous. The Israeli-Palestinian conflict has a lot to do with the dwindling Jordan River. Iraqis, Syrians, and Turks all have issues over the Tigris-Euphrates river basin, while Indians and Bangladeshi are quarrelling over the sacred but sparse waters of the Ganges.[35]

Complicating the shortage of water is an increased purity problem. Slowly but inevitably, surface water seeps down to water tables and aquifers, bringing nitrates from fertilizer and animal excrement as well as petrochemicals and pesticides. When sewage contaminates the water supply, bacteria and viruses make their way into our drinking supply, and impure water is a major health hazard in many portions of the world.[36]

Can anything be done about this growing crisis? First, there are several economic complications. As mentioned in chapter 13, privatization of water distribution is bringing better quality water more efficiently to some middle-class customers, but it is frequently depriving poor people of regular supplies. In many parts of the world, water is provided to farmers far below its actual cost or value, providing an invisible subsidy to agriculture, while city dwellers are paying the full cost. Clearly, a rational basis needs to be found for the problem of paying for water.

Second, much can be done to improve "water productivity," which means getting water precisely to where it is needed with a minimal amount of loss. For example, most municipal water systems lose vast amounts of water through leaky pipes. There are drip irrigation systems, for example, that deliver just the right amount of water to the roots of a plant being cultivated, avoiding massive losses through evaporation or absorption into the soil.[37]

These solutions sound easier than they are. Rebuilding urban water delivery systems all over the world would cost more money than any government wants to spend, and people in the developed world have grown accustomed to their swimming pools and sprinkler systems for lawns and golf courses. Where people are practicing survival agriculture, farmers will pump from the water table or an aquifer without much thought about the future. We may be nervous about water supplies in a decade, but the farmer's family will starve this year if they don't get a crop out of the ground. Hence, water conservation is hard to do, sometimes because people are self-indulgent, and sometimes because they are desperate.

The bottom line? While predictions about the future are always nervous, we are well into a period of unsustainability in our use of water. Given the importance of water for agriculture, our future ability to feed ourselves depends upon increasing water productivity, clearing up sources of pollution, and practicing restraint in our uses of this finite resource. Past experience suggests that we won't do this voluntarily because it will be expensive and difficult. This means that governments may have to regulate water consumption domestically and practice greater levels of cooperation internationally. When something needs to be done and isn't, inaction is itself a political decision.[38]

Portraits of the Real World:
The Sub-Saharan Water Crunch

One of the authors of this book, Richard Collin, once visited a village of about a thousand very poor black Africans in the southeast of the Sudan near the Eritrean border. This community suffered from deprivations in every possible dimension, but what struck him most was the endless, daily struggle to bring water to the village. The work was done by girls and women who walked downhill about two kilometers to a murky, disagreeable stream with a languid trickle of very dubious-looking water. There they filled plastic four-liter jugs, or sometimes ancient tin containers, and carried them back up the hill for cooking, washing, and the irrigation of their kitchen gardens. There was no modern sanitation or sewage system in the village; some human waste must have ended up in the same stream from which the community drew its water.

Climatologists can argue about whether desertification is related to global climate change, or whether it is a cyclical phenomenon that will pass in time. What is beyond argument is that rainfall patterns in northeast Africa have changed dramatically over the course of the past half century, and the situation is worse today than it has ever been. Sudan, Eritrea, Ethiopia, and Somalia were never the Garden of Eden, but they once got enough rain to get a meager crop in the ground. The rains began to fail in the 1960s and have become increasingly sporadic ever since.

In the United States, we are more conscious of the impending oil shortage because we complain when we fill up our jeeps and SUVs with increasingly expensive gasoline. There will certainly be a fuel crisis of some sort, but it will be global in character because we have huge systems for moving crude oil around the world. When it hits, the gasoline shortage will hit the whole planet more or less simultaneously. If the price of crude oil rises in Shanghai, it rises in Chicago the same day.

Water, on the other hand, is only expensive when you haven't got it, and it can't be easily moved around the planet on the basis of market forces. It needs to be produced and used locally. There is a lot of water in Mauritius, but that doesn't help anybody in east Africa, because there is no cost-effective way of getting it there.

That Sudanese village contained the poorest people Richard had ever met, but they were incredibly hospitable. The older men got him into the shade under a canvas tarpaulin and produced a single bottle of a lukewarm cola drink. One of the women brought a half-dozen chipped glasses, and with a few teaspoons apiece of soft drink, they toasted Richard's arrival the same way Europeans or Americans would toast a guest with Champagne. Later, Richard and the other men ate roasted chicken and boiled rice. The women ate the leftovers and then walked back down the hill to fetch water to wash the dishes and prepare for another day.

Forests and Biodiversity

In the analysis of climate change in section 2 below, we will see that plant life, by absorbing carbon dioxide, plays a crucial role in global temperature stability. Forests and jungles also store, recycle, and purify water. When sustainably logged, forests are a source of timber. Humans live in the world's forests, often indigenous or native peoples who have adapted well to life in this sheltering environment and who—in turn—play an important role in protecting it. And there is the biodiversity factor: the woods are a sanctuary for animal and plant life, including as yet undiscovered species that may be useful to us as medicines or other products. About a quarter of all pharmaceutical products used today come from tropical forest plants.

Despite their importance, however, forests have been the target of a ferocious attack by humans. Centuries ago, Europeans and North Americans cut down most of their woodlands, and the developing world is now swinging an axe at its own trees, many of them hard-to-replace tropical rain forests. About half of the planet's original forests have now permanently disappeared as humankind clears land for farms, cities, roads, parking lots, and golf courses. At the beginning of the twentieth century, the planet contained approximately five billion hectares of forest. By the start of the twenty-first century, this number had dropped to 2.9 billion hectares, and less than half of this is natural, undisturbed, and original forests.

In west Africa, Southeast Asia, and the rain forests of Central and South America, deforestation has often taken the form of the environmentally catastrophic "**slash-and-burn**" variety. To create cropland for grain or coffee, or pastureland for beef cattle, developers cut down the valuable hardwood trees (such as teak and mahogany) for sale to furniture makers in wealthy societies, and then burn the rubble.

Despite its lush appearance, a tropical rain forest typically grows out of relatively poor earth; an environmentalist once quipped that a jungle is a desert looking for a place to happen. After a slash-and-burn operation, the resulting ash provides just enough nitrogen to get a few years of cultivation out of the thin layer of topsoil. When this soil is exhausted through overuse and rapid erosion, entrepreneurs move further into the jungle and begin a new round of slashing and burning. Since the land originally cost little or nothing, it can be abandoned without serious financial consequences for the owners.

The environmental cost of deforestation, on the other hand, is considerable. First, the actual combustion creates smog that can be devastating to human health. In 1997–1998, the mass burning of forests on the island of Borneo treated Southeast Asia to catastrophic smog that blocked the sun and blighted the air in Indonesia, Thailand, Malaysia, and Singapore. We will look in more detail at global warming below, but for now, note that smoke particles rising into the atmosphere act like greenhouse gases and contribute to climate change. Obviously, every tree that falls reduces the earth's ability to recycle carbon dioxide back into oxygen. The environmental consequences for land and water are even more calamitous. The remaining topsoil is quickly washed away through erosion, and the now-barren land loses its ability to store and filter water. This can quickly contribute to devastating floods, such as the crippling inundation that struck Mozambique in 2002 and the drought experienced in east Africa in 2006 and 2011.[39] Tribal peoples are driven out, and plant and animal species are decimated. Slash-and-burn is a total loss for everybody except the entrepreneurs who commit this eco-felony.

Biodiversity is simply the range or number of different species of plants and animals existing naturally within a given ecosystem (e.g., a tropical forest). One of the worst consequences of deforestation is the loss of biodiversity. The relentless human expansion into previously uninhabited territories also reduces the number of plants and animals and, in some cases, drives them out of existence. Dollo's Law (named after Belgian scholar Louis Dollo) states that once a species becomes extinct it cannot be re-evolved. Species that die are gone forever, and we are losing many of these life forms before we understand what role they play in the environment or what benefits they could have for us.[40] Should we be concerned? As environmental guru Lester Brown explains,

> As various life forms disappear, they alter the earth's ecosystem, diminishing the services provided by nature, such as pollination, seed dispersal, insect control, and nutrient cycling. This loss of species is weakening the web of life . . . leading to irreversible and potentially unpredictable changes in the earth's ecosystem. . . . As we burn off the Amazon rainforest, we are burning one of the great genetic storehouses.[41]

The Brazilian case is instructive, particularly since the Amazon Basin contains about 30 percent of the world's remaining tropical rain forest and a huge portion of surviving plant and animal species. Unfortunately for biodiversity, the rain forest is being cut down with reckless speed, often by the agents of large multinational corporations. The Brazilian government has passed legislation criminalizing most slash-and-burn deforestation, but it has put little effort into enforcement, even though about 80 percent of Brazil's logging is actually illegal.

Concerned about a range of similar environmental problems, the United Nations staged the 1992 UN Conference on Environment and Development (UNCED) in Brazil's Rio de Janeiro. Sometimes called the "Rio Conference" or sometimes the Earth Summit, the meeting produced a series of resolutions, conventions, and multinational treaties. At this history-making conference, the world's environmentalists turned their attention to a host of problems, including the two issues that hinge on deforestation—the future of the forests themselves, and the problem of declining biodiversity.

As far as forests are concerned, agreement was hard to reach. The developed world wanted those tropical countries with large forests to preserve them for all the usual environmental reasons; developing countries with the world's remaining stands of tropical forest refused to accept orders from rich people who had financed their own prosperity by slaughtering their own forests centuries before. The document that came out of the Rio Conference was a compromise called "The Forest Principles" that encouraged reforestation and the reduction of pollution without actually committing anybody to anything. In the years following the Rio Conference, efforts have been made to create a fund to pay off some of the debts of forest-owning countries in exchange for a promise to refrain from massive deforestation.

The environmentalists at Rio were determined to get further with a basic binding agreement on biodiversity, and they prepared the "Convention on Biological Diversity" for ratification by all the world's governments.[42] In general, the treaty obligates signatories to preserve biological diversity on land and sea, but specific parts of the convention commits technologically advanced states to refrain from establishing patents on naturally

Figure 14.3. Dirty Water
Currently, 65 percent of Ecuador's Amazon is zoned for oil activities. Since the 1970s oil boom, multiple partnerships have formed between the state oil company, now called Petroecuador, and transnational oil companies. The country boasts two oil pipelines that traverse its Amazonian rain forest over the Andes Mountains to the coast. These activities have not gone without conflict as will be discussed below. Most notably, the lasting environmental impact of Texaco (now Chevron-Texaco) on the northern Amazon is still to be determined by a court of law in Lago Agrio, Ecuador. Suffering from oil spills and seepage into groundwater systems that rival the Alaskan Exxon Valdez disaster, local and indigenous peoples demanding a cleanup opened a 1993 multibillion dollar lawsuit against Chevron-Texaco in New York. The case was moved to Ecuador in 2003, where plaintiffs were awarded $16 billion in damages. Chevron-Texaco has appealed this ruling in The Hague, Netherlands, as well as in Ecuador. This photo was taken by Pamela Martin on a trip to Ecuador's Amazon to visit oil spills in 2006. For more on this near-twenty-year battle between indigenous and local communities, and Chevron-Texaco, see Patrick Radden Keefe's "Reversal of Fortune," *The New Yorker*, January 9, 2012, 38–49.

occurring substances. In other areas, intellectual property rights would be commonly shared. The United States detected a threat to U.S. commercial interests and refused to participate in the treaty, along with Thailand.

In September 2008, the **UN-REDD Programme (United Nations Collaborative Initiative on Reducing Emissions from Deforestation and Forest Degradation in Developing Countries)** was formed to combat the devastating loss of our planet's forests. The Programme was launched to assist developing countries prepare and implement national REDD+ strategies, and coordinates with the Food and Agriculture Organization of the United Nations (FAO), the United Nations Development Programme (UNDP), and the United Nations Environment Programme (UNEP).

Essentially, this program places a value on stored carbon in trees and provides financial income based on this value. REDD involves *developed* countries paying *developing* countries carbon offsets for their standing forests. It is a cutting-edge forestry initiative that aims at tipping the economic balance in favor of sustainable management of forests so that their formidable economic, environmental, and social goods and services benefit countries, communities, biodiversity, and forest users while also contributing to important reductions in greenhouse gas emissions.

The UN-REDD Programme was originally funded by Norway and is now funded by various European countries and Japan. While controversial because it employs market strategies of buying and selling carbon bonds to protect forests—something that some argue allows developed countries to continue to pollute and buy UN-REDD bonds to pay for it—it is part of the UN Framework Convention on Climate Change (UNFCCC) mechanisms to encourage protection of our surviving pristine plots of forest. This initiative is a good example of global governance in that it was spearheaded by citizen activists and NGOs from Costa Rica and Papa New Guinea and implemented through the UN FCCC as newly recognized international norms and rules for climate change. It also highlights the tensions between market approaches and nonmarket approaches in combating climate change. Some environmentalists believe that paying to protect the environment only encourages pollution for those who can pay, while others feel that employing market incentives creates a new, green economic tool to save the planet. What do you say?[43]

All of this sounds like science, but it's really politics. Protecting the world's forests and jungles is a political decision, something governments can either do or not do. Most of the world's remaining woodlands are publicly owned and therefore under the direct control of elected officials. Unfortunately, governments tend to undervalue forestland. Inhabited by politically powerless indigenous people, these huge tracts of environmentally crucial land are either left open to poorly restricted logging, given away, or sold at bargain-basement prices, often to foreign interests.

Portraits of the Real World: Paying to Preserve the Amazon? Ecuador's Yasuní National Park

Aside from clear-cutting South America's Amazon rain forest, the world's largest carbon sink, another threat of destruction comes from what lies below its surface: oil and other natural resources. In the case of Ecuador's Amazonian Yasuní National Park, a United Nations Man and Biosphere Reserve, the country's president, Rafael Correa, is proposing that the world pay *not* to drill for oil in this pristine patch of land.[44] Leaving "oil in the soil," as some NGO activists proclaim, not only protects what you might first think of in the Amazon—lush trees and monkeys or exotic pink dolphins—but it also protects two groups, and possibly more, of indigenous peoples that live deep in this national park but have remained out of contact and isolated from the outside world. The Taromenane and Tagaeri are some of the last humans on the planet to live in voluntary isolation from the modern world. As more illegal timber loggers and oil companies expand into this area of the Amazon, these isolated tribes have sent signals to the outside world that they do not want further encroachment. As a result of logging and new roads, unfortunate deaths have occurred, including a 2009 slaying of a mother and her three children as they walked on a new road being clear-cut into their area of the forest. Only days after the sad news, scientists released a study determining that Yasuní National Park is one of the most biodiverse plots of land on our planet, with more tree species than all of North America combined.

So, would you pay to protect Yasuní National Park and its peoples? The price tag is $350 million per year over a thirteen-year time period (approximately $4.55 billion, not including interest earned on the accrued contributions), which would result in half of the expected earnings had Ecuador extracted the oil there. Ecuador (one of South America's poorest countries) says that it's donating half of its earnings to protect the Amazon and lower carbon emissions for the planet. It is proposing the Yasuní-ITT (which stands for Ishpingo-Tambococha-Tiputini, a block within the park) Initiative as a new addition to climate change agreements beyond the Kyoto Protocol, which ends in 2012.[45] The idea is that extremely biodiverse and fossil-fuel-rich countries could be paid by the world community to avoid hydro-carbon emissions, thus lowering emissions for all of us and protecting some of our most diverse and unique environmental hot spots. In light of the BP oil spill in the U.S. Gulf of Mexico in 2010 and the utter devastation that many around the world have witnessed, such an investment seems more urgent.

The problem is that most of us in the industrialized world will continue to use oil for our cars, home heating and cooling, and a myriad of everyday products. If we pay to leave oil underground in these places, won't we just extract more of it somewhere else? That may be the case, unless we also invest in alternative en-ergy sources, which Ecuador is also proposing to the United Nations Framework Convention on Climate Change (UNFCCC), the UN body that discusses climate change agreements.[46] Is this an investment you'd make, or would you encourage your government to contribute to this fund? To learn more about the initiative, go to http://www.yasuni-itt.gov.ec/.[47]

POWERING THE PLANET

This first section concludes with a look at the intensely controversial issue of energy use and supplies. The technologies with which we heat and cool our homes, power our cars, and run our computers and cellular phones are partly the result of political and corporate decisions and partly a consequence of scientific and economic realities. At the start of the twenty-first century, the scientists and the politicians were in confusing conflict with one another. Former president George W. Bush told Americans they needed to create more power by pumping more crude oil and thinking again about nuclear energy. President Barack Obama had authorized offshore drilling for gas and oil just before the 2010 BP disaster in the Gulf of Mexico, after which his power policy shifted more to sustainable fuels. Many scientists argued that burning more fossil fuels was environmental suicide and that nuclear power had inherent waste disposal problems that would not go away. We can only summarize the broad outline of the debate, talking about sources of supply here and environmental consequences in section 2 below.

Population is again at the heart of the problem. Per capita energy consumption has soared globally since the mid-1800s, and grown dramatically in the last half century from 0.9 megawatt hours in 1850, up to 8.2 megawatt hours in 1950, and to 17.1 megawatt hours in 2000.[48] Remember that over the same time span global population has increased by a factor of six, which makes the total increase in energy consumption even greater.

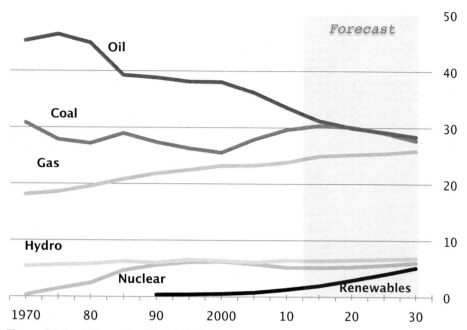

Figure 14.4. Where the World Gets Power
James Clark, data from BP Energy Outlook, http://www.bp.com/sectiongenericar-ticle800.do?categoryId=9037134&contentId=7068677.

Where the World Gets Energy

In a very approximate way, figure 14.4 provides a rough guide to our present approach to powering the planet. The largest single source is crude oil and its derivatives, closely followed by coal and the increasingly popular natural gas. These three together are commonly called fossil fuels or sometimes hydrocarbons. That 1 percent of "Other" comes from two opposite ends of the power spectrum: traditional peoples gather and burn wood, peat, or animal dung for cooking and heating, while modern "green" enthusiasts use high-tech micro-systems such as wind and solar energy. The "water" category includes hydroelectric and geothermal power as well as some very early experiments in harnessing the tides.

Nuclear energy is important but problematic. As early as the 1940s, scientists understood that a controlled nuclear reaction could heat water, producing steam that could create electrical current by powering a turbine generator. Encouraged by the U.S. government under President Eisenhower, Americans and Europeans became enthusiastic about nuclear-generated electrical power. Over one hundred plants were built in the United States, today producing about a fifth of America's electricity, while countries such as France put nuclear power at the heart of their national energy programs. There were many perceived advantages: power from the atom seemed cheap, environmentally friendly, and safe.

The presumption of safety was shattered by several accidents. In 1979, a problem at the Three Mile Island nuclear power plant sent a relatively small amount of radioactive gas hissing into the Pennsylvania countryside. In 1986, a defective nuclear power plant in the Ukrainian city of Chernobyl actually caught fire, spewing horrific amounts of radio-activity into the atmosphere over Eastern Europe and Scandinavia. Three Mile Island and Chernobyl convinced many Americans and Europeans that nuclear power plants involved unacceptable risks, despite some contrary scientific evidence.[49] In 2011, the tsunami that hit Japan and the subsequent malfunction of their Fukushima nuclear power plant and associated radiation exposure renewed public fears about this energy source and its consequences to our health.

Nuclear power, once considered the solution in Europe, is now under a moratorium in countries such as Germany. Governments and industry have never been able to solve the problem of nuclear waste either. While "irradiated" (or spent) nuclear fuel can be reprocessed for subsequent use, there is some waste left over after reprocessing, and no one has ever worked out what to do with it. Radiation from this waste remains harmful to organic life for thousands of years and can leak into the water supply or the atmosphere. Thus, if you add the as-yet-unsolved problem of waste disposal to the cost of generating nuclear power, it becomes more expensive than energy generated by the burning of fossil fuels.

While some Asian countries are still investing in nuclear power, no new nuclear power plants have been built in the United States since 1980, and many European countries are closing down the industry altogether. Environmentalists are relentlessly opposed to nuclear power, and a NIMBY ("Not in My Backyard") reaction appears wherever a waste storage site is proposed. There is very little reprocessing happening in the United States presently, and no definitive agreement on how and where long-term radioactive waste storage should take place. On the other hand, some energy specialists do argue cogently that nuclear power does not contribute to global warming or damage the biosphere and that it can somehow be made safe. Some would even argue that nuclear power is indispensable if we are ever going to wean ourselves from our environmentally punishing diet of fossil fuels such as coal, natural gas, and petroleum, but the "greens" counter that there are better ways to kick the hydrocarbon habit.

The Fossil Fuel Dilemma

At the start of the twenty-first century, most energy is still being created by the combustion of hydrocarbons. The popularity of fossil fuels has less to do with science than with economics. We normally use power either in the form of electricity or the mechanical energy generated by internal combustion engines. Cars, trains, and planes almost universally run on derivatives of crude oil, and electrical power is mostly produced by private companies who burn fossil fuels to create steam to turn electricity-generating turbines. In both the developed and developing world, society is overwhelmingly predicated on the use of fossil fuels to energize modern life, and it will be expensive to convert wholesale to some other form of energy generation. Furthermore, if you count only the specific, short-term costs of generating power—electricity, for example—fossil fuels (especially coal) are currently cheaper than any alternative power production system.

Environmentalists complain that this accounting system fails to include the **externalities** of power production, that is, the environmental costs, present and future, of burning all those hydrocarbons. The pay-at-the-pump price of gasoline, for example, does not reflect the cost of maintaining armed forces all over the world to protect crude oil supply lines. Furthermore, burning all that gasoline is increasing global warming, but we won't know the cost of fixing that environmental reality for a half century.

What is the future for fossil fuels? There is an enormous supply of unused coal, but in developed nations, the use of coal has leveled off because it is, by far, the dirtiest fuel in environmental terms, contributing massively to both global warming and atmospheric pollution. Both India and China, however, have enormous reserves of coal and rely heavily upon it; as these two countries strive for continued economic growth, they will probably ignore environmental concerns and use more coal in the future. Environmentalists Christopher Flavin and Gary Gardner report that the extensive use of coal-fired power generators in China has created an atmospheric public-health hazard.[50] Of the twenty cities globally with the worst quality air, sixteen are Chinese urban centers.

Natural gas, on the other hand, is the least polluting of the three fossil fuels. There are considerable natural gas reserves in many parts of the world, and some scholars believe that natural gas could provide a temporary bridge to some sustainable energy system in the future.[51] The Obama administration in early 2012 announced its support of fracturing, or "fracking," the shale deposits thousands of miles below the earth to release deposits of natural gas. The Marcellus Shale Deposit is noted as one of the largest natural gas deposits in the world covering West Virginia, Pennsylvania, Ohio, and New York. The question is whether this process will also leave residents with contaminated air and water. Following "fracking" for natural gas, we still have the world's dominant energy source, crude oil, and its many derivatives.

There are three limiting factors connected with our continued use of this resource:

- The Finite Resource: In a famous 1972 book called *The Limits to Growth*, a team of MIT-based globalists tried to think simultaneously about population, power, and resources. They built a computer model that forecast short-term catastrophic systems failures for the planet if we continued to breed recklessly and consume increasing amounts of natural resources. While the MIT group was dramatically wrong in most of its specific predictions, the study did drive home the essential point that some resources—such as crude oil—were nonrenewable. Their petroleum prophecies actually turned out to be self-negating in the short term, because worried oil companies promptly went out and discovered more oil. The world's known oil resources are greater today than they were in 1972, and crude oil is still relatively cheap despite spikes between 2004 and 2006, but it is now firmly fixed in our global consciousness that—if present rates of consumption continue to increase—we will start to run out of this finite resource at some point in the future, with rising oil prices and increasing scarcity of deposits.

  How soon is this liable to happen? Petroleum specialists talk pessimistically about Hubbert's Peak (named after M. King Hubbert, who accurately predicted that domestic U.S. production would peak in 1970 and decline steadily after that point). Hubbert's Peak will occur when half of all the known petroleum reserves have been consumed, after which, production will steadily decline in the face of rising demand. When we reach Hubbert's Peak depends a lot on our ability to limit our population and turn to other, more sustainable energy resources, but some scholars believe that crude production will start to decline after 2015 and begin to run out around 2050. As yet, we have nothing technologically equivalent ready to take its place.

The problem is that we need to do more than merely maintain current levels of production, but China and India (to name merely the two most dramatic examples) are going through incredible growth spurts, and both countries will be needing hugely increased oil supplies in the future. In a major study of the connection between resources and political conflict, Michael Klare concludes that the unstable Persian Gulf region will need to double production between now and 2025 to satisfy growing global demand.[52]

- The Unreliable Resource: In the 1970s, the world went through a two-phased oil shock. The 1973 Arab-Israeli War (the Yom Kippur or Ramadan War) finished with oil producers sharply reducing the amount of oil made available to the West and jacking up the price. A few years later, the shah's Tehran government tumbled out of power in oil-rich Iran, raising worries about ultimate supplies and triggering a rapid rise in price. The West reacted by reducing its energy needs and expanding its sources of supply, succeeding so well that the real price of crude today (after adjusting for inflation) is lower than it was before the 1973 war. But the 1970s left many people wondering whether the fate of civilization should forever be linked to a power source that can be switched off by some vengeful Middle Eastern potentate or attacked by terrorists.

- The Dirty Resource: Until recently, our concern had been focused on availability of petroleum, but—as we will see in section 2 below—the growing Green Movement began to attack the oil industry from a new angle, arguing that the burning of oil products (as well as other fossil fuels) was placing an unsustainable burden on the earth's atmosphere. As Seth Dunn observes:

> The salient question . . . is not whether the world will run out of oil—or fossil fuels more generally—but how much more carbon dioxide from burning these fuels can be absorbed by the atmosphere before dangerous climatic disruptions take place.[53]

At the start of the twenty-first century, some industrialists and some American politicians were claiming that we needed to drill for more oil to increase supply and keep prices down. This supply-oriented approach generally pleases those who drive big cars and SUVs. The notion offended environmentalists, however, who offered a variety of creative solutions to the energy problem that did not involve burning more fossil fuels. If we can't increase our dependence on fossil fuels, or choose not to, what will we do instead?

What We Could Do Instead

Few scholars believe that current energy policy is sustainable, but there is considerable disagreement over what path to follow into the future. Students of the issue have suggested a variety of solutions, none mutually exclusive and all capable of simultaneous implementation.

- Economize: As a direct consequence of the rapid rise in oil prices in the 1970s, the world actually made some substantial strides toward more-efficient use of energy.[54] A great deal more could be done, however, to conserve existing stocks of fossil fuels by using them more sparingly. It is generally cheaper to save energy than to generate it. We could insulate our houses better, economizing on both heating and air conditioning costs. Rather than conventional incandescent bulbs, we could use compact fluorescent bulbs that cost more to buy but less to operate, and last much longer. And we could work to reduce the amount of gasoline we consume in cars. American cars have actually grown—on average—larger and thirstier in recent years. The average American vehicle today gets 24.5 miles per gallon, a discouraging decrease from the late 1980s, when vehicles got 26.2 miles per gallon.[55] Putting higher taxes on gasoline and "Yank tanks" would force down consumption of gasoline, but elected officials would probably regard this proposal as political suicide. The development of public transportation systems (rather than individual cars) would create a substantial energy savings.

- Develop Sustainable Sources of Energy: There are too many sustainable sources of energy to review the whole field here. Hydroelectric power is normally included in the list of "clean energy" sources, although every new dam drowns forests or farmland, making the technology somewhat less friendly to the environment. Drawing on the heat of the earth's core, geothermal power is still in the experimental stage, but works well in Iceland. Solar power is among the most promising, using a photovoltaic (PH) cell to generate electrical power. Solar panels could be particularly useful in rural areas too remote to be economically attached to a national power grid. Perhaps the most promising technology is wind power; several European nations are already generating significant quantities of electricity from wind, and the price per kilowatt-hour has dropped. According to conventional accounting techniques, both solar and wind-generated electrical energy are still more expensive than is burning coal or oil to drive generators, and there has been little pressure from political leaders to revamp our global energy structure. Once we begin accounting for the externalities of oil (e.g., cost of pollution, global climate change, military involvement in the Middle East, ocean pollution from oil spills, exhaustion of a finite resource, etc.), it can be argued that wind and solar power could be significantly cheaper than oil is.

- Move toward a Hydrogen-Based Energy Economy: This is not the place to explain the science of fuel cells in any detail, but the technology exists to combine hydrogen and oxygen to produce electricity with only pure water as a "waste" product. It is possible to use fuel-cell devices either in mobile installations, such as cars and trucks, or as small, stationary power stations. The potential problem in hydrogen energy is the difficulty in creating hydrogen. You can "electrolyze" water by using electricity to split water into hydrogen and oxygen, a process that is environmentally harmless. If you use coal or oil to run generators to create the necessary electricity to make the hydrogen, however, the environmental consequences may be almost as bad as using fossil fuels directly to provide electrical power and locomotion for vehicles. In order for the technology to become totally green, we will need to create the hydrogen with sustainable energy such as wind power.

Fuel cell technology is slowly growing more popular, and Honda, Toyota, and DaimlerChrysler are experimenting with fuel-cell powered vehicles. The market for vehicles powered by fuel cells is limited by the continuing high cost of hydrogen and the lack of a distribution network. As with all new technologies, fuel-cell-driven machinery is still somewhat more expensive than are conventional internal combustion engines, but many regard it as the wave of the environmentally friendly future. Blessed with abundant sources of geothermal power, which can be used to create hydrogen, Iceland will perhaps be the first modern society to kick the hydrocarbon habit.[56]

Governments tend to be responsive to the demands of present industries rather than future ones, and the companies hiring lobbyists and making campaign contributions are the conventional automobile, oil, and fossil-fuel interests. The result is that most governments continue to give subsidies to "old" technologies rather than to new and sustainable ones. Even the World Bank continues to advocate fossil-fuel solutions to parts of the underdeveloped world where power is a problem, despite the economic and environmental advantages of sustainable energy solutions. Global figures are hard to get, but Janet Sawin estimated that governments were giving fossil fuel and nuclear power companies as much as one-quarter trillion dollars annually in subsidies, with just a pittance going to companies developing "new" and sustainable technologies.[57]

2. The Environmental Controversy

There is an inherent conflict between long-term protection of the environment and short-term economic development, particularly if financial progress is measured by crude statistics such as the gross domestic product. Burning cheap coal to generate electricity to power industry may boost the economy in the short term while it produces acid rain and contributes to global warming, which will damage the economy in the long term. Ironically, modern technology has made it possible for us to destroy nature with brisk efficiency. With advanced mining equipment, we can quite literally move mountains to extract coal, while huge mechanized trawlers vacuum fish from the ocean.

Environmentalist Lawrence Slobodkin notes that there is no serious likelihood of returning the world to the way it once was when there were fewer of us on the planet. Humankind has fundamentally altered the globe.[58] The question now is how to halt environmental deterioration and how to address the most pressing problems. This is a complex issue, with both scientific and political ramifications, and in this section, we can offer only a few prominent examples of the tension between economic growth and the protection of the environment. Let's start with the whole vexed issue of alterations in our climate, a dilemma that seems to be getting worse, before moving our attention to the ozone layer, a serious problem that is slowly finding an intelligent solution.

GLOBAL CLIMATE CHANGE

First, we need to make a distinction between old-fashioned air pollution and this new-fangled business of global **climate change**, two related but essentially different problems. Atmospheric pollution is caused when human activity spills harmful gases and particles into the air we breathe, at or near ground level. As mentioned above, power stations in most parts of the world burn fossil fuels to turn their generators, and many of them still use inexpensive coal. Over half the electricity in the United States is generated by burning coal and the percentage rises to 75 percent in China and 93 percent in South Africa.[59] The combustion of any hydrocarbon, particularly coal, puts sulfuric acid and nitric acid into the air. Automobile emissions are another source of nitric acid. Moisture in the air collects these poisons and bring them to earth in the form of **acid rain**, which sometimes falls hundreds or thousands of miles from the offending power plant.

Acid rain has decimated forests and croplands in all parts of the world. After damaging the woodlands, the poisoned rain seeps into streams, rivers, and lakes, where it increases the acidity of water, killing off fish and other marine life. When inhaled, sulfur and nitrogen oxides can cause pulmonary diseases and shorten human life.

In the Western world, smog and evil-smelling air have motivated voters to demand improved technology and more stringent legislation to improve the quality of air. In countries with responsive governments, industries have been forced to "scrub" smokestack emissions in order to reduce atmospheric pollution. Most modern automobiles now roll out of the factory equipped with catalytic converters to limit pollution from exhaust fumes. On the other hand, green activists in Europe and the United States maintain strenuously that industrial polluters are taking advantage of legal loopholes to avoid paying for the environmental externalities of business. Matters are even worse in the developing world where economic growth has always been a higher priority for people and governments. As a result, the air in some Third World cities can be hard to see through, much less inhale. India's Chennai (formerly Madras), Turkey's Ankara, and Mexico City are all good examples of beautiful cities with epically bad air. And atmospheric problems in the developing world have a way of blowing through the gardens of the rich; brown clouds from Asia eventually degrade the quality of North American and European air.

Weird Weather

The related phenomenon of what is variously called climate change (or, less accurately, "global warming") is actually quite different and more difficult to remedy. At a simplistic level, here is the relevant science: temperature stability on earth is the result of solar radiation passing through the atmosphere, warming the earth's surface, and then partially escaping back off into space. It gets cooler after sundown, but we don't freeze at night. Why? Carbon dioxide and other gases trap some of this solar energy so that the biosphere has—in the past—remained within normal temperature limits.

The gases that trap solar radiation are called "**greenhouse gases**" because they behave like the glass in a gardener's greenhouse in keeping the air inside the greenhouse artificially warm by trapping some of the sun's energy. In recent decades, however, human activity has increased the presence of greenhouse gases (particularly carbon dioxide) in the upper atmosphere, trapping more and more solar energy, and gradually increasing the temperature on the earth's surface.

Human activities (such as exhaling and burning fires) have always created some carbon dioxide, but as part of the process of photosynthesis, vegetation in the world's forests has always been able to reabsorb a roughly equivalent amount. Green plants and some other organisms produce the glucose they (and we) need to live through the process of photosynthesis. Drawing power from the sun, plants absorb and combine water and atmospheric carbon dioxide to produce chemical energy in the form of glucose and carbohydrates. Oxygen is the most important by-product of this life-sustaining operation, and trees generally do this better than any other form of green plant. Hence, even if trees provided no other benefits, we would need a lot of forest cover simply to reabsorb and recycle the CO_2 that we produce.

For most of human history, the amount of CO_2 in the atmosphere remained roughly static, which means that the amount of heat trapped on the earth's surface remained

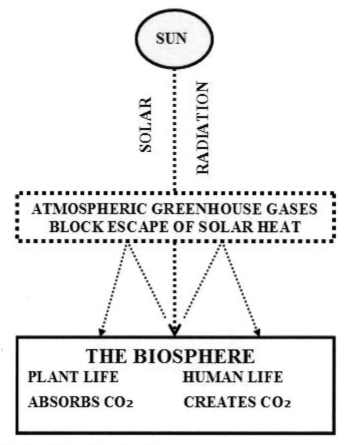

Figure 14.5. The Global Warming Phenomenon
Global warming results from putting more greenhouse gases, particularly carbon dioxide, into the atmosphere than can be absorbed by the planet's diminishing forest acreage. More solar radiation is then trapped and retained on the earth's surface, slowly but surely changing our climate.

relatively stable. By the middle of the 1800s, however, the Industrial Revolution got us hooked on hydrocarbons, which—when burned—produce carbon dioxide. The economic expansion of the twentieth century was fueled first by burning coal, later joined by natural gas and petroleum.

Over the course of the last two centuries, the carbon dioxide content of the atmosphere has increased by about 30 percent and is now at the highest point in recorded history. To make matters worse, we have been systematically slaughtering the world's forests, reducing the planet's ability to recycle carbon dioxide back into breathable oxygen, which results in the accumulation of so much CO_2 in the atmosphere that more solar energy is trapped on the earth's surface.[60] Some oil companies have argued that it is possible to "sequester" or trap some CO_2 before it filters into the atmosphere, pumping it underground or under the seabed. Environmental activists counterargue that sequestration technology does not exist, might not work, and would be more expensive than switching to sustainable sources of energy.

During the same period, human activity added other gases to the atmosphere, increasing the greenhouse effect. Methane, for example, is a component of natural gas and a by-product of the process of refining petroleum; methane also comes from the decomposing residue of rice production and from the intestinal tracts of domestic animals (such as the world's one billion cows). Nitrous oxide increased, thanks to intensive use of those nitrogen-based fertilizers mentioned above, along with some of the chlorofluorocarbons we will discuss below in connection with the ozone layer.[61]

About twenty-five years ago, scientists began noticing a slight warming trend in the oceans and the atmosphere. By the 1980s, this trend seemed to have accelerated with the melting of glaciers and the thinning of Arctic ice; the warmest years in recent human history have happened since the 1990s. In 1988, the United Nations created the Intergovernmental Panel on Climate Change (or IPCC) to coordinate and publish the basic research on the issue. A few scientists and a lot of politicians expressed doubts about the reality of global warming, but this skepticism was effectively silenced in 2001 by a report by the U.S. National Academy of Scientists (NAS).[62] Chartered by Congress but free of governmental constraints, the authoritative NAS announced that global warming was a dangerous reality with the following kinds of likely future effects.

- Gradual Temperature Rise: The earth's surface is between 0.5 percent and 1.25 percent warmer today than it was a century ago. How much warmer the future will be depends on how energetically we deal with the problem in the next few decades. A minimalist prediction from the National Academy of Scientists suggests another 2.5 degrees Fahrenheit hike by the end of the twenty-first century, but that number could rise as high as 10.4 degrees if we take no serious steps toward limiting carbon dioxide emissions. It doesn't take much of a change in global temperature to alter the human environment in a radical way; during the last ice age, the world was only a few degrees colder than it is today. A continued temperature rise will disrupt present patterns of plant and animal life in unpredictable ways, and may exacerbate the shortage of freshwater. A toastier climate will also make the world a friendlier place for mosquitoes, ticks, rats, and other disease-bearing critters. Malaria, still a major scourge of the tropics, could migrate north as rising temperatures make the Temperate Zone less temperate.
- Rising Sea Levels: Much of the world's existing freshwater is trapped in ice, and rising temperatures will melt glaciers and polar ice, raising general oceanic levels and flooding shorelines around the world. Some scholars have forecast a twenty-inch rise by 2050, which would put much beachfront property under water. Catastrophists have produced much larger estimates, arguing that some very large Pacific island countries could disappear altogether while impoverished South Asian societies such as Bangladesh could lose almost all of their agricultural land to an intrusive sea. Florida's Everglades could disappear completely. Rising sea levels might also decrease the amount of freshwater available, since salt water would invade and salinate freshwater coastal aquifers.
- Climate Instability: A generally warmer world seems destined to have more extreme weather, with bigger and more frequent storms, cyclones, and hurricanes, freakish cold snaps in the winter and blistering drought in the summer. The last years of the 1900s

and the first half of this decade have been characterized globally by strange distortions in normal weather patterns. Southern Europe, South Asia, and Southeast Asia have all been hit by heat waves so extreme that children and elderly people died of heat stroke and dehydration. At the same time, the mercury broke records going down in some frigid portions of northern Europe. For several decades now, rainfall in east Africa has been unreliable, and droughts have made agriculture untenable for tens of millions of Eritreans, Somalis, and Ethiopians.

THE POLITICS OF CLIMATE CHANGE

In order to give global focus to a wide range of environmental issues, the United Nations convened the 1992 Rio Conference on Environment and Development (UNCED) described above. Perhaps the most significant result of UNCED was a Framework Convention on Climate Change.

Unfortunately, this Convention on Climate Change relied upon a program of voluntary reductions in carbon dioxide emissions that utterly failed to materialize in the years following the Earth Summit. In order to put some teeth in the convention, thirty-eight leading industrialized countries met five years later in the Japanese city of Kyoto. The result was what diplomats call a **protocol**, a multilateral treaty intended to expand or provide an enforcement mechanism for an earlier treaty. In what became known as the Kyoto Protocol, signatories tentatively agreed to reduce their greenhouse emissions to at least 5 percent below their 1990 levels. The countries of the former Soviet Union and less-developed countries generally were allowed more time to comply.

Despite the fact that the United States is the second-largest producer of total greenhouse gas emissions, the American government refused to ratify Kyoto, arguing that the treaty allowed poorer countries more time for compliance. A resentful Third World counterargued that high HDI countries such as the United States had filled the sky with carbon dioxide, not them, and their fragile economies could not go "cold turkey" where cheap fossil fuels were concerned. The U.S. decision to reject Kyoto continues to be a source of sore feelings within other industrialized countries that are still prepared to make sacrifices to achieve Kyoto's goals.

As you can see in table 14.1, the United States is a massive producer of greenhouse gas emissions, rivaled now by China. Despite U.S. hostility, Kyoto entered into force

Table 14.1.   World Carbon Emissions in Tons

Rank	Country	Tons (millions)	Per Capita
1	China	7,710.50	5.83
2	U.S.	5,424.53	17.67
3	India	1,602.12	1.38
4	Russia	1,572.07	11.23
14	Brazil	420.16	2.11
77	Ecuador	28.71	1.97
152	Uganda	1.93	0.06

Source: The International Energy Agency (U.S. EIA), http://www.eia.gov/iea/carbon.html.

February 16, 2005, although it legally binds only the countries that have signed it, and not the United States. Note that Europe and North America have decreased their overall emissions, while Asia (particularly China and India) and the Middle East have increased their emissions. Some, such as author Bill McKibben, argue that the planet cannot even be called "earth" anymore. He refers to it in his latest book as *Eaarth*.[63] If we all continue our carbon-bloated trend, some fear that the planet will be irreversibly affected.

The scientific community, meanwhile, became increasingly convinced that global climate change was a dangerous reality. The UN's Intergovernmental Panel on Climate Change's *Climate Change 2001 Synthesis Report* asserted that the combustion of fossil fuels needed to be sharply reduced if the world was to avoid catastrophic alterations in weather patterns.[64] Fossil-fuel producers swing a big bat when it comes to political contributions, however, and the oil companies have worked hard to persuade the public that global warming is just an unproven theory that does not require an immediate response. Former president Clinton periodically talked about the problem, but sidestepped a brawl with the fossil-fuel industry and never pushed the Kyoto Protocol. Moving into the White House in 2001, George W. Bush unilaterally declared that the Kyoto Protocol was dead because it would harm American prosperity. In 2001, Vice President Dick Cheney and other senior members of the U.S. government produced a *Report of the National Energy Policy Development Group*, which concluded that America had no option but to find and exploit new resources of coal, natural gas, and crude oil.[65]

Whatever their private convictions, other politicians apparently preferred to avoid explaining to an uncomprehending public why we might need to sacrifice billions of dollars to fix something that might not become a serious problem for another generation and might already be unstoppable.[66] As an environmentalist, Al Gore did a lot to publicize the danger of global warming in his 1992 book *Earth in the Balance* (Boston: Houghton Mifflin).[67] As vice president, he was a driving force behind the Kyoto Protocol, but Gore's defeat in 2000 may have convinced other politicians that the issue was a vote loser.

The Obama administration took strides to lead the United States in the UNFCCC climate change talks in Copenhagen, Cancun, and Durban without much success. While a $100 billion mega-fund for adaptation to and mitigation of climate change impacts was formed by the developed world for developing countries, no new framework for climate change has been established. Countries cannot agree on carbon emission levels, whether the North and the South (developed and developing countries) should have differing standards, or how the world should subsume the economic costs for such a drastic change in our carbon diets. We currently have the European Union Emissions Trading Scheme (EU ETS) formed in response to the Kyoto Protocol, which trades carbon emissions. It allows those European firms that keep their carbon emissions under their quotas to trade what is left to those firms that have overproduced. It's a complicated system that puts a price on carbon, and the jury is still out on whether it has been effective at lowering carbon emissions and should be continued beyond 2012.

While it seems that the world agreed in 2011 at the UNFCCC meeting in Durban, South Africa, to lower carbon emissions, and, to the delight of the United States, China and emerging market countries agreed to join a future treaty. Canada—once a leader in climate change—removed itself from the Kyoto Protocol. Is this treaty dead in the water if industrialized nations such as the United States and Canada haven't signed on? What will a future post-Kyoto treaty look like?

Does the dilemma of the Kyoto Protocol mean that the world is incapable of dealing prudently and effectively with an environmental challenge? Maybe, but before proceeding with more global doom and gloom, let us glance briefly at the planetary response to the ozone crisis.

ORGANIZING THE OZONE

The ongoing saga of the ozone layer is a good rebuttal to the charge that international law never works and the world community is too anarchic to cooperate for the common good.

To understand what went wrong and how the UN took the lead in putting it right, let's be scientific for a moment and describe the stratospheric ozone layer or ozonosphere, which begins about six miles above the earth's surface and extends to about thirty miles up. This layer of air contains a quantity of what is called stratospheric ozone (O_3), which is a variant of the normal oxygen molecule (O_2) but has an extra atom. The function of this ozone is to absorb some of the ultraviolet (UV) radiation emitted by the sun; a little UV helps our bodies generate vitamin D; too much of it, particularly UV-B, causes skin cancer such as the frequently fatal malignant melanoma, plus immune-deficiency problems, cataracts, and genetic mutations. It may also be killing off oceanic plankton, tiny organisms that form the base of the food chain.

In the 1980s, scientists realized that the ozone layer had grown very thin, particularly over the South Pole. The incidence of skin cancer had been rising quickly, and the scientific community discovered that we had been emitting gases and industrial substances capable of destroying stratospheric ozone. The leading culprit was a class of chemicals with the formidable title of chlorofluorocarbons (CFCs), which are also greenhouse gases. Used in air-conditioning systems and refrigerators, solvents and aerosol sprays, fire extinguishers and insulating material, CFCs had a very wide range of industrial uses, but when they escape in a gaseous form, they make their way quickly to the stratosphere where they neutralize ozone. Other "ozone-killers" are the nitrous oxides that emanate from fertilizer, and methyl bromide, a common pesticide. To make matters worse, all these gases also have a greenhouse effect and thus contribute to global warming.

Alarmed, the United Nations Environment Programme (UNEP) convened interested countries in Vienna in 1985, where they created the Convention for the Protection of the Ozone Layer, committing themselves to investigate the crisis and to do something about it.[68] That winter, a cavernous hole in Antarctica's ozone cap was discovered, and evidence mounted that CFCs were to blame. In September of 1987, all the leading producers of CFCs (including the United States) signed the Montreal Protocol on Substances That Deplete the Ozone Layer.[69] Now ratified by virtually every country in the world, the protocol created an international secretariat to monitor compliance and plan subsequent meetings every few years for renegotiations.

No one anticipated that the Montreal Protocol would be a quick fix. Actual emissions of CFCs and other ozone eaters have declined dramatically, but an enormous amount of stratospheric pollution had already happened, and CFCs are still munching ozone, albeit more slowly than before.[70] While the scientific community is confident that long-term news will be good, NASA estimates that it will be 2020 before things stop getting worse

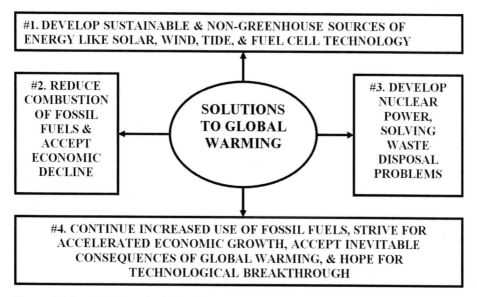

Figure 14.6. Solutions to Global Warming
None of these are easy choices or happy ones. Environmental purists would opt for a combination of #1 and #2, and shudder at #3. Commercial forces and inertia are driving us toward option #4.

and start getting better, and roughly 2050 before the ozone layer returns to normal. One complication is the brisk illegal CFC trade, mostly from China and India, to satisfy the needs of people with older automobiles and refrigerators.

Why did Montreal work when Kyoto didn't, or at least hasn't thus far? The Kyoto Protocol on Global Warming was based on science that is now broadly accepted by the scientific community but was controversial at first and is still not easily understood by the general public. Kyoto demanded that extraordinarily powerful economic interests take a huge financial hit to repair climate problems that have just begun to appear and will not become severe for an indeterminate amount of time. While responsible for about a quarter of the problem, Americans were reluctant to make financial and lifestyle sacrifices in order to be part of the solution.

In contrast, the conclusions reached at Montreal's Ozone Conference were based on fairly simple science about which there never really was much controversy. Replacing all those CFCs with ozone-friendly chemicals has been moderately expensive, but (unlike those potent petroleum people) the refrigerator industry couldn't swing a presidential election. Furthermore, the problem affected the wealthy in a particular way. People of European ancestry are in a high-risk category, and sun-loving Australians have the highest skin-cancer rates in the world. Malignant melanoma is a particular hazard for people with the money and the leisure to enjoy golf, tennis, sunbathing, and sailing. To preserve their safe suntans, Americans signed on enthusiastically, told the U.S. Environmental Protection Agency to hunt down CFC smugglers, and helped persuade the developing world that cooperation was in their long-term interest. Ultimately, the bill for this clear and present danger was manageable, and the time frame was reasonable.

3. Thinking Globally about the Globe

One of the great surprises at the end of World War II was the number of people who had managed to survive German concentration camps. Some of these "die-hards" later described a life of sleeping on crowded cement floors, getting no medical attention, and eating stale bread and watery soup once a day. Millions had perished before liberation came in 1945, but some of the survivors were in reasonable health, albeit psychologically traumatized and physically emaciated.

The concentration camp experience poses some fundamental questions. Given all the facts and all the speculation presented thus far in this chapter, what kind of lifestyle do we envision for humankind in the year 2050? If we are content to live like Dachau prisoners, the planet can support a great many of us, although we're not going to enjoy the loss of liberty or being crammed into limited space on a diet of mice and insects. If we all want to be rich, free, and well fed, then the desired top population number drops dramatically. Or can those who live in the very high HDI countries of North America and Europe arrange to go on living in Disneyland, while the rest of the world dwells in Dachau?

In this context, it's worth remembering that the conflict over future population keeps coming back to an argument about the unequal distribution of resources. From the perspective of the United States, there are too many Pakistanis, and the reckless Pakistani birthrate is fueling religious fanaticism, political instability, and poverty in South Asia.

From the perspective of Pakistan, however, there are too many Americans. Although the United States has less than 5 percent of the world's population, U.S. citizens consume approximately 25 percent of global resources and create about one-fourth of the planet's waste and pollution.[71] The American national obsession with buying, consuming, and throwing away is robbing the world of precious resources and filling the atmosphere with climate-changing pollutants.

Is there any serious likelihood that the world's economies will be less unequal in 2050? If the high HDI societies are not disposed to become any poorer, is there any chance that the low and middle HDI world will become significantly richer? While some progress is both urgently needed and possible, no one believes that the world's economy can be restructured to bring Asian, Latin Americans, and Africans up to the standard of living enjoyed by the people of the high HDI world.

Even vague and conditional answers to this kind of conundrum dictate some policy choices for us as voters and for our political leaders. Do we focus on a decrease in global population? A decrease in individual consumption and prosperity? A better distribution of the world's resources? Or all three?

VISIONS OF THE FUTURE

As we have seen, predictions about future population growth have tended to be wrong, either frighteningly too high or comfortingly too low, but wrong in either case. If you check back at chapter 13, you can see there is a 3.2 billion gap between the UN's highest and lowest estimates of global population in 2050, a date only forty years in the future.

This 3.4 billion-person question mark reflects a serious disagreement among scholars and demographers about how high the population will go and consequently what level of resources and environmental pollution will be involved. Scholars can generally be divided into two groups. There are optimistic Cornucopians, who feel that existing resources will satisfy the needs of a population that will soon level off. A "cornucopia" is a goat's horn filled with food, a Greek symbol of prosperity. On the other side, we have pessimistic Cassandras, who fear continuing high birthrates will overwhelm the earth's resources. In Greek mythology, Cassandra was a female prophet of doom with some strong reservations about that Trojan Horse the Greeks had left outside the city gates during the Trojan War. Cassandras are sometimes called "Catastrophists" and sometimes "neo-Malthusians" because of their belief that Malthus will turn out to be have been right in his pessimistic prediction that overpopulation will doom humankind.

The Cassandras

The first and most famous Cassandra was a dour English clergyman named Thomas Malthus, the author in 1798 of an *Essay on the Principle of Population.*[72] Noting that resources only increase arithmetically while unchecked population grows exponentially, Malthus famously predicted that the human race would eventually breed itself into starvation. Malthus disapproved of birth control, doubted that the working classes were capable of sexual self-restraint, and opposed what we would today call welfare because it would allow people to "get away" with having children they could not support, making the population situation even worse for the next generation.

Modern neo-Malthusian Cassandras worry about the economic and social consequences of continued rapid population growth, fearing that we will stabilize at a population far in excess of what the planet can support. Contemporary neo-Malthusian thinking became famous thanks to the work of two Stanford University biologists working in the 1960s. Garret Hardin's famous essay, "The Tragedy of the Commons" (1968), and Paul Ehrlich's *The Population Explosion* (1968) both mixed Malthusian pessimism with the more contemporary concern that rapid population growth was destroying the environment.[73]

Even if we manage to feed a lot of extra people, some Cassandras have argued that population density will make human civilization more brutal and violent. Researchers often point to a landmark 1962 study involving the deliberate overcrowding of mice. When the mouse population in a restricted environment became too large, mother mice stopped caring for their young, and the males spent almost all their time fighting even though there was enough food.[74] Others have maintained that overpopulation and crowding produce, ironically, loneliness and alienation because the more of us there are, the less we seem able to connect with one another. Looking at life in the United States, author Robert D. Putnam wrote the highly acclaimed *Bowling Alone* in which he described a crowded and lonely society where social networks had broken down, leaving us to do alone the things we once did together.[75] Based on his extensive field studies, author Robert D. Kaplan predicts that overpopulation is helping to destroy the social fabric of the planet.[76]

In the United States, the Washington-based Worldwatch Institute specializes in establishing the intellectual linkage among politics, environmental studies, and demography. In addition to producing extraordinarily useful topical studies, Worldwatch provides a home to a group of moderate Cassandras. In a Worldwatch study entitled *Beyond Malthus,* Lester Brown made the following case:

- The number of people the world can support is a function of the resources available to support those people. Brown argues that Malthus has already been proven substantively right because in important parts of the world, the population already exceeds locally available food, land, freshwater, and financial support.
- This situation will worsen because population growth is not slowing fast enough to counter the "avalanche effect" of too many women having babies. They maintain that even the UN's "most probable" medium variant scenario would see a global expansion from our current 7.0 billion to 8.9 billion in forty-four years, growth destined to occur mostly in already poverty-stricken countries. Hence, we are not just getting 2.6 billion new people, but 2.6 billion very poor people.
- This population surge, Brown argued, will become the primary global problem for the twenty-first century, causing human misery, increased levels of regional undernutrition, political instability, and a devastating burden on the environment. Cassandras put relatively little confidence in future technological developments. Clearly, there have been scientific advances in the past (such as the miracle grains of the 1960s and 1970s and the more recent genetic modification technology) that made an enormous difference to the quality of many lives. But our Cassandras want us to get global population under control first, and then enjoy future technological successes, if and when they occur. Furthermore, they note that most cutting-edge high-tech developments have merely enhanced the lives of already comfortable people. It is difficult to use many new technologies to the benefit of the world's poorest citizens; modern corporations have little incentive to develop products for the penniless.[77]

The early Cassandras came from the field of biology and were familiar with nature's grim "overshoot and die-back" syndrome. A given species will take advantage of a temporary change or improvement in its living environment to "overshoot," breeding beyond the normal carrying capacity of its ecological home. When conditions change, deteriorate, or simply return to normal, the species goes into "die-back" with a sudden increase in mortality, until its numbers are once again in harmony with the carrying capacity of the environment.[78] Cassandras worry that medical modernization has provided a change in the human living environment that has encouraged us to overshoot the carrying capacity of the planet. They believe that a massive die-back will be nature's inflexible punishment.

The Cornucopians

Most academics and nearly all political liberals worry about these forceful Cassandra arguments, but there are a few professors and quite a few pundits who would qualify as Cornucopians, believing that population pressure can be managed and even reversed. The Cornucopian prophet was the late Julian Simon, who argued that the resources available to an expanding population were greater than anyone realized, and human creativity would generate answers to the resource dilemmas of the future.[79] Cornucopians tend to come from the more conservative side of the political spectrum and their arguments are roughly as follows:

- Malthus was wrong because food production has always outdistanced population. If there are people starving today, it's because they lack the money to buy available food. The problem is therefore economics, not fertility, and economics can be fixed. Food is actually cheaper today than in the past, a sure sign that there is no global shortage.
- The population explosion is almost over because demographic transition will soon work in the poorer sections of the world as it has in the developed world. The PC/GDP is rising almost everywhere, and we know from experience that it only takes modest increases in income to produce surprisingly large drops in fertility. While the African total fertility rate is not declining as far or as fast as might be desired, it is undeniably coming down, which suggests that conditions will eventually improve in the most desolate of the world's continents.
- By 2050, Cornucopians argue, we may even see the beginnings of population decline. They argue that there is nothing about demographic transition theory that makes zero population growth a natural resting place. When people have enough money, babies will be the result of love and accidents, not economics. The fertility rate will drop below that magic replacement level of 2.1, and negative population growth (NPG) will send the world's population sliding downward.

Who is right? In a disagreement like this, there is a tendency to assume that the correct answer is somewhere in the middle, an intellectual halfway point between Cassandras and Cornucopians. But the future is a tough neighborhood; in reality, one side could be almost completely right and the other mostly wrong. If the Cornucopians win the argument historically, then things will be fine, but if the Cassandras are even remotely on target, then the world is headed for some serious misery. Perhaps it would be prudent for us to assume that the existing imbalance between resources and people is going to get worse, and start thinking seriously about controlling population and using resources sustainably. If the Cornucopians turn out to be right, we will have improved our habitat. If the Cassandras are correct in their grim forecast, we can perhaps mitigate the worst of the crisis by beginning to address the problem now.[80]

The word "sustainability" has become the mantra of the Green Movement in recent years. An economic system is said to be sustainable if it replaces resources at the same rate it consumes them. Sustainability means supporting ourselves in ways that deny neither our neighbors nor our descendents the ability to support themselves. In recent years, Columbia University has joined forces with the World Economic Forum to create the environmental sustainability index (ESI), which rates the countries of the world on the basis of their ability to combine human development with sound resource management.[81]

THE ENVIRONMENTAL CONTROVERSY: THE DATA

The lead agency for the United States is the Environmental Protection Agency (at www .epa.gov), which is supposed to enforce complicated U.S. statute law. At the international level, the UN's green focus is led by the UN Environment Programme or UNEP, which maintains a useful site at www.unep.org. Not to be outdone, the European Union has its own European Environment Agency with a website at www.eea.eu.int. Described in both chapters 13 and 14, the sometimes-gloomy Worldwatch Institute (www.worldwatch.org) is a research institute financed by charitable contributions and dedicated to the holistic study of the planet's ecosystems. This site not only contains a wealth of information but also offers links to other similar organizations. The Natural Resources Defense Council website (www.nrdc.org) is always timely and interesting.

CONCLUSIONS AND REFLECTIONS

If scholars take the environment seriously, why do politicians spend so little time talking about it? The answer is partly related to the fact that neither side in a conventional Western two-party system has much electoral interest in asking the kind of questions posed in this chapter. For example, most democratic political systems have at least one right-of-center political party representing generally wealthier people and commercial interests. Paying the bill for rectifying environmental damage would fall mostly on the shoulders of their constituents, who may feel that their short-term financial interests are best served by leaving environmental questions to some future generation.

There will typically also be a left-of-center party representing labor union members, farm workers, minorities, and poor people generally. The task of creating high-paying and stable jobs might be perceived by these liberals as more important than preserving nature, or worrying that low-lying Pacific islands might be swamped by rising ocean levels. At least in the short term, it is not necessarily in the interests of sheep and cattle farmers to worry about the dwindling population of grey wolves. From loggers to carpenters, people who depend upon large quantities of timber want inexpensive supplies of wood and may not be able to afford to lament the disappearance of exotic birds that once lived in pristine forests. And the poorer people are, the less time and energy they have to worry about the environment. As Joel Cohen commented trenchantly, "Those who want firewood to cook a meal today will break branches from the last tree standing if they believe that otherwise their children may not survive to lament the absence of trees 20 years hence."[82]

The essence of democracy, furthermore, is frequent elections, and politicians have only a few years to serve before again facing the judgment of the voting public. Many environmental problems are slow to grow and even slower to put right, and a member of the U.S. Congress or the Japanese Diet or the Italian Chamber of Deputies might be tempted to focus on dramatic and popular issues that are capable of a "quick fix."

Consequently, democracies routinely produce governments that are relatively indifferent to the problems of the environment. In nondemocratic regimes, the situation is even more catastrophic, because less-free societies will often be administered by corrupt politicians who are looting their country's common property. Dictators have little time for environmental concerns and will quickly silence a green activist.

This tends to leave concern for the natural world largely in the hands of tiny green parties, NGOs, and civil society groups such as the Sierra Club and Greenpeace.[83] Universities are meant to go where politicians fear to tread, but the academic world sometimes has difficulties in tackling the big environmental issues. Increasingly, the academic world has fragmented the world's knowledge along the organizational lines of their departments: conventional political life belongs to the PoliSci Department, while population growth is deeded to the sociologists. The biologists "own" biodiversity and global climate change, but only the economists over in the School of Business know anything about fossil fuels. In the real world, all these problems all have an environmental core, although it may be tough to find a professor who can explain the interconnectedness of it all.

What We're Going to Need

Since politics is the business of deciding who gets what, when, and how much, we have spent some time in this chapter in deciding what we need now, and what we will have to have in the future. Table 14.2 is an attempt to summarize these currently unmet needs. Bear in mind that the majority of the world's current inhabitants come nowhere near meeting these requirements; a fully resourced world is still a work in progress.

Clearly, we are going to need more food as our numbers increase. We currently have an average global supply of about twenty-eight hundred calories per person per day, and something like three thousand calories per person per day would provide a better safety net. Producing the raw global quantity of food is likely to be less of a technical challenge than actually organizing its distribution to those who are currently trying to survive on much less. Consequently, the gross total food production of the planet needs to be increased, and—if we really care about feeding everyone—we will probably need to move toward more fruits and vegetables and less meat in our diets.

Our future food supplies are contingent upon achieving sustainability in our consumption of water. Estimates vary, but it is probably safe to assume that we need something like twenty liters of water per person per day for personal use, and perhaps ten times that amount for agriculture and industry. If the population continues to increase and we continue to waste water, this may be difficult to achieve.

Table 14.2. Minimum Basic Human Needs

1. Nutrition:	Three thousand calories a day, plus essential vitamins, minerals, and other nutrients.
2. Water:	Twenty liters a day of clean water for personal consumption, plus about two hundred liters for agriculture, industry, and sewage systems.
3. Energy:	One thousand kilowatt-hours per person per year in energy consumption, providing enough power for minimal household use and shared public transportation.
4. Material Services:	Adequate housing, furniture, paper, clothing.
5. Social Services:	Health care, education, welfare, physical security from war and criminality, emergency disaster relief, etc.
6. Prosperity:	$10,000 PC/GDP in real 2005 dollars adapted for purchasing power parity.
7. Non-material Needs:	Personal and political freedom, education, cultural opportunities (such as orchestras, libraries, Internet facilities), human space (uncrowded living areas, access to nature, forests, parks, waterways).

As discussed above, our energy needs will also be difficult to satisfy. As we saw in section 2 above, we not only need to generate more power, but we will also need to power the planet in ways that do not destroy its environment. This will call for a wholesale shift to sustainable energy resources within a generation, a trend that is only slowly beginning.

We have not discussed in detail all our future physical needs, but it should be clear that even a modest population growth will strain our existing supplies of material resources, elements such as timber and minerals.

As table 14.2 suggests, furthermore, we are going to need some interrelated things discussed in earlier chapters. If governments are going to be responsive to human needs, there must be true popular sovereignty in society. In practice, that means that even those who live in democracies cannot rest on the assumption that they have the best possible form of government. Even in advanced Western democracies, commercial interests can sometimes persuade elected officials to act in their interests rather than in the common social good. In the "social services" section of table 14.2, we see that people really do need health care, education, protection, and assistance when disaster strikes. All over the world, we find governments spending vast amounts of the people's money on things that have little to do with the welfare of the citizenry. Can a better-educated citizenry rethink its priorities and force their governments to act accordingly?

And finally, of course, we need money, which means that economic development needs to continue, particularly in the medium and low HDI portions of the planet. The assumption in table 14.2 that a global per capita GDP of ten thousand real dollars would do is a wild guess and nothing more, but the very poor 2.4 billion people on the planet need to have a few more pennies in their pockets or those who live in the high HDI world will never be able to relax and enjoy being economically comfortable.

Throughout this book, we have made the case that the world is interconnected, with no firm frontier between the political universe and the everyday world in which we live. Decisions we make at the polling booth affect the kind of politicians we choose to represent us, and their decisions about poverty, population, and the consumption of resources will have profound implications for our own lives as well as for future generations. In his prophetic 1968 "Tragedy of the Commons" essay, Garrett Hardin distinguished between problems that had technical or scientific solutions, and those that did not. As we look at the interrelated issues of controlling population growth, increasing global prosperity, limiting damage to the environment, and deploying the world's resources intelligently, we find that these are only scientific and technical problems up to a point, after which they become exquisitely political. Since they are not exclusively technical problems, we cannot sit back and wait for technicians to solve them. Political problems in an increasingly democratized world need to be addressed by citizens and voters using the political process. And doing nothing is not an option, since—as Hardin observed—even nonaction is a kind of choice because important consequences also flow from maintaining the status quo.

Tough Choices: Your Role in the Future

On top of being well fed, clothed, and housed, we need to be happy, and chapter 12 noted that happiness is best assured by making people secure, rather than rich. It is not for a couple of professors to suggest what is likely to make you happy. Speaking for ourselves, we like theaters, libraries, and access to nature in the form of forests and rivers. What makes you happy? What do you want that you haven't got? Do you want politicians to make the decision for you? How can you make the political system give you what you want?

Voters in democratic societies have crucial decisions to make about how the future is going to be structured, and people who live in powerful countries get to make some decisions that affect weaker countries around the world. Readers of this text are probably residents of a high HDI country, and while there will be challenges in your future, you are unlikely to go hungry or thirsty for any extended period of your lives. On the other hand, we have learned that about 35 percent of the world's population lives on less than $2 a day and experiences chronic food insecurity.

For a moment, stop and ask yourself how you feel about that level of global deprivation. Maybe you think we ought to do more, and what we do, we should do more effectively, but in the 2008 presidential election campaign, neither party clamored for more aid to the underdeveloped world. Neither presidential candidate thought they could win votes by advocating that America feed a hungry planet. But we're talking about you. Are you comfortable being comfortable in an uncomfortable world? Or are you one of the people analyst Steven Radelet was describing when he commented, "Poverty and inequality around the world simply run counter to the values of many Americans who believe that the widening income gap and high levels of absolute poverty in poor countries are morally unacceptable."[84]

And you don't have to be a passive witness to the future, because you can be involved in shaping the planet you will bequeath to your children and grandchildren. To react creatively to these challenges over the decades to come, we will all need to start thinking "out of the box," breaking down disciplinary frontiers, trying to understand and interrelate what we know about foreign policy and economy and economics and engineering and comparative religion and environmental science. All this will be hard to do, but it needs to be done if you expect to make a difference. We've spent a lot of time speculating on what the world will be like in 2050, and—as we mentioned in the introduction—by 2050, you're probably going to be in your sixties. In what kind of world do you want to grow old? What can you do in the meantime to shape your destiny and the planet that you will leave to your children and grandchildren? Some things are beyond our control, but there is a great deal we can do right now.

And—trust us on this—forty years will go by in a hurry, so you don't have as much time as you think. Get busy.

4. The Wrap: What Have We Learned?

This has been a wide-ranging and detailed chapter, and we've attempted to mingle politics with a series of questions about present and future resources. In section 1, we addressed the whole vexed question of global food supplies, looking at factors such as the loss of land to erosion and pollution, some of the controversies surrounding aquaculture or fish farming, as well as the epic battle over genetically modified plants and animals.

We need more than food to sustain modern life, however, and we also addressed a series of questions involving the kinds of resources we need now and will need more of in the future: water, forest cover, and biodiversity. There are a lot of serious issues involving the energy supply, and we took a quick look at both the supply and the environmental problems surrounding continued use of fossil fuels such as coal, oil, and natural gas.

Inevitably, a lot of people means a lot of pollution and environmental damage, and in section 2, we looked at the biggest environmental issue of them all, the question of global climate change, and speculated on what the weather reports will be like in 2050. The political universe has thus far been unable or unwilling to react coherently to the threat of global warming, but the international community showed that it was capable of responding to an environmental threat when faced with the breakup of the ozone layer. In this connection, we reviewed the Montreal Protocol, and the prospects that the world's stratospheric ozone might be back to normal by 2050.

Sometimes, political scientists can come up with accurate answers, but often it's tough enough just to ask the right questions. When looking into even the near future, the forty-four years between now and the mid-century mark, we tried in section 3 to identify at least what the critical decisions are going to be when dealing with population increase, the exhaustion of raw materials, the effects of environmental destruction, and the unknowable impact of developing technologies.

What's next? This is only the beginning, really, for your journey. Hopefully, by the end of this book, you've discovered that the world may be complicated, but there is room for cooperation and innovative norms and new ideas. It's fitting, and intentional, that we end the book with an in-depth look at our biosphere. In fact, "whole earth politics" might more aptly describe the global challenges that face not just nation-states and their quest for power, but the planet on which we live together as a global community and the resources we share. In each chapter, we emphasized the human struggle for freedom on a small planet with finite resources. Our hope is that you take the tools that you've learned here and apply them to your daily lives—maybe read the world section of the paper and think hard about the way you vote for both local and global issues—and see their connections, and visit your local recycle center. Beyond that small application, the sky's the limit.

Notes

1. Lewis Carroll, *Alice's Adventures in Wonderland* (Boston: Lee and Shepard, 1869), 95.
2. Garrett Hardin, "The Tragedy of the Commons," *Science* 162 (1968): 1243–48.
3. UN Food and Agriculture Organization, www.fao.org.

4. World Resources Institute, *World Resources 2002–2004: Decisions for the Earth: Balance, Voice, and Power* (Washington, D.C.: World Resources Institute, 2003); Worldwatch Institute, *Vital Signs 2003: The Trends That Are Shaping Our Future* (UK: Earthscan Publications Ltd., 2003), 28–29.

5. Gary Gardner and Brian Halweil, "The Overfed and Underfed: Escaping Hunger, Escaping Excess," *World Watch* 13, no. 4 (2000): 25–35.

6. Food and Agriculture Organization (FAO), *The State of Food Insecurity 2003* (Rome, Italy: United Nations Food and Agriculture Organization, 2003); the World Food Programme, www.wfp.org.

7. Vaclav Smil, *Feeding the World: A Challenge for the Twenty-First Century* (Cambridge, Mass.: MIT Press, 2000), 13.

8. Worldwatch Institute, *Vital Signs 2003: The Trends That Are Shaping Our Future*, 28; World Health Organization (WHO), Nutrition Facts, *http://www.who.int/nutrition/topics/3_foodconsumption/en/index6.html*.

9. Caroline Henshaw, "World Food Prices Remain High," *The Wall Street Journal*, May 22, 2011, http://online.wsj.com/article/SB10001424052748703859304576304932662054022.html.

10. Rhett Butler, "Deforestation in the Amazon," Mongabay Environmental News Service, accessed July 10, 2010,, http://www.mongabay.com/brazil.html.

11. World Bank, *World Development Indicators 2003* (Washington, D.C.: World Bank, 2003), 128.

12. Lester R. Brown, *Eco-Economy: Building an Economy for the Future* (New York: Norton, 2001), 60–62.

13. James Gasana, "Remember Rwanda?" *World Watch* 15, no. 2 (2002): 24–33.

14. Wangari Maathai, "Trees for Democracy," *The New York Times*, December 10, 2004, http://www.nytimes.com/2004/12/10/opinion/10maathai.html.

15. Brian Halweil, and Danielle Nierenberg, "Watching What We Eat," in Worldwatch Institute, *State of the World 2004* (New York: Worldwatch Institute/Norton 2004), 70.

16. A. D. Rogers, and D. d'A. Laffoley, "International Earth System Expert Workshop on Ocean Stresses and Impacts," IPSO Oxford, 2011, http://www.stateoftheocean.org/ipso-2011-workshop-summary.cfm.

17. Janet L. Sawin, "Making Better Energy Choices," in Worldwatch Institute, *State of the World 2004* (New York: Worldwatch Institute/Norton, 2004), 29.

18. Rogers and Laffoley, "International Earth System Expert Workshop on Ocean Stresses and Impacts"; John C. Ryan, "Feedlots of the Sea." *World Watch* 16, no. 5 (2003): 22–29.

19. The Aquaculture Network Information Center (www.aquanic.org) is maintained by a consortium of American universities and is the authoritative place to start thinking fish; for an up-to-date expert analysis of this issue, see Beth De Sombre and J. Samuel Barkin, *Fish* (New York: Polity Books, 2011).

20. Robert Paarlberg, "The Global Food Fight," *Foreign Affairs* 79, no. 3 (2000): 21–25; Brian Halweil, "The Emperor's New Crops," *World Watch* 12, no. 6 (1999): 21–29.

21. For more information, see the World Health Organization site at http://www.who.int/foodsafety/publications/biotech/20questions/en/; Paarlberg, "The Global Food Fight," 28.

22. The World Trade Organization, www.wto.org.

23. Brian Halweil, "Biotech, African Corn, and the Vampire Weed," *World Watch* 14, no. 5 (2001): 26–31.

24. Nobody agrees with anybody else where GM is concerned. If you want to be convinced, go to Monsanto's BioTech Knowledge Center at www.biotechknowledge.com and learn to love Frankenfood. GeneWatch at http://www.genewatch.org is critical of the big-business aspects of GM, but their reporting is balanced and informed.

25. See more on Vandana Shiva at www.vandanashiva.org.

26. Already famous for her *Stolen Harvest: The Hijacking of the Global Food Supply*, (Cambridge, Mass.: South End Press, 2000), India's radical Vandana Shiva has produced *Water Wars: Profits Pollution, and Privatization* (Cambridge, Mass.: South End Press, 2001), which argues again that multinational corporations are exploiting scarce natural resources to the detriment of the poor.

27. Smil, *Feeding the World: A Challenge for the Twenty-First Century*, xxiii.

28. Worldwatch Institute, "Is Meat Sustainable?" January 2, 2012, http://www.worldwatch.org/node/549.

29. Joel E. Cohen, *How Many People Can the Earth Support?* (New York: Norton, 1995), 311–12.

30. Halweil and Nierenberg, "Watching What We Eat," 76.

31. Food and Agriculture Organization (FAO), *The State of Food Insecurity 2003* (Rome, Italy: United Nations Food and Agriculture Organization, 2003), 13.

32. UNDP, *Human Development Report 2011*, http://hdr.undp.org/en/media/HDR_2011_EN_Tables.pdf; UNDP, *Human Development Report 2003*, 257.

33. Janet L. Sawin, "Water Scarcity Could Overwhelm the Next Generation," *World Watch* 16, no. 4 (2003): 8.

34. United Nations World Water Assessment Programme, "World Water Development Report 2011," http://www.unesco.org/new/fileadmin/MULTIMEDIA/HQ/SC/pdf/WWDR3_Facts_and_Figures.pdf.

35. Michael T. Klare, *Resource Wars: The New Landscape of Global Conflict* (New York: Holt, 2001), 138–89.

36. Payal Sampat, *Deep Trouble: The Hidden Threat of Groundwater Pollution*, Worldwatch Paper No. 154 (Washington, D.C.: Worldwatch Institute, 2000).

37. Sandra Postel and Amy Vickers, "Boosting Water Productivity," in Worldwatch Institute, *State of the World 2004* (New York: Worldwatch Institute/Norton, 2003), 48.

38. For global issues and institutions working in this area, see the authoritative analysis of Ken Conca, *Governing Water: Contentious Transnational Politics and Global Institution Building Global Environmental Accord: Strategies for Sustainability and Institutional Innovation* (Boston, Mass.: MIT Press, 2005).

39. Brown, *Eco-Economy: Building an Economy for the Future*, 55–57; ENS Environmental News Service, "Deforestation, Climate Change, and East African Drought, January 16, 2006, http://www.ens-newswire.com/ens/jan2006/2006–01–16–02.asp.

40. Lawrence B. Slobodkin, *A Citizen's Guide to Ecology* (New York: Oxford University Press, 2003), 101.

41. Brown, *Eco-Economy: Building an Economy for the Future*, 68–69.

42. See the Convention on Biological Diversity at www.cbd.int.

43. For more on the UN-REDD Programme, see http://www.un-redd.org/; for analysis of the market initiatives of UN-REDD, see the UN-REDD Monitor at: http://www.redd-monitor.org/.

44. Learn more about the initiative at http://www.liveyasuni.org/.

45. See the Kyoto Protocol at http://unfccc.int/kyoto_protocol/items/2830.php.

46. See the UN Framework Convention on Climate Change at http://unfccc.int/resource/docs/convkp/conveng.pdf.

47. See also Pamela L. Martin, *Oil in the Soil* (New York: Rowman and Littlefield, 2011).

48. U.S. Energy Information Administration (U.S. EIA), www.eia.org.

49. Brown, *Eco-Economy: Building an Economy for the Future*, 115.

50. Christopher Flavin and Gary Gardner, "China, India, and the New World Order," in Worldwatch Institute, *State of the World 2006* (New York: Worldwatch Institute/Norton, 2006), 7.

51. Brown, *Eco-Economy: Building an Economy for the Future*, 97.

52. Michael T. Klare, *Blood and Oil* (London: Penguin, 2004), 64; also see Daniel Yergin, *The Quest: Energy, Security, and the Remaking of the Modern World* (New York: Simon and Schuster, 2011); Daniel Yergin's 1991 Pulitzer Prize–winning *The Prize: The Epic Quest for Oil, Money and Power* (New York: Simon and Schuster, 1991) is a classic.

53. Seth Dunn, *Micropower: The Next Electrical Era*, Worldwatch Paper No. 151 (Washington, D.C.: Worldwatch Institute, 2000), 52.

54. Sawin, "Making Better Energy Choices," 25–26.

55. Brown, *Eco-Economy: Building an Economy for the Future*, 101.

56. Dunn, *Micropower: The Next Electrical Era*, 24–26; Brown, *Eco-Economy: Building an Economy for the Future*, 106.

57. Sawin, "Making Better Energy Choices," 39.

58. Slobodkin, *A Citizen's Guide to Ecology*, 8.

59. U.S. Energy Information Administration, *Electric Power Monthly Data Tables*, http://205.254.135.7/electricity/monthly/; Power Scorecard, http://www.powerscorecard.org/tech_detail.cfm?resource_id=2.

60. Slobodkin, *A Citizen's Guide to Ecology*, 156–61.

61. Firor and Jacobsen, *The Crowded Greenhouse: Population, Climate Change, and Creating a Sustainable World*, 115–116.

62. See the Intergovernmental Panel on Climate Change (IPCC) at http://www.nasonline.org/site/PageServer; see the National Academy of Scientists (NAS) at http://www.nasonline.org/site/PageServer.

63. Bill McKibben, *Eaarth: Making a Life on a Tough New Planet* (New York: Times Books, 2010); see also Thomas Princen, *Treading Softly* (Cambridge, Mass.: MIT Press, 2010).

64. IPCC (Inter-governmental Panel on Climate Change), *Climate Change 2001: Synthesis Report* (Cambridge, UK: Cambridge University Press, 2001).

65. See the report of the National Energy Policy Development Group at: http://www.pppl.gov/common_pages/national_energy_policy.html.

66. Ruth Greenspan Bell, "What to Do about Climate Change," *Foreign Affairs* 85, no. 3 (2006): 105–14.

67. Al Gore, *Earth in the Balance* (Boston: Houghton Mifflin, 1992).

68. Convention for the Protection of the Ozone Layer, http://www.unep.org/ozone/pdfs/viennaconvention2002.pdf.

69. Montreal Protocol on Substances That Deplete the Ozone Layer, http://www.unep.org/ozone/pdfs/montreal-protocol2000.pdf.

70. Zoë Chafe, "Ozone Layer Making Tentative Improvements," *World Watch* 16, no. 8 (2003): 8.

71. Gary Gardner et al., "The State of Consumption Today," in Worldwatch Institute, *State of the World 2004* (New York: Worldwatch Institute/Norton, 2004), 11.

72. John Malthus, *Essay on the Principle of Population* (London: St. Paul's Church Yard, 1798), http://www.esp.org/books/malthus/population/malthus.pdf.

73. Garrett Hardin, "The Tragedy of the Commons," *Science* 162 (1968): 1243–48; Paul Ehrlich, *The Population Bomb* (New York: Ballantine, 1968).

74. J. Calhoun, "Population Density and Social Pathology," *Scientific American* 206 (1962): 139–48.

75. Robert D. Putnam, *Bowling Alone: The Collapse and Revival of American Community* (New York: Touchstone Books, 2001).

76. Robert D. Kaplan, "The Coming Anarchy," *The Atlantic Monthly*, February1994: 44–76.

77. Lester R. Brown, Gary Gardner, and Brian Halweil, *Beyond Malthus: Sixteen Dimensions of the Population Problem*, Worldwatch Paper No. 143 (Washington, D.C.: Worldwatch Institute, 1998).

78. John R. Weeks, *Population: An Introduction to Concepts and Issues*, 9th ed. (Belmont, Calif.: Wadsworth, 2011).

79. Julian Simon, *The Ultimate Resource* (Princeton, N.J.: Princeton University Press, 1981).

80. Jared Diamond (already well-known as the author of 1997's *Guns, Germans, and Steel*) claims that the survival of human societies is closely linked to environmental factors in his *Collapse: How Societies Choose to Fail or Succeed* (New York: Viking, 2005).

81. Environmental sustainability index, http://epi.yale.edu/.

82. Cohen, *How Many People Can the Earth Support*, 369.

83. See the Sierra Club at http://www.sierraclub.org/; see Greenpeace at http://www.greenpeace.org/usa/.

84. Steven Radelet, "Bush and Foreign Aid," *Foreign Affairs* 82, no. 5 (2003): 110.

Glossary

absolute majority: In multiparty legislatures, an absolute majority gives you more votes than all the opposition parties put together; in contrast, a "relative majority" just means more votes than any other single party.

acid rain: Precipitation impregnated with industrial waste products such as sulfuric and nitric acids, which damage forests and crops, and pollute waterways.

African Union: Once called the Organization of African Unity and relaunched in 2002, the African Union (AU) is meant to evolve into a multinational organization that closely resembles the European Union (EU).

anarchism: A political philosophy that argues that small communities should manage their own affairs and that national **governments** should be abolished.

animist: Tribal or folk **religions** involving the worship of spirits or inanimate objects.

anomic: From Greek roots meaning "without reason," anomic describes behavior that is illogical, unreasoned, spontaneous, and sometimes violent. Anomic behavior is typically confused in intent and not clearly related to any specific or identifiable objective.

anticipated election: A feature of **parliamentary systems** in which an election is held earlier than the law demands in order to achieve some desired political purpose.

anti-Semitic: In common usage, to be anti-Semitic is to hate those of Jewish faith or ancestry.

apartheid: The Afrikaans word for separateness, apartheid was the systematic denial of civil liberties to non-Caucasians in South Africa.

aquaculture: The process of "fish-farming" or raising fish on land in tanks, artificial lakes, or in sections of coastal ocean that have been made into fish pens with nets.

Arab: In the ordinarily understood sense of the word, Arabs are members of an Arabic-speaking kinship group who perceive themselves to be biologically related to other Arabs in tracing their collective ancestry back to the followers of Mohammed who conquered the Middle East in the 600s and 700s. A minority of Arabs are Christians, and the Muslim **religion** has spread far beyond the Arabic world, but most Muslim Arabs would regard **Islam** as part of their core self-identification as Arabs.

asymmetrical warfare: Combat between two military forces in which there are significant differences in tactics, weaponry, and attitudes about casualties.

autarky: The **theory** that a country should strive for complete resource and economic independence from other countries.

authoritarian: A system of **government** that denies fundamental political and personal rights at a very serious level, but is not gratuitously cruel toward citizens who do not threaten its authority.

ayatollah: In the **Shi'ite** variant of the Islamic **religion**, an ayatollah is a senior clergyman, similar in rank to an archbishop in the Christian community.

balance of payments: The difference between the quantity of money a country exports for imported goods and services on one hand, and the amount of money the same country receives in exchange for its own exported goods and services.

Balkan Peninsula: The strip of land running south from the main portion of Europe and containing the former Yugoslavia, Albania, Bulgaria, and Greece.

Battle of Kosovo: A 1389 fight during which the Ottoman **Empire** defeated and conquered the Serbs, occupying the same sentimental place in Serbian history that the Alamo has for Texans.

Ben-Gurion, David: Leader of the Jewish people in **Palestine** prior to their independence in 1948, and first prime minister of Israel afterward.

bicameral: A legislature with an upper and lower house or chamber is called bicameral.

bilateral: Having two sides, as in negotiations between two countries.

biodiversity: Measured by the number of different species, biodiversity is the range or variety of animal and vegetable life that exists naturally within a given ecosystem.

biosphere: Sometimes called the "zone of life," the biosphere is a global ecosystem in that portion of the earth's surface where life of any sort is possible, extending from the deepest seabed to several miles up into the atmosphere.

bipolar: With two overwhelmingly important poles, a bipolar state system functioned during the years of the **Cold War** (1945–1991) with the planet divided between the United States and the USSR.

bourgeoisie: From a root word meaning "city dweller," bourgeoisie describes that entrepreneurial class of tradesmen, merchants, and professionals (lawyers, architects, etc.) in the medieval period who were neither aristocrats nor peasantry.

Bundestag: In Germany's **bicameral** legislature, the Bundestag is the lower but politically more significant chamber.

capitalism: A system of economic activity in which goods and services are created and sold by profit-making, privately owned corporations generally free from undue **government** control. Capitalist or free-market societies typically create legal institutions to promote private over public enterprise. In circumstances where "capitalism" has a **pejorative** ring, "**free market**" and "free enterprise" are alternate terms for the same system.

carrying capacity: The number of people who can be supported at some level of prosperity by the natural resources of a given environment.

chauvinism: The belief in your nation's inherent cultural superiority to all other nations.

childhood mortality index or **under five mortality rate (U5MR):** The number of children per one thousand born that die before their fifth birthday.

citizenship: The legal relationship between an individual and a **sovereign state**, with a set of reciprocal rights and responsibilities as defined by law.

civil disobedience: The act of openly and deliberately breaking a law and accepting the legal penalty (such as prison or a fine) in order to publicize a political or social cause without violence.

civil society: In democracies, civil society is the realm of voluntary public organizations playing a significant role in the ordering of public affairs. Civil society includes clubs, advocacy organizations, pressure and special **interest groups**, lobbies, churches, labor unions, charities, political parties, and other voluntary, **nongovernmental organizations** that affect public policy at both the national and the international level.

civil war: Sometimes called "intrastate" or "domestic" conflicts, civil wars are those fought within the boundaries of a given **sovereign state** by residents of that state.

climate change: A growing trend for CO_2 and other so-called **greenhouse gases** to accumulate in the upper atmosphere, trapping solar heat on the earth's surface and creating a global warming trend as well as other abnormal weather patterns.

coalition: When no single party wins a majority of the seats in a **parliamentary system**, the result may be a coalition or partnership of several parties that agree to pool their votes to support one compromise candidate as prime minister.

cognate: From the Latin for cousin, cognates are closely related **languages** from the same subfamily such as German and Dutch.

cognitive isolation: The state of being intellectually cut off from your neighbors and surroundings.

Cold War: Beginning at least by 1946 and clearly over by the time of the dissolution of the USSR in 1991, the Cold War was a period of global competition and intense hostility between the United States and its allies, and the Soviet Union and its satellites, characterized by massive investment in weapons and a series of proxy wars in countries like Korea, Vietnam, Angola, and Afghanistan.

combination system: The division of executive duties between a powerful president who handles foreign affairs and defense and a politically significant prime minister who supervises the ordinary administration of the **government**.

command economy: See **Marxist**.

Commonwealth of Nations: A voluntary international organization uniting many of Britain's former colonies, the Commonwealth of Nations links ex-colonies to the mother country for **culture**, commerce, and sport.

communist: Today generally synonymous with **Marxist**, a communist believes in violent revolution to create a command or Marxist economy.

comparative politics: The study of how different political systems confront common or universal political problems.

conditionality: In the context of **foreign aid** or low-interest developmental loans, "conditionality" means that the recipient is expected to conform to the donor's desires, for example, in opening its economy to foreign competition or reducing spending on social services.

confidence bills: In **parliamentary systems**, the passage of major bills proposed by the **government** indicates the legislature's confidence in the prime minister and cabinet, and allows them to continue in office.

constituency: In elections, a constituency is a specific district or territory that elects one candidate to a legislative body.

constitution: The word refers both to the political institutions and structures of a given society, and to any authoritative legal document describing how the political system in question should function.

constitutional monarch: Any royal head of state who has lost most authentic political power but continues to perform certain largely ceremonial functions.

constructivism: The study of the **normative** (or ethical) foundations and identities of states and world leaders to better understand relationships.

consulate: A diplomatic office that performs functions related to immigration, passports and visas, commerce, and the safety of home-country citizens abroad.

containment: George Kennan's **theory** of containment argued that the United States could not destroy the Soviet Union but could keep it contained within its own boundaries until it collapsed under the weight of its own contradictions.

convention: In **international law**, a convention is a **multilateral treaty** dealing with some fundamental issue.

conventional weapons: The standard explosive weaponry employed by armed forces is considered conventional if it is nonnuclear and does not involve chemical or biological agents.

coup d'état: From the French, the phrase literally means a "blow at the state," and is normally used to suggest a sudden and sometimes violent seizure of political power by a relatively small group.

Creole: In Latin America, the term refers generally to people directly descended from the original European settlers. When used to describe a **language**, the word refers to a dialectalized form of some original language, such as the French spoken in Louisiana and Haiti.

critical theorists: Members of this school contend that the theories of realism, idealism, and **constructivism** misrepresent the true foundations of power in the international system and, according to Marxist scholars, impose ways of thinking that create inequalities in the world.

culture: A network of acquired characteristics like **religion**, **language**, literature, music, social interaction, and dress that distinguish one national or **ethnic** community from another.

deficit: A budget deficit occurs when a **government's** expenditures in a given fiscal year are more than its revenue and borrowing is required to make up the difference.

deflation: An increase in the value of goods and services in relation to a given currency, that is, a general reduction in prices.

democracy: An imprecise term describing any society that is considered to be under the political control of its citizens.

demographic transition: A **theory** that attempts to explain why a society's population will expand rapidly for a period and then stabilize if and when the society is modernized by economic, social, and medical changes.

demography: The science of population in general, including the growth or decline of specific **ethnic** communities, age and gender ratios, and other changes in the composition of a specific group.

dependency ratio: A statistic generated by adding those who are deemed for statistical purposes to be too young (below fifteen years of age) or too old (above sixty-five years of age) to be economically productive, dividing this sum by the number of those who are presumed to be working (i.e., those between fifteen and sixty-four years of age), and then multiplying the product by one hundred.

desertification: The process by which formerly arable land is degraded by overplanting or overgrazing, sometimes exacerbated by irrigation with poor-quality water. When the water table drops to an unusable depth, the land becomes desert, a process that happens to about thirty thousand square miles of land a year.

détente: From a French word meaning relaxation, "détente" suggests a period when tensions between two countries decline and warmer relations begin.

devaluation: Devaluation occurs when something loses value in relation to something else. In economics, a currency is devalued or depreciated when it declines in value when traded for other currencies. The same terms, devaluation and depreciation, are used to describe the results of **inflation**, which is when a currency loses value in terms of the goods and services it can purchase.

devolution: The process by which a sovereign **government** relinquishes or hands down certain political powers to some level of **sub-sovereign** government.

dialect: A nonstandard or divergent way of speaking a given **language** with differences in pronunciation, vocabulary, and grammar.

dictatorship: A vague phrase describing any society where the citizenry does not control the operations of **government** or does not enjoy basic civil liberties.

diplomacy: The principal formal process by which **sovereign states** communicate with one another and the methods by which diplomats attempt to serve their **governments**.

diplomatic immunity: Once a custom and now enshrined in **multilateral** treaties, diplomats are immune to arrest in the host country to which they are accredited.

doctrine: The teachings of a **religion** or similar belief system.

double-ballot system: Sometimes called the runoff system, the double-ballot system utilizes a preliminary election to narrow the field of contenders to two, and then provides a second and separate election in which voters choose between the two top voter-getters from the preliminary election. Under this procedure, the winner must necessarily get more than 50 percent of the direct popular vote.

doubling time: The number of years it will take a given population group to double in size if the current rate of growth remains unchanged.

dynasty: A royal or monarchical family passing **sovereignty** or political authority down through the generations.

egalitarian: A social system in which wealth is distributed equally is said to be egalitarian.

elite dictatorship: A less-free **government** in which power is exercised by the top echelon of religious, political, **ethnic**, or other clearly defined social group.

empire: Now mostly a negative term, an empire is a state that conquers and colonializes other **ethnic** groups. The adjective for this behavior is "imperialistic."

empirical data: Information that is based on real-world observation.

epistemology: The branch of philosophy that asks questions about how we know what is really true.

ethnic: A word susceptible of diverse meanings, "ethnic" refers to a human population displaying enough common physical and/or cultural characteristics to be considered an identifiable social group.

ethnic cleansing: The deliberate use of violence to exterminate or drive into exile an unwelcome **ethnic** or national group.

ethnocentricity: An intense focus within a given **ethnic** or national community on the virtues and interests of that group, often combined with a dislike or disrespect for other ethnicities.

exceptionalism: The sense among some Americans that the uniqueness of American society frees it from any obligation to conform to the behavior expected of other societies.

exchange rate: The rate or cost at which one national currency can be traded for another national currency.

executive agreement: A peculiarity of the American political system, executive agreements are binding commitments made by the president with one or more foreign **governments** without seeking congressional approval.

externality: In both economics and environmental science, an externality is a cost or financial consequence of the production of a good or service that is not accounted for in the price of that good or service.

failed state: A country whose central **government** has either ceased to exist or is no longer able to exercise meaningful control over the national territory.

fascism: An incoherent jumble of political ideas conceived as a reaction to World War I by Italy's Mussolini and later imitated by Hitler and others, fascism involves extreme nationalism and/or **racism**, an attraction to militarism, war, and violence, a generalized hatred of the left, especially Marxist and trade-union movements, anti-intellectualism, and the preference for personalized **dictatorships** over democratic institutions.

fatwa: An order or command issued by an Islamic authority.

federal system: Any governing system in which political authority is **constitutionally** divided among national, regional, and local levels of **government**.

feminism: While capable of many different meanings, feminism basically describes any sociopolitical philosophy that demands an improvement in the status of women, and their essential social and legal equality with men.

fiscal conservative: People who demand a balanced budget and oppose **deficit** spending, which is paying out more in benefits than the **government** collects in revenues.

flat tax: A system of taxation in which all citizens, rich and poor, pay the same percentage of their income in taxes.

Food and Agriculture Organization (FAO): The UN agency with headquarters in Rome that works to improve and create sources of food.

foreign aid: The efforts of a donor country to assist a poorer one may consist of funds, credits, low-cost loans, advisory teams, or material resources like food; international charity may be made **bilaterally** and directly from one country to another, or **multilaterally**, from one country to an international agency, such as the UN, charged with the subsequent distribution of aid to individual recipient countries.

foreign exchange: Money from other countries, particularly a **hard currency**, which is held by a given country and can be used for purchases on the international market or the repayment of debts.

fossil fuels: Because they are believed to have been created from the remnants of dead plant life, oil, coal, and natural gas are commonly called fossil fuels or sometimes hydrocarbons.

Fourth World: A category of very destitute nations, many in Africa, whose populations suffer from life-threatening levels of poverty. Many Fourth World countries are economically static or actually getting poorer.

franchise: In **politics**, the franchise is simply the right to vote in public elections.

Francophobe: The "-phobe" suffix on any word indicates fear or mistrust, so you are a Francophobe if you dislike the French.

Francophone: A speaker of the French **language**.

free market: See **capitalism**.

functionalism: The **theory** that the world community should focus on practical, achievable solutions to everyday problems before tackling the great issues of war and peace.

GDP: See **gross domestic product**.

genetic modification (GM): Also called "genetic engineering" and "biotechnology," genetic modification is a series of related technologies in which the genetic code of a species is altered to increase its resistance to insects and disease or otherwise improve the quality or salability of the product.

genocide: The deliberate attempt to kill off an entire **ethnic**, national, or religious group, or to murder large numbers of people specifically because of their ethnicity.

Gini index or Gini coefficient: In **politics**, the Gini index measures the extent to which income distribution in a society deviates from a theoretically perfect equality; more simply, it is an attempt to **quantify** economic inequality. Results range from 1 to 100, with more unequal societies getting higher scores.

global climate change: A widely accepted **theory** that the waste products of modern industrial society are changing the earth's weather, that is, producing generally warmer temperatures, changing patterns of rainfall, and raising sea levels.

global governance: The implementation of policies at global and local levels crafted by a myriad of actors from governmental, private, and nongovernmental spheres, such as ministers, NGO activists, and multinational corporation representatives. An example would be the International **Convention** to Ban Landmines, which was crafted by NGO and **government** leaders and implemented through a UN-sponsored convention that states have adopted.

globalization: The ongoing worldwide process of establishing interconnections among disparate population groups; also, the creation of an increasingly Westernized global **culture**, wider economic and commercial relationships, the rapid global movement of people and information, and the increased influence of the United States and Europe through political, economic, and military power.

governance: The ability of **government** officials to create and deliver honest and effective public policies and services.

government: In **parliamentary systems**, the term "government" refers specifically to prime ministers and their cabinets, while in most **presidential systems**, the word means the whole national-level bureaucracy.

greenhouse gases: When they filter into the atmosphere, gases such as carbon dioxide, methane, nitrous oxide, and chlorofluorocarbons have the effect of trapping the sun's warmth, raising the surface temperature of the earth and altering global weather patterns in unpredictable ways.

gridlock: When branches of the same **government** disagree and prevent each other from functioning.

gross domestic product (GDP): The total output or sum total of all the goods and services produced by a given economy (typically a **sovereign state**) within a given year.

gross national income (GNI): See **gross national product (GNP)**.

GLOSSARY

gross national product (GNP): The GNP is similar to the GDP but it adds earnings created by residents of the country abroad and returned to the country. It subtracts earnings created within the country by foreign nationals and exported abroad. The World Bank now refers to this statistic as the gross national income (GNI). Since the GDP and GNP are somewhat different measurements, it is important not to confuse them. This text only uses the GDP.

guerrilla warfare: In real-life conflicts, guerrilla warfare can be hard to distinguish from terrorism, but the term is normally used to describe irregular forces (sometimes called "partisans") who use unconventional hit-and-run tactics against superior conventional armies in the hope of wearing them down, winning public support, and eventually making the transition to conventional warfare.

hard currency: Any currency that is freely convertible in banks around the world is called a hard currency, and the U.S. and Canadian dollars, the Euro, the British pound, and the Japanese yen are all examples.

hat trick: No one is quite sure why, but in sports, a hat trick is winning three events in a row. In political parlance, it means success in three consecutive national elections.

HDI: See human development index.

hegemon: When used in politics, the word refers to the dominant player in a given conflict, the world power that calls the shots. Americans sometimes like to think of the United States as a global hegemon.

high-intensity conflict (HIC): An increasingly popular technical phrase to indicate a conventional war involving professional military units and fought with standard military weaponry. See also low-intensity conflict.

Holocaust denial: The belief that the mass slaughter of Jews by the Nazis during World War II did not actually take place but was fabricated after the war by Zionists to justify the establishment of Israel and generate sympathy for the Jewish people. While every serious scholar is familiar with the evidence that the Holocaust did take place, Holocaust denial is a remarkably persistent strain of anti-Semitism.

human development index (HDI): Divided into high, medium, and low, the human development index is the UN's attempt to grade the success or failure of countries and governments. It creates a simple summary measurement of three key dimensions: living a long, healthy life; being educated; and having a decent standard of living.

humanism: A secular philosophy that attempts to create a human ethical code without specifically affirming or denying the existence of a Supreme Being.

hung parliament: In multiparty systems, when no party achieves a majority and the several parties in the legislature cannot agree on terms for a coalition, the parliament is said to be "hung."

hyperinflation: A rapid and destructive decline in the purchasing power of a currency, sometimes involving a generalized rise in prices of over 50 percent per month.

hypothesis: A statement that posit the relationship between concepts within the theory.

idealist: One who believes that humankind will evolve into a more peaceful species, overcoming war, intolerance, and poverty. In most political systems, idealists gravitate to the liberal end of the spectrum.

ideology: A philosophy or interconnected set of ideas and convictions about politics or public affairs, like fascism, Marxism, or Western liberalism.

IMF: See International Monetary Fund.

Industrial Revolution: The term refers to a technology-driven social change that began in Britain in the mid-1700s, featuring mechanized agriculture, modern banking, and the creation of a factory system for industrial production. Associated with modern **capitalism**, the revolution spread to North America, Western Europe, and Japan in the 1800s.

infant mortality rate (IMR): The number of babies per one thousand born alive that die before their first birthday.

inflation: The decrease in the value of a given currency in relation to the goods and services it will purchase, that is, a general rise in the average level of prices.

interdiction: A military term suggesting cutting off people or goods from crossing a border; interdiction in law-enforcement terms means a focus on preventing illegal drugs from entering the United States.

interest group: Any formally organized collection of people, clubs, or institutions working together to achieve certain specified public policy objectives.

intermestic: A worthy newcomer to the vocabulary, "intermestic" describes a phenomenon that is both international and domestic.

International Bank for Reconstruction and Development (IBRD): See **World Bank**.

International Bill of Human Rights: The combination of three UN-sponsored multinational treaties: the Universal Declaration of Human Rights, the welfare-oriented ESC Covenant, and the CPR Covenant on civil rights.

International Labour Organisation (ILO): A UN agency meant to study and improve the conditions of working people.

international law: A set of rules, customs, treaties, judicial rulings, and understandings that regulate the interaction among **sovereign states**.

International Monetary Fund (IMF): The Washington-based UN agency that attempts to stabilize currencies and domestic economies.

international relations: The study of those aspects of **politics** that transcend national borders with special reference to the interaction on the world scene of **sovereign states**.

intifada: An Arabic word meaning "uprising" or "shaking off," used to describe periods of intensely confrontational resistance by **Palestinians** to **Israeli** authority.

Inuit: Traditionally called "Eskimos," Native Americans who live near the Arctic Circle prefer to be called "Inuit."

irredentism: The belief that a portion of your natural national territory has been taken away and needs to be restored.

Islam: Religion established in what is now Saudi Arabia by the Prophet Mohammed in the seventh century. It is divided into **Sunni**s and **Shi'ite** Muslims. Islam is a global **religion**, predominating in the **Arab** world but extending across parts of South Asia and into Indonesia.

Islamism: A belief in the legal and social reordering of secular society on the basis of Islamic religious thinking, specifically that ordinary **statute** law should be made to conform with the **Sharia**, or Islamic religious law.

Israeli: Overwhelmingly, Israelis are Jewish or practitioners of the Judaic **religion** who are citizens of the modern state of Israel. A number of **Arab Palestinians** also hold Israeli **citizenship**, but are normally called "Israeli Arabs" or "Israeli Palestinians."

Jew: Members of a religious and cultural group, Jews see themselves as descendents of Abraham and the ancient Hebrew people of the Bible. Although many Jews have become secular, most subscribe to the tenants of the Judaic **religion** and are culturally Jewish in terms of lifestyle. Jews who live in Israel also self-identify in nationalist terms as citizens of Israel.

jihad: Controversial in meaning and application, "jihad" is the Arabic word for "struggle." In its military sense, the word was originally applied to the expansionist campaign against non-Muslims in Arabian and Ottoman history. While the term can also suggest an inner personal struggle against sin, it is routinely used by Islamist leaders as a declaration of war against foreign or domestic enemies.

judicial review: The power of a court to rule on the **constitutionality** of an act of the executive or the legislature.

junta: A group, normally military, who have seized power through a **coup d'état**.

jurisdiction: The right of a given level of **government** to regulate behavior within a specific area. For example, the South Carolina state government has jurisdiction over traffic offenses committed within the state of South Carolina.

kleptocracy: A **government** in which a corrupt majority of senior officials abandon normal **governance** in favor of looting the **public sector** and extracting bribes. Economists often use the term "rent-seeking" to describe this pattern.

Knesset: Israel's 120-seat **unicameral legislature**.

Kosovar Albanians: A Muslim, Albanian-speaking people who live in Serbia's province of Kosovo rather than in Albania itself. Kosovo is currently under UN **governance** since the 1999 NATO air war against Serbia.

language: The systematic use of sounds, gestures, written scripts, and symbols that allows members of a given linguistic community to communicate with one another.

legitimacy: One of the core words in **political science**, legitimacy is a feeling we have that our **government** came into existence through the appropriate procedures and has the right to exercise power.

Leninist: Any Marxist with an activist approach to revolution who hopes to achieve a **communist** society through armed revolt, **guerrilla warfare**, or **terrorism**.

liberalization: In the economic sense of the word, "liberalization" means free trade and the free movement of capital across national boundaries, the reduction of **tariff** barriers, and legislation prohibiting foreign ownership of business interests. Confusingly, enthusiasts for market liberalization often describe themselves as "neo-liberals."

life expectancy: The average number of years of life predicted or anticipated for a newly born child in a given society.

lobbyist: An employee of an **interest group** who tries to persuade public officials to act or vote in favor of policies favored by the interest group.

low-intensity conflict (LIC): Low-intensity conflict refers to any serious political violence ranging from rioting to **terrorism** and **guerrilla warfare** that remains short of full-scale war.

majlis: In Muslim countries a majlis (or majles) is an assembly that may be elected or appointed, and may either advise the ruler or enact legislation.

Maoist: Any Marxist movement that emulates the revolutionary tactics of Mao Zedung (1893–1976) in emphasizing a mobilization of the rural peasantry against a capitalist **government**.

Marxism: A political philosophy associated with Karl Marx (1818–1883) that maintains that **capitalism** is a fatally flawed system that will inevitably be replaced by a **com-**

mand economy in which the **government** would own and control all significant economic resources and manage the economy for the benefit of the people.

median age: In **demography**, the median age is the age at which one-half the population is older and one-half is younger.

Mestizos: In Latin America generally, Mestizos are persons of mixed European and Native American ancestry.

micro-credit: The policy of making small loans to village-level entrepreneurs to start socially useful businesses.

mixed member proportional (MMP) system: Combining SMC and PR in some proportion produces the German-style MMP system.

Montenegro: The only one of the original six republics that once made up Yugoslavia that is still linked to Serbia.

Mossadegh Crisis: In 1951–1953, Iran endured a **constitutional** crisis that saw the end of Prime Minister Mossadegh's career and the creation of a royal **dictatorship**.

mujahideen: An Arabic term meaning "holy warriors," used to describe the Afghan resistance to the USSR, and more generally, any Muslim who makes war on non-Muslims.

mullah: More common in **Shi'ite** than **Sunni Islam**, a mullah is a seminary-trained clerical official, who often exercises some political authority within an Islamic community.

multiculturalism: The belief that we should welcome and study **ethnic** diversity within our society.

multilateral: Having several sides, as in negotiations among three or more countries.

multinational state: When significant elements of two or more nations live in the same **sovereign state**, the result is a multinational state.

multipolar: Featuring a limited number of **sovereign states** or allied clusters of sovereign states, a multipolar state system prevailed roughly from the **Treaty of Westphalia** to World War II.

multi-state nation: An **ethnic** or national group divided into two or more separate **sovereign states**.

mutual intelligibility: Two speech communities are mutually intelligible when a speaker of one community can be understood by another. For example, the British and American variants of English are mutually intelligible.

nation: While the word is commonly used as a synonym for country, "nation" actually describes communities who may or may not be organized into a **sovereign state** but who share all or most of the following six characteristics: **language**, kinship, national **culture**, **religion**, **territoriality**, and national self-identification.

national debt: The sum total of money borrowed by a **government**, but not yet paid off, to cover past **deficits**.

national missile defense (NMD): Variously called "Stars Wars" and the Strategic Defense Initiative, the NMD is being developed to shoot down incoming ballistic missiles.

nationalism: The belief that a given nation should be governed by its own citizens rather than foreigners. At a more intense level, nationalism may also involve an assumption of superiority by members of a given nation over other nations.

nationalization: The action of a sovereign **government** in taking or purchasing ownership of what were previously private-sector economic resources.

nation-state: A **sovereign state** providing a homeland for one dominant national group and containing no significant presence of another national group.

natural law: The **theory** that an inherent code of conduct flows from our basic nature as human beings, constituting an unchangeable law that is distinct both from religious and **statute** law.

negative population growth (NPG): While any population shrinkage would technically qualify as NPG, demographers reserve the term for a serious and sustained pattern of population decline in a given society.

neo-fascist: Any post–World War II movement that has inherited violently racist and antidemocratic ideals from the Mussolini-Hitler era.

neo-liberal: A vague phrase used by American politicians, such as Bill Clinton and Al Gore, to suggest a residual interest in liberal themes such as unions and minorities combined with a new enthusiasm for business, welfare reform, and other traditionally conservative causes.

neo-Nazi: Beyond a heightened reverence for Hitler, neo-Nazis do not differ significantly from **neo-fascists**.

NGO: See **nongovernmental organization**.

nominal: In **politics**, something is said to be nominal if it exists in name but not in reality. In economics, a nominal statistic is one that has not been adjusted for **inflation**.

nongovernmental organization (NGO): A voluntary organization like Amnesty International or Greenpeace, involving citizens of several different countries acting in concert to achieve some political, social, or environmental goal.

non-state actor: A political entity (like a church, a charity, or a political action group) that plays a significant role in international **politics** but is not a **sovereign state**.

normative: An attempt to establish norms or **values** or standards.

oligarchy: From the Greek, an oligarchy is the undemocratic rule by a few, or an **elite dictatorship**.

Oslo Accords: Agreements signed by Israel and the **Palestinian** Liberation Organization in Oslo in 1993 and 1994 to create institutions for limited Palestinian self-**government** in the form of a Palestinian National Authority (PNA). Hailed at the time as a diplomatic breakthrough, Oslo had collapsed by September of 2000.

Palestine: First applied by the Romans to the eastern shore of the Mediterranean, the term "Palestine" has changed its geographical definition over the years. **Arab**s today use the term to describe what was once the old British mandate of Palestine, which included what is today Israel, the West Bank, and the Gaza Strip.

Palestinian: While anybody living in what was once **Palestine** could legitimately be called a "Palestinian," the word universally refers to speakers of the Arabic **language** who trace at least part of their ancestry back to the original Arabian conquerors of Palestine and who self-identify with the territory once called Palestine. Most Palestinians are **Sunni** Muslims; a small but influential minority is Orthodox Christian.

paradigm: In political analysis, a paradigm is a working **theory**, a tested concept that is assumed to be true.

paramilitary: A vague but frequently used word employed to describe a semi-legal organization, more often right than left, that operates on the margins of the law, perhaps with the tacit consent of the real military.

parliamentary system: Any **government** that divides responsibility between a ceremonial chief of state (either a **constitutional monarch** or a ceremonial president), and a chief executive/prime minister and cabinet who are indirectly elected by the legislature.

partisans: Since the word "guerrilla" has a slightly **pejorative** ring, irregular forces are often approvingly called "partisans," but there is no real distinction.

PC/GDP: See **per capita gross domestic product**.

pejorative: A word is pejorative if it is always used in a critical or negative sense.

per capita gross domestic product (PC/GDP): The **gross domestic product** of a country divided by its population, an individual's theoretical share in the wealth of a society.

perspective: A way of seeing the world—like the lenses in eyeglasses.

pidgin: A simplified version of a **language** that features a modified grammar and reduced vocabulary, typically used by nonnative speakers for limited, practical communication.

plebiscite: An election in which individual voters are asked to make some fundamental decision about their national destiny, typically involving independence from, or union with, some other **sovereign state**.

plurality: In an election, a plurality means winning more votes than any other candidate, but not necessarily a majority.

plutocracy: Another phrase for economic **oligarchy**, a plutocracy is a **regime** that keeps a small group of rich people rich and everybody else poor.

political conflict: A clash of views or interests among two or more groups in society that may be resolved or brokered through the normal processes of elections or court decisions, or may escalate to significant levels of political violence.

political science: The academic study of **governments**, **politics**, and the ordering of public affairs.

politics: Politics is the set of structures and procedures human societies use to order or organize public affairs and moderate conflict.

popular sovereignty: The citizens of a **sovereign state** are said to have popular **sovereignty** when they collectively possess ultimate control over their **government** and can participate meaningfully in the ordering of public affairs.

populist: Related to the Latin word for "people," a populist is a man-of-the-people politician who purports to defend the interests of the "the common man" against big **government** and big business.

PPP US$: See **purchasing power parity**.

PR: See **proportional representation**.

praetorianism: A belief among military leaders that they have the right and the obligation to intervene in political life in order to safeguard the destiny of their country.

precedent: In judicial systems, a precedent is a decision reached in a similar case by some previous judge. In some systems, these precedents are regarded as binding on subsequent judges dealing with comparable cases.

presidential system: Any **government** in which a directly or semi-directly elected president combines both ceremonial and real executive powers, and is not elected by nor is simultaneously a member of, the legislature.

private sector: That portion of a society's economic activity that is carried out by private individuals, commercial corporations, and other nongovernmental entities.

privatization: The sale to the **private sector** of resources that had previously been nationalized.

progressive taxation: A tax system that demands a greater percentage of income from wealthier citizens, and a lesser percentage from poorer taxpayers.

proportional representation (PR): Any system for electing legislators that creates a rough equality between the number of votes cast for a given political party and the number of seats that party receives in the legislature.

protectionism: The use of **tariffs**, subsidies, or import quotas to protect a domestic industry from foreign competition.

protocol: A specific nuts-and-bolts **multilateral treaty** that usually follows some earlier and more general international agreement, which commits its signatories to specific and binding obligations.

public sector: That portion of a society's economic activity done by the **government**, such as building roads or financing the military.

purchasing power parity (PPP US$): A method of calculating **exchange rates** that factors in the difference in the cost of living between the United States and the country generating the currency under consideration. The PPP US$ technique allows meaningful **transnational** comparisons of statistics such as the **gross domestic product** and others.

quantify: In the social sciences, to quantify is to put reality into numbers, and ask "how much?" and "how many?"

racism: A deeply engrained belief that certain racial or kinship groups are naturally or biologically superior to others in terms of intelligence, strength, morality, physical beauty, or other attributes.

rapid population growth (RPG): While no universally accepted definition exists, rapid population growth is generally regarded as any demographic increase significantly greater than the average global rate of population growth, currently 1.2 percent per year. Any rate of growth above 2 percent per year is clearly RPG.

ratification: The final step in **treaty** making, ratification occurs when a **sovereign state** completes its legal process for approving a treaty and announces its adherence to it.

real GDP: To distinguish real economic growth from the consequences of **inflation**, economists factor out inflation when calculating the real GDP or real PC/GDP.

realist: A person who does not believe that humankind is capable of much improvement and anticipates that war and crime will always be part of the human condition. Political realists tend to be political conservatives in most societies.

referendum: A style of voting in which voters decide a specific issue of general concern, rather than electing officials to make the decision for them. In some legal systems, a referendum generates a specific **statute**, which becomes law without (or even in opposition to) action by the legislature. The plural is sometimes "referendums" and sometimes "referenda."

regime: Technically, a regime is simply the **government** of a given country, but the word is often used as a term of disapproval, suggesting an undemocratic or perhaps even illegitimate government. In other contexts, it means a set of rules followed by the international community when addressing a given problem.

regressive taxation: A pattern in some societies where poor people actually pay a higher percentage of their income in taxes than do wealthier citizens.

religion: A cultural and/or institutional belief system affirming the existence of a supernatural order and providing both an explanation of the meaning of human life as well as a code of conduct.

representative democracy: Most modern democracies are "representative" in the sense that the voters elect politicians to make and execute most real decisions.

republican: In European **politics** generally, a republican is someone who wants elected **governments** rather than monarchies. The Irish Republican Army wants Britain's royal government to leave Ireland alone.

resource wars: Typically fought for control of economic wealth in the form of mineral resources or water supplies; in causality, these conflicts can sometimes differ from armed robbery in scale only.

royal executive regime: A royal executive **regime** is an inherently undemocratic system in which a member of a royal family exercises substantive political power.

sectarian: From the word "sect" or **religion**, an individual or a society strongly committed to one sect, or religious denomination, and sometimes hostile to others.

Secularist: A person who seeks key answers to crucial questions about everyday life from science and rationality rather than from revealed **religion**.

secularization: The social and psychological process of reducing the role of **religion** in our lives.

Semitic: Any one of the **languages** belonging to what is usually called the Semitic subfamily of languages, including modern-day Arabic and Hebrew, as well as Amharic, which is spoken in Ethiopia. By extension, the term sometimes refers to the population groups (primarily **Arabs** and **Jews**) who speak these languages.

separatism: The idea that the land where you live has been unjustly integrated into the territory of some other nation and needs to be returned to the homeland of your nation.

Serbo-Croatian: Once regarded as one **language** with two principal **dialects**, Serb and Croatian are now more usually considered by the independent Croatia and Serbia to be two separate languages, although there continues to be a high level of **mutual intelligibility** between them.

sex ratio: The number of males per one hundred females in a given society.

sex-selection abortion: The systematic use of tests to determine fetal gender, coupled with abortion, usually to prevent the birth of an unwanted female.

Sharia: The body of Islamic law, drawn from the Koran, the recorded sayings of Mohammed, and the teachings of Muslim jurists.

Shi'ite: The minority community within the Muslim faith, whose members revere the memory of Mohammed's son-in-law Ali and his sons. Shi'ites feel persecuted by the outside world and often regard non-Shi'ites with some hostility. This branch of the Islamic faith is often called Shia or Shiah, and the word "Shii" is sometimes used as an adjective.

shock therapy: The **theory** that an economy—either Marxist or simply corrupt and inefficient—can be transformed quickly into a prosperous free-market system by means of financial austerity, opening of the domestic market to foreign competition, and the rapid **privatization** of publicly owned resources.

short wave: All radios measure their spectrum in kilohertz and megahertz; short-wave radio broadcasts between 0.1 and 30 MHz.

single member constituency (SMC) system: Any procedure for electing candidates to a legislature in which the national territory is divided into constituencies or electoral districts, with one candidate from each being elected by at least a **plurality** of votes cast.

single transferable vote (STV) system: The STV system allows voters to express a first and second preference; when there is no outright winner, the top two candidates are allowed to add their second preferences to their first preferences to produce a majority victor.

Sinhala or **Sinhalese:** The **language** spoken by the generally Buddhist Sinhalese population of Sri Lanka.

Sinn Fein: The legal political party that represents the illegal Irish Republican Army.

Six-Day War: Fought June 5–10, 1967, the Six-Day War ended with the **Israeli** conquest of the Sinai Peninsula (returned to Egypt after the 1978–1979 Camp David Accords), as well as all of Jerusalem, the West Bank, the Golan Heights, and the Gaza Strip.

slash-and-burn: A ruinous land-clearing technique in which trees and vegetation are cut or bulldozed and then burned to create crop or pasture land.

SMC: See **single member constituency.**

social conservatives: People preoccupied with what they view as declining moral **values**, lack of patriotism, illegitimate children, pornography, abortion, divorce, homosexuality, and other social issues.

social democracy: A democratic political system that attempts to reduce poverty and promote an **egalitarian** society by means of **government**-financed social services and by the ownership of some nationalized industries. Also called "mixed economies" or "welfare states."

socialization: A term that cuts through all the social sciences, socialization is the process of learning how to behave in a given society.

societal mayhem: A collapse of social structures, such as police and **governmental** authority, accompanied by **multilateral** violence so widespread and intense that it becomes the leading cause of mortality.

sovereign state: In the **language** of world **politics**, a sovereign state is an independent, self-governing political entity, often called a "country."

sovereignty: The independent political and physical control **governments** exercise over their territory; the right to make and enforce laws in a given territory.

spinning: Controlling a story by briefing journalists, often "off-the-record" in an attempt to put the best possible light on a situation.

stateless nations: Significant **ethnic** communities who live as minorities in one or more **sovereign states.**

statism: The **theory** that a country's **government** should take charge of the general future direction of its economy by planning, directing, coordinating, and stimulating the activities of individual firms in both the public and **private sector.**

statute: To distinguish them from other kinds of laws (moral, etc.), laws regularly passed by a legislature are called statute laws.

sub-sovereign: Any governmental or administrative structure that is subordinate to a truly sovereign **government**, such as an American state or a British county or a municipal government anywhere. Some authors use the term "subnational."

subsidy: A payment from a **government** to a domestic producer to help stabilize prices, maintain a predictable supply of the product in question, and help the domestic producer to compete with foreign commercial rivals in the same field.

successor state: When a large **sovereign state** breaks up into smaller states, the surviving entities are called successor states. Bosnia is one of the Yugoslav successor states.

summit: A meeting among the national leaders or senior diplomatic officials of two or more countries to settle some **multilateral** political problem.

Sunni: Sunnis are the majority group within the Islamic community, and Sunni practice is generally standardized around the world.

supra-sovereign: Any **transnational** organization, such as the United Nations, created voluntarily by a group of **sovereign states** to accomplish a specified range of functions.

surplus: A budgetary surplus occurs when a **government** takes in more revenue or income than it spends in a given fiscal year.

sustainability: An economic system is said to have sustainability if it replaces resources at the same rate that it consumes them, so that the ability of an environment to support a given population remains constant over time.

Taliban: From the Pushtun word for "student," the Taliban were a group of Islamic fundamentalists originally based in Afghanistan's Kandahar who took over the Afghan **government** in Kabul in a lightning 1994–1995 campaign. The Taliban imposed a ruthless and primitive form of **Islam** over their country, offering sanctuary to Osama bin Laden's al-Qaeda network and ruling until the winter of 2001, when American forces removed them from power.

tariff: A tax imposed on goods and services being imported into a given country.

territoriality: An emotional identification with a given geographic area coupled with the belief that this territory rightfully belongs to one's nation.

terrorism: The use of violence or the threat of violence, usually by **non-state actors**, to achieve political objectives through the dissemination of fear.

theocracy: An undemocratic **government** dominated by religious or clerical leaders.

theory: A set of propositions and concepts that seeks to explain phenomena by specifying the relationships among the concepts.

think tank: Any research institution that investigates a given range of issues can be described as a think tank, although some are really lobbies in disguise, producing policy documents that defend the commercial interests of their corporate sponsors. Others are nonpartisan and noncommercial, and are broadly financed by public contributions.

third way: A phrase associated with Britain's Tony Blair and Germany's Gerhard Schröder to suggest a traditional social democrat who remains interested in welfare but is less willing to become involved in the **nationalization** of industry and is willing to embrace various traditionally conservative ideas.

Third World: A shorthand phrase for the world's poorer countries, sometimes casually used to describe all poor societies but employed by political scientists to describe a large category of relatively poor countries who are increasing their national wealth. In this more precise sense, the Third World needs to be distinguished from the **Fourth World**.

total fertility rate (TFR): The estimated average number of children each woman will produce in the course of her lifetime.

totalitarian: A system of **government** in which an extremely repressive leadership elite, often driven by some pervasive **ideology**, invades every aspect of the citizen's life, ruling with extraordinary cruelty.

transliteration: Not to be confused with "translation," transliteration is the process of taking a given word from one writing system and expressing it in another.

transnational: A cultural phenomenon (like a **language** or a **religion**) is said to be transnational if it flows across the borders of two or more countries.

transparency: A **government**, corporation, or other organization has "transparency" when it conducts its business honestly and openly, permitting public scrutiny of its internal finances and operations.

treaty: A formal agreement, between or among two or more **sovereign states**, that signatories regard as binding.

Treaty of Westphalia: Named after the German region where it was negotiated, the 1648 Treaty of Westphalia ended the Thirty Years War, destroyed the power of the Holy Roman **Empire**, and created a new Europe with several dozen well-defined sovereign **governments**, somewhat clearer borders, and countries more frequently organized around **ethnic** or national groups.

Ulster: The geographical term, more often used by Protestants than by Catholics, to describe Northern Ireland, one of the four provinces of the United Kingdom.

under five mortality rate (U5MR): The number of children per one thousand born alive that fail to celebrate their fifth birthday.

unicameral legislature: A parliament or legislature with only one house, that is, it is not divided into upper and lower houses.

UNICEF: See **United Nations Children's Fund**.

unipolar: A state system (like the era of the Roman **Empire**) where one very large **sovereign state** dominates and dwarfs a series of smaller political entities on its periphery.

unitary system: Any governing system in which most political authority is **constitutionally** given primarily to the national level of **government**, which then gives limited authority to regional and local levels of government to carry out specific functions.

United Nations Children's Fund (UNICEF): Preserving its initials from when it was called the UN International Children's Emergency Fund, UNICEF collects charitable contributions and administers a wide range of health and educational projects for children in the poorer parts of the world.

United Nations Educational, Scientific, and Cultural Organization (UNESCO): Entrusted with the care of the global cultural patrimony, UNESCO is headquartered in Paris.

United Nations High Commission for Refugees (UNHCR): The UN agency in charge of caring for refugees and displaced persons.

Partition Plan: A strategy devised by the UN in 1947 to divide **Palestine** into two separate **sovereign states**, one Jewish and one Arabic.

(UN-REDD Programme) United Nations Collaborative Initiative on Reducing Emissions from Deforestation and Forest Degradation in Developing Countries: Formed to combat the devastating loss of our planet's forests, this program essentially places a value on stored carbon in trees and provides financial income based on this value. REDD involves developed countries paying developing countries carbon offsets for their standing forests.

urbanization: The process of population groups moving from the countryside into cities and towns.

utilitarianism: Associated with Jeremy Bentham, utilitarianism suggests that social rules should be based on what observably makes most people happy rather than on abstract philosophical or religious principle.

values: Fundamental, deeply engrained ideas about the nature of the universe and the meaning of our own individual lives.

Wahhabism: A strict and puritanical form of **Sunni Islam** practiced in Saudi Arabia.

Washington Consensus: The shared belief on the part of most American, some European and Japanese political leaders, and international lending institutions such as the

World Bank/IMF complex that poor countries can prosper by opening their markets to foreign trade, selling off public enterprises, and bringing austerity into their domestic financial affairs.

weapons of mass destruction (WMD): An imprecise phrase, WMD implies nuclear, chemical, or biological weapons in the hands of untrustworthy states or terrorist groups that are targeted against civilian populations.

wire services: Information-gathering organizations, like the Associated Press (AP), that produce news stories for newspapers, radio, television, and the Internet.

World Bank: Technically called **International Bank for Reconstruction and Development**, the World Bank is a UN agency that makes low-interest loans to generate economic growth.

World Trade Organization (WTO): Successor to the General Agreement on Tariffs and Trade (GATT), the WTO works for freer trade worldwide and acts as arbitration agency for international disputes over international commerce.

WTO: See **World Trade Organization**.

xenophobic: Hate or fear of foreigners.

zero population growth (ZPG): While no precise definition exists, the term "zero population growth" is typically used to describe a population in which population increase or decrease is insignificant, perhaps no more than half a percent above or below zero.

zero-sum: A concept derived from **political science** game **theory** and used to describe a situation (like two-handed poker) in which every event is seen as good for one side and bad for the other, or irrelevant. In a zero-sum conflict, there is no theoretical possibility of both sides winning or both sides losing. In two-handed poker, for example, one player can only win if the other player loses; there is no possibility of both finishing the game with more money than they collectively brought into it.

Zionist: One who believes that the Jewish people should have a **nation-state** in what was their ancient ancestral homeland.

Bibliography

Abraham, Henry J. *The Judicial Process*. 7th ed. New York: Oxford University Press, 1998.

Achebe, Chinua. *Things Fall Apart*. New York: Heinemann, 1958.

Acosta, Alberto. *Desarrollo Global: Con la Amazonia en la Mira*. Quito: Corporación Editora Nacional, 2005.

Acton, Thomas, and Gary Mundy. *Romani Culture & Gypsy Identity*. Hatfield, UK: University of Hertfordshire Press, 1999.

Adelman, Carol C. "The Privatization of Foreign Aid." *Foreign Affairs* 82, no. 6 (2003): 9–14.

al-Khalil, Samir. *Republic of Fear*. Berkeley; University of California Press, 1989.

Al-Khalili, Majid. *Oman's Foreign Policy: Foundation and Practice*. New York: Praeger, 2009.

Alan, George. *Jordan: Living in the Crossfire*. London: Zed, 2005.

Allawi, Ali A. *The Occupation of Iraq: Winning the War: Losing the Peace*. New Haven, Conn.: Yale University Press, 2008.

Allen, Beverley. *Rape Warfare: The Hidden Genocide in Bosnia-Herzegovina and Croatia*. Minneapolis, Minn.: University of Minnesota Press, 1996.

Allen, Calvin H. Jr., and W. Lynn Rigsbee II. *Oman under Qaboos: From Coup to Constitution*. London: Cass, 2000.

Allison, Graham. *Nuclear Terrorism: The Ultimate Preventable Catastrophe*. New York: Time Books, 2004.

Almond, Gabriel A. *A Discipline Divided: Schools and Sects in Political Science*. Newbury Park, Calif.: Sage, 1989.

———. *Comparative Politics: A Theoretical Framework*. 4th ed. New York: Longman, 2004.

Almond, Gabriel A., et al. *Comparative Politics Today: A World View*. 8th ed. New York: Longman, 2004.

Almond, Gabriel A., and Sidney Verba. *The Civic Culture*. Boston: Little Brown, 1965.

Almond, Gabriel Abraham, and Sidney Verba. *The Civic Culture: Political Attitudes and Democracy in Five Nations*. San Francisco: Sage, 1963.

Alter, Karen J. *Establishing the Supremacy of European Law*. New York: Oxford University Press, 2001.

Amnesty International. "Lives Blown Apart: Crimes against Women in Times of Conflict." http://web.amnesty.org/library/Index/ENGACT770752004.

Anderson, Benedict. *Imagined Communities: Reflections on the Origin and Spread of Nationalism*. New York: Verso, 1991.

Anderson, Fred. *Crucible of War: The Seven Years' War and the Fate of Empire in British North America, 1754–1766*. New York: Knopf, 2000.

Ansari, Ali. *Confronting Iran*. New York: Basic, 2006.

Arceneaux, Craig L. *Bounded Missions: Military Regimes and Democratization in the Southern Cone and Brazil*. University Park: Pennsylvania State Press, 2001.

Arendt, Hannah. *The Origins of Totalitarianism*. New York: Meridian Books, 1958.

Arjomand, Said Amir. *The Turban for the Crown: The Islamic Revolution in Iran*. New York: Oxford University Press, 1988.

Armatta, Judith. *Twilight of Impunity: The War Crimes Trial of Slobodan Milosevic.* Raleigh, N.C.: Duke University Press, 2010.

Armstrong, Karen. *A History of God: The 4000-Year Quest of Judaism, Christianity.* New York: Ballantine Books, 1994.

———. *The Battle for God: A History of Fundamentalism.* New York: Ballantine, 2001.

———. *Muhammad.* London: Phoenix, 2001.

———. *Islam: A Short History.* New York: Random House, 2002.

Atkinson, Hugh, and Stuart Wilks-Heeg. *Local Government from Thatcher to Blair: The Politics of Creative Autonomy.* London: Polity, 2001.

Auletta, Ken. "Battle Stations: How Long Will the Networks Stick with the News?" *The New Yorker,* December 10, 2001, 60–67.

Aung, San Suu Kyi. *Letters from Burma.* New York: Penguin, 1998.

Aust, Stefan. *Baader-Meinhof: The Inside Story of the R.A.F.* Oxford, UK: Oxford University Press, 2009.

Austin, Granville. *The Indian Constitution: Cornerstone of a Nation.* New York: Oxford University Press, 2000.

Avritzer, Leonardo. *Participatory Institutions in Democratic Brazil.* Baltimore: Johns Hopkins Press, 2009.

Axelrod, Robert, and Robert O. Keohane. *Achieving Cooperation under Anarchy: Strategies and Institutions, Cooperation under Anarchy.* Edited by Kenneth Oye. Princeton: Princeton University Press, 1986.

Ayres, Ed. "The Expanding Shadow Economy." *World Watch* 9, no. 4 (1996): 11–23.

Bagdikian Ben H. *The Media Monopoly: With a New Preface on the Internet and Telecommunications Cartels.* 6th ed. Boston, Mass.: Beacon Press, 2000.

Balfour, Sebastian. *Castro: Profiles in Power.* 2nd ed. New York: Longman, 1995.

Ball, Terence, and Richard Dagger. *Political Ideologies and the Democratic Ideal.* 5th ed. New York: Longman, 2003.

Bamford, James. *Body of Secrets.* New York: Anchor, 2002.

Baradat, Leon P. *Political Ideologies: The Origins and Impact.* 8th ed. Upper Saddle River, N.J.: Prentice Hall, 2003.

Baran, Stanley J. *Introduction to Mass Communication.* Mountain View, Calif.: Mayfield, 2001.

Barber, Benjamin. *Jihad vs. McWorld.* New York: Random House, 1995.

———. *Consumed: How Markets Corrupt Children, Infantilize Adults, and Swallow Citizens Whole.* New York: W. W. Norton, 2007.

Bardon, Jonathan. *A History of Ulster.* Belfast: Blackstaff, 1992.

Barfield, Thomas. *Afghanistan: A Cultural and Political History.* Princeton, N.J.: Princeton University Press, 2010.

Barnett, Tony, and Alan Whiteside. *AIDS in the Twenty-First Century: Disease and Globalization.* New York: Palgrave, 2003.

Bartlett, Thomas. *Ireland: A History.* Cambridge, UK: Cambridge University Press, 2010.

Beah, Ishmael. *A Long Way Gone: Memories of a Boy Soldier.* New York: Farrar, Straus and Giroux, 2007.

Becker, Jillian. *Hitler's Children: The Story of the Baader-Meinhof Terrorist Gang.* New York: Lippincott, 1977.

Beech, Matt, and Simon Lee. *Ten Years of New Labour.* New York and London: Palgrave Macmillan, 2008.

Bell, Ruth Greenspan. "What to Do about Climate Change." *Foreign Affairs* 85, no. 3 (2006): 105–14.

Bellamy, Alex J. *Responsibility to Protect.* New York: Polity, 2009.

Bellia, Anthony J. *Federalism.* New York: Aspen, 2010.

Bentham, Jeremy. *Introduction to the Scientific Principles of Morals and Legislation.* Amherst, N.Y.: Prometheus Books, 1998.

Bergen, Peter L. *Holy War: Inside the Secret World of Osama bin Laden.* New York: Free Press, 2001.

———. *The Osama bin Laden I Know: An Oral History of al Qaeda's Leader.* New York: Free Press, 2006.

———. *The Longest War: The Enduring Conflict between America and al-Qaeda.* New York: Free Press, 2011.

Berlin, Isaiah. *Liberty: Incorporating Four Essays on Liberty.* 2nd ed. New York: Oxford University Press, 2002.

Berridge, G. R. *Diplomacy: Theory and Practice.* New York: Palgrave, 2002.

Berridge, G. R., and Alan James. *Dictionary of Diplomacy.* New York: Palgrave, 2000.

Betancourt, Ingrid. *Even Silence Has an End: My Six Years of Captivity in a Colombian Jungle.* New York: Penguin Press, 2010.

Betts, Richard K. "Fixing Intelligence." *Foreign Affairs* 81, no. 1 (2002): 43–59.

Bhagwati, Jagdish. "Coping with Antiglobalization: A Trilogy of Discontents." *Foreign Affairs* 81, no. 1 (2002): 2–7.

Bickerton, Ian J., and Carla L. Klausner. *A Concise History of the Arab-Israeli Conflict*. 6th ed. Upper Saddle River, N.J.: Prentice Hall, 2009; 4th ed., 2002.

Bill, James A., and Robert Springborg. *Politics in the Middle East*. 5th ed. New York: Longman, 2000.

Birdsall, Nancy, ed. *Population Matters: Demographic Change, Economic Growth, and Poverty in the Developing World*. New York: Oxford University Press 2001.

Birdsall, Nancy, and John Williamson. *Delivering on Debt Relief: From IMF Gold to New Aid Architecture*. Washington, D.C.: Center for Global Development, 2002.

Birnbaum, Jeffrey H. *The Lobbyists: How Influence Peddlers Get Their Way in Washington*. New York: Crown, 1992.

Blackburn, Robert. *The Electoral System in Britain*. New York: St. Martin's Press, 1995.

Blasi, Joseph R., et al. *Kremlin Capitalism: Privatizing the Russian Economy*. Ithaca, N.Y.: Cornell University Press, 1999.

Blondel, Jean. *Comparative Legislatures*. Englewood Cliffs, N.J.: Prentice Hall, 1973.

——. *Thinking Politically*. New York: Penguin, 1978.

Bogdanor, Vernon. *The Monarchy and the Constitution*. Oxford, UK: Oxford University Press, 1998.

——. *The New British Constitution*. Oxford, UK: Hart, 2009.

Borjas, George J, and Lawrence F. Katz. "The Evolution of the Mexican-Born Workforce in the United States." National Bureau of Economic Research (NBER) Working Paper No. 11281 (2005). www.nber.org/papers/w11281 (accessed October 15, 2006).

Bose, Sumantra. *Kashmir: Roots of Conflict, Paths to Peace*. Cambridge, Mass.: Harvard University Press, 2003.

Bowen, Jeremy. *Six Days: How the 1967 War Shaped the Middle East*. New York: Simon & Schuster, 2003.

Bowler, Shaun, and Todd Andrew Donovan. *Demanding Choices: Opinion, Voting, and Direct Democracy*. Ann Arbor, Mich.: University of Michigan Press, 2000.

Boyle, Francis A. *The Tamil Genocide by Sri Lanka: The Global Failure to Protect Tamil Rights under International Law*. Atlanta, Ga.: Clarity Press, 2009.

Bradley, John R. *Saudi Arabia Exposed: Inside a Kingdom in Crisis*. New York: Palgrave Macmillan, 2005.

Brady, Bernard V. *Essential Catholic Social Thought*. New York: Orbis, 2008.

Braunthal, Gerard. *Parties and Politics in Modern Germany*. Boulder, Colo.: Westview Press, 1996.

Bremer, Paul L. *My Year in Iraq: The Struggle to Build a Future of Hope*. New York: Simon & Schuster, 2006.

Bright, Chris. "A History of Our Future." In Worldwatch Institute, *State of the World 2003*, 3–13. New York: Worldwatch Institute/Norton, 2003.

Brinkley, Douglas. *Rosa Parks: A Life*. New York: Penguin, 2005.

Brooks, Stephen. *Canadian Democracy: An Introduction*. 3rd ed. New York: Oxford University Press, 2000.

Broomhall, Bruce. *International Justice and the International Criminal Court*. New York: Oxford University Press, 2004.

Brown, Archie. *The Gorbachev Factor*. Oxford: Oxford University Press, 1996.

Brown, Lester R. *Eco-Economy: Building an Economy for the Future*. New York: Norton, 2001.

Brown, Lester R., Gary Gardner, and Brian Halweil. "Beyond Malthus: Sixteen Dimensions of the Population Problem." Worldwatch Paper No. 143 (1998). Washington, D.C.: Worldwatch Institute, 1998.

Brown, Michael T., et al. *Going Nuclear: Nuclear Proliferation and International Security in the 21st Century*. Cambridge, Mass.: MIT Press, 2010.

Bryson, Bill. *Mother Tongue*. London: Penguin, 1991.

Buchta, Wilfried. *Who Rules Iran? The Structure of Power in the Islamic Republic*. Washington, D.C.: Institute for Near East Policy, 2000.

Bull, Hedley. *The Anarchical Society: A Study of Order in World Politics*. New York: Columbia University Press, 1995.

Burgess, Michael. *Comparative Federalism: Theory and Practice*. London: Routledge, 2006.

Burke, Edmund. *Reflections on the Revolution in France*. New York: Dover, 2006.

Burkhalter, Holly. "The Politics of AIDS." *Foreign Affairs* 83, no. 1 (2004): 8–14.

Bushnell, David. *The Making of Modern Colombia: A Nation in Spite of Itself*. Berkeley: University of California Press, 1993.

Butler, Rhett. "Deforestation in the Amazon." Mongabay Environmental News Service. http://www.mon gabay.com/brazil.html (accessed July10, 2010).

Byman, Daniel L. *Keeping the Peace: Lasting Solutions to Ethnic Conflicts*. Baltimore: Johns Hopkins University Press, 2002.

Calhoun, J. "Population Density and Social Pathology." *Scientific American* 206 (1962): 139–48.

Campbell Bruce B., and Arhur D. Brenner. *Death Squads in Global Perspective: Murder with Deniability*. New York: Palgrave, 2000.

Carey, Peter. *Burma: The Challenge of Change in a Divided Society*. New York: St. Martin's, 1997.

Carment, David, John F. Stack, and Frank P. Harvey. *The International Politics of Quebec Secession*. Westport, Conn.: Praeger, 2001.

Carroll, Lewis. *Alice's Adventures in Wonderland*. Boston: Lee and Shepard, 1869.

———. *Through the Looking Glass: And What Alice Found There*. New York: Macmillan & Co., 1875.

Carroll, Rory. "Nigerian Woman Escapes Death by Stoning." *The Guardian*, September 26, 2003, www .guardian.co.uk/world/2003/sep/26/rorycarroll?INTCMP=SRCH.

Carter, Jimmy. *Palestine: Peace Not Apartheid*. New York: Simon & Schuster, 2006.

Casey, Terrence, ed. *The Blair Legacy: Politics, Policy, Governance, and Foreign Affairs*. New York: Palgrave Macmillan, 2009.

Castañeda, Jorge G. *Campañero*. New York: Knopf, 1997.

———. "Latin America's Left Turn." *Foreign Affairs* 85, no. 3 (2006): 28–44.

Castells, Manuel. *The Rise of the Networks Society*. New York: Blackwell Publishers, 2000.

Chafe, Zoë. "Ozone Layer Making Tentative Improvements." *World Watch* 16, no. 8 (2003): 8.

Chamey, Jonathon I., and J. R. V. Prescott. "Resolving Cross-Strait Relations between China and Taiwan." *American Journal of International Law* 94, no. 3 (2000): 453–78.

Chandler, J. A. *Explaining Local Government*. Manchester, UK: University of Manchester Press, 2008.

Charney, Jonathon I, and W. Michael Reisman. "Agora: Breard." *American Journal of International Law* 92, no. 4 (1998): 666–74.

Charney, Michael W. *A History of Modern Burma*. Cambridge, UK: Cambridge University Press, 2009.

Chesterman, Simon, ed. *Civilians in War*. Boulder, Colo.: Lynn Rienner, 2001.

Chomsky, Noam. *The Failed States: The Abuses of Power and the Assault on Democracy*. New York: Metropolitan Books, 2006.

———. *9–11: Was there an Alternative?* New Edition. New York: Seven Stories Press, September 2011.

Chomsky, Noam, and Doug Stokes. *America's Other War: Terrorizing Colombia*. London: Zed, 2005.

Christensen, Loren. *Riot: A Behind-the-Barricades Tour of Mobs, Riot Cops, and the Chaos of Crowd Violence*. New York: Paladin, 2008.

Chua, Amy. *World on Fire: How Exporting Free Market Democracy Breeds Ethnic Hatred and Global Instability*. New York: Doubleday, 2003.

Clark, John D. *Worlds Apart: Civil Society and the Battle for Ethical Globalization*. Bloomfield, Conn.: Kumarian, 2003.

Clawson, Patrick, and Michael Rubin. *Eternal Iran: Continuity and Chaos*. New York: Palgrave, 2006.

Clemons, Walter C. Jr. *Dynamics of International Relations: Conflict and Mutual Gain in an Era of Global Interdependence*. 2nd ed. Boulder, Colo.: Rowman & Littlefield, 2004.

Clifford, John. *The Sri Lanka Reader: History, Culture, Politics*. Raleigh, N.C.: Duke University Press, 2011.

Coale, Ansley, and Judith Bannister. "Five Decades of Missing Females in China." *Demography* 32, no. 3 (1994): 459–80.

Cobb, Clifford, et al. *The Genuine Progress Indicator 2000 Update*. Oakland, Calif.: Redefining Progress, 2001.

Cockett, Richard. *Sudan: Darfur and the Failure of an African State*. New Haven: Yale University Press, 2010.

Cohen, Joel E. *How Many People Can the Earth Support?* New York: Norton, 1995.

Cohen, Stephen P. *India: Emerging Power*. Washington, D.C.: Brookings, 2002.

Cole, Alistair, and Peter Campbell. *French Electoral Systems*. Brookfield, Vt.: Gower, 1987.

Collin, Richard Oliver. *The De Lorenzo Gambit: The Italian Coup Manquè of 1965*. Sage Research Papers in the Social Sciences. London: Sage, 1976.

———. "Breaking the Police: Mussolini's Use of Terrorism." *Violence Aggression Terrorism* 1, no. 1 (1987): 1–13.

———. *La Donna Che Sparò a Mussolini*. Milan: Rusconi, 1988.

———. "When Reality Came Unglued: Antonio Savasta and the Red Brigades." Originally published in *Violence Aggression Terrorism* 3, no. 4 (1989): 269–96. Reprinted in Schechterman, Bernard, and Martin Slann, *Annual Editions: Violence and Terrorism 91/92*. Washington: Dushkin 1991.

———. "When Irish Eyes Stop Smiling." *International Counterterrorism*, Winter 1990/1991, 18–26.

———. "Words of War: The Iraqi Tower of Babel." *International Studies Perspectives* 10, no. 3 (2009): 245–64.

———. "Revolutionary Scripts." In *Culture and Language: Multidisciplinary Case Studies*, edited by Michael Morris, 29–67. Frankfurt: Peter Lang, 2011.

Collin, Richard Oliver, and Gordon L Freedman. *Winter of Fire: The Abduction of General Dozier and the Downfall of the Red Brigades*. New York: Dutton/Penguin, 1990.

Collins, Robert O. *A History of Modern Sudan*. Cambridge, UK: Cambridge University Press, 2008.

Collins, Roger. *The Basques*. Oxford: Blackwell, 1986.

Commoner, Barry. *Making Peace with the Planet*. New York: Pantheon, 1990.

Comrie, Bernard, ed. *The World's Major Languages*. New York: Oxford University Press, 1987.

Conca, Ken. *Governing Water: Contentious Transnational Politics and Global Institution Building Global Environmental Accord: Strategies for Sustainability and Institutional Innovation*. Boston, Mass.: MIT Press, 2005.

Corrales, Javier, and Michael Penfold. *Dragon in the Tropics: Hugo Chavez and the Political Economy of Revolution in Venezuela*. Washington, D.C.: Brookings, 2010.

Cox, Harvey. "The Market as God." *The Atlantic Online*, March 1999. http://www.theatlantic.com/past/docs/issues/99mar/marketgod.htm (accessed July 10, 2011).

Crystal, David. *The Penguin Dictionary of Language*. 2nd ed. London: Penguin, 1999.

Dahl, Robert A. *How Democratic Is the American Constitution?* New Haven: Yale University Press, 2002.

Dalai Lama. *My Land and People*. New York: Warner, 1997.

Danner, Mark. *Torture and Truth: America, Abu Ghraib, and the War on Terror*. New York: New York Review of Books, 2004.

Darwin, Charles. *Origin of the Species*. Edited by Greg Suriano. New York: Grammercy, 1998.

De Lange, Nicholas. *An Introduction to Judaism*. Cambridge, UK: Cambridge University Press, 2000.

DelliCarpini, Michael X., and Scott Ketter. *What Americans Know about Politics and Why It Matters*. New Haven, Conn.: Yale University Press, 1996.

Denov, Myriam. *Child Soldiers: Sierra Leone's Revolutionary United Front*. Cambridge, UK: Cambridge University Press, 2010.

Denver, David, Christopher Carman, and Robert Johns. *Elections and Voters in Britain*. Revised 3rd ed. New York: Palgrave Macmillan, 2012.

De Sombre, Beth, and J. Samuel Barkin. *Fish*. New York: Polity Books, 2011.

Deutsch, John. "A Nuclear Posture for Today." *Foreign Affairs* 84, no. 1 (2005): 49–60.

Diamond, Jared. *Collapse: How Societies Choose to Fail or Succeed*. New York: Viking, 2005.

Dolnick, Edward. "Super-Women." *Health*, July/August 1991, 42–48.

Douglas, Amy J. *Real Choices/New Voices: How Proportional Representation Could Re-vitalize American Democracy*. New York: Columbia University Press, 2002.

Dowty, Alan. *Israel/Palestine*. Cambridge, UK: Polity, 2005.

Drake, Richard. *The Aldo Moro Murder Case*. Cambridge, Mass.: Harvard University Press, 1995.

Drysdale, John. *Whatever Happened to Somalia? A Tale of Tragic Blunders*. London: Haan, 2002.

Duffy, Quinn. *The Road to Nunavut: The Progress of the Eastern Arctic Inuit since the Second World War*. Toronto: McGill-Queens University Press, 1988.

Dugger, Celia. "Senegal Curbs a Bloody Rite for Girls and Women." *New York Times*, October 16, 2011, A13.

Dunn, Seth. *Micropower: The Next Electrical Era*. Worldwatch Paper No. 151. Washington, D.C.: Worldwatch Institute, 2000.

Dupree, Louis. *Afghanistan*. Princeton, N.J.: Princeton University Press, 1978.

Eagleton, Terry. *Ideology: An Introduction*. New York: Verso, 2007.

Easton, David. *A Framework for Political Analysis*. Englewood Cliffs, N.J.: Prentice Hall, 1965.

The Economist. "The Big Mac Index." July 28, 2011. http://www.economist.com/blogs/dailychart/2011/07/big-mac-index

———. "Sri Lanka and War Crimes: Keep Quiet and Carry On." April 11, 2011. http://www.economist.com/node/18561107.

Ehrlich, Paul. *The Population Bomb*. New York: Ballantine, 1968.

English, T. J. *Havana Nocturne: How the Mob Owned Cuba and Then Lost It to the Revolution.* New York: Morrow, 2009.

Enloe, Cynthia. *Globalization and Militarism: Feminists Make the Link.* Lanham, Md.: Rowman and Littlefield, 2007.

———. *Nimo's War, Emma's War: Making Feminist Sense of the Iraq War.* Berkeley: University of California Press, 2010.

ENS Environmental News Service. "Deforestation, Climate Change, and East African Drought." January 16, 2006. http://www.ens-newswire.com/ens/jan2006/2006–01–16–02.asp (accessed October 23, 2011).

Esposito, John L. *Islam: The Straight Path.* New York: Oxford University Press, 1988.

———. *Unholy War: Terror in the Name of Islam.* New York: Oxford University Press, 2002.

Evans, Gareth. *The Responsibility to Protect: Ending Mass Atrocity Crimes Once and for All.* Washington, D.C.: Brookings, 2009.

Falk, Richard A. *Human Rights Horizons: The Pursuit of Justice in a Globalized World.* New York: Routledge, 2000.

Fallows, James. *Breaking the News: How the Media Undermine American Democracy.* New York: Vintage, 1997.

———. *Blind into Baghdad: America's War in Iraq.* New York: Vintage, 2006.

Falola, Toyin. *Violence in Nigeria: The Crisis of Religious Politics and Secular Ideologies.* Rochester, N.Y.: University of Rochester Press, 1998.

Falola, Toyin, and Matthew Heaton. *The History of Nigeria.* Westport, Conn.: Greenwood Publishing Group, 2008.

FAO (Food and Agriculture Organization). *The State of Food Insecurity 2003.* Rome, Italy: United Nations Food and Agriculture Organization, 2003.

Farouk-Sluglett, Marion, and Peter Sluglett. *Iraq since 1958: From Revolution to Dictatorship.* Revised. New York: I. B. Tauris, 2001.

Favarel-Garrigues, Gilles. *Policing Economic Crime in Russia: From Soviet Planned Economy to Privatization.* New York: Columbia University Press, 2011.

Feshback, Murray, and Alfred Friendly. *Ecocide in the USSR: Health and Nature under Siege.* New York: Basic, 1992.

Finnegan, William. "The Economics of Empire." *Harper's Magazine,* May 2003: 41–54.

Firor, John, and Judith E. Jacobsen. *The Crowded Greenhouse: Population, Climate Change, and Creating a Sustainable World.* New Haven: Yale University Press, 2002.

Fishlow Albert. *Starting Over: Brazil since 1985.* Washington, D.C.: Brookings, 2011.

Flavin, Christopher. "Rich Planet, Poor Planet." In Worldwatch Institute, *State of the World 2001,* 3–20. New York: Worldwatch Institute/Norton, 2001.

Flavin, Christopher, and Gary Gardner. "China, India, and the New World Order." In Worldwatch Institute, *State of the World 2006,* 3–23. New York: Worldwatch Institute/Norton, 2006.

Flint, Julie, and Alex de Waal. *Darfur: A Short History of a Long War.* London: Zed, 2008.

Fonseca, Isabel. *Bury Me Standing: The Gypsies and Their Journey.* New York: Knopf, 1996.

Franklin, Jonathan. "Chile's Commander Camila, the Student Who Can Shut Down a City." *The Guardian,* August 24, 2011, www.guardian.co.uk/world/2011/aug/24/chile-student-leader-camila-vallejo.

Freeden, Michael. *Ideology: A Very Short Introduction.* New York: Oxford University Press, 2003.

Freedom House. "Freedom in the World 2011: The Annual Survey of Political Rights and Civil Liberties." http://freedomhouse.org/template.cfm?page=363&year=2011 (accessed November 21, 2011).

Freeland, Chrysta. *Sale of the Century: Russia's Wild Ride from Communism to Capitalism.* New York: Crown, 2000.

Friedman, Thomas L. *The Lexus and the Olive Tree.* New York: Farrar, Straus, Giroux, 1999.

———. *The World Is Flat.* New York: Farrar, Straus and Giroux, 2005.

Friedman, Thomas L., and Michael Mandelbaum. *That Used to Be Us: How Americans Fell Behind in the World We Created and How We Come Back.* New York: Farrar, Straus, and Giroux, 2011.

Friedrich, Carl J., and Zbigniew Brzezinski. *Totalitarian Dictatorship and Autocracy.* Cambridge: Mass.: Harvard University Press, 1956.

Fukuyama, Francis. *America at the Crossroads: Democracy, Power, and the Neo-conservative Legacy.* New Haven: Yale University Press, 2006.

———. "The End of History?" *National Interest,* 1989, 3–18.

———. "Women and the Evolution of World Politics." *Foreign Affairs*, September/October 1998.

———. *The End of History and the Last Man*. New York: Free Press, 2006.

Funderburk, Charles, and Robert G. Thobaben. *Political Ideologies: Left, Center, Right*. New York: Harper & Row, 1989.

Gandhi, Mahatma. *Non-violent Resistance: Satyagrah*. New York: Schocken, 1972.

Gandolfo, Luisa. *Palestinians in Jordan: The Politics of Identity*. London: I. B. Tauris, 2012.

Ganesan, N., and Kyaw Yin Hlaing. *Myanmar: State, Society, and Ethnicity*. Singapore: Institute of Southeast Asian Studies, 2007.

Ganguly, Sumit. *Conflict Unending: India-Pakistan Tensions since 1947*. New York: Columbia University Press, 2002.

Ganguly, Sumit, and Rahul Mukherji. *India since 1980*. Cambridge, UK: Cambridge University Press, 2011.

Gardner, Gary, et al. "The State of Consumption Today." In Worldwatch Institute, *State of the World 2004*, 3–21.

Gardner, Gary, and Brian Halweil. "The Overfed and Underfed: Escaping Hunger, Escaping Excess." *World Watch* 13, no. 4 (2000): 25–35.

Gardner, Richard N. "The One Percent Solution." *Foreign Affairs* 79, no. 4 (2000): 2–11.

Gasana, James. "Remember Rwanda?" *World Watch* 15, no. 2 (2002): 24–33.

Gellner Ernest. *Nations and Nationalism*. Ithaca: Cornell University Press, 1983.

Gerges, Fawaz A. *The Rise and Fall of al-Qaeda*. New York: Oxford University Press, 2011.

Ghandhi, P. R. *Blackstone's International Human Rights Documents*. 2nd ed. London: Blackstone, 2000.

Gheissari, Ali, and Vali Nasr. *Democracy in Iran*. New York: Oxford University Press, 2006.

Giddens, Anthony. *The Third Way: The Renewal of Social Democracy*. Cambridge, UK: Polity, 1999.

Gilbert, Martin. *Israel: A History*. New York: Morrow, 1998.

Gillingham, John. *European Integration 1950–2002: Superstate or New Market Economy?* New York: Cambridge University Press, 2003.

Gills, Barry. "Empire vs. Cosmopolis: The Clash of Globalizations." *Globalizations* 2, no. 1 (May 2005).

Gilpin, Robert. *War and Change in World Politics*. Cambridge: Cambridge University Press, 1981.

Ginsborg, Paul. *Silvio Berlusconi: Television, Power, and Patrimony*. New York: Verso, 2004.

Glenny, Misha. *The Balkans: Nationalism, War, and the Great Powers 1804–1999*. New York: Viking, 2000.

Goldman, Marshall. *Petrostate: Putin, Power, and the New Russia*. New York: Oxford University Press, 2010.

Gore, Al. *Earth in the Balance*. Boston: Houghton Mifflin, 1992.

Gourevitch, Philip. *We Wish to Inform You That Tomorrow We Will Be Killed with Our Families*. New York: Farrar, Straus & Giroux, 1998.

Greenberg, Edward S, and Benjamin I. Page. *The Struggle for Democracy*. 5th ed. New York: Longman, 2001.

Gresser, Edward. "Toughest on the Poor." *Foreign Affairs* 81, no. 6 (2002): 9–14.

Grigsby, Ellen. *Analyzing Politics: An Introduction to Political Science*. Belmont, Calif.: Wadsworth, 1999.

Guardian. "Marie Colvin." February 23, 2012, 18.

Guevara, Ernesto "Che." *Guerrilla Warfare*. Lincoln, Nebr.: University of Nebraska Press, 1983.

Gunlicks, Arthur. *The Lander and German Federalism*. Manchester, UK: Manchester University Press, 2003.

Gurr, Ted Robert. *Peoples versus States: Minorities at Risk in the New Century*. Washington, D.C.: U.S. Institute of Peace, 2000.

Habibullah, Wajahat. *My Kashmir: Conflict and the Prospects of Enduring Peace*. Washington, D.C.: Institute of Peace, 2008.

Hafez, Mohammed M. *Suicide Bombers in Iraq*. Washington, D.C.: Institute of Peace, 2007.

Halberstam, David. *War in a Time of Peace: Bush, Clinton, and the Generals*. New York: Scribner, 2001.

Hall, Duncan. *The British Commonwealth of Nations*. Toronto, Canada: University of Toronto Press, 2011.

Hall, Thomas J., and Rodney Bruce Biersteker. *The Emergence of Private Authority in Global Governance*. Cambridge: Cambridge University Press, 2002.

Hallaq, Wael B. *An Introduction to Islamic Law*. Cambridge, UK: Cambridge University Press, 2009.

Halweil, Brian. "The Emperor's New Crops." *World Watch* 12, no. 6 (1999): 21–29.

———. "Biotech, African Corn, and the Vampire Weed." *World Watch* 14, no. 5 (2001): 26–31.

Halweil, Brian, and Danielle Nierenberg. "Watching What We Eat." In Worldwatch Institute, *State of the World 2004*, 68–85.

Haney, Patrick, and Walt Vanderbush. *The Cuban Embargo: Domestic Politics of American Foreign Policy*. Pittsburgh: University of Pittsburgh Press, 2005.

Hardin, Garrett. "The Tragedy of the Commons." *Science* 162 (1968): 1243–48.

Harris, Ian. *Buddhism in Twentieth-Century Asia*. London: Cassel, 1999.

Harris, Marvin. *Our Kind: Who We Are. Where We Came From. Where We Are Going*. New York: Harper Perennial, 1989.

Hartley, Paul, and Ronald Bland, eds. *South Sudan: Challenges and Opportunities for Africa's New Nation*. New York: Nova, 2012.

Hashim, Ahmed. *Insurgency and Counter-Insurgency in Iraq*. Ithaca: Cornell University Press, 2006.

Hasso, Frances Susan. *Resistance, Repression, and Gender Politics in Occupied Palestine and Jordan*. Syracuse, N.Y.: Syracuse University Press, 2005.

Haufler, Virginia. *A Public Role for the Private Sector*. Washington, D.C.: Carnegie Endowment for International Peace, 2001.

Havel, Vaclav. "Havel Smells Trouble." *Harper's* 285, no. 1708 (1992): 27.

Hawkes, David. *Ideology*. London: Routledge, 2003.

Heaney, Seamus. *New Selected Poems 1966–1987*. London: Faber & Faber, 1990.

Hearn, Adrian H. *Cuba: Religion, Social Capital, and Development*. Raleigh, N.C.: Duke University Press, 2008.

Henderson, James D. *Why Colombia Bled: A History of the Violencia in Tolima*. Tuscaloosa, Ala.: University of Alabama Press, 1985.

———. *Conservative Thought in Twentieth Century Latin America: The Ideas of Laureano Gómez*. Athens, Ohio: Ohio University Press, 1988.

———. *Modernization in Colombia*. Gainesville: University Press of Florida, 2001.

Henderson, James D., et al. *A Reference Guide to Latin American History*. Armonk, New York: Sharpe, 2000.

Hennessy, Peter. *The Prime Minister: The Office and Its Holders since 1945*. New York: Palgrave, 2001.

Henshaw, Caroline. "World Food Prices Remain High." *The Wall Street Journal*, May 22, 2011. http://online.wsj.com/article/SB10001424052748703859304576304932662054022.html (accessed June 10, 2011).

Hicks, Alexander M. *Social Democracy and Welfare Capitalism: A Century of Income Security Politics*. Ithaca: Cornell University Press, 2000.

Hill, Steven. *Fixing Elections: The Failure of America's Winner Take All Politics*. New York: Routledge, 2003.

Hinrichsen, Don. "Ladies, You Have No Choice." *World Watch* 17, no. 2 (2004): 24–30.

Hirsch, John L. *Sierra Leone: Diamonds and the Struggle for Democracy*. Boulder, Colo.: Lynn Rienner, 2000.

Hirsch, John L., and Robert B. Oakley. *Somalia and Operation Restore Hope*. Washington, D.C.: U.S. Institute of Peace Press, 1995.

Hoffman, Bruce. *Inside Terrorism*. Revised edition. New York: Columbia University Press, 2006.

Holbrooke, Richard. *To End a War*. New York: Random House, 1998.

Holland, Jack. *Hope against History: The Course of the Conflict in Northern Ireland*. New York: Holt, 1999.

Horowitz, Donald L. *The Deadly Ethnic Riot*. Berkeley, Calif.: University of California Press, 2003.

———. *Ethnic Groups in Conflict*. Updated ed. Berkeley: University of California Press, 2000.

Hourani, Albert. *A History of the Arab Peoples*. 2nd ed. Cambridge, Mass.: Harvard University Press, 1991.

Housman, A. E. *The Collected Poems of A. E. Housman*. London: Wordsworth, 1994.

Hulse, Frederick S. *The Human Species: An Introduction to Physical Anthropology*. New York: Random House, 1971.

Huntington, Samuel J. *Who Are We? The Challenges to America's Identity*. New York: Simon and Schuster, 2005.

Huntington, Samuel P. "The Hispanic Challenge." *Foreign Policy*, March/April 2004. http://cyber.law.harvard.edu/blogs/gems/culturalagency1/SamuelHuntingtonTheHispanicC.pdf.

Hwang, Ann. "Exportable Righteousness, Expendable Women." *World Watch* 15, no. 1 (2002): 24–31.

Ignatieff, Michael. *Human Rights as Politics and Idolatry*. Princeton: Princeton University Press, 2001.

ILO (International Labour Organization). *Employment Trends 2010*. http://www.ilocarib.org.tt/portal/index.php?option=com_content&task=view&id=1330&Itemid=1209 (accessed July 1, 2011).

ILO (International Labour Organization). *The End of Child Labour: Within Reach*. International Labour Conference, 95th Session 2006, Report I (B). Geneva: International Labour Office, 2006.

International Monetary Forum (IMF). Reform Press Release. November 5, 2010. http://www.imf.org/external/np/sec/pr/2010/pr10418.htm.

IPCC (Inter-governmental Panel on Climate Change). *Climate Change 2001: Synthesis Report*. Cambridge, UK: Cambridge University Press, 2001.

Isbister, John. *Promises Not Kept: Poverty and the Betrayal of Third World Development*. 6th ed. Bloomfield: Conn.: Kumarian, 2003.

Jacobson, Jodi L. "Improving Women's Reproductive Health." In Worldwatch Institute, *State of the World 1992*, 83–99.

Jenkins, Philip. "The Next Christianity." *The Atlantic Monthly*, October 2002, 53–68.

Johnson, Chalmers. *Blowback: The Costs and Consequences of American Empire*. New York: Holt, 2000.

Jones, Seth G. *In the Graveyard of Empires: America's War in Afghanistan*. New York: Norton, 2000.

Joppke Christian. *Immigration and the Nation-State: The United States, Germany, and Great Britain*. New York: Oxford University Press, 2000.

Joshi, Manoj. *The Lost Rebellion: Kashmir in the Nineties*. New York: Penguin, 1999.

Judah, Tim. *Kosovo: What Everybody Needs to Know*. New York: Oxford University Press, 2008.

Judge, David, et al. *The European Parliament*. 2nd ed. New York: Palgrave Macmillan, 2008.

Juergensmeyer, Mark. *Terror in the Mind of God: The Global Rise of Religious Violence*. 3rd ed. Berkeley, Calif.: University of California Press, 2003.

Kaplan, Robert D. "The Coming Anarchy." *The Atlantic Monthly*, February 1994, 44–76.

———. "Was Democracy Just a Moment?" *The Atlantic Monthly*, December 1997, 55–80.

Kashi, Ed. *When the Borders Bleed: The Struggle of the Kurds*. New York: Pantheon, 1994.

Katz, Alan M., ed. *Legal Traditions and Systems: An International Handbook*. Westport, Conn.: Greenwood, 1986.

Katznelson, Ira, and Helen V. Milner, eds. *Political Science: The State of the Discipline*. New York: Norton, 2002.

Keay, John. *India: A History*. Boston, Mass.: Atlantic, 2000.

———. *China: A History*. New York: Basic, 2011.

Keck, Margaret E., and Kathryn Sikkink. *Activists beyond Borders: Advocacy Networks in International Politics*. Ithaca, N.Y.: Cornell University Press, 1998.

Keegan, John. *The Iraqi War: The 21-Day Conflict and Its Aftermath*. London: Pimlico, 2005.

Keen, Benjamin. *Latin American Civilization*. 8th ed. Boulder, Colo.: Westview Press, 2004.

Kenez, Peter. *A History of the Soviet Union from the Beginning to the End*. 2nd ed. Cambridge, UK: Cambridge University Press, 2006.

Kennan, George F. "The Sources of Soviet Conduct." *Foreign Affairs* (1947).

Kennedy, Paul. *Preparing for the Twenty-First Century*. New York: Random House, 1993.

Kennedy, Robert F., and Arthur Schlesinger Jr. *Thirteen Days: A Memoir of the Cuban Crisis*. New York: Norton, 1999.

Keohane, Robert O., and Joseph S. Nye. "Transnational Relations and World Politics." *International Organization* 25, no. 3 (Summer 1971).

———. *Power and Interdependence*. 3rd ed. New York: Longman, 2001.

Keown, Damien. *Buddhism: A Very Short Introduction*. New York: Oxford University Press, 2000.

Kepel, Gilles. *The War for Muslim Minds: Islam and the West*. Cambridge, Mass.: Harvard University Press, 2004.

Ker-Lindsay, James. *Kosovo: The Path to Contested Statehood in the Balkans*. New York: Vintage, 2008.

Khagram, Sanjeev, James Riker, and Kathryn Sikkink, eds. *Restructuring World Politics: Transnational Social Movements, Networks and Norms*. Minneapolis: University of Minnesota Press, 2002.

Khan, Yasmin. *The Great Partition: The Making of India and Pakistan*. New Haven, Conn.: Yale University Press, 2008.

Khandker, Shahidur R. *Fighting Poverty with Microcredit: Experience in Bangladesh*. Published for the World Bank. New York: Oxford University Press, 2003.

Kim, Jim Yong, et al. *Dying for Growth: Global Inequality and the Health of the Poor*. Monroe, Maine: The Institute for Health and Social Justice/Common Courage Press, 2000.

King, Anthony. *The British Constitution*. Oxford, UK: Oxford University Press, 2011.

King, Gary, Robert O. Keohane, and Sidney Verba. *Designing Social Inquiry*. Princeton: Princeton University Press, 1994.

King, Iain, and Whit Mason. *Peace at Any Price: How the World Failed Kosovo*. Cornell, N.Y.: Cornell University Press, 2006.

King, Martin Luther. *Where Do We Go from Here? Chaos or Community?* New York: Harper Collins, 1967.

Kingstone, Peter, and Deborah J. Yashar, eds. *The Routledge Handbook of Latin American Politics*. London: Routledge, 2012.

Kinzer, Stephen. *All the Shah's Men: An American Coup and the Roots of Middle Eastern Terror*. London: John Wiley, 2003.

Kissinger, Henry. *Years of Renewal*. New York: Simon & Schuster, 1999.

Klare, Michael T. *Resource Wars: The New Landscape of Global Conflict*. New York: Holt, 2001.

———. *Blood and Oil*. London: Penguin, 2004.

———. *Rising Powers, Shrinking Planet: The New Geopolitics of Energy*. New York: Metropolitan, 2008.

Klein, Naomi. *No Logo: Taking Aim at the Brand Bullies*. New York: Picador, 1999.

———. *Shock Doctrine: The Rise of Disaster Capitalism*. New York: Metropolitan Books, 2007.

Knightley, Phillip. *First Casualty: From the Crimea to Vietnam*. New York: Harcourt Brace, 1975.

Knott, Kim. *Hinduism, A Very Short Introduction*. New York: Oxford University Press, 2000.

Koerner, Lisbet. *Linnaeus: Nature and Nation*. Cambridge, Mass.: Harvard University Press, 1999.

Krasner, Stephen D, ed. *Problematic Sovereignty: Contested Rules and Political Possibilities*. New York: Columbia University Press, 2001.

Kreppel, Amie. *The European Parliament and Supranational Party System*. New York: Cambridge University Press, 2002.

Krieger, Joel, ed. *The Oxford Companion to Politics of the World*. 2nd ed. Oxford: Oxford University Press, 2001.

Kristof, Nicholas, and Sheryl Wudunn. *Half the Sky*. New York: Knopf, 2009.

Krueger, Anne O. *The WTO as an International Organization*. Chicago: University of Chicago Press, 1998.

Krugman, Paul. "For Richer." *The New York Times Magazine*, October 20, 2002.

———. "The Tax Cut Con." *The New York Times Magazine*, April 14, 2003, 54–62.

———. *The Conscience of a Liberal*. New York: Norton, 2009.

———. *The Return of Depression Economics and the Crisis of 2008*. New York: Norton, 2009.

Kuhn, Thomas. *The Structure of Scientific Revolutions*. 3rd ed. Chicago: University of Chicago Press, 1996.

Kupchan, Charles A. "Independence for Kosovo: Yielding to Balkan Reality." *Foreign Affairs* 84, no. 6 (2005): 14–21.

Kurlansky, Mark. *The Basque History of the World*. New York and London: Penguin, 2001.

Kymlicka, Will. *Finding Our Way: Rethinking Ethnocultural Relations in Canada*. Toronto: Oxford University Press, 1998.

Lacey, Robert. *Inside the Kingdom: Kings, Clerics, Modernists, Terrorists, and the Struggle for Saudi Arabia*. New York: Viking, 2009.

Lancaster, Carol. "Development in Africa: The Good, the Bad, the Ugly." *Current History* 104, no. 682 (2005): 222–27.

Landes, David S. *The Wealth and Poverty of Nations: Why Some Are So Rich and Some So Poor*. New York: W. W. Norton, 1999.

Laqueur, Walter. *A History of Zionism: From the French Revolution to the Establishment of the State of Israel*. New York: Random House, 1972.

———. *Guerrilla Warfare: A Historical and Critical Study*. Piscataway, N.J.: Transaction, 1988.

———. *A History of Terrorism*. Piscataway, N.J.: Transaction, 2001.

———. *After the Fall: The End of the European Dream and the Decline of a Continent*. New York: Thomas Dunne, 2012.

Lasswell, Harold D. *Who Gets What, When and How*. New York: McGraw Hill, 1938.

Last, Jonathan V. "The War against Girls." *Wall Street Journal* Book Review, June 18, 2011. http://online.wsj.com/article/SB10001424052702303657404576361691165631366.html (accessed June 24, 2011).

Lawrence, Quil. *Invisible Nation: How the Kurds' Quest for Statehood Is Shaping Iraq and the Middle East*. New York: Walker Books, 2009.

Layard, Richard. *Happiness: Lessons from a New Science*. London: Penguin, 2005.

Ledbetter, James. *Made Possible By: The Death of Public Broadcasting in the United States*. New York: Verso, 2005.

Lee, Martin, and Norman Solomon. *Unreliable Sources: A Guide to Detecting Bias in News Reporting.* New York: Lyle Stuart, 1991.

Leech, Gary. *Beyond Bogota: Diary of a Drug War Journalist in Colombia.* Boston: Beacon, 2007.

———. *The FARC: The Longest Insurgency.* London: Zed, 2011.

Lenin, Vladimir. *State and Revolution.* New York: International Publishers, 1932.

LeoGrande, William M. *Our Own Backyard: The United States in Central America, 1977–1992.* Durham: University of North Carolina Press, 1998.

Lester, Toby. "Oh, Gods!" *The Atlantic,* February 2002, 37.

Levine, Bertram J. *The Art of Lobbying: Building Trust and Selling Policy.* Washington, D.C.: CQ Press, 2008.

Levitt, Matthew. *Hamas: Politics, Charity, and Terrorism in the Service of Jihad.* New Haven, Conn.: Yale University Press, 2006.

Levy, Jacob T. *The Multiculturalism of Fear.* New York: Oxford University Press, 2000.

Lewis, Bernard. *The Arabs in History.* New York: Oxford University Press, 2002.

Liddell Hart, B. H. *History of the Second World War.* London: Pan, 1970.

Lijphart, Arend. *Parliamentary versus Presidential Government.* Oxford, UK: Oxford University Press, 1992.

———. *Electoral Systems and Party Systems.* New York: Oxford University Press, 1994.

Livi-Bacci, Massimo. *A Concise History of World Population.* 3rd ed. Oxford, UK: Blackwell, 2001.

Luciak, Ilja A. *The Sandinista Legacy.* Gainesville, Fla.: University Press of Florida, 1995.

Maathai, Wangari. "Trees for Democracy." *The New York Times,* December 10, 2004. http://www.nytimes.com/2004/12/10/opinion/10maathai.html (accessed November 22, 2011).

MacArthur, John R. *Second Front: Censorship and Propaganda in the Gulf War.* Berkeley, Calif.: University of California Press, 1993.

Machel, Graça. *The Impact of War on Children.* New York: Palgrave, 2002.

Mackey, Sandra. *The Iranians: Persia, Islam and the Soul of a Nation.* New York: Penguin, 1998.

Macridis, Roy C. *Contemporary Political Ideologies: Movements and Regimes.* 3rd ed. Boston: Little, Brown, 1985.

Maier, Karl. *This House Has Fallen: Midnight in Nigeria.* Boulder, Colo.: Public Affairs, 2000

Malthus, Thomas Robert. *Essay on Population.* London: St. Paul's Church Yard, 1798. http://www.esp.org/books/malthus/population/malthus.pdf (accessed November 23, 2011).

Mamdani, Mahmood. *The Myth of Population Control.* New York: Monthly Review Press, 1972.

———. *When Victims Become Killers.* Princeton, N.J.: Princeton University Press, 2001.

Mander, Jerry. *Four Arguments for the Elimination of Television.* New York: William Morrow, 1974.

Manheim, Jarol B. *Empirical Political Analysis: Research Methods in Political Science.* New York: Addison Wesley Longman, 1998.

Mann, Michel. *Fascists.* Cambridge, UK: Cambridge University Press, 2004.

Manning, Bayless. "The Congress, the Executive and Intermestic Affairs." *Foreign Affairs* 57, no. 1 (1979): 308–24.

Maren, Michael. *The Road to Hell: The Ravaging Effects of Foreign Aid and International Charity.* New York: Free Press, 1997.

Marger, Marvin N. *Race and Ethnic Relations.* Belmont: Calif.: Wadsworth, 1991.

Marks, Jonathon. *Human Biodiversity: Genes, Race, and History; Foundations of Human Behavior.* New York: De Gruyter, 1995.

Marmot, Michael. *Status Syndrome: How Social Standing Directly Affects Your Health and Life Expectancy.* London: Bloomsbury, 2004.

Marr, Phoebe. *The Modern History of Iraq.* 3rd ed. Boulder, Colo.: Westview, 2011.

Marsden, Peter. *The Taliban: War, Religion, and the New Order in Afghanistan.* London: Zed Books, 1998.

Martin, Pamela L. "Global Environmental Governance from the Amazon." *Global Environmental Politics,* MIT Press Journals 11, no. 4 (November 2011): 22–42.

———. *Oil in the Soil.* New York: Rowman and Littlefield, 2011.

———. "Pay to Preserve: The Global Politics of Ecuador's Yasuní-ITT Proposal." In *International Development Policy: Energy and Development,* edited by Gilles Carbonnier, 117–36. Hampshire, England: Palgrave Macmillan, 2011.

Martin, Pamela L., and Franke Wilmer. "Transnational Normative Struggles and Globalization: The Case of Indigenous Peoples in Bolivia and Ecuador." *Globalizations* 5, no. 4 (December 2008): 583–98.

Martin, Randolph. "Sudan's Perfect War." *Foreign Affairs* 81, no. 2 (2002): 111–27.

Mazower, Mark. *No Enchanted Place: The End of Empire and the Ideological Origins of the United Nations.* Princeton, N.J.: Princeton University Press, 2010.

McCarty, Nolan, Keith T. Poole, and Howard Rosenthal. *Polarized America: The Dance of Ideology and Unequal Riche.* Cambridge, Mass.: MIT Press, 2008.

McClintock, Cynthia. *Revolutionary Movements in Latin America: El Salvador's FMLN and Peru's Shining Path.* Washington, D.C.: U.S. Institute of Peace, 1998.

McGinn, Anne Platt. "The Resurgence of Infectious Diseases." *World Watch* 8, no. 4 (1995): 26–32.

———. "Malaria, Mosquitoes, and DDT." *World Watch* 15, no. 3 (2002): 10–17.

McGreal, Chris. "Barak Obama to Push Israel for Two-State Pledge." *The Guardian*, May 17, 2009. http://www.guardian.co.uk/world/2009/may/17/barack-obama-israel-palestine?INTCMP=SRCH.

———. "Israeli PM Binyamin Netanyahu." *The Guardian*, May 24, 2011. http://www.guardian.co.uk/world/2011/may/24/binyamin-netanyahu-israel-palestinians-congress?INTCMP=ILCNETTXT3487.

McGuckin, John Anthony. *The Orthodox Church: An Introduction to Its History, Doctrine, and Spiritual Culture.* Hoboken, N.J.: Wiley-Blackwell, 2008.

McKay, Betsy, Jonathan D. Rockoff, and Mark Schoofs. "AIDS Drugs Can Prevent Infection, Studies Show." *Wall Street Journal*, July 14, 2011. http://online.wsj.com/article/SB10001424052702303367870457644290 1100190640.html?mod=dist_smartbrief (accessed July 15, 2011).

McKibben, Bill. *Eaarth: Making a Life on a Tough New Planet.* New York: Times Books, 2010.

McKittrick, David, and David McVea. *Making Sense of the Troubles: The Story of the Conflict in Northern Ireland.* Chicago: New Amsterdam, 2002.

McLuhan, M. *Understanding Media: The Extensions of Man.* New York: McGraw-Hill, 1964.

McWhorter, John. *The Power of Babel: A Natural History of Language.* New York: Freeman, 2002.

Mearsheimer, John. "Back to the Future: Instability after the Cold War." *International Security* 15, no. 1 (Summer 1990): 5–56.

———. *The Tragedy of Great Power Politics.* New York: W. W. Norton, 2001.

———. *Why Leaders Lie: The Truth about Lying in International Politics.* New York: Oxford University Press, 2011.

Meisler, Stanley. *United Nations: The First Fifty Years.* Boston: Atlantic Monthly, 1997.

Mill, John Stuart. *Principles of Political Economy with Some of Their Applications to Social Philosophy.* London: J. W. Parker, 1848.

Mills, Anthony. *Press Freedom in an Age of Barbarity.* WPFR: Global Overview, IPI (February 9, 2010). http://www.freemedia.at/publications/world-press-freedom-review/singleview/4761/ (accessed November 1, 2011).

Milner, Henry. *Sweden: Social Democracy in Practice.* New York: Oxford University Press, 1990.

Milton-Edwards, Beverley. *Islamic Fundamentalism since 1945.* London: Routledge, 2005.

Milton-Edwards, Beverley, and Stephen Farrell. *Hamas: The Islamic Resistance Movement.* London: Polity, 2010.

Milton-Edwards, Beverley, and Peter Hinchcliffe. *Jordan: A Hashemite Legacy.* London: Routledge, 2001.

Mingst, Karen A. *Essentials of International Relations.* 4th ed. New York: W. W. Norton, 2008.

Mitchell, George J. *Making Peace.* New York: Knopf, 1999.

Moin, Baqer. *Khomeini: Life of the Ayatollah.* New York: St. Martin's, 2000.

Montesquieu, Charles Louis. *Spirit of the Laws.* Cambridge, UK: Cambridge University Press, 1989.

Moore, Patrick Albert. *Confessions of a Greenpeace Dropout: The Making of a Sensible Environmentalist.* Vancouver, BC, Canada: Beatty Street, 2010.

Moravcsik, Andrew. *The Choice for Europe: Social Purpose and State Power from Messina to Maastricht.* Ithaca, N.Y.: Cornell University Press; London: Routledge/UCL Press, 1998.

Morris, Benny. *Righteous Victims: A History of the Zionist-Arab Conflict: 1881–2001.* New York: Vintage, 2001.

———. *Birth of the Palestinian Refugee Problem Revisited.* 2nd ed. Cambridge, UK: Cambridge University Press, 2004.

———. *One State, Two States: Resolving the Israel/Palestine Conflict.* New Haven, Conn.: Yale University Press, 2010.

Moruzzi, Peter. *Havana before Castro: When Cuba Was a Tropical Playground.* Layton, Utah: Gibbs Smith, 2008.

Moynihan, Daniel P. *On the Law of Nations.* Cambridge: Harvard University Press, 1992.

———. *Pandaemonium: Ethnicity in International Politics.* Oxford and New York: Oxford University Press, 1993.

Mudde, Cas. *The Ideology of the Extreme Right.* Manchester, UK: Manchester University Press, 2003.

Mulaj, Kledja, ed. *Violent Non-state Actors in World Politics.* New York: Columbia University Press, 2010.

Mulholland, Marc. *Northern Ireland: A Very Short Introduction.* New York: Oxford University Press, 2003.

Mulloy, Darren. *American Extremism: History, Politics and the Militia Movement.* New York: Routledge, 2004.

Munton, Don, and David A. Welch. *The Cuban Missile Crisis: A Concise History.* New York: Oxford University Press, 2006.

National Commission on Terrorist Attacks. *The 9/11 Commission Report: Final Report of the National Commission on Terrorist Attacks upon the United States.* New York: Norton, 2004.

Natsios, Andrew S. *Sudan, South Sudan, and Darfur: What Everyone Needs to Know.* New York: Oxford University Press, 2012.

Nettle, Daniel, and Suzann Romaine. *Vanishing Voices: The Extinction of the World's Languages.* New York: Oxford University Press, 2000.

Newell, James L. *The Politics of Italy: Governance in a Normal Country.* Cambridge, UK: Cambridge University Press, 2010.

Nierenberg, Danielle. "Correcting Gender Myopia: Gender Equity, Women's Welfare, and the Environment." Worldwatch Paper No. 161. Washington, D.C.: Worldwatch Institute, 2002.

Nigosian, S. A. *World Faiths.* New York: St. Martins, 1990.

Nord, Mark, Alisha Coleman-Jensen, Margaret Andrews, and Steven Carlson, "Household Food Security in the United States." Washington, D.C.: U.S. Department of Agriculture, 2009. http://www.ers.usda.gov/Publications/ERR108/ERR108_ReportSummary.pdf (accessed October 15, 2011).

Norton, Philip. *The British Polity.* 3rd ed. New York: Longman, 1994.

NPR News. "A Historical Moment, the Saudi Women Challenging a Government by Driving." June 18, 2011. http://www.npr.org/blogs/thetwo-way/2011/06/19/137271964/a-historical-moment-the-saudi-women-challenging-a-government-by-driving (accessed June 18, 2011).

Nye, Joseph S. "Globalization's Democracy Deficit." *Foreign Affairs* 80, no. 4 (2001): 2–6.

Osaghae, Eghosa E. *Crippled Giant: Nigeria since Independence.* Bloomington: Indiana University Press, 1998.

Osiel, Mark J. *Mass Atrocity, Ordinary Evil, and Hannah Arendt: Criminal Consciousness in Argentina's Dirty War.* New Haven, Conn.: Yale University Press, 2002.

O'Shaughnessy, Hugh. *The Priest of Paraguay: Fernando Lugo and the Making of a Nation.* London: Zed, 2009.

Owtram, Francis. *A Modern History of Oman: Formation of the State since 1920.* London: I. B. Tauris, 2004.

Paarlberg, Robert. "The Global Food Fight." *Foreign Affairs* 79, no. 3 (2000): 21–38.

Packer, George. *Assassin's Gate: American in Iraq.* New York: Farrar, Straus & Giroux, 2005.

Paden, John N. *Faith and Politics in Nigeria.* Washington, D.C.: Institute of Peace, 2008.

Paxton, Robert O. *The Anatomy of Fascism.* New York: Knopf, 2004.

Peck, Don, and Ross Douthat. "Does Money Buy Happiness?" *The Atlantic Monthly*, January–February 2003, 42–43.

Pérez, Louis A. Jr. *Cuba: Between Reform and Revolution.* 2nd ed. New York: Oxford University Press, 1995.

Perlmutter, Amos. *The Military and Politics in Modern Times.* New Haven: Yale University Press, 1977.

Perritt, Henry H. *Kosovo Liberation Army: The Inside Story of an Insurgency.* Champaign, Ill.: University of Illinois Press, 2008.

Peterman, Amber, Dara Kay Cohen, and Tia Palermo. "Rape Reporting during War." *Foreign Affairs*, August 1, 2011. www.foreignaffairs.com/articles/68008/amber-peterman-dara-kay-cohen-tia-palermo-and-amelia-hoover-gree/rape-reporting-during-war (accessed January 20, 2012.

Peterson, V. Spike, and Anne Sisson Runyan. *Global Gender Issues.* Boulder, Colo.: Westview, 1993.

Petraeus, David. *The Field Manual.* Chicago: Chicago Press, 2007.

———. *US Army/Marine Corps Counterinsurgency Field Manual.* Chicago: University of Chicago Press, 2007.

Phillips, Kevin. *Wealth & Democracy: How Great Fortunes and Government Created America's Aristocracy.* New York: Broadway Books, 2002.

Phillips, Thimothy. *Beslan: The Tragedy of School No. 1*. London: Granta, 2008.

Philpott, Daniel. *Revolutions in Sovereignty: How Ideas Shaped Modern International Relations*. Princeton: Princeton University Press, 2001.

Pierce, Roy. *Choosing the Chief: Presidential Elections in France and the United States*. Ann Arbor: University of Michigan Press, 1995.

Pinder, John. *The European Union: A Very Short Introduction*. New York: Oxford University Press, 2008.

Pipes, Richard. *Communism: A Modern History*. New York: Modern Library, 2001.

Politkovskaya, Anna. *Putin's Russia: Life in a Failing Democracy*. New York: Metropolitan Books, 2005.

———. *A Small Corner of Hell: Dispatches from Chechnya*. Chicago: University of Chicago Press, 2007.

Polk, William R. *Understanding Iraq*. London: Tauris, 2005.

———. *Understanding Iran*. New York: Palgrave Macmillan, 2011.

Pope, Robert. *Dying to Win: The Strategic Logic of Suicide Terrorism*. New York: Random House, 2005.

Postel, Sandra, and Amy Vickers. "Boosting Water Productivity." In Worldwatch Institute, *State of the World 2004*, 46–65. New York: Worldwatch Institute/Norton, 2003.

Poulsen, Thomas M. *States and Nations: A Geographic Background to World Affairs*. Englewood Cliffs, N.J.: Prentice-Hall 1995.

Power, Samantha. *A Problem from Hell: America and the Age of Genocide*. New York: Basic, 2002.

Prabhat, Jha, Rajesh Kumar, Priya Vasa, Neeraj Dhingra, Deva Thiruchelvam, and Rahim Moineddin. "Low Male-to-Female Sex Ratio of Children Born in India: National Survey of 1.1 Million Households." *The Lancet* 367, no. 9506 (2006): 211–19.

Princen, Thomas. *Treading Softly*. Cambridge, Mass.: MIT Press, 2010.

Prugh, Thomas, and Erik Assadourian. "What Is Sustainability Anyway?" *World Watch* 16, no. 5 (2003): 10–21.

Prunier, Gerard. *Africa's World War: Congo, the Rwandan Genocide, and the Making of a Continental Catastrophe*. New York: Oxford University Press, 2011.

Putin, Vladimir. *First Person: An Astonishingly Frank Self-Portrait by Russia's President*. New York: Public Affairs, 2000.

Putnam, Robert D. *Bowling Alone: The Collapse and Revival of American Community*. New York: Touchstone Books, 2001.

Quester, George. "The Future of Nuclear Deterrence." *Survival* 34, no. 1 (Spring 1992): 74–88.

Radden Keefe, Patrick. "Reversal of Fortune." *The New Yorker*, January 9, 2012, 38–49.

Radelet, Steven. "Bush and Foreign Aid." *Foreign Affairs* 82, no. 5 (2003): 104–17.

Ramirez, Maria Clemencia. *Between the Guerrillas and the State: The Cocolero Movement, Citizenship, and Identity in the Colombian Amazon*. Raleigh, N.C.: Duke University Press, 2011.

Randal, Jonathan C. *After Such Knowledge What Forgiveness? My Encounters with Kurdistan*. Boulder, Colo.: Westview, 1998.

Rasenberger, Jim. *The Brilliant Disaster: JFK, Castro, and America's Doomed Invasion of Cuba's Bay of Pigs*. New York: Scribner, 2011.

Rashid, Ahmed. *Taliban: Militant Islam, Oil and Fundamentalism in Central Asia*. New Haven, Conn.: Yale University Press, 2000.

Rather, Dan. *Deadlines & Datelines*. New York: Morrow, 1999.

Raymond, Susan. "Foreign Assistance in an Aging World." *Foreign Affairs* 82, no. 2 (2003): 91–106.

Remnick, David. *Resurrection: The Struggle for a New Russia*. London: Picador, 1998.

Renner, Michael. "Ending Violent Conflict." Worldwatch Paper No. 146. Washington, D.C.: Worldwatch Institute, 1999.

Ricks, Thomas E. *Fiasco*. 6th ed. New York: Penguin, 2006.

———. *The Gamble: General David Petraeus and the American Military Adventure in Iraq, 2006–2008*. New York: Penguin, 2009.

Riedel, Bruce. *The Search for al Qaeda: Its Leadership, Ideology, and Future*. Washington, D.C.: Brookings, 2008.

Risse-Kappen, Thomas, Stephen C. Ropp, and Kathryn Sikkink. *The Power of Human Rights: International Norms and Domestic Change*. Cambridge: Cambridge University Press, 1999.

Rogers, A. D. and D. d'A. Laffoley. "International Earth System Expert Workshop on Ocean Stresses and Impacts." IPSO Oxford, 2011. http://www.stateoftheocean.org/ipso-2011-workshop-summary.cfm (accessed November 21, 2011).

Rogers, Henry. *Writing Systems: A Linguistic Approach*. Oxford: Blackwell, 2005.

Roodman, David Malin. "Still Waiting for the Jubilee: Pragmatic Solutions for the Third World Debt Crisis." Worldwatch Paper No. 155. Washington, D.C.: Worldwatch Institute, 2001.

Roosevelt, Kermit. *Countercoup: The Struggle for the Control of Iran*. New York: McGraw-Hill, 1979.

Rosenberg Weinreb, Amelia. *Cuba in the Shadow of Change: Daily Life in the Twilight of the Revolution*. Gainesville, Fla.: University Press of Florida, 2010.

Roskin, Michael G. *Countries and Concepts: An Introduction to Comparative Politics*. 8th ed. Englewood Cliffs, N.J.: Prentice Hall, 2004.

Ross, Robert J. S., and Anita Chan. "From North–South to South–South." *Foreign Affairs* 81, no. 5 (2002): 8–13.

Rotberg, Robert I. "Failed States in a World of Terror." *Foreign Affairs* 81, no. 3 (2002): 127–40.

Rousseau, Jean Jacques. *Du contract [sic] social, ou, Principes du droit politique*. Amsterdam: Chez M. M. Rey, 1762.

Roy, Arundhati. *The God of Small Things*. New York and London: HarperCollins, 1997.

———. *The Cost of Living*. New York: Modern Library, 1999.

———. *Field Notes on Democracy: Listening to Grasshoppers*. New York: Haymarket, 2009.

———. *Walking with the Comrades*. New York: Penguin, 2011.

Roy, Joaquín. *Cuba, the United States, and the Helms-Burton Doctrine*. Gainesville, Fla.: University Press of Florida, 2000.

Rubin, Barnett R. *The Fragmentation of Afghanistan*. New Haven, Conn.: Yale University, 1995.

Rushdie, Salman. *The Satanic Verses*. Ringwood, Vic., Australia: Viking, 1987.

Rutherford, Kenneth R. *Disarming States: The International Movement to Ban Landmines*. New York: Praeger, 2010.

Ryan, John C. "Feedlots of the Sea." *World Watch* 16, no. 5 (2003): 22–29.

Sachar, Howard M. *A History of Israel: From the Rise of Zionism to Our Time*. New York: Knopf, 1988.

Sachs, Aaron. "Child Prostitution: The Last Commodity." *World Watch* 7, no. 4 (1994): 25–30.

Sachs, Jeffrey D. *The End of Poverty: Economic Possibilities for Our Time*. New York: Penguin, 2005.

Sachs, Jeffrey, et al. *Implementing Debt Relief for the HIPCs*. Cambridge, Mass.: Harvard University Center for International Development, 1999.

Sampat, Payal. "Deep Trouble: The Hidden Threat of Groundwater Pollution." Worldwatch Paper No. 154. Washington, D.C.: Worldwatch Institute, 2000.

Sanchez, Yoani. *Havana Real: One Woman Fights to Tell the Truth about Cuba Today*. New York: Melville House, 2011.

Sanger, David E., and Peter Baker. "Obama Limits When U.S. Would Use Nuclear Arms." *New York Times*, April 5, 2010, A1.

Sapolsky, Robert. "How the Other Half Heals." *Discover*, April 1998, 46–52.

Sassoon, Donald. *Mussolini and the Rise of Fascism*. New York: HarperCollins, 2008.

Sassoon, Joseph. *Saddam Hussein's Ba'ath Party: Inside an Authoritarian Regime*. Cambridge, UK: Cambridge University Press, 2011.

Sawin, Janet L. "Water Scarcity Could Overwhelm the Next Generation." *World Watch* 16, no. 4 (2003): 8.

———. "Making Better Energy Choices." In Worldwatch Institute, *State of the World 2004*, 24–43.

Schaefer, Robert W. *The Insurgency in Chechnya and the North Caucasus*. New York: Praeger, 2011.

Schmidt, Diane. *Writing in Political Science*. 3rd ed. New York: Longman, 2004.

Schofield, Victoria. *Kashmir in Conflict*. London: Tauris, 2000.

———. *Kashmir in Conflict: India, Pakistan, and the Unending War*. 3rd ed. London: I. B. Tauris, 2010.

Scholte, Jan Aart. *Globalization: A Critical Introduction*. 2nd ed. New York: Palgrave, 2005.

———. *Building Global Democracy? Civil Society and Accountable Global Governance*. Cambridge, UK: Cambridge University Press, 2011.

Schumaker, Paul D., and Burdett A. Loomis, eds. *Choosing a President: The Electoral College and Beyond*. Washington, D.C.: CQ, 2002.

Schwab, Peter. *Cuba: Confronting the U.S. Embargo*. New York: Palgrave Macmillan, 2000.

Seldon, Anthony, and Daniel Collings. *Britain under Thatcher*. New York: Longman, 1999.

Sell, Louis. *Slobodan Milosevic and the Destruction of Yugoslavia*. Raleigh, N.C.: Duke University Press, 2002.

Sen, Amartya. *Development as Freedom*. New York: Random House, 1999.

———. *The Argumentative Indian: Writings on Indian History, Culture, and Identity.* New York: Farrar, Straus, and Giroux, 2006.

———. *Identity and Violence.* New York: Norton, 2006.

Sen, K. M. *Hinduism.* London: Penguin, 1961.

Shadid, Anthony. *Night Draws Near: Iraq's People in the Shadows of America's War.* New York: Holt, 2005.

Shea, Dorothy. *The South African Truth Commission: The Politics of Reconciliation.* Washington, D.C.: U.S. Institute of Peace, 2000.

Shiraev, Eric. *Russian Government and Politics.* New York: Palgrave Macmillan, 2010.

Shiva, Vandana. *Stolen Harvest: The Hijacking of the Global Food Supply.* Cambridge, Mass.: South End Press, 2000.

———. *Water Wars: Pollution, Profits, and Privatization.* Cambridge, Mass.: South End Press, 2001.

Shively, W. Philip. *The Craft of Political Research.* 5th ed. Upper Saddle River, N.J.: Prentice Hall, 2001.

Shugart, M. A., and Martin P. Wattenberg. *Mixed Member Electoral Systems: The Best of Both Worlds.* New York: Oxford University Press, 2001.

Sick, Gary. *All Fall Down: America's Tragic Encounter with Iran.* New York: Random House, 1995.

Simon, Julian. *The Ultimate Resource.* Princeton, N.J.: Princeton University Press, 1981.

Simons, Geoff. *Colombia: A Brutal History.* New York: Palgrave, 2004.

Singer, Peter. *Marx: A Very Short Introduction.* New York: Oxford University Press, 2001.

Skaine, Rosemaire. *Female Genital Mutilation: Legal, Cultural and Medical Issues.* New York: McFarland, 2005.

Slobodkin, Lawrence B. *A Citizen's Guide to Ecology.* New York: Oxford University Press, 2003.

Slomanson, William R. *Fundamental Perspectives on International Law.* 6th ed. Stamford, Conn.: Wadsworth, 2010; 4th ed. Belmont, Calif.: Thomson/West, 2003.

Smil, Vaclav. *Feeding the World: A Challenge for the Twenty-First Century.* Cambridge, Mass.: MIT Press, 2000.

Smith, Adam. *The Wealth of Nations.* New York: Simon & Brown, 2011.

Smith, Anthony D. *Myths and Memories of the Nation.* New York: Oxford University Press, 2000.

Smith, Stephen C. *Ending Global Poverty: A Guide to What Works.* New York: Palgrave MacMillan, 2005.

Smith, Tony. "Peso's Devaluation Gives Argentina Cost Advantages." *New York Times*, October 24, 2002. http://www.nytimes.com/2002/10/24/business/peso-s-devaluation-gives-argentina-cost-advantages.html ?pagewanted=all&src=pm (accessed November 2, 2003).

Sparks, Allister. *Beyond the Miracle: Inside the New South Africa.* Chicago: University of Chicago Press, 2009.

Sridhar, Lalitha. "India: Killing in the Cradle." *Populi: The UNFPA Magazine* 28, no. 2 (2011): 10–11.

Staab, Andreas. *The European Union Explained: Institutions, Actors, Global Impact.* 2nd ed. Bloomington, Ind.: Indiana University Press, 2011.

Staten, Clifford L. *The History of Cuba.* New York: Palgrave Macmillan, 2005.

Stearns, Jason. *Dancing in the Glory of Monsters: The Collapse of the Congo and the Great War of Africa.* New York: Public Affairs, 2011.

Stein, Philip L., and Bruce M. Rowe. *Physical Anthropology.* 3rd and 9th ed. New York: McGraw-Hill, 1982, 2005.

Steinberg, David. *Burma/Myanmar: What Everyone Needs to Know.* New York and Oxford: Oxford University Press, 2009.

Steinberg, David I. *Burma: The State of Myanmar.* Washington, D.C.: Georgetown University Press, 2001.

Steinberg, Jonathan. *Why Switzerland?* Cambridge, UK: Cambridge University Press, 1976.

Stern, Jessica. "Pakistan's Jihad Culture." *Foreign Affairs* 79, no. 6 (2000): 115–26.

———. "The Protean Enemy." *Foreign Affairs* 82, no. 4 (2002): 27–40.

———. *Terror in the Name of God: Why Religious Militants Kill.* New York: Ecco, 2003.

Stiglitz, Joseph. *Globalization and Its Discontents.* London: Norton, 2002.

———. "Odious Rulers, Odious Debts." *The Atlantic Monthly*, November 2003, 39–45.

Stiles, Kendall W. *Case Histories in International Politics.* 4th ed. New York: Pearson Longman, 2006.

Suberu, Rotimi T. *Federalism and Ethnic Conflict in Nigeria.* Washington, D.C.: U.S. Institute of Peace, 2001.

Sullivan, Michael J. *Comparing State Polities: A Framework for Analyzing 100 Governments.* Westport: Greenwood, 1996.

Sunstein, Cass R. *Designing Democracy: What Constitutions Do.* New York: Oxford University Press, 2001.

Swain, Geoffrey. *Tito: A Biography.* London: I. B. Tauris, 2010.

Swain, Geoffrey, and Nigel Swain. *Eastern Europe since 1945*. New York and London: Palgrave Macmillan, 2009.

Sweet, Alec Stone. *Governing with Judges: Constitutional Politics in Europe*. New York: Oxford University Press, 2000.

Sweig, Julia E. *Cuba: What Everybody Needs to Know*. New York: Oxford University Press, 2009.

Takeyh, Ray. *Hidden Iran: Paradox and Power in the Islamic Republic*. New York: Holt, 2007.

Talberg, Jonas. *Leadership and Negotiation in the European Union*. Cambridge, UK Cambridge University Press, 2006.

Talbott, Strobe. *Engaging India: Diplomacy, Democracy, and the Bomb*. New York: Random House, 2002.

———. *The Russia Hand: A Memoir of Presidential Diplomacy*. New York: Random House, 2002.

Tamimi, Azzam. *Hanas: A History from Within*. London: Oliver Branch Press, 2011.

Tanner, Stephen. *Afghanistan: A Military History from Alexander the Great to the War against the Taliban*. Philadelphia: DaCapo/Perseus, 2009.

Taras, Raymond C., and Rajat Ganguly. *Understanding Ethnic Conflict: The International Dimension*. 2nd ed. New York: Longman, 2002.

Taylor, Ben Heaven, and Tanja Schuemer-Cross. *The Right to Survive: The Humanitarian Challenge in the Twenty-First Century*. Oxford, UK: Oxfam Publishing, 2009.

Taylor, Brian D. *State Building in Putin's Russia: Policing and Coercion after Communism*. Cambridge, UK: Cambridge University Press, 2011.

Tazmini, Ghoncheh. *Khatami's Iran: The Islamic Republic and the Turbulent Path to Reform*. London: I. B. Tauris, 2012.

Thant, Myint-U. *The Making of Modern Burma*. Cambridge: Cambridge University Press, 2001.

Thiranagama, Sharika. *In My Mother's House: Civil War in Sri Lanka. The Ethnography of Political Violence*. Philadelphia: University of Pennsylvania Press, 2011.

Thomas, David M., ed. *Whistling Past the Graveyard: Constitutional Abeyances, Quebec, and the Future of Canada*. New York: Oxford University Press, 1997.

Thurow, Lester. "Why Their World Might Crumble." *New York Times Magazine*, November 19, 1995.

Tickner, J. Ann. "Feminist Perspectives on 9/11." *International Studies Perspectives* 3 (2002): 333–50.

Tiersky, Ronald. *François Mitterrand: A Very French President*. Boulder, Colo.: Rowman & Littlefield, 2002.

Tolstoy, Leo. *Anna Karenina*. New York: Thomas Y. Crowell & Co., 1899.

Torres Perez, Aida. *Conflict of Rights in the European Union: A Theory of Supranational Adjudication*. New York: Oxford University Press, 2009.

Tran, Mark. "Global Development: The Millennium Development Goals." *The Guardian*, July 7, 2011. http://www.guardian.co.uk/global-development/2011/jul/07/millennium-development-goals-2011-report (accessed July 20, 2011).

Trask, R. L. *Language: The Basics*. London: Routledge, 2004.

Trechsel, Alexander, and Hanspeter Kriesi. *The Politics of Switzerland: Continuity and Change in a Consensus Democracy*. Cambridge, UK: Cambridge University Press, 2008.

Tripp, Charles. *A History of Iraq*. New York: Cambridge University Press, 2000.

Trudgill, Peter. *Sociolinguistics: An Introduction to Language and Society*. London: Penguin, 1995.

Tutu, Desmond. *The Rainbow People of God*. New York: Doubleday, 1994.

———. *No Future without Forgiveness*. New York: Doubleday, 1999.

U. S. Department of State. *Patterns of Global Terrorism, 2001*. Washington, D.C.: U.S. Department of State, 2002.

Udovicki, Jasminka, and James Ridgeway, eds. *Burn This House: The Making and Unmaking of Yugoslavia*. Raleigh, N.C.: Duke University Press, 1997.

UN AIDS. *Global Report Score Card 2010*. http://www.unaids.org/globalreport/AIDSScorecards.htm (accessed December 27, 2011).

UN WFP (United Nations World Food Programme). "Many Bangladesh Children Malnourished News Report." http://www.wfp.org/content/un-many-bangladesh-children-malnourished (accessed January 3, 2012).

———. "Sub-Saharan Africa's Promise is Growing." http://www.wfp.org/content/guest-column-sub-saharan-africas-promise-growing (accessed January 5, 2012).

UNDP (United Nations Development Programme). *Human Development Report 1998*. New York: Oxford University Press for the United Nations Development Programme (UNDP), 1998.

——. *Human Development Report 2000*. New York and Oxford: Oxford University Press, 2000.

——. *Human Development Report 2002*. New York and Oxford: Oxford University Press, 2002.

——. *Human Development Report 2003*. http://hdr.undp.org/en/reports/global/hdr2003/ (accessed November 20, 2004).

——. *Human Development Report 2011*. http://hdr.undp.org/en/media/HDR_2011_EN_Tables.pdf (accessed November 11, 2011).

——. *Statistical Annex Human Development Report 2011*. http://hdr.undp.org/en/media/HDR_2011_EN_Tables.pdf (accessed December 26, 2011).

UNDP-Arab (United Nations Development Programme). *The Arab Human Development Report: Creating Opportunities for Future Generations*. New York: United Nations Development Programme, Regional Bureau for Arab States, 2002.

UNFPA (United Nations Population Fund). *State of the World Population 2003*. New York: United Nations Population Fund, 2003.

——. *Missing—Mapping the Adverse Child Sex Ratio in India*. New York: United Nations Population Fund, 2004.

——. *Report 2011*. http://www.unfpa.org/public/home/factsheets/pid/3856. (accessed December 5, 2011).

UNICEF (United Nations Children's Fund). *State of the World's Children 2003*. New York: United Nations Children's Fund, 2003.

——. *Progress for Children: A Report Card on Nutrition* (Number 4). New York: UNICEF, 2006.

——. *Children Living in Poverty 2011*. http://www.unicef.org/sowc05/english/poverty.html (accessed October 3, 2011).

——. *The Convention on the Rights of the Child*. http://www.unicef.org/crc/ (accessed November 14, 2011).

UNIFEM (United Nations Development Fund for Women). *Progress of the World's Women 2000*. UNIFEM Biennial Report. New York: UNIFEM, 2000.

United Nations. *From Beijing to Beijing + 5*. New York: United Nations, 2001.

United Nations. "Millennium Development Goals Report 2010." http://www.un.org/millenniumgoals/pdf/MDG%20Report%202010%20En%20r15%20-low%20res%2020100615%20-.pdf (accessed November 15, 2011).

——. "Millennium Development Goals Report 2011." http://unstats.un.org/unsd/mdg/Resources/Static/Products/Progress2011/11–31339%20(E)%20MDG%20Report%202011_Book%20LR.pdf (accessed November 15, 2011).

United Nations Food and Agriculture Organization. *Report 2010*. http://www.fao.org/docrep/012/al390e/al390e00.pdf (accessed May 10, 2011).

UNPD (United Nations Population Division). *World Population Prospects: The 2002 Revision*. New York: United Nations, 2003.

Valeri, Marc. *Oman: Politics and Society in the Qaboos State*. New York: Columbia University Press, 2009.

van Schaik, Sam. *Tibet: A History*. New Haven, Conn.: Yale University Press, 2011.

Veigel, Klaus Friedrich. *Dictatorship, Democracy, and Globalization: Argentina and the Cost of Paralysis 1973–2001*. University Park, Pa.: Penn State University, 2009.

Vermeer, Jan P., ed. *In "Media" Res: Readings in Mass Media and American Politics*. New York: McGraw Hill, 1995.

Villiers Negroponte, Diana. *Seeking Peace in El Salvador: The Struggle to Reconstruct a Nation at the End of the Cold War*. New York: Palgrave Macmillan, 2012.

Vogel, David. *The Market for Virtue: The Potential and Limits of Corporate Social Responsibility*. Washington, D.C.: The Brookings Institution, 2006.

von Glahn, Gerhard. *Law among Nations: An Introduction to Public International Law*. 7th ed. New York: MacMillan, 2009.

Wallace, William. *Non-state Actors in World Politics*. New York: Palgrave Macmillan, 2002.

Wallerstein, Immanuel. *The Modern World-System in the Longue Duree*. Boulder, Colo.: Paradigm Publishers, 2004.

——. "The Fantastic Success of Occupy Wall Street." Commentary No. 315, October 15, 2011. http://www.iwallerstein.com/fantastic-success-occupy-wall-street/ (accessed November 4, 2011).

Walter, Carl, and Fraser Howie. *Red Capitalism: The Fragile Financial Foundation of China's Extraordinary Rise*. New York: Wiley, 2011.

Walzer, Michael. *Politics and Passion: Toward a More Egalitarian Liberalism.* New Haven, Conn.: Yale University Press, 2006.

Waterman McChesney, Robert. *Rich Media, Poor Democracy: Communication Politics in Dubious Times.* Champaign, Ill.: University of Illinois Press, 1999.

Weatherby, Joseph N. *The Middle East and North Africa: A Political Primer.* New York: Longman, 2001.

Weatherby, Joseph N., et al. *The Other World: Issues and Politics of the Developing World.* 5th ed. New York: Longman, 2003.

Weeks, John R. *Population: An Introduction to Concepts and Issues.* 9th ed. Belmont, Calif.: Wadsworth, 2011.

Weidenbaum, Murray L. *The Competition of Ideas: The World of the Washington Think Tanks* Piscataway, N.J.: Transaction Publishers, 2011.

Weiss, Gordon. *The Cage: The Fight for Sri Lanka and the Last Days of the Tamil Tigers.* London: Bodley Head, 2011.

Weiss, Thomas G. and Sam Daws. *The Oxford Handbook on the United Nations.* New York: Oxford University Press, 2009.

Weiss, Thomas G., David P. Forsythe, and Roger A. Coate. *The United Nations and Changing World Politics.* Boulder, Colo.: Westview, 2009.

Wendt, Alexander. "Anarchy Is What States Make of It: The Social Construction of Power Politics." *International Organization* 46, no. 2 (Spring 1992): 391–425.

Weyler, Rex. *Greenpeace: How a Group of Ecologists, Journalists, and Visionaries Changed the World.* New York: Rodale, 2004.

WHO (World Health Organization). *World Report on Violence and Health.* Geneva: WHO, 2002).

Wiebe, Robert H. *Who We Are: A History of Popular Nationalism.* Princeton: Princeton University Press, 2001.

Wilson, Frank L. *European Politics Today: The Democratic Experience.* 3rd ed. Upper Saddle River, N.J.: Prentice Hall, 1999.

Wilson, James Q. *American Government: Institutions and Policies.* 5th ed. Lexington, Mass.: D.C. Heath, 1992.

Wolchik, Sharon L., and Jane L. Curry. *Central and East European Politics: From Communism to Democracy.* 2nd ed. Boulder, Colo.: Rowman & Littlefield, 2010.

Wolpert, Stanley. *A New History of India.* 6th ed. New York: Oxford University Press, 2000.

Wood, David M., and Birol A. Yeşilada. *The Emerging European Union.* 2nd ed. New York: Longman, 2001.

Woods, Larry J. *Military Interventions in Sierra Leone: Lessons from a Failed State.* Fort Leavenworth, Kans.: Combat Studies Institute, 2011.

World Bank. *Global Development Finance 2011: External Debt of Developing Countries.* http://issuu.com/world.bank.publications/docs/9780821386736 (accessed November 3, 2011).

World Bank. *World Development Indicators.* Washington, D.C.: The World Bank, 2003.

World Bank. *World Development Report 2000.* New York: Oxford University Press, 2000.

World Resources Institute. *World Resources 2002–2004: Decisions for the Earth: Balance, Voice, and Power.* Washington, D.C.: World Resources Institute, 2003.

Worldwatch Institute. "Is Meat Sustainable?" January 2, 2012. http://www.worldwatch.org/node/549 (accessed January 12, 2012).

Worldwatch Institure. *State of the World 2003.* New York: Worldwatch Institute/Norton, 2003.

———. *State of the World 2004.* New York: Worldwatch Institute/Norton, 2004.

———. *State of the World 2006.* New York: Worldwatch Institute/Norton, 2006.

Worldwatch Institure. *Vital Signs 2003: The Trends That Are Shaping Our Future.* UK: Earthscan Publications Ltd., 2003.

Wright, Lawrence. *The Looming Tower.* New York: Vintage, 2007.

Wright, Robin. *The Last Great Revolution: Turmoil & Transformation in Iran.* New York: Random House, 2001.

———. *Dreams and Shadows: The Future of the Middle East.* New York: Penguin Publishers, 2011.

Yergin, Daniel. *The Prize: The Epic Quest for Oil, Money, and Power.* New York: Simon & Schuster, 1991.

———. *The Quest: Energy, Security, and the Remaking of the Modern World.* New York: Simon and Schuster, 2011.

Yoal, Gerard, and Carl T. Dahlman. *Bosnia Remade: Ethnic Cleansing and Its Reversal.* New York: Oxford University Press, 2011.

Index

Page numbers in *italic* indicate figures; numbers followed by *g* indicate glossary entries.

Cold War, 2, 577
Colombia: communists of, 356–60; U.S. relations
    with, 49, 360–61
colonialism, in poverty, 451–52
colonies: as sub-sovereign entities, 112–13; use of
    term, 113
Columbia Journalism Review, 42n32
Colvin, Marie, 37–39, 332
combatants, in high-intensity conflict, 328
combination system, 245–47, *246, 247,* 248;
    definition of, 577; legislatures in, 250–51; *vs.*
    parliamentary system, 248–49
command economy. *See* Marxism
commercial globalization, 469
commercials, in television news, 23, 24
Commonwealth of Nations, 113–14, 577
commonwealths, as sub-sovereign entities, 112–13
communication: diplomats in, 157; globalization
    of, 469
communist, 220, 577
comparative politics: definition of, 577; as
    discipline, 61; *vs.* international relations, 147–
    48; results of, 232
Comprehensive Test Ban Treaty, 165
computer, radio over, 29
concentration camps, 562
conditionality: definition of, 577; in foreign aid,
    456
confederacy, EU as, 181
confidence bills, 239, 577
conflict: civil disobedience as, 315–16; doctrine
    in, 92; environment in, 533; feminism in, 76;
    freedom and, 192–93, 268; high-intensity, 326–
    34, 582; about homosexuality, 77–79; in human
    experience, 1–2; language in, 87–90; levels of,
    310–14; low-intensity, 319–26, 584; median
    age in, 489; nonviolent adversarial, 314–15;
    overpopulation in, 69; in political science, 45–
    46; poverty in, 73; religion in, 91–99; with sub-
    sovereign entities, 112; terminology associated
    with, 13; world interconnectedness in, 1–3
Confucianism, 95
Congo, 331, 333
Conservative Party (Canada), 138–39
Conservative Party (U.K.), 206–7, 218, 230n24,
    252, 252–53
conservatives: on capitalism, 212; in China, 225;
    gay rights and, 78; use of term, 210–11; in U.S.
    politics, *207,* 209–10
consonantal systems, 90
constituency, 577
constitution: definition of, 578; of India, 259; of
    Iraq, 344; power allocated under, 236; of Russia,
    298; types of, 234

constitutional monarch, 240–41, *241,* 578
constructivism, 58, 578
consulate, 153, 578
Consumed (Barber), 46
containment, 158, 578
contraception, 497, 515–20
convention, 161, 578
conventional weapons, 328, 578
conventional wisdom, in news media, 36
"Convention on Biological Diversity," 545–46
Convention on the Rights of the Child, 81, 165
cooperation, idealist perspective on, 56–57
core countries, in critical theory, 59
core nation, 116, 369, 414
core rights, 197–98
corporations, news media controlled by, 33
corruption: development and, 494; in dictatorships,
    271; in foreign aid, 456; in Russia, 302
cost of living: adjustments for, 435–36; inflation
    in, 440
The Cost of Living (Roy), 213
The Council of Europe, 229n10
Council of Guardians (Iran), 292
counties, as sub-sovereign entities, 111–12
countries. *See* states
Country Reports on Human Rights Practices, 196–97
coup d'état: in Burma, 282–84; definition of, 578;
    in Iran, 291; oligarchy after, 295–96; reasons
    for, 281–82
courts, 255–59
Cox, Harvey, 46
Creole, 578
crime: in Russia, 302; in social modernization, 496;
    U.S. conservatives on, *207,* 210; U.S. liberals
    on, *207,* 208
criminality, in international law, 162
critical media studies, 33
critical theorists, 58–60, 578
Croatian language, 87
Crowe, William, 34, 154
Crystal, David, 84
C-Span, 25
Cuba, *362;* BBC transmission in, 29; conflict with
    U.S., 362–67; economy in, 363, 366, 367–68;
    foreign debt of, 459; freedom in, 195–96;
    history of, *363,* 363–66
Cuban Missile Crisis, 364–65
culture: definition of, 578; in ethnic groups, 82;
    globalization of, 468–69; in nationalist conflicts,
    312; in nationality, *83;* in nationhood, 117
currency: in ALBA countries, 227; in European
    Union, 180; exchange rates for, 440–42;
    national, 442
Current History, 41n18

About the Authors

Richard Oliver Collin began his doctorate in politics at Harvard and finished it at Oriel College, Oxford. He is an author and academic whose books include *Imbroglio*, *Winter of Fire*, *Contessa*, and *The Man with Many Names*, as well as scholarly articles on ethnic, ideological, and linguistic conflict. After an early career as an official of the U.S. Department of Defense, Dr. Collin taught at Coastal Carolina University for thirty years and is now Distinguished Professor Emeritus. He has been active in the peace movement over the past two decades, and now lives in East Yorkshire.

Pamela L. Martin is a professor of politics at Coastal Carolina University in Conway, South Carolina. She has authored various works on global environmental governance and the Amazon, including *Oil in the Soil: The Politics of Paying to Preserve the Amazon* (2011). She is the recipient of a Fulbright Scholar Award to Ecuador and the International Studies Association Deborah Gerner Award for Innovative Teaching. Dr. Martin teaches courses in international relations, international organizations, and environmental governance, and is the advisor of the Model United Nations program.